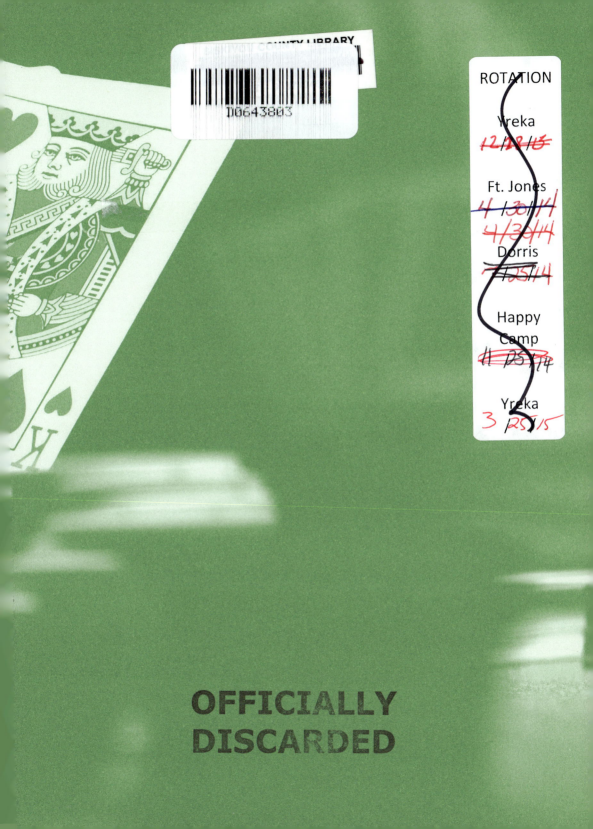

THE STEP-BY-STEP GUIDE TO PLAYING

250 WORLD'S BEST
CARD GAMES

INCLUDING BRIDGE, POKER, FAMILY GAMES AND SOLITAIRES

THE STEP-BY-STEP GUIDE TO PLAYING

250 WORLD'S BEST CARD GAMES

INCLUDING BRIDGE, POKER, FAMILY GAMES AND SOLITAIRES

- Learn how to play classics such as Baccarat, Cribbage, Go Fish, Gin Rummy and Kaluki
- Clearly explained with more than 1200 easy-to-follow photographs and illustrations

- With a special focus on poker games, rules and winning strategies, skills and tactics, and useful tips for players at all levels as well as expert guidance for professional players

JEREMY HARWOOD AND TREVOR SIPPETTS

LORENZ BOOKS

This edition is published by Lorenz Books, an imprint of
Anness Publishing Ltd, Hermes House, 88–89 Blackfriars Road,
London SE1 8HA; tel. 020 7401 2077; fax 020 7633 9499
www.lorenzbooks.com; www.annesspublishing.com

Anness Publishing has a new picture agency outlet for images for
publishing, promotions or advertising. Please visit our website
www.practicalpictures.com for more information.

UK agent: The Manning Partnership Ltd; tel. 01225 478444;
fax 01225 478440; sales@manning-partnership.co.uk
UK distributor: Book Trade Services; tel. 0116 2759086;
fax 0116 2759090; uksales@booktradeservices.com;
exportsales@booktradeservices.com
North American agent/distributor: National Book Network;
tel. 301 459 3366; fax 301 429 5746; www.nbnbooks.com
Australian agent/distributor: Pan Macmillan Australia;
tel. 1300 135 113; fax 1300 135 103;
customer.service@macmillan.com.au
New Zealand agent/distributor: David Bateman Ltd;
tel. (09) 415 7664; fax (09) 415 8892

Publisher: Joanna Lorenz
Editorial Director: Helen Sudell
Project Editors: Rosie Gordon and Elizabeth Young
Cover Designer: Nigel Partridge
Proofreading Manager: Lindsay Zamponi
Production Controller: Mai-Ling Collyer

Designed and produced for Anness Publishing by
The Bridgewater Book Company Limited

ETHICAL TRADING POLICY
At Anness Publishing we believe that business should be conducted
in an ethical and ecologically sustainable way, with respect for the
environment and a proper regard to the replacement of the natural
resources we employ.
    As a publisher, we use a lot of wood pulp to make high-quality
paper for printing, and that wood commonly comes from spruce
trees. We are therefore currently growing more than 750,000 trees in
three Scottish forest plantations: Berrymoss (130 hectares/320 acres),
West Touxhill (125 hectares/305 acres) and Deveron Forest (75
hectares/185 acres). The forests we manage contain more than 3.5
times the number of trees employed each year in making paper for
the books we manufacture.
    Because of this ongoing ecological investment programme, you, as
our customer, can have the pleasure and reassurance of knowing
that a tree is being cultivated on your behalf to naturally replace the
materials used to make the book you are holding.
    Our forestry programme is run in accordance with the UK
Woodland Assurance Scheme (UKWAS) and will be certified by the
internationally recognized Forest Stewardship Council (FSC). The
FSC is a non-government organization dedicated to promoting
responsible management of the world's forests. Certification ensures
forests are managed in an environmentally sustainable and socially
responsible way. For further information about this scheme, go to
www.annesspublishing.com/trees

A CIP catalogue record for this book is available from the
British Library.

Previously published in two separate volumes, How To Play the
200 Best-Ever Card Games and The Complete Practical Guide to
Poker and Poker Playing

PUBLISHER'S NOTE
Although the advice and information in this book are believed to be
accurate and true at the time of going to press, neither the authors
nor the publisher can accept any legal responsibility or liability for
any errors or omissions that may be made.

CONTENTS

INTRODUCTION

Playing cards are used all over the globe and are every-day objects that we all take for granted. But there is much more to these cards than the 52-card deck that most of us are familiar with: there are variations in suit systems, patterns and even the number of cards in a pack, depending on where you are in the world and the game you are playing.

The actual origin of playing cards is unknown. There are many divided opinions, theories and speculation, but it is believed that the earliest playing cards originated in Central Asia. China is a strong candidate as that was where paper was first developed. How playing cards made their way to Europe and throughout the world is also a mystery.

Today, countless games can be played with a pack of cards. In this book, you will find comprehensive instructions to more than 200 of the best-known card games that are still played today, including Rummy, Cribbage, Texas Hold'em, Spanish Mus, German Whist, and Chinese Ten just to name a few. There has been a huge increase in the popularity of card games over the last few years, especially with poker. It is likely that the surge of interest has been generated from televised tournaments and online gaming, making poker one of the most widely played gambling games in the world.

HOW TO USE THIS BOOK

The book is divided into two easy-to-use sections. The first, Card Games, covers all the popular card games from around the world. There are games for friends and family, games to play by oneself, and games for two or more players. You'll find all the traditional games included, such as Baccarat, Blackjack, Kaluki, Bridge, Cheat and Brag, as well as many lesser known games such as Briscola, Crazy Eights, Forty-One and Skat.

Apart from instruction, there is a summary of each of the types of games available to play, as well as their conventional rules, along with some exceptions and variations. Card game rules and strategies are clearly explained and regularly illustrated with simple, detailed diagrams showing example hands in various states of play. Where relevant, a 'D' button is shown, indicating the position of the dealer in relation to the rest of the players, who are referred to in the diagrams and text as 'Player A', 'Player B' etc. With each game, there is also a handy information box that provides a general overview of what you will need to play the game, be it a score sheet or gambling chips, as well as information on how many and what kind of cards are used, an age level for each game and the ranking of the particular cards.

Left: Ian Fleming's secret agent creation James Bond favoured the game bacarrat, and is seen playing the game in several of the films. In the movie Thunderball, James Bond (Sean Connery) encounters his enemy Emilio Largo (Adolfo Cell) over a game of baccarat in the casino. In the recent film adaptation of Casino Royale, baccarat was replaced with Texas Hold'em as it is a much more popular game.

Left: Cribbage is one of Britain's oldest card games, dating back to the 1600s. Today, it is still popular all over the world. Cribbage boards come in different styles, but they all have the same total number of points to achieve.

Far left: Playing card games on the Internet is an increasingly popular pastime. With an hour to spare, you can log on and join a game immediately.

The second section, Poker Games, begins by looking at the history of poker, its origins and evolution throughout the 20th century, and how it has evolved into the game it is today. The fascinating exploits of some of the world's famous poker players are shared, from Johnny Chan to the Hendon Mob.

Having located poker in a contemporary context, the book continues to explain the many aspects of the game that have helped to establish it as one of the more enduring of human pastimes. There are chapters which explain the basic poker skills with an extra focus on the essential knowledge required to enable anyone to play with a degree of confidence, on the assumption that the reader has no actual playing experience. From the deal to the showdown, there will be explanations of how to play, how to bet, and how to distinguish a potential winning hand from a likely loser. Other important facets to be covered are simple tactical play, betting strategies and the elements involved in bluffing opponents. Since poker has a vocabulary all its own, the terminology will also be explained.

The final chapters continue to develop some of the basic concepts and highlight more sophisticated elements of poker play with a view to helping regular players improve their game. The difference between playing in tournaments and playing cash games will be considered, along with the contrasting features of fixed-limit, pot-limit and no-limit poker. These stylistic differences present any serious poker player with a wealth of options when it comes to choosing which game to play and for how much. An appreciation of their impact on any poker game is especially important now that the boom in online poker has extended its reach into so many homes.

The illustrations and comments throughout are intended to supplement the text and underline key points regarding play. Finally, a guide to other publications and a comprehensive and detailed glossary of all the terms used in the many card games covered is included at the back of the book for further reference.

Right: Casinos can be a good setting for enjoying a game of cards. They are safe, friendly and smoke-free environments. The dealers are also trained to run the games professionally.

CARD GAMES

Hundreds of card games have been devised over the centuries, but only a few have had a lasting appeal. Some have very complex rules requiring a lot of practice and great skill, while others are simply a game of luck.

HISTORY OF PLAYING CARDS

Where, when, how and why playing cards originated is still a matter of considerable historical controversy. What is now known for certain is that on New Year's Eve 969, the Chinese Emperor Mu-tsung enjoyed a game of 'domino cards' with his favourite wife. It has also been discovered that what the Chinese called 'money cards', which seem to have originated around the same time as 'domino cards', did bear a close resemblance to their later Western counterparts.

Whatever the exact circumstance of their origins, it is clear that the knowledge of playing cards spread gradually westwards – either across Central Asia and through Persia or, according to some scholars, via India – to reach the Islamic world. It was from there, probably from Egypt, that knowledge of cards eventually crossed the Mediterranean to reach Spain and Italy at about the same time in the late 1300s.

As far as is known, the first brief mention of playing cards comes in a Catalan document dating from 1371, where they are termed *naip*. In 1377, the Italian city of Florence passed a statute regulating the playing of 'a certain card game called *naibbe*, which has been recently introduced into these parts'. That same year, Johannes van Rheinfelden, a monk based in Basle, described playing cards in more detail, writing of a deck of 52 cards. Each of the deck's four suits consisted of 10 numbered cards from One to Ten and three court cards – a King and two Marshals and no Queen or Jack.

Although no physical evidence of it survives, the card deck Johannes was describing had more than a passing resemblance to the decks the Egyptians devised. These consisted of 52 cards, divided into four suits – swords, polo sticks, cups and coins. Each suit consisted of 10 'spot' cards from One to Ten, which were identified by the number of suit symbols or 'pips' on each one, plus three court cards: *Malik* (King), *Na'ib Malik* (Viceroy or Deputy King) and *Thani Na'ib* (Second Under-Deputy).

SUITS AND SUIT SYSTEMS

The composition and design of playing cards varied as knowledge of them spread across Europe. Although the number of cards in a deck was not a constant, the inclusion of numbered cards and court cards plus the division into different suits were standard features from early on.

Early Italian decks contained 56 cards, including four types of court cards – King, Queen, Knight and Knave – and were split into suits of swords, cups, batons and coins. The Spanish soon replaced the Queens with *Caballeros* (mounted knights), while the Germans dropped the Queen in favour of *König* (King), *Obermann* (Upper Man) and *Untermann* (Lower Man). The Germans also replaced the Italian suit symbols with bells, hearts, leaves and acorns. In fact, they went on to experiment with a wide variety of suit symbols, including wine flagons, drinking cups, books, printers' pads and animals, well into the 16th century and beyond.

Left: The Death tarot card, from the Gringonneur pack, a 15th-century Italian set of tarot cards. Tarot cards were originally simply regular playing cards, and were not used as fortune-telling aids until at least the 18th century.

Centre: The Moon, an Italian tarot card, *c.*1490. Italy has a long-standing reputation for beautiful tarot decks derived from the first models of the 15th century.

Far left: The Page of Coins, from a pack of tarot cards (*c.*1483). Traditional Italian playing cards of the 15th century used swords, batons, cups and coins.

Left: 16th-century European playing card designs featuring acorns and trees. The four suits (Spades, Hearts, Diamonds and Clubs) used in most of the world today originated in France in 1480. The *trèfle* (Club) was probably copied from the acorn; the *pique* (Spade) from the leaf.

Below: Various cards from a Chinese game, including a fish and a stiltwalker. Chinese playing cards are thin and long so that several cards can be held at the same time, overlapped in a vertical arrangement.

NAMING THE COURT CARDS

The French paid particular attention to the design and naming of the court cards, often giving them the names of specific heroes and heroines from history and fable. In Rouen, a major centre of French card manufacture until this was moved to Paris, early choices for the identities of the Kings included King Solomon, the biblical ruler of the Israelites; the Roman emperor Augustus; Clovis, ruler of the Franks; and the Byzantine emperor Constantine the Great. By the time of Henri IV (1557–1610), the Kings were widely considered to be representations of King David, Alexander the Great, Julius Caesar and the Holy Roman Emperor Charlemagne.

The Knaves, or Jacks, as they were eventually to become, were the Trojan hero Hector; *La Hire* (Etienne de Vignolles), comrade-in-arms of Joan of Arc; Ogier, one of Charlemagne's knights; and Sir Lancelot from Arthurian legend. The Queens were the warrior-goddess Minerva (who was thought to represent Joan of Arc); Rachel, Joseph's biblical mother; Argine, which is an anagram of Regina (the Latin for 'queen'); and the Old Testament prophetess Judith.

THE ANGLO-AMERICAN DECK

The French suit system became the standard in England, from where it was exported to the British colonies in America, and is thus the ancestor of the 52-card deck that is in international use today. Modern card players know these as Anglo-American cards.

The Anglo-American deck consists of 13 ranks of each of the four suits – Spades, Hearts, Diamonds and Clubs. The court cards are modelled on the ones first produced by the celebrated French card makers in Rouen of the late 16th and early 17th centuries. Each suit includes an Ace, King, Queen and Jack with the remaining cards

in each suit being numbered from Ten down to Two. The court cards bear single pips (symbols of their suit) while the numbered cards carry the appropriate number of pips. Originally, Kings were always the highest cards in a suit, but, by the late 1400s, the previously lowest cards – the Aces – ranked over them (although in some games, players can specify whether Aces are high or low).

Two Jokers complete the standard deck. These were a 19th-century innovation, which card historians believe were devised by Euchre players – Euchre was thought to have originated in Alsace and been brought to America during the 1860s. In some games, the joker serves as a 'wild card' (which can be used to represent any other card) or as an additional trump (card of a suit nominated to be of higher value). Most card games, however, require one or both Jokers to be removed from the pack before play can start. Other 19th-century practical refinements introduced by the Americans include corner and edge indices (identifying marks), which enabled players to hold their cards close together in a fan in one hand as opposed to two; varnished surfaces, for ease of shuffling; and rounded corners, to reduce wear and tear. Finally, court cards became reversible and Knaves became Jacks.

Games for Friends and Family

The world of card games is endlessly fascinating. There are games available to suit practically any taste or age. Some are intuitive; others are intellectually challenging. What the majority of them have in common is that they are action-packed and speedy. Unlike board games, card games do not keep their players hanging on in suspense waiting for their turn to come around.

Patience and Solitaire Games

Card games for a single player are generically termed Patience in Europe and Solitaire in America. Playing them successfully demands clear thinking and concentration during play. David Parlett, the British card authority, described such games as 'the mental equivalent of jogging'.

Typically, the aim in solitaire games is to play out all the cards in the pack by arranging them in a specific order – usually in suit sequences, starting with the Ace and leading up to the King – with the aid of a preset layout. This acts as a workspace for the cards so that they can be sorted. When this is accomplished, the game is said to have 'come out'.

Trick-taking Games

For many people the attraction of cards lies in playing against other players. Outplay games, as they are termed by experts, make up by far the largest category of card games. Each player is dealt a hand of cards and each in turn plays one or more cards to the table. The game ends when one or all players run out of cards to play.

Above: A 17th-century French painting (artist unknown) depicting the making of playing cards, reproduced by means of hand-coloured woodcuts.

Above: A child turns over a card in the hope of finding a match in the Memory game, a quintessential family game that tests card-recall skills.

Most outplay games are trick-taking games, in which each player in turn plays a card face up to the table. This round of cards is called 'making a trick', and playing the first card is termed 'leading'. The card that wins the trick is either the highest of the suit originally led, or, if 'trumps' (cards of a suit nominated to be of higher value) are played, the highest card of that trump suit. Winning a trick often wins that round of cards and allows that player to choose which suit to lead next.

The way in which the trump suit is selected varies. In some games, the choice of trumps is random. They are selected by cutting the deck and exposing a card, usually at the end of the deal. In other games, the winner of the auction – in which the players bid against each other to make a certain number of tricks or points – decides what the trump suit is to be. Winning the right to choose trumps is therefore a powerful incentive in encouraging players to bid.

There are two ways of scoring such games. In what are termed point-trick games, the value of the tricks is affected by which cards they contain. The players are rewarded or penalized for capturing certain cards, each one of which has a pre-assigned value. This type of game includes Manille. In plain-trick games such as Ombre, on the other hand, it is only the number of tricks taken that matters. Play ends when some or all of the players run out of cards, at which point scores are totalled. The winner places the trick face down on the table and leads to the next trick. In games such as Piquet, the aim is both to win tricks and to score for card combinations.

Non-trick Games

Many card games are based on principles other than the taking of tricks. Some are children's classics, passed down through generations, and many are for adults, but they are all worth investigating. For example, Cribbage, an adding-up game in which the aim is to score or avoid scoring certain totals, is generally thought to date from the early 17th century.

In catch and collect games, the objective is to capture all the cards. Games such as Snap and Happy Families are simple children's games, while others such as Gops are far more complex. Fishing games such as Casino are particularly appealing. They are matching games in which each player competes to match the cards in hand with the ones laid out face up on the table. If the cards match, they are placed face down in front of the player who captured them. If there is no match, the card that was played is added to the layout on the table.

In shedding games, such as Michigan, the object is to get rid of all the cards as quickly as possible or to avoid being the last player holding cards. In collecting games, the object is to collect sets of matched cards (melds). The most popular of such games is undoubtedly Rummy – specifically, Gin Rummy, whose enormous popularity stems from the fact that, while it is simple to pick up, play can become very skilled and challenging. Rummy-type games are also known as draw and discard games, because each player has a hand of cards which he tries to improve through drawing and discarding. The player can either draw a card from the face-down stock of cards or from the face-up discard pile, and ends his turn by placing a card on the discard pile.

Above: Card play has a long-established set of procedures amounting almost to ritual. The shuffle is among them – it cannot be taught in words, only copied from watching good practitioners.

In banking games, such as Blackjack and Baccarat, an element of gambling is introduced. One player, the banker, takes on each of the other players individually to see who has the best hand.

Playing the Game

Card-playing involves many rituals and conventions, but they are worth following because they are mostly designed to stop anyone having an unfair advantage. You should establish whether you're playing for money or not, what the penalties are for cheating, and at what point the game will cease (after a target score is reached or after a number of deals, for example). When choosing a game to play, look for one that suits the number of players and their card-playing abilites. It is customary to shuffle and cut the cards before each deal.

Far left: A 19th-century playing card trimmer (c.1870). Early playing cards were printed on uncoated stock and were occasionally trimmed to eliminate the frayed edges.

Left: *The Illustrated Book of Patience Games* by Angelo Lewis (a.k.a. Professor Hoffman), published in 1917 and reprinted several times.

PATIENCE AND SOLITAIRE GAMES

PATIENCE GAMES, KNOWN AS SOLITAIRE GAMES IN THE USA, FALL INTO TWO MAIN CATEGORIES. SOME ARE DEVISED FOR A SINGLE PLAYER, THE AIM GENERALLY BEING TO SORT CARDS INTO SUIT SEQUENCES ON A LAYOUT OR TABLEAU. IN COMPETITIVE PATIENCE, SEVERAL PLAYERS COMPETE TO BE THE FIRST TO COMPLETE A GAME. SPECIFIC RULES GOVERN HOW THE CARDS CAN BE ARRANGED AND REARRANGED. THESE SOLITARY GAMES ARE ESPECIALLY SUITABLE FOR PLAY AGAINST A COMPUTER.

Since the first Patience games were devised in the mid-19th century, they have mushroomed. When Britain's Lady Cadogan produced her *Illustrated Games of Patience* in 1874, she was able to list only 24 of them. In contrast, what is generally regarded as today's standard reference, David Parlett's *Penguin Book of Patience,* covers over 250 forms (500, with variations). Even that is not the end of the story. The *Solitaire Central Rulebook* on the Internet currently offers 1,713 different games, and although the list includes some duplication, its compilers conservatively estimate there to be around 1,500 different types of patience.

The aim of the game is to change the position of the cards by 'building' – that is, transferring cards around the tableau. Some can be played immediately, others not until certain blocking cards have been removed. In most games, play starts by placing the cards known as 'foundations', generally the four Aces, into position. After this,

the aim is to build on each foundation in sequence and in suit from the Ace through to the King. The gap that is created by moving cards is called a 'space' and knowing how to take advantage of this is a major factor in manipulating the tableau to best advantage. If a player is successful in building the entire pack on to the foundations, the patience 'comes out' and the game is won. If it becomes impossible to sort the cards further, the game is lost and must be abandoned.

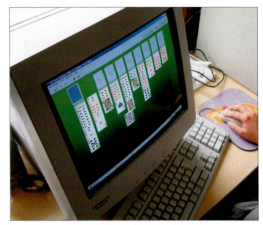

Above: Solitaire is particularly suitable for play against a computer. Many Solitaire software programs can be downloaded from the Internet at no charge.

KLONDIKE

This is probably the best-known game of its ilk in the world, so much so, that many people simply call it Patience or Solitaire without realizing that it has its own name.

You will need: 52-card deck; no Jokers	
Card ranking: None	
Players: One	
Ideal for: 4+	

OBJECT
To build all four 'suit stacks' from Ace to King.

THE DEAL
Deal seven cards in a row, left to right, upturning the first card. Beginning one place along each time, deal another row, again exposing the first card, until you end up with a 'tableau' (see below) of seven columns, the first comprising a single card, the second two, the third three and so on up to seven. Each column should end with an upturned card. The remaining cards are left face down to form the 'stock pile'.

PLAY
Three cards are turned face up from the stock, but only the top one can be played. If this can be used, the second of the three cards becomes available for play, and so again with the final one. Any exposed Aces from the tableau or at the top of the three cards are removed and placed above the tableau to form the foundation of a suit stack.

Cards that are within the tableau may be built down numerically, although they must alternate in colour – a black Five may be played on a red Six, for instance – while a sequence of cards can be moved in its entirety from one pile to another. Each time a face-up card

(or sequence) is moved, the next face-down card is turned over and becomes available for play, with the proviso that in the event an empty space is created on the tableau, only a King can fill it. Exposed cards can be laid in sequence on top of a stacked Ace provided that they are of the same suit.

When all options have been exhausted, any card or cards remaining from the three taken from the stock are placed face up on a 'waste pile' and another three cards turned up, this process being repeated until the stock is exhausted. At any point, the lowest exposed card in a column can be played onto the foundations, or another pile. If the stock becomes exhausted, the waste pile can replace it, but this can happen only twice.

CONCLUSION
The game ends when either all the suits are stacked – the chances of this happening are 1 in 30 – or when no more moves are possible.

Below: In the layout shown, the A♠ should be moved above the tableau to begin a suit stack, with the 2♠ placed on top of it. The card that was under the 2♠ is then turned face upwards. The 9♠ is placed on the 10♦. The card under the 9♠ is then turned face upwards.

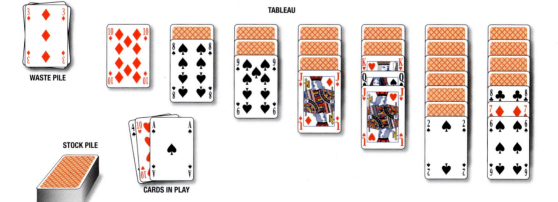

WASTE PILE

TABLEAU

STOCK PILE

CARDS IN PLAY

ACCORDION

It requires persistence to play Accordion successfully, as it takes quite a few deals for the game to come out.

You will need: 52 cards; no Jokers
Card ranking: None
Players: One
Ideal for: 7+

Below: The cards have been dealt in a line from left to right. The repositioned cards, after the moves (King on King, Heart on Heart etc.) have been taken, are shown underneath.

OBJECT

To finish with all the cards in one pile.

THE DEAL

Unlike other games of this genre, there is no tableau – the player simply deals cards singly face up to form a long line from left to right. There is no maximum or minimum number, but experts favour dealing no more than 13 cards at a time.

PLAY

Whenever a card matches the suit or rank of the card immediately to the left of it, it is put on top of the card it matches. This is termed 'packing', after which all the cards to the right are squeezed up to close the gap. Cards can also be moved three places to the left. Packing continues until there is nothing left to pack, at which point more cards are dealt on to the end of the line. Multiple cards must be moved as a complete pile, since matching is limited to the top card. A pile may never be split or separated.

CONCLUSION

The game is won if all the cards can be reduced to a single stack. If not, shuffle the cards and try again.

ACES UP

Somewhat unfairly also known as Idiot's Delight, this is a fast-moving game that requires more skill to play than may be apparent at first glance.

You will need: 52 cards; no Jokers
Card ranking: None
Players: One
Ideal for: 10+

Below: On the left are the four cards dealt at the start of the game. On the right are the two cards left after the lowest two Diamonds have been discarded.

OBJECT

To end up with all four Aces face up in a row and all the other cards discarded in the waste pile.

THE DEAL, PLAY AND CONCLUSION

Four cards are dealt face up in a row. Any card of lower rank and the same suit of another top card can be removed from play. Aces are the highest rank. When all possible cards have been removed, four more cards are then dealt, on top of the remaining ones or on any spaces created. The process continues until all the top cards are of different suits. Four more cards are then dealt on top of these.

If one of the four piles becomes empty, the player can move any top card from any of the other piles into the empty space to create more possible plays. The objective is to remove all cards except for the Aces. The exposed cards precipitate the removal of others as play progresses. The only way to get at cards beneath an Ace is to move the Ace to an empty pile.

Aces Up is easy to play, but it is not easy to win. It all comes down to deciding which card to play into an empty space. To win, you need to end up with just the four Aces face up. If there are any other cards left on the table once the last set of four has been dealt, the game is lost.

LABYRINTH

This is an unusual game in that players are allowed to take the top card of each column as well as the bottom for building on the Ace piles. There may be many gaps in the tableau, giving it the appearance of a labyrinth, as spaces are not filled, except in the first row.

You will need:	52-card deck; no Jokers
Card ranking:	None, but they are stacked in ascending order
Players:	One
Ideal for:	10+

OBJECT

The aim of this game is to build each Ace up into a pile of 13 cards that are arranged in ascending rank order and all in the same suit.

THE DEAL

The four Aces are laid out face up in a row at the top of the table. The rest of the pack is then shuffled and a row of eight cards is dealt face up just below the Aces. Further rows are dealt out during the course of the game.

PLAY

All the cards in the first row are available to start building on the Aces, with new cards being dealt to replace them as needed. When as many cards as possible have been played and any spaces filled, another row of eight cards is dealt. Play proceeds as before, but with one important exception: it is against the rules of the game to fill any more spaces. Instead, once play can go no further, a new row of eight cards must be dealt across the columns underneath the previous row before any further building can take place. All deals must be made in the same direction, usually from left to right.

The last row may consist of fewer than eight cards if cards were used to fill the first row. Strictly speaking this row should be dealt, as far as it can go, in the same direction, but many players prefer to choose which columns to deal the cards to in order to increase the chances of getting the game to come out.

Only the cards in the bottom and top rows are strictly playable. If one can be played from the top row of cards, the card in the bottom row can be played and so on.

Right: The scenario after the deal: the four Aces laid out in a row followed by eight cards dealt from the stock face up underneath.

CONCLUSION

The game ends when the stock has been exhausted and every possible move made. If each stack is complete up to Kings, the player has won. If not, better luck next time.

Right: The 2♠, 3♠ and 2♦ are stacked on the Aces and new cards are dealt to fill in the spaces in the row of eight underneath.

SPITE AND MALICE

This is a competitive Patience game, sometimes known as Cat and Mouse. It is a variation of the late 19th-century Continental game known as Crapette, Cripette, Robuse and Rabouge.

You will need: Two 52-card decks – one without Jokers and another with four Jokers added as wild cards

Card ranking: None, but cards must be stacked in succession; e.g. Two on Ace, Three on Two

Players: Two

Ideal for: 10+

OBJECT

To be the first to get rid of what is termed a 'riddance pile' of 26 cards by playing them to eight piles that are gradually built up in the centre of the table, starting with an Ace and ending with a King. Suits are irrelevant.

THE DEAL

After it has been shuffled thoroughly, each player receives 26 cards from the 52-card pack without Jokers. These are placed face down to form a riddance pile, and the top card (the 'up-card') of each is turned face up. Both players are then dealt five cards from the second 56-card pack (with Jokers), the remainder forming the stock to be used during the course of play and placed face down between the two players. Jokers can represent any card.

Above: Success – the eight piles from Ace to King are complete. In the game, each stack is turned face down after it is finished.

PLAY

A turn consists of a choice of moves. If the up-card is an Ace, the card must be played to start a centre pile. If it is any Two and an Ace has been played, it must be played to that Ace. Playing to a centre pile entitles you to

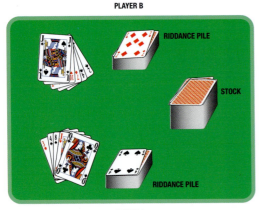

PLAYER B

RIDDANCE PILE

STOCK

RIDDANCE PILE

PLAYER A

Above: The scenario at the beginning of Spite and Malice. Both players have 26 cards in their riddance piles, the top card turned up, plus five cards in their hands. The remaining stock pile is placed between the two players.

another turn. So does playing off all five cards in one's hand, after which you draw five more from the stock pile. Cards in a riddance pile can be played only to one of the centre piles. Once a pile is completed (i.e. up to King), it is turned face down and set aside.

The alternative to playing to the centre is to play any card from your hand to a discard pile, except an Ace, replacing it with a card from the stock pile. Up to four such piles may be started by the same player, otherwise players may add to the top of an existing discard pile, if the rank of the discard matches or is one below that of the current top card. The top discard can be played off at any time to a centre pile. If a player cannot make a move, the opposing player plays alone until such time as the frozen player can play again. If both players freeze, all the cards in play except for those in the riddance piles are shuffled and redealt.

SCORING AND CONCLUSION

The winner scores five points, plus a point for every card the loser has not played from his riddance pile.

When the stock is down to 12 cards, all the completed centre piles are combined with it to form a new one. Play continues until one player succeeds in playing off the last card from his riddance pile.

SPIT

Also known as Speed, there are no turns in this game – opponents play simultaneously. This puts a premium on physical speed and mental agility, both of which are essential if one player is to succeed in playing faster than the other.

OBJECT

The object of the game is to get rid of all your cards faster than your opponent.

THE DEAL

Deal 26 cards to two players from a well-shuffled 52-card pack. Each player deals a layout of five stock piles arranged in a row. The first contains a single card, the second two cards and so on up to five.

All the cards are dealt face down, and the top card of each pile is then turned face up. The 11 remaining cards are the 'spit' cards. These must not be examined before they are played.

You will need: 52 cards

Card ranking: None, but cards can only be played to piles in a certain order (see below)

Players: Two

Ideal for: 10+

PLAY

Both players call 'Spit' while turning over the first spit card in their hands. The two cards are placed side-by-side between the players' respective stock piles to form two spit piles. Players now play simultaneously as fast as they can. They can play the turn-up from any of the stock piles on to either spit pile, provided that the card being played is one rank higher or lower than the turn-up. Suits are irrelevant. Alternatively, if one or more of the stock piles have their top cards face down, these can be turned up, while a turn-up can be moved into an empty stock pile space.

A card counts as played as soon as it touches a pile or space. The opposing player can play on it immediately. If neither player can play, both spit again, turn up the next spit card and place it on top of the particular spit pile they started. Play then continues as before. If neither can play and one player has run out of spit cards, the other spits alone on to either pile.

If one player gets rid of all the stock cards or both of them run out of spit cards, a new layout is dealt. Both players choose a spit pile, ideally the smaller one, by slapping it with their hands. If both choose the same one, the player hitting it first has preference.

Both players then add any remaining spit or stock cards to their respective piles, shuffle their cards and deal new layouts. When the players are ready, they call 'Spit' and play again. If one of the players has fewer than 15 cards, he should deal them into five piles as far as he can and turn each top card over. As this player is unable to spit, there will be only one spit pile, started by the other player.

CONCLUSION

When one spit pile remains and a player runs out of stock cards, the other plays on until he gets stuck. He collects all the cards from the table, deals and spits again. The first to run out of stock and spit cards wins.

PLAYER B

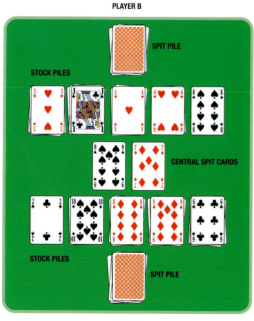

STOCK PILES

SPIT PILE

CENTRAL SPIT CARDS

STOCK PILES

SPIT PILE

PLAYER A

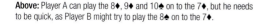

Above: Player A can play the 8♦, 9♦ and 10♠ on to the 7♦, but he needs to be quick, as Player B might try to play the 8♠ on to the 7♦.

NERTS

Also known as Pounce, Racing Demon, Peanuts and Squeal, this is a competitive Patience game that can be played by more than two players if you have enough packs of cards.

You will need: Two (or more) different 52-card packs; no Jokers	
Card ranking: None, but piles must be built in order	
Players: Two (or more)	
Ideal for: 7+	

OBJECT

To be the first player to play all the cards in his 'nerts' pile on to four foundation piles.

THE DEAL

Each player plays with his own pack. Both players deal a nerts pile, 12 cards face down and the last face up, with four more placed face up to form a row of work piles. The remaining cards are kept face down as a stock.

PLAY

Players use the work piles to sort their cards. They are built in descending order and alternating in colour so, for example, a red Six would be placed on a black Seven. The lowest-ranked cards are available to be played on to the foundations. Players may transfer any card from one work pile to another, together with all the cards on top of it. Foundation piles, each of which must be started with an Ace, are built upwards in suit and sequence. Any player can play to any pile when they hold the next card in the sequence. If two players choose the same pile, the fastest one wins and the other player has to take his back. Foundation cards are communal, with all players having access. Cards from nerts piles can be played to empty spaces in work piles, on to existing work piles, or on to foundation piles. As soon as the top card of a nerts pile is played, the next is turned face up. When a player's pile is exhausted, he can call 'Nerts', stopping play. Players, if stuck, are allowed to turn over stock pile cards three at a time and place them in a waste pile, from which the top card can be played. If every player gets stuck, each waste pile is turned to form a new stock, the top card of the stock being transferred to the bottom.

SCORING AND CONCLUSION

One point is scored for each card played to a foundation pile. Two points are deducted for each card left in a player's nerts pile. Deals are played up to an agreed target.

PLAYER B

PLAYER A

Above: Each player has a nerts pile. The top card is face up and there are four face-up cards that form the work piles.

Right: Player A can play the 2♠ from his nerts pile on to the Ace in his foundation pile and the 3♦ from his work pile on to his opponent's foundation pile. Player B can also play the 3♣ from his nerts pile on to his foundation pile.

PLAYER B

PLAYER A

POKER PATIENCE

Also known as Poker Solitaire and Poker Squares, this game is unusual because only 25 cards are actively employed. Unlike most solitaire games, where the aim is to put cards into a preset order, the aim here is to put the cards into certain combinations that correspond to standard Poker hands.

OBJECT

To move cards one at a time out of the stock pile and position them anywhere on a 'grid' of five cards by five cards, so that each of the latter's rows and columns forms the best possible Poker hand ranking. The better the hands that can be created, the higher the score. To win the game, a player needs to score at least 200 points in the American system or 70 points in the English one. The game can be played competitively, in which case the highest score wins.

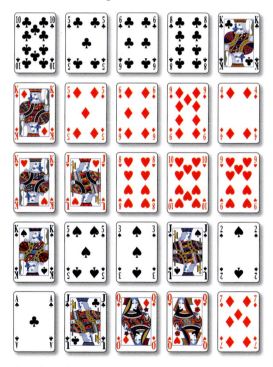

Above: The first four rows here all show a Flush while the final row has a Pair (of Queens). The first column has Three of a Kind (Kings), the second a Full House, the third a Pair (two Sixes), and the fourth a Straight.

You will need: 52 cards; no Jokers
Card ranking: See 'Scoring and Ranking', below
Players: One (or can be played competitively)
Ideal for: 14+

THE DEAL

The player shuffles the pack and deals the first 25 cards face up into a pile to become the stock for the first grid. The remaining cards are kept in reserve for a second one.

PLAY

A typical strategy is to try to establish Flushes on the first four rows and Full Houses, Fours of a Kind, or Straights on the columns. The last row is often used as a dumping ground for cards that do not fit elsewhere in the layout.

Straights are high scoring but are the hardest to create. The alternative is to settle for lower-scoring, but safer, hands, such as Pairs and Three of a Kind. Even the best plans can be spoilt by bad luck. Once a card has been placed, it cannot be moved, nor may the next card in the stock be examined until the turn-up is placed.

SCORING AND RANKING

There are two scoring systems – American and English (given in brackets). Cards are also ranked as follows:

- 100 (30) points for a Royal Flush: A Straight Flush (see below) up to Ace.
- 75 (30) for a Straight Flush: Five cards in sequence and of the same suit.
- 50 (18) for Four of a Kind: Four cards of the same face value.
- 25 (10) for a Full House: Three of a Kind and a Pair.
- 20 (five) for a Flush: Five cards of the same suit.
- 15 (12) for a Straight: A sequence of five cards in any suit.
- 10 (6) for Three of a Kind: Three cards of the same face value.
- 5 (3) for Two Pairs of the same face value.
- 2 (1) for One Pair of the same face value.

CONCLUSION

The game is finished when all the cards have been laid out on to the grid.

POINT-TRICK GAMES

WINNING AND LOSING POINT-TRICK GAMES DEPENDS ON THE POINT VALUES OF INDIVIDUAL CARDS TAKEN WITHIN TRICKS AND NOT ON THE ACTUAL NUMBER OF TRICKS WON OR LOST. A TRICK IS A ROUND OF CARDS, WHERE ONE CARD IS PLAYED BY EACH PLAYER IN THE GAME. A TRICK IS WON WITH THE HIGHEST CARD OF THE SUIT LED OR BY THE HIGHEST TRUMP. MANY GAMES INCLUDE BIDDING, IN WHICH SOME BIDS HAVE AIMS SUCH AS LOSING ALL THE TRICKS.

The games range from France's Manille, which originated as Malilla in Spain, to Stovkahra, the only surviving descendant of a strange Italian game called Trappola, first played in Venice in 1524. Stovkahra is a rare Romanian game, in which the aim is to be the first partnership to win 100 points. On its home turf, it is played with a 32-card German-suited pack (the German suits of Acorns, Leaves, Hearts and Bells correspond to Clubs, Spades, Hearts and Diamonds, repectively). Players score by declaring card combinations, such as Three or Four of a Kind, other than Eights and Nines, taking card points in tricks and winning any trick with a Seven. Winning the first and the last trick with a Seven is worth bonus points – 52 points and 26 points, respectively.

Point-trick games have not just been confined to the West, and many games not mentioned in this book are popular in the East. In Japan, Etoni, or 'capturing pictures', originated in the early 1900s, while Napoleon (not the British game of the same name) is one of the country's most popular games. Mighty, played mostly in Korea, is a related game in which Aces, Kings, Queens, Jacks and frequently Tens are worth a point each. The A♠, which is known in Japanese as *ohrumaita* or simply *maita* ('almighty' or 'mighty'), enjoys a special status. It can beat any other card, including trumps.

Above: Japanese women playing cards (c.1867). The concept of card games was introduced in Japan as early as the 16th century by Portugese traders.

MANILLE

There are a number of versions of this partnership game, of which the most popular are Manille Muette, which is played in silence; Manille Parlée, in which partners are permitted to share a single piece of information about their cards, or suggest what card or suit to lead; and Manille à l'Envers (Reverse Manille). Manille was France's national card game from around 1870 until the end of the Second World War, when Belote finally eclipsed it in popularity.

You will need: 52 cards; no Jokers

Card ranking: The Ten ranks highest, followed by Ace, King, Queen, Jack and Nine to Two

Players: Four

Ideal for: 10+

OBJECT

The aim is to be the first to win two successive deals, or to secure an agreed number of points.

THE DEAL

Each player is dealt eight cards, four at a time, with the dealer turning his last card up to establish the trump suit – that is, the suit of cards that outranks all others – laying it on the table until the first card is led.

PLAY

The player to the dealer's left leads to the first trick. Players have to follow suit if they can; if not, they can play a trump. The highest card of the suit led takes the trick, or the highest trump, if trumps are played. If a player's partner is winning a trick, that player is not obliged to follow suit or trump. If an opponent is winning, however, suit must be followed or a trump played. The highest card of the suit led or the highest trump takes the trick and the winner leads to the next.

SCORING

Each trick taken is worth a point. Five extra points are scored for a trick containing a Ten (*Manille*), four for an Ace (*Manillon*), three for a King, two for a Queen and one for a Jack. If a trick contains more than one of these, points are scored for each.

CONCLUSION

To win a hand, a partnership needs to score a minimum of 35 points. Convention has it that the target score for game is either 100 or 200 points.

PLAYER C

PLAYER B

PLAYER D

TRICK

TRICK

TRUMP

PLAYER A

Above: Player D discards, as his partner is winning the trick with the 10♣. He could have followed suit with the A♣ or J♣, or played a trump with the Q♥, but since his partner is winning, he can hold on to his better cards.

PLAYER C

PLAYER B

PLAYER D

TRICK

TRICK

TRUMP

PLAYER A

Above: Unable to follow suit in this trick, Player D has played the trump (4♣), thus winning it. Player D's partnership scores an extra three points for the King and an extra five for the Ten.

SPANISH SOLO

Widely popular in Spanish-speaking South America as well as in Spain, this game is a cross between Tresillo, the modern form of Ombre, and Manille. Unlike the latter, it includes bidding. Each player puts one of their chips, coins or counters into the pool before starting.

You will need: 36-card pack, Tens, Nines, Eights and Twos having been removed; gambling chips/counters

Card ranking: Seven is highest, then Ace, King, Queen, etc.

Players: Three

Ideal for: 14+

OBJECT

The aim of the game is to fulfil a specified contract and/or score the most points in a hand.

THE DEAL

Each player is dealt 12 cards, four at a time.

BIDDING

There are three bids, which rank in the following order:

- *Juego* (Solo) – a bid to win at least 37 points (36 points if the bidder is the player to the dealer's left). It is worth two game points or four in Diamonds.
- *Bola* (Slam) – a bid to win every trick, having named wanted card and exchanged an unwanted one for it. Its value is eight game points, 12 in Diamonds.
- *Bola sin Pedir* (No-call Slam) – the highest bid, contracting to take every trick without exchanging a card. Its value is 16 points, or 20 in Diamonds.

THE AUCTION

Starting with the player to the dealer's left, each player in turn must either bid or pass. If the former, the bid must be higher than the one preceding it. If a player passes, he puts another chip into the pool and sits out the rest of the auction. The successful bidder becomes the soloist and announces trumps. If these are Diamonds, the value of the bid increases, as shown above. If everyone passes, it is down to the dealer to choose trumps. The hand is still played.

PLAY

The player to the dealer's right leads. The other players must follow suit if possible. Otherwise, they may play a trump or, failing that, any card. The highest card of the suit led wins the trick, or the highest trump if any are played. The most valuable cards in each suit are the Seven (*Malilla*), followed by the Ace, King, Queen and Jack. The soloist now tries to fulfil the bid and other players try to score as many points as they can.

SCORING

- Five points for a trick containing a Seven.
- Four points for a trick containing an Ace.
- Three points for a trick containing a King.
- Two points for a trick containing a Queen.
- One point for a trick containing a Jack.

The winner of each trick scores an extra point.

CONCLUSION

The player scoring the most card points wins the hand. He then receives two chips from the player with the fewest number of points and one chip from the player with the second lowest score. If a soloist's contract is successful, he receives the appropriate number of chips from each opponent, two chips for a successful *Juego*, for instance, and wins the pool. If not, he pays the value of the failed bid to the opposing players and doubles what is in the pool.

Left: With a long strong suit in Diamonds, the natural bid for this player is *Juego* (Solo), naming Diamonds as trumps.

FIFTEENS

This old German game is straightforward to play, but has a twist in its tail concerning the cards that can be led.

OBJECT

To win as many points as possible and end the game with the most chips.

THE DEAL

Players are dealt eight cards each face down.

PLAY

The player to the left of dealer leads to the first trick, and the highest card played wins. The winner of that first trick must lead the same suit to the next, playing his highest card. The next person to win the lead does the same. If he holds no cards of that suit, he must revert to the suit played to take the previous trick or, if still void, the one before that. The next to play also does the same.

You will need: 32-card pack with those below Seven removed; no Jokers; gambling chips/counters

Card ranking: Standard

Players: Four

Ideal for: 10+

A King and Queen of the same suit in a hand is known as a *Zwang* (force). A player holding one declares it upon leading the Queen. This forces the holder of the Ace to play it, leaving the King high. Otherwise, the Ace's holder is free to underplay in the hope of winning the King later.

SCORING AND CONCLUSION

Aces score five, Kings four, Queens three, Jacks two and Tens one. Each player calculates the value of the cards taken in tricks and pays a chip to the pot for every point he is short of 15, or wins a chip for every point that exceeds 15. Players settle up chips at the end of the game.

FORTY FOR KINGS

This 18th-century partnership game was played in France and Germany, where it was known as Quarante de Roi and Vierzig von König respectively.

OBJECT

The aim is to score points for *Cliques* (three or four court cards of the same rank) and for tricks (a round of cards) containing court cards (Kings, Queens, Jacks).

THE DEAL

Players are dealt eight cards in packets of three, two and three face down.

PLAY

The dealer shows his last card to set trumps. Each player then announces and scores for any *Cliques* held. The player to the left of the dealer leads. Players must follow suit or otherwise play any card. The highest card of the led suit or the highest trump takes the trick. The winner leads to the next. Each partnership scores for all the court cards it captures, adding this to its score for *Cliques*.

You will need: 32-card pack, the lowest card is Seven

Card ranking: King, Queen, Jack, Ace, Ten, Nine, Eight, Seven

Players: Four, in partnerships of two

Ideal for: 10+

SCORING AND CONCLUSION

Four Kings score 40 and three score 10, while Queens score 20 and eight, and Jacks score 13 and six. The court cards are worth five, four and three points each when they are captured in tricks. At the end of a trick, the partnerships score all the court cards they have taken and add the total to their scores for *Cliques*. Game is 150 points.

A running total of points is kept, and the first partnership with 150 points (or an agreed amount) wins.

Left: A *Clique* of three Kings is 10 points in Forty for Kings.

TRESSETTE

One of Italy's most popular card games, Tressette, unlike most positive point-trick games, is played without trumps. It is characterized by a distinctive signalling system between partners.

You will need: 40-card deck (Eights, Nines and Tens having been removed from a standard pack)

Card ranking: Three, Two, Ace, King, Queen, Jack, Seven, Six, Five, Four

Players: The standard version is a game for four, playing in partnerships of two, but it can be played by up to eight players

Ideal for: 14+

OBJECT

To score as many points in each hand as possible, until you have reached the winning total, usually 21.

THE DEAL

Each player is dealt 10 cards face down, five at a time.

SIGNALLING

When leading to a trick, three verbal or physical signals are allowed. A call of 'Busso' is a signal to the caller's partner to play the highest card of the suit that has been led, the sign being to tap the card or the table with a fist. Saying 'Volo' means that the caller has no more cards of the suit led, the sign being to glide the card slowly across the table. 'Striscio' means that the lead is the caller's strongest suit, in which case the sign is to flick the card quickly on to the table.

PLAY

The player to the left of the dealer leads. Players must follow suit or otherwise play any card. There are no trumps. The highest-ranking card of the suit led wins the trick, the winner leading to the next trick. The cards rank and count in descending order from Three, Two, Ace, King, Queen and Jack to Seven, Six, Five and Four.

SCORING

Only Aces and court cards have individual point values, but certain card combinations also score. Each Ace is worth a point and each Three, Two or court card scores one-third of a point. The winner of the last trick gets a further point. Any fractions in the end totals are ignored. Scores are rounded down to the nearest whole number.

Certain card combinations must be declared and scored at the end of the first trick. A player holding four Aces, Threes or Twos (Four of a Kind) scores four points, and holding three (Three of a Kind) scores three. A *Napoletana*, when a player holds a Three, Two and Ace of the same suit, is three points. When declaring a *Napoletana*, its suit must be specified. So, too, must the

missing suit be specified when declaring Three of a Kind, otherwise it is invalid. There are several ways to win more points. When a partnership takes all 10 tricks, the points are doubled. This is termed *Cappotto*. When a partership wins all the points, but not all the tricks, the points are trebled (known as *Stramazzo*). *Cappottone*, which occurs when a single player takes all the tricks, wins sixfold. *Strammazzone*, which occurs when one player wins all the points and the opposing partnership wins at least one trick, wins eightfold. *Collatondrione*, which occurs when a single player declares all 10 cards of a suit, wins 16-fold.

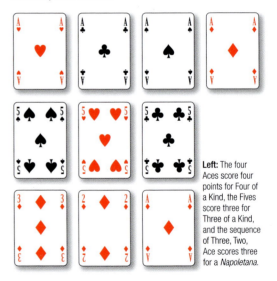

Left: The four Aces score four points for Four of a Kind, the Fives score three for Three of a Kind, and the sequence of Three, Two, Ace scores three for a *Napoletana*.

CONCLUSION

Once all 10 tricks have been played, each partnership scores the value of the cards it has taken in tricks, plus, if applicable, the point for taking the final trick. The partnership that scores 21 points first wins.

TERZIGLIO

Also known as Calabresella, this well-established Italian game is notable, like Tressette, for its unusual card rankings and lack of trumps. Unlike Tressette, there is a round of bidding, and card combinations are ignored and do not score.

You will need: 40-card deck (Eights, Nines and Tens removed from a standard pack)

Card ranking: A Three ranks as highest followed by Two, Ace, King, Queen, Jack and Seven to Four

Players: Optimally three players, although four can play if the dealer sits out the hand

Ideal for: 14+

OBJECT

The overall aim is to be the first player to reach 21 points by capturing tricks containing valuable cards.

THE DEAL

Each player is dealt 12 cards four at a time. The remaining four cards, the *Monte*, are placed face down on the table.

BIDDING AND EXCHANGING

Starting with the player to the dealer's left, each player bids or passes, and a player who has passed may not come in again. Each successive bid should improve on the last. The bids from low to high are:

- *Chiamo* (Call) – if successful, the bidder is entitled to ask if any of the other players is holding a specific card. If one is, he hands it over, getting a card back from the bidder in exchange. If not, the bidder picks up the *Monte*, discarding four cards face down to form a new one. Whoever wins the last trick will win the *Monte* and benefit from any card-points it may contain.
- *Solo* – same as above, but the bidder does not ask the others for a card.
- *Solissimo* – the player plays with the cards as dealt, does not call a card, takes the *Monte* and discards as above.
- *Solissimo Dividete* – here, the player may choose to increase the stakes by calling '*Dividete*' (Half each), whereby the opposing players each take two cards from the *Monte* and discard two.
- *Solissimo Scegliete* – here, by calling '*Scegliete*' (You choose), the four cards of the *Monte* are turned face up and the opposing players agree on the split, 2–2, 3–1, or 4–0, each discarding as many as they take accordingly.

PLAY

The player to the dealer's right leads to the first trick, unless *Solissimo* was bid, in which case the bidder leads. Players must follow suit if possible, otherwise they may play any card. There are no trumps. The person to place the highest card of the suit led wins the trick. The winner of each trick leads to the next one. To win the hand, the bidder must score at least six points, in which case each opponent loses points, depending on what was bid.

SCORING

Each Ace scores a point and each Three, Two or court card one-third of a point. The winner of the final trick not only scores a point for being last but also wins a bonus point for the *Monte*. This counts as an extra trick. *Chiamo* is worth one point, *Solo* two, *Solissimo* four, *Solissimo Dividete* eight and *Solissimo Scegliete* 16. Should the bid fail, the bidder's opponents score the points. If the bidder wins or loses every trick, the amount won or paid to their opponents is doubled. If he wins or loses all the points, the amount won or paid out is trebled.

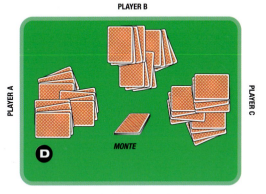

Above: Cards are dealt to each player in three packets of four, the remaining cards forming the *Monte*. Player B will be first to start the bidding, after which Player C leads to the first trick, unless Player B bids *Solissimo*.

CONCLUSION

The game ends when a player scores 21 points, but a target of 31 or 51 may be agreed.

CIAPANÒ

This intriguing game originated in Milan and is the reverse of Tressette. It is also known as Rovescino, Traversone, Tressette a non Prendere, Perdivinci and Vinciperdi.

OBJECT
To avoid taking any trick containing valuable cards, or winning the final trick, which carries an extra penalty.

THE DEAL
Each player is dealt the same number of cards – eight if there are five players, 10 for four, and 13 for three. In the last case, the dealer takes 14 cards and discards one, which is given to the winner of the last trick.

PLAY
The player to the dealer's right leads. Any card may be led, the other players following suit if they can. If not, they can play any card. There are no trumps. The highest card of the suit led takes the trick, the winner leading to the next.

You will need: 40-card deck (Eights, Nines and Tens removed from a standard pack)

Card ranking: Threes rank highest, followed by the Twos, the Aces, the court cards, Sevens, Sixes, Fives and Fours

Players: Three, four or five

Ideal for: 14+

SCORING
In this game, each Ace is worth a point and Threes, Twos and court cards score one-third of a point each. When all the tricks have been played, each player, with the exception of the player who took the final trick, adds up the value of the cards he has taken as penalty points. If there are any fractions left over once the points have been added up, these should be discounted. For instance, a player with three-and-a-third points would score only three points. A player with less than one point would score nothing.

The winner of the last trick scores the total of the other players' scores minus 11. The penalty for winning the last trick varies. It can count for one, two or three points depending on how the other tricks are distributed among the players. If one player wins all the points, this is termed *Cappotto*. He scores zero and the other players score 11 penalty points each. Once a player's cumulative score reaches 31 points or more, he drops out of the game, although by prior agreement this can be raised or lowered by 10 points.

CONCLUSION
When only two players are left in, the one with the lower score wins.

Left: 18th-century French playing cards. Originating in Milan and played widely in France, Ciapanò is typically played with Italian- or French-suited packs.

Below: The 3♠ and 3♥ are the highest cards in this hand, followed by A♠, K♦, Q♦, J♠, the 7♥ and 7♣, the 6♣ and the 2♥.

DA BAI FEN

Roughly translated, Da Bai Fen means 'competing for 100 points', which is the total number of card points in the pack. In China, where the game was invented, there are other versions.

You will need: 52 cards, with the addition of two Jokers as extra trumps

Card ranking: See 'Trumps and Ranks', below

Players: Four players, in partnership

Ideal for: 14+

OBJECT

To win tricks containing counting cards (Kings, Tens and Fives, worth 10, 10 and five points respectively), and to take the last trick of a hand, until your partnership has won a hand of every trump rank, finishing with Aces.

TRUMPS AND RANKS

There are 18 trumps: the two Jokers, the cards of the suit elected trumps during the deal, plus the other three cards of a particular rank (which at the start of the game is the Two). From highest to lowest, trumps rank as follows: red Joker, black Joker, the card of the trump rank and trump suit (2♠ initially, if Spades are trumps), the other three cards of the trump rank (2♥, 2♣, 2♦) and then the remaining cards of the trump suit from Ace down to Two.

At the start, Two is always the trump rank, so the player who first draws a Two in the deal and his partner become the declarers and play first. The player who drew the Two also has the right to declare its suit as trumps. The two players stay declarers until they lose a hand, when their opponents take over. Afterwards, the declarers' current score determines the trump rank. If, for example, they have 10 game points, the trump rank is Tens, 11 means that it is Jacks, 12 Queens, 13 Kings and 14 Aces.

THE DEAL

Players sit crosswise in agreed partnerships. One player at random is designated the 'starter', who shuffles the cards. They are then cut by either opponent before being placed face down on the table. The starter draws first, followed by the next player to the right and so on around the table. The draw continues until everyone has 12 cards in hand, with six remaining on the table.

Once a trump suit has been declared, the player who declared it picks up the six table cards and discards six cards face down. If no trumps are declared, the six table cards are turned up one at a time. The first card of the trump rank to appear determines the trump suit. If none of the trump rank appear, then the trump suit is the highest of the exposed cards (other than Jokers).

PLAY

In the first hand, the player who declared trumps starts; subsequently, each trick's winner leads. The leader can lead one card or several cards of the same suit with the proviso that the latter must all outrank any cards of the same suit held by the other players. If this is not the case, a 'revoke', or penalty, is declared. This stops play and the offended opposing partnership scores as though it had won every trick.

The other players must play as many cards as were led. Suit must be followed if possible, otherwise trumps may be played. The highest card of the suit led or the highest trump wins. As play progresses, all players extract the Kings, Tens and Fives from the tricks they have won and place them face up on the table. Other cards are put face down into a waste pile.

SCORING AND CONCLUSION

At the end of play, the six discards are turned up and its counting cards scored, along with the counting cards the players have won. The number of card points won by the opposing partnership determines the result. This decides who scores how many game points and who will be the declarers for the next hand.

If the opposers score between zero and five card points, the declarers score two game points. However, if the opposers score between five and 35 card points, the declarers score one game point. If the score is between 40 and 75 card points, no game points are scored. In all three instances, the declarers remain the declarers. If, however, the opposers score between 80 and 95 or more than 100 card points, they win one or two game points and become the declarers.

In each hand, a partnership's score is determined by the trump rank when they become declarers. If, for example, a side with a score of nine gains two game points in a hand, their score goes up to 'Jack'. The first partnership to reach Aces (i.e. 14 game points) and win a hand with Aces as the trump rank, wins the game.

Catch and Collect Games

Catching games – card games in which the objective is to capture all the cards – are extremely old. Although many of them are classic children's games, this does not preclude them from being games of skill. As the name implies, collect games revolve around collecting cards. These can be pairs of cards of matching ranks or sets of cards that are matched in rank or by suit.

These types of games can be as simple as Snap (although success here still involves speeds of recognition and reaction), Happy Families (the American version of which is Go Fish) and Authors. The latter is an American game for children, but there is an adult version of the game, called Literature, which is a partnership card game for six or eight players. It revolves around the players questioning their opponents about the cards in their hands and acquiring cards accordingly.

Some more obscure games have their own endearing features. In Pig, players signal the end of a game by touching their noses – the last player to do so is the 'pig' – while in Spoons, they grab for a spoon. Other games, such as Gops or Schwimmen, are more complex. The former is an acronym for 'Game of Pure Strategy', reflecting the tactical skill needed to play the game well. In Schwimmen, the idea is for players to improve their hands in turn by swapping a card at a time for a face-up card on the table. It is particularly popular in Germany and in some parts of Austria.

Whisky Poker was invented in the USA, where it was given its name for fairly self-evident reasons. It was played widely in the late 19th and early 20th centuries, and it still has an American following today. Despite its name and the fact it uses ranking, it is played in an entirely different way to Poker: the chief difference is that no betting is involved.

Above: 19th-century playing cards showing the Baker family from the game Happy Families. The aim is to collect families of four.

CARD-CATCHING GAMES

The simplest and possibly best-known game of this type is Snap, followed by Beggar-My-Neighbour, also known as Beat Your Neighbour Out of Doors. Slapjack is a fun game, which revolves around physically slapping a Jack whenever it appears, while Memory is just what its name implies – a real test of card recall.

SNAP

Players hold their cards face down. Each in turn plays their top card face up to the middle of the table as quickly as possible. When the card played matches the rank of the preceding card, the player who calls 'Snap' first wins the central pool of cards. As players run out of cards, they drop out of play.

If someone calls 'Snap' by mistake – or if two or more players call simultaneously – the pool is placed face up to one side and a new one started. When a card played to the new pool matches the top card of the old one, the player to call 'Snap pool' first wins both pools.

BEGGAR-MY-NEIGHBOUR

Players take it in turns to turn over their top cards and place them face up in the middle of the table. There are two types of card: Ace, King, Queen and Jack are paying cards and the others are ordinary ones.

When a player places a pay card, the opponent has to place four cards for an Ace, three for a King, two for a Queen and one for a Jack. If these cards are all ordinary, the player of the pay card scoops the pool. But if the opponent plays a pay card, the reverse applies. The player who runs out of cards first loses.

Above: Memory involves turning up two pairs from cards scattered face down on the table. Whether through good luck or memory, this player turns up a matching pair, and so keeps the cards.

SLAPJACK

Players hold their cards as face-down piles, each in turn playing the top card face up to the centre of the table. When a Jack is played, the first player to slap it wins the central pile. The winner is the player ending up with all the cards.

In another version, the aim is to lose cards, not win them. Players try to predict what card they are playing by calling out a rank. If card and call match, all the players race to slap the pile. The last one to do so adds the pile to the cards he is holding.

MEMORY

The cards are dealt at random face down over the table, after which each player in turn picks up and announces two of them. If the cards form a pair, that player wins them and has another go; if not, they are replaced face down in the same position and it is the next player's turn. The player with the sharpest memory normally wins.

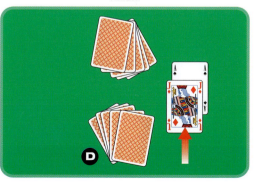

PLAYER B

PLAYER A

Left: In this example of Beggar-My-Neighbour, Player A has laid a Jack, and so does not have to place four cards. This means that Player B has to place one new pay card.

GOPS

This strange game is a test of strategy – its name is an acronym of the term Game of Pure Strategy. It is very popular among game theorists as it is susceptible to logical mathematical analysis. It is also known as Goofspiel.

You will need: 52 cards for three players, but with one suit taken out when there are two players

Card ranking: Standard, Aces low

Players: Two to three

Ideal for: 14+

OBJECT

To win the greatest value of Diamonds, or whichever is the chosen suit, until reaching the required point total.

THE DEAL

The pack is split into its suits, with one – usually Diamonds – being singled out as the so-called competition suit. The remaining suits are divided between the players. If only two are playing, one suit is discarded. The competition suit is shuffled and placed face down on the table, to form the competition stack.

PLAY AND SCORING

Play begins with the top card of the competition suit being turned face up. Players then bid for the card in turn by choosing any card from their hands and placing it face down on the table. When all the cards have been placed, they are turned over. Whichever player has played the highest one wins the competition card. The bid cards, as they are termed, are put aside and the next turn is played.

In the event of a tie between the bidders in a two- or three-player game, the competition card is either discarded or rolled over to the next round, to be taken by the next competition card winner. If there are three players and two tie for best bid, the card goes to the third player.

Gops is difficult to master, since it presents its players with a series of dilemmas that have to be resolved. The skill comes from gauging correctly when to bid high for a card and when to bid low, forcing the opposing players to bid more than they need to take a certain card.

Aces count as one, numbered cards at their face values, Jack 11, Queen 12 and King 13.

CONCLUSION

The game is over once all 13 cards from the competition stack have been taken. In a two-player game, the player scoring 46 points or more wins; in the three-player version, the target score is 31 points.

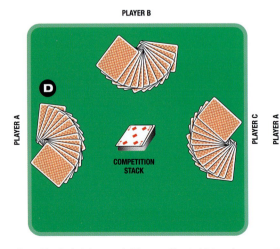

Above: After the deal, the top card of the competition stack is turned over. Players then bid on it by placing one card face down in front of them.

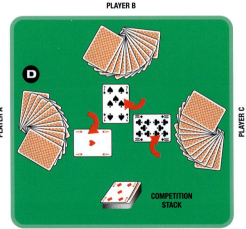

Above: After the deal, all players turn over their bid cards at the same time, and Player C's 10♣ wins over the 5♦.

SCHWIMMEN

Known in English-speaking countries as Thirty-One, Schwimmen is also called Schnautz, Knack and Hosen'runter in Germany and western Austria. Players improve their hands by exchanging cards into a central pool of turned-up cards.

OBJECT

To score nearest to 31 or 32 points by collecting cards of the same suit or holding three cards of the same rank.

THE DEAL

Each player receives an equal number of chips and then is dealt three cards face down, with an extra three being dealt on to the table. The dealer decides whether to play with his dealt hand or exchange it sight unseen with the spare one. The rejected cards are then turned face up.

PLAY

The player to the left of the dealer plays first, the turn to play passing clockwise around the table. Each player is entitled to exchange a card for one of the cards face up on the table, or pass.

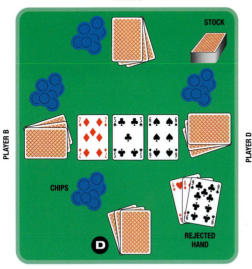

PLAYER C

STOCK

PLAYER B

PLAYER D

CHIPS

REJECTED HAND

PLAYER A

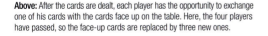

Above: After the cards are dealt, each player has the opportunity to exchange one of his cards with the cards face up on the table. Here, the four players have passed, so the face-up cards are replaced by three new ones.

You will need: 32-card pack created by removing the cards from Two to Six; gambling chips/counters

Card ranking: See 'Scoring and Conclusion', below

Players: Two to eight

Ideal for: 10+

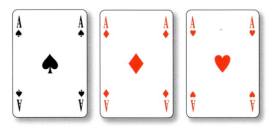

Above: The game ends if a *Feuer* (three Aces) is declared by a player.

If all of the players pass in succession, the face-up cards are then replaced with new ones from the stock pile, and the game continues.

Any player can decide to 'close' at the end of his turn, after which the others have one more chance to play before the hand is over. The hand also ends if certain sets of cards are disclosed. There are two of these: *Feuer* (fire), comprising three Aces (32 points), and *Schnautz*, featuring three cards of the same suit, worth 31 points. Both of them must be declared as soon as they are made.

To score, all player's cards are exposed and the values of cards in any one suit calculated. If play ends because a player closes or declares *Schnautz*, the player with the worst hand loses a chip. If *Feuer* is declared, all the players except the declarer lose a chip. Once a player has lost all his chips, he is said to be 'swimming'. Although he can continue to play, he may do so only until he loses another hand, when he must drop out of the game.

SCORING AND CONCLUSION

Aces are worth 11 points and the court cards 10 each, while the numbered cards count at face value. Only cards of the same suit are scored. Thus, a hand containing the K♣, 7♥ and 9♥ is worth 16 points for the two Hearts – the King does not score. Three cards of the same rank (Three of a Kind) other than Aces score 30.5 points. If scores are tied, a higher Three of a Kind beats a lower one, as does a higher suit, ranked Clubs, Spades, Hearts and Diamonds. The last player in the game is the winner.

WHISKY POKER

In this one-time American favourite, players have the chance to improve their hands by exchanging cards with a spare hand, known as the widow, which is dealt to the table.

You will need: 52 cards, no wild cards; gambling chips/counters
Card ranking: Standard. Hands are also ranked (see below)
Players: Two to nine players
Ideal for: 14+

OBJECT

To collect the best five-card poker hand, the player with the highest hand scooping the pool.

THE DEAL

Before choosing the dealer for each round, every player puts a chip into a communal pot. They draw to decide who deals first, the player with the lowest card having the honour. Five cards are dealt to each player, starting with the player to the dealer's left, with the widow being dealt immediately before the dealer's own hand. The widow is kept face down in the centre of the table. After the first hand, the deal passes to the left around the table.

PLAY

The player to the dealer's left starts by deciding whether to exchange his hand as dealt for the widow. If not, the next player is given the same opportunity and so on round the table. If no one exchanges, the widow is turned face up and play begins.

Each player in turn now has one of three options. He can exchange one card (discarding a card face up and taking a replacement from the widow), exchange all five cards, or knock, signalling the imminent ending of play. The other players have one more turn, after which there is a showdown with the best hand winning the pot.

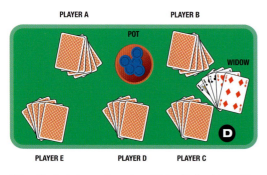

Above: After the deal, no one has exchanged his hand for the widow, so it is turned face up for all players to see before play begins.

SCORING AND RANKING

From lowest to highest, the ranking of hands are:
- High card – a hand with no combinations, but with the highest-ranking card among the hands in play.
- One Pair – two cards of the same value; e.g. 3♦, 3♥ or Q♠, Q♣. If another player holds a Pair of the same value, then whoever holds the highest card in the two hands (called the 'kicker'), wins.
- Two Pairs – two sets of Pairs; e.g. 3♦, 3♥ and Q♠, Q♣. Again, whoever holds the 'kicker' wins if two players hold matching Pairs of the same value.
- Three of a Kind – three cards of the same face value (this is also known as 'trips'); e.g. Q♠, Q♣, Q♥.
- Straight – a sequence of five cards in any suit; e.g. 5♦, 6♣, 7♠, 8♥, 9♣. The highest Straight is one topped by Ace, the lowest starts with Ace. Should two players hold a Straight the one with the highest cards wins.
- Flush – five cards of the same suit. If another player holds a Flush, whoever holds the highest card wins.
- Full House – Three of a Kind and a Pair. When two players hold a Full House, the one with the highest ranking trips wins.
- Four of a Kind – four cards of the same face value (known as 'quads').
- Straight Flush – a combined Straight and Flush, which contains cards in sequence and of same suit.
- Royal Flush – a Straight Flush up to Ace.

The player with the highest-ranking hand takes the pot of chips. Alternatively, each player can start with five chips and the player with the weakest hand forfeits one of these, the first to lose all five chips becomes the overall loser.

CONCLUSION

Depending on the scoring method agreed, a game ends when one player has won all or an agreed number of the chips, or has lost the five chips with which he started.

OTHER COLLECTING GAMES

Games such as Go Fish and Authors are closely related. Their simplicity makes them ideally suited to children. In each, the aim is to collect 'books' – that is, sets of four cards of the same rank – by players asking each other for cards they think might be held. Whoever collects the most books wins the game. The American game Authors gets its name from the fact that, in the 19th century, children played it with cards depicting famous authors. The idea has been extended to include inventors, US presidents, and even well-known baseball players. It is played like Go Fish, but without the stock pile.

GO FISH

OBJECT

To get rid of all of one's cards, by collecting books of four cards of the same rank (i.e. four Tens, Aces or Jacks), or to score more books than any other player.

| You will need: 52 cards |
| Card ranking: None |
| Players: Three to six |
| Ideal for: 4+ |

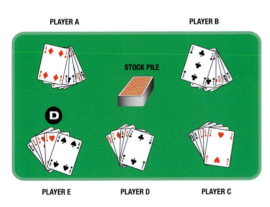

PLAYER A   **PLAYER B**

STOCK PILE

D

PLAYER E   **PLAYER D**   **PLAYER C**

Above: After the deal, Player A asks Player D for a Seven, as he holds one in his own hand and wishes to collect a 'book'. Player D must surrender his 7♦.

THE DEAL

Although special packs of Go Fish cards are available, a standard card pack may be used as a substitute. Five cards are dealt face down to each player, the remainder being placed face down to form a stock.

PLAY

The player to the dealer's left starts the game by asking another player for a card of the same rank as one that appears in his hand. If the player asked does hold such a card (or cards), he must give it (or them) to the asking player, who then gets another turn. If the responding player does not hold any cards of the requested rank, he responds with 'Go Fish!'

The asking player then draws the top card of the stock. If this card matches his initial request, the asking player shows it and gets another turn. If not, the turn passes to the player who said 'Go Fish!', although the asking player must keep his new card. When a player has a book, this must be shown and put aside.

CONCLUSION

The game ends when a player has no cards left and therefore wins, or the stock runs out, in which case, the player who has collected the most books wins.

AUTHORS

OBJECT

To get rid of all one's cards or score more books than any other player.

| You will need: 52 cards |
| Card ranking: None |
| Players: Three to six |
| Ideal for: 4+ |

THE DEAL

The entire pack is dealt singly as far as it will go. Some players may therefore have more cards than others.

PLAY AND CONCLUSION

Each player in turn asks any other player for all the cards they have of a specific rank, or alternatively for a specific card, such as the 7♣. The player who asks must have at least one card of the solicited rank in his own hand. If the player who is asked holds the card, he surrenders it to the asking player, who then gets another turn. If not, he replies 'None' and takes over the turn. When a player gets all four of a given rank, he lays the cards down in a won trick to show the other players.

The game ends when all cards are formed into books. The player with the most books wins. Alternatively, players score a point per book and play to a target score.

FISHING GAMES

FISHING GAMES PROBABLY ORIGINATED IN CHINA, SPREADING FROM THERE TO JAPAN AND KOREA, WHERE THEY REMAIN POPULAR. THEY ARE ALSO WIDELY PLAYED IN TURKEY, GREECE AND ITALY, ALTHOUGH, FOR SOME REASON, THEY HAVE GENERALLY FAILED TO CATCH ON IN THE REST OF THE WORLD. THE IDEA IS TO MATCH THE CARDS HELD IN THE PLAYERS' HANDS WITH THOSE TURNED FACE UP IN A LAYOUT ON THE TABLE.

There is a straightforward difference between Eastern and Western games of this ilk. In the Eastern games (a classic example being Go Stop, a Korean game that is played with flower cards), there is generally a face-down stock, from which players draw. In Western games, cards are played only from players' hands, although a single card can be used to 'capture' several cards simultaneously if their ranks add up to the rank of the card that was played. If a player cannot match a card or cards, he has to add a card to the layout, or to those cards that are already on the table. This card is now ready for the next player to capture or 'catch' it.

Casino is probably the best known fishing game, and is played particularly in the USA and parts of Scandinavia as well as southern Africa, where specific variations have developed in South Africa, Swaziland and Lesotho. In all these variations, however, captured cards remain in play and so can be recaptured and used in 'builds'. Builds are the most complex features of both Eastern and Western fishing games. They take advantage of the rule that a numbered card can capture its fellows on the table, if they are all of the same rank as the card being played. The intention to play such a card must be announced in advance, with its number specified; after this, the cards can be placed together to form the build. Only by playing a numbered card of the rank that was announced when the build was made can another player capture it.

Above: Flower cards are used in Japan and Korea for games of the fishing group. There are 48 cards in a pack, four for each month of the year.

CASINO

Although Casino is generally thought to have originated in Italy, the first evidence of it being played comes from late 18th-century London and subsequently from Germany.

You will need: 52 cards, but only part of the pack is used in any one deal

Card ranking: None

Players: Best with two to four people, the latter playing in opposing partnerships

Ideal for: 10+

OBJECT

To capture opponents' cards by playing a card matching a layout card's number (pairing) or by playing a card that matches the sum of several such cards (summing).

THE DEAL

Each player is dealt four cards, two at a time, with a further four being dealt face up. The dealer sets aside the remaining cards for use in subsequent deals, but no more cards are dealt to the table.

PLAY

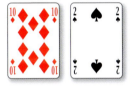

Above: In Casino, the 10♦ is known as the Big Casino and the 2♠ as the Little Casino.

Each player in turn, starting with the one to the dealer's left, plays a card to the table, either capturing one or more table cards or building a combination for capture on a subsequent turn. There are three options during play: to capture, build or trail.

- Capturing – if a player plays a King, Queen or Jack that matches the rank of a card on the table, he can capture that card. If there is more than one matching card on the table – two Queens, say – only one may be captured. A numbered card can capture cards of the same rank and any sets of cards that add up to the rank of the card played. Capturing all the cards on the table is a sweep, which is worth a point to the player making it.
- Building – there are two kinds of build – single and multiple. If a player adds a Three to a Three on the table and announces, 'building Threes' for instance, this is a single build. A multiple build is when more than one card is added. If a player holds two Sixes and there are two Sixes on the table, he plays a Six to the table, puts all three Sixes together, announces 'building Sixes' and captures the combination with the fourth Six on the next turn. The danger of building combinations of cards to be captured subsequently is that an opponent may capture the combination first.

- Trailing – playing a card without building or capturing, when a player can't match any cards in the layout.

SCORING

Only captured cards score. The most valuable are Spades, Aces, the 10♦ (Big Casino) and the 2♠ (Little Casino). At the end of a hand, whoever has the most Spades wins a point. Aces are worth one point each, while Big Casino is worth two points and Little Casino one point. Capturing more than half the pack is worth three points.

The simplest way of scoring is to treat each deal as a separate game. Alternatively, the first player to score 11 points wins a single game, the total being doubled if it takes two deals and quadrupled if this score is accomplished in only one deal.

A third method is known as 21 Up, which is to agree that the first player to win 21 points wins the game, regardless of how many deals it takes.

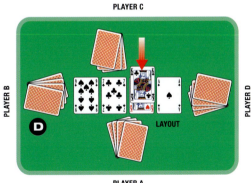

PLAYER C

PLAYER B

PLAYER D

D

LAYOUT

PLAYER A

Above: Player C matches the King in the layout, and so captures it.

CONCLUSION

The game ends when all cards have been played with none remaining in stock, and scores are totalled.

ZWICKER

This popular fishing game from northern Germany originated in the area of Schleswig-Holstein, close to the Danish border. The *Zwick* is the name given to a sweep capturing all the cards on the table.

You will need: 52 cards, to which it is customary to add three (or sometimes four) Jokers

Card ranking: None

Players: Two to four – ideally four playing in partnerships of two

Ideal for: 10+

OBJECT

To capture cards from the layout on the table by playing a card of matching value, and whenever possible score bonus points for *Zwicks* – sweeps that clear all the cards on the table.

MATCHING VALUES

Fixed matching values determine which cards can capture which. Cards from Two to Ten rank at face value, but Aces, Jacks, Queens and Kings have two possible matching values of one or 11, two or 12, three or 13 and four or 14, respectively. The player who captures such a card, plays it to capture other cards, or makes it part of a build, decides the value. If a Queen counts as 13, it can be used to capture a Six and a Seven or a Two, Three and Eight and so on. The three Jokers – Small, Middle and Large – are valued at 15, 20 and 25, respectively. Players agree in advance which Joker is which.

THE DEAL

To start the game, four cards are dealt singly to each player, plus two face up on the table.

PLAY

The player to the dealer's left starts by playing one card face up, next to the two face-up cards on the table. When everyone has played, the dealer deals another four cards to each player, none to the table, and so on until a final deal of five cards each exhausts the pack.

If a player plays a card that matches a card on the table, that card may be captured. Two or more such cards can be captured by 'summing', that is, taking cards that have matching values adding up to the matching value of the card being played. To form a build, a player announces its value and then places his card half over the layout card.

Any build counts as though it is a single card – hence, a Five and Seven makes a build of 12, which can be captured by a Jack. No build can be higher than 14. A build's player is obliged to capture the build eventually, unless another player captures or modifies it first.

SCORING

The values used in scoring differ from those used in matching. The small, medium and large Jokers gain five, six and seven points, respectively; the 10♦ is worth three; and the 10♠, 2♠ and each Ace are worth one. These are the only cards that score. A player capturing more than half the cards in the pack scores three points, and each *Zwick* is worth a point. The highest score wins.

Left: Here, a player captures the 6♠ and 7♣, matching their combined total with the Q♠, which has a matching value of three or 13.

CONCLUSION

Once the final deal (of five cards) has been played, the hand is scored.

Left: The 10♦ is worth three points; the 10♠, 2♠ and each Ace are worth one point.

CUARENTA

In Spanish, *cuarenta* means 'forty'. And it is also the number of cards in the deck used in this game and the number of points needed to win it. What distinguishes Cuarenta from most other fishing games is that matching a card also allows cards in sequence with it to be captured.

You will need: 40 cards (Eights, Nines and Tens having been removed from a standard pack)

Card ranking: None

Players: Two or four in two partnerships. In the latter case, one partner keeps score while the other stores the won cards

Ideal for: 10+

OBJECT

To capture cards by matching them. Alternatively, in the case of numbered cards, to capture them by addition, or by forming an unbroken ascending sequence.

THE DEAL

To choose the first dealer, the cards are shuffled and then dealt face up singly to each player. The first player to be dealt a Diamond becomes the dealer. Five cards are then dealt to each player, the remaining cards being stacked face down on the table.

PLAY

After a deal, a player can make an announcement. If a player is dealt four cards of the same rank (Four of a Kind), the cards are shown (announced) and that partnership wins the game immediately. If a player is dealt three cards of the same rank (Three of a Kind), he calls '*Ronda*' and the declaring partnership scores four points. Although the *Ronda's* rank need not be declared, if one of its cards can be captured by *Caida* – by matching it immediately after it has been played – the opposing partnership scores 10 points if they can remember the event and the rank of the cards at the end of the hand, which is when the bonus can be claimed.

At the start of play, or in the case of *Limpia*, a clean sweep of the table, there is obviously nothing to be captured. The card that was played, either at the start of play or to make *Limpia*, simply remains on the table, as do subsequent cards if no capture is made. *Limpia* is worth two points to the side that is making it.

SCORING

The practice is to use the Eights, Nines and Tens to mark scores – these cards otherwise have no function in the game. When face up, each card represents two points; a face-down card, a *Perro* (dog), represents 10 points. Scoring combinations and card plays are:

- *Ronda* (Three of a Kind) – four points to the declaring partnership.
- *Caida* (capturing a card from *Ronda* by matching it immediately after it has been played) – 10 points to the opposing partnership, claimed at the game's end.
- *Limpia* (a clean sweep of the table) – 2 points to the side making it.
- A team with 20 captured cards scores six points (if there is a tie, only the non-dealing partnership scores).
- If more than 20 cards have been captured, each extra card is worth another point, the total being rounded up to the nearest even number.
- If neither partnership captures 20 cards, the one with the greater number scores two points.
- A partnership with 30 or more points cannot score for *Rondas* or *Caidas*, while one that has 38 points cannot collect for *Limpia*. Game is 40 points.

Above: In Cuarenta, the partnership with Four of a Kind wins immediately.

Left: Three of a Kind is called *Ronda* and scores four points for the declaring partnership.

CONCLUSION

At the end of a hand, each partnership counts its collected cards and scores are calculated.

SCOPA

Originating in Italy around the 18th century, *scopa* means 'sweep' or 'broom'. It is still one of the country's major national card games.

OBJECT
To capture as many cards as possible, particularly Diamonds and high-numbered cards.

THE DEAL
Starting with the player to the dealer's right, each player is dealt three cards face down, after which the dealer deals four cards face up to the table. If the table cards include two or more Kings, it is usual to deal again.

PLAY
Each player in turn, starting with the player to the right of the dealer, attempts to capture one or more of the cards on the table. Only one capture may be made in a turn. If there is no capture, the card played becomes part of the layout and may be captured. There is no obligation to play a card that makes a capture. It is sometimes better to simply add a card to the table. If, however, the card that is played does make a capture, the captured cards must be taken. When everyone has played out their three cards, they are dealt three more, and so on, throughout the game, as long as any cards remain.

CAPTURING
The simplest form of capturing is 'pairing', where one card matches another – a Five and another Five, for example. The second form is 'summing', where the value of the card played is the same as the sum of two or more cards on the table. A Seven can capture a Five and a Two. If there is a card on the table which has a value that is the same as the card being played, only that card may be captured. Only one combination may be captured at a time.

A *Scopa* (sweep) is made when only one card is on the table and a player captures it by pairing, or when all the cards are captured by summing. Although a *Scopa* is worth only one point, its additional value is that it leaves the table empty of cards, so forcing the next player to trail (place a card down without matching it). This leaves the way open for another sweep. The 7♦ is the most important card to capture, as it is worth one point and features in the other three points that may be won.

You will need: Italian 40-card pack or standard pack with Eights, Nines and Tens removed

Card ranking: None

Players: Scopa started off as a game for two, but can be played by three or four

Ideal for: 10+

SCORING
Players sort through their won cards and count their scores. A *Scopa* is worth one point. Single points are also awarded for capturing the most cards, for winning the most Diamonds, capturing the 7♦ – the *Sette Bello* (Best Seven) – and for building the best *Primiera*, in which each player extracts from his won cards the highest-valued card he has taken in each suit.

In order to establish which player's *Primiera* is best, the cards are given special values for this particular purpose. Sevens, the most valuable cards, are worth 21 points, Sixes 18, Aces 16, Fives 15, Fours 14, Threes 13 and Twos 12. The three court cards count for 10 points each. The winner of the point is usually the player with the most Sevens in his *Primiera*.

Above: Cards can be captured by pairing, or by summing, the Seven corresponding to the combined value of the Five and Two.

CONCLUSION
Play continues until no cards remain in hand and the stock is exhausted. Any cards left on the table go to whichever player made the last capture, although this does not count as a *Scopa*. The winner is the first player to score 11 points, or the highest score if more than one player has exceeded that figure. If the scores are tied, the points made on the last deal are counted in strict order, starting with cards and then continuing with points for Diamonds, *Sette Bello*, *Primiera* and *Scopa*.

SCOPONE

This partnership version of Scopa also emerged some time in the 18th century, and is recommended to players seeking something different to the standard trick-and-trump games.

You will need: Italian 40-card pack or standard pack with Eights, Nines and Tens removed

Card ranking: None

Players: Four, in partnerships of two

Ideal for: 10+

OBJECT

To capture as many cards as possible, particularly Diamonds and high-numbered cards, within partnerships.

THE DEAL

Four players sit crosswise, in partnerships. Nine cards are dealt to each player in three batches of three, four cards for the table being dealt two and two after the first and second batches. In Scopone Scientifico (Scientific Scopone), each player is dealt 10 cards, in which case the game has to start with a discard.

PLAY

The rules governing playing, capturing and scoring are broadly the same as in Scopa (see opposite). Partners are not allowed to let each other know which cards they hold in hand, although they can try to signal their intentions by making specific discards in certain situations, such as deciding it is best to avoid capturing a card in favour of trailing one to the table. Captured cards and the cards that captured them are conventionally kept face down in a single pile in front of one of each

partnership's players. The first to play – the player to the dealer's right – has to choose the value of the card he plays carefully so as to reduce the chances of it being captured.

SCORING

If a partnership captures more than 20 cards, it wins a point. If the scores are tied, the point is not given. A partnership with five or more Diamonds also gains a point, with an extra point being awarded for the capture of the 7♦. Each *Scopa*, or sweep of the table, is worth a point, while the partnership with the best *Primiera* (the highest-valued card taken in each suit from the won cards) also scores one for it. The first partnership to score 11 or more points wins the game.

In Scientific Scopone, the target is 21 points. Other differences are that a partnership with the A♦, 2♦ and 3♦ scores *Napoli*, a bonus equal to the value of the highest Diamond in the sequence. A partnership that captures all 10 Diamonds – termed *Cappotto* – wins the game outright.

CONCLUSION

The game is over when a partnership scores the specified number of points, according to the version being played.

PLAYER C

PLAYER B

LAYOUT

PLAYER D

PLAYER A

Above: In Scientific Scopone, a partnership that succeeds in capturing all 10 diamonds scores *Cappotto* and wins the game outright.

Left: In Scopone, three cards are dealt to each player, two to the table, or layout, then three more to each player, two more to the table and finally three more to each player. The player to the dealer's right is first to play.

CICERA

Scopa and Scopone have spawned varying rules and options over the years. Cicera, from the Italian province of Brescia, is the most notable variation to have developed.

You will need: Brescian 52-card pack
Card ranking: None
Players: Four, in partnerships of two
Ideal for: 10+

OBJECT

To capture as many cards as possible, aiming to be the first partnership to score 51 points.

THE DEAL

Each player receives 12 cards, with four being dealt face up to the table.

PLAY

Each player in turn plays a card to the table and makes a capture or leaves it on the table. Capturing is by pairing or summing numbered cards (one to 10 at face value), or pairing court cards.

Making a capture is optional, while if the card played matches a single card and the sum value of several cards, its player can choose which to capture. Once all the cards have been played, the last to capture takes any remaining cards.

SCORING

Points can be scored by *Scúa* (a sweep that captures all the cards on the table in one turn), *Picada* (matching the card previously trailed or left on the table), by an opponent, *Simili* (capturing a card of the same suit) and *Quadriglia* (capturing a set of three or more cards). The side with the majority of cards scores two points, as does the one with the most Spades.

Napula, which is *Napoli* in Scientific Scopone, scores three points, while capturing the 2♣, the 10♦ and the J♥ is worth a point for each capture. Game is 51 points.

CONCLUSION

The game ends when a partnership scores 51 points.

CIRULLA

The preferred version of Scopone in the Ligurian region around Genoa, Cirulla has several quirks.

You will need: Italian 40-card pack or standard pack with Eights, Nines and Tens removed
Card ranking: None
Players: Four, in partnerships of two
Ideal for: 10+

OBJECT

To capture as many cards as possible, aiming to be the first partnership to reach the agreed target score.

THE DEAL

Each player is dealt three cards, and four are dealt face up to the table.

PLAY

Each player in turn plays a card to the table and makes a capture or leaves it to trail. As well as pairing and summing, cards can be captured by 'fifteening' (capturing with a card that makes 15 when added to the cards it captures).

SCORING

If the four cards dealt by the dealer total 15, the dealer scores for a sweep. If they total 30, the score is two sweeps. If the cards dealt to a player total less than 10, the player knocks by showing them. This counts as three sweeps or 10 points if they are three cards of the same rank. The 7♥ may be used as a wild card, which can replace any card.

Players score a point for each sweep, for most cards and most Diamonds. Capturing the 7♦ is worth a point, as is *Primiera* (won by the player with the highest-valued cards taken in each suit in his won cards). *Scala Grande*, the King♦, Queen♦ and J♦, scores five, and *Scala Piccola*, the A♦, 2♦ and 3♦, scores three. If the 4♦ is also held, the score is the value of the highest Diamond held in unbroken sequence. Target scores can be 26, 51 or 101.

CONCLUSION

Capturing all the Diamonds wins the game. The game ends when the agreed target score is reached.

BASRA

This fishing game is widely played in coffee houses throughout the Middle East, sometimes under different names. There are Lebanese, Iraqi and Egyptian versions – the last is described here.

You will need: 52 cards
Card ranking: None
Players: Two; or four, in partnerships of two
Ideal for: 10+

OBJECT

To capture as many table cards as possible, aiming to be the first partnership to reach the agreed target score.

THE DEAL

Each player is dealt four cards. Four more cards are dealt face up to the table. These are the 'floor' cards and must not include any Jacks or the 7♦. If they do, the offending cards are buried in the pack and replacements are dealt.

PLAY

The player to the dealer's right plays first. Each player in turn plays a card face up to the table, the aim being to capture some of the cards that have already been exposed. When the players have all played their first four cards, they are dealt another batch of four each (no more are dealt to the table) and so on until the entire pack has been dealt. The hand is then scored.

CAPTURING

A player can capture by pairing (matching one card with another) or summing (capturing two or more number cards which have a combined value that is the same as that of the card being played).

As Kings and Queens have no numerical value, only pairing may capture them. If a card is able to capture, a capture must be made, but there is no obligation to play such a card.

Capturing all the cards from the floor at once is a *Basra* and scores a bonus 10 points. Playing a Jack also sweeps the table, but does not count as a *Basra* and therefore no bonus is awarded.

If a 7♦ is played, however, it does count as a *Basra*, provided that all the cards on the table are number cards with a combined value of 10 or less. If it is more than 10, or if there are court cards on the table, the Seven still captures all the cards, but there is no bonus.

SCORING AND CONCLUSION

After the last card has been played, any remaining cards are taken by the last player to have made a capture. Each team counts its cards. A team with 27 or more scores 30 points. If there is a tie, the points are carried forward.

Each Jack and Ace is worth one point, the 2♣ scores two and the 10♦ scores three. Generally, whichever side scores 101 or more points first wins the game. If the score is tied, the convention is to play the final game up to a total of 150 points. The game ends when a partnership wins a rubber (five games), or at an agreed time or points total.

PLAYER C

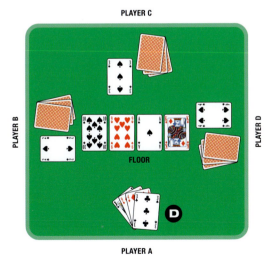

PLAYER B **FLOOR** **PLAYER D**

PLAYER A

Above: Player A, the last to lay to this trick, could play the 4♦, matching Player D's 4♠, or the 3♣, matching Player C's 3♠. Playing his Jack, he would be able to sweep all the cards from the floor, but this would not count as a *Basra*.

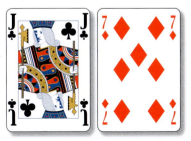

Right: Neither the 7♦ nor the J♣ may be among the face-up cards on the table at the start of the game, but they are both useful during play for capturing cards.

CHINESE TEN

No coverage of fishing games would be complete without an Eastern example such as Chinese Ten. The way a card is flipped from the face-down deck after each play is typical.

You will need: 52 cards; no Jokers	
Card ranking: None	
Players: Two to four	
Ideal for: 10+	

OBJECT

To achieve as high a score as possible, before all the cards on the stock pile are exhausted.

THE DEAL

Depending on the number of players involved, the number of cards dealt varies. If there are two players, they receive 12 cards each; three players receive eight cards each and four players receive six cards. The next four cards are dealt face up to the table and the rest are stacked face down to form the stock.

Above: In this three-player hand of Chinese Ten, Player A (Player C having dealt) can play either the 8♠ or 8♣ to make a value of 10 when added to the 2♦. Alternatively, the Q♠ could be paired with the Q♥.

PLAY

Each player in turn, starting with the player to the left of the dealer, plays a card to the table. To capture a number card, the card played must make up a value of 10 when added to it. For example, an Ace captures a Nine, or a Nine an Ace, and so on. Only pairing can capture Tens and court cards – Ten takes Ten, Jack takes Jack, and so on. At the end of a turn, having either captured a card or trailed, which is to simply place a card on the table, a player then turns the top card of the stock face up. If this captures a card, both cards are taken. If not, it is left on the table for subsequent capture. You can only play one card per turn. Upon making a capture, you place both cards face down in front of you.

SCORING

Players sift all the red cards from their winnings. Low red number cards score at face value, red Nines to Kings score 10 points each, and red Aces score 20. Black cards do not count when two people play. When three or four play, the A♠ counts 30 extra points and the A♣ scores 40 points.

The score is the difference between points taken and the predetermined 'tie' score, which is set at 105 for two players, 80 for three, and 70 for four. For example, in a game between two players, if the points taken are 119 and 90, the former scores +14 and the latter scores -15.

CONCLUSION

The last card from the pack should always capture the last card from the layout. All 52 cards should end up distributed among the players' winning piles.

Left: The red cards in Chinese Ten score at face value, except for Aces (which score 20) and Nines to Kings (which score 10).

LAUGH AND LIE DOWN

A real oddity, Laugh and Lie Down is the oldest fishing game on record and the only one from English sources. Its name is attributed to players laughing at those who must 'lie down'.

You will need: 52 cards; gambling chips/counters	
Card ranking: None	
Players: Five	
Ideal for: 10+	

OBJECT

To make Pairs and Mournivals (Four of a Kind) by matching the cards lying face up on the table.

THE DEAL

Before the deal, each player stakes two chips to the pot and the dealer three chips. Each player receives eight cards, and the remaining 12 are dealt face up to the table. The dealer takes any Mournivals among them.

PLAY

Any player with a Mournival in hand 'wins' those cards and places them face down on the table in front of him. If a player holds a Prial (Three of a Kind), he can do the same with two of the cards. The third is retained in hand.

In turn, each player plays a card to the table to make a capture by pairing. This can also be done by spotting other players' oversights. If, for instance, a player captures only one table card when there are three available, the first opposing player to spot this can take the other pair. If a player cannot make a capture he places his hand face up and drops out of play. This is called 'lying down'.

SCORING

The last player left in a hand wins five chips. A player capturing fewer than eight cards pays a chip for every two cards of the shortfall to the pot. However, a player with more than eight cards receives a chip for every two cards he has gone over.

Left: A Mournival (Four of a Kind). After the deal, any Mournivals found among the table cards are promptly won by the dealer.

CONCLUSION

Play continues until only one player has any cards left in hand, after which chips are settled.

Below: Player D holds a Prial (Three of a Kind) and can place it on the table at the start of play, placing two of the cards face down, and keeping the third card in hand. Player C makes a Mournival of Queens from the two in his hand and two on the table.

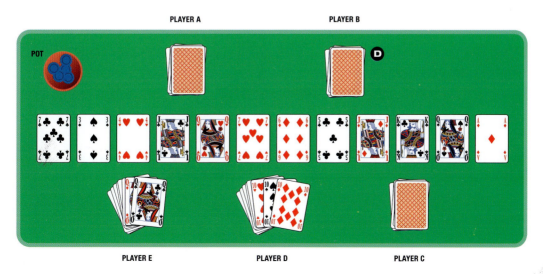

PLAYER A   PLAYER B

POT

PLAYER E   PLAYER D   PLAYER C

ADDING GAMES

THESE ARE ARITHMETICAL GAMES, WHERE THE AIM IS TO REACH OR AVOID SPECIFIC POINT TOTALS. IN A VARIATION OF NINETY-NINE, PLAYERS ARE PENALIZED IF THEY PLAY A CARD THAT CROSSES ONE OF THE THREE 'BORDERS' – 33, 66 AND 99. HISTORICALLY, SUCH GAMES HAVE BEEN MORE POPULAR IN EASTERN EUROPE THAN THE WEST, THE EXCEPTION BEING CRIBBAGE, BRITAIN'S NATIONAL CARD GAME.

Cribbage's history dates back to at least 1630, if not before. Although its invention was, for a long time, credited to Sir John Suckling (1609–42), a notable poet, playwright and wit of the day, there is now little doubt that it actually derived from a game called Noddy, which was popular in the previous century.

The game's fame quickly grew and spread as it was taken up by monarchs and their courtiers. Catherine the Great of Russia, for one, was an enthusiastic Cribbage player, until Whist and then Bridge supplanted it in aristocratic favour. However, it still flourishes in British pubs and clubs; it is estimated that, in Britain alone, there are two million active tournament players. There are two main versions – Six-card Cribbage, which is the standard, and Five-card Cribbage, a game that is older and now far less widely played. They count as adding games because, in their initial stages, the value of the cards played by both players cannot exceed 31.

Ninety-eight, Ninety-nine and One Hundred are similar adding games. In them, the values of the cards are added together as they are played, the aim being to avoid exceeding the target score.

Noddy and Costly Colours are both curiosities. The former appears to date from Tudor times, although the first descriptions date from more than a century later. And, even in its heyday, Costly Colours seems to have been played only in a fairly limited area in Britain.

Above: Russian Empress Catherine II, also known as Catherine the Great, who ruled from 1762–96, was an enthusiastic cribbage player.

NODDY

The undisputed ancestor of Cribbage, dating back to the 16th century, Noddy is so called after the title given to the Jack of the suit turned up at the start of play. 'Noddy' means a fool or simpleton – one who tends to 'nod off' at any opportunity.

OBJECT

To score 31 points over as many deals as necessary, scores being pegged on a board, just as in Cribbage.

THE DEAL

Players cut for the deal, the one with the lower card dealing first. It then alternates. Each player receives three cards singly, the rest of the pack being placed face down on the table, and the top card is turned up. If it is a Jack, the non-dealer pegs two points for 'Jack Noddy'.

PLAY AND SCORING

After the deal, each player in turn announces and scores for (but does not reveal) any combinations that can be made up from his three cards and the turn-up. A Pair pegs two points, a Pair Royal (three of the same rank) pegs six and a Double Pair Royal (four of the same rank) scores 12. Two or more cards totalling 15 points pegs a point for each constituent card, as does three or more cards totalling 25 and four cards totalling 31, known as Hitter.

PLAYER B

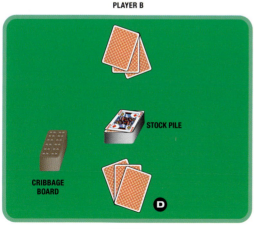

PLAYER A

Above: Non-dealer, Player B, scores two points for the Jack Noddy having been turned up.

You will need: 52 cards; no Jokers; Cribbage board

Card ranking: Standard, Ace low

Players: Two

Ideal for: 7+

Left: Here, the turn up card of the 5♦ means that player A not only completes a run of four (worth three points) but also pegs four more points for a four-card flush.

PLAYER A

Three consecutive cards, such as Two, Three and Four, peg two, and four consecutive cards peg three. Flushes – three or more cards of the same suit – peg a point per card. If the Jack was not turned after the deal, then Jack Noddy is the Jack of the same suit as the turn-up card, and its holder (if any) pegs a point for it.

Any card can be counted more than once, provided that it forms part of a separate combination on each occasion. If either player reaches 31 points from the combination of cards that he holds in his hand, then the game ends and there is no play-off.

If neither player attains 31 points, then the game proceeds to a play-off. The non-dealer plays a card to the table, announcing its face value. The dealer plays in turn, announcing the combined value of the two cards. In the play-off, Aces count for one point, numbered cards count at face value, and court cards score 10 points each. The process continues until 31 points have been pegged, or until neither player can continue without busting (exceeding 31 points).

If one player can continue to play while the other cannot, he plays on alone. If 31 is exceeded, the player who last kept it under 31 pegs one point.

CONCLUSION

Once 31 has been scored – which can happen before a card has been played, when the players announce their combinations – the game is over. Any cards left in hand do not score.

SIX-CARD CRIBBAGE

Whether Six-Card or Five-Card, Cribbage stands out as a unique game. A special Cribbage board is required to play, which uses pegs to record scores. Much of its terminology is also quaint, examples including phrases such as 'one for his nob' and words like 'skunked', used to describe a losing player.

You will need: 52 cards; Cribbage board	
Card ranking: Standard, Ace low	
Players: Two	
Ideal for: 7+	

OBJECT

To score as many points as possible in each hand, being the first after several hands to peg out (complete two circuits of the Cribbage board).

THE DEAL

Both players cut for the deal, the one with the lower card dealing first – Aces are low. Both players, starting with the non-dealer, receive six cards singly. The remaining cards are stacked face down on the table as the stock.

Above: If any Jack is turned up after cutting the pack, the dealer immediately pegs two points 'for his heels'. If a player has a Jack in their hand that is the same suit as the turned-up card, they peg one point 'for his nob' when hands are shown.

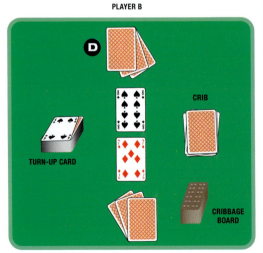

PLAYER B

D

CRIB

TURN-UP CARD

CRIBBAGE
BOARD

PLAYER A

THE DISCARD

After the deal, both players discard two cards face down to form the crib of four cards, aiming to keep a hand that forms scoring combinations. The four crib cards are put aside until the end of the hand, when the cards in it count for the dealer.

The non-dealer cuts the stock. The dealer takes the top card of the bottom half and puts it face up on the top of the pack. This card is the start card. If it is a Jack, the dealer can peg two points, known as 'two for his heels'.

PLAY

Starting with the non-dealer, each player takes it in turn to play a single card, placing the cards in separate face-up piles. They score a running total, the value of each card being added as it is played.

Each time 31 is reached (players must not go above this), the score goes back to zero and another round starts. When a player plays a card that brings the total exactly to that figure, he claims 'thirty-one for two' and pegs two points. If a player cannot play without going over the total, he says 'go' and allows the opposing player to continue. If neither can play, the last player to do so pegs 'one for the go and one for last'. Play goes on until all the cards in hand have been played.

Above: This hand pegs 22 points. There are seven combinations of Fifteen (three times with each Jack, and all the Fives added together), making 14 points, together with a Pair and a Pair Royal (giving two and six points respectively).

Left: Player B lays an Eight after the initial lead of a Seven. The two cards add up to 15, so Player B calls 'fifteen for two' and is able to peg two points.

PLAYER B

CRIB

TURN-UP CARD

CRIBBAGE BOARD

D

PLAYER A

Left: Player B played first here, laying the 7♠. Player A responded with the 4♣. Player B then played the 6♥, allowing Player A to lay the 5♦ and peg four points for a run of Four, Five, Six, Seven.

THE SHOW (SCORING)

Once all the cards have been played, each player picks up the cards they have played and scores them, the start card being counted as part of the hand for both players.

The combinations and scores (shown in brackets) are:

- Fifteen (2): two or more cards totalling 15, counting Ace as one, numbered cards at face value, court cards as 10.
- Pair (2): two cards of the same rank.
- Prial or Pair Royal (6): three of the same rank.
- Double Pair Royal (12): four of the same rank.
- Run (1 per card): three or more cards in ranking order.
- Flush (4 or 5): four or more cards of the same suit.

The same card can be counted as part of different combinations. If a hand contains a Jack of the same suit as the start card, one 'for his nob' is pegged. Finally, the dealer turns over the crib – the four cards the players discarded between them after the deal – and scores it as a five-card hand, exactly as above.

PAIRS AND RUNS

If a player makes any of the following scores in addition to the ones that have already been described, he can peg them immediately. If a card is played that brings the total to 15, its player claims 'fifteen for two' and pegs two points. If a card of the same rank as the previous one is played, the score is 'two for the pair'. If a third card of the same rank is played immediately after this, it is a Pair Royal and its player pegs six points. A 'Double Pair Royal' is awarded if a fourth card of the same rank is played, its player pegging 12 points.

A run is a sequence of three of more cards of consecutive ranks, irrespective of their suits. A player completing a run pegs for the number of cards in it. If, for instance, a Four, Two, Six, Five and Three are played, the player of the Three scores five for a five-card run.

CONCLUSION

The first player to peg out – to exceed 121 points – wins the game. This can happen at any time during play as long as the opposing player's pegs are still on the board. It is usual to play the best of three. If the losing player's score is less than 91, he is 'lurched' or 'skunked' and forfeits double. If it is under 60, it is a 'double lurch' or 'skunk' and he forfeits triple.

Above: This hand pegs 18 points. There are four combinations of 15, making eight points, together with a run of four yielding four points and a flush, giving five points. Finally, there's another point 'for his nob'.

Above: A special Cribbage board and pegs are needed to record the scores in Cribbage. There are two pegs – the forward one showing a player's current score and the rear peg the previous score.

FIVE-CARD CRIBBAGE

F ive-card Cribbage was, for a long time, the standard version of the game and it still features in club, tournament and championship matches, probably because it is partner-friendly.

OBJECT

To be the first to peg 61 points. A player pegging fewer than 45 points is 'in the lurch'.

You will need: 52 cards; Cribbage board

Card ranking: Standard, Ace low

Players: Two

Ideal for: 7+

THE DEAL, PLAY AND SCORING

Four players play as partners, each being dealt five cards and discarding one to the crib. The player to the dealer's left leads first and makes the first show.

At the start of play, the non-dealing partnership pegs 'three for last' as compensation for not having the benefit of the crib.

Hands are played only once until 31 has been reached. Any cards left over remain unplayed.

Four cards of the same suit (a Flush) in hand pegs four – five with the turn-up card. A Flush in the crib (the four cards discarded by players after the deal) only pegs five if it matches the turn-up card's suit.

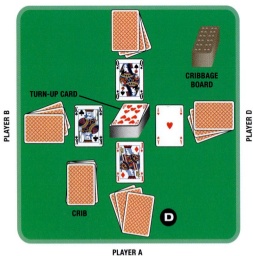

PLAYER C

CRIBBAGE BOARD

TURN-UP CARD

PLAYER B

PLAYER D

CRIB

PLAYER A

Above: In Five-Card Cribbage, if 31 points have been reached, no more cards are laid. Hand points are now calculated.

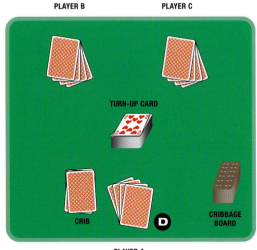

PLAYER B   **PLAYER C**

TURN-UP CARD

CRIB   **CRIBBAGE BOARD**

PLAYER A

Above: In Three-Handed Cribbage, each player receives five cards and one is dealt for the crib. Players must each make one discard, bringing each hand, including the crib, up to four cards.

VARIANTS

In the cut-throat version of Three-Handed Cribbage, each player receives five cards, followed by one to the crib. Players then discard a card each to the crib, after which the player to the dealer's left cuts the pack to reveal the turn-up and plays first. He also shows and counts first, the last player to do so being the dealer. Each player scores for himself.

In the solo version, the dealer's two opponents play as a partnership, each receiving five cards. The dealer takes six cards. Both partners then pass a card to the dealer, who discards four cards to the crib. Play is the same as in the cut-throat game, the one main difference being that each partner scores the amount made by them both. The same applies in Four-Handed Cribbage.

Losing Cribbage is a two-handed six-card game. It is played as the standard version, but the main difference between the two is that every score a player makes is credited to their opponent. The first to score – or rather not to score – 121 points, wins.

In Auction Cribbage, each player states how many points he will subtract from his score in return for the crib, before the starter is turned. The highest bidder deducts that amount and play proceeds as usual.

COSTLY COLOURS

Noted for its complex scoring, Costly Colours is probably a cousin of Cribbage, but relatively little is known about it. Charles Cotton was the first to describe it in his *Complete Gamester*, of 1674. It seems to have survived up to Victorian times, but is no more than a historical curiosity.

OBJECT

To be the first player over a series of games to reach 121 points, by making sequences, combinations and other scoring card plays.

THE DEAL

Both players receive three cards singly, the next card – the deck card – being turned up. Both players use it to help to make sequences and combinations. If it is a Jack or a Two, the dealer pegs four points 'for his heels'.

PLAY

Before play, each player can 'mog', that is, pass a card from his hand face down to the other player. If a player refuses, the other pegs a point for the refusal. If a player mogs (gives away) a Jack or Two, he may first peg two points for it, or four if it is the same suit as the deck card.

The non-dealer plays a card face up to the table, followed by the dealer, who then announces the combined value of the two cards. Play continues until 31 points are scored, or either player cannot play without exceeding that total. This is termed 'busting'. The first player unable to play without doing this has to say 'go', after which the opposing player may add as many cards as possible before he, too, busts. He scores an extra point for the go, plus a point per card if he manages to score 31 exactly. Both players then reveal their cards and peg the value of their scoring combinations, the non-dealer pegging first. The convention is for declarations to be made in the following order – points, Jacks and Twos, Pairs and Prials, Colours and Flushes (see Scoring).

You will need:	52 cards; Cribbage board
Card ranking:	Standard, Ace low or high
Players:	Two
Ideal for:	10+

If either player is left holding cards in hand, the cards played so far are turned down and removed from play. The next in turn to play then starts a new series.

SCORING AND CONCLUSION

Fifteen, 25 and 31, scored in play or in hand, are one point each, a Pair pegs two points, a Prial (Three of a Kind) pegs nine and a Double Prial (Four of a Kind) pegs 18. A Jack or Two of the turned-up suit pegs four; any other Jack or Two pegs two.

Sequences count only in play (one point per card) while Colours (reds or blacks) count only in hand. Three in Colour pegs two; Three in Suit pegs three; Four in Colour, Two in Suit pegs four; Four in Colour, Three in Suit pegs five; Four in Suit – Costly Colours – pegs six. The first to reach 121 points wins.

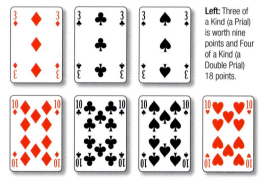

Left: Three of a Kind (a Prial) is worth nine points and Four of a Kind (a Double Prial) 18 points.

Below: With all four cards the same colour, and three of the same suit, this combination would score five points (Four in Colour, Three in Suit). Had the 9♦ been a 9♥, this would have made Costly Colours (four cards of the same suit), scoring six points.

Left: If a Jack or Two is turned up as the deck card, the dealer pegs four points.

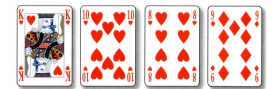

NINETY-EIGHT

This is the first of a set of games known as Adders, in which the card values are added together during play. The aim is to score a set number of points, or to avoid specific totals.

You will need: 52 cards	
Card ranking: See 'Play and Scoring', below	
Players: Two or more	
Ideal for: 7+	

OBJECT
To avoid taking the value of the pile above 98.

THE DEAL
Each player receives four cards dealt singly, the remainder being placed face down on the table to form a stock. Players play their cards face up to the table to create a pile alongside the stock.

PLAY AND SCORING
The player to the dealer's left plays first, with play continuing clockwise around the table. At the moment a card is played to the pile, its player calls out the pile's cumulative value and then draws the top card of the stock to replace the card that was played.

Certain cards change the value of the pile. Playing a Ten reduces its value by 10 points. If a Jack or Queen is played, the value stays the same, whereas playing a King immediately sets the value at 98. All other cards simply add their face value.

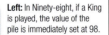

Left: In Ninety-eight, if a King is played, the value of the pile is immediately set at 98.

CONCLUSION
The first player to take the pile above 98 is the loser and, according to convention, has to buy the other players a round of drinks or do a forfeit.

NINETY-NINE

Said to be a Romany game, Ninety-Nine is played along similar conventions to its sister game Ninety-Eight, with some notable exceptions.

You will need: 52 cards; gambling chips/counters	
Card ranking: See 'Play and Scoring', below	
Players: Up to four	
Ideal for: 7+	

OBJECT
To avoid taking the value of the pile above 99.

THE DEAL
Up to four players start with five chips each and receive three cards from a standard 52-card pack. The remaining cards are placed face down on the table to form a stock.

PLAY AND SCORING
The player to the dealer's left plays first and play proceeds clockwise. Each player plays a card face up to a pile on the table, calling out the cumulative value of the pile as they do so. They each then draw the top card of the stock as a replacement.

For each card played, the pile's value goes up by the value of the card, Jacks and Queens counting for 10 points each. An Ace increases the pile's value by one or 11 points, as decided by its player. If a Four is played, the pile value stays the same, but the direction of play reverses. A Nine is worth nothing.

After a Four or Nine, the player calls out the existing value of the pile, saying 'pass to you' or 'back to you', respectively. Playing a Ten increases or decreases the pile's value by 10 points at its player's discretion. Playing a King immediately makes the pile's value 99. Each player loses a point every time they play a card that crosses one of the three 'borders' – 33, 66 and 99.

CONCLUSION
A player unable to play without taking the pile's value above 99 lays down his hand and tosses a chip into the centre of the table. A player with no chips left drops out of the game. The last player left with any chips, wins.

ONE HUNDRED

In certain variations of Adders games, there are individual cards that have special effects; in One Hundred, for instance, playing the A♠ doubles the value of the card pile.

> **You will need:** 52 cards; gambling chips/counters
> **Card ranking:** See 'Play and Scoring', below
> **Players:** Three to six
> **Ideal for:** 7+

OBJECT

To get rid of all your cards without taking the value of the pile above 100.

THE DEAL

Three cards are dealt one at a time to each player. The remainder is placed face down on the table to form a stock.

PLAY AND SCORING

Play starts with the player to the dealer's left and proceeds clockwise around the table. Cards are played singly face up to form a pile, each player calling out its cumulative value as they play, before drawing the top card of the stock to replenish their hands.

A King is worth nothing. The Queens are worth 10 – except for the Q♥, which sets the pile value at zero. Playing a Jack reduces the pile value by 10. Playing a Ten raises the pile value to 100. Most number cards count at face value. Playing a 2♠ doubles the pile value; playing a Four reverses the direction of play. Playing a red Five decreases the pile value by five points. Playing an Ace from a black suit means that its player can set the pile value at any figure between 0 and 100.

If a player makes the pile value equal 100, the only cards the next player can play are black Aces, Fours, red Fives, Tens, Jacks, the Q♥ or Kings.

> ## CONCLUSION
> A player unable to play without taking the pile's value above 100 lays down his hand and tosses a chip into the centre of the table. Players drop out if they lose all their chips; the last with any chips is the winner.

JUBILEE

In this Czech game, played with a 61-card pack, the cards in the black suits score positive points, while those in red suits count as minus points.

> **You will need:** A 61-card pack, containing one full Hearts suit, two Spades suits, two Clubs suits from Ace to Nine (Tens and court cards discarded) and four Jokers
> **Card ranking:** See above, and under Play, below
> **Players:** Two to seven
> **Ideal for:** 10+

OBJECT

To win the most of the 189 points available.

THE DEAL

Each player is dealt eight cards, the remainder of the pack being placed face down on the table to form a stock.

PLAY

Starting with the player to the dealer's left, each player in turn plays a card to a common waste pile. The first to play must play a black card and announce its value. As the players play more cards, they must announce the total value of all the cards that have been played so far in the game. Once they have played a card, they draw replacement cards from the stock, and the procedure continues until the stock is exhausted. No one may bring the total score down to zero. Any player unable to make a legal play must show his hand and pass.

SCORING

Any player who is able to make the running total an exact multiple of 25, by addition or subtraction, scores 10 for a 'Jubilee'. If the total is also a multiple of 100, this score is doubled to 20. But, if a player causes the total to 'jump' a Jubilee rather than hitting it exactly, whether by addition or subtraction, he is penalized five points. It is against the rules of the game to bring the total to below zero.

> ## CONCLUSION
> The game ends when the last card has been played. The final total should be 189 points.

SHEDDING GAMES

THE AIM OF THESE GAMES IS TO GET RID OF CARDS AND TO BE THE FIRST PLAYER TO GO OUT. IN SOME, CARDS MUST BE PLAYED IN ASCENDING SEQUENCE, USUALLY IN SUIT. IN OTHERS, PLAYERS MUST MATCH THE RANK OR SUIT OF THE PREVIOUS CARD PLAYED. ELEUSIS, DEVISED BY GAMES INVENTOR ROBERT ABBOTT IN 1956, IS UNIQUE. PLAYERS SHED CARDS BY MATCHING, BUT THE RULES GOVERNING THIS PROCESS, KNOWN TO ONLY THE DEALER, MUST BE DEDUCED BY OTHER PLAYERS.

Games belonging to the 'Stops' group require that cards be played in ascending order, but also that there is no set order of play. Whoever holds the best card plays it. The 'stops' are the cards that are left undealt and never drawn. This obviously makes it harder to play, since it stops the sequence from following its logical course. In such games, all players are trying to get rid of cards from their hands by playing one or more cards to a discard pile, aiming to match or beat the previous card played.

The oldest of such games is Huc, which was around in the 16th century, followed by Comet a century later. The curiously named Pope Joan game was a middle-class Victorian favourite. The most popular modern game is Michigan, as it is called in the USA. It started off life in Britain as Newmarket.

There are many games within the specific group of shedding games known as 'eights games', but their fundamental objective is the same – to match the rank and suit of the previous card played. Some games are more elaborate than others. In Bartok, for example, the rules about which cards count for what vary from hand to hand. In Eleusis, the dealer invents the rules governing play and the other players try to deduce what it is by noting which plays the dealer rules are legal and which are illegal.

Other games in this group such as Zheng Shangyou and President are known as 'climbing games', as each player in turn tries to play a higher-ranked card than preceding players.

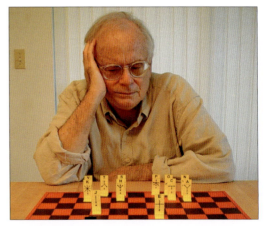

Above: American games inventor Robert Abbott devised the game of Eleusis, which he described as a 'game of inductive reasoning', in 1956.

DOMINO

This long-established game goes by various names, including Card Dominoes, Fan Tan, Parliament and Spoof Sevens.

You will need: 52 cards; no Jokers; gambling chips/counters
Card ranking: None
Players: Any number, but ideally six or seven
Ideal for: 7+

OBJECT

To be the first player to get rid of all one's cards by playing them to a layout on the table.

THE DEAL

Dealer cuts the pack, dealing all the cards out singly to the players. Play starts clockwise from the dealer's left.

PLAY

Before play starts, each player pays an agreed number of chips into the pot. The first to play must then play a Seven – the suit does not matter – or pass. In the latter case, the penalty is a chip to the pot and the turn passes to the next player. Assuming a Seven has been played, that player must play the Six of the same suit to the left of the Seven, the Eight of the same suit to the right, or any other Seven above or below it. The next to play must play another Seven, or the next higher or lower card of the suit sequence. The aim is to end up with four rows of cards, each consisting of 13 cards of the same suit, with the Ace at the far left and the King at the far right. It is best to play Aces or Kings as soon as possible. At each point, if a player cannot go, he must pass and pay a chip.

SCORING

Anyone who fails to play when able to do so, forfeits three chips to the pool. A player who fails to lay a card when he could have played a Seven, forfeits three chips to the pool and five to the holder of the Six and Eight of the suit in question. The first player to get all their cards out scoops the pool. He also collects a chip for each card left in hand from all the other players.

CONCLUSION

The game ends when a player lays the last of his cards.

Above: After players have paid an agreed number of chips into the pot, each game has to begin with a Seven being played.

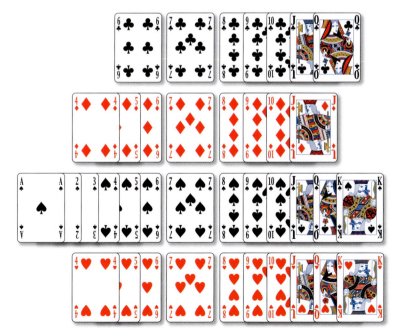

Left: The rows are all well on their way to completion and it's a race now to see who can play their last card first.

MICHIGAN

Also known as Stops, or Boodle, this game is probably descended from the gambling games enjoyed by the 17th-century French nobility, although it is far less serious and the stakes are by no means as high. In Newmarket, the original British version, Aces are low.

OBJECT

To be the first player out, winning stakes by playing specific cards along the way.

BETTING

Before the deal, players stake a certain number of chips on four cards, which are the only ones taken from a second pack, placed face up in the centre of the table to

Above: The four 'pay' cards, or boodle cards, (those that pay out) in Michigan are the A♥, K♣, Q♦ and J♠.

PLAYER C

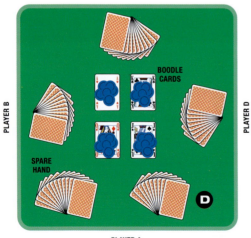

Above: If the dealer decides not to exchange the spare hand for his own, and no one else buys it from him in order to exchange it for his own hand, it is left face down on the table.

You will need:	Two 52-card packs; no Jokers; gambling chips/counters
Card ranking:	None
Players:	Three to eight
Ideal for:	7+

Left: Cardinal Mazarin, pictured here, was an avid card player, and was thought to have used gambling games to his advantage as a 17-century politician in France.

form a layout. The cards in question, A♥, K♣, Q♦ and J♠, are termed 'boodle' cards or 'pay' cards. The dealer stakes two chips on each card and the other players a single chip on each. (In one variant, each player is allowed to distribute his chips freely among the boodle cards, rather than having to stake a fixed amount on each one).

THE DEAL

Each player deals in turn, the deal passing to the left after a hand. All the cards are dealt one at a time, the last card of each round going to form a spare hand, left face down on the table. There are no fixed numbers of cards required to be dealt – the pack is simply dealt out one card at a time to each player. It does not matter if some players get one more card than others.

The dealer can exercise the option of exchanging the hand he was dealt for the spare one. He cannot look at the spare hand before deciding whether to make the exchange – this must take place sight unseen. If the decision is not to exchange, the dealer can auction the spare hand – again, sight unseen – to the highest bidder. Whichever player buys the hand must pay a fixed stake to the kitty. The dealer, however, can exchange his hand for the spare one for nothing. If no one wants to bid, the spare hand is left where it is and it takes no further part in the game. Evidently, whoever deals gets a slight advantage, so the usual practice is to end a game only after all players have had the chance to deal the same number of times.

PLAY

Starting with the player to the dealer's left, each player in turn plays a card face up to the table, announcing what the card is as it is played. Cards that have been played are kept in front of the person who played them until the end of the hand.

The suit that is led depends on which version of the game is being played. In some, any suit may be led, but others specify that Clubs or Diamonds must be played first. Whichever version is followed, the lowest card held in that suit must be led. Whoever holds the next highest card of the same suit must then play it, followed by the next highest, and so on. A player holding more than one card in an ascending sequence may play them at the same time. If, for instance, a player holds the Three and Four of Diamonds, he can play both simultaneously.

During the course of play, any player who plays a card that matches one of the boodle cards wins all the chips staked on that card. The total number of chips staked is usually a set number, but how they are distributed varies. Play continues until either the Ace is played, or no one

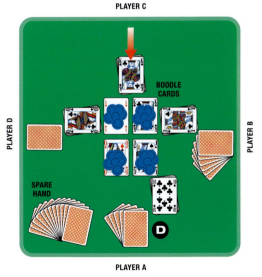

PLAYER C

BOODLE CARDS

PLAYER D

PLAYER B

SPARE HAND

D

PLAYER A

Above: Player C can lay his last card, the K♣, thus receiving gambling chips from other players for each card they hold in their hands – Player C receives two gambling chips if they are boodle cards.

holds the next card in sequence, usually because the card needed has already been played or is in the spare hand. A stop card is one that no one can follow. The last person to play then starts a new round of play. Any suit can be played and the card played must be the lowest one held in that suit, followed by the next one in sequence, and so on.

In one variation of the game, the suit led to restart the game must be different to the previous one. Some versions insist on black after red and red after black. If the player who ended play in the preceding sequence cannot play a card with a different suit, the turn to play passes to the player to his left.

CONCLUSION

There are two possible conclusions. The first is when no one can play another suit, in which case the game ends in a stalemate and there are no forfeits for any cards left in hand. Otherwise, as soon as one player runs out of cards, play finishes. All the other players forfeit a chip for each card remaining in their hand – two chips if any of the remaining cards are unplayed boodle cards. The chips go to the winner. Any chips remaining on the table stay there, the stakes being carried forward to the next hand.

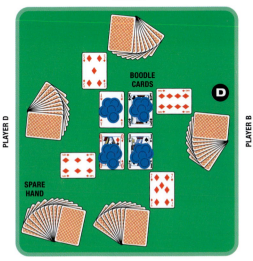

PLAYER A

BOODLE CARDS

D

PLAYER D

PLAYER B

SPARE HAND

PLAYER C

Above: The 8♦ is the last card laid, so the 9♦ is needed next.

CRAZY EIGHTS

When it appeared in the 1930s, this game was called simply Eights. It developed its new name as it became more elaborate. Alternate names include Crates and Swedish Rummy. In Germany, it is Mau Mau (Mao in the USA), in Switzerland Tschausepp and, in the Netherlands, Pesten.

You will need: 52 cards; no Jokers
Card ranking: None
Players: Two to five (or more, using two packs combined)
Ideal for: 7+

OBJECT
To discard as quickly as possible by matching the number or suit of the previous player's discard.

THE DEAL
The dealer deals five cards singly to each player (seven if only two are playing), the remainder being placed face down on the table to form a stock. The top card of the stock is turned up and placed beside it to start a discard pile. If it is an Eight, it is buried in the stock and the next card is turned up to take its place.

PLAY
The player to the dealer's left plays first. Each player in turn must discard a card on to the discard pile. To do so, the card has to match the rank or suit of the previous discard. If this is impossible, the player concerned must draw a card from the stock or, if the stock has run out, pass.

Eights are wild cards. An Eight can be played on any card, its player then nominating the suit that must be played next. It need not be the same suit as the Eight. Some other cards also have a special significance, depending on what form of the game is being played. Sometimes, for instance, playing a Queen means that the next player has to skip his turn, while playing an Ace reverses the direction of play from clockwise to anti-clockwise, and vice versa.

SCORING
If a player gets rid of all his cards, the others score penalties according to the cards they have left in hand. An Eight scores 50, a court card 10 and number cards count at face value. An Ace scores one. If no one can match the last card played, the player with the lowest combined value of cards in hand wins and the remaining players are penalized the respective difference between the value of the cards they hold and the winner's.

CONCLUSION
Play stops when one player has got rid of all his cards or no one can match the last card played, after which scores are calculated.

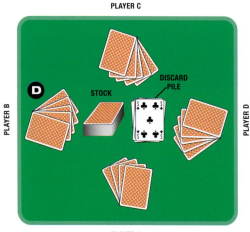

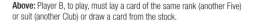

Above: Player B, to play, must lay a card of the same rank (another Five) or suit (another Club) or draw a card from the stock.

Above: If an Eight is turned up, it is buried in the stock and a new card turned up instead.

Left: In Crazy Eights, cards numbered Two to Six and Nine count against players at face value. Eights, however, count as 50, court cards as 10 and Aces as 1.

SWITCH

Also known as Two-Four-Jack or Black Jack, this elaboration of Crazy Eights became so popular in the 1960s and 1970s that it gave rise to a proprietary game called Uno, which is played with special cards of its own.

| **You will need:** 52 cards; no Jokers |
| **Card ranking:** None |
| **Players:** Two to seven |
| **Ideal for:** 7+ |

OBJECT

To be the first player to get rid of all your cards.

THE DEAL

Players receive 12 cards if two or three are playing, but otherwise the deal is 10 cards each. The remainder are stacked face down to form a stock, and the top card is turned face up and placed next to it to start the discard pile. This is the start card for the first sequence of cards.

PLAY

Starting with the player to the dealer's left and continuing clockwise, each player plays a card of the same rank or suit as the previous one face up on top of the discard pile. The alternative is to play an Ace. This is a wild card and its player can specify the suit that must be played next.

If a player cannot play with the cards in hand, he must draw from the stock until he can play. Once the stock is exhausted, all the cards that have been played, with the exception of the last hand, are gathered up, shuffled and laid down as a new stock.

Left: Playing an Ace entitles a player to specify the suit to be played next. Playing a Two forces the next player to play another Two or draw two cards.

Left: A Four must be met with another Four, failing which, four cards are picked up. A Two on a Two or a Four on a Four doubles the penalty cards the next player must pick up, and so on. A Jack switches the direction of play.

TWOS, FOURS AND JACKS

- Playing a Two forces the next player to either play a Two, or draw two cards from the stock and miss a turn. If the player after that also plays a Two, the fourth person must play a Two as well, or draw four cards and miss a turn. The maximum number of cards that a player can be forced to draw is eight.
- Playing a Four is the same, although the number of cards to be drawn goes up to four, eight, 12 or 16.
- Playing a Jack switches the direction of play.

A player with only two cards left must announce 'one left' as he plays the first of them. Otherwise, he misses a turn and has to draw a card from the stock.

SCORING

Aces score 20, Twos, Fours and Jacks 15, Kings and Queens 10. All other number cards count at face value.

CONCLUSION

The first player to get rid of all his cards wins, scoring the value of the cards left in the other players' hands.

PLAYER C

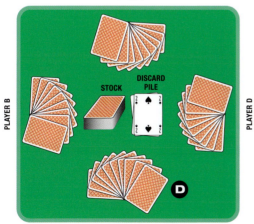

PLAYER A

Left: Player D has laid a Two, meaning that Player A, the next to play, must pick up two cards and miss a turn. If Player A holds a Two, he can play it instead of picking up, meaning that Player B, if he does not have a Two, will have to pick up four cards and miss a turn.

ELEUSIS

This is certainly one of the most mind-bending card games around. Primarily, this is due to the fact that each hand of play is governed by a secret rule, chosen by and known only to, its dealer.

You will need: Three 52-card packs shuffled together; no Jokers

Card ranking: None

Players: Four to eight

Ideal for: 14+

OBJECT

To decipher the dealer's rules and so be the first to get rid of all one's cards.

THE DEAL

The choice of dealer is random, although the convention is that no one deals more than once in the same session of play. Whoever deals receives no cards and does not take part in the game in the conventional way. Each of the other players is dealt 14 cards; then a card is dealt face up on to the table. The remaining cards are stacked face down as the stock.

The dealer's task is to devise a rule governing play that is not too easy or too difficult for the others to deduce and then to enforce it by declaring plays legal or illegal. The rule is never actually revealed during play, although the dealer may choose to give hints as to what it might be. A fairly typical rule would be as follows: if the last card played was from a red suit, the next card to be played must be from a black one, and, if the first card was even, the next card must be odd.

PLAY

The players' aim is to establish a 'mainline sequence' from the starter card across the table to the right, and to get rid of all their cards. A card can be played to the mainline only if it matches the card preceding it. Otherwise, it must be placed in a sideline extending at right angles from the mainline. What is a match varies, depending on the rule each dealer devises. Thus, play is more or less by trial and error until enough evidence has been obtained to suggest what the rule is most likely to be.

As each player plays a card, the dealer calls 'right' or 'wrong'. If the former, the card stays where it was played to the mainline. If the latter, the card is placed in a sideline and the dealer deals the offending player twice the number of cards played – a minimum of two up to a maximum of eight, if the player has tried to play a string of cards.

A player who believes he has discovered the rule, but who has no suitable card to play, can declare 'can't play' and expose the hand, so the dealer can check whether the declaration was right or wrong. If it was right, what happens depends on how many cards are left in hand. If it was wrong, the dealer plays any of the cards that will fit to the mainline and deals the mistaken player five cards. If there are five or more, the dealer places them at the bottom of the stock and deals the player in question four fewer cards than the number they previously held in hand. If there are four or fewer, the game ends.

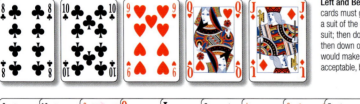

Left and Below: The dealer has devised a rule that cards must go up two in the same suit, then down one to a suit of the opposite colour, then up two in the same suit; then down one to the other red suit; then up four; then down one to the other black suit, and so on. This would make the sequence of cards in the top row acceptable, but that of the row below, unacceptable.

BECOMING 'THE PROPHET'

A player believing he knows the rule may opt to declare himself the prophet in the hopes of bettering his score. There are four conditions:

- The declaration can be made only after successfully adding to the mainline (see 'Play') and before the next in turn starts to play.
- There can be only one prophet at a time.
- No one can be the prophet more than once in a deal.
- At least two other players must still be in play.

The prophet takes over the dealer's functions (telling players if moves are legal or not), and the dealer confirms or negates each decision. If a decision is negated, the prophet is deposed. If there is no prophet, an illegal play means expulsion from the game once 30 cards have been played to the mainline. If there is a prophet, expulsions start once 20 cards have been added to the mainline following the declaration.

SCORING

Every player scores a point for each card left in the hand of the player with the most cards and loses a point for each card in his own hands. A player with no cards in hand wins four points, while the prophet scores a bonus point for every card played to the mainline and two points for each card on any sideline since the declaration.

The dealer scores the same as the highest-scoring player, unless there is still a prophet. If so, the dealer counts the number of cards played since the declaration and doubles the total. If this is less than the highest score, the dealer scores that instead. If the game ends before all players have dealt, those concerned score an extra 10 points each.

CONCLUSION

Play ends and scores are calculated when a player is out of cards, or all, bar the prophet, have been expelled.

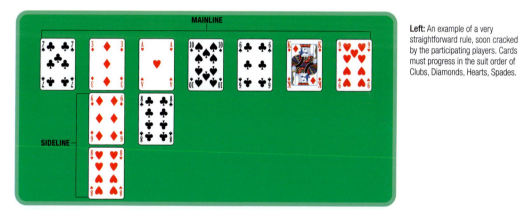

Left: An example of a very straightforward rule, soon cracked by the participating players. Cards must progress in the suit order of Clubs, Diamonds, Hearts, Spades.

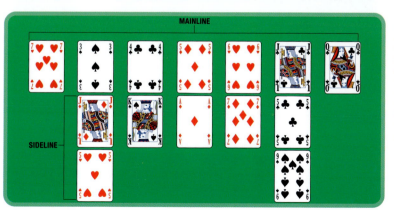

Left: A possible layout on the table during a game of Eleusis. The rule is that, after the first card, a card of the opposite colour must be played next, followed by one of the same colour in sequence. After this, any card of the opposite colour must be played, again followed by a card of the same colour in sequence. Cards breaking this rule are placed in a sideline until the correct card is laid.

POPE JOAN

How this game came to be named after the legendary 13th century female pope is unknown. Traditionally, it was played with a special circular staking board with eight compartments labelled Ace, King, Queen, Jack, Game, Pope (9♦), Matrimony (King and Queen of trumps) and Intrigue (Queen and Jack of trumps). The layout is easy to replicate on paper. Each player starts with a specified number of chips or counters (at least 20).

OBJECT

To be the first player to run out of cards and also to win the most chips.

THE DEAL

The dealer starts by 'dressing the board', which means six chips must be put into the compartment that is labelled Pope, two chips are put into the compartments of Matrimony and Intrigue, and one in each of the other compartments. The cards are then dealt singly to each player, a spare hand also being dealt.

The last card of this hand is turned up for trumps. If it is Pope, Ace, King, Queen or Jack, the dealer wins the contents of the appropriate compartment. The hand plays no further part in the game.

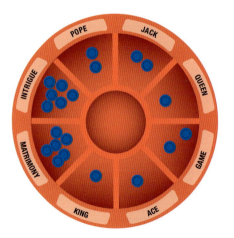

Above: Pope Joan is played on a special staking board with eight different compartments to accommodate the various betting chips, although a makeshift 'board' can easily be reconstructed using paper.

You will need: 51 cards; 8♦ removed; no Jokers gambling chips/counters; paper and pen
Card ranking: See 'Play and Scoring', below
Players: Three to eight
Ideal for: 10+

Above: Assuming Clubs are trumps, whoever plays the Ace wins the contents of the Ace compartment of the staking board. The same applies to the Queen and Jack, in their respective compartments. Whoever plays the 9♦ (the Pope) wins the contents of the Pope compartment. Playing the King and Queen of trumps in succession wins the chips in Matrimony, while playing a successive Queen and Jack wins Intrigue.

PLAY AND SCORING

The player to the dealer's left leads with the lowest card of any suit in his hand. Whoever holds the next highest card of the same suit plays it, and so on, until the sequence cannot be continued. An Ace, for instance, is a natural stop card since it is the highest card in the game. Or, the card required may be in the spare hand, or may have been played already. The cards are played face up to the table, where they stay until the end of the game. The last to play starts a new sequence, again with the lowest card held of a suit of his choice.

Whoever plays the Ace, King, Queen or Jack of trumps, or Pope, immediately wins the contents of the relevant compartment. If the Jack and Queen of trumps are played in succession, their player wins Intrigue. Playing the Queen and King of trumps wins Matrimony, while playing all three wins both compartments.

CONCLUSION

The first person to play the last card from his hand wins the game. The winner scoops the contents of the Game compartment and receives a chip for each card still held in hand from the other players, although a player holding an unplayed Pope (9♦) does not have to pay this. Any unclaimed stakes are carried forward to the next deal.

PRESIDENT

Possibly originating in China, President has several names and many variations. The aim is to be the first player to get rid of all one's cards, so becoming the President. The last player left in is the Donkey. The game's peculiarities include rules governing not only where players should sit, but also what they sit on. In most versions of the game, suits are irrelevant.

You will need: 52 cards, in some versions two Jokers are added as wild cards

Card ranking: Two, highest, then Ace down to Three. If the Jokers are added, they outrank all other cards

Players: Four to seven

Ideal for: 14+

OBJECT

To get rid of all one's cards before anyone else.

THE DEAL

All the cards are dealt singly and the game proceeds clockwise around the table.

PLAY

The player to the dealer's left leads, or, alternatively, the player holding the 3♣. This person leads either a single card or a set of cards of equal rank (for example, three Fives). The others can either pass or play the same number of cards as the preceding player – and all of the same rank, which must be be higher than the ones previously played (for example, three Sixes).

The round continues until, after a play, the other players all pass. The last to play may not play again, but must turn, face down, all the cards that have been played, and then lead to the next round. If he has no more cards left, the lead moves round to the next player who has not run out of cards. Play stops when all bar one of the players have run out of cards.

The first player to run out of cards becomes the President, the next player the Vice-President, and so on. The player who is left with a card or cards still in hand is the Donkey. At this point, the President shifts to the most comfortable seat, and the Vice-President to the next most comfortable one. Other players sit according to their winning or losing status, while the Donkey sits to the President's right (on the least comfortable chair) and the Vice-President to the left.

The Donkey now becomes dealer, dealing the first card to the President. Once the deal has been completed, the Donkey and the President exchange a card, the Donkey giving the President the highest card in his hand and getting back an unwanted one. The President leads to the next round.

In other versions of the game, the names given to players vary. At one time in Europe, King, Nobleman, Poorman and Beggar were popular, as were Boss, Foreman, Worker and Bum in America. In other versions, players are meant to wear appropriate items of headgear.

SCORING AND CONCLUSION

Two points are scored for becoming the President, one for becoming Vice-President; other players score nothing. The first person to score 11 points is the overall winner.

Above: In this scenario, the 7♦ has been laid, so the next player must lay an Eight or higher.

Left: After a deal, the Donkey gives his highest card to the President, in exchange for an unwanted one.

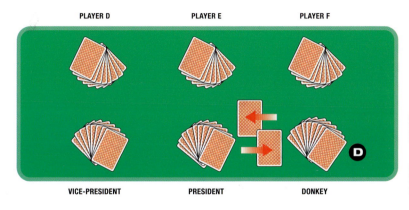

PLAYER D   PLAYER E   PLAYER F

VICE-PRESIDENT   PRESIDENT   DONKEY

ZHENG SHANGYOU

In Chinese, this name roughly means 'Struggling Upstream', but in Britain it has been christened Pits, since the losing players become 'pit dwellers'. It is related to several other Eastern games, such as Big Two, also from China, the Japanese game of Dai Hin Min, and Tien Len from Vietnam.

You will need: 52 cards and two distinguishable Jokers

Card ranking: When laying single cards or a set, the red Joker is highest, followed by the black, the Twos, then Ace down to Three. For single and multiple sequences, Ace is highest, Three lowest. For Twos and Jokers, see below under 'Wild Cards'

Players: Four or more play as individuals. There is also a partnership version

Ideal for: 14+

OBJECT

To be the first or second player to get rid of all one's cards. Players drop out as they lose their cards until only the losing player remains with cards in hand.

THE DEAL

The first player to deal is chosen at random, the next to deal being the loser of the previous hand. The dealer shuffles the cards, places them face down on the table and draws the top card. This is followed by the player to the right. The process continues anti-clockwise around the table until the pack is exhausted.

PLAY

The dealer leads the first of a number of rounds of play. He may lead using any of the following patterns:

- A single card.
- A set of two or more cards of the same rank.
- A single sequence of three or more cards of consecutive rank.
- A multiple sequence (this consists of equal numbers of cards of each of three or more consecutive ranks – for example, 55, 66, 77 or JJJ, QQQ, KKK).

Although suits are generally irrelevant, any single suited sequence is better than any mixed suited one of the same length. If two sequences are mixed, the higher ranking one is the better.

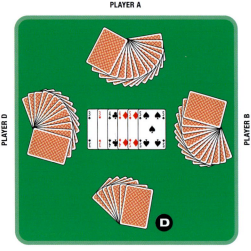

PLAYER A

PLAYER D

PLAYER B

D

PLAYER C

Above: The dealer has laid a multiple sequence – three paired cards of consecutive rank – thus getting rid of six cards.

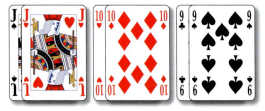

Above: A multiple sequence – three paired cards of consecutive rank. This combination would beat any pair, set or single sequence.

Each player now has to decide whether to pass or to play. There is no penalty for passing even if a play could be made – a player can re-enter the game when his turn to play comes round again. The next player must play the same number of cards as there were in the original lead. The cards must also form the same pattern and have to outrank the cards that were in the preceding play. For example, a pair can be followed only by a higher pair, a single sequence by a single sequence of the same length, but with a higher-ranking top card, and so on.

Tactically, the highest priority is to get rid of the low cards as quickly as possible. It is probably best to avoid leading high cards unless, by doing so, a player can see a sure, safe way of getting rid of all his cards. Often, players holding long sequences find it better to split them up and play them as two or more sequences.

Play goes on until all, bar one, of the players opts to pass in turn. At this point, the last to play turns down all the played cards, which are gathered up and set aside. He then starts the game again by leading with a new playable combination. If that player has no cards left, then the lead passes to the right.

WILD CARDS

Subject to certain restrictions, Jokers and Twos can be played as wild cards to stand for any lower cards. A set containing wild cards loses to an equally ranked natural or pure set. Twos cannot be played in single sequences at all. Jokers can stand in for any card from Three to Ace, but a single sequence reliant on a Joker or Jokers can be beaten by a natural or pure sequence. This also applies to multiple sequences. Although Twos are valid wild cards, they cannot stand for all the cards of a particular rank. At least one must be a natural card or a Joker. For example, 55, 62, 77 is legal, but 55, 22, 77 is not.

SCORING AND CONCLUSION

The first player to run out of cards wins that particular hand and scores two points, while the second player to run out of cards, the runner-up, scores one point.

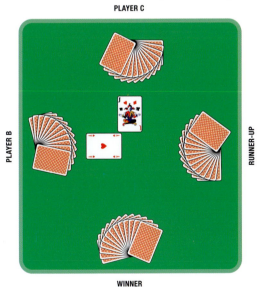

Above: The players who came last and second to last in the previous deal must toss their highest-ranking card face up on to the table. The winner of the previous hand can choose which to pick up, leaving the other card for the runner-up. Both winners discard, and the roles are now reversed, with the second-to-bottom player choosing a card first, followed by the losing player.

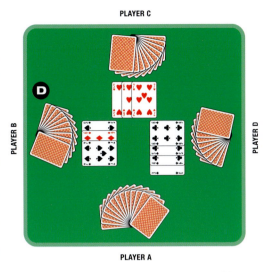

Above: Player B has a mixed sequence of three cards, but Player C beats this with a three-card sequence in the same suit. Player D, however, tops this in turn with a four-card sequence, putting the onus on Player A to lay a higher combination or pass.

No other player can score, although play continues until only one player is left with cards in hand. The last two players become what are known as 'the pit dwellers'. Immediately after the new deal, they must toss their highest-ranking card face up onto the table. If they hold cards of equal rank, they can decide which one of them they prefer to discard. The previous hand's winner is first to pick whichever card he prefers, leaving the second one for the runner-up. Both players then discard one unwanted card each. The second-to-bottom player picks up one of the cards first, leaving the other one for the bottom-placed loser. Play then continues.

The first player to score a total of 11 points wins a rubber. This is card parlance for the match. Typically, it consists of three games and is therefore won by the first player or partnership to win two games.

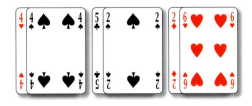

Above: A Two may represent any natural card to accompany an existing card (here Twos represent Five and Six). A Joker may represent any desired card.

TIENG LEN

During the Vietnam War, the Vietnamese national card game reached the USA, where, in a slightly adapted version, it became known as Viet Cong or VC. It is a climbing game, in which Twos rank as the highest card. The highest-ranked suit is Hearts, followed by Diamonds, Clubs and Spades. Rank, however, takes precedence over suit, for example, the 8♠ would beat the 7♥.

OBJECT

To get rid of your cards as quickly as possible by beating combinations of cards played by other players. The aim is to avoid being the last player with cards remaining in hand.

THE DEAL

The first dealer is chosen at random, after which the loser of each deal deals the next game. Cards are dealt one by one, the number depending on the number of players. When there are four, each receives 13 cards; two receive 26; and three receive 17 (the remaining card is left out of play). If more than four play, two packs are used, and the dealer must take care to ensure that an equal number of cards are dealt, and that any left over are discarded.

PLAY

Initially, the player holding the 3♠ plays first – if no one holds this card, it is the player holding the lowest-ranked card. The 3♠ must be played either on its own or as part of a combination. There are six valid 'combinations' that may be played:

- A single card: the lowest card is the 3♠, while the highest is the 2♥.
- A pair (two cards of the same rank).
- A triplet (three cards of the same rank).
- A quartet (four cards of the same rank).
- A sequence (three or more cards of consecutive rank).
- A double sequence (three or more pairs in which the cards rank consecutively, for example, 33, 44, 55). A sequence cannot 'turn the corner' between Two and Three because Twos are high and Threes low.

In two combinations of the same type, the highest-ranked card in them determines which of the two is the better. Each player now has to play to beat the previously

You will need: 52 cards (two packs if more than four players)

Card ranking: Two (highest), then Ace down to Three

Players: Best for four, although it can be between two and eight

Ideal for: 14+

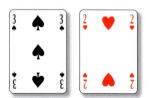

Left: The lowest single card that can be played in Tieng Len is the 3♠. The 2♥ is the highest.

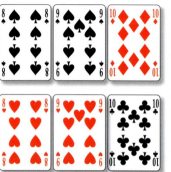

Left: The top three-card sequence would beat that on the bottom, since, when adjudicating between matching sequences, it is the highest-ranking, or top, card that is compared, and Diamonds rank higher in Tieng Len than Clubs.

played card or combination. If a single card is led, only single cards can be played; if a pair, only pairs; and so on. Playing a triplet, therefore, will not beat a pair. Nor will playing a five-card sequence beat a four-card one. A pair consisting of the 7♥ and 7♠ beats one consisting of the 7♣ and 7♦, because Hearts are ranked higher as a suit than are Diamonds. Similarly, 8♠, 9♠, 10♦ beats 8♥, 9♥, 10♣, because it is the Tens that are being compared and Diamonds rank higher than Clubs.

Generally, a combination can only be beaten by one of the same type. However, there are four specific exceptions involving beating Twos, as indicated on the opposite page.

Passing is allowed, even if a player, in fact, could play a card or cards. However, if a player passes, he must continue to pass throughout that round of play. Play continues around the table, omitting players who have passed until another player makes a play that no one else can beat. When this happens, all played cards are set aside and the player whose play was unbeaten starts play again.

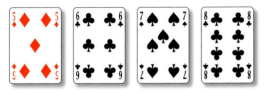

Above: If a four-card sequence is laid, then the next player must also lay a four-card sequence to beat it, topped either by the 8 (Hearts being the highest-ranked suit) or by a Nine.

Above: A four-card sequence, topped by a Two, is the highest-ranking denomination in Tieng Len.

Above: To beat a triplet of Twos requires a double sequence of five, such as the above, a very rare combination.

BEATING TWOS

There are four exceptions to the rule concerning the play of similar combinations. These all involve beating the play of one or more Twos, the highest-ranked card, as follows:

- A single Two is beaten by a quartet.
- A single Two is beaten by a double sequence of three (for example: 55, 66, 77).
- A pair of Twos is beaten by a double sequence of four (for example: 33, 44, 55, 66).
- A triplet of Twos are beaten by a double sequence of five (for example: 33, 44, 55, 66, 77, 88).

CONCLUSION

As players run out of cards, they drop out of play. When it comes to their turn to lead, this passes to the next player to the left around the table still with cards in hand. Play ends when only one player has any cards remaining. He is the loser and has to pay a previously agreed stake to each of the other players.

VARIANTS

Variants of Tieng Len are played in the USA under the name of Viet Cong. The rules vary slightly, as follows:

- A player with four Twos automatically wins the game.
- The player who holds the 3♠ initially must play a combination including that card.
- Twos can be included only in double sequences.
- The highest permissible card in a single sequence is an Ace. Single sequences are called straights and run from Three up to Ace.

There are also special combinations, termed slams, which can beat Twos. The rules for these are:

- A double sequence or a quartet beat one Two.
- A double sequence of five or two consecutive quartets beat a pair of Twos.
- A double sequence of seven or three consecutive quartets beat three Twos.

Another variant involves trading cards before the first lead is played. Any player can exchange any number of cards with another by mutual agreement. If there is no such agreement, the trade does not take place; if it does, a quartet of Twos does not automatically win the game.

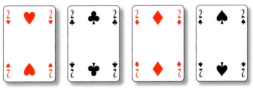

Above: A player with a quartet of Twos in Viet Cong wins the game.

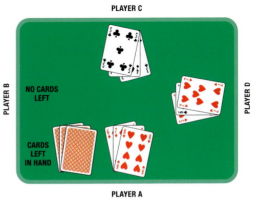

Above: Player B has got rid of his cards so sits out the rest of the hand. Player C lays down a sequence of three, which is topped by Player D and topped in turn by Player A. Players C and D now have no cards left, so Player A is the loser and has to pay an agreed stake to each of the other players.

BEATING GAMES

As a rule, games of this genre are more complex than those discussed so far in this book. In them, players generally take it in turns to be attackers and defenders. Failure to beat an attack means picking up the attacking cards, sometimes others as well, and adding them to your hand. While striving to get rid of one's cards, the primary object is usually to avoid being the last player in, rather than the first one out.

Perhaps the most celebrated example of a game of this kind is Durak, Russia's national card game since Tsarist times. It can be either a multiple or a continuous attack game, in which players take it in turn to attack and defend in what is called a bout. *Durak* means 'fool' and the title is awarded to the player left with cards in hand after all the other players have got rid of their cards.

Shed's origins are uncertain, and it has infinite variations and alternate names. It appears to be closely related to the Finnish game Paskahousu, but unlike the latter, has travelled and is now a favourite in most parts of the Western card-playing world. In all variants, the loser becomes the Shed. He has to perform any menial tasks the other players assign him until someone else succeeds to the role. Elsewhere in Europe, the beating games Rolling Stone and Sift Smoke are both popular.

Mustamaija is another classic beating Finnish game where there is no winner, only a loser. This is the player left holding the Queen when all the other players have run out of cards. A player with the Queen also has to be careful not to play this card too early, or he may be forced to pick it up again. Its holder must therefore carefully judge the best time to play it, which is usually when he thinks that the game is about to end.

Above: An 18th-century Russian woodcut print of two card players. Russia's national card game, Durak, is the most elaborate of the beating games group.

ROLLING STONE

The proverb says that 'a rolling stone gathers no moss', but the opposite can occur here. Players accumulate more cards as the game is played.

OBJECT

To be the first player to run out of cards.

You will need: 52 cards
Card ranking: Standard
Players: The game is best for three to six
Ideal for: 7+

THE DEAL

Each player receives eight cards. All remaining cards are left unused.

PLAY

The player to the dealer's left leads. Players must follow suit, for example, with Clubs; the first player who is unable to do so takes the played cards and leads to the next round. If everyone follows suit, the highest card wins. The winner discards the trick and leads to the next one.

SCORING AND CONCLUSION

The first player to run out of cards is the winner. He scores the value of all the cards held by other players. Number cards and Aces count at face value and the court cards count as 10 each. When playing with young children, you may prefer to start a new game after each hand.

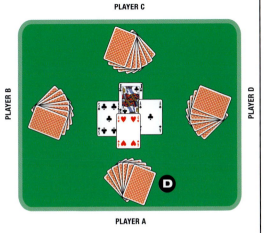

PLAYER C

PLAYER B / **PLAYER D** / **PLAYER A**

Above: Unable to follow suit after the preceding players have laid Clubs, Player A must pick up the played cards and lead to the next round.

SIFT SMOKE

Also known as Linger Longer and Lift Smoke, this game can be accurately classed as the negative version of Rolling Stone.

OBJECT

To be the last player in, not first one out.

You will need: 52 cards
Card ranking: Standard
Players: Three to six
Ideal for: 7+

THE DEAL

Players are dealt 10 cards if three are playing, seven if four, six if five, and five if six. The last card establishes trumps.

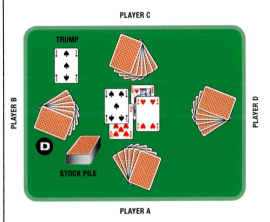

PLAYER C

TRUMP

PLAYER B / **PLAYER D**

STOCK PILE

PLAYER A

Above: Unable to follow suit, Player B can play a trump and win the trick. The cards in the trick are laid down on the table and will only be used again if new stock is needed. He picks up a card from the stock pile and adds this to his hand, which means he will have a card more than the other players.

PLAY AND SCORING

The rules of play are the same as those of Rolling Stone, except that, if trumps are played, the highest trump wins, not the highest card of the same suit. The trick's winner draws a card from the stock. As players run out of cards, they drop out. The winner scores a point for each card in hand.

CONCLUSION

The last player with cards in hand wins. If the stock runs out before this, previous rounds are shuffled to form a new stock. If all players play their last card to the same round, the round's winner wins the game.

DURAK

There are many versions of this celebrated Russian game, which has no winner – only a loser, or a losing side if the game is played with partnerships. One of the most popular versions of this game is Podkidnoy Durak, a game involving a rule which allows other players to join in an attack after it has started by 'throwing in' more cards of matching ranks to those that have been played.

OBJECT

To be the first player out of cards once the stock is exhausted, but, most importantly, to avoid becoming the *Durak*, or 'fool' with the remaining cards.

THE DEAL

Each of the players is dealt six cards one at a time, the next card being turned face up to determine trumps. The remaining cards are placed face down crosswise over the turn-up, so that its rank and value remain clearly visible. These cards form the stock.

PLAY

Initially, the player with the lowest trump (the Six of trumps or, failing a Six, the Seven, and so on) starts play. This consists of a series of bouts, in which there is an attacker, who, in this version, may be aided by the others, and a defender, who plays alone.

Below: This player has been tricked by the *Durak* (fool) into cutting the pack, so must take on the *Durak*'s role, which involves dealing and cutting cards.

You will need: 52-card pack with Twos to Fives removed
Card ranking: Ace highest, down to Six, lowest
Players: Two to six; or four playing in partnerships of two
Ideal for: 10+

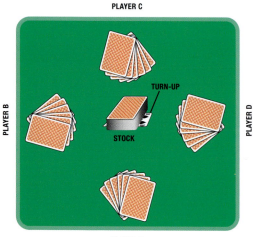

Above: Each player is dealt six cards face down, with the next card turned face up to determine trumps. The remaining cards are placed in a pile face down crosswise over the turn-up card and serve as the stock.

ATTACKERS AND DEFENDERS

The first player is always the attacker, while the player to the attacker's left is always the defender. Although other players can join in an attack, they may do so only with the main attacker's permission, who must indicate whether to go ahead and play, or wait. Before deciding whether to continue with an attack, alone or with others, an attacker also has the right to ask questions regarding another player's proposed attacking cards.

The attacker starts by playing any card face up in front of the defender. To beat off the attack, the defender must play a higher card of the same suit, a trump, or a higher trump if a trump is led. If the defender cannot do this, he must take all the played cards into his hand.

MULTIPLE ATTACKS

If this attack is beaten, more attacks can still be launched, subject to the following stipulations: each subsequent attack card played must be of the *same* rank (it doesn't need to be higher) as a card that has already been played by either the attacker or the defender. The maximum number of attack cards that can be played in any one bout is six. If a defender holds less than six cards before a bout starts, the maximum number of attack cards is the same as the number of cards in the defender's hand.

If a defender cannot beat an attack, he picks up the attack card, together with all the other cards played in the bout until then. All the players entitled to take part in the attack also give the defender the cards they could have played had the attack continued.

Each attack card is placed separately face up in front of the defender, who places each card played in reply on top of it, taking care to position it so that the values of both sets of cards can be seen. A successful defender becomes the new attacker. If the defence is unsuccessful, the role passes to the player to the defender's left, the next player in rotation becoming the next defender.

DRAWING FROM STOCK

After each bout, any player left with fewer than six cards in his hand must replenish it by drawing cards from the stock. Each player in turn, starting with the attacker, takes a card from the stock until either he has six cards or the stock is exhausted with the taking of the trump turn-up. The defender draws last and does not draw if he holds six or more cards. After the stock runs out, play continues without drawing.

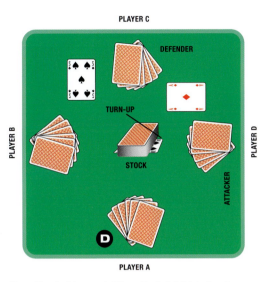

Above: The only defence against Player D's attack (A♦) is to play a trump.

If a player draws the Six of trumps, this card can be exchanged for the turned-up trump, even if another player has already drawn the turn-up, provided that play in the next bout has not yet begun.

ENDING

In the individual version, as each player runs out of cards, he drops out of the game. If the defender's last card beats the attacker's last card, the result is a draw.

In a partnership, if one partner drops out, the other takes over the turn. They decide between themselves which of them will deal the next hand and become the *Durak*, or 'fool'. The other partner will then be the defender. In this scenario, it is often advantageous for the weaker player to deal first, so that the stronger one defends. He may also be able to take advantage of card etiquette.

According to the rules, only the dealer can handle the cards, which is deemed a menial task. If another player can be tricked into touching them – by cutting them, say, after the initial shuffle – that player must take over the dealer's, or *Durak's*, role.

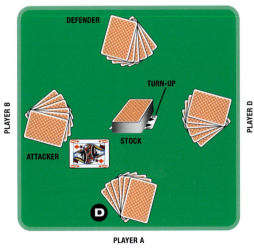

Above: A single attacker, Player B, has led the Q♦. The defender, Player C, must play a K♦ or A♦ or a trump, in this case, a Spade, to beat the attack.

CONCLUSION

Play continues until the last player remains with cards. This player still holding cards is the loser, also known as the *Durak*, or 'fool'.

Svoi Kozyri

This Russian single-attack beating game seems to have been around since the beginning of the 19th century. Its name means 'one's own trumps', which gives an immediate clue to its chief peculiarity. Before the game, each player chooses a different trump suit, cards of which can trump any other cards of any other suit.

Object

Using trumps to avoid being the last to hold any cards.

The Deal

Before the cards are dealt, the players select their trump suits. Each player receives nine cards, dealt singly.

Play

Before play starts, the players check their hands to see if they are holding any Sixes of suits other than their personal trump suit. If they are, they give them to the player whose trump suit they belong to, which means that all the players hold at least one trump.

The player to the dealer's left leads any card face up to the table to start a play pile. The other players try to beat the top card of the pile by playing a higher card of the same suit or a personal trump, followed by a second card of their own choosing. It is not necessary to follow suit.

PLAYER C

PLAYER B | **PLAYER D**

PLAYER A

Above: At the start of play, each player who holds a Six that is not of his chosen trump suit must hand it over to whomever has chosen that suit.

You will need: 52-card pack with Twos to Fives removed

Card ranking: Ace highest, down to Six, lowest

Players: Best for four

Ideal for: 14+

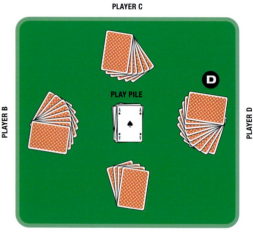

PLAYER C

D

PLAY PILE

PLAYER B | **PLAYER D**

PLAYER A

Above: The play pile is topped by an Ace, led by Player A. If this suit happens to be Player B's personal trumps, he must pick up the entire play pile. Players here hold different-length hands, having had to pick up penalty cards during play.

If a player cannot beat the top card, or elects not to do so, he has to pick up from the pile. If the top card is not one of that player's trumps, the pick-up is three cards, or the whole pile if there are fewer than three cards in it. If it is that player's trump other than the Ace, the pick-up is five cards. If it is the Ace of that player's trump, he must pick up the entire pile.

Before deciding whether to play, the player concerned is allowed to look at the cards that would have to be picked up, including the card that the next to play would have to beat. If the previous player takes the whole pile, the next to play starts a new pile. As players run out of cards, they drop out of the game.

Conclusion

The last player left holding any cards is the loser. If that player, however, has only one card left and can beat the last top card with it, the game is a draw.

DUDAK

This Czech favourite (translated 'bagpipe') can trace its origins back to Durak and Svoi Kozyri, since it incorporates elements from both games. It is fairly straightforward to play, which is presumably why many children in its Bohemian homeland are said to be addicted to it.

OBJECT

The aim is to play out all of one's cards. The last player left holding a card or cards in hand is the loser.

THE DEAL

Each player is dealt eight cards singly from a 32-card pack.

PLAY

The player to the dealer's left leads, playing any card face up to start a play pile. Subsequently, each player in turn may, if possible, play two cards to the play pile. Before doing so, a player may opt to declare a suit to be personal trumps for the rest of the game. Each player will normally choose a different suit, but it is possible for two or more players to choose the same trump. However, having nominated a trump suit, a player may not change his suit for the rest of the game.

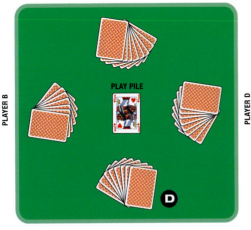

PLAYER C

PLAYER B

PLAY PILE

PLAYER D

PLAYER A

Above: Player B here, the first to play following Player A's deal, has led the J♥. Player C now must lay Q♥, K♥ or A♥, or a trump if trumps have been declared, after which he can lay a second card of his choice.

You will need: 52-card deck with Twos to Sixes removed

Card ranking: Ace highest, to Seven, lowest

Players: Best for four

Ideal for: 14+

Above: With Clubs as trumps and the Q♥ topping the pick-up pile, a player holding this hand would be unable to beat or trump it. He would therefore have to pick up all the cards from the pick-up pile.

The first card to be played must be a higher card of the same suit as the top card of the pile, or a trump, if trumps have been declared. The choice of the second card is up to each player. If a player cannot beat the top card, or elects not to, he must pick it up and continue to pick up cards until one that he can beat or one which he is willing to beat, is uncovered. If the whole pile is taken, that player's turn ends and the next player starts a new pile.

If a personal trump suit has been declared, the procedure is slightly different. Rather than pick up cards one by one, the player is given no option other than to pick up the entire pile. The next to play then starts a new one.

As players play their last cards, they drop out of play. If a player goes out by playing two cards, play continues as normal. If he has only one card left and goes out by beating the top card of the pile with it, the pile is turned face up and put to the side. The next player starts a new one by playing one card, and play continues as before.

CONCLUSION

A round ends when just one player is left with cards in his hand. The overall winner is the one who loses fewest of an agreed number of games. Alternatively, it is the player who has not lost a game when everyone else has lost at least one.

MUSTAMAIJA

This interesting game from Finland is related to several other Scandinavian beating games, in particular the Norwegian game of Spardame ('Spade Queen'), which it closely resembles. In both games, the aim is to avoid being the player left holding the Q♠ (known as 'Black Maria') when all the other players have successfully managed to get rid of their cards.

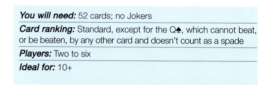
OBJECT

To avoid becoming 'Black Maria', or the loser who is left holding the Q♠.

THE DEAL

Each player is dealt five cards, one at a time. Those remaining are placed face down on the table as the stock.

PLAY

The player to the dealer's left starts the first round by playing between one to five cards of the same suit face up to the table. He may draw the necessary replacements from the stock. The cards may include the Q♠ if the other cards are spades.

Next, the dealer turns the top card of the stock face up to determine trumps. The usual convention is that Spades may not be trumps, so, if the turn-up is a Spade, the dealer places it in the middle of the stock and turns up the next card until another suit appears.

ATTACKERS AND DEFENDERS

The player to the dealer's left is designated as the initial attacker and the player to the attacker's left as the first defender. The latter must beat as many of the attacker's cards as possible by playing a higher card of the same suit, or, if the card is from a non-trump suit, playing a trump.

The attacker's beaten cards, and the ones used to beat them, are discarded and take no further part in the game. Any of the attacker's unbeaten cards must be picked up

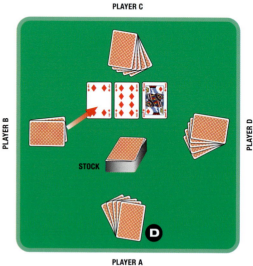

PLAYER C

PLAYER B

PLAYER D

STOCK

PLAYER A

Above: Player B (the player to the dealer's left) launches the first attack. Player C must beat each of the cards with higher Diamonds or trumps in order to defend successfully. If so, all the cards are discarded. Otherwise, Player C must pick up any unbeaten cards.

by the defender and taken into his hand. If the defender beats all of the attacker's cards, he becomes the next attacker. If not, he forfeits the chance to attack, which passes to the player to his left, who otherwise would have been the next defender. The Q♠ can neither beat nor be beaten by any other card, and must therefore always be taken up.

Once the stock is exhausted, a new rule states that an attacker cannot lead more cards than there are in a defender's hand. As players run out of cards, they drop out of play.

Left: The Queen of Spades – a dreaded card in many betting games since the player left holding it loses the game. Known in Mustamaija as 'Black Maria', it can never be beaten, meaning that a defender is forced to pick it up and add it to his hand.

CONCLUSION

The last player left in, who invariably ends up holding the Q♠, is the loser, or 'Black Maria'.

KITUMAIJA

This unusual Finnish game is a cross between Durak and Mustamaija. The chief differences are that there are two classes of card, known as 'bound cards' and 'free cards', and permanent trump suits. Diamonds trump Spades and Hearts, but not Clubs, which are invulnerable.

OBJECT

To avoid being the player left with cards in hand, and thus the holder of the Q♠.

THE DEAL

Players are dealt five cards each, in packets of three and two. The dealer then deals a card face up to the table, to start the first spread. The remainder are placed face down to form the stock.

PLAY

Each player in turn, starting with the person to the dealer's left, must play as follows:

- If the topmost card of the spread is the Q♠, the next player must take it into hand, along with the top five cards of the spread (or as many as there are, if there are fewer than five), and end his turn.
- Otherwise, he must play a bound card – a higher card of the same suit – as the top card of the spread. If this top card is a Spade or a Heart, a Diamond can be played as trump, even if its player could have followed suit.

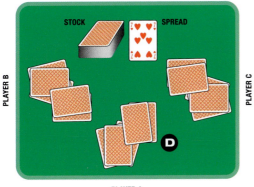

Above: Five cards are dealt to each player, first in packets of three, then in packets of two. The next card is turned face up in the centre, to start what is known as the spread (i.e. the play pile). It is placed beside the stock.

You will need: 52 cards; no Jokers

Card ranking: Standard, except for the Q♠ (see under 'Play', below)

Players: Three to five

Ideal for: 10+

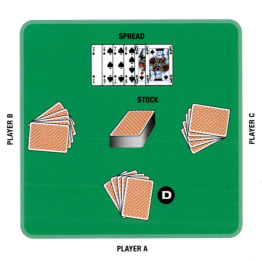

Above: The next player must beat the King with an A♣, or a trump (Diamond) of any rank. If not, he must pick up the spread's first three cards.

- The bound card must be followed by a free card – this is a card of its player's choosing. The Q♠ can be played only as a free card, not as a bound one. Any player who cannot beat the top card has to pick up the first three cards of the spread and take them into hand.
- Until the stock run outs, the players replenish their hands from it, so they always have five cards in hand.

Once the stock has run out, no further free cards may be played. However, to give the Q♠ holder the chance to get rid of it, many players opt to ignore this rule and continue playing bound and free cards, as before. The alternative is to make an exception in the case of the Q♠. Players drop out as they run out of cards.

CONCLUSION

The last player left in, who invariably will be the player left holding the Q♠, is the loser.

HÖRRI

This game is the Finnish equivalent of Durak. Many Finnish card games are related to Russian ones, owing to the fact that Finland was a province of the Tsarist Empire up until the 1917 Revolution.

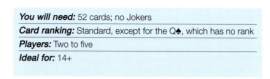

You will need: 52 cards; no Jokers
Card ranking: Standard, except for the Q♠, which has no rank
Players: Two to five
Ideal for: 14+

OBJECT

To avoid being the player left with cards in hand, and thus the holder of the Q♠.

THE DEAL

Instead of dealing cards as normal, the entire pack is placed face down in the centre of the table to form the stock. The dealer then takes the top eight cards of the stock and arranges them face up around it.

THE DRAW

Each player in turn draws a card from the stock. Diamonds trump Spades and Hearts, but not Clubs, which are invulnerable. If a Spade, Heart or Club is drawn, and the turn-up cards include a lower-ranking card of the same suit, the player takes all these cards into his hand. If there is no such card, the drawn card is replaced and the next player draws. If the next player draws a Diamond, and the turn-up cards include a lower-ranking Diamond or any Spade or Heart, all of these are added to the player's hand.

PLAYER C

PLAYER B · STOCK · PLAYER D

PLAYER A

Above: Player B has drawn the 8♥. Since there are no lower Hearts among the turn-ups, the card is replaced and it is Player C's turn to draw.

Once the stock has been exhausted, the last player to take two cards adds any remaining turn-up cards to his hand. Naturally, the players end up with hands of varying length. Some may have no cards at all, in which case they have to sit out play.

PLAY

The player holding the 2♠ plays it face up to the table to start a spread of discards. Each player tries to lead a higher-ranking card of the same suit as the top card, or, if the top card is a Heart or Spade, trump it with a Diamond.

If unable or unwilling to play, the player concerned takes the bottom card of the spread and adds it to his hand. If a player 'completes' the spread – that is, plays a card that makes the number of cards the spread contains the same as the number of players – the spread is turned face down and a new one started.

PLAYER C

PLAYER B · STOCK · PLAYER D

PLAYER A

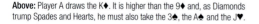

Above: Player A draws the K♦. It is higher than the 9♦ and, as Diamonds trump Spades and Hearts, he must also take the 3♠, the A♠ and the J♥.

CONCLUSION

The last player left in – who invariably will be holding the Q♠ – is the loser.

SKITGUBBE

This is a popular Swedish game, originally for three players. Play is divided into two phases. Skitgubbe means 'dirty old man' (in the sense of unwashed), and is the name given to the loser.

You will need: 52 cards

Card ranking: Standard

Players: Three

Ideal for: 14+

OBJECT

To collect, in the first phase of the game, cards that can be discarded as quickly as possible in the second phase.

THE DEAL

Each player is dealt three cards. The remainder are placed face down in a pile on the table to form the stock.

PLAY

This consists of tricks played by two players at a time, beginning with the two non-dealers. There is no need to follow suit – the highest card takes the trick. If the player who led wins the trick, he leads again with the same player; otherwise, the next trick is contested by the other two players, and so on. Cards from the trick are placed face-down in front of the player who wins them.

If the cards are equal, this is a *Stunza* (bounce). The cards are placed face up on the table, both players draw a card from the stock and the same player leads again. This continues until one of the players takes a trick.

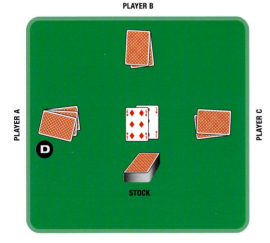

PLAYER B

PLAYER A

PLAYER C

D

STOCK

Above: Player B lays the 3♥, but Player C tops this with the 6♦. Player C must place both cards face-down on the table next to him and lay a fresh card to Player A.

The trick winner takes all the cards that have been played (including those in the *Stunza*), turns them face down in front of himself and leads to the next trick.

Each player draws a card from the stock after playing. Rather than playing from hand, a player can opt to turn up the top card of the stock and play that instead.

Left: If two cards of the same rank, such as these two Kings, are played in the first phase of the game, this is known as a *Stunza*. The cards are placed face up on the table, and both players draw a card from the stock, beginning a new trick. The trick winner takes all the played cards, and begins a new trick.

Once the stock runs out, play carries on for as long as possible. Then, all three players use the cards they have won, together with any cards they may have left in hand, as their playing hands. The aim is to play out all one's cards. The player who drew the last card from the stock leads, its suit determining trumps. Now all three players play in turn, not two at a time as in phase one.

The leader may play a single card, or a sequence of two or more cards in the same suit. For example, the player concerned could elect to lead a Two and a Three or a Three, Four and Five, and so on, provided that whatever cards he decides to play are all of the same suit.

In order to take the trick, the cards that the opposing players play must be better – of the same suit but higher in rank – or, if a non-trump suit has been led, they must be a trump or trump sequence. A player may play trumps even if he is able to follow suit. The winner of the trick leads to the next.

A player who cannot play a better card picks up the last cards to be played. The player to the left then leads.

CONCLUSION

The last player left with cards in hand is the loser.

SHED

Also known as Karma and Palace, among other names, Shed's origins are a mystery. What is clear, however, is its international acceptance.

OBJECT

To avoid being the last player left holding cards.

THE DEAL

The addition of two Jokers to the pack is optional for up to five players, but essential for six. The dealer deals three cards face down to each player. These are the down-cards. Three cards are then dealt face up – the up-cards – and finally three cards to hand. Any remaining cards are placed face down to form the stock.

Before play starts, each player has the option to exchange any of the cards in hand with the up-cards. No one may look at their down-cards until they are played.

PLAY AND CONCLUSION

The first player to declare a Three in his hand leads. He plays any number of cards of the same rank face up to start the discard pile and then replenishes his hand from the stock to keep a minimum of three cards. Each player in clockwise turn must then play a card or cards of equal

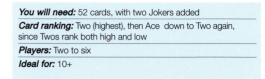

You will need: 52 cards, with two Jokers added

Card ranking: Two (highest), then Ace down to Two again, since Twos rank both high and low

Players: Two to six

Ideal for: 10+

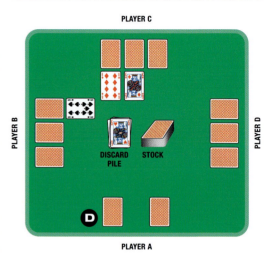

Above: Players B's up-card is not of equal rank or higher to Player A's K♥, so he must pick up the discard pile and revert to playing in hand.

or higher rank to beat the pile's top card. If a player cannot discard, he picks up the discard pile and the next player starts a new one.

A Joker may be played at any time, and simply reverses the direction of play. Twos rank high and low, so one or more may be played at any time – the next player in turn may play any other rank. Tens can be played on any card, in which case, the discard pile is removed from play and the same player gets another turn to start a new one. The discard pile is also removed from play if a set of four cards of the same rank is played.

As players' hands run out, they switch to playing from their up-cards. If a player is forced to pick up the discard pile, he reverts to playing from hand. Once the up-cards are played, the down-cards are played (blind) one at a time. If the flipped card does not beat the top card on the discard pile, the discard pile is picked up. As players run out of cards, they drop out of play.

The winner is the first to discard the last down card and the loser is the last left holding cards – 'the shed'.

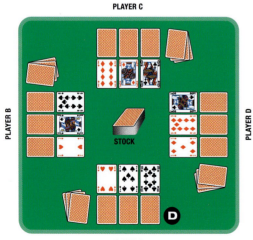

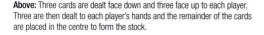

Above: Three cards are dealt face down and three face up to each player. Three are then dealt to each player's hands and the remainder of the cards are placed in the centre to form the stock.

PASKAHOUSU

Verbal declarations and challenges are an integral part of play of this Finnish game. An ability to bluff successfully and a sharp card sense are essential qualities for would-be winners.

OBJECT
To bluff, and avoid being the last left holding cards.

THE DEAL
Each player receives five cards, and the remaining cards are placed face down to form the stock.

PLAY
Starting with the player to the dealer's left, each player can pass, play a card face down claiming it to be a Three (whether or not truthfully), or draw the top card from the stock and play it sight unseen, making the same claim. If everyone passes, the process starts again, although the first discard is now claimed to be a Four.

Declarations and Challenges
Each player in turn plays a card or sequence of cards face down to the discard pile, declaring them to be of equal or higher rank than that of the cards previously announced. This may or may not be true. However, before the next player plays, the most recent declaration can be challenged, in which case, the cards in question must be turned face up.

If the declaration was true, the challenger must add the whole discard pile to his hand. If not, the challenged player must pick up. In either case, play passes to the player to the left of the player who was challenged.

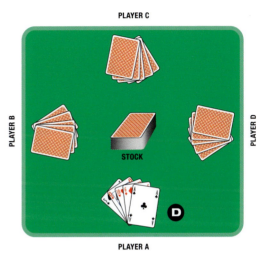

PLAYER C
PLAYER B
STOCK
PLAYER D
PLAYER A

Above: At the start of the game, Players B, C and D have all passed. Having no Three (the card required as an opening lay), Player A can either pass as well or he can play a card from his hand (or the top card of the stock, sight unseen), claiming it as a Three. It's then up to the remaining players to challenge or leave the declaration unchallenged.

Special Rules
- A Jack, Queen or King may not be declared unless the previous declaration was Eight or higher.
- An Ace may not be declared unless the previous call was one of the court cards – or the discard pile is empty.
- A Two may be called at any time, but the next play must be another Two.
- If Tens are called unchallenged, a new discard pile is started. If a Ten is played to an empty table, the next to play must pick it up and miss a turn.
- A player may opt to draw the top card of the stock and add it to his hand (instead of playing from hand).

Left: Jacks, Queens and Kings cannot be declared unless the previous declaration was Eight or higher.

Left: If Tens are declared but unchallenged, the discard pile is moved out of play and a new one is started.

CONCLUSION
The game continues until all the players, bar one, are out of cards. That player is the loser.

CHEAT

Known as I Doubt It, as well as another cruder title in the USA, this children's game remains popular with young people. There are many versions. It is an ideal game for larger groups to play, and 'cheats' or those who wrongly accuse can be given forfeits or dares.

You will need: 52 cards; no Jokers (two packs when more than five are playing)	
Card ranking: None	
Players: Two to 10	
Ideal for: 7+	

OBJECT

To be the first player to get rid of all his cards (using false calls where necessary), but without cheating on the final play. To disrupt others by spotting cheats and making accusations.

THE DEAL

All the cards are dealt out singly to the players (some may end up with one card more than others).

PLAY

The player to the dealer's left plays first, play going clockwise around the table. Each player in turn discards from one to four cards face down, calling out their rank as they do so. The first to play calls 'Aces', the second 'Twos', the third 'Threes' and so on, up through the card ranks. After Tens come Jacks, followed by Queens and Kings, and then it is back to Aces again.

CHALLENGING

The cards a player puts out supposedly belong to the rank that they are declared to be. In practice, however, a player may lie – in fact, lying may be compulsory since you must play at least one card even when your hand does not contain any cards of the required rank.

If any player thinks that call and cards do not match, he can challenge play by calling 'Cheat'. The cards that the player who is being challenged played are then turned face up. If the challenge is false, the challenger picks up the discard pile and takes it into hand. He may also be given a forfeit. If any played card is not of the called rank, the challenge is correct and the person who played the cards picks up the pile and adds them to his hand. The cheat may also be given a forfeit. If there is no challenge, play continues.

The winner of a challenge is the next to play, calling the next rank in sequence, although in some versions of the game, he can choose whichever rank he likes to call.

VARIANTS

Other versions include making the sequence of ranks that have to be played run downwards (for example, Aces, Kings, Queens, Jacks etc.), and allowing players to play, or claim to play, the next rank above or the next rank below the one called by the preceding player.

CONCLUSION

The first player to get rid of all his cards and defeat a challenge arising from his final play wins the game. If there is a successful challenge, he must pick up the pile and play continues until there is a winner.

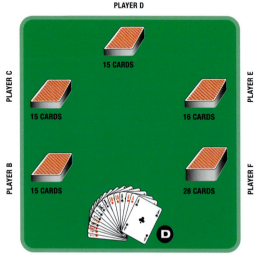

PLAYER D

PLAYER C

PLAYER E

PLAYER B

PLAYER F

15 CARDS

15 CARDS

16 CARDS

15 CARDS

28 CARDS

PLAYER A

Above: Player F has been caught cheating and has had to pick up all the cards previously laid. Player A can legitimately lay the two Aces or Tens face down, announcing them as such, or add a card of a different rank to one of these, announcing 'Three Aces', for example. The onus would then be on one of the other players to make a challenge.

VERISH' NE VERISH'

A cross between Cheat and Old Maid, another children's game, this Russian offering is slightly more complicated, but well worth the effort. The name itself translates as 'Trust, Don't Trust' or, more colloquially, as 'Believe It Or Not'.

OBJECT
To avoid, through bluffs, becoming the last with cards.

THE DEAL
For two to three players, use a 32-card pack; for four to six players, use a standard 52-card pack. After the cards have been shuffled, one card is drawn at random and put face down to the side, after which the rest are dealt singly, face down to all the players in clockwise rotation.

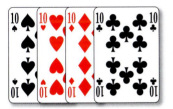

Left: A player starting a new round is allowed to discard any sets of four cards he has been dealt, such as these four Tens.

PLAYER B

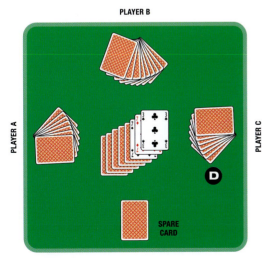

Above: Player C, the third to play, laid down three cards, claiming them to be three Sevens, but Player B challenged, saying 'Ne Verish'. Player C must expose the cards, revealing that one is a Three, and pick up all the cards on the table. A new round then begins.

You will need:	52-card deck with Twos to Sixes removed
Card ranking:	None
Players:	Up to six
Ideal for:	7+

PLAY
A game consists of several rounds and each round is made up of what are termed moves. It is generally played by up to six players. The player to the dealer's left makes the first move by playing up to four cards face down to the table and declaring their rank – although this declaration need not necessarily be true.

The next player has two options. He may say 'Verish' ('I trust you'), or nothing, because trust is assumed, in which case he plays, face down, the same number of cards as the previous player and calls the same rank (truthfully or not), awaiting whether the next player will challenge him or not. Or, he may decide to challenge the previous player, and say instead 'Ne Verish' ('I don't trust you'), and turn the previously played cards face up to discover the truth.

If the cards rank as declared, the unsuccessful challenger has to pick up all the cards so far played in the game. If, on the other hand, the challenge is correct, the player who was challenged must pick up the cards and take them into hand.

This ends the round, the next being started by the player to the left of the penalized player (this should be the challenger himself, if he was correct). Before play starts, that player is entitled to discard any set of four cards of the same rank, showing them to the others before setting them aside. This obviously decreases the number of cards in play.

As play continues, more and more sets of four cards are eliminated. However, because one card is removed from the pack before the deal, the other three cards of this rank necessarily remain in play until the end of the game.

CONCLUSION
The eventual loser is the player who is left holding one or more of the initially discarded ranked cards, while the other players have managed to get rid of all their cards successfully.

RUMMY GAMES

THERE ARE MANY DIFFERENT GAMES OF THIS TYPE, THE ORIGINS OF WHICH SEEM TO BE CHINESE. INDEED, THEY WERE UNKNOWN IN THE WEST UNTIL THE EARLY 20TH CENTURY. THEY ARE KNOWN TECHNICALLY AS DRAW-AND-DISCARD GAMES, IN WHICH THE OBJECTIVE IS TO COLLECT MATCHING CARDS, EITHER OF THE SAME RANK OR SEQUENCES IN A SUIT, AND MELD THEM INTO SETS, WHICH ARE THEN DISCARDED AND COUNTED UP AT THE END OF THE GAME.

In basic rummy games, such as Rummy itself, the aim is simple – to meld an entire hand into groups and then to discard the melds as quickly as possible. This sounds easy enough, but, as is often the case, there can be complications.

Loba (meaning 'she-wolf'), a South American version of Rummy much played in Argentina, can be either a positive or a negative game. In the former, Loba de Más, players score points for the melds they make and lose points for cards remaining in hand at the end of play. The objective is to score as many points as possible. In the latter, Loba de Menos, points are scored for cards in hand when play ends, but the objective is to score as few points as possible. Melds do not score.

In Three Thirteen, an American Rummy game, the number of cards dealt to each player differs from round to round, and there is a different wild card in each round. The number of cards dealt determines which card is the wild card.

What is termed Contract Rummy is played in much the same way as basic Rummy, the fundamental difference being that, in each round, the players' melds have to conform to a specific contract. Each player must also collect a particular combination of groups and sequences of cards before they can start to meld. The contract becomes harder with successive deals.

Contract Rummy is less a single game than a protracted contest: a typical game consists of seven deals.

Above: Tiles for Mah-jong, a game that originated in China. The play in Rummy closely resembles that of the Chinese game, and probably derives from it.

RUMMY

Straight Rummy, as it is sometimes called, first appeared in the early 1900s in the USA, where it also went under other names, such as Coon Can, Khun Khan and Colonel. How it originated is uncertain, though some think that it was derived from a Mexican game called Conquian, the earliest known Rummy game in the Western world, or from Rum Poker.

You will need: 52 cards; scorecards

Card ranking: See under 'Scoring', below

Players: Two to six, but best played with four

Ideal for: 7+

Left: In this hand, the four Fours make up a group and the three court cards form a sequence in Diamonds.

OBJECT

To be the first to get rid of all one's cards by melding, laying off and discarding cards.

MELDS, LAY OFFS AND DISCARDS

There are two types of meld – sequences (runs) and groups (sets or books). Three or more cards of the same suit in consecutive order make up a sequence; a group is three or four cards of the same rank. Laying off means adding a card or cards to a meld you have played face up to the table. Players must discard one card onto the discard pile after each turn. No player may add to another's meld until he has laid down one of his own.

THE DEAL

The first dealer is chosen at random, the deal then passing to the left. If there are two players, each receives 10 cards, three or four get seven and more than four players receive six cards. The cards are dealt singly; then a

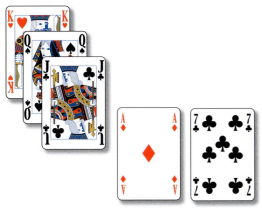

Above: The court cards score 10 points each, the Ace scores one point and the Seven scores its face value. These scores are added to the winner's total.

card is turned face up to start the discard pile and the remaining cards put face down beside it to form the stock. Thorough shuffling is essential before each deal.

PLAY

The player to the dealer's left leads. Each player starts by drawing a card from the top of the stock, or the top card of the discard pile. Each can then play a meld, or lay off. Only one meld may be played per turn. The top card picked up from the discard pile cannot be discarded, but one drawn from the stock can. If the stock runs out, the discard pile is turned face down to form a new stock.

SCORING

In the version of Rummy given here, after a player goes out the remaining players add up the value of any cards that are not melded or that have not been declared and shown. Court cards are worth 10 points each, Aces one point and number cards face value. The cumulative total is added to the winner's score. In some versions, points count against players instead, one variation allowing them to wipe their score by collecting a sequence of seven cards of the same suit. The game should be played to a fixed number of deals or to a target score.

CONCLUSION

Play comes to an end when one player gets rid of all his cards. The winner is the player with the highest score.

RUMMY VARIANTS

O ver time, many modifications have been made to the basic rules and structure of Rummy, so exactly which rules are being played should always be agreed before the start of the first deal. Some games, for instance, allow multiple melds; in others a player who has yet to meld or lay off wins a double score if he succeeds in going out in one turn. This is 'going rummy'.

HOUSE RULES

Practically every player favours a different set of house rules, the majority of which are optional. Some prefer, for instance, that no cards can be laid off on other players' melds unless the player wishing to do so has already laid down at least one meld of his own. In some games, though, a player may lay off cards only to his own or his partner's melds, while others allow cards to be laid off to any meld on the table.

ACE HIGH OR LOW

Whether Aces are played high or low is a perennial debate. In the standard game of Rummy, they are low – so Ace, Two, Three is a valid sequence, while Queen, King, Ace is not. In some games, however, Aces are allowed to count as either, and are worth 11 points each in consequence. Such games are referred to as Round-the-Corner Rummy: this is because, if Aces are high, a sequence may 'turn the corner', as in High-Low Rummy.

Left: Examples of melds when the Ace counts high and low. Some variations allow only one of these options, others both.

STOCK-PILE VARIATIONS

Other variations specify how players can go out, what happens when the stock is exhausted, and how a hand is scored. In Discard Rummy, a player has to discard his last card – it cannot form part of a meld or be laid off. Alternatively, the discard pile is shuffled before being used as the new stock and limits may be placed on how many times this can happen.

Right: A classic family game, Rummy has almost as many house rules as there are homes! All kinds of variations have sprung up, so players choose for themselves the conventions that fit them best.

BLOCK RUMMY

In Block Rummy, the discard pile is not reused at all. Assuming no one wants to pick up the top card of the discard pile, the hand ends once the stock is exhausted. Players score the value of the cards in hand, the winner being the player with the fewest points.

BOATHOUSE RUM AND CALL RUMMY

Both these variants are played much like basic Rummy, but with several important differences. In Boathouse Rum, a player drawing the turn-up from the discard pile must also draw the top card of the stock, or a second turn-up. Either way, he draws two cards. Cards may not be laid off and nobody can meld until one player goes rummy. At that point, the other players lay down as many melds as they can and the hand is then scored in the usual manner.

Call Rummy means just that. If any player discards a card that could be laid off against a meld, any other player can call out 'Rummy', pick up the discard, lay it off himself and replace it with one from his own hand. If two or more players make the call simultaneously, the one who is next in turn to play wins the call.

SKIP RUMMY AND WILD-CARD RUMMY

Both of these versions are played in much the same way as basic Rummy. In Skip Rummy, the principle difference is that sequences cannot be melded, only groups. In addition, once a player has laid down a meld, he is allowed to lay off the fourth card of a rank to his own or to any other player's three cards of the same rank. A player who is left with a pair in hand can go out without discarding as soon as he draws a third card of the same rank. Play ends when one player goes out, or when the number of cards in the stock equals the number of players. The discard pile is not reused.

In Wild-Card Rummy, Twos and Jokers – it is a further option whether the latter are played – are wild. They score 25 points each. Players can steal a wild card from any meld on the table provided that they can replace it with the card it represents, but no one may meld until one player has gone rummy. Scoring works in the normal way.

Right: In this wild-card version of Rummy, the 2♥ and Joker are wild cards so can count as anything. Here they represent Sevens, thus completing a winning meld.

Far right: In this One-Meld Rummy game, having picked up the Q♣, this player completes a second meld and wins the game.

KRAMBAMBULI

Other Rummy games adopting the same principle include Krambambuli, which hails from Germany. In this two- to three-player game, one of the options open to a player is to steal cards from another player's melds. You can do this provided that the theft does not invalidate the meld, that you can combine it with at least two cards from your own hand to make a new meld and that you do not steal more than one card a turn. The lowest score wins.

ONE-MELD AND TWO-MELD RUMMY

The difference between these variants lies in the way players can go out in a hand. In the former, a player can go out only by going rummy, that is, by melding every card in hand at once, with or without the benefit of the discard. The player concerned scores the value of the meld multiplied by the number of players.

In Two-Meld Rummy, going rummy is forbidden. Any player able to do so must keep a meld in reserve to be laid down on his next turn.

Left and Below: In Krambambuli, melds are more or less communal property. In the situation here, with a meld of four Aces on the table, a player holding the hand shown below could pick up the A♠ from the table to make a sequence (Ace, Two, Three).

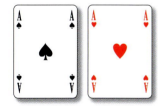

GIN RUMMY

Often referred to affectionately simply as Gin, its countless aficionados consider this to be the only form of Rummy worth playing. Best as a two-player game, it is far harder to master than it appears. When played well, it is a fast, exciting game, some players being expert enough to bring a hand to an end after only six or so draws.

TWO-PLAYER GIN

OBJECT

To end up with a hand in which most or all of the cards can be melded into groups – that is, three or more cards of the same rank – and sequences, which must consist of three or more cards in suit and sequence. Numerals count at face value, court cards 10 each and Aces one.

THE DEAL

In Two-Player Gin Rummy, each player receives 10 cards, dealt singly. After the deal, the next card is turned up to start the discard pile and the remaining cards are placed face down to form the stock.

PLAY

The non-dealing player always plays first. He must start by taking the turn-up or passing, in which case the dealer has the same option. If both players pass, the non-dealing player must take the top card of the stock. Subsequently, each player can take a card from either pile. At the end of his turn, each must discard a card face up on to the discard pile. If a player opts to take the turn-up, this cannot be discarded in the same turn.

KNOCKING

Either player can end play by 'knocking' – that is discarding one card face down to the discard pile and exposing the rest of the hand, arranged as far as possible into sequences and groups. For the knock to be valid, any deadwood (the value of unmatched cards) must not be worth more than 10 points. Knocking with no deadwood

Right: Player A has here knocked and laid down his hand. With just one unmatched card (the Ace, counting for one point), this hand scores 13 points. Player B has unmatched cards worth 14 points. Had the hands been the other way round, Player B would have scored 13 points plus a bonus of 10 for what is known as the undercut.

You will need: 52 cards; scorecards

Card ranking: None

Players: Two

Ideal for: 10+

in hand is called 'going gin' and is worth an extra bonus. Play also stops if the stock is down to two cards and the player who took the third-to-last card discards without knocking. In this case, there is no score and the same dealer deals again. Once a player has knocked, the opposing player shows his cards. Provided that the knocker did not go gin, the opposing player can lay off unmatched cards by extending the melds laid down by the knocker. The reverse, however, is not allowed – the knocker is never permitted to lay off unmatched cards.

SCORING

Each court card is worth 10 points and Aces one, while the number cards count at face value. At the end of the game, both players count the values of their unmatched cards. If the knocker's count is higher than that of his opponent, he scores the difference between the two counts, plus a bonus of 20 points if he went gin, plus the opponent's count in unmatched cards, if any.

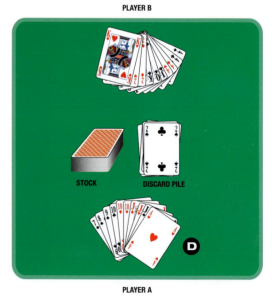

PLAYER B

STOCK   DISCARD PILE

PLAYER A

If the knocker's count is lower than that of his opponent, or if the counts are equal, the opposing player scores the difference between the two, plus a 10-point bonus for what is termed the 'undercut'.

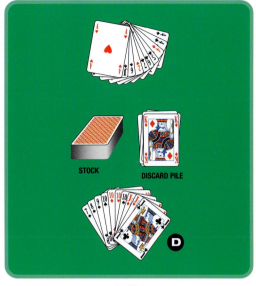

MELDS

Two types of meld (card combination) are used in Gin Rummy:

- A group or set – three or more cards of the same rank.
- A sequence or run – three or more cards of the same suit in consecutive order.

A card can be used only in one combination at a time. It is against the rules of the game to try to use the same card as part of a group and a sequence.

STOCK

DISCARD PILE

PLAYER A

CONCLUSION

A player must reach a cumulative score of 100 points or more to win the game. Both players also receive a bonus 20 points for each hand they won, and the winner adds an extra bonus of a further 100 points for the game – 200 if the losing player failed to score at all. After all the points have been totalled, the player with the lower score pays the winner an amount related to the difference between the two scores, which is doubled if the loser failed to win a single hand.

Above: Had Player A not gone gin, Player B could have laid off the 6♠ on Player A's sequence and the J♠ on the group. As it is, no laying off is permitted, so Player A will score 19 points for Player B's unmatched cards plus another 20 points for going gin.

THREE- AND FOUR- PLAYER GIN

If three players are playing, the dealer deals to the other two players and then sits out the hand, with the loser of the hand dealing the next. There is also a three-player variant called Jersey Gin, in which the winner scores the difference between his hand and that of each opponent.

Four can play as two partnerships, each player in one team playing a separate game with one of the opposing pair. Players alternate opponents from hand to hand, but stay in the same partnerships throughout the game.

If both partners win at the end of a hand, they score their combined total of points. If only one player from a partnership wins, the partnership with the higher total scores the difference. To win the game, a partnership needs to reach a cumulative total of 125 points or more.

PLAYER B

STOCK

DISCARD PILE

PLAYER A

Left: In this game Player A has melded every card before knocking and laying down his hand. Player B is still waiting for a Two. Although the difference between unmatched cards is only five points, Player A scores a bonus of 20 points for going gin.

LOBA

This Argentinian game can be played negatively (Loba de Menos), when the aim is to score as few points as possible, and positively (Loba de Más), when it is to score high. Both versions are played in much the same way, except in Loba de Más, Twos can be used as natural Twos or wild cards.

You will need: Two 52-card decks; four Jokers; scorecards; gambling chips/counters

Card ranking: See under 'Scoring', below

Players: Two to five

Ideal for: 10+

OBJECT
To be the first player to go out in the negative game, or the highest-scoring player in the positive version.

THE DEAL
Each player receives nine cards (11 in the positive version), the next being turned to start the discard pile. The remainder form the stock.

PLAY
Each player draws the top card of the discard pile or the top card of the stock. A card can be drawn from the former only if played immediately. In the positive game, the whole of the discard pile must be taken.

Melding follows. No player may add to another's meld until he has laid down one of his own. In Loba de Más (the positive game), players may add only to their own melds. Finally, a card is discarded face up. Jokers may be discarded only if they are the last cards held.

SCORING
In the negative game, the first to go out scores nothing, the other(s) scoring penalty points. Jokers, Aces and the court cards score 10 points each, number cards face value. Players scoring more than 101 points must drop out unless they elect to buy back in by paying a stake in chips into the pot. This is allowed twice.

In the positive game, melds score positive points, cards in hand negative ones. An Ace in a meld scores three points if high, one point if low, Kings to Eights two and Sevens to Threes score one. Jokers and Twos are worth three if substituting for Aces to Eights, otherwise one. The negative values are three for Aces, Jokers and Twos, two for Kings to Eights and one for Sevens to Threes.

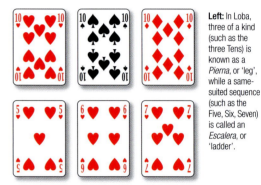

Left: In Loba, three of a kind (such as the three Tens) is known as a *Pierna*, or 'leg', while a same-suited sequence (such as the Five, Six, Seven) is called an *Escalera*, or 'ladder'.

CONCLUSION
A round ends when a player gets rid of all his cards. In Loba de Menos, the game is won when all other players have exceeded 101 points and are prohibited from buying their way back in again, and in Loba de Más when a player reaches 150 or more positive points. The winner takes the pot.

MELDS
There are two types of meld (card combination) that are allowed in Loba:

- A *Pierna* – three or more cards of the same rank, but of different suits.
- An *Escalera* – three or more cards of the same suit in sequence.

Jokers cannot be used in *Piernas*, and *Escaleras* can contain only one. In the positive game, *Escaleras* can contain any number of wild cards, although these cannot all be Jokers.

Above: An *Escalera* in Loba de Más can contain any number of wild cards, but they cannot all be Jokers. Here, the Jokers represent the 6♥ and 7♥.

THIRTY-ONE

Also known as Scat and Blitz, this is a straightforward draw-and-discard game. One of the oldest known gambling games, it has been popular in Europe since the 15th century.

OBJECT

To collect cards of the same suit totalling 31 points, or as near 31 as possible.

THE DEAL

The first dealer is chosen at random. After the deal of three cards to each player, the remaining cards are stacked face down to form the stock, the top card being turned up and placed separately to start a discard pile.

Left: An example of the highest possible hand in Thirty-One: two court cards and an Ace of the same suit, together worth 31 points.

PLAY

The normal practice is to start off with three chips each and all the players deciding which will be their particular points suit. The maximum hand value possible is 31, which would mean holding the Ace and two court cards of the same suit. If a player holds cards of three different suits, the value of the hand is that of

Above: Here, the A♦, 7♠, 3♥, which scores 11 for the Ace but nothing for the other two cards, is beaten by the J♠, Q♠, K♠ (scoring 30).

the highest card. Play rotates to the left. Each player in turn draws the top card from the discard pile or the stock and throws away a single card on to the discard pile. If the top discard is taken, it cannot be thrown away in the same turn, but a card drawn from the stock can be.

SCORING

Aces are worth 11 points, court cards 10 points each and number cards their face value. Winning the game depends on the number of lives lost. (In variations of the game a player scores $30\frac{1}{2}$ points for three of a kind).

Left: This player may hold an Ace and two court cards, but the hand's value is only 11 points, corresponding to the Ace, the highest-ranked card of the three.

CONCLUSION

The game continues until a player succeeds in scoring 31 points, in which case the cards are shown immediately. All the other players lose a life and pay a chip into the pool. The alternative is to knock before reaching 31 points. The knocker stops playing, the others getting one last chance to draw and discard. Then all the players show their hands. The player with the lowest hand value loses a life. If scores are tied, the knocker is safe, but the other player or players involved also lose a life each.

If the knocker is the loser, which can happen because he scores the lowest, or because another player declares 31 after the knock, he forfeits two lives. Players who have lost three lives can play on, but if they lose again, they are out of the game. The last player left in wins.

THREE THIRTEEN

This is Rummy with a difference. In each of its 11 rounds, there is a different wild card, while a differing number of cards, three to 13, is dealt to each player. The number of cards determines which is the wild card. At the end of a round, players arrange as many of their cards as they can into groups, and any cards left over score penalties.

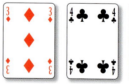

You will need: 52-card deck for two players; two 52-card decks for three or more; scorecards

Card ranking: See under 'Scoring', below

Players: Two or more players

Ideal for: 7+

OBJECT

To form the cards in hand into groups, preferably of high-scoring cards. Groups consist of three or more cards of the same rank, or consecutive sequences of three or more cards in the same suit.

WILD CARDS

There are different wild cards in each round: Threes in the first, Fours in the second and so on up to Kings. Aces, which are ranked low in this game, are never wild cards. A wild card can stand in for any other card – it can even be used to make up a complete group.

THE DEAL

The first dealer is chosen at random, after which the deal passes to the left after each round. In the first of these, three cards are dealt to each player, in the second four,

and so on up to the final round, when, instead of 11 cards, 13 are dealt. The remaining cards are placed face down on the table to form the stock, the top card being turned up and put beside it to start a discard pile.

PLAY

The player to the dealer's left starts and play progresses clockwise around the table. Each player draws a card from the top of the stock or the discard pile and discards a card face up on to the latter. Players arrange as many cards as they can into groups, with penalty points being scored for any unmatched ones. A player can announce that he is out (has matched all his cards into groups) only when discarding, and the other players each get one more turn before the round ends and the scores are calculated.

SCORING

Any unmatched card counts against players. Aces score a point, Tens and the court cards 10 points and other number cards their face value.

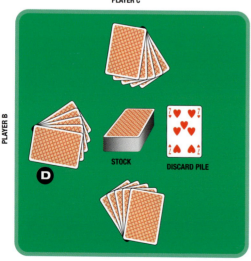

PLAYER C

PLAYER B

STOCK

DISCARD PILE

PLAYER A

Left: As well as wild cards changing in each round, so too does the number of cards dealt. It starts at three and increases by one at a time, until 13 cards are dealt in the 11th round. In the third round, players receive five cards, as here.

Above: Wild cards in Three Thirteen change round by round, ascending one rank after each deal. The cards shown here, therefore, are possible examples of wild cards in each of the first four rounds of the game.

CONCLUSION

The player who has the lowest cumulative score at the end of the game is the winner.

CONQUIAN

Dating from the 1880s, this two-player game is thought to have originated in Mexico. It is considered by some to be the ancestor of all subsequent Rummy games devised in the West, although others say their origin is Chinese.

You will need: 40 cards (52-card deck with Eights, Nines and Tens removed)

Card ranking: Ace, lowest, up to Seven and then Jack, Queen and King (highest)

Players: Two

Ideal for: 7+

OBJECT

To be the first player to go out by melding 11 cards – that is, the 10 cards that are being held, plus the top card of the stock.

THE DEAL

Each player gets 10 cards dealt singly, the remainder being placed face down to form the stock.

MELDS

There are two types of meld (card combination) in Conquian:

- A group or short – three or four cards of the same rank.
- A sequence or straight – three to eight consecutive cards of the same suit.

During play, both players are allowed to rearrange their melds to create new ones, provided that their existing melds still contain the minimum three cards they need to be valid. Melds always have to include a turn-up from the stock. They also must be kept entirely separate. It is against the rules for a player to lay off cards on the other's melds.

PLAYER B

NON-DEALER

STOCK

TURN-UP CARD

D

PLAYER A

PLAY AND CONCLUSION

The non-dealer starts by turning up the top card of the stock and then exercises one of two options. The turn-up must be melded immediately with at least two cards held in hand, after which another card must be discarded face up to serve as the next turn-up. Otherwise the player must pass, after which the dealer must decide whether to do the same or meld with the turn-up.

If he chooses to pass, a new turn-up is drawn from the stock and the process begins again. If a player declines to play a turn-up that could be added to an existing meld, the opposing player can force the meld to be made. A shrewd tactician can take advantage of this to destroy the opposing player's position.

Play continues until a player goes out by melding the turn-up with all 10 cards held in hand. It also stops when the stock runs out. If neither player can make the final meld, the game is a draw and the stakes for the next one are doubled.

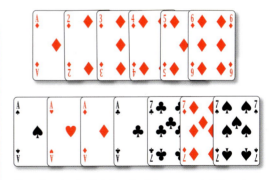

Above: Examples of melds in Conquian: first a sequence of six Diamonds; second, a group of Aces followed by a group of Sevens.

Left: Ten cards have been dealt to each player and, having turned up the Q♦, the non-dealer can pick it up if he is able to meld it with two cards in his hand. Otherwise, he must pass, allowing the dealer the opportunity to meld or pass. If the dealer also passes, a new turn-up card is drawn from the stock.

CONTRACT RUMMY

The oldest known game of this type is called Zioncheck, which dates from the 1930s. Many other variants, such as Hollywood Rummy, Joker Rummy and Shanghai Rummy, have been devised since then. In each game, players contract to make certain melds, dictated by which deal is in progress. Contracts get harder from round to round.

You will need: Two decks of 52 cards with single Joker for three to four players; three packs of 52 cards plus two Jokers for five to eight players; scorecards

Card ranking: Standard, Aces low or high; Jokers serve as wild cards; Twos can also count as wild cards

Players: Three to eight players

Ideal for: 14+

OBJECT

To make the required contract in a given round and end up, after seven deals, with the lowest score.

THE DEAL

There are seven deals in total. In the first three rounds, players receive 10 cards each, and then from the fourth round onwards, 12 cards. The first dealer is chosen at random, after which the deal passes to the left after each round. The deal is also clockwise, each player receiving one card at a time. The remaining cards are placed face down on the table to form the stock pile, the top card of which is turned face up and put alongside to start the discard pile. If the stock is exhausted before any player goes out, the convention is to turn the discard pile down, shuffle it, and use it as a replacement stock pile.

CONTRACTS

The contracts specifying which melds (card combinations) have to be laid down by each player differ in each of the seven rounds, as follows:

- First round – two groups of three cards.
- Second round – a group of three and a sequence of four.
- Third round – two groups of four.
- Fourth round – three groups of three.
- Fifth round – two groups of three cards and one sequence of four.
- Sixth round – one group of three and two sequences of four.
- Seventh round – three sequences of four.

Above: In the fourth round of Contract Rummy, the card combinations needed are three groups (that is, cards of the same rank) of three. The groups shown here are of Kings, Nines and Twos.

Above: An example of the melds required in the final round of Contract Rummy, when three sequences of four cards have to be laid down. Note that the third sequence actually contains five cards, since the 'discard' must be played in addition to the cards in hand in order to go out.

PLAY

The player to the dealer's left plays first. Each player in turn starts by taking the top discard or drawing the top card of the stock. A player deciding to do the latter must wait until the others have had a chance to indicate whether they want to take the discard. A player does this by simply saying 'May I?' If more than one player makes the call, the discard goes to the next to play. Taking the discard like this means drawing an extra card from the stock as a penalty.

The first melds are then laid down. This can be done only once per round, although this does not necessarily have to be during the initial play. The melds must be the ones required by that round's contract (see box left).

Once players have melded, they are free to begin laying off the cards remaining in hand by adding cards to each other's melds, although this process cannot start until the turn after the initial meld has been laid. It is now within the rules to extend sequences, the longest possible one being 14 cards, with an Ace (one low and one high) at either end. To extend a group, players add more cards of equal rank to it.

Right: This sequence of cards would be legal because the two four-card sequences within it are in a different suit.

Right: This sequence of cards in the same suit needs a gap between the Five and Six to be legal. Only one of the four-card sequences within it is valid.

SCORING

The first player to go out wins the round with a score of zero. The others score penalty points for the cards left in hand. Aces and Jokers score 15 points, the court cards 10 points each and the number cards are worth their face values. The scoring is cumulative, the player with the lowest score at the end of the final round winning the game.

PLAYER B

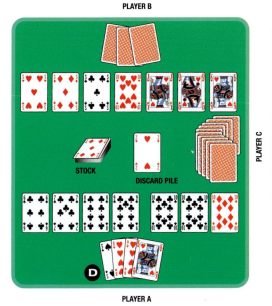

PLAYER A

Above: Players A and B have both laid down the required melds for the second round (a group of three and a sequence of four). Player A has picked up the 5♠ from the stock, which can be laid off on to Player B's group of Fives. Similarly, his 8♥ and 9♥ can be added to Player B's sequence, but the K♥ cannot be laid.

MELDS

As in other forms of Rummy, there are two types of meld: sequences and groups. In this game, sequences must consist of at least four consecutive cards of the same suit.

- An Ace can count as low or high, but not both at the same time. Ace, Two, Three, Four would be a valid sequence, but Queen, King, Ace, Two would not.
- A group consists of three cards of the same rank irrespective of suit.
- Players may not meld two sequences in the same suit that are continuous. To be valid, they must either have a gap between them or overlap: for example, 2♠, 3♠, 4♠, 5♠ and 4♠, 5♠, 6♠, 7♠ would be valid, as would 2♠, 3♠, 4♠, 5♠ and 7♠, 8♠, 9♠, 10♠ but not 2♠, 3♠, 4♠, 5♠, 6♠, 7♠, 8♠, 9♠.
- All the cards held in the last round must be melded simultaneously, and a five-card sequence is allowable, since, in order to go out, the discard must be played as well as the cards in hand.

CONCLUSION

Play ends after the seventh deal, final scores then being calculated.

PUSH

This is the partnership version of Contract Rummy. Although it is played in much the same way, there are differences, notably in the way cards are drawn and discarded.

You will need: Two 52-card decks; four Jokers; scorecards

Card ranking: Standard, Aces high and low; Jokers and Twos are wild cards

Players: Four, in partnerships of two

Ideal for: 14+

OBJECT

To make, as a partnership, the required contract for each deal. The aim during the game is to get rid of all wild cards and valuable cards from your hand during play so that you do not accrue lots of penalty points if you lose the round. The partnership with the lowest number of penalty points at the end of the final round is the winner.

THE DEAL

In each deal there is a minimum requirement for each player's initial meld. There are five rounds: in the first, six cards are dealt to each player and so on until a final deal of 10 cards. The first dealer is chosen at random, after which the turn to deal passes to the left. Once the cards have been dealt, the next card is turned face up to start the discard pile and the remaining cards placed face down

to form the stock. If the first face-up card is a wild card (a Two or a Joker), the dealer will bury it in the stock pile and turn up a replacement card to start the discard pile.

CONTRACTS, MELDS AND WILD CARDS

The contracts specifying which melds (card combinations) have to be laid down by each player differ in each round as follows:

- First round – two groups of three equally ranking cards.
- Second round – one group of three cards and one sequence of four consecutive cards of the same suit.
- Third round – two sequences of four cards.
- Fourth round – three groups of three.
- Fifth round – two sequences of five.

Since two packs of cards are used, there are two of each card, which is why a group cannot contain two identical cards of the same suit. However, it is permissible to meld two groups of the same rank – an 8♣, 8♥ and 8♠ and an 8♥, 8♠ and 8♦, for instance, would be legal.

A sequence consists of three or more cards of the same suit in consecutive order. Aces can be either high or low, but not both at the same time. Once melded, sequences cannot be split up or joined together, but only extended by players laying off cards.

As wild cards, Twos and Jokers can be used to represent any card in any group or sequence. If a meld consists entirely of wild cards or has only one natural card in it, its player must state whether it is meant to be a group or a sequence. If the latter, what each card represents has to be specified, but, in the case of a group, it is necessary only to state the rank.

Below: In Push, the melds that are required change in each of the five rounds, examples being shown here.

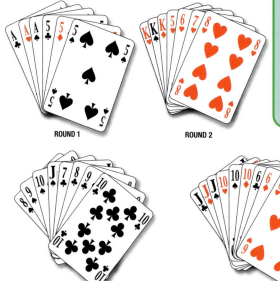

ROUND 1

ROUND 2

ROUND 3

ROUND 4

ROUND 5

PLAY

The player to the dealer's left plays first, play continuing clockwise around the table. Each turn consists of three elements: drawing, melding and discarding.

DRAWING

As far as drawing is concerned, there are two options. If a player wants the top card of the discard pile, he may take it and add it to his hand. If a player does not want the top card, he can take a face-down card off the top of the undealt stock cards. The way this is done gives the game its name. The player takes a card from the stock, places it on the top card of the discard pile and then 'pushes' these two cards to the opposing player to the left, who must take these cards into hand. The first player then draws the next card from the stock pile. Because of the pushing, players can sometimes accumulate quite a large number of cards in their hands.

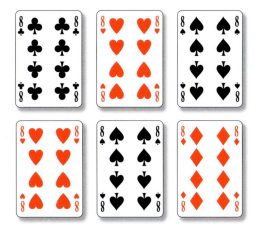

Above: Because two packs of cards are used in Push, it is possible to have two groups of the same rank, as shown here.

Left: If a wild card is turned up after the deal, it is buried in the stock and the dealer turns up a replacement.

MELDING AND DISCARDING

Having drawn, players have the opportunity to lay their first melds face up on the table. Not only must these meet the terms of the contract for the round, but both players in a partnership must meld individually before they can go on to lay down further melds or lay off cards to any meld already on the table made by themselves or by their opponents.

If a player holds a card that is represented by a Joker in any meld, he may exchange it, as long as the Joker can be laid off on to another meld immediately, or used as part of a new one. It cannot be taken into hand. Players end their turns by discarding a card on to the discard pile.

SCORING

The losing partnership counts the value of the cards that both of them are still holding. Each Two or Joker counts for 20 penalty points, each Ace 15, each of the court cards and Tens 10 and the remaining cards five points each. Scoring is cumulative from round to round.

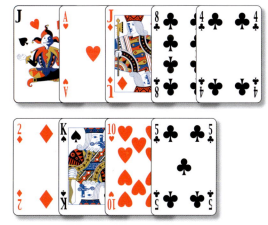

Above: A partnership left holding these cards would lose 100 points: 20 each for the Joker and Two, 15 for the Ace, 10 for the King, Jack and Ten, and five each for the Eight, Five and Four.

CONCLUSION

Play continues until a player succeeds in going out by getting rid of all the cards in hand. This involves melding or laying off the entire hand, or melding all bar one of the cards, which is then the last card to be discarded. It is at this point of the game that the penalty points are counted. The successful player and his partner score nothing – even though that partner will have cards remaining in hand.

KALUKI

Another version of Rummy with a difference, Kaluki, or Kalookie, is always played with a double pack, plus four Jokers as wild cards. The exact rules of play differ from place to place, but the ones detailed below are typical.

You will need: Two 52-card decks; four Jokers; gambling chips/counters

Card ranking: Standard, Aces high and low; Jokers are wild

Players: Two to five

Ideal for: 14+

OBJECT

To combine all cards in hand into groups and sequences. Stakes are agreed beforehand. The call-up is the amount the losers pay to the winner of each hand, while a kaluki is paid to a player who melds all 13 cards simultaneously. An initial stake is paid into the pool. Players may decide to set the stakes as follows: one unit (chip) for a call-up; two for a kaluki; three for the initial stake and five for a buy-in (see below under 'Scoring and Conclusion').

THE DEAL

The dealer shuffles the pack, after which the player to his right cuts the cards. These are then dealt singly to the players until each player has 13. The next card is turned up to start a discard pile. The remaining cards are stacked face down beside the turn-up to form the stock.

PLAY

The player to the dealer's left draws a card from the top of the stock or the top discard. He can then meld or pass before discarding a card to the discard pile. (A meld is three

or four cards of the same rank, or three or more cards in suit and sequence. No meld may contain two identical cards). If the top discard is taken, it must be melded on the first play. Play ends when a player melds all bar one of the cards in hand and discards that card. Each player's first meld must be worth at least 40 points.

Jokers can be used as wild cards, that is, they can represent any other card, in which case they take on that card's value. Once an initial meld has been laid down, its player can build on it by adding cards, or do the same with any other meld on the table. Jokers can also be exchanged for the cards they represent. If the stock runs out, the discard pile is shuffled to form a new one. If this, too, is exhausted, the game is declared void.

SCORING AND CONCLUSION

Losers score penalty points for the cards that remain in their hands. Aces count for 11 points, the three court cards and Tens count for 10, Jokers score 15 points and all other number cards score at face value.

At the end of each hand, the stakes are paid and the losers' penalty points calculated. Players with more than 150 penalty points are eliminated unless they choose to buy in. This involves paying a buy-in stake (the amount must be agreed by all the players at the start of the game) to the pool so that a player may remain in the game. They are allowed to do this twice, but only if there are at least two other players left in the game. The winner is the last player left and he is entitled to scoop the contents of the pool.

Above: A player picking up the 3♦ or 4♦ could exchange them for the Jokers, enabling him to then use the Jokers in another meld.

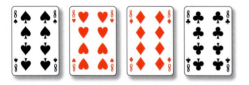

Above: This meld could be laid down by a player with another meld on the table, but not as a player's first meld as it is worth only 32 points, which would be eight points short of the required 40.

Above: A player left holding these cards at the end of a round would score a total of 44 penalty points: 15 points for the Joker, 11 points for the Ace, 10 points for the Jack, and 8 points for the Eight.

VATICAN

No one knows exactly where this game originated, though some card authorities think that it was probably a Czech or Central European invention some time in the mid-20th century. What makes it different from other Rummy games is the way in which melds are treated as communal. They can be arranged and rearranged more or less as the players please.

OBJECT

To be the first player to go out by playing all the cards in his hand to card combinations (melds) on the table. Melds are sequences or groups of three or more cards of the same rank, or in suit and sequence. In a group, the cards must all be of different suits. In a sequence, the Ace can be high or low, so King-Ace-Two is allowed.

THE DEAL

In the initial deal, the two packs of cards are shuffled together with two Jokers, and each player receives 13 cards. The rest are stacked face down on the table to form the stock. There is no turn-up and no discard pile.

PLAY

Each player in turn has the option of drawing a card from the stock or playing at least one card from his hand to any melds that have already been laid on the table. If the stock has run out and a player cannot play, he has no alternative but to pass.

Jokers are wild cards: they can be substituted for any other card, provided that, when one is played, its player states what card it represents. This cannot be changed unless the actual card is substituted for the Joker. After this, the Joker must be used immediately in a new meld.

It is illegal to draw and meld in the same turn. The first time players meld, they must begin by laying down a sequence of three cards of the same suit, all taken from their existing cards. Once they have done this, they can

You will need: Two 52-card packs; two Jokers

Card ranking: Standard, Aces high and low; Jokers are wild

Players: Two to five, though the experts say that it is at its best with three or four

Ideal for: 10+

FIRST MELD

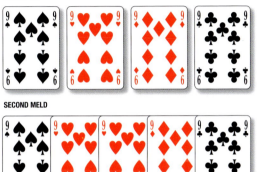

SECOND MELD

THIRD MELD

Above: The first meld here is legal in Vatican, but not the second or third. Five cards of the same rank cannot be melded, nor two of the same rank and suit.

then add more cards and rearrange melds to form groups and sequences at will. The one thing that matters in this game is that every meld laid on the table must consist of at least three cards of the same suit, or three or four cards of the same rank, all of which must come from different suits. More than four of a kind is not allowed.

CONCLUSION

If the stock is exhausted, players must continue to play if they can. Otherwise, they must pass. There is no system of scoring. The first player to run out of cards wins the game.

Right: In Vatican, the first time that players meld, they must begin by laying down a sequence of three cards in suit, all taken from hand.

BANKING GAMES

WHAT MAKES BANKING GAMES DIFFERENT FROM OTHER VYING GAMES IS THE NATURE OF THE VYING THAT TAKES PLACE. INSTEAD OF ALL THE PLAYERS COMPETING AGAINST ONE ANOTHER TO SEE WHO HAS THE BEST HAND, ONE PLAYER, THE BANKER, TAKES ON EACH OF THE OTHER PLAYERS INDIVIDUALLY. FOR THIS REASON, MANY BANKING GAMES ARE CONSTRUCTED TO GIVE THE BANKER A SLIGHT ADVANTAGE.

Many banking games require specialist equipment, such as a betting table marked with a staking layout or a shoe – a long oblong box with a tongue – from which the cards are dealt. To save time and effort, it is also customary to play with several packs of cards shuffled together, rather than just a single deck. Some games, however, can equally well be played off the cuff with a single pack of cards. Also, such games do not necessarily have to be played for money at all.

Banking games are quick to play and are essentially numerical, as suits are often irrelevant. Their widespread popularity is due to the combination of chance and skill. They are mostly defensive, not offensive, and there are two basic categories: turn-up games and point-card games. In turn-up games like Yablon, players bet on winning or losing cards as determined by a card or cards turned up by the dealer, and the bet is on whether a certain card will turn up before another. In point-card games, such as Blackjack, players draw cards one by one, with the aim of creating a hand of a given value, or nearest to that value. The objective in Blackjack is to achieve a hand with a total value of 21 or closer to 21 than the hand held by the dealer, but which does not exceed that figure. To achieve this straight off means being dealt a Ten, Jack, Queen or a King plus an Ace.

Above: Napoleon is known to have played Pontoon, among other card games, while he was held in exile on St Helena, from 1815 until his death in 1821.

PONTOON

This is the long-established British version of the internationally popular banking game Vingt-et-Un, or Twenty-One. Its origins go back at least to the early 19th century – when, to while away the time on the lonely island of St Helena, Napoleon's British captors taught him the game.

OBJECT

To get a hand that adds up to 21, or as close as possible without going over, preferably with just two cards.

SCORING

Number cards count at face value, while the court cards are worth 10 points each. An Ace can be worth one or 11 points. The best possible hand is a Pontoon, which is 21 points in two cards, followed by Five-card Trick, which is five cards worth 21 or less. A hand of three or four cards totalling 21 points beats everything but a Pontoon or a Five-card Trick, while hands of fewer than five cards and worth 20 points or less rank in order of point value. A player with a hand worth more than 21 points is bust.

THE DEAL AND PLAY

The banker deals a card face down to each player. All players bar the banker may examine their cards, then place their initial bets. Players can bet as many chips as they like up to an agreed maximum. When the players have made their bets, the banker looks at his card, and has the right to double. In this event, the players must double their bets. The banker deals another card face down. If any player has a Pontoon it must be declared, in which case the player

You will need:	52-card deck; gambling chips/counters
Card ranking:	See under 'Scoring', below
Players:	Five to eight is considered best
Ideal for:	7+

turns the Ace face up and stakes nothing more. If a player has two cards of equal rank, they can be split into two hands by placing them face up and doubling the existing stake. A player with cards worth 16 points or more may now stick, i.e. keep his cards and stake as they are, and the turn passes to the next player. Otherwise, he may buy another card, which is dealt face down, by adding a chip to his initial stake or he can twist without adding to his stake, when another card is dealt face up. This continues until all the players stick or bust.

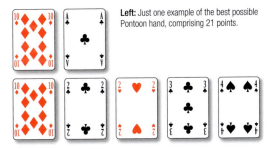

Left: Just one example of the best possible Pontoon hand, comprising 21 points.

Above: An example of a Five-card Trick which, in this case, adds up to 21 points, and is the second-best possible hand a player can have.

CONCLUSION

When all players have either stuck or bust, the game ends with the 'pay-off'. The banker's cards are turned face up, and the banker is free to add more cards to them, dealt face up one at a time, to attempt to bring his score to 21. At any point, the banker can elect to stick. If the banker has a Pontoon, the bank wins outright. If he sticks on a lesser hand, any player with cards worth more wins, and Pontoons and Five-card Tricks are paid double. If the banker goes bust, the bank pays players whose cards add up to 16 or more, the amount that they staked. If no one has a Pontoon, the used cards are added to the stock and a new hand is dealt. If there was a Pontoon, the cards are shuffled and cut before the next deal.

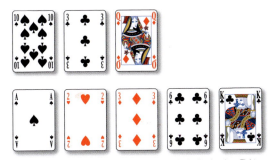

Above: Two examples of hands that have gone bust. In the first hand, an Eight was needed to make 21 points, but the Queen took the total to 23 points. In the second hand, a Five-card Trick looked like it was a real possibility, but the King takes the total just one point too high, at 22.

BLACKJACK

This is an extremely popular game, played in casinos around the world. Its origins go back as far as the 17th century to the French game called Vingt-et-Un. After the French Revolution, Vingt-et-Un migrated across the Atlantic to the USA, where it eventually took its current form.

> **You will need:** 52-card deck; gambling chips/counters
> **Card ranking:** See under 'Scoring', below
> **Players:** Any number, each playing alone against the House (dealer)
> **Ideal for:** 7+

OBJECT

To beat the dealer by building up a hand worth as close as possible to 21 points, but not over that total. If the player busts he loses, even if the dealer also busts.

SCORING

Number cards count at face value, while the court cards (known in Blackjack as face cards) are worth 10 points each. An Ace can be worth one or 11 points. A hand consisting of an Ace plus a court card or a Ten is a Blackjack, or 'natural'. It can win its holder a bonus, since he receives one-and-a-half times the original bet. All other winnings are equal. If, however, the dealer also holds a Blackjack, the hand is tied – this is termed a 'push'. No one wins or loses, and the stakes are carried forward to the next hand.

THE DEAL AND PLAY

Any number can play the game. The rules require all players to place their initial bets on the table before the hand can be dealt. Players simply put the chips they want to bet in front of them inside what is termed the betting circle. After the initial bets have been staked, the dealer deals two cards face up to each player and one card face up and one face down for himself. If a player is dealt a Blackjack and the dealer's turn-up is a number card between Two and Nine, that player is paid off immediately and his cards collected. If the dealer's turn-up is an Ace, court card or Ten, nothing can happen until the dealer's second card is turned.

If the dealer's turn-up is an Ace, a player can bet up to half the original stake that the down card is worth 10 points. In other words, he is betting that the dealer has a Blackjack. This is termed an 'insurance' bet, since it is worth double if it is correct. Similarly, if, after receiving the first two cards, a player thinks that he cannot beat the dealer's hand, he is allowed to 'surrender' – that is, immediately concede half the amount that has been bet. The exception is if the dealer has a Blackjack, in which case the entire stake is forfeit.

STANDING AND HITTING

Players dealt any combination of cards other than a Blackjack have two options. They can either stand (take no more cards) or call for a hit and be dealt additional cards. If the latter, these cards are dealt face up one at a time until the player either stands, or busts by exceeding 21 points. A player who busts loses cards and stake.

Left: Known as a 'natural' in Blackjack, this hand of 21 points wins its holder a bonus. The player receives one-and-a-half times the original bet.

Left: A player dealt two cards of the same rank can split them and play both as independent hands, an option often considered if the dealer has a poor turn-up showing.

DEALER'S CARDS   **PLAYER'S CARDS**

Above: The dealer's cards total an unpromising 17 points, while his opponent has 12 points. The player should hit for a further card here, in the hope of being dealt a card that takes his total closer to 21 than that of the dealer.

Left: Blackjack is one of the most popular casino card games in the world. Enthusiasts are attracted to the fact that success in the game requires a mix of chance with elements of skill. A lot of attention is given to card counting (keeping track of which cards have been played since the last shuffle).

Deciding when to hit or stand is key, as it can improve the odds of winning by more than 3 per cent. The basic rules are to stand on a hand of 17 or more and to hit on a hand of eight or less. If the dealer's turn-up is neither an Ace, nor a Ten or court card, he cannot make Blackjack. If it is a high card (an Eight or Nine), there is an increased chance he will go bust should he draw further cards.

Splitting

Players dealt two cards of the same rank have the option of splitting them and playing both cards as independent hands, though the same stake has to be wagered on the second hand as on the first. The player is then dealt a second card face up to each of them, and thereafter plays them as separate hands. There are two restrictions: if Aces are split, the player concerned can only receive one more card, while, in a split, a two-card 21 does not count as a Blackjack. Despite this, many players consider splitting to be worth doing if the dealer has a poor turn-up showing. In this situation, there is also the option of 'doubling down' (doubling the original bet). Players can also double down on any two cards.

Card Counting

Blackjack can be more rewarding than most casino games since it offers innumerable probability situations and choice of play. By keeping track of the cards that have already been played, a player can make a good estimate of the odds that apply to all the cards left in the deck. For example, the player can increase the starting bet if there are many Aces and Tens so far unseen, in the hope of hitting a Blackjack. If few Ten-cards have appeared to date, the fact the dealer must draw to 16 or less would

mean that his chances of busting are relatively great. Card counting is helpful when used in conjunction with sound basic playing strategy and a good betting technique.

Hard and Soft Hands, or Pairs

Any hand without an Ace, or any with one where the Ace must be counted as one to avoid busting, is defined as a hard hand. Experienced players always hit a hard eight or less and stand on a hard 17 or better. Soft hands are hands that include an Ace, which can always be counted as one. They are so-called because the chances of going bust are reduced. Players should almost always stand on a soft 18 or higher and hit a soft 17 or lower.

Pairs are two cards of the same rank. A player holding one has to decide whether to split the pair and play two hands rather than just one, or to play the hand as dealt as a hard hand. Aces and Eights are always split.

Conclusion

Once all the players have ended their turns by standing or going bust, the dealer turns his face down card face up. If the result is Blackjack, the bank wins the stakes of all the other players. If not, provided that the two cards now on display count for 16 points or less, the dealer can draw more cards, face up and singly. He must stand when the cards are worth 17 points or more.

If the dealer busts, all the players still in the game win. If a player's card count is closer to 21 than that of the dealer, that player wins. If it is less, that player loses. The only way a player can lose without busting is when the dealer is closest to 21.

BACCARAT

Anyone who has read Ian Fleming's *Casino Royale* will be familiar with the climactic game of Baccarat played between James Bond and the chief villain. The game probably originated in Italy in the 1490s. Its name comes from the word *baccara*, meaning 'zero', which refers to the fact that court cards and Tens are worth nothing.

You will need: 52-card deck; gambling chips/counters

Card ranking: See under 'Play', below

Players: Any number, each playing alone against the bank (dealer)

Ideal for: 7+

OBJECT

To beat the banker with a higher hand, the best possible being worth nine points.

THE DEAL

In Baccarat proper, the house is always the bank; in Chemin de Fer, a popular variant, it passes from player to player. Either way, the banker shuffles the cards and passes them to each player in turn, who deals two cards face down separately. The banker finally takes two. Players examine their cards and bet against the bank, which plays against each of them separately.

Right: It is the practice in Baccarat to deal from a shoe, but this is not essential.

PLAY

Number cards count at face value. Aces are worth one point. A two-card total of nine points is termed a 'natural' and cannot lose. A two-card total of eight is the second-best hand. No further cards may be drawn if a player is holding a two-card draw of six or seven. In hands adding up to more than nine, only the second digit counts, i.e. five plus seven is worth two, not 12.

If the count is less than five, a player must call for another card, which is drawn face up, but, if the count is exactly five, he may stand (take no more cards) or

Left: If the two-card total of a player's hand is less than five, that player must call for another card, which is drawn face up.

Left: A two-card total of nine, such as that shown here, is termed a 'natural' in Baccarat, and cannot lose.

draw (call for another card). If the banker's hand is worth less than five points, he must draw. If it is worth three points, the banker draws if the opponent's third card is anything between an Ace and a Ten. If the banker's hand is worth four points, he draws to an opponent's third card between Two and Seven and, if it is worth five points, he draws to a third card which is between Four and Seven. If the third card is worth six or more, the banker draws only to a Six or a Seven.

Even with a hand worth just three points, the banker stands if the opposing player's third card is an Eight. If the banker has four points, the bank stands if the player's third card is an Ace, Eight, Nine or Ten, while, if the bank's cards are worth six points, the bank stands to an Ace or Ten. If the bank's cards are worth seven points or more, the banker always stands, regardless of the value of the third card a player may hold.

CONCLUSION

The hand with a value of nine points, or the one closest to nine, wins. If the hands are tied, there is no winner or loser, and the stakes are carried forward to the next deal.

YABLON

Also often known as Acey-Deucey and In Between, Yablon is a simple gambling game in which suits are irrelevant and only three cards are played per hand. In the USA the game has been recently rechristened Red Dog, which is confusing because there is another gambling game of the same name. Casino play involves anything up to eight packs dealt from a shoe.

You will need: 52-card deck; gambling chips/counters	
Card ranking: See under 'The Deal and Play', below	
Players: Any number, each playing alone against the bank (dealer)	
Ideal for: 10+	

OBJECT

To bet on whether a third card dealt by the dealer will rank between the first two cards.

THE DEAL AND PLAY

Cards from Two to Ten count at face value, Jacks score 11, Queens 12, Kings 13 and Aces 14. In Yablon, players bet that the third card dealt from the top of the pack will be intermediate in rank between the first two cards. All players make an initial stake, after which the dealer deals them two cards face up on the table with enough space between them for a third.

The dealer then places a marker to indicate the spread, the difference between the card values of the cards that have been dealt, and the odds being offered on an additional bet. If a player bets no further, but wins the hand, he wins the original stake at even money.

If they wish, players can now raise their bets, but not by more than the initial bet, the odds being determined by the 'spread' – that is, the number of ranks intermediate between the first two cards. For example, if the 5♠ and the 7♣ are dealt then the spread is one, and the

players are allowed to place a 'raise' bet up to the size of the original bet. If the two cards are consecutive (such as the 5♠ and the 6♣), it is a tie. If they are identical, then the players are not allowed to raise. The number of players is irrelevant, since all players win or lose simultaneously. The only strategy decision that the player is allowed to make is whether or not to double the bet.

SCORING

The odds paid to successful players vary with the 'spread' – the number of ranks between the first two cards. A spread of one has odds of 5:1, a spread of two has odds of 4:1, and a spread of three has odds of 2:1. For spreads of between four and 11, the odds are even.

CONCLUSION

The dealer deals a third card face up. If the card is intermediate, the players win. If not, the bank does. Players who have raised and won get the original stake back, plus the raise at the appropriate odds.

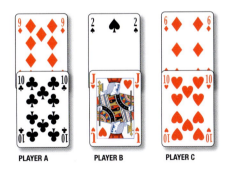

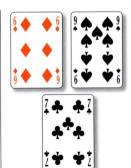

Above: Players bet that the third card from the top of the pack will be intermediate in rank between the first two cards. For Player A, this is impossible, so he will fold. Player B has every chance of success, so he is likely to bet heavily. Player C's chances are limited, so betting will be more circumspect.

Above: On the left, the dealer has turned up a Jack outside the spread of the two cards dealt. All bets placed are lost. In the example on the right, the dealer's card falls in between the table cards, so any player who placed a bet and raised will retrieve his original stake plus the raise at appropriate odds.

SPECULATION

Mentioned by Jane Austen and Charles Dickens in their novels, this, according to the 1847 edition of *Hoyle's Games*, is 'a noisy round game that several may play'. In his *The Card Player*, published 20 years later, Charles Pardon described it as an ideal 'merry game for Christmas parties'. Though it dropped out of favour at the end of the 1800s, it is well worth reviving.

> **You will need:** 52-card deck; gambling chips/counters
> **Card ranking:** Standard
> **Players:** Any number, each playing alone against the dealer
> **Ideal for:** 7+

OBJECT

To end the game holding the highest trump card when all the cards being played have been revealed.

THE DEAL

All players begin with the same number of chips, each anteing one to start the pot. (The ante is the stake that each player must put into the pot before receiving a hand or new cards.) The dealer deals three cards face down in front of each player in a stack, turning the next one up in front of him to establish the trump suit. If it is an Ace, the dealer wins the game immediately.

PLAY

Assuming the dealer hasn't already won, players turn up their top cards, starting with the player to the dealer's left. If a trump card is turned up that is higher than the previous player's, its holder may offer it for sale or retain it. The holder of the highest trump card sits out play until a higher one is turned up. Any player may offer to buy any face-down card or cards sight unseen – they can be revealed only when turned up during play. If no trump card is turned up, the pot carries over to the next round.

Left: If the dealer turns up an Ace, he wins immediately.

Right: In some variations of Speculation, a player turning over a Jack has to pay an extra chip into the pot.

CONCLUSION

The game ends when all the cards have been exposed or if a player turns up the Ace of trumps. Whoever holds the highest trump is the winner.

Left: Writer Jane Austen (1775–1817) mentioned the game Speculation in her novel *Mansfield Park*, as did Charles Dickens (1812–70) in his novel *Nicholas Nickleby*.

LET IT RIDE

This banking game is a variation of the poker game Five-Card Stud. In Let it Ride, players do not have to beat anyone else's hand. It is popular with beginners because it is very easy to learn.

You will need: 52-card deck; gambling chips/counters

Card ranking: See 'Hand Ranking' below

Players: Any number

Ideal for: 7+

OBJECT

To construct a winning Poker hand, the minimum hand being a Pair of Tens. Players win according to how good a Poker hand is made by their three cards combined with the dealer's two cards.

THE DEAL AND PLAY

Each player places three equal stakes before the deal, although subsequently one or two of them may be withdrawn. Each player is then dealt three cards face down, while the dealer takes two.

After the cards have been examined, each player can either withdraw one of the three initial stakes, or let it ride – stay with their stake. The dealer then exposes one of the two cards he has been dealt and the other players

get the same opportunity. This means that, at the most, players will have three stakes in front of them when the dealer's second card is turned and, at the least, one.

The skill lies in knowing when to let a bet ride. It is the best strategy to let it ride on the first bet if you hold a high-card Pair; Three of a Kind; three consecutive cards of the same suit valued Three, Four, Five or better; three of a Straight Flush with one skip – a missing card – and at least one high card, or with two skips and at least two high cards. On the second bet, in addition to the above, let it ride if you have Two Pairs, four of any Flush, four of a Straight or four High Cards.

SCORING

All players with a Pair or better are paid at the following fixed odds, according to their stakes.

- A Pair – evens
- Two Pairs – 2:1
- Three of a Kind – 3:1
- Straight – 5:1
- Flush – 8:1

- Full House – 11:1
- Four of a Kind – 50:1
- Straight Flush – 200:1
- Royal Flush –1,000:1

Left: On the second bet, it is best to let it ride if you have four of any flush.

HAND RANKING

Hands rank from highest to lowest as follows:

- Royal Flush – A Straight Flush up to Ace; i.e. J♦, Q♦, K♦, A♦.
- Straight Flush – A combined Straight and Flush; i.e. cards in sequence and of same suit.
- Four of a Kind – Four cards of the same face value ('quads').
- Full House – Three of a Kind (also known as 'trips') and a Pair. When two players hold a Full House, the one with the highest-ranking trips wins.
- Flush – Five cards of the same suit. If another player holds a Flush, whoever holds the highest card wins.
- Straight – A sequence of five cards in any suit; e.g. 5♦, 6♣, 7♠, 8♥, 9♣. The highest Straight is one topped by Ace, the lowest starts with Ace. Should two players hold a Straight, the one with the highest cards wins.
- Three of a Kind – Three cards of the same face value; e.g. Q♠, Q♣, Q♥.
- Two Pairs – Two sets of Pairs; e.g. 10♦, 10♥ and Q♠, Q♣. If two players hold Pairs of the same value, whoever holds the highest cards in the two hands – the 'kicker' – wins.
- One Pair – Two cards of the same value, Ten or above; e.g. 10♦, 10♥ or Q♠, Q♣. Should another player hold a Pair of the same value, then whoever holds the kicker wins.
- High Card – A hand with no combinations, but having within it the highest-ranking card among the hands in play.

CONCLUSION

The game ends after the dealer's second card has been turned with what's known as the payout. Players show their hands, and the dealer collects the stakes from any players whose three cards plus the dealer's two do not form a Pair of Tens or better. The others are paid according to their stakes at the appropriate odds.

ALL FOURS GAMES

SOME OF THE MOST INTERESTING CARD GAMES IN THE ENGLISH-SPEAKING WORLD CAN TRACE THEIR ANCESTRY BACK TO THE TIME OF CHARLES II'S REIGN IN THE 17TH CENTURY, SPECIFICALLY TO A GAME CALLED ALL FOURS. THIS GAME INTRODUCED THE TERM 'JACK' FOR 'KNAVE', ALTHOUGH IT TOOK MANY YEARS FOR THIS NAME TO BE UNIVERSALLY ADOPTED. WHEN ALL FOURS REACHED THE USA 200 YEARS LATER, THIS SOON SPAWNED VARIANTS.

Despite its origins as a low-class game played mostly in alehouses or by servants and the lower ranks of the British Navy, All Fours rapidly became one of the most popular games in the USA in the 19th century. Despite subsequent competition from other games, notably Euchre and Poker, All Fours has survived, partly by developing more elaborate forms to compete with them for interest. It is the national card game of Trinidad and is still played in the Yorkshire and Lancashire regions of its British homeland.

Over time, quite a few variants of All Fours have developed including Pitch, Smear, Cinch and Don, all of which incorporate some system of bidding.

Pitch originated in the USA, where it is also called Setback or High-Low-Jack. There are two varieties: partnership and cut-throat. In the former, four players play in partnerships, and in the latter players are out for themselves. Smear is also American in origin and uses Jokers as extra trumps. Cinch comes from Colorado, and the aim is to play a trump high enough to beat the Five of Trumps.

Don is yet another version of the all-fours partnership game played in various forms in Ireland, from where it crossed the Irish Sea to reach Britain some time in the late 19th or early 20th century.

Above: The use of the term 'Jack' was considered rather vulgar when first introduced. In *Great Expectations*, Dickens has the character Pip divulge his social status when Estella says snootily 'He calls his knaves *Jacks*, this boy!'

ALL FOURS

The earliest reference to All Fours dates from 1674, when it was recorded in Charles Cotton's *Complete Gamester* as being a game played in Kent, England. From there, it migrated to the USA under the names Seven Up and Old Sledge.

You will need: 52-card deck; scorecards

Card ranking: Standard

Players: Normally four, playing for themselves or in partnership, though two or three can play as well

Ideal for: 14+

OBJECT

To win as many points as possible, thus being the first player to score seven.

THE DEAL

Players cut the pack for the deal: the one with the highest card becomes the first dealer. The deal passes to the right after each hand. Each player is dealt six cards, either singly or in two packets of three, and the next card is turned face up to indicate the putative trump suit for the hand. If the turn-up card is an Ace, Jack or Six, the dealer or the dealing partnership scores a bonus point.

ESTABLISHING TRUMPS

The player to the dealer's right has the option of accepting the trump suit, in which case he says 'Stand', or requesting a change by saying 'I beg'. If the dealer overrides the request, he says 'Take One', in which case the opposing player or partnership scores a point and play begins. If the dealer agrees to change trumps by saying 'Refuse the gift', the turn-up is set aside, each player is dealt three more

cards and the next one is turned up to find a new trump. The procedure is repeated until a new trump suit is established. If the deck is exhausted before this happens, the cards are 'bunched', that is, thrown in, shuffled and then dealt again. The entire process is termed 'running the cards'. Following it, players discard enough unwanted cards face down to reduce their hands to six cards again.

PLAY AND SCORING

The player to the dealer's right leads, and the other players must follow suit, or they must trump. If they cannot do either, they can play any card. The highest card of the suit led or the highest trump wins the trick. There are penalties for playing a card of a different suit to the card that was led when one could have followed suit, or failing to play a trump when one could have been played (termed a revoke or renege). If the offending player failed to follow a trump, despite holding one or more of the five top trumps, the penalty is to forfeit the game. For a revoke on a non-trump lead or failing to play a low trump to a trump lead, the opposing players win a penalty point and the revoking player cannot win the point normally awarded for game. Points are won in each hand as follows:

- One point for High (being dealt the highest trump).
- One point for Low (being dealt the lowest trump).
- One point for capturing the Jack of trumps.
- One point for turning up a Jack (if applicable).
- One point for Game (ending up with the highest total of point-scoring cards). Aces count four, Kings three, Queens two, Jacks one and Tens 10. Each partnership adds up the value of any such cards they have won in tricks, and whichever has the most scores the game point. In the event of a tie, no Game point is scored.

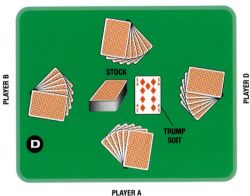

PLAYER C

PLAYER B

STOCK

PLAYER D

TRUMP SUIT

D

PLAYER A

Above: In this scenario after the cards have been dealt, the player to the dealer's right can accept the turned-up trump suit or request a change, in which case it is down to the dealer to make the final decision.

CONCLUSION

Play in each round continues until all cards have been laid. The first player to score seven points wins.

PITCH

This game, which is also known as Setback or High-Low-Jack, is played like All Fours, but with a round of bidding added. Instead of turning a card to establish trumps, the player who wins the auction chooses the trump suit, which is confirmed by 'pitching' – leading a card from the chosen suit to the first trick.

You will need: 52 card-deck; scorecards	
Card ranking: Standard	
Players: Two to seven (four usually play in partnerships of two; six can also play in pairs)	
Ideal for: 14+	

OBJECT

To win a specified number of tricks (rounds of the game) or to score bonus points.

THE DEAL

Each player is dealt six cards three at a time, and the remainder of the pack is placed face down out of play. The deal rotates clockwise after each hand.

BIDDING

Following the deal, there is a round of bidding in which each player can bid up to the maximum number of points that can be won in each hand for High (being dealt the highest trump), Low (being dealt or having captured the lowest trump), Jack (having captured the Jack of trumps) and Game (ending up with the most point-scoring cards). The bids are two, three and four, plus smudge, a bid to win all six tricks. Each bid must be higher than the one

before it, though the dealer, who bids last, can 'steal the deal' by matching the previous bid. If, however, the other players all pass, the dealer is obliged to bid at least two.

PLAY AND SCORING

The winning bidder becomes the pitcher, with the right to choose the trump suit and lead to the first trick. The highest trump played wins each trick, or the highest card in the suit led. Players may use a trump on any trick even if able to follow suit. The trick's winner leads to the next.

A player or partnership that fulfils their bid scores the number of points they have won. Bidding two and making four, for example, scores four points. If they fail to make their bid, they are 'set back' by that amount, that is, they lose the value of their bid.

The opposing player or partnership makes whatever points they earn. If, for instance, the pitching partnership bid two, but their opponents take the Two of trumps, they score a point for Low. Likewise, High, Jack and Game are also worth one point.

Left: Assuming Spades are trumps, if a partnership has bid two but its opponents capture the 2♠, the opponents score a point for Low (having captured the lowest trump).

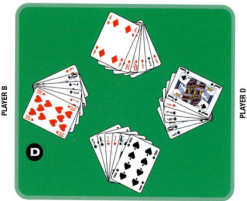

PLAYER C

PLAYER B

PLAYER D

PLAYER A

Above: A scenario after the deal. Player C bids two in an attempt to win a point for High (highest trump) with his Ace. Player D bids three for the same reasons, plus he is hoping to win a point for Low (lowest trump) with his Two. Players A and B decide to pass. As the highest bidder, Player D pitches the Ace, thereby making Clubs trumps.

CONCLUSION

The game is won by the first player or partnership to reach a previously agreed total of points – this can be as low as seven or as high as 21 – but this can be achieved only at the end of a hand in which the partnership made its bid. Paradoxically, this means that the game can be won by a partnership with fewer points than the losing partnership.

SMEAR

This game has four distinguishing features. First, two Jokers can be used as lowest trumps. Second, Low is always won by the holder of the lowest trump other than a Joker, not the winner of the trick containing it. Third, the Jick (the other Jack of the same colour as the trump suit) can be played as an extra trump. Finally, all players must discard after bidding is over.

You will need: 52-card deck; two Jokers; scorecards	
Card ranking: Standard	
Players: Four, in partnerships of two	
Ideal for: 14+	

OBJECT

To be the first partnership to score 52 points by winning tricks containing scoring cards.

THE DEAL

Players are dealt 10 cards each.

BIDDING

The deal is followed by a round of bidding, starting with the player to the dealer's left. Players can pass or bid the number of points (the minimum is four and the maximum 10) that they undertake to win in exchange for the right to name the trump suit. Each bid must be higher than the last.

PLAY

Once trumps have been called, the highest bidder picks up the 14 remaining cards, adds them to his hand and then discards 18 cards. The other players discard four cards from the hands they hold, so that everyone ends up with a six-card hand. A player with more than six trumps must play the excess number to the first trick: he may not include more than one point-scoring trump. The highest bidder plays first. The other players must follow suit if they hold any cards of the suit that was led. A player with no card of the suit led may play any card.

Left: The Jack of the same colour as trumps is called the Jick. So, if Diamonds are trumps, the J♥ is the Jick.

No trump may be played until all such cards have been played. The highest card of the suit led or the highest trump wins the trick.

SCORING AND CONCLUSION

Points are won as follows:
- One point for High, won by the highest trump.
- One point for Low, won by the lowest trump.
- One point for capturing the Jack of trumps.
- One point for taking the Jick.
- One point for playing either of the Jokers.
- One point for Game.
- Three points for Trey, won by the Three of trumps.
- One point for Game (determined by card rankings).

The game point goes to the team taking the highest total in scoring cards. Aces count four, Kings three, Queens two, Jacks and Jokers one and Tens 10. Each partnership adds up the value of any such cards they've won in tricks, and whichever has the most scores the game point.

Some variations do not recognize the Trey point, in which case the maximum bid would be seven, not 10. If the winners of the bid make as many or more points as they bid, they score all the points they made. If not, the amount of the bid is deducted from their score, which may leave them with minus points. The non-bidding partnership scores all the points they take in either case.

The first partnership to score 52 points wins; in the event of a tie, the bidding partnership wins.

Above: With Diamonds as trumps, a player taking a trick with the Three in it scores three points for Trey.

Above: Players score one point for playing either of the Jokers.

CINCH

T his All Fours game, otherwise called Pedro, originated in the USA as a variation of Pitch. Though its popularity has declined, it is still widely played in various parts of the USA and Central America, with variants in Finland and Italy.

You will need: 52-card deck; scorecards
Card ranking: See under 'Play and Scoring'
Players: Four in partnerships of two
Ideal for: 14+

OBJECT
To be the first partnership to reach 62 points through taking tricks containing scoring cards.

THE DEAL
Players are dealt nine cards, three at a time.

BIDDING, DISCARDING AND DRAWING
Each player has one chance to pass or to bid. The minimum bid allowed is seven points and the maximum 14. If the first three players pass, the dealer is obliged to bid seven. The highest bidder announces which suit will be trumps, after which everyone bar the dealer discards their non-trump cards face down and is dealt enough replacements to give them six.

The dealer then discards, goes through the remaining cards and picks up all the trumps they contain. This may mean that he ends up with a hand of more than six cards, in which case more than one card must be played to the first trick, the card on top being the only one that counts.

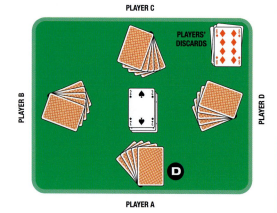

PLAYER C

PLAYERS' DISCARDS

PLAYER B

PLAYER D

PLAYER A

Above: As the dealer has the choice of taking any trumps from those cards left after the deal, he may have to play several cards to the first trick. Only the top card of those played by the dealer is considered to be in play, and he should end up with just five cards left in his hand.

The others are 'buried', that is, discarded and do not count. It is against the rules, however, to bury any of the scoring trumps.

PLAY AND SCORING
The highest bidder leads to the first trick. Players follow suit if they can or they can play a trump. If unable to do either, they can play any card. In the trump suit, cards rank Ace, King, Queen, Jack, 10, 9, 8, 7, 6, 5 (the Pedro), the other 5 of the same colour (the Low Pedro), 4, 3, 2. In non-trump suits the ranking is Ace, King, Queen, Jack, 10, 9, 8, 7, 6, 5 (when the opposite colour to trumps), 4, 3, 2. The highest card of the suit led or the highest trump takes the trick, its winner leading to the next.

If the bidding partnership makes their bid, they score all the tricks they take. If unsuccessful, they must deduct the amount of the bid from their score. The Ace, Jack, Ten and Two of trumps each score one point, while the two Pedros score five points each. The non-bidding partnership scores for everything they make. With the exception of the point for the Two of trumps, which goes to the partnership of the player who was dealt it, the partnership capturing the cards in tricks takes the points.

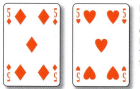

Left: In Cinch, the Five of trumps is called the Pedro and the Five of the same colour the Low or Left Pedro. So, if Diamonds are trumps, the 5♦ is the Pedro and the 5♥ the Left Pedro.

CONCLUSION
If both teams score 55 points or more, the situation is termed 'bidder goes out'. If the bidding team make their bid on the next hand, they win. If not, the hand is scored normally, the result being that the opposing team can often snatch the victory. The winners of the game are the first team to reach or exceed 62 points.

DON

Related to All Fours, this game probably descended from the 19th-century game Dom Pedro, which became popular in Ireland and America, where the name was abbreviated to Don.

You will need:	52-card deck; Cribbage board for scoring
Card ranking:	Standard
Players:	Four, in partnerships of two
Ideal for:	14+

OBJECT
To be the first to reach a predetermined score through wining tricks that contain scoring cards.

THE DEAL
Players cut to establish 'first pitch' – that is, who will lead first and set trumps. In the Irish variant, the player holding the 2♦ pitches or 'pucks out' to the first trick. The player to the pitcher's right then deals nine cards singly in the English version of Don or 13 cards in the Irish version. The remainder are stacked face down.

PLAY
All players now examine their hands, except the pitcher's partner, who cannot touch his cards until after the first card has been led. This is to avoid the risk of the player signalling to the pitcher the suit to make trumps. As in the majority of partnership card games, a player may not signal what cards he holds or what a partner should play.

The pitcher pitches a card to the first trick to start play, its suit establishing trumps. Players must follow suit if they can, trump or otherwise play any card. The highest card of the suit led or the highest trump played wins the trick. The winner of each trick leads to the next.

SCORING AND CONCLUSION
Because the scoring system is somewhat convoluted, it is the custom to keep score by pegging on a Cribbage board. Firstly, each side sorts through its tricks, when all cards have been played. They add up the points scored for winning tricks containing specific trumps or any five, and peg the amount on the board. In nine-card Don, they are scored accordingly: trump Ace = four, trump King = three, trump Queen = two, trump Jack = one, trump Nine = nine, and trump Five = 10. Non-trump Fives are worth five points.

Next, they add together the card values of the Aces, Kings, Queens, Jacks and Tens they hold in each of the four suits, to decide which team scores the extra points for 'Game' at the end of the play. The side that wins the majority of card points in that deal wins eight points. Here, Aces score four points, Kings three, Queens two, Jacks one and Tens 10. If both partnerships tie, then neither scores for Game. The first partnership to score an agreed total of points, customarily 91 or 121, wins.

In the Irish variant, scoring is the same except that the trump Nine ('Big Don') = 18 points; the trump Five ('Little Don') = 10 points and non-trump Nines score nine. The first partnership to score 80 wins.

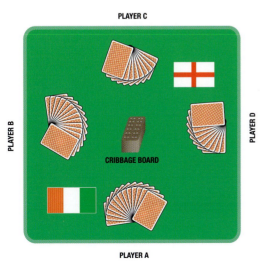

PLAYER C

PLAYER B

CRIBBAGE BOARD

PLAYER D

PLAYER A

Above: In the English version of Don, players receive nine cards; in the Irish version, 13 cards are dealt.

Above: The scoring trumps in Don are Ace, King, Queen, Jack, Nine and Five; the score is usually pegged on a Cribbage board.

SOLO GAMES

THIS TYPE OF GAME DIFFERS FROM OTHER PLAIN-TRICK GAMES, SUCH AS BRIDGE AND WHIST, BECAUSE THE INDIVIDUAL PLAYERS ARE ULTIMATELY OUT FOR THEMSELVES AND FINISH THE GAME WITH A SCORE OF THEIR OWN. THERE ARE NO FIXED OR SET PARTNERSHIPS, ALTHOUGH IF FOUR PLAYERS ARE INVOLVED, TEMPORARY ALLIANCES CAN BE FORMED FOR CONVENIENCE – SOMETIMES THREE PLAYERS AGAINST ONE, BUT MORE OFTEN TWO VERSUS TWO.

Typically, the highest bidder in each deal names trumps and then sets out to win a specified number of tricks. The object of the other players is to prevent this. The bid is termed a solo. Its bidder is often known as the soloist and he leads.

Leading is often advantageous, since it determines the suit that the other players, if able, have to play. Playing last, however, has its merits as well, since the final player can react to what the previous players have played and, in theory, can compute the outcome of the trick for each of his possible plays. The contents of each trick are irrelevant – only the number of tricks taken by the individual players matters.

Some games have a remarkable historical pedigree. Ombre dates back to a 16th-century Spanish card game called Hombre, in which the term was used to denote the solo player. It is thought to be the most significant ancestor of subsequent bidding games, including Whist and Bridge. Boston, although its name suggests a link with the American War of Independence, probably started in France at the end of the 18th century.

Other noteworthy alliance games are Belgian Whist or Wiezen and Colour Whist or Kleurenwiezen, which is its more complex relation. Solo Whist, which developed in Britain into a popular game by the end of the 19th century, was derived from a Belgian game.

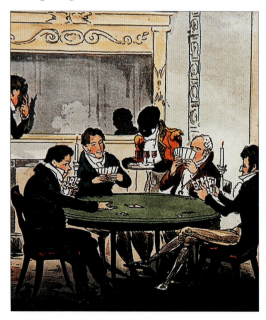

Above: An English engraving entitled *A game of Whist* (c.1821), a classic trick-taking card game that was played widely in the 18th and 19th centuries.

SOLO WHIST

Also known as English Solo, this game became popular in the 1890s, when it reached Britain from Belgium, where it was known as Whist de Gand (Ghent Whist). Players play for themselves, but they form temporary alliances – one against three or two against two – for each hand. There is no running score. Each deal is complete in itself.

You will need: 52-card deck; no Jokers; scorecards or counters
Card ranking: Standard
Players: Four
Ideal for: 10+

OBJECT
To make at least as many tricks (or, in the case of *Misère* bids, at least as few) as bid.

THE DEAL
Whichever player cuts the lowest card deals first. The deal, bidding and play run clockwise around the table. The cards are dealt in four batches of three with the last four cards being dealt singly to each player until everyone has 13 cards. The last card is turned face up to indicate the prospective trump for the trick.

BIDDING
The auction starts with the player to the dealer's left, each player having the chance to bid a contract, or to pass. From lowest to highest, the possible bids are:
- Proposal (or Prop) – a bid to win at least eight tricks in partnership with another player with the suit of the upturned card as trumps (scores one point per trick).
- Cop – an acceptance of another player's prop.
- Solo – a contract to win at least five tricks on his own (scores one point per trick).
- *Misère* or *Mis* – an undertaking to lose every trick (scores two points).
- Abundance – a contract to win at least nine tricks, with trumps of one's own choosing (scores three points per trick).
- Royal Abundance – a contract to win at least nine tricks, with trumps being the suit of the turned-up card (scores three points per trick).
- *Misère Ouverte* – a contract, with one's cards turned face up after the first trick, to lose every trick (scores four points).
- Abundance *Declaré* (or Slam) – a bid to win all 13 tricks solo (scores six points).

PLAY
Once the contract is established, the player to the left of the dealer leads to the first trick, except if a Slam has been called, in which case the lead passes to the soloist. In the *Misère Ouverte* bid, the soloist's hand must be spread face up on the table at the end of the first trick and before the second is led. Players must always follow suit if possible, otherwise any card may be played. The highest card of the suit that has been led takes the trick, unless trumps have been played, in which case the highest trump wins. The winner leads to the next trick.

CONCLUSION AND SCORING
Generally, players settle up in counters or total scores at the end of each hand, when all 13 tricks have been won.

In Prop and Cop, each member of the winning partnership receives a counter for making the bid from both of the other two players, plus a further counter from both for each overtrick. If the contract is broken, each of the bidders pays five counters to the two other players for the failed bid, plus an extra counter to both per undertrick.

In all other bids, the successful soloist is paid by all three opponents, but pays them if the bid fails. The soloist wins three units in total (one from each opponent), for instance, if he makes a Solo, and nine if he makes an Abundance.

PLAYER C

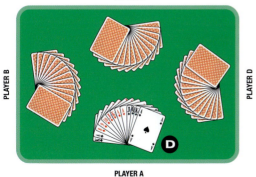

PLAYER B

PLAYER D

PLAYER A

Above: This very strong hand, with Diamonds as trumps, is ideal for a bid of Slam: a contract to win all 13 tricks playing solo.

BELGIAN WHIST

Otherwise known as Wiezen, the Flemish for Whist, Belgian Whist is a descendant of Boston and is similar to Solo Whist. It is closely related to Colour Whist (Kleurenwiezen in Flemish, Whist à la Couleur in French). The difference between them is that in Belgian Whist the trump suit is established by turning up the last card to be dealt. In Colour Whist, it is determined by the bidding.

You will need: 52 cards; no Jokers; gambling chips/counters
Card ranking: Standard, Aces high
Players: Four
Ideal for: 10+

OBJECT

To make at least as many tricks (or, in the case of *Misère* bids, at least as few) as bid.

THE DEAL

Before the deal, each player puts an agreed number of chips or counters into a pool. The cards are then dealt four, four and five to each player. The last card to be dealt is turned face up to indicate the trump suit. The dealer picks it up when bidding is over.

BIDDING

In the bidding, each player can make a proposal, accept a proposal, bid higher or pass. The various bids, from lowest to highest, are as follows:

- Proposal – a contract to win at least eight tricks with the help of a partner (the caller has to take five of these tricks and the partner three).
- Acceptance – agreeing to a proposal, and thus to score eight tricks (at least three oneself) in partnership with the proposer.
- Solo – a bid to take five or more tricks.
- Abundance – a bid to take at least nine tricks, with trumps of one's own choice.
- Abundance in trumps – a bid to take at least nine tricks, where trumps is the suit of the upturned card.

- *Troel* – open only to a player holding three Aces, this is an undertaking to win at least eight tricks with a partner – either the player holding the fourth Ace or the holder of the highest Heart not held by the bidder.
- *Misère* – an undertaking to lose every trick, playing solo with no trumps.
- Solo Slam – a contract to take all 13 tricks.

PLAY

The player to the dealer's left leads, except in Slam or Abundance when the lead is with the soloist. Players must follow suit if they can, otherwise play a trump or any other card. In *Troel* with three Aces, the fourth Ace's holder must lead it to the first trick. If the bidder holds all four Aces, the highest Heart must be played.

SCORING AND CONCLUSION

The scores are totalled at the end of each hand when all 13 tricks have been won. A successful soloist wins the pool, plus a varying amount from the other players depending on the contract. The minimum is three times the contract's value. Partners divide the pool and win a set amount from their opponents. A losing soloist doubles the pool and pays the appropriate amount to each opponent. Losing partners double the pool between them and each pays the appropriate amount to one opponent.

Proposal, Acceptance and Solo bids score one for each trick, plus one for each overtrick. The scores are doubled if all 13 tricks are taken. Abundance scores eight points, *Misère* 10 points, *Troel* two points plus two per overtrick and Solo Slam scores 24 points.

Left: Comprising almost exclusively low cards, this hand is ideal for a bid of *Misère*: a contract to lose every trick, which is played in no trumps.

Left: With all four Aces, long Clubs, and only a slight weakness in Diamonds, this hand is worth a bid of Solo Slam, naming Clubs as trumps.

SOLO VARIANTS

Several solo variants exist, which are all fun to play and present a real challenge. Crazy Solo, of American origin, is a multi-player game – the number of players can vary from three to 12, which affects how it is played. A 36-card deck is used, but sometimes fewer cards are employed, depending on how many play. Knockout Whist is British in origin and it consists of seven hands of diminishing size.

CRAZY SOLO

OBJECT

To make more tricks than one's opponents, either in partnership with another player or alone.

You will need: 36-card deck, Twos to Fives removed

Card ranking: Ace, Ten, King, Queen, Jack (scoring 11, 10, four, three and two points respectively), followed by Nine, Eight, Seven and Six (each scoring no points)

Players: Four is ideal

Ideal for: 10+

THE DEAL

All the cards are dealt singly, starting with the player to the dealer's left, who also leads the first trick.

BIDDING

A round of bidding follows the deal to decide who will be the solo player, each bid having to be higher than the last. Players can bid Pass, Solo, Solo in Hearts, Go Alone or Go Alone in Hearts. In Solo in Hearts and Alone in Hearts, Hearts are the trump suit. Otherwise, the successful bidder calls the trumps.

PLAY

If the bid is Solo or Solo in Hearts, the successful bidder calls a card to choose a partner. The player holding that card does not need to reveal his identity until the time comes for the card to be played. The partnership is called the 'solo players' and their opponents are the 'gang'.

The player to the dealer's left leads to the first trick. Suit must be followed if possible or a trump played but there is no requirement to beat the previous card. A player who cannot follow suit or trump may play any card.

The highest card of the suit that has been led takes the trick, unless trumps have been played, in which case the highest trump wins. The winner leads to the next trick. The Ten ranks second, below Ace.

SCORING AND CONCLUSION

At the end of the game, points won by the caller and his partner are totalled to establish the margin of the win or loss. There are 120 points to be won, so scoring 61 or more of them wins the game.

The solo players receive points from (or pay) each member of the gang, the payout being calculated according to which suit was selected as trumps. If trumps are Spades, Clubs or Diamonds, then the payout is two points for every point over 60. However, if Hearts are trumps, it is three points. Each hand ends when all nine tricks have been won.

KNOCKOUT WHIST

OBJECT

To be the player who wins the trick in the final hand.

You will need: 52-card deck; no Jokers

Card ranking: Standard, Aces high

Players: Any number from three to seven

Ideal for: 7+

THE DEAL

Each player receives seven cards. The uppermost of the undealt cards is turned face up to indicate what the trump suit will be. The player on the dealer's left leads the first trick.

PLAY

Players must follow suit if they can, otherwise they may play any card. Each trick is won by the highest trump in it; otherwise by the highest card of the suit led. The winner of the most tricks in subsequent hands chooses the trump suit for the next. The second hand consists of six cards and so on until in the final hand, one card is dealt to each player.

A player who fails to take any tricks in a hand is knocked out of the game. If this occurs in the first hand, he is awarded a 'dog's life' – that is, he is dealt one card and can choose when to play it. If he is successful, he is reinstated into the game.

CONCLUSION

The game is won by the winner of the one trick on the final hand, or before that if one player wins all the tricks in an earlier round.

119

BOSTON

There are many versions of Boston, which won widespread popularity despite its extremely complicated system of calculating payments for bids, overtricks and undertricks. The game is a hybrid of Quadrille and Whist and may have originated in France in the late 18th century.

You will need: 52-card deck; no Jokers; scorecards

Card ranking: Standard, Aces high

Players: Four

Ideal for: 14+

OBJECT

To gain the most points by making no less and no more than the number of tricks bid.

THE DEAL AND BIDDING

Each player is dealt 13 cards. The player to the dealer's left opens the bidding, the highest bidder becoming the soloist, playing alone against the other three players unless one of them agrees to become an ally or supporter. The bids can be positive – an offer to win a stated number of tricks – or negative, in which case the contract is to lose them.

POSITIVE BIDS AND SCORING

Five is the lowest positive bid. This is an undertaking to win at least five tricks with a named suit as trumps. The supporter must win at least three out of the five tricks. If the bid is six, seven or eight, the supporter must take four tricks, that number remaining the same if the bid is nine, 10, 11 and 12. The highest bids are a Boston and a Boston *Ouverte*. In both, the contract is to win all 13 tricks, in the latter with cards face up on the table.

The former scores 100 points and the latter 200. Otherwise, starting from Five, the points that can be scored for each positive bid are: four (plus one for each overtrick or undertrick), six (plus two), nine (plus three), 12 (plus four), 15 (plus five), 18 (plus six), 21 (plus seven) and 24 (plus eight). Overtricks score if the contract is won. Undertricks score if the contract is lost.

NEGATIVE BIDS AND SCORING

The lowest negative bid is *Petite Misère*, in which the contract is to lose 12 tricks with one discard at No Trumps. It is worth 16 points, while a *Grande Misère* is a bid to lose all 13 tricks and is worth 32. A bid of *Piccolissimo* is a contract to take only one trick and scores 24. If the bidder holds all four Aces, the bid is Four-ace *Misère* and scores 40.

PLAY

The player to the left of the dealer plays the first card. Subsequent players must follow suit, if possible, or play a trump. Otherwise, they can play any card. The highest card of the suit led or the highest trump takes the trick, its winner leading to the next one.

CONCLUSION

In a solo contract, bonuses are added for overtricks and undertricks, plus the equivalent of two overtricks if the soloist holds three honours and four if four. The total is doubled if trumps are Clubs, trebled if Diamonds and quadrupled if Spades. The honours are Ace, King, Queen and Jack of Trumps. If the contract is supported, the total for each partner is halved. If only one member of the partnership makes the contract, he scores zero, while the losing partner loses half the value of his contract plus half the value of that part of the contract that has been won. Play ends when the final trick has been won or lost.

PLAYER C

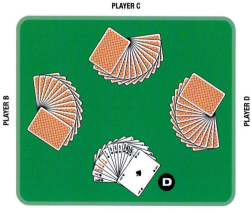

PLAYER B

PLAYER D

PLAYER A

Left: This hand, which is strong both in top cards and Spades, is perfect for declaring a bid of Boston *Ouverte*, naming Spades as trumps. The contract will be played with the bidding player's cards laid face up on the table, and will score 56 points if it is successful.

QUADRILLE

A four-handed adaptation of Ombre, Quadrille ousted Ombre in popular affection, only to be replaced by Partnership Whist. At least 160 chips of four different colours are needed to play it.

You will need: Standard pack with Eights, Nines and Tens removed; at least 160 gambling chips/counters of four colours

Card ranking: See below under 'Bidding'

Players: Four

Ideal for: 14+

OBJECT

To win at least six tricks after nominating trumps, either solo or in alliance.

THE DEAL

From the 40-card deck, the deal is 10 cards per player, usually dealt in batches of four, three and three.

BIDDING

Card rankings vary depending on the colour of each suit and whether the suit is plain or trumps. The top three trumps are *Spadille* for the A♠ (top trump), *Manille* (the Two if the trump suit is black or the Seven if the trump suit is red) and *Basta* (the A♣). They are collectively known as *Matadors*. The two black Aces are always trumps, regardless of what trump suit has been declared.

Each player takes it in turn to bid, pass or overcall – that is, to outbid a previous bid. In the simplest version of the game, the bids start with an alliance, in which the aim of the declarer is to take at least six tricks after nominating trumps and calling the holder of a specified King into a partnership.

If Solo is bid, the declarer proposes to win at least six tricks playing alone against the other three. *Vole* (slam) is a bid to take all 13 tricks without any support from a partner. A solo bid overcalls an alliance.

PLAY

The player to the dealer's left leads. Players follow suit if possible, otherwise they can play any card. However, a player holding a *Matador* (trump) need not play it to a trump lead unless it is lower in value than the led card.

SCORING

A successful soloist wins the pot, plus bonus chips paid to him by each opponent – four for the solo, one if he held three *Matadors*, two for double *Matadors*, one for *Premiers* (winning the first six tricks straight off) and two for *Vole*. If the contract is lost, the soloist forfeits the same number of chips to the other players.

PLAYER C

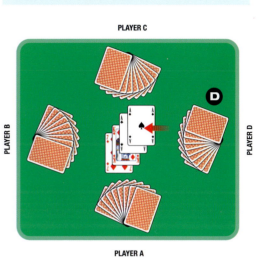

PLAYER A

Above: Here, Player C looked set to win the trick after trumping with the A♣ before Player D played the highest trump of all, the A♠, and took the trick.

Losing partnerships divide losses according to how many tricks each partner won. If the declarer wins less than three tricks, he has to pay the total loss. The same goes if a player calls a partner.

If the declarer wins only five tricks, this is called *Remise*. If four or less, it is *Codille*. In the first instance, the declarer must double the stake and pay the opponents for any *Matadors* held. In a *Codille*, the stake is divided between the opposing players.

CONCLUSION

If the declarer wins the first six tricks, or *Premiers*, he has won the game. Alternatively, the declarer can decide to lead a seventh trick, in which case the bid becomes a *Vole* and all players must pay three more chips into a second pool. If the contract fails, the other players split this, but the declarer still gets paid for the *Premiers* and for winning the game.

OMBRE

This fast-moving trick-taking game was originally for four players – even though the player opposite the dealer took no active part in the game. It was therefore as a three-hander that the Ombre craze swept Europe until it was superseded by Quadrille. It was one of the first card games to introduce the notion of bidding, in which one player tries to fulfil a contract while the other two players try to prevent this.

You will need: 40-card deck (Eights, Nines and Tens removed from a standard pack); gambling chips/counters
Card ranking: See under 'Card Ranking'
Players: Three
Ideal for: 14+

OBJECT

The successful bidder aims to fulfil his contract by winning more tricks than any of his opponents. Their aim is to stop him by winning a majority of the tricks themselves, or to draw, in which case the bidder still loses.

CARD RANKING

The ranking of the cards varies with the colour of their suit and whether they are trumps. The top three trumps are called *Matadors*: the *Spadille* (the A♠), *Manille* (the Two of a black trump suit or the Seven of a red trump suit) and *Basta* (the A♣). The two black Aces are always trumps, regardless of what trump suit has been declared.

THE DEAL AND AUCTION

Before the deal, the dealer puts five chips in the pot. Each player is then dealt nine cards in packets of three. The remaining cards form the stock pile, which is placed face down on the table and used for exchanging cards.

Ombre has a language all of its own. The first dealer, chosen at random, is called backhand, the player to the right is forehand and the one to the left is middlehand.

Each hand begins with an auction. The winner of the bidding becomes the declarer (*Ombre*), and plays alone against the other two players (defenders) in partnership. The three calls that can be made in the auction are:

- Pass, in which case a player can take no further part in the bidding, and gives up his chance of being declarer.
- Bid, when a bid is made that outranks any bid previously made in the auction.
- Self, in which a player can equal a bid made previously by a player who is after him in rotation. Forehand can call self over the other two players, but middlehand can call self only over backhand.

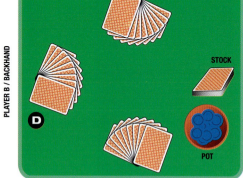

Above: The dealer in Ombre is called 'backhand', the player on the left 'middlehand' and the player on the right 'forehand'.

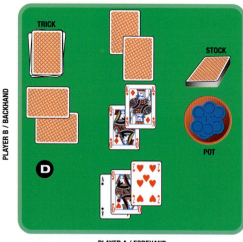

Above: Player A here can either trump by laying the *Spadille* (A♠), or renege with the 7♥. Doing the latter will leave the Queen a bare singleton, significantly reducing its chances of winning a trick.

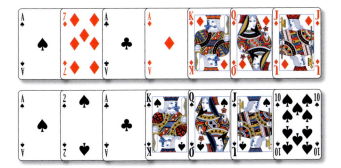

Left: With Diamonds as trumps, the top-ranking card is the A♠ (*Spadille*), followed by the 7♦ (*Manille*) and A♣ (*Basta*). In a red trump suit, the fourth highest is its Ace A♦ (*Punto*), but it is not a *Matador*. The remaining Diamonds follow in rank in descending order.

Left: With Spades as trumps, the top-ranking card is the A♠ (*Spadille*), followed by the 2♠ (*Manille*), A♣ (*Basta*), and then the remaining Spades in descending order, beginning with the King.

Only forehand and middlehand are involved initially in the auction, which ends when both players have called and one of them has passed. Backhand can then join in the auction, which continues until the contract is settled.

BIDDING AND CONTRACTS

The final bid by the declarer determines the contract. He plays either a Game or *Nolo* contract. In the former, he aims to take more tricks than either defender, and in the latter, he aims not to take any tricks at all. The players take turns exchanging cards with the stock pile, subject to restrictions relating to bids and corresponding contracts as follows:

- A simple game: the declarer names trumps, by naming the suit or turning the top card of the stock pile face up. All players can change their cards; the declarer goes first.
- A Spade game: Spades are automatically trumps.
- A *Tourné* or *Grand Tourné*: both game contracts, in which the top card of the stock pile is turned up. If *Grand Tourné* is bid, the bidder must hold *Spadille* (the A♠) and *Basta* (the A♣) in his hand.
- Solo: game contract where the declarer has to play his hand as dealt, but the defenders can exchange up to eight cards with the stock pile.
- Spade Solo: like Solo with Spades as trumps.
- Simple *Nolo*: *Nolo* contract. Only the declarer can exchange cards.
- Pure *Nolo*: like Simple *Nolo*, but neither the declarer nor defenders exchange cards with the stock pile.
- *Nolo Ouverte*: like Pure *Nolo* but when the declarer plays his first card, he also turns his hand face up for both defenders to see.

PLAY

Following the card exchange, the nine tricks are played. Forehand always leads to the first trick, regardless of who was dealer. Players have to follow suit if they can, unless one of them is holding a *Matador*, in which case he may

choose whether to play it or keep it back and play a card from another suit. If the lead card is a higher *Matador*, a player holding a lower one must play it. The trick is taken by the highest card of the suit led or by the highest trump, the winner of the trick leading to the next.

SCORING AND CONCLUSION

Play continues until all nine tricks have been won. If the declarer wins, he takes the pot, and from each player:

- One chip for simple games and *Tourné*.
- Two chips for *Nolo*, *Grand Tourné* and Solo.
- Three chips for Pure *Nolo* and Spade Solo.
- Five chips for *Nolo Ouverte*.

In Game contracts, the declarer wins outright if he takes the first five tricks. The alternatives are:

- *Bête*, in which the declarer scores the same number of tricks as one of the other players.
- *Puesta*, where no one wins a majority of tricks.
- *Codille*, when the declarer takes fewer tricks than one of his opponents.
- *Tout*, when the declarer takes all nine tricks. In this case, he has to declare the decision to try to do so in advance before leading for the sixth trick.

Winning *Tout* means the others have to pay the declarer an extra chip each. In the case of *Bête*, the declarer pays the other players according to which contract was bid. In *Codille*, there is an extra penalty: one chip for low contracts, two for Pure *Nolo* and Spade Solo and three for *Nolo Ouverte* with only the higher-scoring opponent being paid. If the declarer fails to win a *Tout*, he gives both the others a chip, but still gets chips for winning.

In Solo contracts, the declarer wins outright when he takes no tricks. The alternatives are:

- *Bête*, when one trick is taken.
- *Codille*, when the declarer takes two tricks or more.

PREFERENCE

This three-handed game is played in various parts of Europe, notably in Austria, Russia and the Ukraine, where it used to be the national game. Hearts is the highest suit, followed by Diamonds, Clubs and Spades. The game is played with either German-suited cards – a 32-card pack, the suits of which are Hearts, Bells, Acorns and Leaves – or a standard pack stripped of Sixes down to Twos. The main version of the game described here is called Austrian Preference.

OBJECT

To win at least the predetermined number of tricks. In each hand, one player (the declarer) chooses trumps and tries to take six out of the possible 10 tricks. The other two players (the defenders) try to stop this happening, but they are also obliged to take two tricks each. If a defender believes it will be impossible to do this, he is allowed to drop out of the hand.

THE DEAL

Players cut to decide who will be the first dealer, after which the deal passes to the right. The cards are dealt clockwise, three to each player, two face down on the table to form a stock, four to each player and then a final three. All three players put the same stake into the pot – in Austrian Preference, it is the custom to use money, rather than chips or counters. At the outset, each player contributes an equal sum to the pot.

BIDDING

The player to the left of the dealer opens the bidding. Players can either bid or pass, but if they pass they can take no further part in the auction. The possible bids are:

- One, two, three, four, representing Clubs, Spades, Diamonds and Hearts respectively.
- Game, which indicates that the bidder does not want to pick up and use the cards in the stock.
- Hearts, which is a Game bid in Hearts.

Players are only allowed to bid one higher than the previous bid or pass, so the first player to bid can only bid one, Game or Hearts. The other players can then bid two over the one, followed by three and then four.

You will need: 32-card deck (Sixes down to Twos removed from a standard pack); gambling chips/counters

Card ranking: Ace, King, Queen, Jack, Ten to Seven

Players: Three

Ideal for: 14+

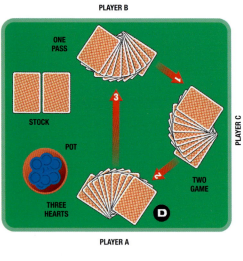

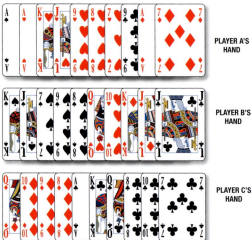

Above: A possible bidding sequence in Preference. Player B begins by contracting to make six tricks, but Player C bids higher, only to be outbid by Player A who goes higher again. After Player B makes the decision to pass, Player C then bids Game, forgoing the right to pick up the stock, but Player A contracts for Game in Hearts, the highest bid.

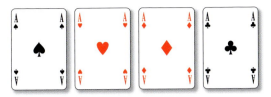

Above: A player holding all four Aces is paid an extra 10 points by each of his opponents if he wins the first six tricks.

Once game has been bid, only another bid of game or Hearts can outbid it. In the first instance, both bidders must declare what they are proposing as trumps. The one declaring the higher suit wins. If a player bidding a number is outbid, he can opt to hold. This is the equivalent to matching the other player's bid. If the second bidder does not raise the bid, the initial bidder wins.

A bid of one, if successful, means that the declarer can name any suit as trump. Two means that Clubs cannot be nominated, Three stops Clubs and Spades from being trumps, and Four means that Hearts are trumps.

PLAY

In a numerical contract, the declarer picks up the stock, adds it to his hand and then discards two cards face down. He then says what will be trumps, following which each opponent must decide whether or not to play the hand. If only one of them decides to play, he has the option of inviting the other to play with him, though it is his responsibility to win the four tricks the partnership needs, not that of his partner.

If both defenders concede, the declarer automatically wins all 10 tricks. If not, play proceeds with the declarer playing the first card of the first trick. The others must follow suit, playing a higher card, if possible. If not, they must trump or discard. The highest card of the suit led takes the trick, or the highest trump if any are played.

If, when both of the other players are defending, the first of them can beat the lead, he must do so with the lowest suitable card in his hand. This is termed 'indulging' and it provides the opportunity for the defending partner to take the two tricks he needs.

Failing to indulge when able to do so constitutes a revoke, when play stops and settlements are made without recourse to the pot. A revoking declarer pays the other players the equivalent of three-tenths of the pot, or five-tenths if only one defender was playing. If a defender revokes, he pays the declarer the full amount of the pot and four-tenths of its value to his partner.

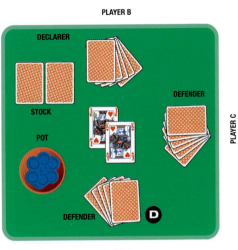

PLAYER B

DECLARER

STOCK

POT

DEFENDER

DEFENDER

PLAYER C

D

PLAYER A

Above: With the declarer having led Hearts, the first of the two defenders, Player C, is obliged to beat the card if he can. Called 'indulging', it gives the defending partner the opportunity to take on the two tricks he needs to make.

RUSSIAN PREFERENCE

There are four types of Russian Preference – Sochi, St Petersburg, Classic, and Rostov or Moscow. Other versions of the game are played in Croatia, Serbia, Slovenia and Trieste. The main difference between Russian and Austrian Preference is that, as well as being more complicated, the declarer in the former can contract to win more than six tricks.

SCORING AND CONCLUSION

When 10 tricks have been played, the players are paid from the pot according to the number of tricks they have made. First the declarer takes 10 points and pays any defender who did not drop out one point for each trick taken. If a declarer has taken less than six tricks, he pays a penalty of 20 points to the pot. The following bonuses apply, depending on the bid:

• Hearts bonus: in a Hearts game, a successful declarer receives an extra 10 points from each of his opponents, although he has to pay 10 to each of them if the bid fails.

• Four Aces bonus: a declarer who held four Aces receives a bonus of 10 points from each opponent if successful, but does not pay anything if he fails to fulfil his contract.

• No Ace bonus: a declarer who held no Aces and declared the fact before leading to the first trick, receives a bonus of 10 points from each opponent if successful, but pays them an extra 10 each if not.

ASSZORTI

This compelling three-player game was invented in Hungary. In many respects, it is similar to Preference, but it is simpler to play. Like many other Hungarian card games it uses a German-suited 36-card pack, the suits of which are Hearts, Bells, Acorns and Leaves, but a standard pack can be used when stripped of Fives down to Twos.

You will need: 36-card deck (standard pack with Twos, Threes, Fours and Fives removed); scorecards

Card ranking: Ace down to Six

Players: Three

Ideal for: 14+

OBJECT

To win at least the specified number of tricks bid. A bid is an offer to win at least six tricks after exchanging three, two, one or no cards with the stock.

THE DEAL

Players cut the pack to establish who deals first. Each player receives 11 cards, three each first then four batches of two. A further three cards are dealt face down on to the table to form a stock.

BIDDING

After the deal, players bid or pass in turn, starting with the player to the left of the dealer. If a player bids, he is undertaking to win at least six tricks after exchanging three, two, one or no cards with cards from the stock. Players are only allowed to bid one higher than the previous bid, or pass, so the first player to bid can only bid three. The next player can bid to exchange two and so on. The highest bidder becomes the soloist, drawing as

Below: Examples of the Hearts and Acorns suits in a German-suited pack of cards. The other two suits are Bells and Leaves.

many cards as were bid (if any) from the stock, discarding the same number and naming the trump suit or deciding the hand will be No Trumps.

ARRIVÁZS AND DOUBLING

If trumps are to be played, the soloist can also bid *Arrivázs*. This is an undertaking to win the last three tricks of the hand, for which he gets a bonus of eight points. This is doubled if the hand is No Trumps or if the tricks are captured without a trump being played. Game and *Arrivázs* are scored separately. Either or both can be doubled and redoubled up to five times, the levels being announced as *Kontra* (two), *Rekontra* (four), *Szubkontra* (eight), *Hirskontra* (16) and *Mordkontra* (32). If the soloist announces *Rekontra*, only the partner of the player who announced *Kontra* can respond by calling *Szubkontra*.

PLAY

Players must follow suit if they can, or trump if unable to follow suit. They may renounce, that is, play any other card, only if they are unable to do either. The player to the right of the soloist leads, the trick falling to the player of the highest card of the led suit, or to the highest trump if any are played.

SCORING

The basic scores for bids of three, two, one and hand are two, four, six and eight points respectively, the scores being doubled if the hand is No Trumps. Obviously, doubling and redoubling affects these basic scores. Over-tricks count for half the above values, while undertricks score minus the full values in the first and second possible bids and half values in the remainder.

CONCLUSION

Play continues until all the tricks have been won or the soloist has won six or more tricks.

OH HELL!

In this popular game, also known as Niggle, the objective is to bid to win an exact number of tricks – a player winning more or less is penalized. There are various ways of playing and scoring.

You will need: 52-card deck; no Jokers; scorecards
Card ranking: Standard, Aces high
Players: Three to seven players
Ideal for: 10+

OBJECT

To win an exact number of tricks, no more or less.

THE DEAL

Players draw to establish who will deal first. If there are three or four players, the initial deal is 10 cards, if six play it is eight, while if seven play it is seven. (In the USA, each successive hand is dealt with one card fewer down to one, then one card up again back to the starting number. In Britain, the reverse happens, with the initial deal being just a single card.) The next card is turned face up to establish trumps and the remaining cards are stacked face down with the turned-up trump on top of the pile. The turn to deal passes to the left.

BIDDING

Bidding starts with the player to the dealer's left – the dealer always bids last. No player can pass, though a bid of *Nullo* (zero) is allowed. The dealer, however, cannot bid a number that would enable all players to fulfil their bids.

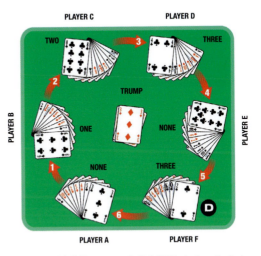

Above: A possible bidding sequence in Oh Hell! With six players involved, each receives eight cards, meaning that the final total of bids must not equal eight. Player F therefore, who is the last to bid here, cannot bid Two, so contracts instead to make three tricks. At least one player will fail to make the number of tricks he bids.

PLAY

The player to the dealer's left plays the first card, the other players following in turn. They must follow suit if they can, or, if they cannot, play a trump, assuming that they are holding trumps in their hands. Only if neither is the case can they play a card from any other suit.

SCORING

For making a bid, a player scores 10 points for each trick bid and won – just 10 points in total for a bid of zero. A player failing to make his bid has to deduct 10 points for each trick under the total.

CONCLUSION

Play continues until all tricks have been played and won. The final cumulative score decides the winner.

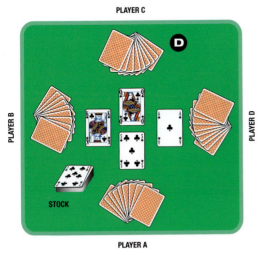

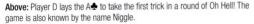

Above: Player D lays the A♣ to take the first trick in a round of Oh Hell! The game is also known by the name Niggle.

NINETY-NINE

Devised by British card authority David Parlett in 1967, this ingenious game revolves around its players bidding secretly, using bid cards, to win an exact number of tricks by removing cards from their hands. The suit of each bid card represents a different number of tricks: for example, Clubs represents three tricks.

OBJECT

To win exactly the number of tricks bid by discarding three cards representing that number. Players use the suits to represent the number of tricks bid as follows: ♣ = 3 tricks, ♥ = 2 tricks, ♠ = 1 trick, ♦ = 0 tricks. For example, a player bids nine tricks by laying aside ♣♣♣ (3 + 3 + 3 = 9), or three tricks by laying ♣♦♦ (3 + 0 + 0 = 3).

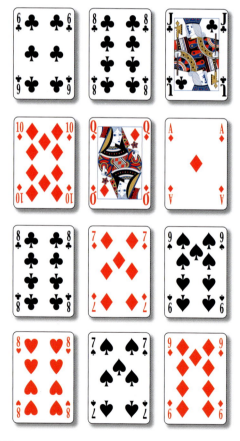

You will need: 36-card deck, (standard pack with Fives to Twos removed); scorecards
Card ranking: Standard, Aces high
Players: Three ideally, although can be two to five
Ideal for: 14+

THE DEAL

Assuming there are three players, each player is dealt 12 cards, three of which become bid cards. Normally, the bid cards are left face down until play ends. However, a player can decide to up the stakes by offering to 'declare' by exposing these cards at the start of play, or 'reveal' – that is, to also play with his actual hand exposed.

Only one player is allowed to declare or reveal at a time. If more than one player wishes to declare, the player nearest to the dealer's left has priority. An offer to reveal always supersedes an offer to declare.

PLAY

The first deal is played without trumps. Subsequent deals are played with a trump suit, which is determined by the number of players who fulfilled their previous contract. If all three did, the trump suit is Clubs, Hearts if two, Spades if one, or Diamonds if none. The player to the left of the dealer plays first. Players must follow suit, if possible, or otherwise trump or play any card. The highest card of the suit led or the highest trump takes the trick, its winner leading to the next.

SCORING AND CONCLUSION

Each player scores a point for each trick taken regardless of his bid, 10 points if all three players make their contracts, double if two players succeed and treble if only one does. A successful premium bidder scores an extra 30 for a declaration and 60 for a revelation. If the bid fails, the other players score the appropriate premium.

Play continues until all the tricks have been played and won. A game is 100 points with a further 100 being added to the winner's score. A rubber is three games.

Left: Players lay down three cards (bid cards) to show the number of tricks they aim to make with the nine cards in their hands. Each card in Clubs indicates three tricks, in Hearts it indicates two, in Spades one, and in Diamonds none. These four sets of cards from the top down, therefore correspond to: nine tricks (3 + 3 + 3 = 9); no tricks (0 + 0 + 0 = 0); four tricks (3 + 0 + 1 = 4) and three tricks (2 + 1 + 0 = 3).

Piquet Games

VARIOUS FACTORS MAKE THIS INTERESTING FAMILY OF CARD GAMES STAND OUT. POINTS CAN BE SCORED FOR VARIOUS COMBINATIONS OF CARDS (WHICH, IN PIQUET, IS TERMED MAKING MELDS). IN ADDITION, PLAYERS MAKE ADDITIONAL SCORES BY TAKING TRICKS. PIQUET ITSELF IS THE OLDEST OF THESE GAMES, WITH A HISTORY THAT DATES BACK TO AT LEAST THE 16TH CENTURY, AND A STRONG FOLLOWING AMONG CARD GAME AFICIONADOS.

Though Piquet has a long and venerable history, its exact origins are somewhat obscure. What seems the most likely is that it originated in France, where its unknown inventor devised it to entertain Charles VI. It later became an English game by adoption from the time of Charles I onwards. Piquet is regarded by many as one of the best card games for two players, but its association with the aristocracy and literate upper classes, and the complexity of its rules may partly explain why it has lost its popularity since the end of the First World War.

In France, Imperial emerged in the 16th century as a two-player hybrid of Piquet and another old game dating back to the 15th century, known as Triomphe. It still has its adherents, particularly in the Midi region of the southern part of the country, and offers many points of interest to card game enthusiasts. Variants for three players or more became popular as well.

One of the earliest three-player variants is 'the noble and delightful game' of Gleek, an English game that reached the height of its popularity between the 16th and the early 18th centuries. Its name may be related to the German word *gleich*, meaning 'equal' or 'alike', for Gleek is the term used in the game to describe a set of three Aces, Kings, Queens or Jacks. Individual cards have unusual titles: the Ace is Tib, Jack is Tom, while Six, Five and Four are called Tumbler, Towser and Tiddy.

Above: *A Game of Piquet* (c.1861) by Meissonier. References to the game date back to 1534, making it one of the oldest card games still being played.

PIQUET

Modern Piquet can be played in two ways – American style and English style – though in practice there is little difference between the two. Two 32-card decks are usually used at a time – one in use and the other shuffled ready for the next deal. A game is known as a *partie* and usually consists of six deals.

You will need: Two 32-card decks (Sixes down to Twos having been removed from two standard decks – see below)

Card ranking: Ace down to Seven

Players: Two

Ideal for: 14+

OBJECT

To score the most points by capturing tricks and collecting card-scoring combinations.

THE DEAL

The players cut for first deal, after which it alternates between them. The dealer is called Younger and the non-dealer Elder. The former deals 12 cards for himself and 12 for the opposing player in packets of two or three, spreading the eight cards that are left over face down on the table to form a stock.

DISCARDING

The first stage involves the discarding and exchanging of cards, but, before this, a player can claim what is termed *Carte Blanche* if there are no court cards in his hand. This is worth 10 points. Otherwise, Elder discards up to five cards face down and replaces them from the stock.

Below: A standard pack of 52 cards is used in Piquet, but all of the cards below seven are removed – with the exception of the Aces. Of the remaining 32 cards, the Aces count for 11 points, followed by Kings, Queens and Jacks, which score 10 points each, and then Ten, Nine, Eight and Seven.

American rules say this is optional, but English ones state that at least one card must be discarded. Younger may then discard and exchange up to as many cards as are left in the stock, but he has the freedom to decline to do so. If Younger does discard and exchange any cards, he may then inspect any remaining cards in the stock, but this means Elder can inspect them as well. Both players may examine their own discards at any stage during play.

DECLARING COMBINATIONS

Depending on their cards, both players can declare three types of combination, namely:

- A point, which is a collection of cards all of the same suit.
- A sequence, which is a run of three or more cards in one suit in rank order.
- A meld, when a player holds three or four cards of the same rank but in different suits.

It is not obligatory to announce the best combination – or to declare a weak one – if the player concerned believes that such concealment will serve his tactics the better. This is termed 'sinking a declaration'.

Elder declares first, announcing his best combinations in each category, saying 'A point of…', 'A sequence of…' or, in the case of a meld, 'A three or four of…'. After each announcement, Young says 'good', meaning that Elder's hand is better and can be scored, 'not good' if Younger has a better combination, or 'equal', in which case the points go to the player with the higher-ranking cards. Aces score 11; the court cards and Tens 10 each; and Nines, Eights and Sevens their face value.

PLAYING

Once the declarations have been completed, Elder announces the score he has made thus far and leads to the first trick, scoring an extra point for leading. Younger responds by announcing his total score. If he has failed to score anything and Elder's score reaches 30 as the result of leading to the trick, the Elder wins a *pique*, a bonus of 30 points. Elder then plays the first card to the next trick. Younger follows suit, if possible, or otherwise discards. Trumps do not feature in Piquet. Players must follow suit. Each trick is worth a point if the player who led to it wins it, otherwise it is worth two. A player taking seven to 11 tricks gets a bonus of 10 points 'for cards', while taking all 12 tricks means a bonus of 40 'for *Capot*'. Winning the last trick scores an extra point.

Right: Piquet became a popular card game among the aristocracy in England during the reign of Charles I (1625–49).

SCORING

In a point combination, the player with the longest suit scores a point for each card in it. Thus:

- Point of three scores three.
- Point of four scores four.
- Point of five scores five.
- Point of six scores six.
- Point of seven scores seven.
- Point of eight scores eight.

Scoring for sequences is as follows:

- A *Tierce* (three cards) scores three.
- A *Quart* (four) scores four.
- A *Quint* (five) scores 15.
- A *Sixième* (six) scores 16.
- A *Septième* (seven) scores 17.
- A *Huitième* (eight) scores 18.

Scores for melds are as follows (sets of Nines, Eights and Sevens do not count):

- *Quatorze* (four Aces, Kings, Queens, Jacks or Tens) scores 14.
- *Trio* (three Aces, Kings, Queens, Jacks or Tens) scores three.

If a player scores 30 points before the other has scored, he is awarded a bonus of 60 points. This is a *repique*.

CONCLUSION

At the end of the sixth deal, the scores are totalled. If a player has scored under 100 points, he is deemed to be 'Rubiconed'. His opponent wins and scores 100 plus the two final scores. If a player has scored more than 100 points, he 'crosses the Rubicon' and wins the game, scoring 100 plus the difference between the two final totals. In a tie, two more deals are played as a tiebreaker.

Above: An unbeaten set of four Queens is known as a *Quatorze* and is worth a total of 14 points to its holder.

Above: Elder's starting and finishing hands before and after discarding his cards. Elder has so many weak cards in his hand that it is worth exchanging the maximum five cards for five new ones.

Above: Younger's starting and finishing hands. After Elder discards five cards, Younger is left with three cards to exchange with those from the stock in the hope of picking up some better ones.

IMPERIAL

In this game, players use counters to keep score. Each player starts with five red counters and six white to their left, moving one of the white ones to the right to signify each point won in play. Six points equals an imperial. This is marked by a red counter and the six white counters are moved back again to the left.

You will need: 32-card deck, Sixes down to Twos having been removed; red and white counters

Card ranking: Ace down to Seven

Players: Two

Ideal for: 14+

OBJECT

To score the most points by capturing tricks and collecting point-scoring card combinations.

THE DEAL

The dealer deals two hands of 12 cards each in packets of two, three or four. The next card is turned face up to establish trumps. The remaining cards are placed face down across it. If the turn-up is an 'honour card' (an Ace, King, Queen, Jack or Seven) the dealer scores a point for it. If it is an Ace or a King, the dealer can exchange a Seven for it, assuming that he holds one in his hand.

PLAY AND SCORING

Before play starts, both players work out and announce how many points they have according to the values of the cards they hold in any one suit. An Ace scores 11, the court cards 10 each and the Ten, Nine, Eight and Seven are at face value. The player with the higher score wins a point, but, if the scores are tied, the point goes to the non-dealing player. Both players also score any *Impériales* they may be holding in their hand, which can be:

- An *Impériale d'Alout* (King, Queen, Jack and Ten), worth 12 points if they are trumps, six points if they are non-trumps.
- An *Impériale d'Honneur* (all four of one of the following ranks plus one of the other cards: Ace, King, Queen, Jack or Seven), worth six points.
- An *Impériale Blanche* (all four cards of any rank other than court cards with one other card, again not a court card), worth 12 points.

They must be declared strictly in the above order and shown if the opposing player requests it.

After the *Impériales* have been declared, play begins with the non-dealing player leading. The dealer must follow suit with a higher card, play a trump or revoke if unable to do either. The trick is taken by the highest card of the suit led or the highest trump if any are played. The winner of each trick leads to the next.

A player scores a point for leading an honour to a trick and one for capturing a trick containing one. At the end of play, a player winning more than six tricks scores a point for each of them. If one player takes all 12 tricks, this is *Capot*, which is worth 12 points, but, if the tricks are divided, neither player scores.

Whenever a player scores six points, the opposing player's points are forfeited. The sole exception is when an *Impériale Blanche* is declared, when the opposing player's points are not forfeited. Scores can be written down but counters are preferable.

HAND 1

HAND 2

HAND 3

Above and left: Examples of scoring Imperials: (1) An *Impériale d'Alout*, worth 12 points in trumps or otherwise six points (2) an *Impériale d'Honneur*, worth six points and (3) an *Impériale Blanche*, worth 12 points.

CONCLUSION

Game is 36 points. The first player to shift all 11 counters from left to right is the winner.

GLEEK

This is a somewhat elaborate game in which there are four main stages. In the first, players bid for the chance to improve their hands by discarding cards and replacing them with ones from the stock. They then bet as to who holds the longest suit, followed by declarations of Gleeks (Three of a Kind) and Mournivals (Four of a Kind) before getting down to the final stage of trick play.

You will need:	44-card deck (Threes and Twos removed from a standard pack); scorecards; gambling chips/counters
Card ranking:	Ace down to Four
Players:	Three
Ideal for:	14+

OBJECT

To score the most points by capturing tricks and collecting certain cards or card-scoring combinations.

THE DEAL

The players cut the pack to establish who will be the dealer. The lowest card wins. Each of the players is dealt 12 cards in packets of four, the remaining cards being placed face down to form the stock. Players put an equal number of chips into a pot. The dealer turns up the top card of the stock to establish trumps.

BIDDING

All players start with the same number of chips. After the deal has been completed, they bid for the right to discard seven cards in exchange for the stock, although the turned-up trump is excluded. The player to the dealer's left bids first, starting the bidding with 10 chips. The other players can either raise the bid by two chips or pass, so dropping out of the bidding. When two players have passed, the winning bidder pays half the final bid to each of them. Without showing any cards, he discards seven cards and replaces them with the stock.

VYING

The players now bet to see who holds the best 'ruff' – the highest card value in a single suit. This is determined by adding up the cards. Aces count 11, Kings, Queens and Jacks 10 each and all the other cards at face value. The players start by putting two chips each into a pot, after

which they have several options. They can pass, decide to match the previous bet, or raise it by a further two chips. The process continues until two players pass or there is a showdown. The holder of the best hand wins the pot.

Finally, all the players declare and score for any Gleeks and Mournivals they may hold, each opposing player paying the holder the appropriate number of chips. In Gleeks, Aces are worth four chips, Kings three, Queens two and Jacks one. In Mournivals, Aces are worth eight chips, Kings six, Queens four and Jacks two.

PLAYING THE TRICKS

The player to the left of the dealer leads. Players must follow suit if possible, trump or otherwise play any card. The highest trump or the highest card of the suit led wins the trick, and the winner leads to the next.

Every trick taken scores three points for its winner, plus bonus points for the top trumps. These have their own names and special point values. An Ace is Tib and worth 15 points, Kings and Queens score three points each, a Jack is Tom and worth nine points, while Six (Tumbler), Five (Towser) and Four (Tiddy) score six, five and four points respectively. Tumbler and Towser are optional inclusions. If the turned-up card is an Ace or any of the court cards, the dealer counts it in as part of his total score.

CONCLUSION

A game consists of 12 tricks. At the end, any player scoring less than 22 puts a chip into the pot for every point of the shortfall, while any player scoring more than 22 takes a chip out of the pot for every point scored in excess of that figure.

Left: The top trumps won in tricks (here, assuming trumps are Spades) have their own names and special point values. An Ace is known as Tib and is worth 15 points, Kings and Queens are each worth three points, a Jack (Tom) scores nine points, while Six, Five, Four, known as Tumbler, Towser and Tiddy respectively, score just their face value.

ADVANCED CARD GAMES

Dedicated card players are always on the lookout for games they have not played before. The card games in this section of the book require more skill than the average, and so will appeal to the more sophisticated player rather than the complete beginner. This is not to say that a novice should never experiment – only that it is a good idea to master the principles of simpler trick-taking games, such as Whist, before trying to tackle a more complicated bidding game such as Contract Bridge.

Excellent Contract Bridge players have almost always started off with Whist, its 17th-century antecedent. Indeed, many experts believe that, while any good Whist player can become a good Bridge player once the elements of bidding have been mastered, many who pass as good Bridge players could be quite out of their depth at Whist. In fact, the British card authority David Parlett is of the opinion that 'nobody should learn Bridge without prior experience of Whist', going as far as to say that 'many Bridge players would improve their game by going on a crash diet of Whist only'.

QUICK-TRICK GAMES

Quick-trick games can also be very challenging. As in Bridge, many of these games include an element of bidding, but the element that makes them particularly demanding is that, as opposed to many other card games, not all the cards are dealt. Naturally, this makes it harder for players to deduce what cards their opponents may be holding.

Above: Well-dressed players taking part in a Whist drive, *c.*1906. The players change tables every few deals and face several different pairs of opponents.

Euchre, for which the modern Joker was invented, is the most sophisticated of these games, although Nap, or Napoleon, a simplified version, is probably more popular, being played throughout northern Europe under different guises. The author Jerome K. Jerome mentioned the game in his comic masterpiece *Three Men in a Boat*, when he described his three leading characters – J, the book's narrator, George and Harris – settling down to indulge in a game of 'Penny Nap after supper'. The game was probably named after the French emperor Napoleon III, who is thought to have played a version of it.

HEARTS AND ITS RELATIVES

Games in the Hearts family stand the usual scoring conventions of card games on their head. The aim in these games is to *avoid* winning tricks, and so amass points. This makes Twos and Threes as valuable as Aces and Kings often are in other card games, while holding middle-ranking cards, such as Sevens and Eights, can mean positive danger, if not complete disaster.

Playing games like Hearts well means cultivating a special kind of card sense. Often, it is best to aim not to take any tricks at all, especially in games where holding or winning certain cards means incurring a penalty. Two variants (not included in this book) illustrate this point well. In Black Maria, the player ending up with the

Above: A fashionable group play a game of Bridge, 1912.

Jack-Nine games, the Jack is promoted to become the highest trump, followed by the Nine. The three classic examples of this type of game are Belote, Klaverjas and Schieber Jass, the national card games of France, the Netherlands and Switzerland, respectively.

POKER AND ITS ORIGINS

Of all these more advanced games, Poker stands alone. This is a five-card vying game in which players bet money or gambling chips into a communal pot during the course of a hand; the player who has the best hand at the end of the betting wins the pot, in a 'showdown'. It is also possible for the pot to be won by a hand that is not the best, by bluffing the other players out of play.

It is believed that Poker emerged early in the 19th century, probably in New Orleans, on board the great Mississippi paddle steamers. It seems likely that its immediate ancestor was a French game called Poque, which itself was a version of the German game Poch. According to American card authority Louis Coffin, 'the French name was pronounced 'poke' and Southerners corrupted the pronunciation to Pokuh or Poker'. Brag, a vying game based on three-card hands, is also thought to have been an influence.

By Victorian times, Draw and Stud Poker had emerged. Then came further variants in which the notion of one or more communal cards was introduced. By that time, Poker had become what American card historian Allen Dowling aptly termed 'the great American pastime'. It is now a favourite throughout the card-playing world.

Above: An international Bridge tournament in New York in 2005. Played socially by many, Bridge is also a seriously competitive game, with championship matches held across the world.

Queen of Spades scores an extra 13 points, and each Heart counts for a single point, although a player with the Jack of Diamonds deducts 12 points from his score. In Pink Lady, the other variant, ending up with the Queen of Hearts means a 13-point penalty.

In Jacks and its close relative Polignac, the Jacks, as might be expected, are the high-scoring danger cards.

ACES, TENS AND OTHER CARDS

Some card games give specific cards particular values. In games such as Skat, Germany's most popular card game, Aces count for 11 points, Tens 10, Kings four, Queens three and Jacks two. The aim is to win at least 61 card points in tricks (the number of tricks taken is in itself immaterial). So-called King-Queen games are governed by the same principles, and, in them, declaring the 'marriage' of a King and Queen of the same suit in the same hand wins bonus points. This makes games like Sixty-Six exciting because it introduces an element of unpredictability into the game. Declaring a 'marriage' can transform the scoring situation, turning a losing player into a winning one.

Games like Bezique, Marjolet and Pinochle use the same principles, with an extra 'marriage' being allowed between a specified Queen and a Jack of a different suit. They differ in the fact that players win most of their points by collecting and melding certain sequences and combinations of cards. In

Right: Classic image of a joker or court jester, wearing a cap and bells, carrying a ninny stick, or jester's wand, from a 15th-century manuscript.

BRIDGE AND WHIST GAMES

BRIDGE AND WHIST BELONG TO TRICK-TAKING CARD GAMES, IN WHICH THE OBJECTIVE IS TO WIN A SPECIFIED NUMBER OF TRICKS; AS MANY TRICKS AS POSSIBLE; OR OCCASIONALLY A SPECIFIED ONE, SUCH AS THE LAST TRICK OF A HAND. IN SOME GAMES, THE AIM IS TO LOSE RATHER THAN WIN TRICKS, WHILE IN POINT-TRICK GAMES, THE TOTAL POINT VALUE OF THE CARDS TAKEN DETERMINES THE RESULT, RATHER THAN THE NUMBER OF TRICKS.

As far as most trick-taking games are concerned, the rules clearly state what can be led and when. The most common requirement is the need to follow suit. In certain games, players are required to ruff – that is, to play a trump – if they are unable to follow suit and hold a trump card or cards in their hands.

In trick play, each player is normally dealt the same number of cards and plays a card in turn face up to the table. The player with the best card, usually the highest-ranking card of the suit that has been led or the highest trump, wins all the others. These constitute a trick which the winner places face down in a winnings pile; he then plays the first card of the next trick. Who leads initially is normally decided by cutting the cards. The other players play in order according to their positions around the card table, typically clockwise in games from English-speaking countries. In positive trick-taking games, players aim to take as many tricks as possible. Exact prediction trick-taking games, such as Bridge, involve a contract, in which players aim to win a set number of tricks. There are two scoring systems. In what are termed plain-trick games, it is only the number of tricks taken by each player that matters. The points on the cards making up the tricks are irrelevant. In point-trick games, however, players are rewarded or penalized for capturing certain cards, each of which has a pre-assigned value.

Above: Harold Vanderbilt (1884–1970), American multi-millionaire, revised the rules of bridge in 1925, thus turning auction bridge into contract bridge.

BRIDGE BASICS

Four players take part in a game of bridge and are conventionally known in bridge literature as North, East, South and West. The players in the North and South seats form one partnership and sit opposite one another. They will compete against East and West, who form the other partnership.

For each deal, one of the players is the "dealer". (In a social game, the dealer for the first deal is chosen by a cut of the cards. Thereafter, the deal passes clockwise to the next player. In tournament bridge, the plastic or wooden board containing the cards indicates who is the dealer.) The dealer deals the pack of 52 cards in a clockwise direction, one card at a time. When the whole pack has been dealt, each player will hold a "hand" of 13 cards. It is customary to sort these into suits, with the cards in descending order within a particular suit. For example, you might sort out your hand like this:

♠A Q 9 5 4   ♥A 8 5 3   ♦K 9 4   ♣5

Above: West has five spades to the ace–queen, four hearts to the ace, three diamonds to the king and a singleton club.

You have sorted all the spades to be together. The rank (order of importance) of the cards is: ace (highest), king, queen, jack, 10, 9, 8, 7, 6, 5, 4, 3, 2 (lowest). As you see, the five cards in the spade suit are arranged in descending order of rank, with the ace on the left and the 4 on the right. If someone were to ask you afterwards what hand you held, you would reply

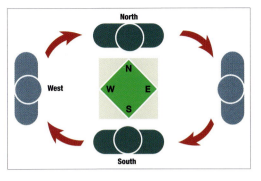

Above: For both the bidding and play, the action takes place in a clockwise direction. If South makes the first call in the auction, for example, West will make the second call. If West later leads to the first trick, the second card will be played by North.

"I had five spades to the ace–queen, four hearts to the ace, three diamonds to the king and a singleton club". A "singleton" is a holding of just one card in a suit; a "doubleton" would be a holding of two cards. When you describe a hand, you cannot be expected to remember the low cards (known as "spot cards") and would usually name only the "picture cards" (aces, kings, queens or jacks) that you held.

So, each of the four players holds a hand of 13 cards. These are held close to the chest, so that the other three players can see only the backs of the cards. The subsequent action consists of two parts: the "bidding" and then the "play" of the cards.

Although the bidding occurs before the play when you are actually engaged in a game of bridge, it is not possible to understand the bidding until you know how the play will go. For that reason the play will be described first here. So that you can understand the basics, if you are new to the game, the idea of tricks and trumps will be addressed first. Later the bidding will be described and a sample complete deal of bridge will give you a general idea of how the game is played.

Above: Bidding sequence. In tournament bridge each player creates a line of all his calls during the auction. Here, the player has made three bids.

What is a trick?

The play of the cards, at bridge, is very similar to that in the old game of whist. It consists of a sequence of "tricks". A trick consists of four cards, one played by each player. The highest card played will "win the trick".

This is a typical trick, with the cards played in a clockwise direction around the table:

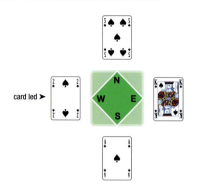

West plays first to the trick and chooses to play the ♠2. You might also say that "West leads the ♠2". (You will see later how it is decided who leads to the first trick and to each of the subsequent tricks.) West "leads" the ♠2, then, and North plays the ♠5. East plays the ♠K and South "wins the trick" with the ♠A. He wins the trick because his card is the highest one played in the suit that was led. Remember that the ranking of the cards is: ace (highest), king, queen, jack, 10, 9, 8, 7, 6, 5, 4, 3, 2 (lowest). Because South won the trick, he will lead to the next trick. It will be his choice whether to lead another spade or to play some different suit.

A ROUND OF TRUMPS
♠ ♥ ♦ ♣

The term "round" is similar in meaning to "trick". If declarer plays a "round of trumps", this means that he leads a trump and the other three hands play a card to the trick. If, for example, both defenders hold at least one trump, this round of trumps will draw two trumps from the defenders' hands. For that reason, you might also say "declarer draws a round of trumps". You might also say "declarer draws trumps in three rounds", meaning that he had to lead trumps three times, on three successive tricks, in order to remove all the defenders' trumps.

If you hold a card in the suit led, you must "'follow suit". In other words, if a spade is led you must play a spade if you have one. When you cannot follow suit, you must play a card in a different suit. Unless you play a card from the suit chosen as the "trump suit", your card in a different suit cannot win the trick, however high it is. Suppose the trump suit is spades and South leads the ♣J here:

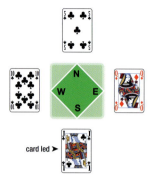

South, who won the previous trick, leads the ♣J. The next two players follow with lower cards in the same suit and East has no clubs left in his hand. He "discards" the ♦Q. South's ♣J wins the trick because it is the highest card in the suit that was led.

What are trumps?

During the bidding, which will be explained in a moment, a suit may be chosen as "trumps". This suit then becomes more powerful than the other three suits. A low trump, such as the two, will defeat even the ace of a different suit. When you have no cards left in the suit that has been led, you can play any card in the trump suit and win the trick with it. Let's assume that spades are trumps and this trick arises:

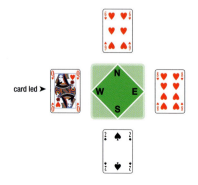

West, who won the previous trick, leads the ♥Q. The next two players follow with lower hearts. South, who has no hearts left, plays the two of trumps. Even though his trump is a lowly two, he wins the trick. Bridge players would say "South trumped with the two" or (more commonly) "South ruffed with the two".

Sometimes two players have no more cards in the suit that was led and both choose to play a trump. In that case the higher trump will win the trick:

card led ➤

West leads the ♥10 and North beats this with the ♥J. East has no more hearts and attempts to win the trick by ruffing with the ♠3. South "overruffs" with the ♠4. He wins the trick because his card is the higher of the two trumps played.

You can see how useful trumps are. You can use them to prevent the other side from winning tricks with their high cards in other suits. You can also use them to score extra tricks of your own – by ruffing low cards of a non-trump suit, cards that would otherwise not win a trick.

NOTATION FOR CARDS IN BRIDGE
♠ ♥ ♦ ♣

When a suit symbol precedes a number, or a letter that denotes a picture card, this represents a card. It is the accepted shorthand for representing a card in print, perhaps in a bridge book or article or in a newspaper. So, ♠ 3 is short for the card known as the "three of spades". ♦ K is the "king of diamonds". ♠ A J 7 6 is the written form of a spade suit containing four cards: the ace, jack, seven and six.

The bidding

During the bidding each partnership tries to assess how many tricks they will be able to make during the play, also which trump suit they should choose. (The trump suit is the most powerful suit during the play of the cards, remember. Any trump, however low, will win against a card from any other suit). A further option is to play the hand in "no-trumps", in other words without a trump suit.

We will see in a moment how you make a bid. For the moment, let's suppose that the bidding ends with South announcing that he, in conjunction with his partner's hand opposite, can make ten tricks with spades as trumps. The cards are then played and South must attempt to score ten tricks out of the 13 that are available. The other two players, known as the defenders, will try to prevent him from achieving this target.

That is the purpose of the bidding, then. One side, usually the one with the most high cards (aces, kings and queens) between them, will set themselves a target of tricks and choose whether they want a particular suit to become trumps.

What is a bid?

During the "bidding", or "auction", each player may make a "bid" when it is his turn to speak. He may instead choose to "pass". (There are two other possible calls, "double" and "redouble", which will be explained later.)

The first actual bid, as opposed to a pass, is known as the "opening bid". To open the bidding, you need slightly better than an average hand. The strength of a hand consists of two main factors – the quantity of high cards (such as aces and kings) and the length of your suits. A hand with plenty of high cards will obviously offer a good prospect of scoring several tricks when the time comes for the play. So will a hand that contains one or more long suits – seven spades, for example. That is because you can make such a suit trumps and score several tricks with it.

To measure the high-card strength of a hand, a point-count system is used. An ace is worth 4 points, a king 3 points, a queen 2 points and a jack 1 point. As a rough guide, you can open the bidding when you hold at least 12 points. Suppose you are the dealer and therefore have the first chance to bid. Your hand is:

♠A J 9 4   ♥K Q   ♦A K Q 7 5   ♣6 3

You have 19 points (5 in spades, 5 in hearts and 9 in diamonds) and this is easily enough to make an opening bid. You will bid 1♦ (one diamond), since diamonds is your longest suit and at this stage it is therefore your best guess as a satisfactory trump suit.

Above: Since you have a strong hand, you will open the bidding. Your longest suit is diamonds and you will open 1♦.

During the play there will be 13 tricks available. A bid at the one-level says that you think you can score seven tricks with your chosen suit as trumps. In other words, you will make seven tricks and the defenders will make six tricks; you will score more tricks than the other side, but only just. The first six tricks are known as "the book" and your bid says how many extra tricks, over the book, you think you can make in conjunction with your partner's hand opposite. Here your bid of 1♦ means that you think you can make seven tricks with diamonds as trumps. A bid of 2♥ would mean that you thought you could make eight tricks with hearts as trumps. Similarly, a bid of 3NT (three no-trumps) would mean that you thought you could make nine tricks in no-trumps, in other words with no suit as trumps.

Once someone has made an opening bid, the auction continues in a clockwise direction around the table. Each player, when it is his turn, has the chance to pass or bid. If he chooses to bid, he must make a higher bid than the last one that was made. This is why the bidding is also called the "auction". You can make a bid at the same level, here the one-level, provided your suit is ranked higher than the suit bid previously.

This is the ranking order of the five possible "denominations":

NT no-trumps (highest)
♠ spades
♥ hearts
♦ diamonds
♣ clubs (lowest)

So, a bid of 1♥ (one heart) is a higher bid than 1♦ (one diamond) because hearts are ranked above diamonds. Spades and hearts are known as the "major suits"; diamonds and clubs are the "minor suits". If all the possible bids were stretched out from the lowest to the highest, this would be the order: 1♣, 1♦, 1♥, 1♠, 1NT, 2♣, 2♦, 2♥, 2♠, 2NT, etc… 7♣, 7♦, 7♥, 7♠, 7NT.

An opening bid of 1♣ is the lowest possible bid, meaning that you think you can score seven tricks with clubs as trumps. A bid of 7NT is the highest possible bid, meaning that you think you can score 13 tricks (seven plus the "book" of six) with no trump suit.

Look again at the line of bids. Suppose someone, either your partner or an opponent, has already bid 1♠ and you have a hand on which you want to make a bid in clubs. You cannot bid 1♣ because this bid is lower than 1♠. You would have to bid 2♣. (You might also choose to bid 3♣, or some higher bid in clubs, on certain types of hand.)

The auction continues until there are three consecutive passes. The last bid then determines what is known as the "contract". If the last bid was 4♠, for example, the partnership making that bid would then try to make ten tricks (four plus the book of six) with spades as trumps. So, the bidding sets a target number of tricks for one of the partnerships.

NOTATION FOR BIDS
♠ ♥ ♦ ♣

When a suit symbol is placed after a number, this represents a bid (rather than a card). So, 2♥ is short for the bid of "two hearts". This would mean that the bidder thought his partnership could score eight tricks (the book of six, plus two) with hearts as trumps. Similarly, 3NT is short for "three no-trumps". If you read in a bridge article that "West led the ♦6 against 4♠", this would mean that West led the six of diamonds (a card) against four spades (the contract, determined by the final bid in the auction).

The play

It is an unusual aspect of bridge that one player becomes the "declarer" (the player trying to make the number of tricks specified in the contract). Suppose, as in the previous section, that the contract is 4♠. The player who first made a bid in spades becomes the declarer. The player to his left (one of the defenders) will lead the first card of the first trick. This play is known as the "opening lead".

Once the opening lead has been made, declarer's partner lays his entire hand face-up on the table. The hand, known as the "dummy", is arranged in four lines facing towards the declarer, with the trump suit (if any) on the left. Declarer's partner will take no further part in this deal. The declarer will play the cards from the dummy as well as from his own hand.

Above: The dummy is arranged in four vertical lines, one for each suit, with the cards in descending order of rank (highest at the top).

For the rest of the play, the dummy (and its remaining cards) will be visible to declarer and to each of the defenders. Whichever of the four hands wins a particular trick, this will be the hand from which the first card is led to the next trick.

Bidding a game

Even in this basic summary of the game, it is necessary to mention something about the scoring. That is because it has a critical effect on the bidding. If you make the contract determined in the auction you score these points for each trick bid and made:

When ♦ or ♣ are trumps: 20 points for each trick
When ♠ or ♥ are trumps: 30 points for each trick
In no-trumps, 40 points for the first trick and 30 points for each subsequent trick

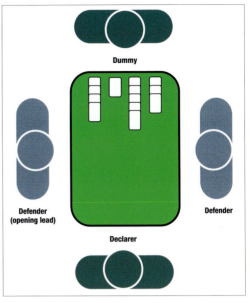

Above: The four players. The defender on declarer's left makes the opening lead and declarer's partner (the dummy) displays his hand face upwards on the table. Declarer plays a card from dummy, the other defender plays a card and declarer completes the trick with one of his cards.

One of the main aims in bridge is to "make a game". To achieve this, you need to score at least 100 points. In no-trumps this can be done by bidding and making the nine-trick contract of 3NT, since 40+30+30 = 100. When the trump suit is spades or hearts (known as the "major suits", remember), you need to bid the ten-trick contract of 4♠ or 4♥, since 4 times 30 is 120. Most difficult is to make a game with diamonds or clubs (known as the "minor suits") as trumps. You would then need to bid 5♦ or 5♣, since 5 times 20 is 100. This will require you to make 11 of the available 13 tricks.

During the auction the partnership that holds the majority of the high cards will have two main decisions to make. They must decide which suit to make trumps, or perhaps to play in no-trumps. They must decide also whether their combined strength merits attempting a "game contract". In very rough terms, since suit lengths are also important, a partnership can make a game contract when they hold 25 of the available 40 high-card points between them. During the bidding they will attempt to discover if this is in fact the case.

A typical hand of bridge

The time has come, in this brief summary of the game, to see a complete hand of bridge (see below).

North, who was the dealer and holds the 19-point hand that we saw earlier, opens 1♦. East has a poor hand and passes. South holds 6 points. To "respond" to an opening bid at the one-level (in other words, to make a bid when your partner has already opened the bidding), you need 6 points or more. South has enough to respond and bids 1♠, suggesting spades as trumps. This is a higher bid than 1♦ because the spade suit is ranked higher than diamonds.

West has a strong club suit and decides to enter the bidding. He cannot bid 1♣, since this would be a lower bid than 1♠. He therefore overcalls 2♣. The word "overcall" means to make a bid after the opponents have already bid. North is pleased that his partner has bid spades because he also holds spade length. This means that spades will make a good trump suit. He plans to "agree spades as trumps" by making a further bid in spades himself. He will have to choose how high to bid in spades – the higher he bids, the stronger the hand he will show.

Since his own hand is very strong, North judges that the partnership can make a game in spades. (As a

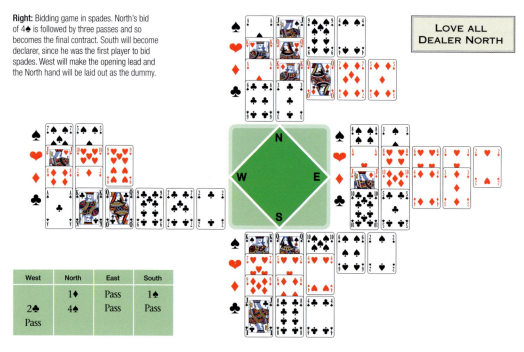

FINDING A TRUMP FIT
♠ ♥ ♦ ♣

To make a satisfactory trump fit, you usually need at least eight of the available 13 cards in a particular suit. On this deal North holds four spades and knows, from his partner's 1♠ response, that South holds at least four spades too. The North–South partnership has therefore "found a trump fit". North confirms that spades will be trumps by "raising his partner's suit". Because his hand is so strong he raises it to 4♠, a game contract. If he held a minimum opening bid of around 12 points, he would instead raise to just 2♠.

---

rough guide, 25 points between the hands will be enough to make a game contract. Here North holds 19 points and expects his partner to hold at least 6 points for his response.) North jumps to 4♠ because this will be worth 120 points and is therefore a game contract.

The next three players pass and the auction is over. The "final contract" is 4♠ and South will be the declarer since he was the first player to bid spades. West, the player to the dealer's left, will make the opening lead.

Right: Bidding game in spades. North's bid of 4♠ is followed by three passes and so becomes the final contract. South will become declarer, since he was the first player to bid spades. West will make the opening lead and the North hand will be laid out as the dummy.

LOVE ALL
DEALER NORTH

West	North	East	South
	1♦	Pass	1♠
2♣	4♠	Pass	Pass
Pass			

We will now see the play of the cards. South, the declarer, must attempt to score ten tricks with spades as trumps. West, the player to declarer's left, makes the "opening lead" of the ♣A. North lays his cards on the table, displaying the dummy. From now on, declarer will play a card from the dummy to each trick as well as a card from his own hand.

Trick 1: The other three players follow with lower clubs and West's ♣A wins the trick.

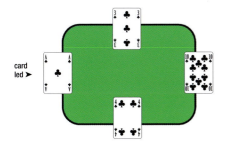

Above: Trick 1. West wins the first trick with the ♣A, the other three players following suit.

Trick 2: Since West won the trick he will lead to the second trick. He leads the ♣K and again the other three players follow with lower clubs. East–West (known as the "defenders") now have two tricks.

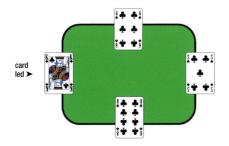

Above: Trick 2. West leads the ♣K, everyone following, and wins the trick.

Trick 3: West leads the ♣Q. Since the dummy has no clubs left, declarer can "ruff in the dummy". If he carelessly ruffs with the ♠4, East (who also has no clubs left) will overruff with the ♠8. That will be three tricks for the defenders and the ♥A would then give them a fourth trick to defeat the contract. Declarer therefore ruffs with the ♠9. He knows that neither defender holds a higher trump than this, so he has prevented an overruff.

Above: Trick 3. West leads the ♣Q and declarer ruffs with the ♠9. East cannot overruff and discards a heart.

Trick 4: Declarer now starts to "draw trumps". In other words, he will play sufficient rounds of trumps to remove the defenders' trumps. They will not then be able to ruff any of his tricks. Declarer leads dummy's ♠4 to his ♠K and both defenders follow.

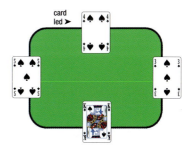

Above: Trick 4. Declarer leads dummy's ♠4 to his ♠K and both defenders follow suit.

Trick 5: Declarer leads the ♠2 to dummy's ♠A and both defenders follow again. Since there were only four trumps missing, he has now drawn trumps.

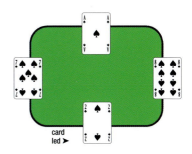

Above: Trick 5. Declarer draws a second round of trumps, everyone following suit.

Tricks 6/7/8: Declarer scores tricks with the ace, king and queen of diamonds. On the third round he has no diamond to play from the South hand and discards one of his hearts. West also "shows out", discarding a club. If the diamond suit had "broken 3–2" (in other words, one defender had held three diamonds and the other had held two), the ♦7 and the ♦5 would have scored two further tricks and declarer would have been able to discard his two remaining hearts.

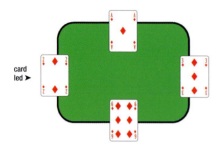

Above: Trick 6. Declarer scores a diamond trick by leading dummy's ace.

Above: Trick 7. Declarer continues with dummy's ♦K, scoring a second diamond trick.

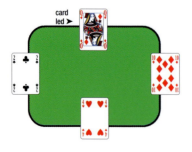

Above: Trick 8: Declarer discards a heart on the dummy's ♦Q and is disappointed to see West show out, throwing a club.

Trick 9: As it is, declarer leads the ♥K and East wins with the ♥A. Declarer has "knocked out" the ♥A, as bridge players say, and "established" the ♥Q as a winning card.

Above: Trick 9: Declarer leads the ♥K to East's ♥A, thereby setting up the ♥Q as a winner.

Trick 10: East leads a heart and the trick is won with dummy's ♥Q.

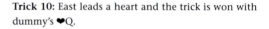

Above: Trick 10. Declarer wins East's heart return in the dummy.

The last three tricks will be taken with the three trumps remaining in declarer's hand. In total, declarer scored ten tricks: five trump tricks, one club ruff in the dummy, three diamond tricks and one heart trick. He therefore made his game contract of four spades. We will look at scoring in some detail, later in the book. For the moment, we will just say that North–South will score 120 for making four spades and a bonus of 300 for bidding and making a game. That is a score of +420 for North–South. The defenders, East–West will score -420 because the game was made against them. Scorepads (social bridge) and scorecards (competition bridge) have a plus column and a minus column.

PLAYING BRIDGE AGAINST THE COMPUTER

By using the Internet, you can play with human players from around the world. Alternatively, without needing to access the Internet, you can play bridge on your own computer. Your partner and your opponents will be provided by software that runs on your machine. They will bid and play their cards automatically. The early bridge-playing programs were disappointingly weak, making poor bids and even worse plays. However, they have greatly improved in the last few years and can now give you an entertaining game.

There are many such software packages on the market (including Jack, Q-Plus, Bridge Baron and GIB). The saved screen below reflects the bidding of a hand on GIB. The human player (South) was playing

Below: A screen from the GIB computer-playing software, taken at a moment South is about to bid.

with three computer-generated players, and the deal came from a supplied library of deals from real tournaments. In this case it was from the 2002 Cap Gemini tournament. The human player decided to double 3♠ at this stage. He led the ♥Q against 3♠ doubled and declarer lost two clubs, a diamond and three trump tricks, going two down for a 500 penalty.

USER PROFILES
♠ ♥ ♦ ♣

When becoming a member of an online bridge club, you are invited to create a "profile" that describes yourself. For example, you may choose to disclose your real name (rather than your screen "nickname"). You may also declare that you are a novice, an expert or world class.

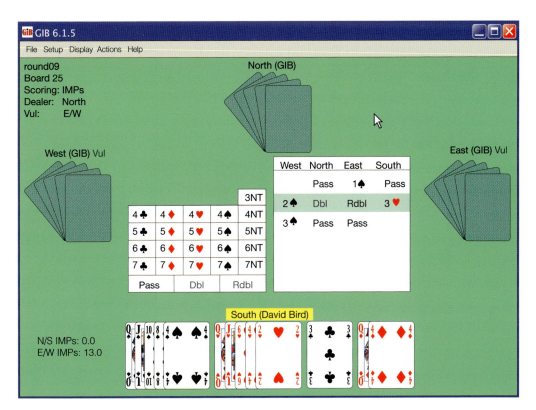

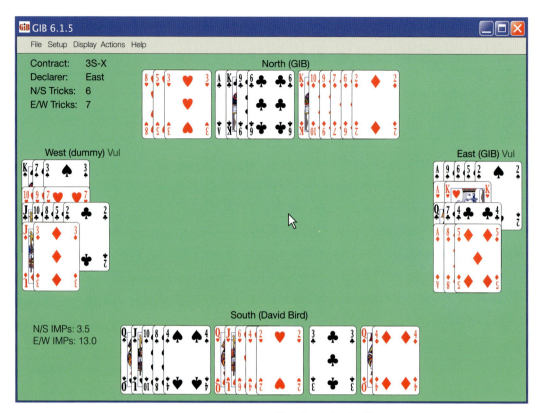

Above: A screen from the GIB computer-playing software, just after completion of the play.

This was the screen at the end of play (above). The score-sheet from the original event reveals that +500 is worth +3.5 International Match Points (IMPs) when compared with the average result. A good bridge-playing package will offer you some means of judging how well you have performed. In other words, you need other scores for a comparison. Either the software can replay the deal, with four computer players, or it can use deals from real tournaments, as we have just seen.

You may wonder how such packages are programmed. GIB decides which card to play by creating several sets of random hands for the two unseen players – hands that match the bidding and the play so far. It then sees which card will produce the best result, by playing each random deal to its conclusion. For example, if playing the ♠9 wins on 15 of the 20 random deals and playing the ♠Q wins on only 12, it will play the ♠9. This is much more effective than trying to program general rules such as "second hand low". Indeed, when a super-powered version of GIB competed against world-class players at

a recent world championship, it was placed halfway up the field. This was a phenomenal achievement when you bear in mind how weak bridge-playing programs were in the early days.

North	East	South	West	Contract	Declarer	Result	Score	IMPs
Chagas	Pszczola	Brenner	Kwiecien	3S-X	East	down 3	+800	+9.5
SaelensmindeSacul	Brogeland	Versace	Karwur	3S-X	East	down 2	+500	+3.5
Ravenna	Gawrys	Madala	Jassem	3C-X	West	down 2	+500	+3.5
Westra	Stansby	Leufkens	Gitelman	3S-X	East	down 2	+500	+3.5
GIB 6.1.3	GIB 6.1.3	David Bird	GIB 6.1.3	3S-X	East	down 2	+500	+3.5
Garozzo	Muller	Versace	De Wigs	2H	South	made 3	+140	-5.37
Robson	Auken	Mahmood	Reps	2D	North	made 4	+130	-5.87
Verhees	Gromov	Jansma	Peturin	2D	North	made 4	+130	-5.87
Helness	Weinstein	Helgemo	Gamer	2D	North	made 3	+110	-6.37

Click OK to continue to next deal,
click on a line to see the hand record
or select from the menus.

OK

Above: By comparing your own result with those obtained by the players in the original tournament, you can assess how well you fared.

CONTRACT BRIDGE

Love it or loathe it, Bridge has long been one of the most popular card games in the world: its origins date back to the 1880s. Auction Bridge made its debut in 1904 and Contract Bridge in 1925. The latter soon became the dominant form of the game, thanks largely to two Americans – Harold Vanderbilt, who codified its rules, and master player Ely Culbertson, the great popularizer of the game.

You will need: 52-card deck; no Jokers; scorecards
Card ranking: Standard, Aces high
Players: Four, playing in partnerships of two
Ideal for: 14+

Above: Ely Culbertson (1891–1955) built on the efforts of the founders of Contract Bridge by developing the game's first comprehensive bidding system. The vast publicity campaign he orchestrated for Bridge was instrumental in establishing its popularity.

OBJECT

To make, in tandem with one's partner, a specified number (contract) of tricks – or more – scoring enough points over a sequence of deals to make game and then win a rubber without giving away a greater number of points in doing so. A rubber is card parlance for a match. It usually consists of three games and is won, or taken, by the first partnership to win two of them.

SPECIAL FEATURES

Establishing Partners

Partners are determined by social agreement, or by a cut, in which the cards are fanned out face down on the table. Each player in turn draws a card. The two players with the highest-scoring cards become the lead partnership; the player with the higher card becomes the dealer. The convention is to sit around the table according to the points of the compass – North and South form one partnership and East and West the other.

Dummy

After the first card of a hand has been led, the cards of the declarer's partner are laid face up on the table and he takes no active part in that particular hand. The declarer is the highest bidder at the auction (see page 135).

Ruffing

In Bridge, playing a trump is termed ruffing. Usually the declarer and the dummy (see above) control the majority of trumps between them since they chose the suit to be played. Thus, one of the declarer's aims is to draw off the opposing partnership's trumps, leaving them with none. The declarer normally has enough trumps left to make sure that the defending partnership is not given the opportunity to win tricks with what are termed long

cards, as these will simply be trumped. Long cards are the cards remaining in a suit after all the cards of the other players have been exhausted.

SCORING

Both partnerships keep running scorecards, which are divided into two columns headed 'WE' and 'THEY' with a horizontal line partway down each sheet. Points can be scored 'above the line' and 'below the line'.

If a partnership wins a contracted number of tricks or more, it is deemed to have fulfilled its contract and a score is awarded accordingly. If not, the contract is said to be defeated and points are awarded to the defending partnership. Each partnership aims to win the most points in the best of the three games that make up a rubber.

Points per Trick

Trick points (only given for each trick over 'the book', which consists of the first six tricks) are entered below the line. Only the declaring partnership can score them and then only if it has fulfilled the contract for the deal. If trumps are Clubs or Diamonds, the partnership scores 20 per trick, and 30 per trick if trumps are Hearts or Spades. If there are No Trumps, it scores 40 for the first trick after the book and 30 for each subsequent one. Clubs and Diamonds are termed minor suits, while Hearts and Spades are the major suits.

Doubles and Redoubles

If the contract is doubled, scores are doubled in turn. If it is redoubled, points are multiplied by four. If the declaring partnership succeeds in winning a doubled contract, it wins an extra 50 points above the line. This is sometimes known as '50 for the insult'. The bonus above the line for a redoubled contract is 100 points.

SCORES AT CONTRACT BRIDGE

Contract made: the declarer scores below the line for each trick bid and won

Suit bid and won	Points	Doubled	Redoubled
Minor suit (♦ ♣)	20	40	80
Major suit (♠ ♥)	30	60	120
No Trump (NT) for 1st trick	40	80	160
NT for subsequent tricks	30	60	120

Declarers may also score above the line
(TV= trick value, V=Vulnerable)

For each overtrick	TV	100	200
For each overtrick (V)	TV	200	400
For making a doubled/ redoubled contract	50	100	
For making a small slam	500/750 (V)		
For making a grand slam	1000/1500 (V)		

Contract defeated: the defenders score above the line

Undertricks	Points	Doubled	Redoubled
First	50	100	200 (if not vulnerable)
or	100	200	400 (if vulnerable)
Second/Third	50	200	400 (If not vulnerable)
or	100	300	600 (if vulnerable)
plus for each subsequent trick	0	100	200 (if not vulnerable)

Honours: scored above the line

Any four of A, K, Q, J, 10 of trumps	100
All five of A, K, Q, J, 10 of trumps	150
All four Aces at No Trumps	150

Rubber scores at the end of play

Winning the rubber, opponents winning one game	500
Winning the rubber, opponents winning no games	700
Winning the only game in an unfinished rubber	300
For the only part-score in an unfinished game	100

Bonus and Penalty Points

Bonuses for tricks made in excess of a contract, or points awarded to a defending partnership if the contract is defeated, are also recorded above the line. These are termed overtricks and undertricks. Overtricks are scored the same as bid tricks. If, however, a declaring partnership wins fewer tricks than it bid, neither side scores anything below the line, but the defending partnership scores above the line for the number of tricks by which the declaring partnership falls short of its target. The value of such scores varies, depending on whether a partnership is what is termed 'vulnerable'. If it is, the scores are increased. A partnership is deemed vulnerable once it has won a game towards a best-of-three rubber. Once the two partnerships have each won a game, they are both vulnerable.

Slams

A contract to make all 13 possible tricks is termed a Grand Slam, while a contract to make 12 is a Small Slam. If a declaring partnership is vulnerable, it wins a bonus of 750 points above the line for making a Small Slam and 1,500 for a Grand Slam. If it is not vulnerable, it wins 500 points or 1,000 points.

Honours

Bonus points are awarded to players holding honours in their hands before any cards are played, although these are not actually scored until the end of the hand. Honours are the top five trumps: Ace, King, Queen, Jack and Ten. If a player holds all of these, he scores a bonus of 150 points above the line for the partnership. Four honours in one hand score 100. If there are No Trumps, but a player holds four Aces, the partnership scores 150 points for honours.

Points when Vulnerable

A partnership that has won a game is deemed vulnerable, meaning that any penalty points incurred against it are significantly increased (see scoring table, left). Both partnerships can be vulnerable at the same time.

Game and Rubber

A rubber typically consists of three games, so is won by the first side to win two. If a partnership wins two games without reply, it scores 700 bonus points for the rubber, this being reduced to 500 points if the opposing partnership has won a game. Victory in the rubber, however, goes to the partnership with the highest total after trick and premium points have been added together.

HAND A

HAND B

HAND C

Above and left: In adding up the value of hands, Aces are worth four points, Kings three, Queens two and Jacks one. An extra point is added in Hand A for the doubleton (just two cards in a suit), two points for Hand B for the singleton (just one card) and three points for Hand C for the void (where one suit is absent).

THE DEAL

Each player is dealt 13 cards, the dealer distributing the cards clockwise, one at a time. After each hand, the deal passes to the player to the left of the previous dealer.

A hand needs to contain at least 12 points to be worth an opening bid, i.e. to be considered a winning hand. An Ace is worth four points, a King three, a Queen two and a Jack one. Some players allow an extra point for a five-card major suit, or for a 'doubleton' (two cards in a particular suit), adding two points for a 'singleton' (just one card in a suit) and three for a 'void' (where one suit is absent).

THE AUCTION AND CONTRACT

After the deal, the starting point is an auction, often termed bidding, which ends with the establishment of a contract. By this, the winning partnership commits itself to taking a minimum number of tricks, either with a specific suit as trumps or with No Trumps. The auction is started by the dealer when all the players have evaluated the cards in their hands, other players calling in clockwise order.

There are four types of call – bid, double, redouble and pass. A bid indicates the aim of making six tricks, the book, with one's partner, plus a stated number of extra ones, from one to seven, 'the levels'. A bid of 3♦ would mean that the bidder anticipates the partnership can take nine tricks in all (the book plus three), with Diamonds – the denomination – as the trump suit. An alternative would be 3NT (No Trumps), in which case the target is still nine tricks, but the hand is played without a trump suit.

A player can double the last bid by an opponent and redouble if the opponent's last bid was a double. If a doubled bid becomes the contract, the score for making it, plus any overtricks, is doubled, but penalty points are

doubled likewise if the contract is not made. A pass means no bid. The auction is over if three passes in succession follow a bid, double or redouble, or if all four players pass in the first round of bidding. In the latter case, all the cards are thrown in and the player to the dealer's left shuffles and deals again.

When first bidding, the key aim is to find the strengths and weaknesses of other players' hands as well as trying to making a contract. All kinds of bidding systems have been devised to this end. Players must state which system they are using at the start of a rubber before play begins.

There are 35 possible bids in all. Each bid has to be higher than the previous one. The level – that is, the number of tricks the bidding partnership undertakes to win – can obviously be increased, in which case any denomination can be specified, or the denomination can be changed to a higher one, with the level remaining the same. Denominations are ranked, from lowest to highest, as Clubs, Diamonds, Hearts, Spades and No Trumps (NT). The lowest possible bid is 1♣, while 7NT is the highest.

PLAY

Once the auction is over and the contract established, the player in the contracting partnership who first bid No Trumps or a trump suit becomes the declarer, playing his partner's hand (the dummy) as well as his own. The partner lays his cards down face up on the table, trumps to the right and other suits ranked in rows, as soon as the first card is played, and this player takes no further active part in the hand. The defending player to the declarer's left leads, followed by the other players clockwise round the table. The dealer plays a card from the dummy hand followed by one from his own hand after the opponent to his right has laid a card. Players must follow suit unless unable to do so, in which case a card from another suit, or a trump, may be played. The highest card of the suit led, or the highest trump, wins the trick.

CONCLUSION

Winning a game in bridge does not mean the contest is over. Game is awarded to a partnership that amasses 100 points or more below the line (either in a single contract or by adding together the scores of two or more). Partnerships must then score again from scratch in another game. The first partnership to win two out of the three games takes the rubber.

PARTNERSHIP BRIDGE VARIANTS

Various forms of Bridge have developed over the years, including Duplicate Bridge, the game normally played in clubs, tournaments and competitions, Chicago Bridge, where a game is completed in four deal; and Auction Bridge, the precursor of Contract Bridge. Although the rules of bidding and play are the same in Auction and Contract Bridge, the scoring system is different.

AUCTION BRIDGE

In Auction Bridge, the notion of vulnerability does not exist, so there is no extra penalty for failing to fulfil a contract if your partnership has won a game already. Odd tricks – that is, tricks over the book – are scored below rather than above the line and count towards winning a game.

Clubs count for six points, Diamonds seven, Hearts eight and Spades nine. If the contract is doubled, so is the number of points. If it is redoubled, Clubs are worth 24 points, Diamonds 28, Hearts 32 and Spades 36. Undertricks are scored above the line, as are bonuses for completing the contract and making a Grand or Small Slam. The first partnership to score 30 points below the line wins that game and the first one to win two games takes the rubber, and is awarded another 250 bonus points.

CHICAGO BRIDGE

The advantage of Chicago Bridge is that it is complete in four contracts. Vulnerability (whereby a side, having won a game towards the rubber, is subject to increased scores or penalties) varies from hand to hand in a fixed pattern. In the first hand, neither partnership is vulnerable. In the second, North and South are vulnerable; and in the third, East and West are vulnerable. In the final hand, both partnerships are vulnerable.

To determine the score for a successful contract, players first work out the score for the number of tricks made, including overtricks and taking any doubling into account. If the value of the contract was less than 100 points, 50 points are added for a part-score. If it was more than 100, 300 points are added if the partnership is not vulnerable; 500 are added if it is. The score for defeating a contract is the same as in Contract Bridge. There is no score for honours, nor extras for the rubber.

At the end of the fourth and deciding deal, if either side has a part-score – that is, points greater than zero but less than the magic 100 below the line – it receives a bonus of 100 points above the line.

VARIANTS

In Rubber Bridge, each hand is freshly dealt at random, and scores depend as much on the run of the cards as on the skills of the players.

In Duplicate Bridge, rather than trying to win more points than the opposing partnership, the aim is to do better than others playing the same cards. Each partnership is known as a pair and the final scores are calculated by comparing each pair's result with those of the others playing the same hand. Special four-way card holders called bridge boards are used to pass each player's hand to the next table to play it, while so-called bidding boxes, invented in Sweden in the 1960s, are also often used. At times, players are split into teams of four.

Other forms of Bridge include Reverse Bridge, where all cards rank back to front (in other words, Twos are the highest cards, followed by Threes, Fours and so on down to Aces, which are the lowest); Nullo Bridge, in which partnerships bid to lose tricks rather than to win them, and Brint, a variant of Bridge devised in the late 1920s, which is distinguished by its extremely elaborate – some would say over-sophisticated – scoring system. Basically, the higher the bid, the more each trick is worth. These three Bridge variants are rarely played.

Left: Bidding boxes carry a set of cards, each bearing the name of a legal call in Bridge. This allows the player to make a call by displaying the appropriate card from the box, rather than speaking aloud and chancing others hearing the bid.

PIRATE BRIDGE

This type of Bridge certainly seems to be a contradiction in terms, since, instead of playing in fixed partnerships, players switch alliances between deals.

Bridge authorities claim that Pirate Bridge was developed by R. F. Foster in 1917, but it seems likely that the occultist Aleister Crowley (1875–1947) devised it and Foster put the rules into definite shape. Crowley thought that what he had devised was 'such an improvement on the ordinary game', but it suffers from the fact that players with the best-matched hands inevitably manage to identify each other and make their contract easily as a result.

Pirate replaces fixed partnerships by floating alliances made from deal to deal. The dealer is the first to bid. Each player in turn has the choice of whether to accept the bid, so signalling his willingness to become dummy in partnership with the bidder, or passing. If all players pass, the hands are thrown in and the deal starts again. The player to the left of the previous bidder takes up the bidding. If the bid is accepted, each player in turn from the acceptor's left around the table may bid higher, pass, double or, if a double has been bid, redouble. If all players pass, the bid becomes the contract. A player may choose to make a new bid, which can be accepted or rejected by the previous bidder or acceptor. The latter can also try to break an alliance by naming a new contract when it is his turn to play, but, if no higher bid is accepted, that alliance must stand.

A double reopens the bidding. Making this bid gives sometime allies the chance to bid themselves out of their alliance by naming another bid in the hopes that another player will accept it. Or, if they are sufficiently confident, they can choose to redouble the accepted bid.

Once the contract is established, the declarer leads the opening trick, his partner laying down his hand as dummy. Play then proceeds in strict rotation around the table, even if declarer and dummy are seated next to rather than opposite one another. Scores are recorded below or above the line for each player. The game is scored in the conventional way (see scores at Contract Bridge), with individual scores noted above or below the line by each player involved.

Above: Aleister Crowley, occultist and probable inventor of Pirate Bridge.

THREE-HANDED BRIDGE

Aficionados of Bridge have ways of playing, even without the regulation four players. Three-Handed Bridge has many devotees, particularly to the following two games.

CUT-THROAT BRIDGE

In this simple version of Three-Handed Bridge, the dealer deals four hands, leaving one hand face down on the card table to eventually form the dummy. The declarer is the person who bids the highest. He turns the dummy face up between the two defenders after the left-hand opponent has led. Alternatively, players can mutually agree to turn one or more of the dummy cards face up after each bid.

TOWIE AND BOOBY

In Towie, a three-handed variant that two American players devised in 1931, six of the dummy cards are dealt face up. The highest bidder becomes the declarer, turning up and playing the whole of the dummy hand.

In Booby, each player is dealt 17 cards, with one extra card being dealt face down. Each makes four discards face down to complete the dummy. Bidding follows the conventional pattern, with the addition of a *Nullo* bid. Ranking between Hearts and Spades, this is a bid to lose a specified number of tricks, playing at No Trump. A bid of two *Nullos* is a bid to win no more than five tricks, while seven *Nullos* corresponds to a *Misère*, i.e. losing all tricks. *Nullo* bids are valued at 30 points per trick.

WHIST

Whist was the game of choice for many serious card players until Bridge took over from it in the early 20th century. Its popularity dates from the mid-1700s, when Edmond Hoyle described it in the first-ever rulebook of card games that was published in 1746. There is no bidding in classic Whist, but there are sufficient nuances in the play to make it a fascinating game.

> **You will need:** 52 cards; no Jokers; scorecards
> **Card ranking:** Standard, Aces high
> **Players:** Four, in partnerships sitting opposite each other
> **Ideal for:** 10+

OBJECT

To win as many of the 13 tricks as possible.

CONVENTIONS

Like Bridge, Whist has its own accepted conventions, or 'conventional leads' as they are strictly termed, worked out when the game was most in vogue. These have been condensed and simplified in the table below. Leading to the first trick gives the player the advantage of setting the pace and being able to make the best use of the cards in hand to try to signal to a partner which cards are held. This signal is used if the player concerned does not hold the Ace or King of that suit.

Conventions include finessing (playing the third highest card of a suit while also holding the highest, to draw out opponents' highest cards); leading with a trump (to indicate that you are holding five or more in your hand), and forcing (leading with a suit you believe one of the other players does not hold).

CONVENTIONS

In plain suits			
When holding	**1st lead**		**2nd lead**
• A, K, Q, J	K	then	J
• A, K, Q	K	then	Q
• A, K–J	K	then	A
• A, K	A	then	K
• K, Q, J, x	K	then	J
• K, Q, J, x, x	J	then	K
• K, Q, J, x, x and more	J	then	Q
• A, x, x, x, x and more	A	then	4th highest of remainder
• K, Q, x and more	K	then	4th highest of remainder
• A, Q, J	A	then	Q
• A, Q, J, x	A	then	Q
• A, Q, J, x, x	A	then	J
• K, J, 10, 9	9	then	K (if A or Q fails)
• Q, J, x	Q		
• Q, J, x, x and more	4th highest		

In trump suits			
When holding	**1st lead**		**2nd lead**
• A, K, Q, J	J	then	Q
• A, K, Q	Q	then	K
• A, K, x, x, x, x and more	K	then	A
• A, K, x, x, x, x	4th highest		

THE RULE OF ELEVEN

A further convention – leading the fourth best of your longest suit (counting from the top down), enables a player to apply what is termed the 'rule of eleven' to gauge the lie of the cards. Assuming your partner has led his fourth highest card, you subtract its face value from 11, to establish (in theory), how many of the higher cards are lacking from his hand. By further subtracting the number you hold yourself, you can deduce the number of higher cards held by the opposing side.

To show that he is holding an Ace, for instance, a player will lead a King. If a player leads the Seven of a suit in which his partner holds the Jack and King, this means that there are four cards above the Seven against him, of which his partner holds two. The partner cannot hold the Ace, or he would have played it, so his hand must include any four cards from Queen and Ten down to Seven, while the opposing partnership must hold the Ace and any one of Queen, Ten, Nine and Eight between them.

REVOKES

If a player does not follow suit when able to do so, a penalty is imposed. The cost of this (known as a revoke) is three game points, which can either be added to the opponents' score or subtracted from that of the revoking partnership. If both partnerships revoke, the hand is abandoned and a new one dealt.

PLAYER C

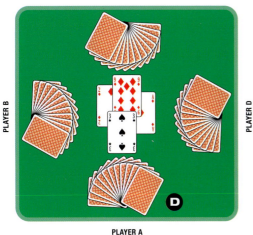

PLAYER A

Above: With Diamonds having been played by Player B, Players C and D follow suit. The A♦ seems set to win the trick, but Player A is out of Diamonds, so wins the trick with a low trump.

THE DEAL

Who deals first is determined by cutting the pack. The player to the dealer's left shuffles and the one to the right cuts the cards before the deal is made. Each player is singly dealt 13 cards face down except for the last card, which is turned up to denote trumps for that hand. The dealer claims the card when the trick is led. Otherwise, players can agree trumps in advance, in which case the convention is to follow a fixed sequence: Hearts, Diamonds, Spades and Clubs. No Trumps can also be introduced, so every fifth hand is played without trumps. Subsequent deals pass clockwise to the next player, who shuffles as before.

PLAY

Play starts with the person seated to the dealer's left, moving clockwise around the table. The first card becomes the suit for the trick. The other players must follow suit if they can. If they cannot, they can play a trump or discard any card. The player playing the highest card of the suit that has been led or the highest trump, if any are played, takes the trick. To claim it, he turns it face down in front of him. The winner leads play for the next trick.

Right: Player D, the first to lead, played the K♠, indicating that he also holds the A♠. His partner, Player B, lays the Q♠, almost certainly indicating he holds either a singleton (just one card) or doubleton (just two cards) in Spades.

SCORING

The partnership that gets to or exceeds five game points first – seven game points in the USA – wins the game. A rubber is a match that consists typically of three games, and is therefore won by the first side to win two. The match is won by the partnership with the highest number of game points at the end of the rubber.

In a five-point game, points can be won from tricks, honours and revokes. The first six tricks do not score, while tricks from seven to 13 are worth one game point each. If a partnership holds all the honour cards, the Ace, King, Queen and Jack of trumps, it gains four game points. If three honour cards are held, two extra game points are given. The winning partnership is also given a game point if its opponents make three or four tricks, two points if they make only one or two, and three points if they fail to score at all. In the seven-point system, players who revoke concede two game points to the opposing partnership. The final score is the difference between seven and the number of game points, if any, won by the losers. The final hand is played even after seven points have been won, and the points are added to the final score.

CONCLUSION

The game continues until all 13 tricks have been won. If one partnership takes all tricks, it is termed a Slam.

PLAYER C

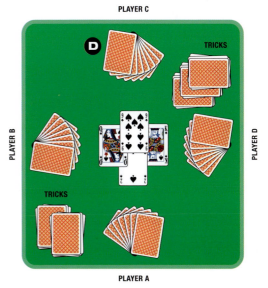

PLAYER A

BID WHIST

Many other games have developed from Whist, often with some element of bidding added. Perhaps the most significant of these is Bid Whist, which is widely played by the African-American community in the USA. Other interesting bidding variants include Norwegian Whist, in which the aim can be to lose tricks rather than win them, and Contract Whist, which is much like Bridge but without the dummy.

OBJECT

To fulfil the contract as bid and so score the points that are necessary to win the game.

THE DEAL

The player who draws the first Diamond deals first. Each player is dealt 12 cards, the remaining six being placed face down on the table to form a kitty.

TAKING THE KITTY

What happens after the deal depends on whether trumps are being played. If they are played, the successful bidder 'sports' the kitty, turning it up so the cards can be seen, and adds it to his hand before discarding six cards. Once sported in this way, the kitty counts as the first book to be won by the partnership. If there are No Trumps, the kitty is not shown to the other players.

You will need: 52 cards plus two Jokers, marked (or differentiated) the 'Big' Joker and the 'Little' Joker; scorecards

Card ranking: In high bids ('uptown'), cards rank Ace down to Two. In low bids ('downtown'), cards rank Ace up to King. In trump bids, cards rank Big Joker, Little Joker, Ace down to Two (uptown) or up to King (downtown)

Players: Four in partnerships, sitting opposite each other

Ideal for: 14+

BIDDING

Each player can bid only once, or pass. Each bid must be higher than the last. If the first three players pass, the dealer must bid. A bid consists of a number from three to seven, indicating the number of tricks (called 'books') above six that the bidder's team contracts to make.

Adding 'uptown' to a bid means that a trump suit will be named once the bidding is over and that high cards will win, while adding 'downtown' means that low cards will. When bidding No Trumps, a player waits until the end of bidding before specifying whether high or low cards count for more.

PLAY

Any card may be led, players following suit if possible. If not, they can play a trump or a card from a different suit. The ranking of the cards depends on what has been specified in the bid. If a player fails to follow suit despite holding an appropriate card, this is a renege and the reneging side is penalized. If it has won enough books, three are taken away from it. If not, the non-reneging team is deemed to have won 13 books.

SCORING AND CONCLUSION

Players score points by bidding for and winning books. A game consists of 13 books, and each book won above six is worth a point, but, in order to score, the bidding side must make at least as many points as it has bid. If it fails, the points that were bid are subtracted from the score. If the winning bid is No Trumps, scores are doubled. Winning all 13 books is termed a 'Boston', in which case, scores are quadrupled. The game continues until all 13 tricks have been won.

PLAYER C

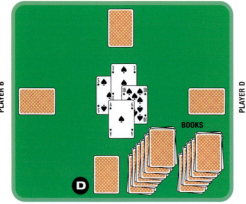

PLAYER A

Left: This trick takes the A–C partnership to 12 tricks (or books, as they are called in Bid Whist). If they can win the last trick, they will have made a 'Boston', in which case, scores are quadrupled.

SPADES

Devised in the USA during the 1930s, Spades came of age globally with the coming of the Internet and the mushrooming of online card rooms. It is a plain-trick game (that is, one in which the winner or loser is determined solely by the number of tricks scored) in which Spades are always trumps. There are numerous variations in the rules, but what follows is the most generally accepted one.

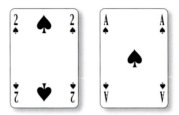

Left: The lowest and highest trumps in Spades. The A♠ will always win whatever trick it is laid to, while the 2♠ will win only when used to trump and no higher Spade is played to the trick.

OBJECT

To win at least as many tricks as bid for, or no tricks at all.

THE DEAL

The first dealer is chosen at random, after which the deal rotates clockwise. The cards are dealt singly, starting with the player to the dealer's left. Each player receives a total of 13 cards.

BIDDING

Players contract to win a specified number of tricks, the non-dealer partnership declaring first. Each pair's bids are added, the total being the number of tricks that

PLAYER C

PLAYER B

PLAYER D

PLAYER A

Above: Some versions of Spades stipulate that players must lead their lowest Club, as here. Surprisingly, the last player to play has won the trick with the 2♠, meaning that he must be void in Clubs. Laying the first spade like this is known as 'breaking Spades'.

partnership must win in order to make the contract. Once made, bids cannot be changed. Nor are players allowed to pass, although a player who believes that he can lose every trick may declare 'nil'. If that is the case, his partner must state how many tricks he is prepared to win.

PLAY

The player to the dealer's left leads. Any card, except a Spade, can be led, and other players must follow suit if they can. Some versions of the game stipulate that players must lead their lowest Club on the first trick and that anyone void in Clubs must discard a Diamond or a Heart.

Spades may not be played until either a player plays one because he cannot follow suit – this is known as 'breaking Spades' – or until the leader has nothing but Spades left. If no Spades are played, the player of the highest card of the suit that has been led wins the trick. Otherwise, the highest Spade wins.

SCORING AND CONCLUSION

The side scoring 500 points first wins the game. Taking at least as many tricks as were bid means that the bidding partnership scores 10 times what it bid, and an extra point for each overtrick. These overtricks are known as 'bags'.

If a nil bid succeeds, the bidding players' side scores an extra 50 points, which are added to the score his partner makes for tricks taken. If the bid is unsuccessful, the partnership forfeits 50 points, but any tricks taken by the unsuccessful bidder count towards fulfilling their partner's contract. The game continues until all 13 tricks have been won.

KAISER

Although Kaiser is German for 'emperor', this intriguing trick-taking game did not originate in Germany. Ukrainian immigrants to Canada are thought to have developed it half a century or so ago, although whether they brought it over from their homeland or devised it for themselves is a mystery. The side that bids highest chooses the trump suit, unless playing No Trumps.

OBJECT

To win at least as many tricks as bid, or to bring down the opposing partnership's bid.

THE DEAL

The deal and play are both clockwise. The first dealer is chosen at random, with the deal passing to the left after each hand. All the cards in the pack are dealt singly, so that each player ends up with a hand of eight cards.

BIDDING

Once the deal has been completed, each player, starting with the player to the dealer's left, has one chance to bid or to pass. The possible bids are from five to 12 points.

You will need: 32 cards including Sevens to Aces, but with the 3♠ replacing 7♠ and 5♥ replacing 7♥; scorecards

Card ranking: Standard, Aces high

Players: Four, in partnerships of two

Ideal for: 14+

Each must be higher than the one before it, although the dealer only needs to equal the highest bid to win the bidding. It is unnecessary to specify a trump suit in a bid, but a player who wants to play No Trumps must say so. If all the players pass, the hands are thrown in and the deal passes to the next player.

PLAY

The highest bidder chooses trumps and leads to the first trick, the other players following suit if possible, or playing any other card. The trick is taken by the player of the highest card of the suit that has been led, or by the player of the highest trump, if trumps are being played.

SCORING AND CONCLUSION

When all the cards have been played, the tricks are counted and scored. Each team gets one point for each trick it takes, plus five points for winning a trick containing the 5♥.

If it wins a trick containing the 3♠, it loses three points. If the side that chose trumps makes as many points as it bid, it adds that number of points to the score. If it took fewer, the bid is subtracted. If No Trumps was played, the figures are doubled.

If the bidding team's opponents have a cumulative score of less than 45 points, they score what they took. If it is 45 or more, the score is pegged, unless they end up with a negative score. In that case, the points are deducted from their total. Fifty-two points are needed to win the game.

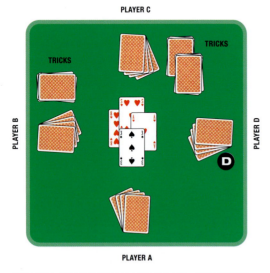

Above: Player C here looks to be on target to score a five-point bonus for his partnership by winning a trick containing the 5♥. However, Player A, unable to follow suit, plays the 3♠, thus reducing the trick's value to three points (one for the trick, plus five for the 5♥, minus three for the 3♠).

Left: Winning a trick containing the 5♥ scores the player concerned an extra five points. One containing the 3♠ loses three points.

FORTY-ONE

This game originated in the Middle East, where it is a favourite among Syrian and Lebanese card players. Players partner each other as in Bridge; North and South play against East and West. Hearts is the permanent trump suit.

You will need: 52-card deck; no Jokers; scorecards

Card ranking: Standard, Aces high

Players: Four, in partnerships of two

Ideal for: 14+

OBJECT

For one member of a partnership to win 41 points or more, and for all players to retain a positive score. A running total score is kept for each individual player.

THE DEAL

Each player gets 13 cards, dealt anti-clockwise around the table. The deal also rotates anti-clockwise. The first card is dealt singly, but others are dealt in twos.

Right: Forty-One is a much played card game in Syria, and to some extent in Lebanon. Even though it is a parnership game, a running total score is kept for each individual player.

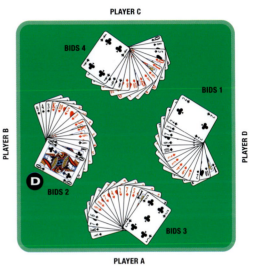

Above: The bidding shows that Player A aims to make three tricks, Player B two, Player C four and Player D one. As this falls one short of the minimum 11 tricks needed, the hands must be thrown in and the cards dealt again.

BIDDING

The bidding starts with the player to the right of the dealer. Each player gets one chance to bid, stating the minimum number of tricks he expects to make. When added up, the bids must reach a minimum total of 11. Otherwise, the hands are thrown in and there is a new deal.

Bids of one to six score a point per trick if successful, otherwise they lose one point per trick. Bids of seven or more win or lose two points per trick bid. The common practice is to bid between two and six tricks. The dealer then decides whether to play the hand or not, and can bid to take the total up to the 11 needed for play to commence or he can over or under bid for a new deal.

PLAY

The player seated to the dealer's right leads. Any card of any suit may be led, but subsequent play must follow suit if possible. If not, a player can discard from another suit or trump with a Heart. If no trump is played, the highest card of the suit that has been led wins the trick. Otherwise, the highest Heart played wins. The winner of each trick then leads to the next.

SCORING AND CONCLUSION

Each player's score is recorded cumulatively. A player who takes as many tricks as he bid scores the value of the bid. There is no bonus for taking tricks over and above the bid. A player who bids and takes seven or more tricks scores twice the number of tricks bid. If that player fails to take enough tricks in a subsequent hand, he loses the doubled points, i.e. 14. This can be important. Although it is only one player who has to reach the magic total of 41 points or more, the partnership can win the game only if the other partner's cumulative score is positive rather than negative. Play continues until all 13 tricks have been won.

VINT

This game originated in Tsarist Russia. It is thought to be an ancestor of Bridge, although there is no dummy and the tricks taken by both partnerships count towards a game. Vint in Russian means 'screw', which alludes to the way in which players force bids up by outbidding each other in the first of the two auctions that start off the game.

OBJECT

To make as many tricks as bid for and to score 60 below the line for game. The first partnership to win two games scores a bonus of 400 points, the winners of the remaining four deals scoring 600, 800, 1,000 and 1,200 points, respectively.

THE DEAL

After the players have cut, the pack is dealt out to each player one card at a time.

BIDDING

The dealer begins the bidding. A bid is the number of tricks a player aims to take above six. A suit must be specified. If a player's bid is overcalled, he can make a higher one in the next bidding round, even at the expense of a partner.

The highest bidder becomes the declarer and starts the second auction, which ends when both partners have passed twice. The suit named in the highest-ranking bid becomes trumps unless the winning bid is No Trumps.

PLAY

The declarer leads, with each of the other players following with a card of the same suit. If a player cannot follow suit, he can play a trump or discard. The winner of the trick leads the next one.

Below and Right: Three Aces, or a same-suited sequence of three, is termed a coronet and scores 500 points. If the sequence is in the trump suit, it is termed a doubled coronet and scores 1,000 points.

You will need:	52 cards; no Jokers; scorecards
Card ranking:	Standard, Aces high
Players:	Four, in partnerships of two
Ideal for:	14+

Scores are recorded above and below the line, but the scorecard is split into four columns as opposed to two. The higher the bid, the more each trick is worth, with both partnerships scoring for the value of the tricks they take. On a bid of one, a trick is worth 10 points, on a bid of seven, it is 70 points. The total score is termed the game score and is entered below the line. Once a partnership scores 500 below-the-line points, the game is over.

SCORING AND CONCLUSION

All undertricks – tricks fewer than the numbers bid – incur a penalty of 100 times the trick value, entered above the line as a minus score. So, too, are bonus points for winning a game, rubber, Grand Slam (every trick) or Little Slam (every trick bar one), and honour points, which, in Vint, are the four Aces and top five trumps – there are nine in all, since the Ace of trumps counts twice.

They can be scored by either partnership, regardless of winning or losing, but whichever one holds the majority of them scores the number held multiplied by 10 times the value of the contract. For example, assuming that the contract is five, a partnership holding the Ace of trumps, two other Aces, and the King, Queen and Ten of trumps between them scores for the seven honours and five for the contract. They multiply this total by 10, so ending up with a score of 350 points. In No Trumps, they score 25 times the trick value.

If a player holds three Aces or a same-suited sequence of three, he scores 500 points, known as a coronet. If the sequence is in trumps, the score is doubled, and this is known as a doubled coronet. Play continues until all 13 tricks have been won.

QUINTO

In the early 1900s, Angelo John Lewis, better known as the stage magician 'Professor Hoffman', invented this imaginative variant of Whist. Quinto derives its name from the 'quints' that feature in the game – that is, the Joker, the Five of each suit, and two cards of the same suit totalling five. Points are gained for winning tricks, and especially for any quints that they may contain.

You will need: 52-card deck; one Joker; scorecards

Card ranking: Standard, with suits also ranked, Spades (lowest), Clubs, Diamonds, Hearts (highest)

Players: Four, in partnerships of two

Ideal for: 14+

OBJECT

The object of the game is to score 250 points in as many deals as it takes.

THE DEAL

Each player is dealt 12 card singly, the remaining five being left face down on the table. Hoffman referred to these as the 'cachette'.

Above: Also known as the Quint Royal, the Joker has no trick-taking value. However, it is worth 25 points to the partnership that wins it.

BIDDING

Once the cards have been dealt, and before play begins, each player has the opportunity to pass, double or redouble an opponent's double. Doubling, as the name suggests, doubles the value of each trick won from 5 to 10 points, while redoubling raises it still further to 20 points. If this happens, the relative value of quints to tricks is reduced. Quints can be the Joker, which is worth 25 points, the Five of each suit or two cards of the same suit totalling five in the same trick. A quint in Spades is worth five points, Clubs 10, Diamonds 15 and Hearts 20.

PLAY

Play starts with the player to dealer's left, partnerships competing to win tricks containing quints. The winner of a trick leads to the next. If possible, players have to follow suit, although if they cannot, they can play any card from their hands.

The game is played without trumps. The suits, however, are ranked, from low to high, starting with Spades followed by Clubs, Diamonds and Hearts. A player may discard from a lower suit if unable to follow the suit led. Equally, he may win the trick by playing a card from a higher suit. This inevitably means that the highest card of the highest suit played takes the trick. A player whose hand contains the Joker at the 11th trick must play it if the only other option is to win the trick.

SCORING

Each trick is worth five points, with bonuses for any quints in it. The top-scoring quint is the Joker – the Quint Royal. It is worth 25 points. It cannot be led to a trick, nor can it win a trick, but otherwise it may be played at any time. If a partnership wins a trick with a quint in it, it scores the quint immediately. Its value depends on its suit.

Left: This trick would be worth 20 points: 10 points for the 2♣ and 3♣ (making a quint in Clubs) and another 10 for the 5♣ (another quint). The points are scored immediately after the trick is taken.

Left: This trick also has two quints within it: the 5♥ as well as the 4♥ and A♥. Here, though, because the suit is Hearts, each quint would score 20 points, making 40 points in total.

CONCLUSION

If scoring a quint means that the partnership has reached the 250-point target, play stops. If not, the side taking the final trick also wins the *cachette*, which counts as a 13th trick and scores for any quint or quints it may contain. All the tricks are then scored to ascertain if there is a winner. If not, or if the two sides are tied, there is a new deal.

WIDOW WHIST WHIST FOR THREE PLAYERS

Whist is flexible enough to be adapted to suit three or even two players. This classic version of Three-handed Whist is aptly termed Widow Whist. It gets its name from the extra hand that is dealt just to the left of the dealer. This is the widow, which players are given the chance to play rather than their own hands. In Widow Whist, Clubs are always trumps and each player is out for himself – there are no partnerships.

You will need: 52 cards; no Jokers; scorecards	
Card ranking: Standard, Aces high	
Players: Three	
Ideal for: 10+	

OBJECT

To win as many tricks as possible by playing the highest card of the suit led, or the highest trump.

THE DEAL

To establish who deals first, the players cut the deck for the highest card. The dealer then deals 13 cards each to the active players plus 13 cards face up for the widow.

PLAY

The player to the left of the dealer has first choice of playing the widow rather than his hand. If he decides not to play the widow, it is passed to the next person on the left, and so on, around the table. If a player takes the widow, the original hand is passed on.

SCORING AND CONCLUSION

If the player to the dealer's left decides to play the widow, he has to take only three tricks to break even – in other words, a point is awarded for every trick taken over three. Any other player taking the widow has to take four tricks before he starts scoring. Play continues until all 13 tricks have been won.

GERMAN WHIST WHIST FOR TWO PLAYERS

Two-handed versions of Whist include German Whist, in which players start with either 13 or six cards each. Despite the name, the game is thought to have originated in Britain.

You will need: 52 cards; no Jokers; scorecards	
Card ranking: Standard, Aces high	
Players: Two	
Ideal for: 7+	

OBJECT

To win high-ranking cards in the first phase of the game in order to win the majority of the tricks in the second.

THE DEAL

Thirteen cards are dealt to each player; the remaining cards are placed face down on the table to form the stock. The top card of the stock is turned up for trumps.

PLAY

The non-dealer leads and the dealer must follow suit. If unable, he may discard any card or play a trump. The highest card of the suit led wins the trick unless it is trumped. The trick's winner picks up the face-up card from the top of the stock and adds it to his hand. The loser takes the next face-down card. The trick's winner leads, turning up the top card of the stock. Players aim to add as many good cards from the stock to their hand as they can, which means they try to win tricks only if they think that the exposed card on top of the stock is likely to be worth more than the one beneath. Once the stock is exhausted, the two players aim to win the majority of the remaining 13 tricks.

SCORING AND CONCLUSION

The only tricks to score are those won in the second phase of the game, after the stock has run out. Whoever wins the most tricks (seven or over) wins the game, or, if a succession of games are being played, the difference between the two totals at the end of the last trick. Play ends when all of the final 13 tricks have been won.

CALYPSO

Invented in the West Indies in the early 1950s, this is a partnership game in which each player uses the cards he wins to form 'calypsos' – all 13 cards of a given suit. Who partners whom is established by cutting the deck. Players with the highest cards partner each other against the ones with the lowest. Whoever cuts highest of all becomes the dealer and chooses where to sit, thus determining his own and the other players' personal trumps. In Calypso, North's trumps are always Hearts, South's are Spades, East's are Diamonds and West's are Clubs.

You will need: Four 52-card decks; scorecards
Card ranking: Standard, Aces high
Players: Four, in partnerships of two
Ideal for: 10+

OBJECT

To build calypsos – all 13 cards of a given suit – in one's own trump suit, to help one's partner build his own, and to hinder the opposing partnership's attempts at calypso building.

THE DEAL

The player who cut the highest, deals first. There are four deals in all, one by each player. Each player is dealt 13 cards singly, the rest of the pack (containing all four packs shuffled together) being placed face down to one side of the table. These cards are gradually used up in subsequent deals.

PLAY

Tricks are played for, with players following suit where possible. If not, they can discard, or trump each trick using their personal trump suit. The only cards that can be used to construct a calypso are those won in tricks. Each calypso must be complete before a player can start building another, the process being made harder by the fact that any cards within a trick that duplicate ones already in a calypso cannot be retained for building any future calypsos.

The player who wins a trick takes the cards he needs from it and hands over any his partner requires. The remaining cards – those played by the opposing partnership and those unusable cards from the winning partnership's hands – are stacked face down in a winnings pile. When complete, the calypso is laid face up in front of the player who made it.

SCORING

Each partnership scores points as follows:
- 500 for each partnership's first calypso.
- 750 for each partnership's second calypso.
- 1,000 for each partnership's subsequent calypsos.
- 20 per card in an unfinished calypso.
- 50 for each card in the winnings pile.

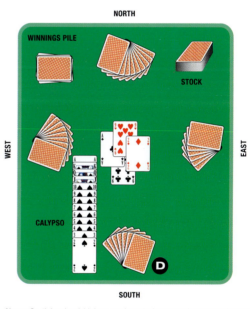

Above: South has just laid down a calypso in the appropriate personal trump suit (Spades) and led to a new trick. West seemed on course to win this, until North laid a personal trump, only to be trumped again by East, whose personal trump suit is Diamonds.

CONCLUSION

After 13 tricks have been taken, the deal passes to the player to the left of the previous dealer and new hands are then dealt. The procedure continues until four deals have been completed, after which the game is scored.

Quick-trick Games

What distinguishes most quick-trick games is that not all the cards are dealt out, thus making it hard for players to deduce what their opponents are holding. The games range from sophisticated ones with an established historical pedigree, requiring an advanced level of skill, such as Euchre, to Truc, a Spanish and Provençal game in which tricks are won by bluff rather than by calculation.

Most quick-trick card games involve gambling. In most of them, each player is dealt three cards, the aim being to win a single trick; or five cards, in which case he has to take at least three tricks; or bid a minimum number. Bidding is the hallmark of games of skill such as Euchre, Five Hundred and Napoleon (or Nap as it is more commonly known). In their day, all three games attracted a fanatical following.

Although it is French by origin, and thought to descend from a game called Juckerspiel that was formerly played in Alsace, Euchre was, at one time, the most popular trumps game in the USA. Originally brought to Pennsylvania by German immigrants known as the Pennsylvania Dutch, Euchre has the distinction of being the first game to use the Joker. This was introduced at some time during the 1850s, to serve as the highest trump. The Joker started to appear in the well-known guise of the court jester around 1880.

The origins of Napoleon or Nap are particularly interesting. Some authors suggest that it derived its name from the French Emperor Napoleon III, the nephew of the great Napoleon, who popularized a version of it in the mid-19th century. Others trace its roots back even further, to the First French Empire (1804–14), pointing out that the names of Wellington and Blücher, Napoleon's successful adversaries at the Battle of Waterloo in 1815, feature in it as possible bids, as does Napoleon himself.

Above: This classic image of a jester playing a flute, with a ninny stick attached to his belt, appeared on cards around 1880.

EUCHRE

This popular partnership game is played widely in Canada, the north-eastern USA and in England's West Country. Although the essentials are fairly consistent, the game has a wide range of variations. In North America, it is customary to play with a 24-card deck, but in British Euchre, a Joker, known as Benny or Best Bower, is added.

You will need: 24-card deck (Eights and below having been removed from a standard pack); one Joker; scorecards

Card ranking: See under 'Card Ranking' below

Players: Four, in partnerships of two

Ideal for: 14+

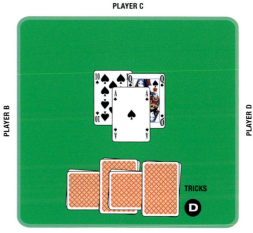

PLAYER C

PLAYER B

PLAYER D

TRICKS

D

PLAYER A

OBJECT

To win at least three of the five tricks, in which case the score is one point. If the same partnership takes all five tricks, they score two points.

CARD RANKING

Aces are the highest-ranking cards and Nines the least valuable ones, but there are two exceptions. The Joker (Benny or Best Bower) is the highest trump, followed by the Jack of the trump suit, the so-called Right Bower, and the other Jack of the same colour, which is the Left Bower.

THE DEAL

Each player is dealt five cards, the remaining cards being placed face down on the table. The dealer, chosen at random, turns the top card face up to set the trump suit.

BIDDING

Starting to the left of the dealer, players bid to establish which side will win at least three tricks with the face-up card's suit as trump. As soon as a player says, 'I accept', taking the face-up card and replacing it with one of his own face down, the bidding is over. The alternative is to pass. If everyone passes, a new bidding round ensues.

The partnership that chooses trumps is known as the 'makers' and the other as the 'defenders'. However, a player with a strong hand may bid to 'go alone' – that is, to play the hand without a partner. This means that the other player places his cards face down on the table and sits out the hand.

PLAY

The player to the dealer's left leads, unless someone has decided to go alone, in which case the lead passes to the player on that person's left. If two players go alone, the player of the team that did not choose trumps leads.

Above: Player A, going alone, wins the final trick, thus taking all five tricks (a March). His partnership scores five bonus points.

Players must follow suit if possible, otherwise they may play any card. The highest card played in the led suit wins the trick, unless trumps are played. If so, the highest trump wins, and the winner leads to the next trick.

SCORING

If all four players take part, the makers score a point for taking three or four tricks. If they take all five – termed a 'March' – they get a bonus point. If they fail to win three, they are 'euchred' and the defenders score two points.

If a maker goes alone and wins all five tricks, the partnership scores five points, or one point if the score is three or four tricks. If a defender does so and wins three or more tricks, that partnership scores four points.

CONCLUSION

The winning partnership is the first to score an agreed number of points (such as 10, 11 or 21).

PEPPER

T he modern descendant of a game called *Hasenpfeffer* (Jugged Hare), this fast-paced game is closely related to Euchre. The chief differences are that, in Pepper, all the cards are dealt, and an element of bluffing is also encouraged. As in Euchre, the top trumps are the Right and Left Bowers (Jack of trumps and Jack of the same colour), but there is an additional No Trumps bid in which the Ace in every suit ranks the highest.

OBJECT

To make at least the number of tricks bid and to score 30 or more points. If both sides reach this total in the same hand, the result is a draw.

CARD RANKING

The Jack of the trump suit, the so-called Right Bower, is the highest trump, followed by the other Jack of the same colour (the Left Bower). Aces are the next highest-ranking cards and nines the least valuable. In a No Trump bid, cards rank Ace to Nine in all suits.

THE DEAL AND BIDDING

Six cards are dealt to each player singly, after which the player to the dealer's left bids, or passes, first. Players have one chance to bid, the choice being to pass or to

You will need:	24 card-deck (Twos to Eights having been removed from a standard pack); no Jokers; scorecards
Card ranking:	See under 'Card Ranking' below
Players:	Four, in partnerships of two
Ideal for:	10+

raise the bidding. Bids can be for one, two, three, four, or five tricks. The highest bids are Little Pepper and Big Pepper. Both are bids to take all six tricks, but the former is more conservative than the latter. A bid of Little Pepper means that the score for taking all six tricks is six. A bid of Big Pepper doubles the score to 12 points for winning all six tricks, but the penalty for failing to do so is also doubled.

PLAY

Players must follow suit, if possible, or otherwise play a trump or any card. The highest card of the suit led takes the trick, or the highest trump if trumps are played. The winner of each trick leads to the next.

SCORING AND CONCLUSION

The bidding side scores a point for each trick it takes if it makes its contract, but is set back (loses) six points if it fails. If the bid is Big Pepper, the bidders are set back 12 points. Their opponents score a point for each trick they take. The first partnership to score 30 or more points wins.

VARIANT

Some enthusiasts favour a different version of the game, in which the defenders can challenge or concede the hand at the end of bidding. If the decision is to challenge, actual play is restricted to the winner of the bidding and the two defenders, the remaining player sitting out the hand. If the defenders concede, the bidders score the value of the bid.

There is only one round of bidding, with the two highest bids becoming Pepper and Pepper Alone. They are worth seven and 14 points, respectively. Unless the bid is Pepper Alone, the successful partners exchange a card. Neither is allowed to look at the card until the exchange is completed. The main difference in the scoring system is that the defenders lose points if they fail to take any tricks, the amount varying with the bid's value, as do the penalties for not making the contract.

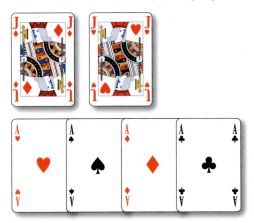

Above: As in Euchre, the Jack of trumps (here, it is Diamonds) is the top-ranking card and the other red Jack ranks second. The two Jacks are called the Right and Left Bowers, respectively. In a No Trumps contract, Aces are the highest cards, with Jacks ranking below Queens.

FIVE HUNDRED

R elated to Euchre and Pepper, this fascinating game was originally devised and copyrighted by the United States Playing Card company in 1904. While still played in the USA, it has since become extremely popular in Australia and New Zealand.

You will need: 32-card deck (Sixes and below having been removed from a standard pack); one Joker; scorecards

Card ranking: See under 'Card Ranking' below

Players: Three is optimal

Ideal for: 10+

Left: Although holding the Ace, this player's long suit in Spades makes this an excellent hand for bidding *Open Misère* – a contract played out with the declarer's cards face up on the table.

OBJECT

To achieve a score of 500 points or more as a result of winning a contract.

CARD RANKING

The rank order for trumps is Joker, Right Bower (Jack of trumps), Left Bower (Jack of the same colour suit) and then Ace down to Seven. In No Trump hands, there are no Bowers. The Joker becomes the highest-ranking card in whatever suit is chosen by the player holding it and so will win any trick in which it is played.

THE DEAL

Who deals first is established by cutting the pack, Kings ranking highest, Aces second to lowest and the Joker the lowest. The player making the lowest cut wins the deal. Each player is dealt 10 cards in packets of three, two, three and two, or three, three, three and one. The three cards left over are placed face up to form a kitty.

BIDDING

Starting with the player to the dealer's left, each player bids in turn. The options are to name a contract with a higher value than the preceding one, or to pass. Each step upward in the bidding is termed a 'jump'.

When bidding, players must state how many tricks they expect to make, (the highest number that can be bid is 10 and the lowest six), and nominate trumps or

No Trumps. A No Trump bid ranks the highest, followed by one in Hearts, Diamonds, Clubs and Spades. This makes the most valuable contract 10 No Trumps and the least valuable one six Spades. If the bid is *Misère*, the contract is to lose every trick at No Trumps. An Open *Misère*, the same bid but with cards exposed, scores double.

PLAY

The winning bidder, the contractor, starts by picking up the kitty and discards three cards face down to take its place. He can discard any three cards, including the ones he has just picked up. What happens next depends on the nature of the contract. If it is *Misère* or Open *Misère*, the contractor's partner takes no part in play, simply putting his hand face down on the table. The contractor leads to the first trick. The other players must follow suit if they can or, if they cannot trump, must play any card. The highest trump or the highest card of the suit led takes the trick, its winner leading to the next.

SCORING AND CONCLUSION

If the bidder wins the contract, the score is the value of the bid. A contract of 10 No Trumps scores 520 points, while one of six Spades is worth 40 points. If the contract fails, its value is deducted from its bidder's score.

The opposing players score 10 points for every trick they take. At *Misère*, they score 10 for each trick taken by the bidder. If a player contracted to take eight tricks or fewer manages to win all 10, a Grand Slam, the bonus is 250 points, or double the value of the contract. Play continues until all 10 tricks have been taken.

SCORES FOR CONTRACT MADE

	♠	♣	♦	♥	No Trumps
Six	40	60	80	100	120
Seven	140	160	180	200	220
Eight	240	260	280	300	320
Nine	340	360	380	400	420
Ten	440	460	480	500	520
No tricks/No trump		*Misère* 250		Open *Misère* 500	

ECARTÉ

This elegant two-hander, derived from a French 15th-century game called Triomphe, was once extremely popular in casinos, largely because onlookers placed sizeable side-bets on the outcome. It is fast, skilful and extremely enjoyable to play, despite a somewhat convoluted scoring system involving whether cards are exchanged or not after the deal.

OBJECT
To score five points in order to win a game.

THE DEAL
The deal alternates, and each player is dealt five cards in packets of three then two, or two then three. The remaining cards are placed face down on the table to form a stock, and the dealer turns the top card up to determine which suit will be trumps. If the card is a King, the dealer scores a point. If this takes his total from previous games to five points, he wins automatically and there is no actual play.

EXCHANGING OF CARDS
If the non-dealer believes that he can make at least three tricks, he leads to the first trick, or otherwise can 'propose' that both players exchange some of their cards. What happens next is for the dealer to decide: he can accept the proposal or refuse it. If the dealer accepts, the non-dealer, followed by the dealer, discards at least one card and draws the same number of replacement cards from the top of the stock.

If the dealer's decision is to refuse the proposal, the hand is played without any exchange of cards. However, the dealer is now obliged to take at least three tricks and a failure to do so is reflected in the scoring.

The process can continue until the non-dealer decides to lead, the dealer refuses a proposal, or the stock is exhausted, in which case play must start immediately with the non-dealer leading to the first trick. Neither player may discard more cards than remain in the stock and the trump card may not be taken in hand.

> **You will need:** 32 card-deck (Sixes and below having been removed from a standard pack); scorecards
>
> **Card ranking:** Kings highest, then Queens, Jacks and Aces down to Sevens
>
> **Players:** Two
>
> **Ideal for:** 14+

SHOWING THE KING
If either player holds the King of trumps, he may show it before play and score a point, provided that he has not already played some other card to the first trick.

PLAY
At the start, the non-dealer plays first. The other player must follow suit and win the trick if possible, either by leading a higher card of the same suit or by trumping a non-trump lead. If he can do neither, he can play any card. The winner of each trick leads to the next.

SCORING
Taking three or four tricks wins a point, while taking five, a '*Vole*', wins two points. If the player who rejected an exchange fails to take three tricks with the hand he was originally dealt, two points go to the opponent. Further deals ensue until one player scores 5 points. At the end of a game, if one player ends up with only one or two points, the other wins a double stake, which becomes a treble if the loser's score is zero.

CONCLUSION
The first player to score five points wins a game.

Left: A strong Ecarté hand. With the top card (King) in two suits, and strong cards in the others, it is likely to win at least three tricks unless the opponent's hand is almost all trumps. A player with these cards would have no need to countenance exchanging cards.

Right: If either player holds the King of trumps, he may show it before play and score a point. If the turn-up after the deal is a King, the dealer scores a point.

TWENTY-FIVE

T he national card game of Ireland, Twenty-Five was originally called Spoil Five or Five Fingers, since the aim is to prevent anyone from winning three of the five tricks played. It is descended from a game called Maw, reputedly the favourite of James VI of Scotland (later James I of England). What makes the game unique is its peculiar card ranking, although this is soon mastered with a little practice.

OBJECT

To win at least three tricks – better still, all five – and sweep the kitty, or to stop opposing players from doing so (known as 'spoil five').

You will need: 52-card deck; no Jokers; gambling chips/counters
Card ranking: See under 'Suits and Ranking' below
Players: Five considered ideal, although can be two to ten
Ideal for: 14+

SUITS AND RANKING

The game is always played with a trump suit, the highest trumps being the Five of trumps (Five Fingers), Jack of trumps, A♥, and Ace of trumps if a trump other than Hearts is being played. The remaining cards rank according to the colour of their suit. Hearts and Diamonds rank from King and Queen down to Two and Ace, while Spades and Clubs rank King, Queen, Jack, Ace and from Two to Ten.

THE DEAL

Each player starts with a total of 20 chips and puts one into the kitty. Players then cut for the deal: the one to cut the lowest wins. Starting with the player to the dealer's left, five cards are dealt face down to each player in packets of two and three. The remaining cards are stacked face down, the dealer turning the top one up to determine trumps.

If the turned-up card is an Ace, the dealer may pick it up and exchange it for any unwanted card in his hand. This is termed 'robbing the pack'. Similarly, if a player is dealt the Ace of trumps, he may declare it, then rob the pack, by taking the turn-up and discarding an unwanted card face down, before playing to the first trick.

PLAY

The player to the dealer's left leads. If the lead is a plain suit, the other players must follow suit or trump. If they cannot, they may discard. If trumps are led, the same ruling applies, unless the only trump a player holds is one of the top three – a Five or Jack of trumps or the Ace of Hearts. In this case, assuming that the trump that was led is lower in value, the player can choose to discard from another suit rather than play the trump.

CONCLUSION

A player taking the first three tricks can choose to take the kitty or 'jinx' – that is, try to win the two tricks that remain. If successful, as well as taking the kitty, each player pays the jinxer a chip. If not, the jinxer loses the kitty and the tricks are 'spoilt'. The same applies if no one takes three tricks: the kitty is carried forward to the next hand, each player raising it by one chip.

Above: In Twenty-Five, the highest-ranking trump (here, Diamonds) is the Five, known as Five Fingers. The Jack of trumps ranks next, followed by the A♥ and Ace of trumps if a trump other than Hearts is being played.

Right: Descended from a game called Maw, Twenty-Five was reputedly the favourite card game of James VI of Scotland.

AUCTION FORTY-FIVES

This variant of Twenty-Five is a Canadian favourite, the ranking of the cards, the way in which tricks are played and the right to renege being the same as in the Irish original. The difference is that a bidding element is introduced, in which bids are made in multiples of five up to 30 without a suit being declared. The winning bidder names trumps.

OBJECT
To win, as a partnership, the requisite number of tricks to score 120 and so take the game, or, if not, to prevent the opposing partnership from doing so.

SUITS AND CARD RANKING
The game is always played with a trump suit, the highest trumps being the Five of trumps (Five Fingers), Jack of trumps, A♥, and Ace of trumps if a trump other than Hearts is being played. The other cards rank according to the colour of their suit. Hearts and Diamonds rank from King and Queen down to Ace, while Spades and Clubs rank King, Queen, Jack, Ace and from Two to Ten.

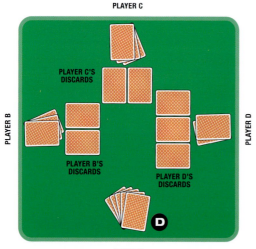

Above: Once bidding is over and trumps have been declared, each player in turn, starting with the player to the dealer's left, can discard as many cards as he wishes from his hand. Before dealing the required number of replacements, the dealer has the option of 'robbing the pack' – that is, examining all the cards that have not been dealt and adding any he wants to his hand.

You will need: 52 cards; no Jokers; scorecard

Card ranking: See under 'Suits and Card Ranking' below

Players: Four to six, in partnerships of two (in alternating seats)

Ideal for: 14+

THE DEAL
Each player is dealt five cards in packets of three and two or two and three. Once bidding is over and trumps have been declared, each player in turn, again starting with the player to the dealer's left, may decide to discard as many cards as he wishes from his hand face down on the table. Before dealing the required number of replacements, the dealer has the option of 'robbing the pack' – that is, to examine all the cards that have not been dealt and pick out whichever ones he wants in his hand.

BIDDING
The bidding starts with the player to the dealer's left and continues clockwise around the table. Each player in turn may bid or pass, although the player who passes may not re-enter the bidding at a later stage. Each bid must be higher than the one that preceded it, although the dealer has the privilege of opting to say, 'I hold'. This means that the last bid is equalled. The next player to bid must therefore raise the bid or decide to pass.

PLAY
The player to the left of the winning bidder leads. If the lead is a plain suit, other players must follow suit or trump. If they cannot, they may discard. If trumps are led, the same rule applies, unless the only trump a player holds is one of the top three and ranked higher than the led trump. In this case, the player may discard from another suit.

SCORING AND CONCLUSION
Each trick taken scores five points, as does the highest trump in play. If the bidding partnership takes at least the amount of the bid, it scores all the tricks won, but, if not, the amount of the bid is deducted from the score. The other partnership always scores what it has taken in tricks. If a partnership bids and makes 30 (the maximum number of possible points in a hand) the score is doubled to 60. A partnership that has won 100 or more points is not allowed to bid less than 20. The game is over when a partnership reaches 120 points.

NAPOLEON

In spite of its name, this is a British card game, which was extremely popular in Victorian times. A straightforward trick-taking game, the convention is to play Nap, as it is usually known, for small stakes and settle up after each hand. Although usually played with a standard deck, some players prefer to strip out the low cards of each suit to increase the skill factor. A Joker can also be added, in which case it becomes the highest trump, or in *Mis* – a bid to take no tricks – the only trump.

You will need: 52-card deck (occasionally with lower ranks removed or a Joker added); gambling chips/counters

Card ranking: Standard, Aces high

Players: Four to five is best

Ideal for: 14+

Left: The author Jerome K. Jerome mentions Victorian favourite Penny Nap in his celebrated book *Three Men in a Boat*.

OBJECT

To make at least the number of tricks bid or to stop another player from doing so.

THE DEAL

It is standard practice to shuffle the cards only at the start of a game and after a successful bid of five. Otherwise, they are simply cut by the player to the dealer's right before each deal. Each player is dealt five cards in packets of three and two or two and three. The deal passes to the left after each hand.

BIDDING

Each player bids to win a number of tricks if given the lead and choice of trumps, starting with the player to the dealer's left, moving clockwise round the table. There is only one round in which each player must bid higher than the last one, or pass. The lowest bid is two, which is worth two points, followed by three, which scores three, *Mis* (lose every trick), also worth three, four, worth four, and Nap, which is worth five. A Wellington is worth five for doubled stakes and, if a Blücher follows, this is redoubled. A Wellington can be bid only if another player has already bid Nap and a Blücher can only follow a Wellington.

PLAY

The highest bidder leads to the first trick. The suit of the card that is led automatically becomes trumps, except in a *Mis* if it has been agreed that the bid should be played at No Trumps. Players must follow suit, if possible, or trump or, otherwise, play any card. The highest card of the suit led, or the highest trump if any are played, takes the trick, the winner leading to the next.

SCORING AND CONCLUSION

If the bidder is successful, each of the opposing players has to pay him the value of the bid. If the bidder wins insufficient tricks, or, in the case of *Mis*, takes any at all, he must pay each opponent the same amount that would have been won had the contract been successful.

In some games, the payments for Nap, Wellington and Blücher are doubled if they are won, but not if they are lost. The game continues until all tricks have been played.

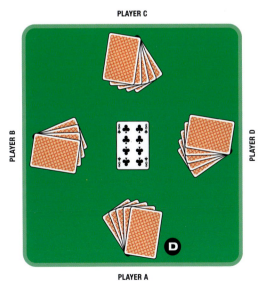

Above: Player B leads to the first trick, so Clubs automatically become trumps.

BRANDELN

This attractive game is the German equivalent of Nap. Its name in English means 'to smoulder'. Two of the bids – *Bettel* and *Herrenmord* – are for No Trump games. In the others, the successful bidder nominates trumps before he leads.

You will need: 28 card-deck (Eights, Sixes and below having been removed from a standard pack); scorecard

Card ranking: Ace, King, Queen, Jack, Ten, Nine, Seven in every suit except trumps (Jack, Seven, Ace, King, Queen, Ten, Nine)

Players: Four

Ideal for: 14+

OBJECT

To take at least three tricks, the lowest possible bid, up to a maximum of seven. There is no bonus for overtricks.

BIDDING AND PLAY

Players are dealt seven cards. They may bid or pass. Each bid must be more than the previous one, unless an earlier bidder decides to 'hold' the bid of a later one, forcing that player to raise or pass. Bidding a *Brandeln* means taking three tricks and a score of a point. Four tricks wins two points, five wins three, and six wins four, while *Bettel*, (a *Mis* bid), *Mord* and *Herrenmord* score five, six and seven.

The successful bidder announces trumps on leading to the first trick. The others must follow suit, trump or overtrump or otherwise play any card. The highest card of the suit led or the highest trump wins the trick. If successful, the bidder wins the value of the bid from each opponent; if unsuccessful, he deducts it from his score.

Left: In plain suits (left), card ranking is standard, Ace high. In the trump suit, (right, here ♣), the Jack and Seven are the top trumps.

RÖDSKÖGG

This is the Swedish version of Nap, the name of which translates as Redbeard. It is also known as Fem Opp (Five Up), probably because of the five-point penalties that feature in various stages of the game. It is played without trumps.

You will need: 52 cards; scorecard

Card ranking: Standard, Aces high

Players: Three to seven

Ideal for: 14+

OBJECT

To shed enough points to end up with a score of zero from an opening score of 12.

THE DEAL

Players are each dealt six cards in two packets of three, after which the dealer 'knocks' with the words 'Knock for cards and misdeal'. Any player picking up his cards before the dealer knocks goes five up – that is, has five penalty points added to his score.

BIDDING, PLAY AND SCORING

Players, who each start with scores of 12, can bid from one to six, or pass. A bid of six can be overcalled by a bid of Redbeard, which is an all-or-nothing bid and cannot be overcalled. The successful bidder becomes the soloist and leads to the first trick. Other players must follow suit, or otherwise play any card. The highest card of the suit led takes the trick, the winner of each trick leading to the next.

A successful bidder of Redbeard sheds as many points as the bid, or, if unsuccessful, goes five up. The other players shed one point per trick. If they take no tricks at all, they go five up, unless they take the option the soloist must give them to drop out after the fourth trick. If they do so, no penalties are incurred, but if they play on, they must take at least one of the final two tricks.

CONCLUSION

The player who is the first to reach zero wins. If he fails to announce this by saying 'Knock for going out' and another player subsequently makes the announcement, he goes five up.

BOURRÉ

This game owes its present popularity in the American South to its successful revival as a Cajun game in Louisiana. It probably descends from a French three-card game, which, in turn came from the Spanish game Burro, meaning donkey.

You will need: 52-card deck; no Jokers; gambling chips/counters
Card ranking: Standard, Aces high
Players: Two to eight, but five and over is optimal
Ideal for: 14+

OBJECT

To win as many of the five tricks as possible. A player who wins three tricks scoops the pool.

THE DEAL AND PLAY

Each player puts the same number of chips into the pot, and is then dealt five cards singly face down. The dealer's last card is dealt face up to indicate trumps. The player to the dealer's left now decides whether to pass or play. This is announced in turn around the table. Players who have decided to play undertake to win at least one trick. They state how many cards – if any – they want to discard, the dealer dealing the replacements from the stock.

The player to the dealer's left leads. Tricks are played for as in Whist, with players having to follow suit, discarding or trumping if they cannot do so. Any player holding the Ace, King or Queen of trumps is obliged to play it as soon as possible.

SCORING AND CONCLUSION

Holding cards that will ensure winning three tricks is termed a 'cinch' and guarantees winning the pot. A player who does not take any tricks is *bourréd* and must pay into the pot the same number of chips as is already there. If two players win two tricks each – this is a split pot – the hand is tied and the pot is carried forward to the next deal.

JULEP

Originally from Spain, this game is firmly established throughout South America. The name literally means 'a sweet drink'.

You will need: 40 card-deck (Tens, Nines and Eights removed from a standard pack); gambling chips/counters for juleps
Card ranking: Ace, Three, King, Queen, Jack, Seven, Six, Five, Four, Two
Players: Three to seven, five to six being ideal
Ideal for: 14+

OBJECT

To take at least two tricks to avoid having to pay sweeteners, *juleps*, as forfeits of chips to other players or into the pot.

THE DEAL

Each player is dealt five cards, the dealer turning up the topmost undealt card to establish trumps. The remaining cards form a stock.

PLAY AND SCORING

Each player can choose to pass, in which case he throws in his hand, or bid to play. This means taking at least two tricks. Players must follow suit or trump. Only if they can do neither can they discard. The highest card of the suit led, or the highest trump, takes the trick. Players who bid to play can discard as many cards as they like, drawing replacements from the stock. If only one player bids, any one player who passes may offer to 'defend the pack' by drawing six new cards from the stock and discarding one of them. The player to the dealer's right leads.

Any player who fails to take a minimum of two tricks has to pay an agreed forfeit, the *julep,* into the pot. If only one player succeeds, he wins the pot plus a *julep* from the other players. If two players win two tricks, they split the pot and *juleps*.

CONCLUSION

If the pack was defended unsuccessfully and lost, the lone bidder wins the pot, but no *julep*. If the defender wins, he gets the pot and a *julep* from the lone player.

FIVE-CARD LOO

This is a typical example of a plain-trick game in which players who think they will be unable to take a single trick or reach a minimum quota of tricks can drop out of the hand before play begins. There are five- and three-card versions, the latter being covered later. The J♣ is known as Pam. It always belongs to the trump suit and beats every other card in the pack, including the Ace of trumps. As well as Loo, other games of this kind include Rams in France and Blesang in Switzerland.

OBJECT

The object is to win at least one trick, each trick earning the player taking it a fifth of the pot.

THE DEAL

Players cut to see who deals first, the player with the lowest card winning – Aces are low for this purpose. The dealer puts five chips into the pot and deals five cards to each player in packets of three and two. The remaining cards are stacked face down to form the stock, the topmost being turned face up to indicate trumps.

FLUSH

A Flush is five cards of the same suit – a plain suit or trumps – or four of a suit plus Pam. The highest Flush is four of a suit plus Pam, followed by a Flush in trumps and then by a plain-suit Flush containing the highest top card. Whoever holds the best Flush 'looes the board', taking all five tricks by default and so winning the game.

SCORING

All the players have the opportunity to stay in or to drop out. Any player who stays in wins a share of the pot in proportion to the number of tricks he takes, but a player failing to win a single trick is deemed to be 'looed' and has to double what is already in the pot.

You will need: 52 cards; no Jokers; gambling chips/counters
Card ranking: J♣ highest, then standard, Aces high
Players: Three to eight
Ideal for: 14+

BIDDING, PLAY AND CONCLUSION

Each player in turn announces whether to pass or to play. All the active players then have the right to discard as many cards as they choose in exchange for replacements from the stock. The player to the dealer's left leads. The others must follow suit, if they can, or otherwise play a trump. Only if they can do neither are they permitted to discard. The highest card of the suit led or the highest trump, if any trumps are played, wins the trick.

If the Ace of trumps is led, its leader may say 'Pam, be civil', in which case anyone holding Pam may not play it if there are any other trumps in his hand. Each trick a player takes wins a fifth of the pot, but anyone failing to take a trick must pay a forfeit into it. The winner of each trick leads to the next and must lead a trump if possible.

Below: The J♣ in Five-Card Loo is known as Pam, and beats every other card in the pack, including the Ace of trumps. In this case, if Clubs were trumps, the player holding Pam would beat the A♣.

Left: A Flush is five cards of either a plain suit or trumps, or four of a suit and the J♣ (Pam). The best Flush is four of a suit plus Pam, then a Flush of trumps, then a plain-suit Flush with the highest top card. The player with the best Flush (if any), wins all five possible tricks without play.

NORRLANDSKNACK

The name of this game from the far north of Sweden means 'North Country Knock'. It is related to Ramina, which is played in Finland.

You will need:	52-card deck; gambling chips/counters
Card ranking:	Standard, Aces high
Players:	Three to five
Ideal for:	14+

OBJECT

To lose tricks rather than to win them. The winner is the first player to reach zero points.

THE DEAL

The dealer deals three cards to each player, turns up the next card to establish trumps, and then deals the final two cards. Each player can either knock, so undertaking to take at least one trick, or, on the first deal, say 'I lurk'. This means he won't be penalized for failing to win a trick. Subsequently, the choice is to knock or pass. In the opening deal, a draw follows the initial knock. Every player, except the dealer, who has to take the turned-up trump, can discard and exchange as many cards as he likes. After that, players choose whether to drop out or play.

PLAY, SCORING AND CONCLUSION

Each player puts a chip into the pot and is given a score of 10 points, which goes down a point for every trick a player takes. The player to the left of the dealer leads, playing the Ace of trumps if he holds it. Otherwise, the lead can be any card. In the opening hand, if a knocker fails to

take any tricks, he is 'loafed'. This means either adding five to his score, or raising it to 10 if that would make the score more. In subsequent hands, the same penalty applies to all players. They must also put a chip into the pot. The player who reaches zero first, takes the pot.

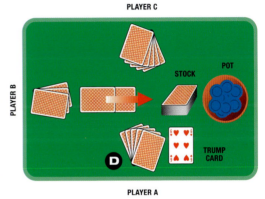

Above: After the deal and knock, every player, except the dealer, who has to take the turned-up trump card, can discard and exchange as many cards as he likes. Here, Player B exchanged two cards.

FEMKORT

The name of this Swedish game translates as Five Cards. It is unusual, as it does not matter how many tricks are won until the last trick is played, and any player may call for 'better cards' during the course of play. There are no trumps.

You will need:	52-card deck; no Jokers; gambling chips/counters
Card ranking:	Standard, Aces high
Players:	Two to ten
Ideal for:	14+

OBJECT

The object is to take the final trick and so win the pot.

THE DEAL

Each player puts an equal number of chips into the pot; this is agreed prior to the start of the game. They are then dealt five cards each in packets of two and three.

PLAY AND CONCLUSION

Each player plays to a trick by laying a card face up on the table. The card is left like that for the remainder of the game, so that all the players can see who has played what. The player to the left of the dealer leads first, play following suit if possible. The highest card of the led suit takes the trick, the winner leading to the next.

If a player calls for 'better cards' and no other player objects to the call, the hand is void and a new deal follows. Otherwise, play continues with the cards as held. The game is won by whoever takes the final trick.

THREE-CARD LOO

This is the older version of Loo, which can trace its origins back to the 17th century. It was a notorious gambling game in the 19th century, when, unless stakes were deliberately limited, fortunes were quickly lost on the turn of a few cards. The rules, conventions and card etiquette are broadly the same as in Five-Card Loo, but there are some important differences. Initially, the dealer puts three chips into the pot – this is termed a 'single'. If the pot contains chips left over from a previous hand, it is a 'double'.

OBJECT

To win at least one trick. A player who fails to win a trick is said to be 'looed' and, as a penalty, must add three chips to the pool.

You will need: 52 cards; no Jokers; gambling chips/counters
Card ranking: J♣ highest, then standard
Players: Up to 17, but five to seven is optimal
Ideal for: 14+

THE DEAL

Everyone starts with an equal number of chips. Each player receives three cards, which are dealt singly, while a spare hand, called Miss, is also dealt. The remaining cards are stacked face down, and the top one is turned up to indicate trumps.

Right: In Three-Card Loo, the first to lead must play the Ace of trumps (here, Spades) if he holds it. If the Ace is the turned-up trump, he must, if possible, lay the King of trumps instead.

PASSING AND EXCHANGING

Each player decides whether to play, in which case the undertaking is to take at least one trick, or to throw in the hand. Any player offering to play is entitled to ask if he can exchange the hand he has been dealt for Miss, but only the first player to request this can actually do so. He does this without looking at Miss (sight unseen) and afterwards cannot drop out or exchange back again.

Above: Although Three-Card Loo had a bad reputation for being a vicious gambling game, it was also played in the 19th century as a mild domestic pastime, and appeared frequently in the novels of Jane Austen.

If every player passes, the dealer scoops the pool, as does the exchanging player if everyone else passes. If only one player plays before the dealer without exchanging, the dealer must either play for his hand – exchanging or not – or elect to 'defend Miss'. In this case, he must still play, but cannot win or lose.

PLAY, SCORING AND CONCLUSION

The leading player must lead the Ace of trumps if he holds it, or, if the Ace is the turned-up trump, the King of trumps, if he has it. Otherwise, he must still lead a trump if he holds more than one in hand. The other players must follow suit and play a higher card if they can. If not, they must trump. Only a player holding no cards of the suit led and no trumps can discard. The highest card of the suit led or the highest trump wins the trick. The winner leads to the next trick, which he must lead with a trump, if possible.

Each trick earns the player who took it a third of the pool. A player who is 'looed', i.e. one who takes no tricks at all, pays three chips into the pot (or an amount agreed in advance before play starts), which is then taken forward as a double. Otherwise, a player who is looed must put in whatever the pool contained at the start of the deal.

TOMATO

This Spanish equivalent of the game Loo is extremely popular in its homeland.

OBJECT

The first player deciding to play after the cards have been dealt must take two tricks, while the others must take at least one trick each to avoid being 'tomatoed'. Each trick taken wins a third of the pot.

THE DEAL

The dealer puts three chips into the pot, after which each player is dealt three cards. Before looking at his hand, the dealer must say 'pass' or 'play'. If the latter, the next card is turned up to establish trumps, after which the dealer discards a card (sight unseen) and picks up the upturned one. This commits him to taking two tricks, and only then does the dealer look at his hand. If the dealer passes, the first to say 'play' goes through the same procedure, though only one trick has to be taken. If all pass,

> **You will need:** 40-card deck (Eights, Nines and Tens having been removed from a standard pack); gambling chips/counters
>
> **Card ranking:** Ace, Three, King, Queen, Jack, Seven, Six, Five, Four and Two
>
> **Players:** Three to ten
>
> **Ideal for:** 14+

the hands are scrapped and the pot is carried forward. The other possibility is for a player to 'defend the pack', which he does by drawing a new hand from the stock. If he takes a trick, the pot is carried forward to the next hand.

PLAY, SCORING AND CONCLUSION

The first active player to the right of the dealer leads. Players must follow suit and beat the card if posssible or, if unable to follow, must trump or overtrump. They may pass only if unable to do either. Each trick taken wins a third of the pot, while a player who wins no tricks is 'tomatoed' and has to double it.

ZWIKKEN

This is the Dutch version of an old Austrian game, Zwicken, once widely played throughout the old Hapsburg Empire until it was banned. Players can decide whether to play for the entire pot or just for part of it, or to pass. Anyone holding a *Zwikk,* three of a kind, automatically wins the game.

OBJECT

To win by either getting the highest *Zwikk*, or taking two tricks, or winning a trick that is worth more card points than those of the other two players added together.

THE DEAL

Players each put a chip into the pot and are dealt three cards – first one, then two – from a 20-card pack. The next card is turned up to set trumps.

PLAY, SCORING AND CONCLUSION

The player offering to play for the highest amount becomes the shooter, the person who undertakes to win by either of the three ways detailed under Object. Before play,

> **You will need:** 20-card deck (Nines and under removed from a standard pack); no Jokers; gambling chips/counters
>
> **Card ranking:** Ace, King, Queen, Jack, Ten
>
> **Players:** Three
>
> **Ideal for:** 14+

a player holding the Ten of trumps may exchange it for the turned-up card. Any player holding a *Zwikk* declares it, and wins the pool. If there are two *Zwikks*, the higher-ranking one wins. If no one has a *Zwikk*, the player to the dealer's left leads. Players must follow suit if possible, otherwise trump, or overtrump. The highest card of the suit led, or the highest trump, wins the trick.

An Ace is worth four points, a King three, a Queen two and a Jack one. A successful shooter wins the stake he played for, but, if not, the same amount must be added to the pot, probably because of the high stakes involved.

Left: One of the aims in Zwikken is to secure three of a kind, the highest being three Aces.

TOEPEN

This noisy cheating game is very popular in Dutch cafés and bars, as the loser has to pay a forfeit, which is usually a round of drinks.

You will need: 52-card deck with Twos to Sixes removed

Card ranking: Ten (highest), Nine, Eight, Seven, Ace, King, Queen and Jack (lowest)

Players: Three to eight

Ideal for: 10+

OBJECT

To lose as few lives as possible, starting with 10, and to take the last trick. The winner of that trick becomes the next dealer.

THE DEAL

From the 32-card deck, four cards are dealt two at a time. Any player with a hand consisting of an Ace and the three court cards may exchange it for a new one, but this opens up the possibility of a challenge from another player, who can insist on turning up the discarded hand.

Left: A player in Toepen with three Tens in his hand must whistle or sing, while one with four Tens must stand up.

If the discarded hand contains cards other than the ones specified, the discarder loses a life for cheating. If not, the challenger loses one. A player with three Tens must whistle, or sing, or, if holding four, stand up. For a player holding three or four Jacks, both conventions are optional.

PLAY AND CONCLUSION

The player to the dealer's left leads and the winner of the final trick deals the next hand; each other player losing a life. Play then follows convention, but a player may knock the table to raise the stakes by an extra life at any stage. Once a player has knocked, he may not do so again until someone else has done so. The others can stay in at the risk of losing a further life for each subsequent knock, or fold.

The game ends when a player loses 10 lives and has to pay an agreed forfeit.

AGURK

This Danish game is popular throughout the Baltic region – *agurk* is Danish for cucumber. Suits have no significance; what counts is the face value of each card. The twist comes in the last trick, when the player taking the trick is penalized.

You will need: 52 cards; no Jokers; gambling chips/counters

Card ranking: Ace is 14, King 13, Queen 12, Jack 11 and the other cards as marked

Players: Three to seven

Ideal for: 10+

OBJECT

To end up with the lowest number of penalty points.

THE DEAL

Players pay the same stake into the pot and are each dealt six cards.

PLAY

The player to the dealer's left leads. Each player after that can play a card with a rank that is at least as high as the highest card previously played, or play his lowest-ranking card. Whoever plays the highest card or, if the cards are of equal value, whoever is the last to play, leads to the next trick.

SCORING AND CONCLUSION

The player taking the final trick is penalized according to its face value (the sum of the cards that make up the trick). Once a player has accumulated 30 penalty points, he is 'cucumbered' and drops out of play. The player can elect to come in again, but, if so, starts with the same number of penalty points as the player with the next highest total. This can be done only once. The pot goes to the player with the lowest total of penalty points when only two players are left in the game.

TRUC

There are several versions of this Spanish game, the one played in Catalonia being the most popular. It is also played with slight variations in the south of France. Played with a Spanish pack, the cards in each suit run from Ace to Seven and Ten to Twelve – the Ten is the Valet, the Eleven is the Horse and the Twelve the King. Suits are Coins, Cups, Swords and Batons. The dealer and the player to the dealer's left are the captains of their respective partnerships, which sit opposite each other at the table.

OBJECT

In each deal, the aim is to win two tricks, or, the first if both sides win one. The first partnership to reach 12 points wins.

BETTING AND SIGNALLING

The hand, and the bets associated with it, is won by the partnership taking two out of the three possible tricks. If there is a tie, the non-dealing partnership wins. While a hand is in progress, players are allowed to talk freely and even signal to their partners. Winking, for instance, means that the player holds a Three, pouting means a Two, and showing the tip of the tongue means an Ace.

THE DEAL

The deal passes to the right after every hand. Three cards are dealt to each player singly. Provided that neither partnership has yet scored 11 points from previous hands, the non-dealing one may propose a one-card deal, in which there is no raising of the stakes. The partnership's captain requests this by tapping on the pack instead of cutting it after shuffling. The dealer can accept or reject the proposal.

Below: Played with a 40-card Spanish pack, the cards used in Truc in each suit run from Ace to Seven and Ten to Twelve, with the Ten called *Sota* (Valet), the Eleven *Cavall* (Horse) and the Twelve *Rei* (King).

You will need: Spanish 40-card pack
Card ranking: Three (highest), Two, Ace, King, Horse, Valet, Seven, Six, Five and Four (lowest)
Players: Four, in partnerships of two
Ideal for: 14+

PLAY

The player to the dealer's right leads. The highest card takes the trick, unless both teams play two or more cards of equal value. In this case, the trick is drawn and goes untaken. The winner of a trick leads to the next.

SCORING AND CONCLUSION

Each hand is initially worth a point, but any player can double this to two by calling '*truc*' either before or after playing a card. The captain of the opposing partnership decides whether to accept the call, or concede. The alternative is for either player in that partnership to call '*retruc*', so raising the stakes by a further point.

When a partnership reaches 11 points – the game is 12 points – the players must decide whether or not they want to play the next hand. If they play, the hand is automatically worth three points and no raising is allowed. If not, the opposing partnership scores a point.

TREIKORT

Treikort is a three-player game that was at one time widely played in Iceland, where it originated. It is closely related to Alkort, another Icelandic card game.

OBJECT

To win as many tricks as possible and take the title of Pope. This means winning 13 tricks over three games.

THE DEAL AND PLAY

Each player is dealt nine cards, three at a time. The player to the dealer's left leads to the first trick. Whichever player plays the highest card takes the trick and leads to the next. Any card may be led at any time with the exception of a Seven. A player cannot lead a Seven until he has taken a trick. The first player to take five tricks scores a point.

BECOMING POPE

A player who wins 13 tricks over three games takes the title of Pope. This gives him the right to get one of the two other players to give up his highest card and to take a Seven from the third player – if that player has one in his hand – in exchange for any cards he elects to discard. If the first player has no Seven, the Pope must do without.

The title of Pope is lost as soon as its holder fails to take 13 tricks in any further three consecutive games.

Left: The Sevens in Treikort are unusual in that they cannot be beaten if led but otherwise are worthless.

CONCLUSION

The highest cumulative trick taker at an agreed point wins the game.

PUT

This English version of Truc traces its origins back to the 16th century. Its name derives from the call 'put', made when a player is about to play a card.

OBJECT

To be the first player to score five points.

THE DEAL AND PLAY

Both players contribute the same stake before they cut for the deal, which subsequently alternates. Each player receives three cards, which are dealt to them singly.

The non-dealer leads, the higher ranking of the two cards played winning the trick. If both cards are of equal rank, the trick is tied and the cards discarded.

SCORING AND CONCLUSION

A player winning two tricks or one trick to two ties scores a point. If the score is one trick each and the third is tied – this is termed 'trick and tie' – the hand is a draw, as it is if all three tricks are tied. The first player to score five points wins the game. A player can call 'put' while playing a card, in which case the opposing player may either resign and concede the point or play on, in which case the winner of the trick automatically scores five points and so wins the game. If the call of 'put' is made and the result is a tie, no one scores any points.

Left: In Put, any card may be played to a trick, which is taken by the higher-ranking of the two. If both are equal, the trick is tied and discarded.

ALUETTE

Otherwise known as Le Jeu de Vache (The Cow Game), Aluette is played along the French Atlantic coast, where its likely cradle was Nantes. It has many unusual features, including the way cards are ranked and the signalling system employed to indicate which cards individual players hold.

OBJECT

To ensure that just one partner takes more tricks than any other single player.

THE DEAL

Each player is dealt nine cards three at a time, the rest being stacked face down on the table.

RANKING AND SIGNALLING

The card rankings in Aluette are complex. Eight individual cards rank the highest. The first four are termed *Luettes* and consist of the 3♦ (*Monsieur*), the 3♥ (*Madame*), the 2♦ (The One-eyed Man) and the 2♥ (The Cow). Players signal that they are holding these cards by looking up, placing a hand on the heart, closing one eye and pouting respectively. *Doubles* consist of the 9♥ (Big Nine), the 9♦ (Little Nine), the 2♣ (Two of Oak) and the 2♠ (Two of Script). The signals are lifting a thumb, raising a little finger, raising an index finger and pretending to write.

These cards are followed in order by Aces, Kings, Queens, Jacks and Nines down to Threes. Suits do not feature in the game. This means that all Aces are equal in value and will beat Kings, which beat Queens and so on.

PLAY

The player to the left of the dealer leads, after which any card can be played since there is no compulsion to follow suit. The highest card takes the trick and the winner leads to the next. If a trick is tied, it is discarded.

MORDIENNE

This is not compulsory, but is a commonly played extra. If a player is confident that he will not only win the most tricks, but also take them in unbroken succession, he

You will need: 48-card Spanish-style pack, or conventional pack with the four Tens removed

Card ranking: See under 'Ranking and Signalling' below

Players: Four, in partnerships of two

Ideal for: 14+

Above: 19th-century playing cards from the Aluette deck. Aluette is also called Le Jeu de Vache, from the picture of a cow depicted on the Two of Cups.

signals this by biting his lip. If his partner nods back, the bidder says '*Mordienne*' and the contract is made. A successful bid wins its bidder two game points, but, if it fails, they are awarded to the opposing partnership.

SCORING AND CONCLUSION

The player who takes the most tricks individually scores a game point for his partnership. In a tie, the partnership to reach that number of tricks first scores a game point. The first side to score five game points wins the game.

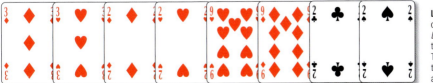

Left: The highest-ranked cards in Aluette are *Luettes* and consist of the 3♦, 3♥, 2♦ and 2♥. These are followed by the *Doubles*, the 9♥, 9♦ and the 2♣ and 2♠.

HEARTS GAMES

WHAT MAKES GAMES OF THIS FAMILY UNIQUE IS THAT THE BASIC AIM IS TO NOT WIN TRICKS, OR AT LEAST TO NOT WIN THOSE THAT CONTAIN CARDS CARRYING A PENALTY. THE SKILL LIES IN KNOWING WHEN TO PLAY YOUR HIGH CARDS AND WIN SAFE TRICKS, LEAVING THE BOGUS CARDS FOR YOUR OPPONENTS TO TAKE. PENALTY CARDS ARE USUALLY HEARTS PLUS THE Q♠, ALTHOUGH IN JACKS AND POLIGNAC, JACKS ARE THE CARDS TO AVOID.

It takes a particular type of card sense to successfully play Hearts and other games in this fascinating family. Cards such as Twos and Threes are as valuable as Aces and Kings in many of these games, and the middle ranks such as Sevens and Eights can be quite dangerous. Most of these games seem straightforward enough on the surface, and all of them are fun to play, but many have an added sting that can sometimes take an unwary player by surprise.

Generally, the best strategy is to aim to take no tricks at all, or at least avoid winning tricks that contain penalty cards. However, this is not necessarily always the case. In some Hearts games, it can pay a player to try to take every trick because if he is successful, his score is reduced rather than increased.

In the Italian game Coteccio ('reverse' in Italian), for instance, the aim is either to avoid taking the greatest number of card penalty points or to win all five tricks. In the latter case, the successful player wins outright. Hearts, the classic trick-avoidance game, has an interesting possible twist. If a player wins all the scoring cards, termed 'hitting the moon', his penalties are reduced by 26 points, or all the other players' scores increase by the same amount.

Above: In Hearts, capturing all the scoring cards, plus the Q♠, is known as 'hitting the moon', and reduces a player's penalties by 26.

HEARTS

irst recorded in the USA in the 1880s, Hearts is an extremely popular game with literally dozens of possible variations. Thanks to its success as a computer game, the four-handed version may reasonably be regarded as standard. There are no partnerships as such, although sometimes it pays for two players to collaborate informally. There are no trumps.

OBJECT

To avoid taking any tricks containing penalty cards (the entire Hearts suit and the Q♠) or to capture all 14 of them (termed 'hitting the moon').

You will need: 52-card deck; no Jokers	
Card ranking: Standard, Aces high	
Players: Three to eight, but four most commonly	
Ideal for: 10+	

THE DEAL

Each of the players receives 13 cards dealt singly.

PASSING OF CARDS

After the first deal, each player passes three cards face down to the player to the left and gets the same number from the player to the right. Each player must place the cards to be passed – there is no restriction on what these can be – face down on the table, ready to be picked up by the receiving player. Only then may players pick up the cards that have been passed to them.

The process is repeated on the second and third deals, the difference being that, on the second deal, the cards are passed to the right and received from the left. On the third deal, the players seated opposite each other exchange them. The cycle is repeated until the game is over.

PLAY

Any player holding the 2♣ must lead it to the first trick. If possible, players must follow suit, otherwise playing any card. The person playing the highest card of the led suit takes the trick and leads to the next.

It is against the rules to lead a Heart until one has been discarded – this is 'breaking Hearts' – unless a player holds nothing but Hearts or the only alternative is to lead the Q♠. Nor can any penalty card be played to the first trick unless there is no alternative. Normally, all non-penalty

cards won in tricks are discarded on to a waste pile, and penalty cards are turned face up on the table and laid in front of the players who won them. This allows players to work out which penalty cards are still to be played.

SCORING

Every Heart is worth one penalty point, while the Q♠ scores 13 points. If a player manages to 'hit the moon', he can either deduct 26 points from his total, or elect to have all the other players' scores increased by 26 points.

CONCLUSION

The game continues until one player reaches or exceeds a score of 100 penalty points at the end of a hand. The player with the lowest score is the winner.

Left: A typical trick in Hearts. Unable to follow suit, Player C gleefully discards the Q♠. Player D also cannot follow suit, so discards the A♥. Player B unexpectedly finds he has 14 penalty points counting against him.

Below: The cards to avoid in Hearts games are usually Hearts and the Q♠.

JACKS

Sometimes called Knaves, this penalty-trick game is best described as a cross between Hearts and Polignac. In this game, tricks with Jacks in them score minus points, while tricks without Jacks win plus points.

You will need: 52 cards; no Jokers	
Card ranking: Standard, Aces high	
Players: Three, easily adaptable for more	
Ideal for: 10+	

OBJECT

To take as many tricks as possible without Jacks in them.

THE DEAL AND PLAY

Each player gets 17 cards, the remaining card being turned up to establish trumps. The player to the dealer's left leads, the others following suit if possible. A revoke – that is, not following suit nor playing a trump when able to do so – costs the player concerned three plus points. The trick goes to the player of the highest trump, or the highest card of the led suit.

SCORING

At the end of a hand, each player scores one plus point for every trick he has taken. If, however, he has any Jacks in his tricks, he scores minus points – one for the J♠, two for the J♣, three for the J♦ and four for the J♥.

Left: In Jacks, there is a penalty for each Jack taken in tricks, so the aim is to avoid winning tricks with Jacks in them.

CONCLUSION

The first player to score 20 plus points wins.

POLIGNAC

The French version of Jacks, Polignac dates back to the early 19th century. Its German equivalent is Slobberhannes (Slippery Hans).

Deck: 32 cards for four players, Twos to Sixes removed; 28 cards for five or six players, Twos to Sevens removed	
Card ranking: Standard, Aces high	
Players: Four to six	
Ideal for: 10+	

OBJECT

To avoid taking any tricks with Jacks in them – especially the J♣ (the Polignac).

THE DEAL AND PLAY

The cards are dealt evenly in batches of two or three. The player to the dealer's left leads, the others following suit if they can, otherwise playing any card. The highest card of the led suit takes the trick.

Left: In Polignac, the aim is to avoid taking tricks containing Jacks. The J♣, known as the Polignac, incurs two penalty points, while other Jacks, such as the J♦ here, incur just one penalty point.

SCORING

After each hand, each player scores penalty points for any Jacks taken. If a player takes Polignac, the score is two penalty points. The other Jacks score a point each.

If a player decides to take all the tricks – which is known as 'general' – this must be declared before play. If successful, the other players are penalized five points each. If not, the 'general' gets the penalty and the Jacks are scored as usual.

CONCLUSION

The player with the fewest points after an agreed number of hands wins. Alternatively, the first person to score ten points is the loser.

Barbu

In this complex and skilful game, players take it in turns to be dealer and declarer, each playing seven possible contracts once. This means 28 hands must be played in all to make up a game.

You will need: 52-card deck; no Jokers; scorecard

Card ranking: Ace down to Two

Players: Four

Ideal for: 14+

Object
To make one's contract, or prevent other players from making theirs.

The Deal and Contracts
The dealer deals 13 cards to each player, then declares which of the seven contracts (see box) is to be played. It takes some experience to decide when to declare each contract. It is best to play No Tricks close to the last hand, when playing it with a weak hand is unlikely to prove a disaster. Trumps is best left to last, so that the declarer can be sure of having a hand with four trumps in it.

Doubling and Redoubling
After a contract has been declared, each player in turn may double all or some of the other players, or elect not to do so at all. It is what amounts to a side-bet between two players in which one of them is confident that he will outscore the other, though in the two positive contracts, players are only allowed to double the declarer.

The declarer can only double players who have doubled him, though, over each sequence of seven deals, each player has to double the dealer at least twice. A player who is doubled can redouble the player who doubled him. Saying 'Maximum' means that the player making the announcement is doing that and at the same time doubling any players who have not already doubled him.

Play and Scoring
The declarer starts play. Players must not only follow suit but also play a higher card than the preceding one if possible. If unable to follow suit, any card can be played in a negative contract, or trumps in a positive contract. The highest card played takes the trick, its winner leading to the next. At the end of each hand, all players record the points they have taken in plus or minus columns.

Following this, the results of any doubling are calculated pair by pair, doubles having been recorded on the scorecard as they were made. By convention, the declarer's doubles are ringed to make it easier to check that each

Negative Contracts
The five contracts (all in No Trumps) are as follows:
- No Tricks – each trick is worth minus two points.
- No Hearts – each Heart scores minus two with the exception of the Ace, which scores minus six. The declarer cannot lead a Heart unless there is nothing else but Hearts in his hand.
- No Queens – each of the four Queens scores minus six points and the hand ends when the last one has been taken.
- No King – the K♥ scores minus 20.
- No Last Two – taking the last trick of the hand scores minus 20, while the penultimate trick is worth minus 10.

Positive Contracts
The two contracts are as follows:
- Trumps – the declarer selects a trump suit.
- Dominoes – the declarer announces a starting rank – e.g. Dominoes from Eights – and plays a card accordingly. The next player must play either a card of the same rank from a different suit or a card of the same suit and adjacent rank to the one that has already been played. These cards are placed face up in a pattern on the table. So, if the card that is led is the 8♠, the next player places a 7♠ or 9♠ to the appropriate side of it or an Eight of a different suit above or below it. A player without such a card has to pass. The first player to lay down all of his cards scores plus 40, the second, plus 20, and the third plus 5. The final player scores minus five.

player has made the two doubles required by the rules. If neither of the two players doubled the other, there is no side-bet. If only one of a pair doubled the other, the difference between their scores is calculated and then added to the score of the player who did better and subtracted from the score of the one who did worse. If one player doubled and the other redoubled, the procedure is the same, but the difference is doubled before being credited to the one and subtracted from the other.

Conclusion
Play continues until every trick has been taken. The highest cumulative score at an agreed point wins.

TËTKA

Also known as Tyotka, this game hails from Russia and is widely played throughout eastern Europe. The word *tëtka*, which means 'auntie' in Russian, refers to the Queen of the 'bum suit' in each hand. Both the card and the suit are best avoided or penalty points are incurred. It is virtually impossible to escape all of them, particularly as the game progresses.

OBJECT

To play your hand tactically so that you win only tricks that contain no 'bum cards'. The lowest score (which is the lowest number of penalty points) wins.

THE DEAL

Each player takes it in turn to deal. The first is chosen at random by cutting the pack; and the player with the highest card wins. Four players are dealt 13 cards each singly, the last card being turned up before the dealer adds it to his hand. This becomes the so-called 'bum card'; its suit is the 'bum suit' for that particular deal, and its rank is the 'bum rank'. Play proceeds to the left and a game is any agreed multiple of four deals.

PLAY AND SCORING

The player to the left of the dealer leads, and the other players follow suit if possible. Otherwise, any card may be played. There are no trumps involved. The player of the highest card of the suit that was initially led takes the trick and then leads to the next.

Each penalty incurred scores one point. Penalties are given for the following: for taking a Queen; for taking the Queen of the bum suit (*tëtka*); for taking the bum card in a trick; for winning the 'bumth trick' (i.e. the first if the bum card is an Ace, the second if it is a Two, and so on); for taking the last trick; and for winning the most tricks.

You will need: 52-card deck; scorecard

Card ranking: Standard

Players: Four

Ideal for: 10+

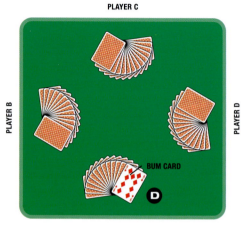

PLAYER C

PLAYER B

PLAYER D

BUM CARD

D

PLAYER A

Above: The last card, turned up by the dealer, becomes the 'bum card', meaning that its suit is the 'bum suit' for that particular deal and its rank the 'bum rank'. Here, then, Diamonds are the bum suit and Nine is the bum rank.

Tactically, it is well worth remembering that several different penalties may be incurred during the course of a single deal. This is a common feature of many so-called compendium games in the Hearts family, of which Tëtka is a classic example. Each of the four Queens, for instance, is worth one penalty point. If more than one Queen is played in a trick, the penalties soon start to mount up. Equally, if a King is the bum card, for example, and a player leads a King at trick 13 (the bumth trick), he would incur two penalty points.

CONCLUSION

Play continues until every trick has been taken. The lowest cumulative score at an agreed point wins the game, a game being any agreed multiple of four deals.

Left: Taking a Queen of any suit incurs a penalty. If a player takes a Queen of the 'bum suit' (*tëtka*), he incurs an extra penalty point.

SCHIEBERAMSCH

This is a trick-avoidance game, the name of which comes from the German word *Schieben* (shove) and *Ramsch* (rubbish). Its complex scoring is similar to that of Skat. Here, however, the undesirable cards (*Skat*) are 'shoved' round from player to player. Jacks are the trump suit.

OBJECT

To avoid winning the most card points in tricks. However, before play begins, each player has the chance to bid 'grand hand', whereby he undertakes to win at least 61 points in tricks and without picking up the *Skat*.

THE DEAL

Each player is dealt 10 cards as follows: one batch of three (then two extra cards are placed face down on the table to form the *Skat*), then batches of four and three.

DISCARDING AND CALLING

The player to the dealer's left may pick up the *Skat*, add one or both cards to his hand, and discard an equal number of cards face down in its place to form a new one. Each player in turn may repeat the process. A player with sufficient confidence in his hand can pass the *Skat* on unseen, in which case the loser's eventual score is doubled.

If a player calls 'grand hand', he becomes the soloist, playing against the other two players in partnership. In this case, the *Skat* is not used, but is turned up and added to the soloist's won tricks at the end of play. Either opponent may call '*Kontra*' to double the contract and the soloist can respond with '*Rekontra*', redoubling it.

PLAY

The player to the dealer's left plays the first card. The others follow suit if possible. The highest card of the suit led or the highest Jack wins the trick. The winner of each trick starts the next round. If a non-trump suit is led, a player cannot follow suit by playing its Jack but may trump with another Jack if unable to follow. The player who wins the last trick must take the *Skat*.

SCORING

Each Jack is worth two points. Aces score 11 points, Tens are worth 10, Kings four and Queens three. Nines, Eights and Sevens score zero. The number of points scored by each player is divided by 10, and fractions are rounded down. If all take tricks, the player with the most card points scores that number as a penalty score, increased by as many doubles that apply, then rounded down to the nearest 10. For example, if two players doubled by not taking the *Skat*, and the loser took 64 card points, he scores 4 x 64 = 256 ÷ 10 = 25 (ignoring the remainder). If one player takes no tricks, the player with the most card points scores double (before rounding down). In the event of a tie, both players count the same penalty. If one player takes all the tricks, his penalty score is then reduced by 120.

Grand hand is scored with the 'base value' set at 24 points and multiplied by a 'multiplier' calculated as follows: each Jack is worth a point; two are added for game; and one point for either side getting 90 or more card points (a *Schneider*) or taking all the tricks (a *Schwarz*).

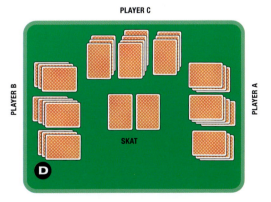

Above: The layout of the cards after the deal, with two cards for the *Skat*.

CONCLUSION

The player with the cumulative lowest score over an agreed number of hands wins the game.

BASSADEWITZ

Originating in Germany, this uncomplicated game is thought to be a precursor to Ramsch, itself the original version of Schieberamsch. It is still played in parts of German-speaking Europe.

OBJECT

To take as few as possible of the 120 card points available in each hand, and win the pool.

THE DEAL

The dealer puts 12 chips into the pool (or all four players contribute three) and deals eight cards to each player.

PLAY

The player to the dealer's left leads to the first trick, the other players following suit if they can. Otherwise, they play any card. The highest ranked card or highest card of the led suit takes the trick. The winner of each trick leads to the next. There are no trumps.

SCORING AND CONCLUSION

Cards rank and score as follows: each Jack is worth two points, Aces score 11 points, Tens are worth 10, Kings four and Queens three. Nines, Eights and Sevens score zero.

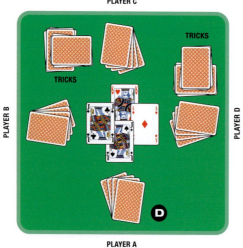

Above: Player C, having just won a second trick, leads the K♥. Player D tops it with the A♦, Player A tops it again with the J♠, but Player B takes the trick with the J♣, the highest-ranked card.

You will need: 32-card deck (Sixes down to Twos having been removed from a standard pack); gambling chips/counters

Card ranking: Jacks (in descending order J♣, J♠, J♥, J♦), followed by Ace, Ten, King, Queen, Nine, Eight and Seven

Players: Four

Ideal for: 10+

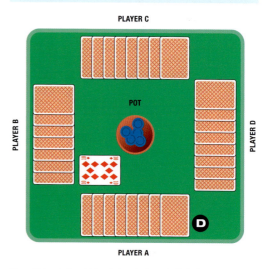

Above: Before dealing eight cards to each player, the dealer has to put 12 chips into the pot (or, upon agreement, each player can put in three).

The player with the lowest number of card points wins five chips from the pool, the second lowest four chips and the third lowest three chips. In the event of a tie, the player who led to the trick wins. A player taking no tricks can beat a player who scores no card points.

If a player takes every trick, he receives four chips from each of the other players. If a player scores 100 card points or more and fails to take all the tricks, he pays four chips to each of his opponents. In both cases, the pool is carried through to the next hand and the same player deals again. This also happens when everyone takes the same number of card points.

VARIANT

In an earlier version of the game, an Ace would count for five penalties instead of 11, and each player would add one per trick to his card-point total. This meant that the maximum score would be 88 when four played.

COTECCIO

The name Coteccio or Cotecchio is applied to various negative point-trick games in Italy. The version that is described here is played in Trieste. It uses the card-points system that is associated with the ancient game of Trappola.

You will need: 40-card deck (Tens, Nines and Eights having been removed from a standard pack); gambling chips/counters

Card ranking: Ace down to Jack, then Seven down to Two

Players: Two to seven

Ideal for: 14+

OBJECT

To avoid taking the most card points in tricks; alternatively to win all the tricks, when the winning player takes the contents of the pot.

THE DEAL AND PLAY

All the players pay agreed equal stakes into the pool and start the game with a notional four 'lives'. Five cards are then dealt to each player in turn, and the remaining spare cards are put to one side.

The player to the dealer's right leads to the first trick. Play proceeds anti-clockwise. The other players must follow suit if possible, or they may play any card. The player who places the highest card of the leading suit wins the trick. The trick is then placed face up in front of the player taking it. The winner of each trick leads on to the next. There are no trumps.

SCORING

Aces score six points, the Kings five, the Queens four and the Jacks three. The remaining cards, from the Sevens downwards, score zero. The winner of the last trick scores six. The player with the most points at the end of a hand normally loses a life. If two or more players tie for the most points, they each lose a life. If one player takes all of the first four tricks, he has two options. He can elect to annul the hand, in which case no one loses a life, or he can try to win the fifth trick by leading to it. If his card wins the trick, he gains a life and the other players each lose one. If not, he loses a life and the winner of the trick gains one.

If all four players tie for most of the tricks, which means that they will 'die' at the same time, the entire game is anulled. Players re-start the game with four lives each, and a new pool is added to the old one.

CONCLUSION

In theory, players drop out once they have lost four lives. By agreement, though, a player in this position can opt to 'call the doctor' after paying an extra stake into the pool (provided at least two other players remain alive) and receive as many lives as remain to the player who has the second fewest. Those left alive continue until only one player remains. The last player wins and collects the contents of the pot.

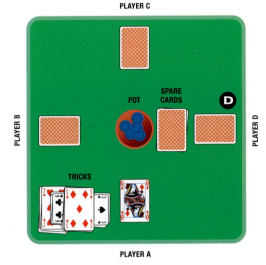

PLAYER C

SPARE
POT   CARDS   D

PLAYER B   PLAYER D

TRICKS

PLAYER A

Above: Player A, having taken the first four tricks, can annul the hand, in which case no one loses a 'life', or he can lead the last card. If this wins, he gains a life and the other players lose one. If not, he loses a life and the trick's winner gains one. Here, he gambles on winning the final trick.

Above: Coteccio is unique among Italian card games for its points system. Of the top four cards, Aces score six points, the Kings score five points, the Queens four points and the Jacks score three.

ACE-TEN GAMES

MANY OF EUROPE'S BEST-KNOWN CARD GAMES ARE TERMED ACE-TEN GAMES, THAT IS, ONES IN WHICH ACES COUNT FOR 11 POINTS, TENS SCORE 10, KINGS FOUR, QUEENS THREE AND JACKS TWO. THE OTHER CARDS ARE USUALLY VALUELESS, AS ARE TRICKS. IT IS SCORING CARD POINTS THAT COUNTS. GAMES ARE USUALLY WON BY TAKING AT LEAST 61 CARD POINTS IN TRICKS, AND PLAYERS ARE ALMOST ALWAYS PENALIZED FOR TAKING FEWER THAN 31 POINTS.

The first Ace-Ten game in card-playing history is Brusquembile, recorded as being played in France as early as 1718. The most celebrated of all is Skat, Germany's national card game. There are many others, each with unique characteristics. In games such as Schafkopf, for instance, some of the Queens and Jacks are permanent trumps whereas in Klaverjas, which originated in the Netherlands, Jacks and Nines, rather than Aces and Tens, are the highest trumps. Players holding the King and Queen of the same suit, Four of a Kind, or sequences of three or more cards in a suit score bonuses. In southern European countries, most notably in Italy and Spain, local packs do not include a Ten. This has not stopped games like Briscola and Madrasso, the latter being a favourite in Venice and the surrounding area, from becoming widely popular. Another card, which is usually the Three, but sometimes the Seven, takes the Ten's place.

All these games are played with stripped-down packs, containing 40, 36, 32, 24 or 20 cards. Reducing the size of the pack has several advantages. It obviously speeds up the game, and has led to the invention of new games ideally suited to three players.

Having fewer cards also introduces variety into trick play and trick-taking. Some tricks are worthless, while others may contain enough high-scoring cards to win the game outright after only a few tricks have been played. Some of these games are extremely complicated to play but are worth the effort.

Above: Skat, which was invented in 1810 in Germany, is now the country's national card game and one of the most celebrated of all Ace-Ten games.

SCHAFKOPF

Widely played in southern Germany, notably in Bavaria where it was invented in 1811, this three- or four-player game exists in many forms. It is played with a 32-card German-suited pack, but here French suits have been substituted.

You will need: 32-card deck (Sixes and below having been removed from a standard pack); scorecard

Card ranking: Queens and Jacks (*Wenzels*) are the highest trumps, ranked Q♣, Q♠, Q♥, Q♦, J♣, J♠, J♥, J♦. Other trumps and non-trumps: Ace (highest), Ten, King, Nine, Eight and Seven

Players: Three or four, with ad hoc partners from deal to deal

Ideal for: 14+

OBJECT

The aim of the game is to win at least 61 card points of the 120 available. A bonus is awarded for taking 90 or more (*Schneider*), or winning all eight tricks (*Schwarz*).

THE DEAL AND PLAY

Each player is dealt eight cards four at a time. Each in turn says 'Pass' or 'Play'. If all pass, the deal is annulled. If one or more bids, they declare their contract (see box). The player to the left of the dealer leads to the first trick. Players must follow suit if possible, otherwise they may play any card. The highest card of the led suit wins the trick, or the highest trump if played. The winner of each trick leads to the next. Whoever holds the called Ace (see below) must play it when its suit is led, or must lead with it the first time he leads from its suit, unless he holds four or more other cards of the same suit.

Left: If a player bids Call-Ace, and asks for the A♦, the holder of this hand will become his partner for the deal, assuming that no other player bids higher. The bidder's hand must contain a Diamond, other than a Q, J or A.

CONTRACTS AND BIDDING

After the deal, players either pass or compete for bidding. From lowest to highest, the bidding contracts are:

• Call-Ace – Hearts and *Wenzels* are trumps. The bidder 'calls the Ace' by naming the Ace of a suit other than Hearts (and must be a suit in which he holds a card other than the Q, J and A) and the player holding it becomes the bidder's partner (which is only revealed by play).

• *Wenz* – Jacks are trumps, ranking in their normal order.

• *Suit Solo* – the bidder can nominate a trump suit, which, headed by all the *Wenzels*, forms a series of 14 trumps. The bidder cannot hold any trumps other than *Wenzels*.

• *Solo-Tout* – a bid to take all eight tricks.

• *Sie* – a bid to take eight tricks, using all the *Wenzels*.

• *Kontra* – an opponent may double a contract by saying 'Kontra' at any time up to the playing of the opening trick's second card. The soloist, or soloist's partner, can in turn redouble. In both cases, the side concerned must score at least 61 in order to beat the contract.

SCORING AND CONCLUSION

Aces are worth 11 points, Tens score 10, Kings four, Queens three and Jacks two. 'Runners' are the top three trumps held in one hand, or by one partnership, together with any more trumps held in downwards succession. They score 10 points each, and this is increased if there is any doubling.

In Call-Ace, the losing players pay 10 points to each of their opponents, or 20 points if they are *Schneidered* (their opponents have taken 90 or more), or 30 points if they are *Schwarzed* (their opponents have won all eight tricks).

In *Wenz* and *Suit Solo*, the soloist can win or lose 50 points or get a bonus of 60 points for *Schneider* and a bonus of 70 points for *Schwarz*. Winning or losing *Solo-Tout* is 100 points, *Sie* is 200 points. Play continues until all the tricks have been played. A game is any multiple of four deals.

Left: German-suited double-headed picture cards. Queens and Jacks are permanent trumps, ranking above Aces.

Skat

Invented in around 1810 in Germany, Skat has spread across the world. Basically it is a three-handed trick-taking game. Each hand begins with an auction, the winner becoming the declarer and playing alone against a partnership of the other two players. The player to the dealer's left is called Forehand, the one to Forehand's left Middlehand, and the player to Middlehand's left Rearhand.

> **You will need:** 32-card pack (Sixes and below having been removed froma standard deck); scorecards
>
> **Card ranking:** Trumps (except in a Grand game, see below): J♣ (highest), J♠, J♥ and J♦, Ace, Ten, King, Queen, Nine, Eight and Seven. Non-trumps: Ace, Ten, King, Queen, Nine, Eight and Seven
>
> **Players:** Three (or four, with dealer sitting out hand)
>
> **Ideal for:** 14+

Above: In a Suit game, the four Jacks are the highest trumps, ranking from high to low according to suit ♣, ♠, ♥, ♦. In a Grand game, only the Jacks are trumps, whereas in a Null game there are no trumps at all.

Object

Usually to win at least 61 card points. There are options to take at least 90 points, or to win or lose all 10 tricks.

The Deal

Each player receives 10 cards in packets of three, four and three. The last two cards of the deck, the *Skat*, are placed face down on the table. This takes place after the players receive their first three cards and before the second and third packets of four and three cards are dealt to them.

Types of Game

Which player will be the declarer, playing alone against the other two players in partnership, is determined by an auction. The declarer's aim is usually to win at least 61 card points, although there are the options of aiming to take at least 90, or to win or lose all 10 tricks. It all depends on which type of game the declarer elects to play – Suit, Grand or Null. In a Suit game, the four Jacks are the highest trumps regardless of suit, followed by the remaining seven cards of the chosen suit. In a Grand game, only the Jacks are trumps, while Null is a bid in which there are no trumps, to lose every trick.

The declarer can also elect to play with the *Skat* or without it. No one else may examine the *Skat* until after the last trick has been played, but any card points it may contain count for the declarer.

Game Values

Players bid by announcing the minimum score of the contract they wish to play (and *not* the name of the contract), which they calculate in advance as follows.

In Trump games, what is termed the 'base value' of the suit chosen as trumps is multiplied by additional factors known as 'multipliers'. The base values are nine for Diamonds, 10 for Hearts, 11 for Spades and 12 for Clubs. The base value for a Grand – that is, when only the four Jacks are trumps, is 24.

The multipliers are always taken in the following order, all being added together as you go. *Spitze* (Tops) is based on the number of consecutive top trumps (*Matadors*), from the J♣ downwards, held or not held in hand. If a player holds the J♣, he is 'with' as many *Spitze* as there are in hand. The maximum possible holding is 'with 11' in a Suit game and 'with four' at Grand. If the J♣ is not held, that player is playing 'without' as many of the top trumps that rank above the highest trump in hand. If that trump is the J♠, the player concerned is 'without one' and so on up to a possible maximum of 'without 11' in a Suit game or 'without four' at Grand.

A point is then added for game – 'one for game' – by which the player undertakes to win at least 61 card points. Another point can be added if the intention is to reach *Schneider* (90 points or more) and another point for *Schwarz* (winning every trick).

If a player intends to play from hand without taking the *Skat*, he adds another point – 'one for hand'. If this is the case, then he can also increase the game value by adding one or two extra points for declaring he will win *Schneider* or *Schwarz* as well as the points gained for actually winning either. If declaring *Schwarz*, game value can be further increased by a point for playing *Ouvert* – that is, with the hand exposed on the table.

The lowest possible game value is 18, the highest valued Suit game 216 and the highest Grand is 264. Null games, by contrast, have set values, which never vary. These are 23 for Null with *Skat*, 35 for Null hand, 46 for Null *Ouvert* and 59 for Null *Ouvert* from hand.

BIDDING

Middlehand starts by bidding against Forehand, by announcing successive game values, starting with 18, to which the response is 'Yes' until either Middlehand decides not to bid higher or Forehand passes. Jump bids are allowed (jumping from 18 straight to 33, say), but it is illegal to announce anything but a specified game value.

With the first stage of the auction concluded, Rearhand takes over the bidding. The last player not to pass becomes the declarer. If using the *Skat*, the declarer picks it up, discards two cards and announces what the game is to be. If playing from hand, the word 'hand' is added, together with any other declaration, *Schneider*, *Shwarz* or *Ouvert*. In the last instance, the declarer lays his hand face up on the table before leading the trick.

CONCEDING THE GAME

The declarer has the right to concede the game at any time before he plays to the first trick. There are various reasons for this, the commonest one being that, when playing with *Skat* exchange without two or more *Matadors*, the declarer finds one or more higher *Matadors* in the *Skat*. Suppose, for instance, there is a successful bid of 30, its bidder intending to play in Hearts (Hearts 'without' two, game three, x 10 = 30). If the *Skat* includes the J♣ or J♠, this revalues the bid at 20 ('with' or 'without' one, game two, x 10 = 20).

The declarer now has three choices. He can announce Hearts, as he intended, and attempt to win *Schneider* for the extra multiplier that will increase the game value to 30. He can choose a different game – Spades (22), Null (23), Clubs (24) or Grand (48). If none of these options is playable, then the game is conceded without play.

PLAY AND SCORING

The player to the dealer's left (Forehand) leads and the winner of each trick leads to the next. Suit must be followed if possible, but otherwise any card can be played. The highest card of the suit led or the highest trump, if any are played, takes the trick. All the cards won by the partners should be kept together in a single pile. All 10 tricks have to be played – except if the declarer

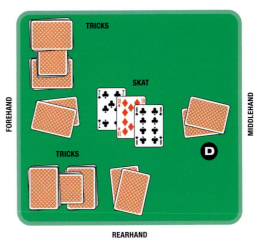

Above: Middlehand here, going for a Null contract, is caught out when the dealer leads the 7♣ and Forehand discards, as he is unable to follow suit. Middlehand's 8♣ wins the trick, meaning that the contract is lost. There is no need to play out the remaining two tricks.

wins a trick and the contract is Null. Once all the tricks have been completed, the *Skat* is turned face up so the game can be valued correctly.

For the declarer to win the game, he must take at least 61 card points – 90 points if the bid was *Schneider*, every trick if the bid was *Schwarz* or no tricks at all if the bid was Null – and the game as revalued after the end of play is worth at least the amount that he bid.

Assuming all these conditions are satisfied, the declarer adds his actual game value to his aggregate score. The *Skat* counts as part of the hand for the purposes of game valuation. This means that it is possible to be 'with' or 'without' 11, even though only 10 cards are actually held in hand.

If the declarer loses a game worth at least the amount bid, its full value is doubled and deducted from his aggregate score. If the value of his game is less than the amount bid, the value to be doubled is defined as the nearest appropriate multiple of the relevant base value that exceeds the bid or equals it, i.e, if his bid was 36, and the game was 30, he loses 40, doubled to 80. If he is *Schneidered*, no extra penalty is applicable.

CONCLUSION
Play continues until all the tricks have been played.

DOPPELKOPF

The north German equivalent of Schafkopf, Doppelkopf is played with a double pack and has an unusual system of 26 trumps. There are a number of somewhat arcane variations.

You will need: Two 24-card decks (Eights and below having been removed from two standard packs); scorecards

Card ranking: Trumps: 10♥, 10♥, Queens, Jacks, A♦, A♦, K♦, K♦, 10♦, 10♦, 9♦, 9♦. Clubs and Spades: Ace, Ten, King, Nine. Hearts: Ace, King, Nine

Players: Four, in variable partnerships

Ideal for: 14+

OBJECT

To take at least 121 card points by capturing valuable cards in tricks.

THE DEAL

Each player is dealt 12 cards each in batches of three. Any player dealt five or more Kings, eight or more Aces and Tens or just one trump, may demand a redeal.

Above: The first hand here has five Kings, while the second has four Tens and four Aces. In each case, the player holding such a hand can demand a redeal.

BIDDING

Players announce 'Gesund' ('healthy'), meaning that they are happy to play a normal game in which players with the Queens of Clubs ('the grannies') partner each other, or 'Vorbehalt' ('reservation'), meaning that they want to play some other type of game. In Vorbehalt, the first two options are Hochzeit (Marriage) or Armut (poverty), in both of which the player seeks a partner. A player who, despite holding both grannies, is not confident of playing solo, bids Hochzeit. The first player other than the bidder to take a trick becomes the bidder's partner. A player holding three or fewer trumps, which must be placed face down on the table, can bid Armut. The partner is the player who picks up these discards and exchanges the same number of cards with the bidder.

The third option is to choose one of eight types of solo. In Trump Solo, the bidder names the trump suit, while in Queen and Jack Solo only Queens or Jacks are trumps. Ace Solo is a No Trumps bid. In Hearts, Spades, Clubs and Diamonds Solo, the respective suits are trumps.

PLAY, SCORING AND CONCLUSION

In a Gesund game, the partnership with the Queens of Clubs is dubbed the Re team; in a Vorbehalt game, it is the partnership or soloist specifying the game that is Re. The opposing players are know as the Kontra team. Announcing 'Re' or 'Kontra' doubles the amount of points to be won.

Once a double has been announced, there can be further announcements. 'No 90' is an undertaking to win at least 151 card points, 'No 60' at least 121 and 'No 30' at least 211. Schwarz means the players intend to win every trick that is played. If successful, each member of the announcing team wins an extra game point, but if they fail they lose the game. Re team players each score a game point for winning at least 121 card points. If the Kontra team takes 120 card points, each player wins two game points.

'Catching a fox', won by the team capturing the A♦ (the fox), is worth one game point for each player. Karlchen Müller (Charlie Miller),which is winning the last trick with the J♣, scores the same, as does Doppelkopf, which is taking a trick where all the cards are Tens and Aces. Note that neither catching a fox or Karlchen Müller can be scored in Solo contracts.

Above: Two players holding the Q♣ have the option of partnering with each other, in which case they are dubbed the Re team.

Above: Winning a trick containing the A♦ is termed 'catching a fox', and is worth one game point for each player in a partnership. Winning the last trick with the J♣ is termed Karlchen Müller (Charlie Miller) and, again, scores a point for both players.

AVINAS

This partnership game hails from Lithuania. It is played in two ways, depending on whether or not Sevens are exposed during the deal.

You will need: 32-card deck (Sixes and below having been removed from a standard pack); scorecard

Card ranking: Q♣ (highest), Sevens, Q♠, Q♥, Q♦, J♣, J♠, J♥, J♦, Aces, Tens, Kings, Nines, Eights

Players: Four, in partnerships of two

Ideal for: 14+

OBJECT

The aim of the declaring side is to take at least 61 of the 120 card points available.

THE DEAL

Each player is dealt eight cards in batches of four, and the dealer exposes everyone's fourth and eighth cards. If no Seven is turned up, the player to the dealer's left chooses a trump suit and states how many trumps he holds without revealing the name of the suit. The other players either pass or quote a higher number of cards held in a suit of their own choosing. The player stating the greatest number of trumps becomes the declarer and leads to the first trick. This is a No Sevens game.

If one of the exposed cards is a Seven then its suit is trumps; if more than one card is a Seven, then the last one dealt becomes the trump suit for that deal. The player who was dealt the Seven of trumps is declarer and will lead to the first trick. This is a Sevens game.

PLAY

In a No Sevens game, the declarer must lead a trump to the first trick. If a Queen or Jack is led and it is unclear what the trump suit is, the player at his left must ask and be answered. The first trick's winner must lead a trump to the second if one is held. All other tricks can be led by any card, and players must follow suit if possible. The declarer may stop play when he realizes he has won or lost.

In a Sevens game, the declarer knocks the table if he aims to take all eight tricks, doubling the value of the game. Opposers can knock to redouble. All the tricks are played but, if the game is doubled, the declarer loses as soon as his opponents take a trick.

The declarer leads to the first trick. Players must follow suit if possible. The highest card of the suit led, or the highest trump, wins the trick. Normally all eight tricks are played. The declarer wins if he scores more than 61 points, and his opponents are penalized. If not, he is penalized.

Right: As no Sevens feature in the dealt cards, the player to dealer's left chooses a trump suit. The other players can pass or announce a trump suit in turn. He who bids the longest suit sets trumps and becomes the declarer.

SCORING AND CONCLUSION

Aces score 11, Tens 10, Kings four, Queens three and Jacks two. Both games are scored negatively, i.e. marking or cancelling penalties against the losers and winners.

A Sevens game is scored by means of circles called *Avinas* (Rams). If the declarers win, their opponents are penalized by as many *Avinas* as there were Sevens in the deal. If the declarers lose, they are doubly penalized. In subsequent hands, *Avinas* are scored by cancelling those of the opposing side.

A No Sevens game is scored in Pips, written down as a running total. Pips cannot be cancelled. If the declarers win, opponents are penalized one Pip if they score between 31 and 59 card points, two Pips if they take 30 or fewer, and three if they score zero. If the declarers score between 32 and 59, they are penalized two Pips; if they score between two and 31, they are penalized four Pips, and they are penalized six if they score zero.

Play lasts until one side has 12 Pips, while the other has none. If both sides have scored Pips, the game goes to the side with fewer penalty *Avinas*.

PLAYER C

PLAYER B

PLAYER D

PLAYER A

SIX-BID SOLO

This is one of three American games – the others are Crazy Solo and Frog – derived from Tappen, which first appeared in southern Germany, western Austria and Switzerland in the early 1800s.

You will need: 36-card deck (Fives and below having been removed from a standard pack); scorecards

Card ranking: Ace (highest) down to Six

Players: Three

Ideal for: 14+

OBJECT

The player who bids the highest value game plays solo against the other two players, competing to win tricks containing valuable point-scoring cards.

BIDDING

There are six possible bids, the bidding starting with the two players to the dealer's left. Only after one of them has dropped out is the dealer allowed to participate.

THE DEAL

Each player is dealt seven cards in packets of four and three, then three are dealt to the table to form a widow, or stock, then each player gets a final four. The widow is left untouched until the end of the game.

PLAY

Except in Spread *Misère*, when it is the player to the right, the player to the bidder's left always plays the opening lead. Players must follow suit or play a trump card if they can. The highest card of the led suit or highest trump played takes the trick and the winner leads to the next.

SCORING

Aces score 11, Kings four, Queens three, Jacks two and Tens 10. The Eight, Seven and Six are valueless. If the bid is Solo, a successful soloist wins two points from each opponent for every card point taken over 60, but loses two points for every card point taken short of that total if the contract fails. A Heart Solo scores three points, *Misère* 30, Guaranteed Solo 40, Spread *Misère* 60, Call Solo 100 and Call Solo in Hearts 150. Except in *Misère* bids, any card points the widow may contain are added to the soloist's final score.

BIDDING

The bids, from lowest to highest, are as follows:

- Solo – an undertaking to win at least 60 card points with any suit other than Hearts as trumps.
- Heart Solo – the same as Solo but with Hearts as trumps.
- Guaranteed Solo – an undertaking to win at least 74 points if playing in Hearts, or 80 if in another suit.
- Call Solo – an undertaking to win 120 points, the soloist having the right to name any card, upon which the holder must surrender it in exchange for a card of the soloist's choice.
- *Misère* – an undertaking to lose every trick (there are no trumps).
- Spread *Misère* – the same as *Misère*, but with the soloist's cards exposed.

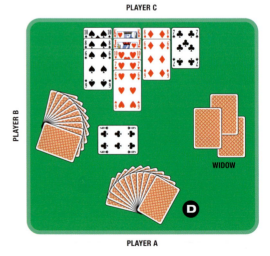

Above: Player C has bid Spread *Misère* (undertaking to lose every trick with his hand exposed). Player B has led the 6♣. Player C will have to play the 7♣ to this, but Player A will have to play higher unless unable to follow suit.

HAFERLTAROCK

This is one of several German games that are obviously derived from Tarock, as Tarot is termed in German-speaking countries, but with the 22 *tarocks* that make up the fifth suit in true Tarot left out. It is definitely not as old as its venerable Italian ancestor, the origins of which date back to the 15th century, but it is a stimulating game to play in its own right.

OBJECT

To win at least 61 of the 120 card points available after naming trumps and playing alone against the other two players.

THE DEAL

Each player gets 11 cards in packets of four, three and four, with three cards being placed face down on the table as a widow (stock) before the final packet is dealt.

BIDDING

As a preliminary, the three players each contribute 100 chips into the pot. Starting with the player to the dealer's left, each player decides whether to pass or say 'Play'.

PLAYER A

PLAYER B

PLAYER C

Above: With poor cards, Player A passes immediately, but Players B and C indulge in a bidding battle. Player B's strong Clubs, however, coupled with support in other suits, provides enough incentive to outbid Player C, who finally passes as well.

Player A	Player B	Player C
Pass	Play	Play/Hand
—	And Five	And Ten
—	And Fifteen	And Twenty
—	And Twenty-five	Pass

You will need: 36-card deck (Fives and below having been removed from a standard pack); gambling chips/counters

Card ranking: Ace, Ten, King, Queen, Jack, Nine down to Six

Players: Three

Ideal for: 14+

The latter is a bid to take at least 61 of the 120 card points, playing solo against the other two players and nominating trumps. The next player can take the game off him by bidding 'Hand'. The first bidder can then bid 'Hand' to reassert his bid, or pass. 'And Five', which raises the bid to 66 points, then 'And Ten' and so on, raises the bidding in multiples of five.

This continues until there is a winning bid. The soloist now declares whether the intention is to play a Pick-up or a Hand game. In the former, the soloist picks up the widow and discards three cards before naming trumps. The latter means he will play his dealt hand.

PLAY

The player to the left of the dealer leads to the first trick and play follows convention, with the highest card of the led suit (or the highest trump if any are played) taking the trick. The winner of the trick leads to the next.

SCORING

The scoring cards are Aces, worth 11 points, Tens 10, Kings four, Queens three and Jacks two. The other cards are valueless. Any points in the widow go to the soloist, whether he fulfils his contract or not.

If successful, the soloist wins a basic five chips, plus five chips for every five points in excess of the contract. If the contract fails, the soloist loses five chips for every five points of the shortfall.

If successful in a Pick-up game, the soloist takes the appropriate number of chips from the pot. In a Hand game, the opponents each pay the soloist one chip per point, plus five points for every five points the contract was raised above 61 during the bidding.

CONCLUSION

The game ends when the pot is empty, or by mutual agreement. The winner is the one with the most chips.

EINWERFEN

Einwerfen is a long-established German partnership game and a good one to start with if you are new to Ace-Ten games.

OBJECT

To win a single game by taking 61+ card points, a double game (90+ points) or a treble for taking every trick.

THE DEAL

Players are dealt eight cards each, the dealer turning up the last one for trumps. The player to the dealer's left leads to the first trick.

SCORING

Aces score 11, Kings four, Queens three, Jacks two, and Tens score 10. The other cards do not score. A partnership scoring 61+ card points wins a single game, a double for 90+, a treble for every trick. If the scores are tied, the value of the next deal is doubled. Any subsequent deal that has the same trumps as the first is doubled in value.

You will need: 32 card-deck (Sixes and below having been removed from a standard pack); scorecard

Card ranking: Ace down to Seven

Players: Four, in partnerships of two

Ideal for: 10+

Right: This trick scores four points for the King, 11 for the Ace and three for the Queen, used as a trump: 18 points in all.

Right: This trick scores 10 for the Ten, two for the Jack and 11 for the Ace: 23 points in total.

PLAY AND CONCLUSION

Players must follow suit if they can, play a trump or else play any card. The trick is taken by the highest card of the suit led or the highest trump. The trick's winner leads to the next. Play ends once all tricks have been chased.

YUKON

This Canadian game is a curious blend of elements drawn from Skat and Scotch Whist.

OBJECT

To become the first side to score 250 card points.

THE DEAL

The players receive four cards each. The rest of the pack is placed face down to form the stock, from which players draw the top card after each trick to replenish their hands.

PLAY

The player to the dealer's left leads to the first trick. Players must follow suit if possible or otherwise trump. The Yukons (Jacks) are permanent trumps and they all rank higher than the other cards.

The J♠, the Grand Yukon, takes any trick in which it is played, as does the first played of two or more Yukons (i.e. if two Yukons are played to the same trick, the first one laid wins). Otherwise the highest card of the suit led wins.

You will need: 52 cards; no Jokers; scorecards

Card ranking: Grand Yukon (J♠), the other Yukons (Jacks), Tens, Aces, Kings, Queens and then Nine to Two

Players: Four, in partnerships of two

Ideal for: 10+

Above: The Jacks are the highest-scoring trumps in Yukon.

SCORING AND CONCLUSION

The highest-scoring card is the J♠, worth 15 points, followed by the other Jacks, which score 10, as do Tens. Aces score five, Kings three and Queens two.

The game ends when a partnership scores 250 points. If the stock is used up, play continues until players run out of cards, when the side with the most points wins.

SCOTCH WHIST

In this straightforward partnership point-trick game, players cut the deck to determine partners – the two high cuts play the two low cuts.

You will need: 36-card deck, Fives and below having been removed; no Jokers; scorecard

Card ranking: Standard, Aces high

Players: Four

Ideal for: 10+

OBJECT

To score points by winning tricks, especially those including the top five trumps.

THE DEAL

The person with the lowest cut deals a hand of nine cards to each player. The last card is turned up and its suit is trumps. It belongs to the dealer, but it stays face-up on the table until the dealer plays to the first trick.

PLAY

The player to the dealer's left leads to the first trick. Players must follow suit if they can, or trump or discard. The highest card of the suit led wins. If a trump is played, the highest trump wins. The winner of the trick sets it aside and leads the next trick. Each trick taken after a team 'makes book' (wins six tricks) counts for one point.

SCORING AND CONCLUSION

The Jack of trumps scores 11 card points, followed by the Ace, worth four, King three, Queen two and Ten scores 10. No other cards count. Players score the point value of any top trumps that they may take in tricks, plus an extra point per card for each card they end up with in excess of the number they were dealt. The first partnership to score 41 points wins the game.

Left: Also known as Catch-the-Ten, this interesting game has a venerable history. In his biography of Samuel Johnson, author James Boswell (pictured) referred to Scotch Whist as Catch-Honours.

REUNION

This 18th-century game from the Rhineland consists of three deals – one by each player.

You will need: 32 cards, Sixes and below having been removed; gambling chips; scorecard

Card ranking: Jack of trumps (Right Bower), the other Jack of the same colour (Left Bower), Aces, Tens, Kings, Queens, non-trump Jacks, Nines, Eights and Sevens

Players: Three

Ideal for: 10+

OBJECT

To win the most card points and to avoid ending up with a score of less than 100, as this carries penalties.

THE DEAL

The player who cuts the lowest deals 10 cards in packets of three, four and three, turning up the second of the final two cards for trumps. The dealer discards two cards – not a Bower or an Ace – face down. Any card points they may be worth go to the dealer at the end of the game.

PLAY

The turn-up is left in place until the second trick has been played. The player to the dealer's left leads. Players must follow suit, if possible, or otherwise trump if possible.

SCORING AND CONCLUSION

Each Bower scores 12 card points, Aces 11, Tens 10, Kings four, Queens three and the other Jacks two. The last trick is worth an extra 10 points. If both Bowers are taken in the same trick, the Left Bower's holder immediately pays a chip to the Right Bower's player.

Play continues until the third deal has been completed. Any player with a score of between 100 and 150 pays the winner a chip. If the score is under 100, the penalty is two chips and, if under 50, three.

Madrasso

Across between Tressette and Briscola, Madrasso is the most popular card game in Venice and its environs. It is usually played with the Venetian patterned 40-card Italian pack, with suits of Swords, Batons, Cups and Coins, equivalent to ♠, ♣, ♥, ♦.

You will need: 40-card deck (Tens to Eights having been removed from a standard pack); scorecard
Card ranking: Ace, Three, King, Queen, Jack and Seven to Two
Players: Four, in fixed partnerships
Ideal for: 14+

Object

A game consists of at least 10 *Battutes* (deals) and the winning partnership is the first to reach the target score of at least 777 points.

The Deal

For the first hand, the dealer is chosen at random; in subsequent hands, the deal passes to the right. Each player is dealt 10 cards, starting with packets of three and two. The next card is turned face up on the table to establish trumps. Three cards each are then dealt to the players, the dealer taking only two, followed by a packet of two cards.

The dealer's face-up card stays on the table until it is played to a trick. However, a player holding the Seven of trumps has the option of exchanging it for the turn-up before playing a card to the first trick.

Scoring

At the end of each deal, each side calculates its score, totalling the point value of the cards it has taken in tricks. The scoring cards are Aces, which are worth 11 points, Threes 10, Kings four, Queens three and Jacks two. In the event of a revoke (that is, if a player fails to follow suit when holding a card of that suit), play stops and the revoking partnership is penalized 130 points. The winners of the last trick receive a 10-point bonus.

Play and Conclusion

The player to the dealer's right leads to the first trick. Players must follow suit if possible, otherwise any card can be played. Each trick is won by the highest trump in it, or, if no trumps are played, by the highest card of the suit led. The winner of each trick leads to the next. Each hand is played until all 10 tricks have been won.

After 10 hands have been played, any player can make a declaration claiming to have reached the 777-point target immediately after taking a trick. Play stops immediately, the claim is checked, the score of the non-scoring partnership being calculated by subtracting the scoring side's total from 1,300. If the claim is upheld, the declaring partnership wins. If it is not upheld, it loses. If neither has reached that total, the game resumes until one does, or one partnership declares that it is out.

Another way of winning is termed *Cappotto*, which means taking all of the 10 tricks in a hand. This is why declarations are not allowed until 10 hands have been played. Even if one partnership has scored 777 points by the eighth or ninth hands, the other could still make *Cappotto* and so steal the game.

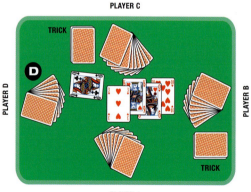

Above: Players B and C here have both won a trick. The dealer's turn-up card (used to determine trumps), the Q♣, is still exposed on the table. Player B lays the 10♥, which is topped by the Queen, King and Three in succession. Player A wins the trick, as Three is highest.

Right: The scoring cards in Madrasso are Aces (worth 11 points), Threes (10), Kings (four), Queens (three) and Jacks (two).

BRISCOLA

One of Italy's most popular card games, Briscola is most notable for the various facial expressions that are allowed as a way of signalling between partners.

OBJECT

To be the first player or partnership to score a game (at least 61 cards points) or a rubber (three games).

THE DEAL

The player cutting the lowest card is the first to deal – the deal subsequently passes to the right. Each player is dealt three cards face down, the next card being turned face up to set trumps. The remaining cards are placed face down on the table to form the stock.

PLAY

The player to the dealer's right leads to the first trick. Unlike most other card games, there is no obligation to follow suit for as long as any cards remain in the stock. The winner of each trick takes the top card from the stock to replenish his hand, followed by all the other players in turn.

When the stock is exhausted, the next to play draws the turn-up and the game continues until all the cards have been played.

Above: A group of men playing cards in Palermo, Sicily, 2004. Briscola remains one of Italy's most popular card games.

You will need: 52-card deck with Tens to Eights removed; plus a Two removed if three are playing; scorecards

Card ranking: Ace highest, then Threes, Kings, Queens, Jacks and Sevens to Twos

Players: Two to three playing solo, or four in partnerships

Ideal for: 10+

SCORING AND CONCLUSION

Aces score 11 points, Threes score 10 points, Kings four points, Queens three points and Jacks score two. The remaining cards are valueless. A two-way or three-way split of card points at the end of a game is a draw. A rubber is the best of five games, a game equating to at least 61 points.

Play continues in each hand until all the tricks have been won. The player or partnership taking the majority of the 120 card points available wins a game.

SIGNALS

When four people play, certain signals are allowed in Briscola so that partnerships can signal certain trump holdings to each other, when neither opponent is looking. These conventional signs are codified as follows:

- Ace – go tight-lipped.
- Three – twist the mouth sideways.
- King – raise eyes upwards.
- Queen – show the tip of the tongue.
- Jack – shrug shoulders.

VARIANT

A chief five-player variant of Briscola is Briscola Bastarda. The chief differences are the introduction of a round of bidding and a secret partnership between the winning bidder and another player.

In the bidding, players estimate the number of points they will take in the game. The highest bidder names a specific card to establish the trump suit and who his partner will be. This is the holder of the specified card. The scores of the caller and holder count together. If the total equals or exceeds the bid, the caller wins two points, the holder a point and each opponent is penalized a point. If the bid is lost, each opponent wins a point, the holder is penalized a point and the caller two.

KING-QUEEN GAMES

AS THE SAYING GOES, MARRIAGES ARE MADE IN HEAVEN. IN KING-QUEEN GAMES ANY PLAYER DECLARING THE 'MARRIAGE' OF THE KING AND QUEEN OF THE SAME SUIT IN THE SAME HAND WINS BONUSES. TYPICALLY, A NON-TRUMP MARRIAGE SCORES 20 POINTS, WHILE A TRUMP (ROYAL) ONE SCORES 40. SUCH GAMES ARE EXCEPTIONALLY FASCINATING BECAUSE, AS EVERY EXPERIENCED CARD PLAYER KNOWS, THEIR OUTCOME IS SO UNPREDICTABLE.

There are several games that share the same basic system of trick-taking and card values, although some introduce an extra element of bidding. Of these intriguing games, the German game Sechsundsechzig (Sixty-Six) – and its Austrian equivalent Schnapsen – is probably one of the best known. It is an exciting game because nearly every card in the deck counts. This means that a player who looks sure to lose can suddenly turn a game on its head and emerge as its winner.

The basic aim is to win points by capturing the most valuable cards and to score bonuses by melding Marriages (matching Kings and Queens). However, there are specific features that make play even more challenging and stimulating. For instance, in many games, players are not allowed to keep scorecards, so they need really clear heads in order to keep track of what is going on as well as good card sense to make the most of the cards.

In Spain and some Latin American countries, Tute is a popular card game. In it, declaring a Marriage is referred to as 'singing' it. A player is only allowed to 'sing' immediately after he has taken a trick. Mariás is the most popular card game in the Czech Republic and Slovakia. Tysiacha, an Eastern European game, is less well known than it should be. Its peculiarity is that bidding must start at 100 points, which means that higher bids can only be fulfilled by declaring King-Queen marriages.

Above: Melding Marriages of the King and Queen of the same suit gains a player bonuses in this group of games.

SECHSUNDSECHZIG (SIXTY-SIX)

This is one of the best card games for two players. Although there is some doubt as to when and where it was invented, Sixty-Six has probably been played at least since the 17th century.

You will need: 52-card deck with Eights and below removed
Card ranking: Ace (highest), Ten, King, Queen, Jack and Nine
Players: Two
Ideal for: 14+

OBJECT

To make Marriages of King and Queens in the same suit or score tricks containing certain cards, and thus to be the first player in each deal to take 66 points.

THE DEAL

Each player gets six cards, dealt in two packets of three. The next card is turned up to establish trumps and half covered with the rest of the cards (the stock) face down.

PLAY

Initially, suit need not be followed, the winner of each trick being the higher card of the suit led or the higher trump. Once a trick has been played, both players (starting with whoever won the trick) replenish their hands with a card from the stock.

After the stock has run out, suit must be followed and no more Marriages may be melded. The stock is often closed before this by a player who thinks 66 points can be won with the cards as they stand. Either player may close when it is their turn to lead by flipping over the turn-up and placing it face down on top of the stock.

TRUMPS AND MARRIAGES

A player with the Nine of trumps can exchange it for the turn-up, provided it is still covered by at least two cards and he has taken a trick. If a player is dealt a Marriage or melds one with a card from the stock, he can claim 20 points for a non-trump Marriage and 40 for a trump one, provided that he has taken a trick, is about to lead to a trick, and at least two cards remain in the stock. The declaring player must lead one of the Marriage cards to the trick. If a player declares a Marriage but fails to take any subsequent tricks, its score is cancelled.

SCORING AND CONCLUSION

Players must keep a mental note of their running score. The Ace, Ten, King, Queen, Jack and Nine count for 11, 10, four, three, two and zero points, respectively. After the last trick, or earlier if either player claims to have

reached 66 points, the hand is scored. In the first case, the player with the most points wins. In the second, if 66 points have been scored , the declarer scores a game point if the opposing score is 33 points or more, two if under 33, and three if zero. If the claim is incorrect, the other player scores two game points, or three if he has not taken a trick. If a player closes and subsequently fails to score 66 points, the penalties are the same. The first player to take seven game points wins the game.

Play in each hand continues until all tricks have been played or until a player claims to have scored 66 points.

Above: The scoring cards are Aces (worth 11 points), Tens (worth 10), Kings (worth four), Queens (worth three) and Jacks (worth two).

PLAYER B

STOCK   TURN-UP

TRICK

D

PLAYER A

Above: A player who is holding the Nine of trumps (the 9♥) can exchange it for the turned-up card, provided he has already taken a trick and that the stock contains at least three cards.

BONDTOLVA

This is a traditional Swedish favourite, the name of which translates as 'farmer's dozen'. Roughly speaking, it is the Swedish equivalent of Sixty-Six, but with a few quirks of its own. The simplest version is for two players.

You will need: 52-card deck with Eights and below removed
Card ranking: Ace, Ten, King, Queen, Jack and Nine
Players: Two
Ideal for: 14+

OBJECT

To be the first to get to 12 points by melding Marriages (King and Queen of same suit), winning *Matadors* (Aces and Tens) and taking the last trick.

THE DEAL

The two players are dealt six cards each, three at a time, the other cards being stacked face down to form the stock.

PLAY

The first player to declare a Marriage establishes which suit is trumps. The non-dealer leads. Each trick is taken by the higher card of the suit led, or by the higher trump once trumps have been fixed, but players do not have to follow suit or trump. The winner of each trick draws the top card of the stock, followed by the other player, and leads to the next trick. Once the stock is exhausted no Marriages are allowed; the second to play must follow suit, playing a higher card if possible, or play a trump.

Above: In Bondtolva, Aces and Tens, the top- and second top-ranking trumps, are known as *Matadors.*

SCORING

Aces score four points, Kings three, Queens two and Jacks one. The Nine is valueless. The first Marriage to be declared scores two points; subsequent Marriages score a point. The bonus for winning the last trick is a point, as is the bonus for taking the majority of Aces and Tens. If the scores are equal, the point for the latter goes to the player with the most card points. If the scores are still equal, neither player scores the bonus point. To win the game, a player needs to score exactly 12 points.

CONCLUSION

Play in each hand continues until all tricks have been played or until a player scores 12 points. A player scoring over 12 must deduct the excess from his previous total.

VARIANTS

There are three- and four-player versions of the game, which are played in much the same way with a few minor differences. The four-player version is played in partnerships. Before trumps are established, the player leading the trick can ask if his partner holds a Marriage, or, if holding one card of a Marriage, if the partner can pair it. The next trick must then be started, if possible, from the declared Marriage. Once trumps are fixed, a player can ask the first question again, in which case that suit must be led to win the point, or lead a King or a Queen and ask the partner to wed it.

PLAYER B

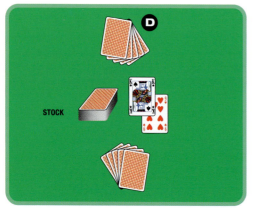

PLAYER A

Above: Player A has led the 9♥ to the first trick. Since no Marriages have been melded yet, there are no trumps, so Player B, unable to follow suit, discards the K♠. Player A therefore wins the trick and picks up a card from the stock, followed by Player B.

TUTE

One of the most popular card games in Spain and in Spanish-speaking Latin America, Tute exists in many forms. The two-player version called Tute Corriento is the oldest form of the game and is the one described here.

You will need: 52-card deck with Tens to Eights removed

Card ranking: Ace, Three, King, Queen, Jack and then Seven to Two

Players: Two

Ideal for: 14+

OBJECT

To be the first to score 101 points by winning tricks, declaring Marriages and taking the last trick.

THE DEAL

The two players deal in turn, six cards to each player. The next card is placed face up on the table to determine the trump suit. The remaining cards are placed face down across it to form the stock.

PLAY

The non-dealer leads to the first trick. Until the stock is exhausted, there is no need to follow suit or trump. The winner of a trick draws the top card of the stock and the loser draws the next. The face-up trump forms the last card of the stock. When the stock runs out, the second to play must follow suit, playing a higher card if he can, or, if possible, trumping.

EXCHANGING AND SINGING

A turned-up Ace, Three or court card (a King, Queen or Jack) can be exchanged for the Seven of trumps. If a Four, Five, Six or Seven, it can be exchanged for the Two of trumps. To signal an exchange, a player places the appropriate card under the turned-up one, and the exchange occurs when that player takes a trick. If the stock runs out before then, the original card is reclaimed.

A player who holds the King and Queen of the same suit can score extra points by declaring ('singing') them, and showing the two cards. This can only be done immediately after winning a trick and before leading to the next. A player having more than one such combination must win another trick before being allowed to declare it. However, if a player holds four Kings or Queens (a *tute*), he can sing them after winning a trick and immediately wins the game. If a player has a Marriage in a trump and a non-trump suit, the trump suit must be declared first. When declaring a Marriage in a non-trump suit, the suit should be named.

SCORING

Aces score 11 points, Threes 10, Kings four, Queens three and Jacks two. Ten points are awarded to the player taking the last trick. A non-trump Marriage (King and Queen of same suit) scores 20 points and a trump Marriage (King and Queen of trump suit) scores 40.

PLAYER B

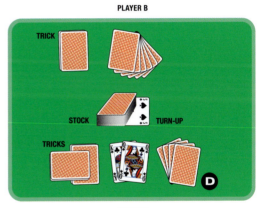

PLAYER A

Above: Player A here, having just won a second trick to Player B's one, sings a Marriage by showing a King and Queen of the same suit. Trumps being Spades, this is a non-trump Marriage, which scores 20 points.

CONCLUSION

Declaring a *Tute* wins the game outright. Otherwise, after the last trick, both players count the points they have won for cards in tricks, singing Marriage and for taking the last trick. If neither has scored 101 points, there is a second deal, the points won in that being added to those taken in the first. If either player thinks that he has scored 101 points, this can be declared and play stops. Such a declaration must be made immediately before leading a trick. If the claim is correct, the declaring player wins; if not, he loses.

TYSIACHA

In Russian-speaking countries, this three-player game is known by the above name. In Poland, it is called Tysiac. Both words mean '1,001' – the target score needed to win the game, and are basically the same game, but with slight variations.

You will need: 24 card-deck (Eights and below having been removed from a standard pack); scorecard

Card ranking: Ace, Ten, King, Queen, Jack and Nine

Players: Three, or four with dealer sitting out the hand

Ideal for: 14+

OBJECT

To be the first to score 1,001 points or more.

THE DEAL

Seven cards are dealt singly to each player. Three cards, termed the *prikup*, are then dealt face down on the table.

BIDDING

Following the deal, players bid to determine who will be the soloist against the other two players. The first bid must be at least 100 points, following which bids go up in fives. Bids over 120 are not allowed unless the player making the bid has a Marriage in hand.

The soloist takes the *Prikup*. He can increase the bid, or, if he decides there is little likelihood of honouring it, he can declare *Rospisat* (that he concedes). In this case, each opposing player scores 60 points. A player declaring *Rospisat* is not penalized on the first two occasions, but on the third, and every third time thereafter, 120 points are deducted from his score.

The soloist passes a card face down to each opponent, so that all three players have eight cards in hand. Any player holding the four Nines can now opt to show them and ask for a new deal.

PLAY

Trumps are established when the first Marriage is declared, although they can be changed by the declaration of a subsequent Marriage. Declaring a Marriage involves showing both cards, announcing their suit and leading either of them to the next trick.

SCORING AND CONCLUSION

An Ace scores 11, Ten 10, King four, Queen three, Jack two and Nine zero card points. A Marriage (King and Queen of same suit) scores 100 points in Hearts, 80 in Diamonds, 60 in Clubs and 40 in Spades. If the soloist scores at least the value of the bid, this is added to his score. If not, the value is subtracted from it. The other

Left: If a player holding this hand is passed a fourth Nine by the soloist, he can call for a new deal.

players score the full value of card points taken in tricks, rounding them up or down to the nearest five, plus the value of any Marriages they may have melded.

Scoring between 880 and 1,000 is against the rules. If this happens, the player is said to be 'on the barrel', a fact indicated by drawing a box on his scorecard. The score is pegged at 880 and the player is given three chances to score 120 points and win the game. In the event of failure, the player 'falls off the barrel' and is penalized 120 points. If either opposing player fails to take any points in tricks three times, he is penalized 120 points on the third occasion. From that point onward, he loses 120 points every third time this occurs. Play continues until all the tricks have been played.

Right: In Tysiacha, a Marriage of the King and Queen of Spades scores 40 points, in Hearts 100 points, in Diamonds 80 points and in Clubs 60 points.

GAIGEL

This game has spread from southern Germany and Switzerland to the USA, where it has been adapted for two players. It is a three- or four-player game, the latter played in partnerships. There is no universally accepted set of rules, and the game is played differently from place to place. The partnership version is described here.

OBJECT

To be the first side to win or exceed 101 points in counters and Marriages, or to detect that the opposing side has done so and failed to claim their win before leading to the next trick.

THE DEAL AND PLAY

After shuffling the two 24-card packs together, each player is dealt five cards, and the next card is turned up to establish trumps. The cards left over form the stock. As long as there are cards left in the stock, there is no necessity to follow suit, but when it is exhausted, players must do so, head the trick if possible (play a higher card than any so far played to the trick), or otherwise trump and overtrump. A trick's winner draws the top card of the stock, the other players then drawing in turn.

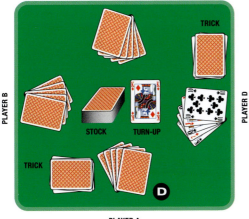

PLAYER C

TRICK

PLAYER B

STOCK   TURN-UP

PLAYER D

TRICK

D

PLAYER A

Above: Holding the Seven of trumps (known as the *Dix*), Player D can exchange it for the turn-up at any time, provided the partnership has taken at least one trick and the stock contains at least three cards.

You will need: Two 52-card decks, each with Nines, Eights and cards below Seven removed; counters

Card ranking: Ace (highest), Ten, King, Queen, Jack, Seven

Players: Three, or four playing in partnerships. The partnership version is explained here

Ideal for: 14+

When players play to a trick, they are allowed to declare a Marriage (King and Queen of same suit) if they hold one, but no more than one Marriage in the same deal. Such a declaration can be made only if the declaring partnership has already taken a trick, or if the card to be played takes the trick for them. The declaring player shows both cards and then plays one of them. A non-trump Marriage scores 20 points, a trump one 40.

TAKING THE TURN-UP

A player with the Seven of trumps, the *Dix*, can exchange it for the turn-up at any time, provided that the partnership has taken at least one trick and at least three cards remain in the stock.

Alternatively, the player can place the Seven under the turn-up for his partner to pick up if he holds the other Seven. His partner may decide to take the turn-up and pass across the other Seven. If he is not holding the other Seven and one of the opposing partners then plays it, the first player can pick up the turn-up immediately.

SCORING

Aces score 11 points, Tens 10 and the court cards – Kings, Queens and Jacks – score four, three and two points respectively. Sevens are worthless and count for nothing.

CONCLUSION

Play stops when either side claims to have taken 101 or more points, or when the opposing partnership has done so but neglected to declare it before leading to the next trick. If correct, the claiming partnership wins a single game. If its opponents have not taken a trick, they win a double game or *Gaigel*. If the claim is wrong, the other side wins a *Gaigel*. Claiming a win incorrectly is known as 'overgaigling' and failing to claim a win is 'undergaigling'.

MARIÁS

Closely related to the Hungarian game Ulti, the most popular version of Mariás is for three players, although four can play it. In the three-player game, one player becomes the soloist, playing against the other two in partnership. In its Czech homeland, Mariás is customarily played with a 32-card German-suited pack, but here a reduced standard pack has been substituted.

OBJECT

To win a clear majority of the points available. This is at least 90, but can rise as high as 190 when Marriage declarations are taken into account.

You will need: 52-card deck with Sixes and below removed

Card ranking: Aces, Tens, Kings, Queens, Jacks, Nines, Eights and Sevens

Players: Three, or four with the dealer sitting out the hand

Ideal for: 14+

THE DEAL

The first dealer is chosen at random, after which the deal passes to the left for each subsequent hand. Before the deal, the player to the dealer's right must cut the 32-card pack. The dealer then gives a packet of seven cards face-down to Forehand (the player to the dealer's left) and continues dealing clockwise in packets of five, so that after two rounds of dealing, Forehand has 12 cards and the other two players each have 10. At this stage, Forehand is only allowed to pick up and look at the first seven cards dealt; Forehand's other five cards are left face down on the table until trumps have been chosen. The other players may look at all 10 of their cards.

Right: In Mariás, Aces and Tens are the only scoring cards. Known as 'sharp cards', they are worth 10 points each. Points are also scored for melds and winning the last trick.

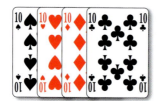

Below: After the deal, Forehand can only look at the first seven cards he has been dealt and choose a trump suit from them should he wish. The strong Diamond suit looks a good bet.

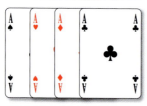

CHOOSING TRUMPS

Forehand proposes a trump suit, bids first and leads to the first trick, the next being Middlehand and the third Rearhand. To choose trumps, Forehand examines the first seven cards in his hand. If he elects to choose the trump suit from them, he turns up the appropriate card. If not, he can 'choose from the people' – that is, by selecting any card from the five remaining ones sight unseen, turning it up as before. He then takes all the cards except for the turn-up and discards two, face down. An Ace or Ten cannot be discarded and if the discards include a trump, Forehand must say so.

CHOOSING THE CONTRACT

Forehand starts by bidding Suit, a game with trumps, that only he can play as soloist. Either opponent can veto this by bidding *Betl* or *Durch*. Both are no-trump bids. In *Betl*, the opposing players win if they can force the soloist into taking a trick. In *Durch*, the soloist loses if his opponents win a trick. There are open options for each bid in which players' cards are placed face up on the table after the first trick has been played. Such bids double the score. In Suit, the soloist has to win more points than the combined scores of the opposing players.

Various bonuses augment scores. For the soloist, Seven is an undertaking to win the last trick with the Seven of trumps; Hundred is one to win 100 points or more without melding more than one Marriage.

Both bids can be combined. A Double Seven is an undertaking to win the last trick with a Seven and the trick before that with another one. The opposing players can make identical announcements by adding 'Against' to the bids.

DOUBLING AND REDOUBLING

To double, either of the opposing players can call '*Flek*', the soloist having the option of redoubling by calling '*Re*'. The opponents can then double again by saying '*Tutti*', which the soloist can redouble by announcing '*Retutti*'. How this is done depends on the type of contract.

If *Betl* or *Durch* is to be played, the option to double goes hand in hand with the final determination of the contract. There are three possible responses to its announcement: 'Good', which means that it is accepted as it stands; 'Bad', which means that the player making the call is prepared to play higher; and '*Flek*', which doubles the contract's value as explained above. In a Suit contract, the opponents simply answer 'Good' or 'Bad'. As well as starting the doubling processes, players can now announce for which bonuses they intend to play.

PLAY

In Suit contracts, following suit, playing a higher card of the same suit to lead to the trick or playing a trump is obligatory, if possible. In non-trump contracts, the first two conditions apply. In a Suit contract, any player announcing a Marriage (King and Queen of same suit) must play the Queen and announce the appropriate score before playing the King. The cards of a Marriage

Above: An example of 18th-century German playing cards showing the four suits of Acorns, Leaves, Hearts and Bells. In its Czech homeland, Mariás is traditionally played with a 32-card German-suited pack.

are kept separate from the trick and left face up in front of the player scoring them, so that they can be checked afterwards when scores are totalled.

SCORING AND CONCLUSION

Play continues until all tricks have been played. Aces and Tens, known as the 'sharp cards', are the only cards to score and are worth 10 points each. Melding a non-trump Marriage scores 20 points, and melding a trump Marriage scores 40. A further 10 points are awarded for taking the last trick. A successful Suit contract scores a point for game, while *Betl* scores five points and *Durch* scores 10 points.

Unannounced bonuses are worth a point for Quiet Seven and Killed Quiet Seven – that is, when the Seven of trumps is beaten on the last trick – and two for Quiet Hundred. In this, every extra 10 scored over 100 is worth another two points. Announced bonuses – Seven, Seven Against, Killed Seven, Hundred and Hundred Against – score double. All bonus scores are also doubled if the trump suit was Hearts. Revoking costs the offender 20 points – 10 to each of the other players – or the value of the contract plus bonuses, whichever is more. If Forehand bids the basic game and no extras are added or doubles made, it is taken that the opposing players have conceded, and Forehand scores accordingly.

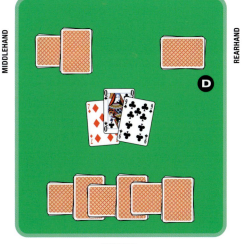

Above: Forehand not only takes the final trick (winning seven to his opponents' combined total of three) but does so with the Seven of trumps (in this case, Diamonds). If he had announced during the bidding the intention of winning the last trick with the Seven of trumps, he would have scored two bonus points. Unannounced, he scores a single extra point.

Queen-Jack Games

GAMES SUCH AS BEZIQUE AND PINOCHLE STAND THE CONCEPT OF MARRIAGE ON ITS HEAD BY ALLOWING MELDS (SETS OF MATCHING CARDS) BETWEEN THE Q♠ AND THE J♦. THESE ARE KNOWN AS BEZIQUES AND CAN BE EITHER SINGLE OR DOUBLE. THERE ARE ALSO SCORES FOR HOLDING FOUR OF A KIND, OR SAME-SUIT SEQUENCES. IN BEZIQUE, EVEN IF A PLAYER STARTS WITH POOR CARDS, SKILFUL BUILDING OF MELDS MEANS THAT HE MAY WELL END UP A WINNER.

Although originally conceived for only two players, other versions of Bezique for more players developed, while the size of the deck, originally 32 cards, also increased to make games last longer. Two-pack Bezique was all the rage in Paris in the 1840s, while Rubicon Bezique, which is played with four decks totalling 128 cards, originated in London slightly later. Chinese Bezique, which was Sir Winston Churchill's favourite card game, is played with six packs.

Pinochle, the American counterpart of Bezique, remains one of the country's most popular card games. Its basic form is Two-handed Pinochle, although Partnership Pinochle, Partnership Auction Pinochle and Double-Pack Pinochle are all games for four players, two against two as partners. Auction Pinochle is the most popular form of the game for three. In general terms, players score for melds and tricks that contain specified scoring cards. The game can seem over-complex, particularly in the second stage of the game, when players have to take back the cards in the melds they have previously declared, but it more than repays the effort of learning it.

Marjolet is an elegant game for two players that is popular in southwest France. As in other games of this genre, part of the excitement comes from the balancing of the cards that are played to tricks against those that are kept in hand in the hope of making melds. To heighten the tension, some players allow the scoring of only one meld after winning a trick.

Above: Original boxed set of the Royal game of Bezique, which was manufactured by Godall & Son, London (1910).

BEZIQUE

A game called Hoc, played at Louis XIV's court at Versailles, may be the origin of Bezique. The improved two-pack version then became the height of fashion in Paris in the 1840s.

You will need: 64 cards (two standard packs with all cards below Seven removed)

Card ranking: Ace, Ten, King, Queen, Jack, Nine, Eight and Seven

Players: Two

Ideal for: 14+

OBJECT

To be the first to reach 1,000 points over as many deals as necessary, dealing alternately.

THE DEAL

Eight cards are dealt to each player in packets of three, two and three. The next card is turned up to establish trumps and the remaining cards are placed face down to form the stock. If the turn-up is a Seven, the dealer scores 10.

PLAY

The non-dealer leads. The trick is taken by the higher-ranking card of the suit led, or by a trump. At this stage, there is no need to follow suit. If both players play the same card, the leading card takes the trick. The winner of the trick can declare a scoring combination, laying the cards face up. These can still be used to take future tricks and to help to form new combinations, although they cannot be used twice in the same combination. The declaring player draws the top card of the stock followed by the opposing player, and leads to the next trick.

A player with the Seven of trumps may exchange it for the trump turn-up after taking a trick as an alternative to declaring a combination.

SCORING

Brisques (Aces and Tens) taken in tricks score 10 points. Scoring combinations, from highest to lowest, are:

- Double Bezique (two Q♠ and two J♦): 500 points.
- Same-suit sequence of Ace, Ten, King, Queen and Jack of trumps: 250 points.
- Any four Aces: 100 points.
- Any four Kings: 80 points.
- Any four Queens: 60 points.
- Any four Jacks: 40 points.
- Single Bezique (between Q♠ and J♦): 40 points.
- Royal Marriage (between the King and Queen of trumps): 40 points.
- Common Marriage of a non-trump King and Queen: 20 points.

Also, any player may show a Seven of trumps and win 10 points. There are 10 bonus points for winning the last trick.

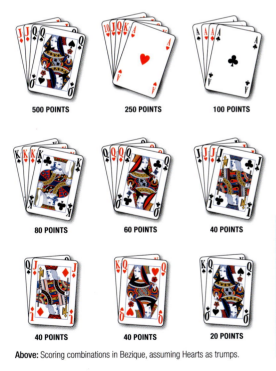

500 POINTS	250 POINTS	100 POINTS
80 POINTS	60 POINTS	40 POINTS
40 POINTS	40 POINTS	20 POINTS

Above: Scoring combinations in Bezique, assuming Hearts as trumps.

CONCLUSION

Once the stock is exhausted, suit must be followed and trumps played if this is impossible. The player taking the final trick wins a bonus 10 points. No further declarations are allowed. Play continues until one player has reached or exceeded a total of 1,000 points. If the losing player has scored under 500 points, he is 'rubiconed', and the winner scores a double game.

MARJOLET

Simpler to play than Bezique, Marjolet allows the Jack of trumps – the Marjolet – to be melded (matched) to the four different Queens. Indeed, a Queen may be melded to the Marjolet and to her matching King at the same time.

You will need:	52-card deck with Sixes and below removed
Card ranking:	Ace, Ten, King, Queen, Jack and Nine to Seven
Players:	Two
Ideal for:	14+

OBJECT

To score points by taking Aces and Tens, so-called *Brisques*, in tricks and by declaring melds (sets of matched cards).

THE DEAL

Both players receive six cards. The next card turned up sets trumps; the remainder of the pack forms the stock.

PLAY

There is no need to follow suit. The trick is taken by the higher card of the suit led, or by a trump played to a non-trump lead. Both players take a card from the stock. The player who won the trick leads to the next. Before this, the winner can declare any meld. All melds are placed face up in front of the declaring player. His cards can still be used in trick play and to make other melds.

Once the stock runs out, both players take their melds into hand. For the last six tricks, suit must be followed and a higher card played, if possible. Otherwise, a trump must be played, again if possible. Melds may still be declared.

SCORING

If the Seven of trumps (the *Dix*) is turned up at the start of play by the dealer, he wins 10 points, while a player holding it can exchange it for the turn-up after taking a trick. The score for the exchange is 10 points. If the player opts not to exchange, the *Dix* still scores 10 when it is played, regardless of whether the trick is won or lost.

Winning the last trick is worth a bonus of 10 points, while, should a player succeed in taking all six tricks, he receives a bonus of 50 points. Each player then sorts through the cards he has won and scores 10 for each *Brisque* he has taken.

> ## MELDS
>
> The winner of a trick can declare any of the following melds:
>
> - Four Aces – 100 points.
> - Four Tens – 80 points.
> - Four Kings – 60 points.
> - Four Queens – 40 points.
> - Marriage between the King and Queen of trumps – 40 points.
> - Marriage between the King and Queen of a non-trump suit – 20 points.
> - Marriage between the Jack of trumps and any trump or non-trump Queen – 20 points.

100 POINTS	80 POINTS	60 POINTS
40 POINTS	40 POINTS	20 POINTS	20 POINTS

Above: Scoring combinations in Marjolet, assuming Hearts as trumps.

CONCLUSION

Play continues until all tricks have been taken. The winning score can be either 500 or 1,000 points.

Above: in Marjolet, it is possible to meld the Jack of trumps (in this example, Clubs) with any of the four Queens.

PINOCHLE

Closely related to Bezique, Pinochle started life in the USA as a two-player game, but there are now three- and four-handed versions, plus ones for five or more players. Auction Pinochle, described here, is the most popular three-handed form.

You will need: Two 24-card decks (Eights and below having been removed from two standard packs)

Card ranking: Ace, Ten, King, Queen, Jack and Nine

Players: Three in this version, although can be two to five

Ideal for: 14+

OBJECT

To make as many points as bid from melds (matches) declared from hand after taking the widow. Card points are made in tricks, with extra for winning the last trick.

THE DEAL AND BIDDING

Each player is dealt 15 cards three at a time. Three cards are placed face down to form the widow (stock). The player to the dealer's left bids first. All bids must be multiples of 10 and the opening one must be at least 300 (unless agreed otherwise). The highest bidder takes the widow, discarding three cards face down, announces trumps and declares any melds. If these fulfil his bid, there is no play and he scores the value of his game.

The bidder can also concede if he doubts he can fulfil his bid in play. He loses only his game value, as opposed to twice the game value if he plays and fails.

PLAY

The bidder leads to the first trick. Suit must be followed and, if possible, a player has to 'kill', that is, play a higher card of the same suit. If not, a trump must be played. Otherwise, a player can 'slough' or discard any card. The highest card of the suit led, or the highest trump if any are played, wins the trick. The trick's winner leads to the next.

SCORING

There are two ways of scoring points, through melding combinations and winning scoring cards in tricks. Aces, Tens and Kings are called counters and are worth 10 points each, while Queens, Jacks and Nines count for nothing. The winner of the last trick scores an extra 10 points.

If the bid is made, the bidder scores the points taken in melds and play. If not, the bidder 'goes out' with the bid being deducted from his score. The other players score the same way, provided that they have captured at least one counter. If not, they score nothing. All scores are doubled when Spades are trumps. Frequently, although not always, Hearts as trumps triple the scores.

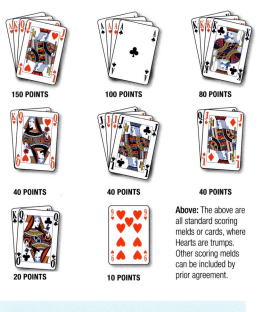

150 POINTS   **100 POINTS**   **80 POINTS**

40 POINTS   **40 POINTS**   **40 POINTS**

20 POINTS   **10 POINTS**

Above: The above are all standard scoring melds or cards, where Hearts are trumps. Other scoring melds can be included by prior agreement.

CONCLUSION

Play continues until all tricks have been taken. The first player to score 1,500 or more points wins.

JACK-NINE GAMES

WHAT DIFFERENTIATES THESE GAMES FROM OTHERS OF THE MARRIAGE FAMILY IS THE PROMOTION OF THE JACK TO THE HIGHEST-RANKING TRUMP, WITH A VALUE OF 20, FOLLOWED BY THE NINE WITH A VALUE OF 14. BELOTE IS THE NATIONAL GAME OF FRANCE, AND KLAVERJAS THE FAVOURITE IN THE NETHERLANDS, WHILE IN SWITZERLAND AND AUSTRIA, JACK-NINE GAMES ARE UNIVERSALLY POPULAR. THE GAMES ARE SO SIMILAR THAT IF YOU MASTER ONE IT IS EASY TO LEARN ANOTHER.

Although authorities on the history of card games agree that the first Jack-Nine games probably originated in the Netherlands, it was undoubtedly the Swiss who honed them until they reached their present sophisticated status. Indeed, these so-called Jass games have become so popular in Switzerland that others which have nothing to do with them have been classified as kinds of Jass, while Swiss cards have come to be known as Jass cards.

A standard Jass pack consists of 36 cards in suits of Bells, Shields, Acorns and Flowers. The French-suit equivalents are Hearts, Diamonds, Clubs and Spades. The name Jass (pronounced 'yass') is thought to originate from Jasper, which was the Dutch name for the knave in the 18th century.

The French version, Belote, became the most popular card game in the country in the mid-20th century. A close relative of Klaberjass and of Klaverjas, the Dutch national card game, it has spawned many variants of its own. Of these, the most interesting is probably Coinche, which now rivals its precursor in the popularity stakes. It has one particularly novel feature. In order to make a declaration during the bidding stage of the game, players have to bang their fists on the table. Schieber Jass, a long-established Swiss game for four players playing in partnerships, also has an unusual feature – an elaborate scoring system, in which, at least traditionally, scores are chalked on a slate painted with two Zs.

Above: A Swiss card deck, also known as Jass cards, which consist of 36 cards in suits of Bells, Shields, Acorns and Flowers.

KLABERJASS

This popular two-hander is known in Britain as Clob, Clobby or Clobiosh, while in the USA it is known as Klob, Kalabriasze or Klabber. It is also sometimes called Bela. In trumps, the Jack and Nine – the *Jass* and the *Menel* or *Mi* – are promoted over the Ace. As well as the two-player version, there are three- and four-player variants.

OBJECT

To reach or exceed a total of 500 points.

THE DEAL

Each player receives six cards three at a time. The next card is turned up to establish a possible trump suit and the remainder placed face down to form the stock. Once trumps have been decided (see below), three more cards are dealt to both. A player holding the Seven of trumps, the *Dix*, can then exchange it for the trump turn-up.

BIDDING

The bidding that follows establishes whether either player accepts the turned-up suit as trumps. The non-dealer can either pass, say 'Take it' or say '*Schmeiss*'.

Left: In trumps (here, assumed as Spades) the Jack (known as the *Jass*) and Nine (known as the *Menel*, or *Mi*), rank above the Ace.

Below: A same-suit sequence of three in Klaberjass is a *Terz* and scores 20 points, but it would score nothing if the other player holds a better sequence. This could either be one of three cards running Queen, King or Ace, or a sequence of four cards or more, known as a *Halbe*, which counts for 50.

You will need: 32-card deck (Sixes and below having been removed from a standard pack); scorecards

Card ranking: Ace, Ten, King, Queen, Jack, Nine, Eight, Seven, except in trumps, where the *Jass* (Jack of trumps) ranks highest, followed by the *Menel* (Nine of trumps)

Players: Two (though three to four versions exist)

Ideal for: 14+

Schmeiss is an offer to become the Maker with the turned suit as trumps and has to be agreed by the dealer. Otherwise, the deal is annulled. If the non-dealer passes, the dealer has the same choices.

PLAY AND SCORING

Before the trick is led, either player holding a sequence of three or more cards must announce the fact. A *Terz*, a sequence of three cards, is worth 20 points, while a *Halbe*, a sequence of four or more, counts for 50. It is only the player with the best sequence who can score. Any *Halbe* beats a *Terz*, a *Terz* with a higher top card beats one with a lower top card, and a *Terz* in trumps is better than one in a plain suit. To determine who has the best sequence, the non-dealer announces 'Twenty' or 'Fifty' on leading to the first trick. The dealer replies 'Good' if he cannot match the number, or 'Not Good' if he can beat it. The questions 'How many cards?', 'How high?' and 'In trumps?' can also be asked.

A *Belle*, the King and Queen of trumps, is worth 20 points. Unlike the preceding melds, or matches, it is not announced until one of its cards is played to a trick. A 60-*Terz* is the term applied to describe a *Terz* of the King, Queen and Jack of trumps. It is worth 60 points.

Winning the last trick scores 10 extra points. The *Jass* is worth 20 points, Nines 14, Aces 11, Tens 10, Kings four, Queens three and the other Jacks two.

CONCLUSION

At the end of the hand, both players declare their totals. If the Maker has scored higher, both players score the points they made. If not, his opponent scores the total made by both players. If equal, the Maker scores nothing and the opposing player scores what he took. The first to score 500 or more points in melds and card points wins.

BELOTE

Although it came to France only in about 1914, Belote is now the country's most popular card game. Two, three or four players can play it, but the four-player partnership version described here is the one most often played.

You will need: 52-card deck wtih Sixes and below removed

Card ranking: Trumps: Jack, Nine, Ace, Ten, King, Queen, Eight and Seven. Plain suits: Ace, Ten, King, Queen, Jack and Nine to Seven

Players: Two to three, or four in partnerships of two, as here

Ideal for: 14+

OBJECT

To score as many points as possible through taking tricks and making melds (matches).

THE DEAL

Five cards are dealt to each player three and two at a time. The next card is turned face up. The player to the dealer's right can now 'take' (that is, choose the suit of the turned-up card as trumps) or pass. If the latter, each player gets the same option. If all pass, each has another chance to 'take', this time, naming a trump suit other than the turn-up. If everyone passes again, there is a new deal but the pack is not shuffled. The player who 'takes' becomes the Taker and picks up the turn-up. The others are dealt three more cards, with the Taker getting two.

PLAY

The player to the dealer's right leads. Players must follow suit, trump, over- or undertrump, or discard any card.

SCORING AND CONCLUSION

The Jack of trumps is worth 20 points, the Nine of trumps 14, Aces 11, Tens 10, Kings four, Queens three and the other Jacks two. The other Nines, Eights and Sevens are valueless. When declaring *Belote* and *Rebelote*, *Belote* is

---

MELDS

Various types of meld score, namely:

- *Carré* (Four of a Kind – can consist of all four Jacks, Nines, Aces, Tens, Kings or Queens) – four Jacks scores 200 points, four Nines 150 and the others 100 points each.
- *Cent* (a sequence of five or more cards of the same suit) – 50.
- *Cinquante* (a sequence of four cards of the same suit) – 50.
- *Tierce* (a sequence of three cards of the same suit) – 20.
- *Belote* and *Rebelote* (the King and Queen of trumps) – 20.

---

declared first, followed by *Rebelote* when the Queen is played. Apart from this, only the partnership with the highest declaration can score.

The last trick scores an extra 10 points, the *Dix de Der*, for the partnership winning it. If the taker's partnership wins at least as many points as its opponents, both sides score all the points they have made. If not, they are *dedans* (inside). Their opponents score 162 points, to which they add the value of the taking side's declarations plus their own. If the taker's partnership wins all nine, it scores *Capot* (100 points) not *Dix de Der*.

Play continues until one partnership has scored 1,000 or 1,500 points (as agreed before play starts).

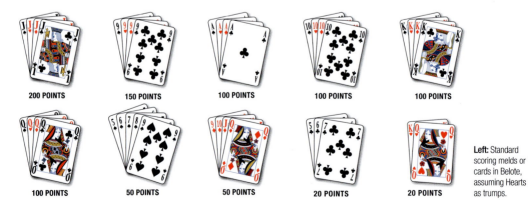

| 200 POINTS | 150 POINTS | 100 POINTS | 100 POINTS | 100 POINTS |

| 100 POINTS | 50 POINTS | 50 POINTS | 20 POINTS | 20 POINTS |

Left: Standard scoring melds or cards in Belote, assuming Hearts as trumps.

COINCHE

This is a popular version of Belote, with the unique feature that players have to bang the table to signal a declaration. Its name derives from the twist that players can *coincher* (double) and redouble each other's bids.

You will need: 52-card deck minus Sixes and below; scorecards

Card ranking: Trumps: Jack, Nine, Ace, Ten, King, Queen, Eight and Seven. Plain suits: Ace, Ten, King, Queen, Jack and Nine to Seven

Players: Four, in partnerships of two

Ideal for: 14+

OBJECT

To score points through taking tricks, holding the King and Queen of trumps, or achieving the highest meld.

THE DEAL

The players are dealt eight cards before bidding starts.

BIDDING

Whether or not there is a trump suit depends on the contract to be played – a suit contract, a no trump contract or an all trump one. In the bidding, the aim is to take more than half the trick points available and to score more points in tricks and melds (matched set of cards) than the other partnership. The convention is to bid a number followed by a contract, the lowest permissible number being 80. Subsequent bids go up in multiples of 10. Bidding ends when the other players all pass, or when an opponent doubles the bid, unless the bidding partnership redoubles. The traditional way of signalling a double is to bang a first on the table – in fact, *coinche* means 'fist' in French.

When declaring *Belote* and *Rebelote*, *Belote* is declared first, followed by *Rebelote,* when the Queen is played. Apart from this, only the partnership with the highest declaration can score. If two declarations appear equal, the second to declare asks 'How high?' and the previous declarer must give a clearer and truthful indication accordingly.

MELDS

On playing to the first trick, players announce their highest meld – the possible combinations are the same as in Belote, namely:

- *Carré* (Four of a Kind) – four Jacks scores 200 points, four Nines 150, and four Aces, Tens, Kings or Queens 100 points.
- *Cent* (a sequence of five or more cards of the same suit) – 50.
- *Cinquante* (a sequence of four cards of the same suit) – 50.
- *Tierce* (a sequence of three cards of the same suit) – 20.
- *Belote* and *Rebelote* (the King and Queen of trumps) – 20.

PLAY

If the lead is a trump, players must follow suit, playing a higher card if possible. If a plain suit is led, it is not necessary to head the trick (play a higher card). If an opponent is winning with a trump, a higher one must be played, but if it is a partner any card can be discarded.

SCORING AND CONCLUSION

At the end of play, both partnerships calculate how much they have won in trick-points and melds. Aces are worth 200 points, Tens 150, and Kings, Queens, Jacks 100 each. Taking the last trick is worth 10 points, while announcing *Belote* and *Rebelote*, the King and Queen of trumps, scores 20 points, except in a non-trump contract.

If the declaring partnership is successful, both sides score the points that they have made and the declarers add the value of the contract to their total. If not, they score zero, their opponents winning 160 trick points, the value of their melds and the value of the lost contract. All scores are affected by any doubling. Game is 3,000 points.

Left: An unusual feature of Coinche is that players have to bang the table to signal a declaration.

Left: When declaring *Belote* and *Rebelote* (the King and Queen of trumps, which here are Clubs), *Belote* is declared first, followed by *Rebelote* when the Queen is played.

BOONAKEN

Closely related to another Dutch game called Pandoeren, this is faster, less complicated and decidedly less serious. In all probability, it gets its name from the Dutch for the three highest trumps – *Boer, Nel, Aass*, or Jack, Nine, Ace.

You will need: 32-card deck (Sixes and below having been removed from a standard pack); scorecard

Card ranking: Trumps: Jack (highest), Nine, Ace, King, Queen, Ten, Eight, Seven. Plain suits: Ace (highest) down to Seven

Players: Five is optimal

Ideal for: 14+

OBJECT

To find a loser, who has to pay for a round of drinks.

BIDDING

The player to the left of the dealer bids first. A number bid is an undertaking to win that many points in tricks and *Roem*, which are specific card combinations (see Scoring). A no-trump bid to lose every trick is *Misère* and a bid to take them all is *Zwabber*. *Boonaak* is the same as *Zwabber* but with trumps. *Boonaak* plus a number is a bid to win all the tricks plus that score in *Roem*. Bidding continues until three players pass in succession.

THE DEAL

Six cards each are dealt three at a time, and two cards are placed face up on the table, one after each packet has been dealt. The successful bidder uses these cards to improve his hand by exchanging and discarding. If the bid is a number or a *Boonaak*, he also chooses the trump suit.

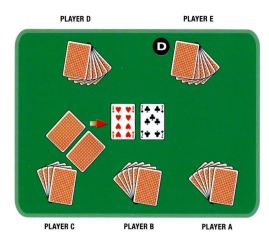

PLAYER D   **PLAYER E**

PLAYER C   **PLAYER B**   **PLAYER A**

Above: The declarer (Player C), can improve his hand by exchanging up to two cards with the two in the centre. Having bid *Misère*, Player C in this instance discards two high cards and picks up the 8♥ and 7♣.

PLAY

The successful bidder leads to the first trick. If the bid is a number bid, he must also announce *Roem* at this stage. The amount announced must be equal to or more than the number bid. If an opposing player has *Roem* in hand worth at least as much as the *Roem* the successful bidder has announced, he announces it as well. If it is worth more than the bidder's, the latter's *Roem* is cancelled and does not count towards winning the contract.

If a trump is led, the other players must follow suit, unless the only one held is the Jack of trumps, when any card can be discarded. When a plain suit is led, that suit must be followed or a trump played. A player is allowed to trump even though suit could have been followed.

SCORING

In the trump suit, Jack scores 20, Nine 14, Ace 11, King three, Queen two, Ten 10, while Eight and Seven score zero. Plain suits (those that are not trumps) score 11 for the Ace, three for the King, two for the Queen, one for the Jack and 10 for the Ten, cards below Ten not scoring. There are no bonus points for taking the last trick.

Roem also scores, provided that the *Roem* held by any opposing players are not higher. A sequence of three cards in a suit scores 20, four 50, five 100 and six 200. Four Jacks are worth 200 points, Aces, Kings and Queens 100 points and the King and Queen of trumps (*Stuk*) 20 points.

CONCLUSION

In a number contract, the declarer wins if trick-points and *Roem* equal or exceed the amount of the bid. Other contracts are scored as might be expected. All scores are entered on a scorecard, a win being marked by a plus and a loss by a minus. A player with two pluses is a winner and can sit out the game. A player with two minuses is the loser.

KLAVERJAS

Extremely popular in its Dutch homeland, Klaverjas is distinguished from other games of this genre because melds (matched sets of cards) are scored as they occur within individual tricks.

You will need: 52-card deck wtih Sixes and below removed

Card ranking: Trumps: Jack, Nine, Ace, Ten, King, Queen, Eight, Seven. Plain suits: Ace, Ten, King, Queen, Jack, Nine, Eight and Seven

Players: Four, in partnerships of two

Ideal for: 14+

OBJECT

To win more than half of the available points in each hand if your partnership has chosen trumps, otherwise to prevent the opposing partnership from scoring these points. Ultimately, the aim is to score as many points as possible over 16 hands.

THE DEAL

From the 32-card deck, each player is dealt eight cards in packets of three, two and three.

CHOOSING TRUMPS

Trumps are determined in either of two ways. Free choice means that the player to the dealer's left can either nominate a trump suit or pass. If he passes, the next player has the same choice. If all four players pass, the player to the dealer's left must decide.

The alternative is to choose trumps at random by turning up the top card of a second deck. The player to the dealer's left either accepts this card as trumps or passes. If he passes, the next player chooses. If everyone passes, a second card is turned up. Its suit automatically becomes trumps.

MELDS

Melds score as follows:

- Three consecutive cards of the same suit – 20 points.
- Four consecutive cards of the same suit – 50 points.
- Four of a Kind (except Jacks) – 100 points.
- Four Jacks – 200 points.
- A Marriage of the King and Queen of trumps (known as *Stuk*) – 20 points.

PLAY

The player to the dealer's left leads to the first trick. The others must follow suit if possible. If no trumps are played, the highest card of the suit led takes the trick. If the trick contains trumps, the highest trump wins. Before leading to the next trick, the winner of the previous one scores the value of any *Roems* (melds).

Signalling between partners is accepted. Discarding a low card of a particular suit, for instance, means the player holds its Ace, while discarding a court card (King, Queen or Jack) is a warning not to lead that suit.

SCORING AND CONCLUSION

In the trump suit, the Jack is worth 20 points, the Nine 14, Ace 11, Ten 10, King four and Queen three. In non-trump suits, Aces score 11 points, Tens 10, Kings four, Queens three and Jacks two. If the partnership choosing trumps wins more than half of the available points, both sides keep the points they have taken. If not, the partnership scores nothing and its opponents take all the points, including bonuses. The winner of the last trick gets a 10-point bonus. Play continues until 1,500 points have been scored.

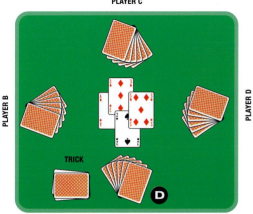

PLAYER C

PLAYER B

PLAYER D

TRICK

PLAYER A

Left: Signalling through discards is a feature of Klaverjas. A low discard, such as the 2♠ played here, is used by Player A to show he holds an Ace of that suit (A♠). Discarding a court card is a warning not to lead that card's suit.

HANDJASS

Like its Swiss and western Austrian counterparts, this Jass game revolves around points, which can be scored for three features known as *Stöck*, *Wys* and *Stich* (Marriages, melds and tricks). In its homeland, it is played with a 36-card Jass pack with its suits of Acorns, Shields, Bells and Flowers.

You will need: 52-card deck with Fives and below removed; scorecards

Card ranking: Jack of trumps (highest), Nine of trumps, Aces, Kings, Queens, other Jacks, Tens, Nines, Eights, Sevens, Sixes

Players: Two to five, although four is optimal

Ideal for: 14+

OBJECT

To score at least 21 game points for melds (matched sets of cards) in hand and counting cards captured in tricks.

THE DEAL

Each player gets nine cards in batches of three. If two are playing, two extra hands of nine are dealt. One of these is spare. This means that each player in turn, starting with the one to the dealer's left, has the right to replace the hand he has been dealt with the spare. The other hand is dead and its top card is turned up for trumps.

If three play, the remaining cards are laid down as a spare hand, but the top card is turned for trumps. If four play, there is no spare hand and the dealer's last card is shown to determine trumps. If five play, each deals in turn and then sits out that hand.

Left: The highest-scoring cards in Handjass are the Jack of trumps (known as the *Puur* and worth 20 points) and the Nine of trumps (known as the *Näll* and worth 14 points). Here, Diamonds are trumps.

MELDS

Same-suit sequences are allowed, as are groups. Only the player with the best meld in hand can score for melds. Four Jacks are worth 200 points, four Nines 150 and four of any other numbered card 100. If there are two quartets of cards worth 100, a higher-ranking one beats a lower-ranking one. A three-card sequence is worth 20, a four-card one 50, five 100, six 150, seven 200, eight 250, nine 300. The sequence order – Ace, King, Queen, Jack, Ten, Nine, Eight, Seven and Six, is the same in every suit, including trumps. A longer sequence beats a shorter one. If equal in length, a higher-ranking one beats a lower-ranking one. A Marriage between the King and Queen of trumps, a *Stöck,* is worth 20.

PLAY

The player to the dealer's left leads to the first trick. If the lead is a trump, the other players must follow suit, unless the only trump a player is holding is the Jack of trumps. In this case, any card may be played. If a plain suit is led, the others are free to follow suit or trump. In neither case can a lower trump be played if a higher one has already been led, unless a player's hand consists of nothing but trumps, in which case any card can be played.

SCORING

The highest-scoring card is the Jack of trumps (the *Puur*), worth 20 points, followed by the Nine of trumps (the *Näll*), which scores 14. Aces score 11, Kings four, Queens three, the other Jacks two and Tens 10. The other Nines, together with the Eights, Sevens and Sixes, do not score.

At the end of a hand, the two players taking the most meld points each score a game point. If scores are drawn, the pack is cut to break the tie. A player scoring less than 21 meld points is penalized by having a game point taken away. Game points are sometimes called 'sticks' and minus points are 'potatoes'.

Left: If two players tie at the end of a hand for the second-best score in meld points, the players concerned cut the pack and whoever draws the highest card scores the game point.

CONCLUSION

A player drops out on reaching either five game points or seven sticks, depending on which version of the game is being played. The last player left in is the loser.

SCHIEBER JASS

Schieber is probably the most popular member of the Swiss Jass family of card games. The game itself is a variant of Handjass, although its precise rules vary. It is played with a 36-card Jass pack, but here the suits of Acorns, Flowers, Shields and Bells have been substituted with the English counterparts Clubs, Spades, Hearts and Diamonds, respectively.

You will need: 52-card deck with Fives and below removed

Card ranking: *Obenabe* ('top-down') no-trumps contracts: Eights (highest), Sevens, Sixes, Nines, Tens, Jacks, Queens, Kings and Aces. *Undenufe* ('bottom-up') no-trumps contracts: Sixes (highest), Sevens, Eights, Nines, Tens, Jacks, Queens, Kings and Aces. Plain suit contracts: Jacks (highest), Nines, Aces, Kings, Queens, Tens, Eights, Sevens and Sixes

Players: Four, in partnerships of two

Ideal for: 14+

OBJECT

To win 3,000 points in total, by melding (matching sets of cards) and winning tricks.

THE DEAL

From the 36 card-deck, each player gets nine cards dealt in threes. The holder of the 7♠ starts the bidding, leads to the first trick and deals the second hand.

BIDDING AND CONTRACTS

The player holding the 7♠ can choose which contract is to be played, or can decide to *schieben* (shove) the responsibility over to his partner. The choice is between suit contracts in Clubs and Spades, which score single; Hearts or Diamonds, which score double; and the no-trump contracts (*Obenabe* – meaning literally 'top-down' – and *Undenufe* – meaning 'bottom-up'), which score treble.

PLAY

The player to the dealer's left leads. If the lead is a trump, the other players must follow suit, unless the only trump a player is holding is the Jack of trumps. In this case, any card may be played. If a plain suit is led, the others are free to follow suit or trump. In neither case can a lower trump be played if a higher one has already been led, unless a player's hand consists of nothing but trumps, in which case any card can be played.

In a no-trump contract, players must follow suit if they can. Each player announces the highest *Weis* (meld) he holds when he plays to the first trick. The partnership with the highest *Weis* scores for it, and for any other *Weis* that it may hold, the score being multiplied by the factor for the contract. Their opponents score nothing. A player holding the King and Queen of trumps may announce 'Stöck' ('Marriage') as the second card is played.

SCORING

In *Obenabe* contracts Aces are worth 11 points, Kings four, Queens three, Jacks two, Tens 10 and Eights eight. Nines, Sevens and Sixes count for nothing. In *Undenufe* contracts, Sixes score 11, Eights eight, Tens 10, Jacks two, Queens three and Kings four. Sevens, Nines and Aces do not score. In plain suit contracts, Jacks score 20, Nines 14, Aces 11, Kings four, Queens three and Tens 10. The other cards are valueless.

After each hand, both partnerships multiply their totals by the factor for the hand. The first partnership to score 3,000 points wins. If the losing partnership has failed to score more than 1,500, the winners are awarded a bonus game. If a side claims a win during the first trick of a hand, their opponents can counter-claim. *Stöck* (Marriage) is scored, followed by *Weis* (meld) and *Stich* (first trick), to establish who won first. Twenty points are awarded for *Stöck* (Marriage), which again is multiplied by the factor for the contract. The winner of the last trick scores a bonus of five points. If either side manages to take all nine tricks, a bonus of 100 for 'match' is awarded.

Left: In an *Undenufe* contract, the meld that contains higher trick winners is the winning three-card sequence. In this instance, 6-7-8 is the higher and Queen-King-Ace the lower meld.

CONCLUSION

A hand continues until all tricks have been taken. The game lasts until one partnership or the other scores at least 3,000 points – this typically takes 12 hands.

CANASTA GAMES

ALTHOUGH THEY ARE MEMBERS OF THE RUMMY GENRE, CANASTA GAMES HAVE ONE IMPORTANT DIFFERENCE. INSTEAD OF USING MELDS (MATCHES) SIMPLY AS A TOOL FOR GETTING RID OF CARDS IN HAND, PLAYERS SCORE POSITIVELY FOR THE MELDS THEMSELVES. CANASTA ITSELF WAS THE MOST POPULAR AMERICAN CARD GAME OF THE 1950s. IT REACHED THE USA FROM LATIN AMERICA IN ABOUT 1948, AND IS STILL PLAYED BY MILLIONS AROUND THE WORLD.

In fact, Canasta – the word is Spanish for 'basket' – was not the first game to introduce a positive scoring system for melds. The honour belongs to a game called Michigan Rum and another called 500 Rummy, both of which were widely played in the 1920s and 1930s. However, Canasta certainly has been the most influential worldwide. Although it is invariably regarded as a partnership game, perhaps because Bridge players invented it, it works just as well for two players.

The story of Canasta goes back to 1939, when well-to-do attorney Segundo Santos and his architect friend Alberto Serrato met in the Jockey Club of Montevideo, Uruguay, to devise an alternative to Bridge. The new game quickly spread throughout South America and then, after the Second World War, to the USA. It was soon played everywhere, from smart resorts on the eastern seaboard to highly fashionable clubs in California. American forces overseas spread the game to Asia, Europe and even the Soviet Union, and for a time in the early 1950s, it came close to displacing Contract Bridge as the world's most popular card game.

The various games Canasta has spawned over the years all have their individual quirks. In Samba, for instance, three packs of cards are used. Hand and Foot is another interesting variant, in which each player is dealt two sets of cards: the hand and the foot.

Above: Originating in Uruguay, Canasta reached dizzying heights of popularity in the USA in the early 1950s.

SAMBA

There are seemingly countless variations on classic Canasta. Some are simple adaptations to suit differing numbers of players, while others have developed into interesting games in their own right. Of these, Samba – also known as Samba-Canasta and, in the Netherlands, as Straat-Canasta (Sequence Canasta) – has been the most influential.

You will need: Three 52-card decks; six Jokers; scorecards

Card ranking: Ace down to Four, with Twos and Jokers serving as wild cards, and Threes having special rules attached to them (see 'Play' for wild cards and Threes)

Players: Two to six. If there are two, three or five, they play independently; if four or six, they play in partnerships

Ideal for: 14+

OBJECT

To be the first player to score 10,000 points by melding (matching sets of cards) in order to win the game.

THE DEAL

With two to five players, the deal is 15 cards to each player; six players get 13 cards each. The remaining cards form the stock, the top card of which is turned up to start the discard pile.

Left: Samba is characterized by allowing same-suit sequences as melds, as well as groups. A sequence, however, is not allowed to contain any wild cards.

MELDS

Same-suit sequences and groups are allowed. A group of seven or more cards is a *Canasta* and a seven-card sequence is a *Samba*. To go out, a player or partnership must have melded at least two *Canastas*, two *Sambas* or one of each. Wild cards – Jokers and Twos – cannot be used in a sequence, while a group may contain only two.

Aces and wild cards count for 20 points, Kings to Eights 10, and Sevens to Fours and black Threes five. Red Threes can be melded only if two *Sambas* or *Canastas* have already been laid, in which case each is worth 100 bonus points (1,000 if all six are melded).

If any are left in hand, they count as 750 penalty points. Black Threes can be melded in groups, but only when going out. Wild cards and Threes block the discard pile if discarded. Using the top card, which is blocking it, to start a new meld, unblocks it.

PLAY

Each player draws two cards from the stock, melds if he can, and discards a card. To use the discard pile, players must hold two natural cards of the same rank as the top discard, or, if they have not yet melded, meet the initial meld requirements. For scores under 1,500 points, this means the cards must be worth 50 points; for up to 3,000, 90 points; for up to 6,000, 120 points; and for 7,000 or more 150 points.

SCORING AND CONCLUSION

Scores are calculated by taking the value of the cards that have been melded and deducting from that the value of cards left in hand. Any bonus points are then added. Each *Samba* is worth 1,500 points. A pure *Canasta* – one made up solely of natural cards – scores 500 and a mixed one 300. Going out is worth 200 points. The first to score 10,000 points wins outright.

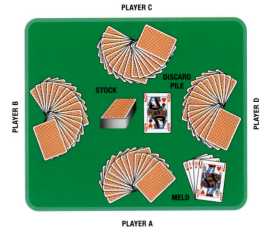

Above: Having already laid down a meld in Hearts, Player A can pick up the discard pile and add the Q♥ to the meld. Had the meld been in hand rather than laid to the table, Player A could not then have picked up the discard pile.

CANASTA

Invented in 1939 in Uruguay, Canasta is one of the great successes of modern card games. The rules vary, but always include laying at least one seven-card meld (matching set) or *Canasta*.

You will need: Two 52-card decks; four Jokers; scorecards

Card ranking: Ace down to Four, with Twos and Jokers serving as wild cards, and Threes having special rules attached to them (see 'Play' for wild cards and Threes)

Players: Four, in partnerships of two

Ideal for: 14+

OBJECT

To make melds – three cards or more of the same rank other than Jokers, Twos and Threes – and build them up into *Canastas*, which are melds of at least seven cards.

THE DEAL

Each player is dealt 11 cards singly, after which the remaining cards are placed face down to form the stock. Its top card is turned face up to start the discard pile. If the turn-up is a Joker, Two or a red Three – Jokers and Twos are wild cards (that is, they can represent any card) – another card is turned up and placed on top of it. A player dealt one or more red Threes must place them face up in front of him and draw replacements from the stock. They are bonus cards that take no part in play.

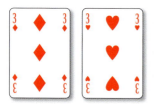

Left: When a red Three tops the discard pile it is placed at right angles over it, meaning it is frozen and no player can take the pile. To unfreeze the pile, a player needs to have two natural cards of the same rank as the turn-up in hand.

Right: Black Threes are stop cards. When one tops the discard pile, the pile cannot be picked up until the Three is covered by another card. They cannot be melded unless a player is 'going out' (getting rid of all cards in hand).

MELDS

Suits are irrelevant in Canasta, so melds consist of three or more cards of the same rank. At least two of these cards must be natural cards as opposed to wild ones. No meld can contain more than three wild cards, although there is no limit to the number of natural cards in one.

If a seven-card meld is all natural, it is termed a natural *Canasta*. If it contains wild cards, it is mixed. Adding a wild card to extend a natural *Canasta* will turn it into a mixed one, but a wild card cannot be shifted from meld to meld. Nor is a partnership allowed to run more than one meld of a given rank or to add cards to a meld laid by the opposing side.

The first meld laid by a partnership must meet or beat a specific points requirement, which is calculated according to that partnership's current score. At the start of play, it is 50 points. If a partnership's score is 1,500 or over, it is 90 points and, if 3,000 or more, it is 120.

INDIVIDUAL CARD SCORES:

- Red Threes – 100 points each.
- Jokers – 50 points each.
- Aces and Twos – 20 points each.
- Kings, Queens, Jacks, Tens to Eights – 10 points each.
- Sevens, Sixes, Fives, Fours and black Threes – five points each.

Left: At the start of play, the value of cards in a first meld must be at least 50 points. The far left meld is unacceptable, as Jacks are only worth 10 points. Aces score 20, so the second meld could be laid.

Right: Twos and Jokers in Canasta serve as wild cards, that is, they can represent any card.

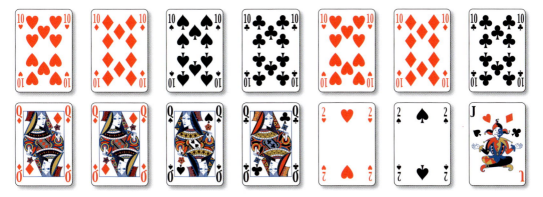

Above: The natural *Canasta* is worth 500 bonus points, plus 70 points as it is comprised of Tens. The mixed *Canasta* is worth 300 bonus points plus a further 130: 10 each for the Queens, 20 each for the Twos and 50 for the Joker.

PLAY

At the start of a turn, the player concerned can draw the top card of the stock or take the discard pile in its entirety. If the player chooses the first option, the card can be added to hand, melded or, if desired, discarded at the end of the turn. The second option applies only if the top discard can be melded at once. Nor may the discard pile be taken if the top discard is a wild card or a black Three. The latter is a stop card. By discarding one, a player can stop an opponent taking the pile until the Three is covered by another card. Moreover, black Threes cannot be melded unless a player is 'going out' – that is, getting rid of all cards in hand.

If the turn-up is a wild card or a red Three, no player can take the pile. It is what is termed 'frozen'. Nor may a partnership take it if it has yet to meld. To unfreeze the pile, a player needs to have two natural cards of the same rank as the turn-up in hand. The three cards can then be used to make a new meld, or be added to an existing one. Players end their turns by making a discard face up to the discard pile. This can be any card except a red Three.

CONCLUSION AND SCORING

Play ends when a player goes out, which can be by melding, laying off, or discarding the last card in hand, provided that the partnership concerned has laid at least one *Canasta*. Each partnership scores the value of the cards it has melded, plus bonuses of 500 points for each natural *Canasta*, 300 for each mixed one and 100 for each red Three declared (800 if all four red Threes are held). There is a further bonus of 100 points for going out, which is doubled if the player is going out 'concealed' – that

PLAYER C/NORTH

PLAYER A/SOUTH

Above: A game of Canasta in progress. The North–South partnership is well on its way to a mixed *Canasta* in Tens, and also has melds in Sixes and Aces, together with a red Three. East–West has two red Threes, and melds in Jacks and Kings. The discard pile is currently frozen by a wild card, meaning that no player can pick up the pile unless he holds in his hand two cards of the same rank as the card topping the discard pile (here, a Seven).

is, without having previously made any melds or lay-offs and doing so by playing a complete *Canasta*.

The value of cards left in hand is subtracted from both totals. If a partnership has failed to lay a single meld, or failed to declare a red Three, each red Three it may hold counts for 100 points against it (800 points if all four are held). The cumulative score needed to win the game is 5,000 points, the margin of victory being the difference between the scores of the two partnerships.

HAND AND FOOT

Invented in North America, this fascinating game has several features that set it apart from other games of its ilk. It uses one more pack than the number of players – up to five can play – plus Jokers. Each player is dealt two separate hands simultaneously and there are three types of combinations – natural, mixed and wild. The last of these consists entirely of Jokers and Twos.

OBJECT

To meld (group) as many cards as possible and either to go out first or to be left with as little 'deadwood' (cards that are not in any meld) as possible. You score points for cards you have melded, and lose points for any cards left in your hand at the end of the play.

THE DEAL

Once it has been agreed which partnership is to deal first and after the cards have been thoroughly shuffled, one partner takes part of the deck and deals four stacks of 13 cards face down from it. This is the Hand. Meanwhile, the partner of the hand dealer does the same with the other part of the deck until each player has a second stack, known as the Foot. The remaining cards are placed face down to form the stock, the top card of which is turned up and placed next to it to start the discard pile. If the turn-up is a red Three or a wild card – a Two or a Joker – it is buried in the stock and the next card turned up.

Above: A feature of Hand and Foot is that matching combinations, known as melds, can consist entirely of wild cards, which are Twos and Jokers.

You will need: Five 52-card decks plus ten Jokers, for four players; scorecards

Card ranking: Ace down to Four, with Twos and Jokers serving as wild cards (see 'Play', opposite, for rules on this and Threes)

Players: Ideally, four, in partnerships of two

Ideal for: 14+

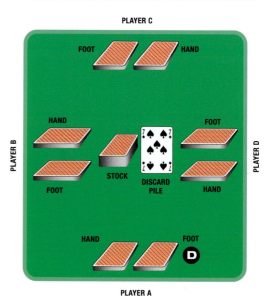

Above: After shuffling the packs, one partner takes part of the deck, deals four face-down stacks of 13 cards and passes them around the table in a clockwise direction until each player has a stack – the Hand. Meanwhile, the dealer's partner takes another part of the deck and deals a further four stacks of 13 cards each, once again passing these in a clockwise direction until each player has a second stack – the Foot.

MELDING

Players score points for the cards that they have melded and lose points for any cards left in hand at the end of play. In this game, a meld is a set of from three to seven cards of the same rank. Once such a meld has been started, either partner is at liberty to add more cards to it until there are seven in place.

There are three valid melds. A natural (or clean) meld contains no wild cards, while a mixed (or dirty) meld contains one or two. There must be at least six cards in such a meld for two wild cards to be included. A wild meld, as its name implies, consists entirely of wild cards. A complete meld of seven cards is called a pile.

PLAY

Players pick up and play the Hand first. The Foot stays face down sight unseen until its owner has played the last card from the Hand. Before each player plays, he must place any red Threes held in the Hand face up and draw replacements from the stock. The player to the left of the person who dealt the hands plays first.

Each player starts by drawing the top two cards from the stock. He then melds some cards or adds to his partner's melds and finally discards one card face up to the discard pile. An alternative to drawing from the stock is to pick up the top seven cards from the discard pile. This option is open only if the top discard is not a Three, and the player is holding two cards of the same rank as the top discard that can be melded with it immediately.

The first meld each partnership makes in each round must meet the minimum meld requirements. Several melds may be made at once to achieve this. In the first round, the requirement is at least 50 points, in the second 90, in the third 120, and in the fourth 150. Jokers are worth 50 points each, Twos and Aces 20, Kings down to Eights 10, and Sevens to Fours score five points.

Neither red nor black Threes may be melded. Red Threes, if declared, are worth a bonus 100 points each, but any left in hand count for 100 penalty points. If discarded, black Threes block the discard pile, so they are often used tactically. Any left in hand count for five penalty points. This means discarding any Threes held in hand one at a time on to the discard pile as quickly as possible.

Below: An excellent, if unlikely, opening hand. The red Three can be declared, earning a bonus of 100 points, while the black Three can be saved to block the discard pile at an opportune moment. The wild Twos and Jokers can be used towards a wild meld, or towards a mixed meld in Queens or Aces.

SCORING AND CONCLUSION

For a player to be allowed to go out, the partnership concerned must have melded two natural, two mixed and one wild meld between them. The other partner must have picked up his Foot and played at least part of a turn from it. The player seeking to go out must also have obtained his partner's permission to do so.

Scores are then totalled, points deducted for cards left in hand, and bonuses awarded. Each natural pile is worth 500 points, a mixed one 300 and a wild pile 1,500. This is why most players, if possible, try to complete this particular pile as soon as they can. There is an additional 100-point bonus for going out.

If the stock is depleted to the point where no player can draw from it, play also ends, although it may be possible to continue for a time as long as each player is able to take and meld the previous player's discard. In this case, both partnerships score for the cards that they have melded, less the points for the cards they have remaining in their Hands and Feet. Obviously, the bonus for going out is not awarded.

The game ends when a partnership has made 10,000 points, or the four rounds have been played. In that case, the partnership winning the most rounds wins the game.

Below: Here, only Player A's hand is shown, along with the table cards. Players A and C have a natural meld of Aces and are well on the way to completing a mixed meld in Queens. Their opponents have nearly completed a wild meld and have started a mixed meld in Nines. Player A, whose turn it is to play, can pick up the discarded J♠ or pick up two cards from the top of the stock.

PENNIES FROM HEAVEN

This variant of Canasta is notable for the highly unusual role played by Sevens. They may not be discarded until each partnership has grouped seven or more cards consisting solely of Sevens. Nor may they be discarded when going out. There are also two deals in this game.

> **You will need:** Four 52-card decks; eight Jokers; scorecards
>
> **Card ranking:** Aces down to Eights, then Sixes, Fives and Fours, with Twos and Jokers serving as wild cards, and Threes and Sevens having special rules attached to them (see 'Play' for wild cards and Threes)
>
> **Players:** Four or six, playing in partnerships
>
> **Ideal for:** 14+

OBJECT

To score points by melding (grouping) cards into four types of *Canastas* (a meld of seven or more cards): natural, mixed, wild and sevens. A team needs one of each of these types to go out.

THE DEAL

Each player receives 13 cards, dealt singly, and followed by a packet of 11 cards, which is kept face down until a player has personally completed a *Canasta* by laying the requisite seventh card from his hand.

The second hand, the so-called 'pennies from heaven', can then be picked up and taken into hand. The remaining cards form the stock, the top card of which is turned up to start the discard pile.

Left: A *Canasta* of Sevens in Pennies from Heaven scores 1,500 points.

MELDS AND CANASTAS

A natural *Canasta* – consisting of seven cards of the same rank with no wild cards – is worth a bonus of 500 points. A mixed one, containing up to three wild cards with all the others of the same rank, counts for 300. A *Canasta* of seven wild cards scores 1,000 points and a *Canasta* made up of Sevens scores 1,500 points.

A meld must consist of a minimum of three cards and a maximum of seven. Depending on a partnership's cumulative score, the first meld to be laid must meet a minimum points requirement. For a minus score, this is 15 points; for a score from zero to 4,995, it is 50 points; and for one from 5,000 to 9,995, it is 90 points. If the score is between 10,000 and 14,995, the requirement is 120 points and 150 thereafter.

A mixed meld in process of construction must contain at least two natural cards and not more than three wild ones. A natural meld can be turned into a mixed one by adding wild cards to it, while, once a meld has been completed, the partnership that melded can start another meld of the same rank.

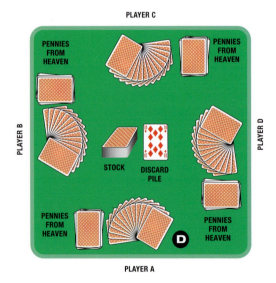

PLAYER C

PENNIES FROM HEAVEN

PENNIES FROM HEAVEN

PLAYER B

PLAYER D

STOCK

DISCARD PILE

PENNIES FROM HEAVEN

PENNIES FROM HEAVEN

PLAYER A

Above: Each player is dealt a batch of 11 cards in addition to his main hand of 13 cards. The second hand cannot be picked up until a player has personally completed a *Canasta* by laying the requisite seventh card from hand.

PLAY

Each player in turn has the option of drawing the top two cards from the stock or taking the entire discard pile. He can then start a new meld or add cards to melds his

Above: The meld at the top is acceptable, containing no more than three wild cards. The second of the two contains four, so would not be allowed.

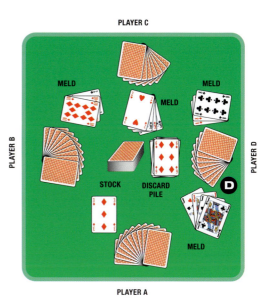

Above: An example of play in progress. Player A has laid down a red Three (and drawn a replacement from the stock) and a meld of Jacks. Player B has begun a meld in Tens, Player C one in Kings, and Player D has, so far, a natural meld in Eights.

partnership has already started constructing. To end a turn, one card from hand is discarded face up on to the discard pile. Whether the discard pile can be taken or not is subject to certain conditions. If its top card is a natural one and the player concerned holds two matching natural cards in hand, the pile may be taken, always provided that the three cards are melded immediately and that the minimum meld requirement has been satisfied previously. It can also be taken if its top card matches an existing meld of fewer than seven cards, provided that it is added immediately to that meld. A discarded wild card freezes the pile.

Twos and Jokers are wild cards. Jokers are worth 50 points each, Twos and Aces 20 points, Kings down to Eights 10, and Sevens to black Threes score five points. Red and black Threes have the same properties as in regular Canasta. Any player who is dealt or draws a red Three must place it face up on the table immediately and draw a replacement from the stock.

Each declared red Three counts for 100 bonus points (1,000 if the same partnership lays out all eight of them). Any left in hand score 100 penalties each (1,000 if all eight are held). Black Threes cannot be melded, except by a player going out. If one is discarded, it blocks the discard pile, as does a red Three if that is the first card to be turned up after the deal.

SCORING

A partnership must have completed all four types of *Canasta* before one of its players can go out by melding all of the remaining cards in hand, or all bar one of them, which is the final discard. This must not be a Seven. It is customary to ask a partner's permission to go out before doing so, in which case the player concerned must abide by that partner's decision.

The partnerships each score all the cards they have melded, plus any bonuses for *Canastas* and a further 100-point bonus for the side that went out first. From this, they deduct the value of any cards left in hand. Scores for red Threes are added or debited as appropriate.

CONCLUSION

If the stock is exhausted, play can continue as long as the players are willing to pick up discards. If not, it ends and the hand is scored as above, although the bonus for going out is obviously not awarded. The first partnership to score 20,000 or more points wins the game. If the scores are tied, a deciding hand is played.

PINÁCULO

This game originated in Spain and is regarded by some as a forerunner of Canasta. Jokers and Twos are wild cards. As well as scoring for groupings (melds) in the same way as Canasta, there are additional scores for specified melds.

You will need: Two 52-card decks; four Jokers; scorecards
Card ranking: Standard, with Twos and Jokers being wild
Players: Four, in partnerships of two
Ideal for: 14+

OBJECT

To score 1,500 points over as many deals as it takes, scoring extra for melds and conceding penalties for 'deadwood', or cards not in a meld.

THE DEAL

After the initial shuffle, the player to the dealer's left cuts the cards. Each player is then dealt 11 cards singly from the bottom half of the cut pack. The remaining cards are stacked face down to form the stock, and the top card is turned up to start the discard pile. If exactly the right number of cards (44) is cut for the deal, the cutter scores a 50-point bonus.

MELDING

A meld contains three or more cards of the same rank, or three or more in suit and sequence. The latter is an *Escalera* and must contain at least two natural (not wild) cards. In addition, Aces count as high and Threes low.

Melds are the property of the player or partnership that played them, and must be kept separate. No two melds may be combined, even if their ranks match or such a combination will complete a sequence.

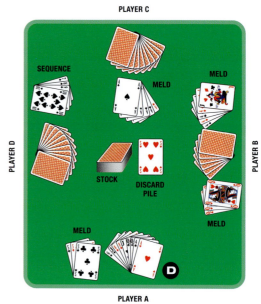

Above: Player A can play the J♠ and 6♠ on to Player D's sequence, the A♥ on to Player C's meld and the 4♣ and Q♣ on to Player B's melds. But first, he must decide whether to pick up the 5♥, together with the rest of the discard pile, adding the Five to his existing meld, or to pick up from the stock.

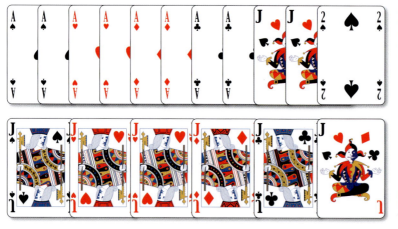

Left: The highest-scoring meld in Pináculo, 11 of a kind, is called a *Pinnacle* and scores either 3,000 points or 1,500 points, depending on whether it was constructed gradually or not.

Left: The lowest-scoring meld in Pináculo is five court cards and a wild card, which scores 120 points.

PLAY

The player to the right of the dealer leads and play proceeds in an anti-clockwise direction. Each player in turn draws a card from the stock or takes the whole discard pile. The player then goes on to start a meld or to lay off cards to a meld that has already been started by the partnership. At the end of each turn, a card is discarded face up to the discard pile.

Above: The penalty points for being left with these two sets of cards contrast sharply. In the first set, the Joker would count for 30 points, the Two for 20, the Ace for 15, and the King and Eight for 10 each, making a total of 85. In the second, each card counts for just five points, making a total of 20.

If a player is holding a natural card that is being represented by a wild card at either end of an incomplete *Escalera*, he may substitute a natural card for the wild one. The wild card is not taken into his hand, but is placed sideways at one end of the *Escalera* as a reminder to score it at the end of play. There is an added twist. A partnership or player with 750 points is said to be *barbelé* (French for caught in the barbed wire). This means that the next meld they lay must be worth at least 70 points. Any meld lower than this must be withdrawn and the offending partnership has to concede a 50-point penalty.

SCORING

Players score positively for cards in melds but lose points for cards left in hand at the end of the game. Jokers score 30 points either way, Twos 20, Aces 15, Kings to Eights 10 and Sevens to Threes five points each.

Scores are calculated at the end of the game. There are points for melds and bonus or penalty points scored during play: there is a bonus of 20 for going out; going out without the use of a wild card doubles the values of all the cards in the final meld; going out 'concealed' (melding all 11 cards) similarly doubles their face values; if they are all natural cards, their values are quadrupled.

> ### SCORING MELDS
>
> Specific melds score a premium number of points, rather than their face value, as follows:
>
> - A *Pinnacle* (a meld of 11 of a kind, declared simultaneously) scores 3,000 points; a *Pinnacle* constructed gradually in one hand scores 1,500 points.
> - A clean *Escalera* (a sequence of 11 natural cards in suit) scores 1,000 points.
> - An unclean *Escalera* (containing a Two of a matching suit) scores 800 points.
> - An unclean *Escalera* (containing two Twos of a matching suit) scores 750 points.
> - A dirty *Escalera* (that is, one containing one or more non-matching Twos) scores 550.
> - A meld of eight natural Aces scores 1,000 points.
> - A meld of eight natural Kings, Queens or Jacks scores 750 points.
> - A meld of seven natural Aces scores 400 points.
> - A meld of seven natural Kings, Queens or Jacks scores 300.
> - A meld of six natural Aces scores 300 points.
> - A meld of six natural court cards scores 200 points.
> - A meld of six Aces that includes a wild card scores 180 points.
> - A meld of six court cards that includes a wild card scores 120 points.

Eight natural number cards score their total face value plus 50. Each Joker replaced by a natural card during the course of play scores an extra 30 points. Each Two that was similarly replaced scores an additional 15 in an *Escalera* or twice face value in a meld of cards of the same rank.

CONCLUSION

When a player has one card left in hand, he must call '*Pumba!*' or be penalized 50 points. The game ends when a player goes out by melding or laying off the remaining cards in hand, with or without discarding. It also ends if the stock is exhausted.

CONTINENTAL RUMMY

There are many different versions of this attractive game, which can be played by up to 12 at a time. What makes Continental Rummy different from other games of its ilk is that no groupings (melds) can be laid until a player can go out by doing so. No cards may be laid off, nor can natural cards be exchanged for wild ones.

You will need: Two packs or more, with Jokers. Five players or fewer use a double pack plus two Jokers; six to eight use a triple pack with three Jokers; more than nine use a quadruple pack with four Jokers; gambling chips/counters

Card ranking: Aces rank high and low, the remaining cards ranking from Kings down to Threes; Twos and Jokers are wild cards

Players: Two to 12

Ideal for: 10+

OBJECT

To meld all one's cards in sequences of the same suit and in only one of the specified patterns, which are 3–3–3–3–3, 3–4–4–4 or 3–3–4–5 (see picture, below).

THE DEAL

If two packs are used, the dealer shuffles. Otherwise, the dealer and another player each shuffle parts of the pack – the dealer has the right to shuffle second, and these packs are then combined. Each player is dealt 15 cards three at a time, the remainder being placed face down to form the stock. In some versions of the game, the dealer is awarded a bonus of 15 chips for lifting off exactly the right number of cards to complete the deal. The top card of the stock is turned up to start the discard pile. Players are given an agreed number of gambling chips.

PLAY

Each player in turn draws either the top card of the stock or the turn-up from the discard pile and then discards one of his cards. Only same-suit sequences count, not matched sets. To go out means melding five three-card

sequences, three four-card and one three-card sequences, or one five-card, one four-card and two three-card ones. Two or more of these sequences may be of the same suit, but a sequence must not 'go round the corner' – that is, an Ace can count as high or low, but not as both.

SCORING

If a player goes out without drawing a single card, there is a bonus of ten chips; for going out after only drawing once, seven chips; and for doing so without playing a Joker or a Two, 10 chips. Melding all 15 cards of the same suit is also worth 10 extra chips.

CONCLUSION

The game ends when a player melds 15 cards in one of the specified patterns and makes a final discard. The winner collects a chip from each of the other players for winning, two for each melded Joker and one for each Two.

Above: The sequences in Continental Rummy must conform to specified patterns, comprising: five sets of same-suit sequences of three; three sets of four and one of three; or two sets of three, together with one of four and one of five. Sequences must be of the same suit, and they must not 'go round the corner' – in other words, a sequence could not run from King through to Two.

500 Rum

This variant of Rummy dates from the 1930s. In it, points are scored for grouped (melded) cards and lost for unmelded ones. Unlike similar games, players are not limited to only taking the top discard: more cards may be drawn, but at least one must be laid off or melded straight away.

You will need: 52 cards (two packs for five or more players); no Jokers; scorecards

Card ranking: Aces high or low, then Kings down to Twos

Players: Two to eight, but three is optimal

Ideal for: 10+

OBJECT

To score points by melding cards, the game being won by the first player to score 500 or more points.

THE DEAL

Players draw for deal, and the person with the lowest card deals first. Each player is dealt seven cards. If only two are playing, the deal is 13 cards each, and the remaining cards form the stock. The top card of the stock is then turned face up to start the discard pile. As play progresses, this should be spread sufficiently for players to see all the cards in it.

HAND 1   HAND 2

Above: To calculate scores, the point values of the cards each player has melded are added up and that of any cards left in hand are subtracted. The first hand here scores 40 points for the meld of four Jacks, but loses 25 points for the number cards, making a total of 15 points. The second hand scores 22 points for the same-suit sequence in Hearts, but loses 22 points for the two Queens and 2♠, meaning that no points are scored.

PLAY

Each player in turn draws the top card of the stock or any card from the discard pile. In the latter case, the desired card must be played immediately, and all the cards lying above it must be taken. The other cards may be melded or laid off in the same turn or added to the hand.

Melds consist of sets of three or four cards of the same rank and sequences of three or more cards of the same suit. Sequences may not 'go round the corner', in other words, a sequence of Ace, King, and Queen is valid, but King, Ace, and Two is not. Each player finishes by discarding a card.

SCORING AND CONCLUSION

Play ends when a player goes out – that is, gets rid of all the cards in his hand, or the stock is exhausted. To calculate scores, the point values of the cards each player has melded are added up and that of any cards left in hand are subtracted. An Ace is worth 15 points if high and a single point if low. The court cards count for 10 points each and the number cards at face value.

The first player to score 500 points wins the game, the winning margin being the difference between that and the final scores of the other players.

PLAYER C

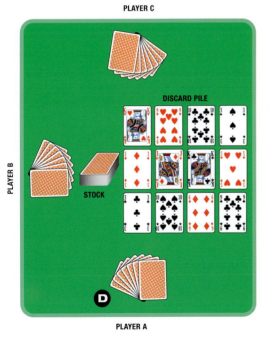

DISCARD PILE

PLAYER B

STOCK

D

PLAYER A

Above: The discard pile in 500 Rum should be spread out, so that all the cards in it can be seen by every player.

VYING GAMES

IN THIS GROUP OF GAMES, PLAYERS BET ON WHO HOLDS THE BEST HAND. MOST GAMES END WITH A 'SHOWDOWN', IN WHICH THE HANDS ARE COMPARED TO SEE WHICH IS THE BEST. VYING GAMES ARE UNUSUAL IN THAT THERE IS NO ACTUAL CARD PLAY, ALTHOUGH PLAYERS HAVE THE CHANCE TO IMPROVE THEIR HANDS BY DISCARDING AND DRAWING NEW CARDS. POKER IN ALL ITS FORMS IS THE BEST KNOWN WILL BE EXPLAINED IN MORE DETAIL IN THE FOLLOWING CHAPTERS.

As well as gambling, what these games have in common is that, to a greater or lesser extent, they all involve an element of bluff. This is why, although a player may be dealt a bad hand, he can still win by superior play. It means having the courage to bet on bad cards in the hope that the other players will lose their nerve and all drop out of play, so that you win by default. This happens when a player raises the stake and the others are not prepared to match the bet in case the stake-raising player has an unbeatable hand.

Vying can take either of two forms. In the first, the oldest type, players pay into a pot to back up the claim that they hold the best hand, or drop out, losing whatever they have staked. When only two players are left in the game, there is a showdown. The way to call this is by matching the previous player's stake. It does not have to be raised further.

In the second, newer form of vying, all the players in the game can force a showdown by matching the previous stake. This means that the player who previously raised the stake is unable to raise it further. The procedure for this can be quite complicated. In the Swedish game Chicago (not to be confused with the Bridge variant of the same name), there are two showdowns between the players before a final trick-taking phase.

Above: The film based on Fleming's *Casino Royale* features a game of no-limit Texas Hold 'em Poker between James Bond (Daniel Craig) and the chief villain.

BRAG

Thought to be derived from a Tudor card game called Primero, which was popular in the days of Elizabeth I, Brag has a long and illustrious history. While it is similar to Poker, the way in which bets are made is different. In the classic game, hands consist of three cards and the highest hand is a Prial (Three of a Kind) of Threes. There are several varieties, but all are what are termed hard-score games – that is, those played for gambling chips or cash.

OBJECT
To finish with the best-ranked hand and scoop the pot.

ANTES
Before play begins, players should agree on several points: the initial stake, or ante, to be put into the pot before each deal; the maximum and minimum initial bet and amount by which bets can be raised; and any variations to the basic rules such as whether or not wild cards are to be played.

You will need: 52 cards; gambling chips/counters

Card ranking: Standard (except for wild cards – see page 226)

Players: Four to eight is optimal

Ideal for: 14+

BRAG HANDS

From highest to lowest, Brag hands rank as follows:

- Prial – A set of three cards of equal rank (a set of Threes is the best possible Prial, followed by a set of Aces down to Twos, the lowest).
- Running Flush – Three cards of the same suit (highest is an Ace, Two, Three).
- Run – Three consecutive cards of mixed suits (highest is an Ace, Two, Three).
- Flush – Three non-consecutive cards of the same suit.
- Pair – Two cards of equal rank.
- High Card – A hand consisting of three cards that do not fit into any of the above combinations. It ranks according to the highest card in it. There is no ranking of suits.

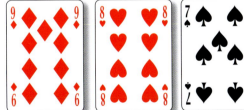

Above: The cards are ranked by suit in the conventional order of ♠♥♦♣, which means a Spade will beat a Heart of the same rank and a Diamond will beat a Club. This is only needed when two players have the same hands but in different suit combinations (as shown). In this case, the combination at the top wins, due to the Ace being a Spade.

Above: In this case, two players have the same hand combination again. The hand at the top wins again, due to the highest card, the nine, being a Spade. Even though the lower combination has two cards that beat the above combination it is the high card that wins the hand and the game.

WILD CARDS

In Brag, wild cards are known as floaters – they were once called braggers or turners. Either all Twos can be wild, or just the black ones. The One-Eyed Jacks, the J♠ and the J♥ (so called because only one eye shows), can also be wild – so can the K♥, known as the Suicide King because the sword the King carries appears to pass through his head.

A Joker or Jokers can be added to the pack to serve as extra wild cards. Such cards can replace any natural card in the pack. If, however, two hands are equal, a hand with no wild cards always beats one with wild cards in it, while a hand with fewer wild cards beats one with more of them. Thus, a hand of three Fives will beat a hand of two Sixes and a wild card, or a Seven and two wild cards.

THE DEAL

The cards are shuffled only for the first deal. In subsequent ones, this happens only if the previous deal was won by a Prial. Otherwise, the cards are simply added to the bottom of the pack as players fold. Each player receives three cards dealt singly face down to the table. However, each player is obliged to contribute one chip into the pot before any cards are dealt.

PLAY AND BETTING

Once dealt, cards may either be examined or left as they are should their holder take the option of playing blind. If a player decides to do this, he takes part in the betting in the normal way, but any bets are worth double.

At any stage, when it is that player's turn to bet, he can decide to look at the cards before making the decision of whether to bet or to fold. In that case, he ceases to be a blind player.

The player to the left of the dealer has the chance to bet first. The options are to bet any amount between the minimum and maximum stakes that have been previously agreed, or to fold.

A player who runs out of chips during the betting, but who still wants to stay in the game, may 'cover the kitty' by placing his hand over the pot. The other players then start a new pot and continue playing.

The process continues until there are only two players left in the game. They carry on betting until one drops out, in which case the surviving player wins the pot without having to show his hand. The alternative is for either to 'see' the other by doubling the previous player's bet. Both players then expose their hands, the one who called for the showdown exposing his hand first.

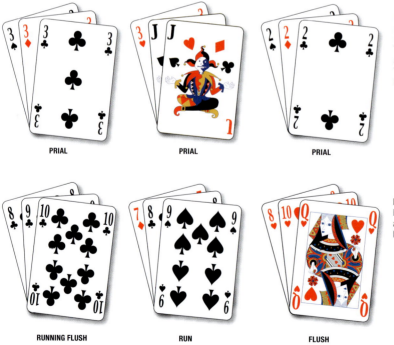

PRIAL

PRIAL

PRIAL

Left: A Prial of Threes is the highest possible hand, and a Prial of Twos is the least strong Prial possible. The second of the three hands, although ostensibly a Prial of Threes, would be beaten by a hand with no wild cards.

RUNNING FLUSH

RUN

FLUSH

Left: Examples of a Running Flush, Run and Flush. After a Prial, these are, in descending order, the next highest hands in Brag.

Above: In this game, player A has a pair three, player B has a pair J, and player C has a high card of 9♣. Player A and B's pair beat player C's high card, with player A being the overall winner as the pair J beats the pair three.

VARIANTS
FIVE-CARD BRAG
In Five-Card Brag, each player receives five cards, discarding two face down before play starts.

SEVEN-CARD BRAG
Seven cards are dealt. The players must choose three cards to play from their hands, or they can make two hands. If they played two hands, they would have to win both hands to win the pot. In Seven-Card Brag, anyone dealt Four of a Kind wins the pot automatically and there is a new deal. Otherwise, each player discards a card to the bottom of the deck and forms the remaining six cards into two hands, placing the higher one to the left and the lower one to the right. The higher hand is played first.

A player may play both hands blind if they wish. One hand can be looked at, and then decided whether to keep or throw it away. If it is kept, and the other hand is discarded the player is now considered open. If the player throws away the cards they have seen and keeps the other hand, the player can still play blind.

Below: In Seven-Card Brag, if a player is dealt four of a kind of any number, they will automatically win the pot and end the game.

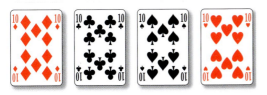

NINE-CARD BRAG
The procedure is the same in Nine-Card Brag; all the players are each dealt nine cards, who then sort the cards into three sets of hands, which are ordered and played from highest to lowest. An ante is then played for each set of hands, with one main pot as well. The winner of each set takes one the ante for the hand, but if a player wins all three sets they also win the main pot.

THIRTEEN-CARD BRAG
In this game, each player is dealt thirteen cards. To play thirteen-card brag, each player may choose three cards to play from the thirteen cards, or another variation involves making four hands from the thirteen cards.

FIFTEEN-CARD BRAG
This can be played as a family game. Each player is dealt fifteen cards, from which they make five sets of three cards. Each player must then lay their cards down in order, beginning with the highest first. The winner is the one who wins the most hands.

You can even play with any number of cards. Just make the best hand, then discard the rest.

CONCLUSION
The player with the highest hand wins the pot. If the two hands are equal, the player who paid to 'see', loses. If a player has covered the kitty, his hand is compared at the end of play to the hand of the 'winner', and the better of the two hands wins it. If one player is playing open and the other blind, the rules state that 'you cannot see a blind man'. The only options are to continue to bet or to fold. If both players are blind, betting twice the blind stake forces the hands to be compared.

Right: During a game, gambling chips are used to keep track of winnings. When betting, players should place their chips immediately in front of them. It can be argued that using chips may detach a player from the actual cash sums involved.

MUS

A game from the Basque part of Spain, Mus is unusual: although its mechanics resemble those of Poker in that cards are drawn and each player then bets on his hand, it is played up to a fixed total of points. And unlike Poker, players are allowed to signal to their partners which cards they hold. Suits are irrelevant. What matters are the cards' ranks and values. In Mus, originally played with a 40-card Spanish pack, Threes count as Kings and Twos as Aces. The cards also have point values – a *Rey* (King), *Caballo* (Horseman) and *Sota* (Ten) are each worth 10 points, while the other cards score at face value. This becomes important in the final betting round of each deal.

OBJECT

To score points through various card combinations. The game is not usually played for money.

You will need: 40-card Spanish pack; 22 stones or counters
Card rankings: *Rey* (King), *Caballo* (Horseman), *Sota* (Ten), and then Seven down to Ace
Players: Four players in partnerships of two
Ideal for: 14+

THE DEAL

The player to the dealer's right, known as the *Mano*, is the person who leads play, and all procedures pass to the right. All players are dealt four cards singly and the remaining cards are stacked face down to form the stock. Players can call '*Mus*' if they want to try to improve their hands by discarding, or can say '*No hay mus*' if happy with the cards as dealt. All four players must agree to the exchange, otherwise none can be made.

The players must then all discard from one to four cards, which are replaced by cards from the top of the stock. The process can be repeated until a player calls a halt to it. If the stock is exhausted before this, a new stock is formed from the shuffled discards.

PLAY AND BETTING

There are four rounds of betting, each for a particular combination of cards, carried out in strict order (see box below). In each round of betting, the *Mano* starts by deciding to pass or to bet. If the former, the next player to the right takes over. If no one bets, the *Mano* starts the next betting round.

If someone bets in the *Grande* and *Chica* betting rounds, the opposing players can fold, match the bet, or raise it. This is when signalling between partners becomes important. Closing the eyes means poor cards,

MUS HANDS

There are four valid card combinations: *Grande*, *Chica*, *Pares* and *Juego*, on which players bet in strict order. They comprise the following:

- *Grande* – a bet that one or the other player in a partnership holds the highest hand.
- *Chica* – a bet that one or the other player in a partnership holds the lowest hand.
- *Pares* – a bet for the best-paired hand, a hand where two or more cards rank equally. Sub-rankings within *Pares* are:
  a. *Par Simple* (the lowest), two cards of equal rank.
  b. *Medias*, three cards of the same rank and one of a different one.
  c. *Dobles* (the highest), two pairs.

If no betting takes place, a *Par Simple* is worth one point, a *Medias* two and a *Dobles* three.

- *Juego* – a declaration that the cards in hand are worth at least 31 points. If no player can declare *Juego*, the alternative is *Punto*, denoting a hand worth 30 points or less.

Above: Mus was originally played with a 40-card Spanish pack, organized into four suits, the Aces of which are shown clockwise from the top: *Bastos* (Clubs), *Copas* (Cups), *Espadas* (Swords) and *Oros* (Golds or Coins). The three distinctive court or face cards in each suit are the *Rey* (King), *Caballo* (Horseman) and *Sota* (Ten).

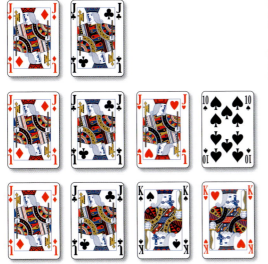

Left: Three examples of *Pares:* a *Par Simple* (the lowest, being two cards of equal rank; a *Medias* (being three cards of the same rank and one of a different one); and *Dobles* (the highest, being two pairs).

Below: After the last betting round, players lay down their hands. Player A has a *Par Simple* as does Player C. Player D has *Medias* (Three of a Kind), but Player B wins with *Dobles* (two pairs).

PLAYER C

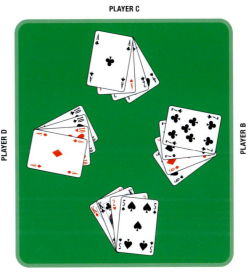

PLAYER D

PLAYER B

PLAYER A

for instance, a hand of Four, Five, Six and Seven. In some versions, a player with these cards can expose them immediately and be dealt a replacement hand, provided that the declaration is made before calling "*Mus*".

Biting the lower lip means three Kings. Pouting the lips means that the player concerned would like to exchange some cards or it can mean that the player is holding three Kings and an Ace. Inclining the head to the right means that the player would prefer not to change cards. Shrugging the shoulder means that a player has a *Punto* of 30, while sticking out the tip of one's tongue means that the player is holding three Aces.

Betting continues until one side or the other folds, or sees the last raise. In the latter case, there is a showdown. Before any bets can be made in the *Pares* and *Juego* stages, each player must say if he actually holds the requisite cards. If at least one player from each partnership says 'Yes', a round of betting follows. If both players in one partnership say 'No', but either or both members of the opposing one say 'Yes', they can score the basic number of points for what they hold, but betting is disallowed. If all four players say 'No', there is no score. Instead, players then bet on who has the best *Punto*, that is, a hand worth 30 or fewer points.

One final bet, an *Órdago*, is a call for an immediate showdown. The opposing players must either fold or see the bet. The outcome of the entire game is determined by who holds the best hand for that particular round.

SCORING

After the last betting round, players all show their cards, and the hand is scored round by round, although only for points that have not as yet been claimed and taken. These are represented by tokens called *piedras* (stones), 22 of which are placed in a saucer in the centre of the table. A minimum bet is two stones.

In each partnership, one player is responsible for collecting the stones. For every five stones won, four are returned to the saucer and one passed to the other partner. Each of these is worth five points.

When the player in charge of the *piedras* has collected seven such stones, he must call '*Dentro*' ('inside') to alert the opposing players to the fact that the team is within five points of winning the game.

CONCLUSION

A match is three games, the side winning two of them winning the contest.

PRIMERO

This intriguing game, which is still played in parts of central Italy as Goffo, or Bambara, originated in Renaissance times. It is thought likely that a variant of it was favoured by Henry VIII of England. It has strong similarities to many aspects of modern-day Poker, although it is based on four-card, rather than five-card, combinations.

OBJECT

To score points through various card combinations and to finish with the highest-scoring hand.

THE DEAL

Before the deal, players each ante an agreed amount to the pot. The ante is the stake that each player must put into the pool before receiving a hand or new cards. Each player is dealt four cards, two at a time. The turn to deal and bet passes to the left.

PLAY AND BETTING

Any player dealt a winning hand can call for an immediate showdown, in which the best hand wins the pot. If no one wins outright, each player makes the necessary discards and is dealt replacements. There may be a further round of betting at this stage.

Otherwise, play starts with the player to the dealer's left, each player in turn having the choice of three options: to stake, bid or pass. In order to bid, the previous bet must be staked, that is, matched, before the new bid can be announced. Any bid must specify a points total, the type of hand and the amount being bid. The hand type must be higher than the one bid by the previous bidder, or the points total must be higher than the

> **You will need:** 40-card deck (standard pack with Eights to Tens removed); gambling chips/counters
>
> **Card ranking:** King, Queen, Jack, Seven down to Two, and Ace
>
> **Players:** Four to eight
>
> **Ideal for:** 14+

preceding one. A player who passes must discard one or two cards and draw replacements. Unlike Poker, it is impossible simply to fold.

Above: A *Primero*, which is the lowest-ranking hand in the game, consists of one card in each suit.

SCORING

Ties are broken in favour of the hand with the highest point count. For this purpose, each rank scores a specific number of points. The court cards are worth 10 points each, and Aces 16. Sixes and Sevens count as three times their face value. Hence, a Six counts as 18 and a Seven as 21. Twos to Fives are worth 10 points plus their face value. Thus, a Four is worth 14 points and a Five 15.

Above: A Fifty-Five, the second-lowest-ranking hand in the game. **Above:** Four of a Kind (Chorus), the highest-ranking hand in the game.

PRIMERO HANDS

There are four possible winning hands, which are detailed below from highest to lowest. Hand ranking wins over the highest score unless in a tie.

- Chorus – Four of a kind.
- Flush (or *Fluxus*) – A hand in which all four cards are of the same suit.
- Fifty-Five (or *Maximus*) – A hand consisting of Ace, Six and Seven of one suit plus one other card.
- *Primero* – A hand consisting of one card of each suit.

CONCLUSION

The game continues until a win is claimed. If there is a tie, the hand with the highest points wins.

POCH

This game is at least 500 years old. It has spread from its German homeland as far as North America, where variants of it are played under the names of Tripoli and Three in One. To play, you need a special board called a *Pochbrett*, which has nine compartments, each of which holds the chips bet on specific winning cards and combinations.

You will need: Standard deck with Twos to Sixes removed; gambling chips/counters; (drawing of a) Pochbrett board

Card ranking: Ace down to Seven

Players: Three to six

Ideal for: 14+

Left: A copy of a cover of a Poch boardgame (*c.*1897), with a picture of the Joker. It is currently on display at the Munich Municipal Museum.

OBJECT
To be the first player to get rid of all his cards.

THE DEAL
Before the deal, players dress the *Pochbrett* board, each putting one chip into each of its nine compartments – Ace, King, Queen, Jack, Ten, Marriage, Sequence, Poch (marked with a Joker on the board) and the unlabelled centre pot. From the 32-card deck, players are dealt five cards each, the next one being turned face up to determine the 'pay suit'. If a ready-made board is not to hand, it is fairly easy to make your own using paper.

Left: A *Pochbrett* board has nine sections for holding gambling chips, which are bet on specific winning cards and combinations.

PLAY AND SCORING
In the game's first stage, holding the Ace, King, Queen and Jack of the pay suit means winning the chips in the matching compartment. Holding the King and Queen wins the Marriage compartment, while holding Seven, Eight and Nine of the pay suit wins the Sequence compartment; if no one declares these, or if an Ace, King, Queen, Jack or Ten is turned up as the pay suit card, the chips are carried forward.

In the second stage, players bet on who has the best combinations of cards. Any set of Four of a Kind beats any set of Three of a Kind, and any set of Three of a Kind beats any Pair. A set of higher-ranking cards always beats the same number of lower-ranking ones. If two players hold Pairs of the same rank, one containing a card from the pay suit is better. Four Eights, for instance, beats three Kings, which beats two Nines, which beats the Queens of Hearts and Diamonds, which beats the Queens of Spades and Clubs, if Diamonds or Hearts is the pay suit.

Players bet by stating '*Ich poche*' and how many chips they are betting. The alternative is to pass. After the initial bet, players can either match it, raise or fold. The winner takes all the chips that were bet, plus the chips in the Poch compartment.

The previous stage's winner starts the final one by placing a card face up on top of the centre compartment on the board. Whoever holds the next higher card of the same suit then plays it, the process continuing until no one can play the next card required. The player of the last card of that sequence starts play again.

CONCLUSION
The first player to get rid of all his cards wins, taking the contents of the centre compartment. Other players forfeit a chip for each card they hold in hand.

BOUILLOTTE

This game was invented at the time of the French Revolution as the official replacement for a game called Brelan, which the Revolutionary government decided to ban. It was popular in France until the late 19th and early 20th centuries, when it was slowly but surely supplanted in French affections by the newly fashionable game of Poker.

OBJECT

To finish with the highest-ranking combination or suit, and so win the pot and/or bonus chips.

STRADDLING

Each player starts with a stack of 30 chips, known as the *cave* (stack). Players ante a chip to the pot, the dealer adding an extra chip. The ante is the stake that each player must put into the pool before receiving a hand or new cards. The player to the dealer's right can now elect to double the size of the pot. This is known as a straddle. The next player can do the same and so on round to the dealer. If a player chooses not to straddle, or does not have enough chips to do so, the straddling ends and the cards are dealt.

THE DEAL

Each player receives three cards, the dealer turning the next card face up to establish the trump suit.

PLAY

Players bet on who has the best hand, the first to bet being the player to the right of the last player to straddle. He can either open or pass. To open, a player must bet at least as many chips as the highest previous stake. The others may call (match) the bet, raise it or fold.

SCORING

Bonus chips from each of the opposing players are given to the holder of a *Brelan Carré* or *Brelan* (see box). If no one holds a *Brelan Carré* or a *Brelan*, the points for the cards held by all the players, including those who folded, are calculated suit by suit. Aces score 11 points, Kings and Queens 10 points each and the others score at face value. The suit with the highest total is the winning suit and the player holding the highest card of that suit wins the pot.

You will need: 20 cards comprising Aces, Kings, Queens, Nines and Eights; gambling chips/counters

Card ranking: Ace highest, Eight lowest

Players: Four

Ideal for: 10+

Above: Bouillotte was invented during the years of the French Revolution.

BOUILLOTTE HANDS

From highest to lowest, Bouillotte hands rank as follows:

- *Brelan Carré* – Three of a Kind of the same rank as the turn-up. It is worth a bonus three chips.
- *Brelan* – Three of a Kind. It is worth one extra chip. If more than one player holds a *Brelan*, the highest wins.

Right: Three of a Kind (*Brelan*). In the event of a tie, the best hand is one that matches the rank of the turn-up, making a *Brelan Carré*. If neither matches, the highest-ranked *Brelan* wins.

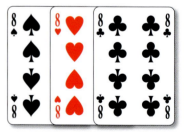

CONCLUSION

Betting continues until there are only two players left, when the first to call a bet forces a showdown.

SEVEN TWENTY-SEVEN

In this American vying game, the court cards are worth half a point each and number cards their face values. Aces can count for either a point or 11 points, depending on whether they are being played low, high – or, indeed, both.

You will need: 52 cards; gambling chips/counters

Card ranking: Ace high or low, remaining cards Kings down to Twos

Players: Four to ten

Ideal for: 10+

OBJECT

To end up with a hand that is as near to seven or 27 points as possible.

THE DEAL

Players ante their initial stakes to the pot. The ante is the stake that each player must put into the pot before receiving a hand or new cards. After this, one card is dealt face up to each player and another one face

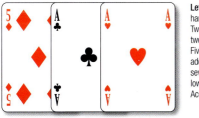

Left: The perfect hand in Seven Twenty-Seven: two Aces and a Five, the cards adding up to seven for Aces low and 27 for Aces high.

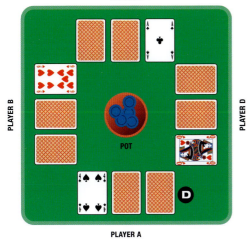

PLAYER C

PLAYER B

POT

PLAYER D

PLAYER A

Above: Once players have examined the face-up and face-down cards they have been dealt, each player, starting with the one to the dealer's left, may ask for an extra face-down card.

down. Once the face-down cards have been examined, each player, starting with the one to the dealer's left, may ask for an extra face-down card to be dealt.

PLAY AND BETTING

The first round of betting follows, initiated by the player to the dealer's left, who may either pass or bet any amount within the agreed maximum and minimum betting limits. If he passes, the chance to open the betting passes to the next player and so on round the table.

Following this, the other players can fold, or call (match) or raise the bet. If all the players but one fold, that player takes all the bets, the cards are thrown in and the next in turn deals. Otherwise, betting continues until the stakes are equalized – this happens, when, after one player has bet or raised, all the other players call or fold.

After each betting round, the remaining players can each ask for an extra card to be dealt to them face down. The alternative is to play the hand as it is. Another betting round follows.

SCORING AND CONCLUSION

When no player asks for an extra card, there is a showdown. Everyone still in the game reveals his cards. There are two winners – the players whose totals are nearest to seven and 27, respectively. They split the pot equally. In the event of a tie, players split the relevant part of the pot. For example, if two players score 6 points and one scores 24, the player with 24 takes half the pot and the players with 6 take one quarter of the pot each. If no one has scored exactly seven or 27 (the perfect hand to do this is Five, Ace and Ace), the nearest wins.

To win, you have to be below or equal to the target. This means that you cannot win the seven pot if your score is more than seven, or anything at all if your score is over 27. Under beats over means that, if the differences are equal, it is better to be under the target, not over it. For example, if the four players have scored 5.5, 7.5, 26 and 28 respectively, the ones with 5.5 and 26 win.

QUASI-TRUMP GAMES

BRITISH CARD GAME AUTHORITY DAVID PARLETT COINED THIS PHRASE FOR A STRANGE GROUP OF TRICK-TAKING GAMES, EACH WITH ITS OWN IDIOSYNCRASIES. PLAYERS NEED NOT FOLLOW SUIT AND INSTEAD CAN PLAY ANY CARD THEY LIKE. THERE IS NO CONVENTIONAL TRUMP SUIT — CERTAIN CARDS, OFTEN WITH SPECIAL NAMES, ACT AS QUASI-TRUMPS OR HAVE SPECIAL POWERS OF THEIR OWN. THIS APPLIES TO SEVENS, WHICH ALWAYS WIN THE TRICK, BUT ONLY WHEN LED.

Until Charles Cotton published *The Complete Gamester* in 1674, rules of card games were rarely written down and, when they were, they were almost always never complete. Generally speaking, they seem to have been transmitted orally. The French comic genius François Rabelais (*c.*1483–1553) noted the names of games, but these were not standardized and varied from place to place. Given all the variations, it is surprising that so many games managed to survive.

It is now accepted that the first trick-taking games probably first appeared in around 1400. Karnöffel is among the first, with reference to it dating back to 1426. Its rules were thought to be totally lost until it was discovered that a game called Kaiserspiel, which fitted Karnöffel's general description almost exactly, was still being played in a few places south of Lucerne in Switzerland. Judging by researchers' reconstructions, Karnöffel was an anarchic affair. Any card could be played to a trick, players could talk freely about the cards in their hand and what they wanted their partners to do. Also, only some of the cards in the suit designated as trumps had trick-taking powers: namely, the Jack, the Seven (if led), the Six and the Two. When it was first introduced, Catholics were outraged that the Pope, as one trump is named, was outranked by the Devil, while royalty were not amused to see Kings being beaten by low cards.

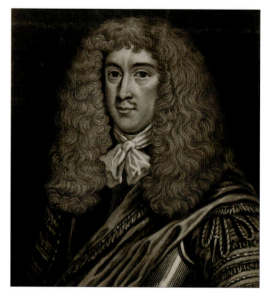

Above: Charles Cotton, 17th-century author of *The Complete Gamester*, was one of the first to write down the rules of several quasi-trump games.

WATTEN

This eccentric game originated in Bavaria, from where it spread to the Tyrol. It started life as a four-player partnership game, but there are versions for two and three players. In Bavaria, it is played with a 32-card German-suited pack; the Tyrolean version introduces the 6♦ as an extra wild card.

OBJECT

To score two or more game points by taking three tricks, or for one partnership to bluff the other into conceding.

TRUMPS AND RANKING

Watten is distinguished in having three permanent top trumps, the K♥, the 7♦ and the 7♣. Individually, these are known as *Maxi*, *Belli* and *Spritzer* and collectively as *Kritischen*. There is also a separate *Schlag* (trump rank) and trump suit. The cards of the trump rank are called *Schläge* (strikers), the highest being the *Hauptschlag* (chief striker) – the card that also belongs to the trump suit. The three other strikers rank immediately below it, followed by the remaining cards of the trump suit. The player to the dealer's left selects the trump rank and the dealer names the trump suit.

PLAYER C

PLAYER B

PLAYER D

PLAYER A

Above: In this hand of Watten, Player B has announced Nine as the trump rank, and the dealer has announced Clubs as the trump suit. Player B leads the *Hauptschlag* (chief striker – the card belonging to both the trump suit and the trump rank), forcing the next player to lay a top trump, another striker or a card from the trump suit. Player C lays the 7♦ (*Belli*), but Player D tops this with the K♥ (*Maxi*). Player A discards, allowing Player D to take the trick.

You will need: Standard pack with Sixes and below removed

Card ranking: Non-trump ranking is Ace down to Seven; for trump ranking, see below

Players: Four, in partnerships of two

Ideal for: 14+

THE DEAL AND PLAY

The dealer shuffles the 32 cards, which are then cut by the player to the right. If the cut card is a top trump, the cutter may take it. If the next one is the second-top trump, the dealer may take that and, if the next card is the third, the cutter can take it again. Each player is dealt five cards in packets of three and two, although the dealer and cutter get fewer if they have added to their hands.

After the deal, the trump rank and suit are announced, and the player to the dealer's left leads to the trick. If the chief striker is led, then a top trump, another striker or suit trump must be played if possible. Otherwise, there is no obligation to follow suit.

Left: There are three permanent top trumps: the K♥, 7♦ and 7♣, collectively called *Kritischen*.

SCORING

The score can be affected by any prior betting, which can take place at any time after the announcement of trump rank and suit by a player saying '*Gehen*' (go). If the opposing side respond with '*Schauen*' (see), the stakes are raised to three game points, or they can concede. Betting can continue indefinitely, although a team with nine or 10 game points is *Gespannt* (tight) and not allowed to bet further. Game is either 11 or 15 points.

CONCLUSION

Hands continue until three tricks are taken (if there is no betting, the team taking them scores two points) or a partnership is bluffed into conceding.

KARNÖFFEL

Claimed to be the oldest trick-taking game in the Western world, Karnöffel was one of the first to have a trump suit, properly termed the 'chosen' suit. This reconstruction is based on the research of US card authority Glenn Overby.

You will need: Standard pack with Aces removed

Card reading: King down to Two, except in trumps (see below)

Players: Four, in partnerships of two

Ideal for: 14+

OBJECT

To take the most tricks out of five to win a hand. Players agree how many hands make up a game at the start.

TRUMP SUIT RANKINGS

The trump suit ranks differently, and certain cards have trick-taking powers. The Jack of trumps (*Karnöffel*) ranks highest, beating all other cards. The Seven of trumps, the Devil, comes second, but enjoys that status only if it is led. Following this is the Six of trumps (the Pope) and the Two of trumps (*Kaiser*), then the Three of trumps (the *Oberstecher*) and the Four of trumps (the *Unterstecher*). These last two cannot beat any of the above trumps. The Three of trumps cannot beat a King, and the Four of trumps cannot beat a Queen or King. A Five of trumps, the *Farbenstecher*, cannot beat any of the court cards or any of the above trumps.

THE DEAL

Each player receives five cards dealt singly, the first face up, the others face down. The lowest-ranking face-up card determines which suit is trumps. In the event of a tie, trumps are set by the first card of that rank to be dealt.

PLAY

The player to the dealer's left leads to the first trick. The person who plays the highest card of the suit led or the highest trump wins the trick and leads to the next. Subsequently, any card can be played, since there is no requirement to follow suit. During the course of play, players are allowed to communicate freely with one another. In fact, most of the important cards have signals linked to them. It is even legal to signal cards that are not held in order to try to confuse the opposition.

PLAYER C

PLAYER B

PLAYER D

PLAYER A

Above: Here, Spades are trumps. Player B leads the 4♠ (*Unterstecher*) but this is not strong enough to beat the Queen played by Player C. Player D plays the 3♠ (*Oberstecher*), winning the trick until Player A tops it with a King.

CONCLUSION

The partnership taking the most tricks out of the five available wins the hand. The player who led to the first trick then deals the next hand. Partnerships agree at the start how many hands will make up a game.

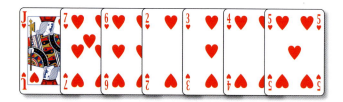

Left: Trumps (here assumed to be Hearts) have special ranks and trick-taking powers. The Jack (*Karnöffel*) ranks highest, followed by the Seven (the Devil), but only if this is led to a trick. Next comes the Six (the Pope), the Two (*Kaiser*), the Three (*Oberstecher*), the Four (*Unterstecher*) and the Five (*Farbenstecher*).

BRUS

A Swedish partnership game, Brus is unique because it is played with a mixture of 18 playable and 14 unplayable cards.

You will need: Standard pack with Fives and below removed

Card ranking: See 'Playable and Unplayable Cards'

Players: Four or six, playing in partnerships of two or three

Ideal for: 14+

OBJECT

To score six strokes (game points) over as many deals as it takes. In each deal, a game point is won by the partnership that wins six tricks.

PLAYABLE AND UNPLAYABLE CARDS

Playable cards are the only ones that can be played to tricks, while the unplayable ones are unusable, the exception being the K♣, which can score if a side that has taken five tricks holds it. For this reason, it is known as the 'outcome card'.

From highest to lowest, all playable cards are the J♣ (*Spit*), the 8♠ (*Dull*) and the K♥ (*Brus*). These cards are the *makadori* (matadors) and are followed by the Nines, Aces, the other three Jacks and Sixes of Clubs, Spades, Hearts and Diamonds, respectively. The 9♣ is commonly called *plägu* – literally, this means 'torture', because playing it may force the next player into leading a *makadori* he would rather have kept in reserve.

Unplayable cards are the remaining Eights, Tens, Queens and the other Kings, although the K♣ can score in a specific instance. Sevens have their own status. They are scoring cards and cannot be beaten, but they cannot beat other cards. They have no rank order.

THE DEAL

From the 36-card deck, each player receives nine cards (or six cards each if there are six people playing), dealt one at a time. Play is to the left.

PLAY

The player to the dealer's left leads, but first he lays any Sevens he may hold face up on the table. Each of these counts by itself as a trick. He then leads a playable card to the first trick. Each of the other players in turn must subsequently play a higher card if they can. If not, they must pass. The highest card played wins the trick and its winner leads to the next, assuming that he holds Sevens or playable cards. If not, the lead passes to the next player in clockwise rotation.

SCORING

Winning six tricks is worth a stroke. Winning six tricks in succession is known as a lurch (*jan*) and is worth two strokes. A no-score draw is a possible outcome.

CONCLUSION

Play continues until a partnership has won a score by taking six tricks – five if they hold the K♣. The latter feature is often called into play when playable cards have been exhausted and neither side has managed to take six tricks. If neither partnership succeeds in taking six tricks, there is no score and the same dealer deals again. Six strokes wins the game.

Below: The so-called playable cards in Brus, ranked in order from the highest to lowest.

Left: The so-called unplayable cards in Brus. They are all unusable, except the K♣, which is the 'outcome card'. Possession of this decides some games which would otherwise be drawn.

ALKORT

This was Iceland's national card game until its place was usurped by Bridge. What adds spice to this game, which can trace its origins back to at least the 18th century, is its unusual card rankings and the fact that, before play starts, it is perfectly legal to show your partner your highest card.

OBJECT

To take as many tricks as possible. Five or more tricks need to be taken in order to win a game.

CARD RANKING

The cards rank as follows. The K♦ is highest, followed by a 2♥, 4♣, 8♠, 9♥ and 9♦, and then Aces, Jacks, Sixes and the remaining Eights, regardless of suit. The Queens, Threes, black Nines, and remaining Fours, Twos and Kings are valueless. The Sevens have a special status. When led to a trick, they are unbeatable, but otherwise they cannot beat another card. A Seven cannot be led unless its player has previously taken a trick.

THE DEAL

Players cut for partners and deal. From the 44-card deck, each receives nine cards three at a time; the remaining cards are placed face down to form the stock. If a player holds no card capable of beating an Eight, he may declare himself *friöufaer* (under eight). He shows all his cards, discards eight and takes eight from the stock.

PLAY

Before play, the partners secretly show each other the highest card in their hands. The player to the dealer's left leads to the first trick. The trick's winner leads to the next.

You will need: Standard pack with Tens and Fives removed
Card ranking: See under 'Card Ranking' below
Players: Two, or four in partnerships of two, as described here
Ideal for: 14+

There is no need to follow suit, and the highest card played takes the trick. If two or more equally high cards are played, the one played first counts as highest.

SCORING

At least five out of the nine tricks need to be taken in order to score a game point. If a partnership takes five tricks before their opponents have taken one, they *múk* their opponents and score five points. If they win six or more tricks in this way, they make a stroke, scoring as many points as there are tricks in the stroke.

CONCLUSION

Play continues until all five tricks have been played for, unless one partnership has taken five tricks in succession. In this case, play continues for as long as it takes to win.

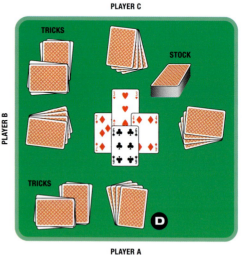

Above: Player B has led the 7♦. Sevens can only be led after having previously taken a trick, and, although worthless otherwise, when led they cannot be beaten, so Player B takes the trick.

Left: This player holds no card capable of beating an Eight, so may declare himself *friöufaer* (under eight). To do this, he must show all his cards, and discard all but one of them, taking eight replacements from the stock.

TAROT GAMES

CONTRARY TO POPULAR BELIEF, TAROT CARDS WERE NOT ORIGINALLY INVENTED FOR FORTUNE TELLING. THEY WERE INTRODUCED INTO THE ITALIAN CARD WORLD IN THE EARLY 15TH CENTURY AS A MEANS OF PEPPING UP TRICK-TAKING GAMES BY INTRODUCING A NEW INGREDIENT INTO THEM – THE NOTION OF TRUMPS. FROM THERE, TAROT GAMES SPREAD THROUGHOUT MUCH OF EUROPE, AND THEY ARE STILL POPULAR THERE TODAY.

The Italian idea was to add a fifth suit of 21 specially illustrated numbered cards called *trionfi* (triumphs) to the then standard pack of 56 cards bearing the standard Italian suitmarks of swords, staves, cups and coins, plus a special card called the Fool or *Excuse*. The original full pack therefore consisted of 78 cards. Despite appearances, the Fool is not the origin of the modern Joker. Originally, it was simply a card that could be played at any time, rather than following suit or trumping. It could not take a trick. Later, in Central Europe, its role changed and it became the highest trump.

The *trionfi* were trick-takers, and their original function was to act as cards that would beat any ordinary card played to the same trick. In English, *trionfi* was to become trumps, but Tarot games never really caught on in Britain in the same way as they did in Spain, Portugal and the Balkans, where they remain popular to this day. It was not until early in the 16th century that card players decided that it was simpler and more economical to pick a card at random from the existing pack and make its suit trumps, so doing away with the complexities of the separate *trionfi* suit. Slightly later, for reasons unknown, the Italians renamed *trionfi* as *tarocchi*. It is from this latter word, however, that the German word *tarock* is derived and subsequently the French and English word tarot.

Above: Most people associate Tarot cards with fortune telling, but, contrary to popular belief, they were not invented for that purpose.

FRENCH TAROT

This, as the name suggests, is the most popular Tarot game in France. The 78-card *Tarot Nouveau* deck consists of the four standard suits, a suit of 21 *atouts* (trumps) and the *Excuse* (the Fool). The *Excuse*, the One and Twenty-one of trumps, are known collectively as *bouts* (ends).

> **You will need:** 78-card *Tarot Nouveau* deck (see opposite)
>
> **Card ranking:** The 21 numbered trumps (from Twenty-one to One); the *Excuse* (depicting a Fool or Jester); the 14 cards in the four suits: King, Queen, Cavalier, Jack and Ten down to One
>
> **Players:** Four, in variable partnerships from hand to hand
>
> **Ideal for:** 14+

OBJECT

The soloist, the successful bidder, aims to win a minimum number of points, the amount of which depends on the number of *bouts* in the tricks he wins.

BIDDING AND THE SOLOIST

The person who will play alone as the soloist against the three others is decided by an auction. Starting with the player to the dealer's right, each player in turn has one opportunity to bid to win a certain number of points with their hand, or to pass. Each bid must be higher than the one preceding it. If all four players pass, the cards are thrown in and the next to deal deals a new hand.

The soloist's objective is to win a set number of points, which varies depending on the number of *bouts* that are contained in the tricks he takes. Three *bouts* means that the soloist needs at least 36 card points to win, two *bouts* requires 41 points to win, and one *bout* 51 points. With no *bouts*, at least 56 card points are needed to win. Each *bout* and King is worth five points, Queens four, Knights three and Jacks two.

DECLARATIONS

Before play, each player in turn can make one or more declarations. The points these score do not count towards winning a bid. They are scored in addition to what is won or lost. A player holding 10 or more trumps can declare *Poignée* (bunch). A single bunch scores 20 points (10–12 trumps), a double (13–14 trumps) 30 and a treble (15 trumps) 40. Declaring *Chelem* (slam) is an announcement of the intention to take all 18 tricks. If successful, it is worth 400 points; there is a 200-point penalty for failure. An undeclared *Chelem* scores 200 points and no penalties.

THE DEAL

Each player receives 18 cards in packets of three, with six cards being dealt face down to form the *chien* (dog). They can be dealt at any stage of the deal, but the first and last three cards of the pack cannot be included. A player who has been dealt the One of trumps and no other trump must declare the deal void. The cards are thrown in and the next dealer deals.

Right: Cards from the Marseilles Tarot pack, one of the standard patterns for the design of tarot cards accepted today. There are 21 trump cards, the first of which is the Magician (*le Bateleur*); the House of God, or Tower (*la Maison Dieu*), is the sixteenth trump. At times, the Fool (*le Mat*), is unnumbered and viewed as separate and additional to the other 21 numbered trumps.

LE BATELEUR
THE MAGICIAN

LA MAISON DIEU
THE TOWER OF DESTRUCTION

LE MAT
THE FOOL

Above: 17th-century French tarot cards: *La lune* (moon), *Le chariot* (chariot), *L'ermite* (hermit) and *Ivsttice* (justice), by an unknown Parisian manufacturer.

The four possible bids are as follows:

• *Petite* (small): if successful, its bidder can use the cards in the *chien* to improve his hand.

• *Garde* (guard): the same bid for a higher score. In both this and *Petite*, the soloist turns up and takes the cards in the *chien* and discards six cards from his hand face down. These discards may not include any trumps, Kings or the *Excuse*.

• *Garde Sans Chien* (guard without the dog): the taker plays without the benefit of the cards in the *chien*, although the card points in it still count towards his score.

• *Garde Contre le Chien* (guard against the dog): the taker plays without the cards in the *chien,* and the card points in it go to the taker's opponents.

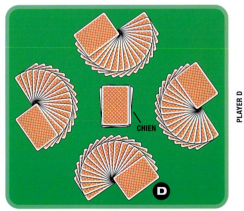

PLAYER C

PLAYER B

PLAYER D

CHIEN

D

PLAYER A

PLAY

The soloist takes the *chien* and discards, moving it to his side of the table if playing *sans le chien*, or, if the bid is *contre le chien*, moving it to the opposite player's side. The player to the dealer's right leads. Players must follow suit if they can, or trump or overtrump. If this is impossible, a trump must still be played even though it will not take the trick. The *Excuse* can be played at any time. It can also be retrieved from a taken trick and replaced by a worthless card. The *Excuse* cannot take a trick unless it is led to the last trick by a team that has won the 17 preceding ones.

SCORING AND CONCLUSION

At the end of the hand, the opponents pool their tricks. The last trick is worth 10 points (*Petit au Bout*) if it holds a One of trumps. The cards are counted in pairs of two non-scoring cards or a non-scoring card and a scoring one. The first scores a point, and the second is worth the scoring card's value. The total is deducted from 91 for the soloist's score. In a *Petite*, the score won or lost is 25 for game, plus the difference between the card points the soloist won and the number needed. The *Petit au Bout* is added or subtracted. In a *Garde*, the total is doubled; in *Garde Sans Chien* quadrupled and in *Garde Contre le Chien* sextupled. The *Poignée* and *Chelem* bonuses are added or subtracted. The soloist wins, or loses, this number of points from all three opponents.

Left: The remaining six cards in the pack, the *chien*, can be dealt at any stage of the deal, but must not include the first and last cards of the pack.

OTTOCENTO

Originating in Bologna in the 16th century, hence its other name Tarocco Bolognese, this partnership game is still played there with a special 62-card pack also known as the *Tarocco Bolognese*. It consists of four 10-card suits (Swords, Batons, Coins and Cups), 21 trump cards, and a wild card called the *Matto*, which is not a trump and has no ranking order.

You will need: Tarocco Bolognese 62-card pack	
Card ranking: See box below	
Players: Four, in partnerships of two	
Ideal for: 14+	

OBJECT

To be the first to score 800 points. There are four ways to score points: for card combinations in individual hands; for card combinations from tricks captured by each partnership; for individual counting cards captured in tricks by each partnership; and for winning the last trick.

THE DEAL

Who deals first is decided randomly, after which the deal passes to the right. The dealer shuffles the cards, and the player to his left cuts them. Each player receives 15 cards five at a time, the dealer discarding two from the seven he would otherwise be left with at the end of the deal. The discards count for the dealing partnership as though they were in tricks, but if the partnership loses every trick, they too are lost. The only cards that may not be discarded are the *Tarrochi* (see box) and the Kings.

PLAY

Immediately before playing to the first trick, each player in turn has the opportunity to declare any scoring combinations by placing the appropriate cards face up on the table. Otherwise, after this, the cards are picked up and returned to that player's hand. The alternative is to score them at the end of the hand. It is not compulsory to make declarations, nor need they be made in full. A player may declare a sequence of four cards, for instance, while actually holding five, without penalty. If either side scores 800 points through declarations alone, the game ends then, without any further play.

Any card may be led, the other players following suit or playing a trump, unless a player holds the *Matto*. This can be played regardless of whether its player holds any

Left: Aces from an Italian playing card set, of the Batons, Cups, Coins and Swords suits. Italian playing cards most commonly consist of a deck of 40 cards (four suits from One to Seven, plus three face cards). Since these cards first appeared in the late 17th century, when each region in Italy was a separately ruled province, there is no official Italian pattern.

cards of the suit led. It is always retained by the partnership playing it – if the opposing partnership takes the trick, it is simply exchanged for a worthless card. It can be lost only if the partnership playing it loses every trick.

Upon leading to a trick, a player can make three signals. *Vollo*, tossing a card in the air, means that this is the last card held in that particular suit. *Busso*, striking the table with the fist, is a signal to play the highest card held. *Striscio*, scraping a card on the table, is a request to lead trumps. It is acceptable to make more than one signal at the same time.

SCORING

The *Tarrochi* (*Angelo*, *Mondo*, *Bègato* and *Matto*) and Kings are worth five points, Queens four, Knights three, Jacks two and all other cards a point each. The winner of the last trick scores six extra points. The cards are counted in pairs, a point being deducted from each pair's value. Including the last trick, there are 93 points available in the pack.

To work out card points, a single one-point card is placed on top of each two-, three-, four-, or five-point one and the values scored. The remaining one-point cards are counted in pairs with the six-point bonus for taking the last trick being added, if appropriate. The other side's score is determined by subtracting the declaring partnership's total from the possible 93 points in the pack. The partnership to score 800 points first wins the rubber.

Below: Cards from the Visconti-Sforza deck, the earliest set of Tarot cards, which was produced in Italy in the mid-15th century. They were commissioned by Filippo Maria Visconti (1392–1447), Duke of Milan. The cards were then still called *trionfi* (trump) cards, From left to right, the cards are the Fool, the Hanged Man, the Magician, and the Empress.

Combinations of three or more cards of the same kind are called *cricche*. A *cricche* of all four *Tarocchi* is worth 36 points, while any three scores 18. Kings score 34 and 17 for four or three respectively, Queens 28 and 14, Knights 26 and 13 and Jacks 24 and 12. If three or more different *cricche* are scored at the same time, the total score is doubled. Combinations of three or more cards in sequence also score. A three-card sequence scores 10 points, with each additional card adding five points to that score.

This is where the *Matto* and *Bègato* shine. As wild cards, they can be used to establish a sequence or to extend one, but can only be used in trump sequences. They can then be used consecutively, except at the end of a sequence. If they are not needed to establish a sequence, they can be added to its length – and increase the score.

CONCLUSION

If any combinations are announced during the first trick, they are scored then. Otherwise, scoring takes place at the end of the hand. Usually, one partnership starts by laying out all the cards it has captured face up on the table, so as to show all the significant cards of each suit, trumps and *Mori* in rank order.

The *cricche* are counted first, remembering to double the score if there are more than three of them, followed by those of the opposing partnership. Sequences are then scored, and the scores are again doubled if there are three or more. Finally, the individual card points are calculated.

POKER GAMES

It was in New Orleans in 1892 that the name Poker was first used for this game. Despite its somewhat insalubrious reputation, it has gone from strength to strength to become one of the world's most popular card games.

PLAYING POKER

In one form or another, poker and its antecedents have been played for over 500 years. The game is such a part of western culture, at least, that many poker-related phrases have found their way into everyday language. The uninitiated may regard it as just a card game, albeit one that particularly engages people who possess an innate desire to gamble. Yet to anyone who has ever played poker, such a basic definition of this challenging and often rewarding pursuit cannot begin to tell the whole story. Indeed, some players regard poker as less of a game and more as a way of life. Now, in the early stages of the 21st century, those elements of poker that have contributed to its longevity are being discovered by a new generation of players every day. All over the world, newcomers are learning how to bluff, bet and rake in the chips, as well as experiencing the heartbreak associated with losing a large pot courtesy of a bad beat.

The rapid increase in the popularity of poker and its elevation from card game to cultural phenomenon has been a notable feature of the past decade. Televised poker tournaments have helped generate more interest in the game than ever before, with professional players and tournament winners now frequently acquiring celebrity status on the back of such media exposure. Magazine articles, books and advertising continue to feed the public's renewed appetite for the game. While poker has often been characterized as glamorous, many stars from the worlds of film, television and sport are keen players whose endorsement helps bolster that image. Poker has simply never been more fashionable.

Helping to keep it that way are the online casinos which, since the launch of PlanetPoker in 1998, have become multimillion-dollar businesses attracting the interest of serious corporate players. ParadisePoker, an early competitor in the market, was bought for US$297.5m by Sportingbet Plc in October 2004 and its share price, quoted on the London Stock Exchange's Alternative Investment Market (AIM), soon increased by 375 per cent. This commercial interest is readily understood given the fact that in April 2005, according to UK bookmakers Ladbrokes, around US$180m was being wagered at online poker tables every day. Interactive gambling online is expected to generate annual turnover of US$100 billion and pre-tax profits of US$11 billion by 2010. There are now hundreds of

Left: Learning poker can be fun and challenging. It can be a fulfilling pastime and one that often becomes a great passion for many players.

Left: Peter Eastgate won the main event of the World Series of Poker on November 11th 2008 in the Rio Hotel and Casino in Las Vegas, Nevada. At just 22 years old, he is the youngest WSOP champion to date. His winnings totalled $9.15 million.

Below: In a game where the wild card is played, four aces and a joker, known as five of a kind, is the highest ranking hand possible.

online sites offering convenient and instant access to a poker game from the comfort of home, allowing hundreds of thousands of players to exercise their skill and judgement simultaneously, around the clock. The one obstacle hampering projected economic growth in online gaming, however, is the legislation enacted in the United States that restricts American financial institutions from processing transactions to Internet gaming operations. The Unlawful Internet Gambling Enforcement Act of October 2006 has not prevented American players from continuing to play online, but has reduced the incentive to playing online by making it difficult for them to access their online gaming accounts to make or receive payments. Given that the United States accounted for just over half of all online poker players when the act became law, the leading companies in the market are expected to consolidate their positions to cope with the expected short-term decline in demand for their product. As more companies chase fewer customers, so mergers and acquisitions are also predicted to occur while attention turns to expanding the market in Europe and the rest of the world.

Despite the legal situation in the United States, the impact of televised poker and online gaming has been to revive interest in playing poker socially, whether in clubs or at home, as the game continues to shed its sometimes dubious reputation in favour of growing respectability. More women are playing, taking advantage of the wealth of online opportunities to practise their skills before tackling opponents away from the virtual poker world. Live poker may still be dominated by men in numerical terms but latest estimates suggest that women represent 40 per cent of the online market. It seems likely that this interest will soon be reflected at the poker tables in casinos and clubs.

THE HISTORY OF POKER

POKER HAS BEEN A POPULAR PASTIME SINCE THE 1800S WHEN IT WAS A NATURAL PART OF EVERYDAY LIFE IN AMERICAN CULTURE, AND HAS OFTEN FEATURED IN THE WESTERN FILM GENRE. TODAY IT IS STILL A WIDELY PLAYED GAME, WITH TELEVISED GAMES BRINGING POKER TO A NEW AUDIENCE.

As the new millennium gathers pace, the status of poker as the game of choice among card players worldwide remains intact. Crucially, poker's image has also undergone a transformation. Television schedules are liberally sprinkled with poker programming offering viewers a chance to see the world's best players, many of whom are young and precociously talented, demonstrating their skills at the table. The result of this recent development is that big-screen representations of the game have also been updated. Poker-playing scenes set in Wild West saloon bars are now rivalled by luxurious settings for the game in which even James Bond, as depicted in *Casino Royale* (2006), does his bit to bolster the popularity of Texas Hold 'em. That poker should feature in such a high-profile cinema release underlines the enduring appeal of a game that has a rich and colourful history like no other.

Right: In the early years of the 21st century, poker has emerged as the world's most popular card game following a massive boost in interest stimulated by television and the Internet. After 200 years of evolution, it now enjoys a much more positive image as the game's association with the lawlessness of the Wild West and the Mafia-run Las Vegas casinos finally begins to wane. Today, poker is big business and has an air of legitimacy that should ensure that the stigma previously associated with playing the game remains a thing of the past.

ORIGINS OF POKER

Determining the exact origins of poker has proved an elusive task for those researching the history of the game. It is widely accepted that poker as it is played today developed rapidly in the United States during the 18th and 19th centuries, following the influx of immigrants seeking work and fresh opportunities in the New World. In his book *An Exposure of the Arts and Miseries of Gambling*, published in 1834, author Jonathan H. Green describes the rules of poker, the so-called 'cheating game'. This refers to a game involving a deck of just 20 cards that had overtaken three-card monte in terms of popularity as a betting medium, ironically because it was considered less prone to manipulation by 'card sharps'. Although he did not identify it as poker, this same game was also described by English actor Joseph Cowell in 1829. He had witnessed it being played in New Orleans and was aware of its popularity on the Mississippi riverboats, which effectively transported it through Louisiana and into the rest of the country.

THE EUROPEAN INFLUENCE

Card games had been growing in popularity throughout France since the 15th century, while in Germany a similar game named pochen or pochspiel held sway. However, the French connection is thought to provide the most tangible link in the evolution of poker, as the colonials who settled in Canada and New Orleans imported a gambling and bluffing game named poque. Both games were played with a deck of either 32 or 36 cards, and winning hands were limited to pairs, three of a kind and four of a kind. Elsewhere in Europe, the Spanish game primero, dating back to 1526, is thought to have been an influence on poque and pochen, although, like France's brelan and the English game of brag, players only received three cards with which to make a hand. Italy played host to il frusso, which incorporated much the same elements as the other European games.

However, though it is impossible to prove beyond doubt, all may owe their origins to a Persian game called Âs Nas. Similar to five-card stud poker, Âs Nas was played with either 20 or 25 cards, depending on

Above: The French connection is thought to be the most tangible link in the evolution of poker. French colonials who settled in Canada and New Orleans imported a gambling and bluffing game called poque. However, some people believe the game may be descended from the German game of pochen, the English game of brag or even the Persian game of Âs Nas.

Left: When gambling fell out of favour in frontier towns such as New Orleans, poker was forced onto the paddle-steamers that chugged along the Mississippi river. Gaming on the paddle steamers travelling the Mississippi effectively transported games such as poker through Louisiana and the rest of America.

the number of players. Yet, although the cards for playing this game were known to exist in the 16th century, no mention is made of the game until 1890, some years after poker itself was already established. Whatever the provenance of poker, it is the impact of post-18th-century American culture on the game that has accelerated its development into the phenomenally popular diversion known today.

PLAYING CARDS

The first playing cards were introduced into Europe in the 14th century by the Saracens and Moors, their origins being traced back to 10th-century China and, latterly, Egypt. These early cards were made of thin slices of ivory or wood and frequently featured colourful, hand-painted designs. As such, they were generally the preserve of the wealthy and it was only with the development of printing from woodcuts and the subsequent invention of the printing press that cheaper decks could be produced. The French influence in North America popularized card games, leading to further evolution in card design as Americans began to make their own modifications in around 1800. These included the addition of indices in the corners (the identifying marks placed in the cards' borders or corners) and double-headed court cards for easier recognition, patterned rather than plain backs as well as rounded corners and varnished surfaces to help reduce wear and tear.

Below: A selection of historic cards showing that the basic design of the court cards and the suits has remained unchanged for centuries. From the left: 18th-century French king of spades and queen of hearts, German double-headed jack of clubs from 1860, a jack of diamonds from Belgium, 1811.

THE SUITS
♦ ♣ ♥ ♠

The suits of clubs, diamonds, hearts and spades are believed to have been standardized by the French, who also introduced the representations of royal court figures for the higher-value cards. Although refined in detail, owing to improvements in printing methods, the basic design of the court cards has remained unchanged for at least 200 years. Traditional Latin and German playing cards feature variations on the theme of the suits. Spanish and Italian playing cards, for example, feature coins, cups, swords and batons while Germanic designs incorporate hearts, leaves, bells and acorns.

Above: A set of three cards showing the modern double-headed court cards of the king, queen and jack. Modern playing cards carry index labels on opposite corners to facilitate identifying the cards when they overlap. Round corners were introduced to eliminate the problem of wear and tear resulting from traditional square corners.

THE AMERICAN GAME

It was not until after the end of the American Civil War in 1865 that poker could be said to have shrugged off the European influences that shaped its development. By 1875, with the 52-card deck widely used and jokers introduced, the game had become a prominent facet of American culture. The 50 years leading up to that point had seen the game move from its original base in the Mississippi delta to the frontier towns of the Wild West and then on to California as a gold rush took hold in 1849. However, five-card draw and five-card stud poker were not as popular with some prospectors as games such as roulette, which offered a quicker route to riches compared to a card game that required patience and a little application in order to earn any reward. Despite the game not proving to everyone's taste as well as meeting opposition from various prohibitionist movements of the 19th century, poker continued to be played by those Americans who accepted risk and speculation as as a natural feature of everyday life.

New Orleans

The first casino to open in the United States was owned by John Davis, whose establishment in New Orleans fed the public desire for gambling by remaining open 24 hours a day. Food, alcohol, dancing girls and popular games like faro and roulette were all part of the casino experience for Davis's clients. Such was the success of his venture that more casinos soon followed, creating a reputation for the 'Big Easy' as the country's gambling capital. This cultural shift made New Orleans attractive to various full-time card players and professional cheats, both groups seeking to exploit the naive and the gullible. The waterfront area, known as 'the swamp', became a virtual no-go area for the law as the gamblers and cheats policed themselves. Those who either won more than seemed polite or who were otherwise exposed as frauds knew that they ran the risk of instant summary justice from their victims, sympathy for their plight being in short supply.

Above: A woman driving a wagon in New Orleans in 1900. The city became the first in America to host a casino when John Davis opened one in 1922. The 'Big Easy', as it was nicknamed, became renowned for attracting gamblers. An attempt was made to outlaw gambling in Louisiana in 1911, but this was never seriously enforced and New Orleans continued to benefit from the tourists who came to try their luck at the gaming tables.

Right: John Doyle hosts a poker party at his Arizona ranch with Judge Brown and Professor Burrison in 1887, illustrating how the popularity of the game had spread north and west from the Mississippi delta area where it initially developed.

Right: Old timers playing poker in a bar, in 1913. Traditionally, bars have always been popular locations for card games, and in America the cultural association of poker with saloon bars developed during the Wild West era when any self-respecting bar owner would provide a poker table for the entertainment of the clientele.

Below right: 'Wooding Up' on the Mississippi by Frances F. Palmer, 1863. The thousands of riverboats that plied the Mississippi and Missouri rivers became havens for poker players in mid-19th-century America as various towns passed legislation prohibiting gambling. It was aboard one such vessel in 1832 that Jim Bowie, inventor of the Bowie knife, came to the aid of a man who was on the verge of suicide having been cheated out of his fortune while playing poker.

Riverboat gambling

The casinos of New Orleans drew many more visitors to the city, boosting its economy and that of the surrounding area. As the riverboats of the Mississippi, the Missouri and the Ohio contributed to the commercial growth of the region, so they provided the means for the professional gamblers to ply their trade and seek fresh markets of their own. This was no easy task since an increasing number of towns were already passing legislation to outlaw various gambling practices in a bid to drive them away. Vicksburg in Mississippi took such action as early as 1835, but the thousands of multi-decked paddle-steamers remained a haven for the poker players and card sharps, who often dressed in fine, fashionable clothes to offset their negative image.

By this time poker had distanced itself from its precursors with players having to negotiate just one round of betting based upon the strength of their five-card hand. Initially, with decks consisting of only 20 cards, the game was limited to four players and there was no draw, the mechanism which enables players to exchange a card in their hand with a fresh

card from the deck. Ever mindful of an opportunity to tip the odds in their favour, card professionals gradually started to implement the use of 52-card decks to play poker and, within a couple of decades, this game had almost completely eclipsed the 20-card version. A bigger deck meant that more players could be accommodated during a game and the introduction of the draw gave them a chance to improve their hand. The price to be paid was an extra betting round, the impact of which was to increase the levels of skill and judgement required to win.

POKER IN THE WILD WEST

The global success of the Western as a Hollywood film genre, albeit one which conveyed a slightly romanticized view of America's past, is obviously the major reason why poker is so often associated with the Wild West. Although sometimes peripheral to the action, the game features in countless saloon-bar scenes, accurately representing its popularity in the staging posts, mining towns and cattle-transit stations of the time. Less accurate are the portrayals of the West's legendary characters whose heroic deeds were exaggerated, if not entirely fabricated, for the entertainment of avid newspaper readers on the East Coast. Writers such as E.Z.C. Judson, publisher of a weekly sensationalist magazine called *Ned Buntline's Own*, helped create the enduring myths about the West and its adventurers. As a result, towns such as Deadwood and Tombstone became more famous for the fatal resolution of betting disputes than for the mineral riches that led to their existence.

Life as a professional gambler was fraught with danger since so many potential sore losers possessed impulsive natures and firearms. Indeed, the invention of the small Derringer pistol, inaccurate beyond six feet, stemmed from the need for gamblers to keep an ace up their sleeve, figuratively speaking. To offset the danger, those with a penchant for a gamble often ran saloons or brothels in order to provide a regular income and, given the prevailing morality of the times, to legitimize their lifestyle. In 1849 the fabled Gold Rush diverted attention further west as prospectors headed for California. Such was the influx of people to the area that San Francisco very soon overtook New Orleans as the nation's biggest gambling centre.

Legality and morality

The call for gambling to be outlawed has been heard regularly throughout history, with gamblers viewed as both morally bankrupt and in need of protection from their perceived weakness. Certainly, bearing in mind that poker was originally called 'the cheating game', it is understandable why those who insisted on playing were so often cautioned by others of a more temperate nature. The sharp practices of the so-called professional gamblers were targeted in western frontier towns towards the end of the 19th century, with certain games either made illegal or strictly controlled. Although few of these laws were ever enforced, a total ban was introduced in the early 20th century in several states.

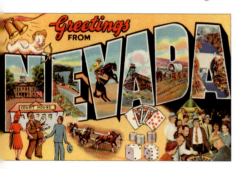

Above: Picture postcard from Nevada, 1941. Along with many other states, Nevada's legislators had sought to ban gambling. In 1931, a ruling from California's attorney general that draw poker was a game of skill and should not be subject to anti-gambling law allowed Nevada to relax its prohibitive stance. In turn, Las Vegas developed into the gambling capital of the world.

Right: Robert Mitchum in *Blood on the Moon*, 1948, watching a tense game of five-card stud in a scene that typifies poker's representation in the Western. In 1968, Mitchum starred in *Five Card Stud*, another Western which centred on events at the poker table.

Above: Prospectors in a gold mining town in Nevada. Gold was discovered at Goldfield, Nevada, in 1902 and six months later there was a bustling frontier town on the site. Note that there are a hotel, theatre, bank, jewellery store, and a horse market already established.

Left: James Butler 'Wild Bill' Hickok, pictured in 1873 as he appeared when performing in one of William 'Buffalo Bill' Cody's Wild West shows. The frontiersman and famed marksman also spent time enforcing the law as a US marshal before being killed in a Deadwood saloon bar by Jack McCall while playing poker in 1876. The cards he was holding at the time – black aces and eights – have since been known as the 'Dead Man's Hand'.

By 1988, Nevada and New Jersey were the only states where gambling was permitted, though the situation has changed radically to the extent that only two, Utah and Hawaii, now actively prohibit gambling.

Apart from the practice being restricted to adults, opportunities to gamble legally are now available to most in the developed world. Yet the varied legislation applicable across different American states, primarily aimed at prohibiting organized gambling, has created a confusing picture that currently renders a friendly game of poker at home potentially illegal. More dramatically, though Americans constitute the majority of online poker players, this activity has effectively been rendered illegal in the US following the successful passage of the Unlawful Internet Gaming Act in October 2006. Various interpretations of the 1961 American Wire Act, originally introduced to prevent racketeers betting by telegraph, have often been made to suggest that online gambling is illegal. Under the terms of the new law, it is now illegal for American banks, credit card companies and other financial institutions to engage in transactions with online gaming companies. As a consequence, online poker players based in the US are now prevented from depositing and withdrawing sums from their online poker accounts.

EARLY RANKING OF HANDS
♦ ♣ ♥ ♠

Throughout poker's evolution the ranking of hands was not as clearly defined as it is today. The introduction of the straight – five cards of differing suits in a numerical sequence, for example 6, 7, 8, 9, 10 – and the flush – five non-sequential cards of the same suit – created problems for poker philosophers of the time. Confusion reigned regarding the validity of these hands and, even when accepted, their value in relation to other hands did not always reflect their true merit in terms of probability. Traditionalists who had grown used to the concept of four aces representing the premium hand found it difficult to acknowledge that the odds against securing a sequence of five cards in the same suit – a straight flush (see below) – were greater, rendering the hand more valuable.

20TH-CENTURY POKER

Draw poker and five-card stud remained the predominant variations well into the 20th century, but to these staples of the genre was added the communal card game, of which Texas Hold 'em is currently the most popular example. Games such as wild widow and spit in the ocean embodied the idea of a common card being dealt and were popular during the 1920s. Another development was the concept of high-low poker in which the pot, the term for the total stakes bet during the playing of each hand, was divided equally between the highest and lowest hands still standing at the time of the showdown, which is the point in the game when the betting has concluded and players reveal their cards to determine the winner. A further development was lowball, which was simply a draw poker game in which the lowest hand, not the highest, took the pot.

By the 1930s, a variation on the theme of stud poker had emerged, with players being dealt seven cards rather than five, a development which, once again, increased the number of betting rounds to be withstood before the conclusion of each hand. The possibility of players securing stronger poker hands using five of the seven cards available to them, working in tandem with more betting opportunities, led to its growth in popularity. It soon eclipsed five-card stud which, by comparison with this relative newcomer, was perceived as a sterile and much less dynamic game. A lowball version of seven-card stud, usually referred to as razz, inevitably evolved and the seven-card game, whether played high or low, became the poker variation of choice for many players. As recently as the 1980s, another popular game emerged in the shape of Omaha Hold 'em, often referred to as simply Omaha. A community card game, the format of Omaha is based on the game that is currently the most popular of all poker variations – Texas Hold 'em.

Cataloguing the game

A sense of how poker had captured the imagination of the American public is gleaned from the efforts to catalogue all that was known of the game in the early 20th century. The fruits of this research materialized in 1905 with the publication of R.F. Foster's book *Practical*

Above: 'Amarillo Slim' Preston (centre) chats with casino owner Benny Binion while playing Bill Lee (far left) in a US$10,000 challenge match at the Hotel Sahara in Las Vegas, 1975. Preston had been eliminated from the World Series of Poker (WSOP) world championship game but quickly found another poker challenge. In this case, Lee emerged victorious when Preston's pair of sixes proved insufficient to beat Lee's pair of queens in the final hand.

Left: Thomas Austin 'Amarillo Slim' Preston, winner of the 1972 WSOP championship, is arguably the first true poker celebrity of the modern era. Regular appearances on American TV chat shows following his WSOP triumph drew attention to the previously obscure world of the professional poker player.

Poker. At around the same time, references to 'dealer's choice' appeared, suggesting that several variations of poker were already widely played, with the nominated dealer deciding which would apply for each individual hand. Over the years, additional publications of Hoyle's famous guide to card games, which originated in 1742, have included numerous poker variations and serve as a record of the latter-day development of the game. More recently, poker literature has expanded to include many books on the theories behind successful poker play, a trend established by Frank R. Wallace in 1968 with his *Advanced Concepts of Poker*. This was the first of many books to analyse the game sufficiently to identify the ruthless and aggressive betting strategies typically adopted by profitable players.

Poker professionals

The poker professionals of the 19th century were an itinerant breed who favoured card games over other forms of gambling since a minimal amount of equipment was required compared to other games like faro and roulette. Armed with a deck of cards, the professional could establish a game almost anywhere and at any time, although the need for some means of self-defence was taken as read. But those who gambled for a living, generally being regarded as crooks themselves, frequently encountered keen poker players among the criminal fraternity. This, of course, presented additional risks. Similarly, the professionals and hustlers of the mid-20th century regularly operated on the edges of legality and often faced opponents with a marked aversion to losing.

NATIVE INDIAN RESERVATIONS
♦ ♣ ♥ ♠

Above: As a pastime, playing cards was not confined to the colonists emanating from Europe since it also proved popular with the indigenous peoples of America.

One of the driving forces behind the expansion of gambling in America has been the Indian Gaming Regulatory Act of 1988, allowing the various Native American tribes to run casinos on their land as a concession to exercising some autonomy over their affairs. Commercially successful, and well run, these operations have fed the appetite for the nation's gamblers and helped generate employment opportunities and better economic prospects for the many local people who work in them.

Right: Poker chips, or poker tokens, are used to keep track during gambling to replace money being handled at the table during a game.

Left: Doyle 'Texas Dolly' Brunson, a contemporary of 'Amarillo Slim', at the launch party of the World Poker Exchange London Open in August 2005. Brunson won the WSOP world championship in 1976 and 1977, following which he collaborated on *Doyle Brunson's Super System: A Course in Power Poker*, a book still regarded as essential reading for the discerning player.

For legendary players such as Johnny Moss, Doyle 'Texas Dolly' Brunson and Thomas 'Amarillo Slim' Preston, being hijacked at gunpoint and forced to hand over the money they had just won was one of the hazards of their chosen profession. Anecdotes about their adventures from the 1950s onwards highlight how many parts of post-war America still resembled the Wild West in terms of their apparent lawlessness.

LAS VEGAS

Though the Wild West imagery associated with poker is familiar to us all, the game has also become inexorably linked with a city that is arguably the gambling capital of the world – Las Vegas. The reasons for its dramatic development from a small crossroads watering hole in the Nevada Desert to the glittering tourist destination of legend are threefold. The relaxation of Nevada's state laws prohibiting gambling in 1931 coincided with the construction of the Hoover Dam 30 miles away, a project that attracted many thousands of labourers, and potential gamblers, in Depression-era America. Organized criminals who had prospered during Prohibition by meeting the public demand for alcohol, gambling and other vices, exploited this attractive opportunity. As a means of laundering their profits, the Mafia gangs

of New York, Detroit, St Louis and Chicago knew that running a casino had proven merit, and money was soon poured into the construction of these pleasure palaces designed to meet the needs of a new market.

Within 20 years, Las Vegas had become a hugely popular destination for people seeking the pleasures offered by legal gambling. Gradually, increasing numbers of professional poker players moved to the city to take advantage of the constant stream of tourists, until the World Series of Poker (WSOP) was established, promoting both the game and the city as a whole. In truth, most casino operators view poker ambivalently since tables take up a substantial amount of room that might otherwise be devoted to games that earn them higher profits. However, the resurgence in poker's popularity means that casinos are again content to welcome players in the knowledge that, once inside, they are likely to spend their money on other diversions.

The Mafia
Benjamin 'Bugsy' Siegel, a Brooklyn-born bookmaker, is the man credited with first visualizing the possibilities offered by Nevada's relaxation of its gambling laws. In league with New York crime boss Meyer Lansky, he set about construction of the

Above: The Fremont Street Experience in Las Vegas boasts 10 casinos and over 60 restaurants, all contained in an area that is covered by a permanent canopy and illuminated by two million lights.

Right: Charles 'Lucky' Luciano, the New York vice king, was deported from America during the war years. He is shown here after a special government commission had placed him under police surveillance. Under the 'admonitory' sentence, Luciano had to spend every night at his home in Naples from 9pm to 7am for the next two years, and was barred from public entertainment places and individuals 'suspected of socially dangerous activities' or who had criminal records. The commission ruled there was a reasonable suspicion that Luciano had contacts in the underworld and was involved in narcotics traffic and race fixing.

Flamingo Hotel and Casino but wound up making an enemy of gangster Charles 'Lucky' Luciano and was murdered in 1947. On the Las Vegas Strip, other hotel-casinos were built using money from the Teamsters Union Pension Fund, under the control of the Mafia. The criminal gangs were soon happily taking a cut from casino profits behind the scenes, despite maintaining a respectable image in public. This was bolstered by the regular presence in Las Vegas of Hollywood's elite, including the legendary Rat Pack, led by Frank Sinatra.

The Mafia's controlling influence in Las Vegas, however, was under attack from two sides, as law enforcement agencies and big business sought to drive them out and take back control of the city. Efforts to prosecute some of the leading crime bosses finally proved successful in the 1980s but, long before then, billionaire recluse Howard Hughes had influenced the Nevada State Government to permit public corporations to own casinos. This led to greater interest from the giants of Wall Street before the speculative commercial boom of the 1980s saw further acquisitions by, among others, Mirage Resorts Inc, owners of the Golden Nugget, the Mirage and Treasure Island. The major leisure corporations have since marketed Las Vegas to tourists previously disturbed by its sleazy image, although, for many, the historic undercurrent of criminality remains part of its appeal.

The Rat Pack

Apart from the gambling on offer, the other great draw in Las Vegas during the early 1960s was the entertainment provided by the top stars of the day. The leading light was Frank Sinatra, who regularly teamed up with Dean Martin, Sammy Davis Jr and comedian Joey Bishop for shows at the Sands Hotel and Casino. Along with actor Peter Lawford, brother-in-law to President John F. Kennedy, they became known as the Rat Pack, a group of entertainers whose talent was matched by their prodigious appetite for drinking, gambling and consorting with a string of attractive and equally famous women. They were the epitome of 'cool' and their association with Las Vegas helped the city maintain its allure.

Above: Howard Hughes, famous aviator and film producer (pictured in 1940), whose efforts indirectly led to the Mafia's grip on Las Vegas being loosened. His lobbying of the Nevada State Government led to a change in state law allowing public corporations, as well as private individuals, to own casinos. One by one, Mafia casino owners sold their interests to powerful leisure and entertainment companies. In 1967, Hughes himself bought the Desert Inn having tired of the owners' insistence that he should leave.

Left: Dean Martin and his friends, Joey Bishop and Frank Sinatra, opened a three-week engagement at the Sands Hotel in Las Vegas, April 1966, determined that their songs, patter and assorted hijinks qualify them as 'The Men from SPREE', (Society for the Prevention of Routine Entertainment Events).

POKER IN THE 21ST CENTURY

Left: Players at Binion's Horseshoe casino Las Vegas during the 2001 World Series of Poker (WSOP) championship – an event begun by owner Benny Binion in 1970. In that inaugural competition, 35 players competed for the unofficial accolade of world champion. By 2001, the WSOP had grown to 26 tournaments spread over five weeks. In May 2001, Carlos Mortensen won US$1,500,000 in the US$10,000 no-limit Texas Hold 'em world championship.

Below: The French Open tournament in 2005 at Casino Barrière de Deauville in France, part of the inaugural European Poker Tour (EPT). Coverage of the WSOP and World Poker Tour (WPT) on cable television had prompted TV director and player John Duthie to instigate a similar operation in Europe. Brandon Schaefer won the €144,000 (US$186,500) prize.

The advent of online poker over the last decade has, of course, been a massive boost to the game's popularity and the establishment of businesses with multimillion-dollar turnover has helped to improve its image. PlanetPoker began the online trend in 1998 but it is PokerStars that currently heads the rankings as the busiest and most popular poker website, eclipsing PartyPoker, which withdrew from the American market following the passage of the Unlawful Internet Gambling Enforcement Act in 2006. Analysts expect the industry's annual turnover to exceed $100 billion by 2010 as interest in poker builds upon the convenience of playing from home. The changing face of the game is underlined by the WSOP championship successes of Chris Moneymaker in 2003 and Greg Raymer in 2004, as both of these players qualified for the main event via online satellite tournaments. Their victories provided a boost for the credibility of online poker and its supporters, as well as keeping alive the dream that anyone can become a world champion.

Poker on television

While online poker offers a convenient means of playing the game, it is television that has boosted poker's profile and helped create a market served by the virtual casinos and gaming rooms of the Internet. Initial attempts to cover the WSOP on television were very limited, there being no way of discovering what cards each player held until or unless there was a showdown. Roving reporters and camera operators from American channel ESPN tried to capture the excitement of the event but it was difficult to retain the interest of viewers other than diehard poker fans. Coverage of the game changed with the introduction of miniature cameras positioned beneath specially designed tables featuring glass panels, pioneered on the UK's *Late Night Poker* in 1999. Now viewers could

see the players' cards and understand the dynamics of the game – invariably no-limit Texas Hold 'em – and the strategies employed by the professionals.

This innovation led to improvements in ESPN's coverage of the WSOP, which is now more extensive than ever and features many of the supporting events as well as the main championship game itself. Encouraging ratings for what was considered a minority interest led to a commission from the Travel Channel, owned by the American company Discovery Communications Inc., to establish the World Poker Tour (WPT) in 2003. The tour comprises several tournaments contested at various locations, primarily in America, highlights of which are then shown on any one of up to 100 channels globally. Crucially, anyone able to pay the entry fee is welcome to participate and several hundred players, both amateur and professional, normally compete in each event. Within a year, the European Poker Tour (EPT) was instigated along similar lines while TV production companies, often sponsored by online poker sites, now stage an increasing number of tournaments specifically for the small screen. Finally, proof that televised poker was a ratings winner came with the launch in March 2005 of the Poker Channel, the first of its kind to broadcast nothing but poker-related programming.

Above: American Chris Moneymaker, pictured with his US$2,500,000 prize for winning the 2003 WSOP championship US$10,000 no-limit Texas Hold 'em tournament. His success boosted the profile of online poker since it was via the PokerStars website that he entered a US$40 satellite tournament that ultimately led to a seat at the world championship game. In beating over 800 other entrants to the title, he confounded the experts because he arrived in Las Vegas with no experience of live tournament poker.

TOURNAMENT POKER
♦ ♣ ♥ ♠

Prior to the inception of the WSOP, tournament poker played on a knockout basis was rarely, if ever, contemplated by regular cash game players. The success of the self-styled world championship of poker, however, stimulated interest in this form of the game throughout Las Vegas, extending later to the rest of the world. By its very nature, tournament poker generates confrontations that are ultimately resolved by one player amassing all the chips. Consequently, the inherent drama of proceedings that conclude with a definitive winner satisfies the requirements of television which now features a great deal of poker programming.

WORLD SERIES OF POKER

The World Series of Poker (WSOP) held annually in Las Vegas is undoubtedly the major event on the poker tournament calendar. Over a period of eight weeks, more than 20,000 players can be expected to take part in around 60 different tournaments encompassing several popular poker variations. Entry to these events comes at a cost, ranging from US$500 for the casino employees' tournament to US$10,000 for the no-limit Texas Hold 'em world championship. The prize pools provide a substantial incentive to play, and each winner also receives a gold bracelet as a memento of their victory. If the entry fees seem prohibitively expensive, then numerous satellite tournaments are also held during the year, offering players the chance to win a place in the main event itself for a much smaller sum. Both Chris Moneymaker and Greg Raymer battled through a series of online poker tournaments for a modest outlay before scooping the top prize in the 2003 and 2004 WSOP tournaments respectively.

The early days

Inspired by the heads-up match between Johnny Moss and Nicholas 'Nick the Greek' Dandolos that he staged in 1949, casino owner Benny Binion revived the idea of a contest to determine poker's world champion in 1970.

He had seen the potential for such an event at the Texas Gamblers' Reunion the year before in Reno. This invitation-only festival at Tom Morehead's Riverside Casino saw a handful of leading professionals play poker against each other and garnered a fair degree of publicity. When Morehead sold his casino, Binion acquired the rights to his tournament and replicated

Above: Joe Hachem proudly displays his WSOP gold bracelet after becoming world champion in July 2005. Born in Lebanon, Hachem moved to Australia in 1972 and settled in Melbourne where he lives with his wife and family. He often played poker at a local casino, but began to take the game more seriously as a source of income when a debilitating physical condition left him unable to continue working as a chiropractor.

Left: The statue of Benny Binion outside Binion's Horseshoe Casino, created following the purchase of the Eldorado Club and Apache Hotel in 1951. Binion's casinos appealed to serious gamblers by allowing games with higher betting limits than those found at the resort casinos and hotels on the Strip. This created friction with some Mafia-controlled concerns but Binion was not intimidated.

the concept at his Horseshoe Casino the following year. Thus, the WSOP was established, with 35 players competing at five poker variations for the accolade of world champion. For the only time in its history, the winner was decided by a vote among the players and Johnny Moss, the doyen of the professional game, was judged the best all-round poker player in the world.

The following year, Binion established the decisive world championship game as a freeze-out tournament with players contributing a US$5,000 fee to buy in to the competition. Significantly, the poker variation he selected for this knockout event was no-limit Texas Hold 'em. Moss won again, beating just five

opponents to take the US$30,000 prize and confirm his status as champion. In 1972, the buy-in was raised to its current level of US$10,000 and on this occasion Thomas 'Amarillo Slim' Preston emerged victorious before starting a series of promotional television appearances that firmly planted the WSOP in the public domain.

The present

From an initial entry of 35 players in 1970, the number competing in the world championship game grew to over 5,000 in 2005. As a result, the prize pool exceeded US$50 million with the winner alone, Australian Joseph Hachem, collecting US$7.5 million. The status of being acknowledged world champion, along with the life-changing prize money on offer is now proving so attractive that a limit of 8,000 entrants has been placed on the 2006 renewal. Sadly, the phenomenal success of the WSOP means that it is no longer staged entirely at Binion's Horseshoe Casino. Harrah's Entertainment acquired the casino in 2004, along with the rights to the WSOP, and moved the tournament to Harrah's Rio Casino, although the final two days of the 2005 event were staged back at Binion's. This proved the swansong for the WSOP's association with its original home which was sold on to the MTR Gaming Group in 2005 and now bears the name of Binion's Gambling Hall and Hotel.

Left: Greg 'Fossilman' Raymer, WSOP champion in 2004, pictured defending his title in the 2005 US$10,000 no-limit Texas Hold 'em world championship.

Above: The legendary Benny Binion, the man who devised poker's unofficial world championship, the WSOP. Though he established the Horseshoe in 1951, he had to sell his share of the family business to pay for legal costs incurred defending a charge of tax evasion, for which he was convicted in 1953 and spent four years in jail. This barred him from ever holding a gaming licence but the family officially employed him as a consultant.

BENNY BINION
♦ ♣ ♥ ♠

Though he lacked a formal education, Benny Binion learned much about human nature while riding the range in Texas as a boy and put these lessons to good use when he arrived in Las Vegas to run his first casino. As a bootlegger and numbers runner, he knew how to survive on the wrong side of the law, somehow even avoiding prison when convicted of first-degree murder. His place in the annals of poker is secure because of the WSOP, of course, but Binion was primarily a gambler who used his insight to provide his fellow gamblers with what they really wanted. Eschewing the glamorous trappings of the hotels and casinos on the Strip, Binion's philosophy for success was simple: "Good food, good whiskey and good gamble. That's all there is to it." He died on Christmas Day, 1989.

JOHNNY MOSS AND NICK DANDOLOS

Earning a living from poker has historically been regarded as a dubious activity. Yet there is no doubt that many famed players retain a sometimes romantic or even heroic status because of their perceived rebelliousness in the face of accepted wisdom. The willingness to back one's judgement with hard cash, relying on one's own wit and resourcefulness in order to prosper, is generally admired. Such qualities have always been found in professional poker players, while exploits on the edges of legality have generated a host of legendary anecdotes. As a result, some of poker's characters have emerged as successful exponents of the game, along with several notable confrontations.

Johnny Moss

Often referred to as the 'Grand Old Man' of poker, Johnny Moss (1907–97) learned how to play the game as a boy when a group of card sharps taught him all the tricks of their trade. As a teenager in Odessa, Texas, his ability to identify foul play saw him employed at a saloon to monitor the card games, giving him the chance to learn about poker strategy. Within a couple of years, he took to the road and led a sometimes hazardous existence as an itinerant gambler – a rounder – travelling the country in order to earn a living from gambling.

As an expert on cheating, Moss took exception to those who lacked respect for the game, always carrying a gun to enforce his stance. On several occasions he ordered opponents to strip at gunpoint to determine whether they were wearing 'holdout machines', devices explicitly designed to conceal cards. Famously, during one particular game he noticed a hole in the ceiling, suggesting that someone on the floor above was looking at his cards. When his suspicions were flatly denied, he shot at the ceiling and wounded the spy, exercising a particularly forceful strategy that confirmed his palpable contempt for poker cheats. Up until his death in 1997, Moss was a regular participant at the WSOP, winning eight gold bracelets and over US$680,000 in tournament prize money. He also won three of the first five world championship events, including the inaugural competition in 1970 when the title was decided by a vote among the contestants.

Above: Johnny Moss, acknowledged as the best poker player in the world by his peers at the first WSOP in 1970 after a series of games encompassing the most popular variations at the time. The following year he won again, though the decisive championship event on that occasion was a knockout Texas Hold 'em tournament.

Moss v Dandolos

This legendary poker confrontation took place in 1949, when America's most notable gambler Nicholas 'Nick the Greek' Dandolos approached casino owner Benny Binion with a proposition. He wanted to play poker for exceptionally high stakes against just one opponent, in what is known as a heads-up confrontation, with a no-limit betting structure in operation. This allows players to bet their entire chip stack at any moment during the play of a hand, there being no upper limit on the size of any bet. Seeing an opportunity to publicize his business, Binion agreed to stage it, provided he could choose the opponent and have the pair play in public. He contacted his old friend Johnny Moss, regarded as the best poker player alive, and invited him to the game, which began almost immediately upon his arrival. Dandolos, flush with a reputed US$10 million in stake money accrued during a successful run in New York, held the upper hand for the first few weeks, but Moss fought back. Apart from breaks for sleep, the marathon contest lasted for five months and regularly drew crowds of interested spectators eager to witness the action. Eventually, it was Dandolos who conceded defeat with the famous words: "Mr Moss, I have to let you go", by by which time his losses were at least US$2 million.

Nicholas 'Nick the Greek' Dandolos

One of the most fearless gamblers of all time, Dandolos was born in Crete in 1883 and moved to North America as a teenager to find his fortune. While based in Montreal, he quickly made his mark as a gambler, striking up a lucrative friendship with jockey Phil Musgrave, whose insight helped him accumulate US$500,000 in a single horse-racing season. From there, he moved to Chicago, where he turned his attentions to cards and dice, having already lost his first fortune. Such was his skill and mathematical acumen that casinos frequently offered him jobs, which he always declined because of a reluctance to accept the likely cut in pay. Although he conceded defeat in the marathon poker confrontation with Johnny Moss, Dandolos remained a keen competitor, whose lifetime's betting turnover is thought to have touched US$500 million dollars. When he died on Christmas Day 1966, this legendary big-time gambler was penniless.

Above: Nicholas 'Nick the Greek' Dandolos (right), outside the Federal Court in Los Angeles. He had been testifying in a case in which three men were accused of extorting money in 1964 from a hotelier named Ray Ryan, a man Dandolos had previously pursued in connection with a gambling debt. Though his gambling exploits were legendary, Dandolos died a pauper.

Left: Action from the WSOP with Stu 'The Kid' Ungar (centre), 'Amarillo Slim' Preston (second right) and Johnny Moss (far right) all involved at the same table. Moss claimed the title of world champion on three occasions, in 1970, 1971 and 1974 while Ungar achieved the same feat with victories in 1980, 1981 and 1997. Preston's world championship bracelet was earned in 1972 when the tournament was played as a 'winner takes all' event.

BRUNSON, HELLMUTH, SMITH AND HOOKS

Doyle 'Texas Dolly' Brunson

Without a doubt, many of the legendary players of contemporary poker history have enjoyed dramatic lives, and Doyle 'Texas Dolly' Brunson is no exception. Born in Longworth, Texas, in 1933, the physically imposing Brunson was an accomplished athlete as a teenager, but his dreams of a career in professional basketball were ended by an industrial accident that broke his leg in two places. After recovering his fitness, he found that regular jobs paid far less than he was consistently able to win at the poker table. So, in partnership with Thomas 'Amarillo Slim' Preston and Brian 'Sailor' Roberts, Brunson set about earning a living in the card rooms of Texas. Six years of hustling together ended ignominiously on their first trip to Las Vegas, when they lost their entire six-figure bankroll, this being the cash players set aside strictly for poker. Later, after miraculously overcoming cancer in the early 1960s, Brunson made his way back to Las Vegas, moving there permanently in 1973. The newly established WSOP attracted his attention and Brunson became world champion in both 1976 and 1977. Famously, he won the final pot in both tournaments

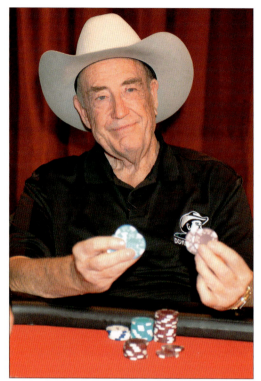

with the same hand – a full house of tens over twos. His book, *Doyle Brunson's Super System: A Course in Power Poker*, was first published in 1978 and is still regarded as a classic treatise on how to play the game. Now into his seventies, Brunson is still competing and winning on the tournament circuit, with today's top players acknowledging that he has probably done more to popularize poker than anyone else.

Above: Veteran Doyle 'Texas Dolly' Brunson promotes a televised tournament in London in 2005. A career in basketball was a possibility for the man from Longworth, Texas, but a serious leg injury curtailed any ambitions Brunson had to become a professional sportsman. He concentrated his efforts on poker and took to the road with 'Amarillo Slim' Preston and Brian 'Sailor' Roberts, the three of them seeking out high-stakes games wherever they could find them. Still a regular participant in tournaments around the world, Brunson is one of the most recognizable and respected characters in the game.

Left: A younger Doyle Brunson takes time out to read *Sklansky on Razz*, one of several poker books by mathematician and gambler David Sklansky, a contributor to Brunson's own book *Super System: A Course in Power Poker*.

Above: Poker professional Phil Hellmuth, the self-styled 'poker brat', holds the record for the greatest number of prize-money finishes at the WSOP and is also the record holder for the most WSOP tournament wins, having secured his eleventh title in 2007. All eleven have been in Texas Hold 'em events.

Above: Chess champion Bobby Fischer prepares for his 1972 duel with Russian grandmaster Boris Spassky in Reykjavik, Iceland. Among the chess experts assisting Fischer during his successful world championship bid was Kenny 'What a Player' Smith who later turned to professional poker.

Phil Hellmuth

Born in Madison, Wisconsin, Phil Hellmuth is arguably the biggest name in poker today. He shot to prominence when he won the ultimate prize at the WSOP in 1989, aged 24. Within seven years, his peers were talking about him as the best tournament poker player in the world. Yet, despite this respect for his ability, Hellmuth has not always endeared himself to opponents. The title of his forthcoming autobiography, *Poker Brat*, highlights his tendency in the past to show plenty of emotion during a game, even churlishly berating other players for their style of play.

Although experience has mellowed him a little, Hellmuth is calculating enough to realize that maintaining this feisty, combative image keeps his profile high at a time when poker is subject to widespread media interest. Since his 1989 triumph, Hellmuth has amassed 50 tournament wins and is currently the second most successful player at the WSOP in terms of prize money accrued. In March 2005, he won the National Heads-Up Poker Championship in Las Vegas, earning US$500,000 in the process, and he also triumphed in series three of *Late Night Poker*, a televised tournament shown on UK television's Channel 4. Married with two sons, Hellmuth is the author of three books on poker and has also produced an instructional video on the game.

Smith versus Hooks

The novelty value of one particular hand contested by these two players is sufficient for it to have entered poker folklore. Kenny Smith, famed for always wearing a silk top hat and shouting "what a player" each time he won a hand, was also a respected chess master who had assisted the late Bobby Fischer during his 1972 world championship campaign. His opponent in this heads-up situation, which emerged during a game of Texas Hold 'em, was Bob Hooks, runner-up in the 1975 WSOP world championship. Hooks called for the amount of the 'blind', the compulsory bet made by the two players to the dealer's left, but Smith made a substantial raise before the 'flop', this being the moment when the first three community cards are revealed. Smith's pre-flop raise prompted Hooks, whose two cards comprised a pair of kings, to bet 'all-in', meaning he pushed his remaining chips into the pot. Smith now faced a massive call, but he simply stared at Hooks, showing no apparent intention of ever making a decision. After several minutes, with everyone beginning to wonder how to resolve the situation, Hooks broke one of the defining rules of the game by calmly looking at Smith's cards himself. Seeing a pair of aces, the only hand that could possibly be ahead of him at this point, he moved Smith's chips into the pot, played out the hand and duly lost.

ULLIOTT, PEARSON AND PRESTON

Dave 'Devilfish' Ulliott

Probably the most famous British poker player currently in action is Dave 'Devilfish' Ulliott, a jeweller from Hull in northern England. His success in the inaugural series of *Late Night Poker* on Channel 4 renewed interest in the game in Britain and brought his talents to a much wider audience. However, his wisecracking style and dry sense of humour disguise a cool and calculatedly aggressive approach to poker. In fact, some observers consider that his self-confident comments, if taken at face value, border on arrogance. However, with over US$5 million in tournament prize money to his name, Ulliott is entitled to consider himself one of the premier players in the world.

On the other side of the Atlantic, Ulliott earned respect at the WSOP in 1997 when winning the US$2,000 pot-limit Texas Hold 'em event made him one of very few non-Americans to claim a WSOP title. Earlier that year, a friend had coined the nickname 'Devilfish'

while Ulliott was playing heads-up in a pot-limit Omaha event against multiple-tournament winner Men 'The Master' Nguyen, the pair of them being the only players left in the competition. If not cooked properly, eating the devilfish can prove fatal and evidently 'The Master' experienced a night of poker indigestion. Since 1997, Ulliott has regularly made the final tables at tournaments and enjoyed a fine run at the 2005 WSOP when he secured three prize-money finishes. Ulliott now appears in televised tournaments regularly.

Walter 'Puggy' Pearson

A colourful character of the Las Vegas poker scene in the 1960s and 1970s, Walter 'Puggy' Pearson, who died in April 2006, was renowned as one of the great hustlers of his day. Apart from playing professional poker, Pearson also learned how to play golf once he discovered the opportunities for betting on various aspects of the game as the round progressed. On the

Left: Men 'The Master' Nguyen in action at the poker table. Feared and respected in equal measure by his peers, Nguyen fled his native Vietnam in 1978 and was granted asylum by the United States later that year, eventually settling in Los Angeles. His first experience of poker came on a trip to Las Vegas in 1984 and by 1987 he had won his first tournament. Married with eight children, Nguyen has won *Card Player Magazine*'s Player of the Year award on four occasions, most recently in 2005.

Below: Dave 'Devilfish' Ulliott, Britain's most successful poker player in terms of tournament prize money won. A pawnbroker and jeweller by trade, Ulliott began to take poker seriously in the early 1990s, travelling around the UK in search of high-stakes cash games. His first visit to the WSOP in 1997 resulted in victory in the US$2,000 pot-limit Texas Hold 'em tournament.

Above: Walter 'Puggy' Pearson (left) with 'Amarillo Slim' Preston before the final game that made Pearson world champion in 1973. Pearson grew up in Tennessee in a large family with nine siblings. His nickname 'Puggy' arose from a childhood accident that left him with a disfigured nose.

Left: 'Amarillo Slim' at the Poker Million tournament held at the Hilton Hotel Casino on the Isle of Man in November 2000. His four WSOP victories include the world championship in 1972, after which his regular television appearances made him a minor celebrity outside the poker world.

putting green he was especially accurate, managing to win money from many of the professional golfers that he challenged to a round. He triumphed in the WSOP no-limit Texas Hold 'em poker world championship in 1973, the first time the tournament was televised, having been runner-up the year before to 'Amarillo Slim' Preston. Perhaps his greatest legacy is the concept of the 'freeze-out' tournament, an idea that he is credited with introducing into Las Vegas and which has been adopted in virtually all major poker tournaments throughout the world. In these events, players start with the same number of chips but they are not allowed to purchase any more during play. Those who lose all their chips are eliminated from the competition.

Thomas 'Amarillo Slim' Preston

If there is one name synonymous with poker in the eyes of the world, that name is undoubtedly 'Amarillo Slim', the pseudonym employed by one Thomas Austin Preston Jr. A renowned storyteller, as shown in his biography *Amarillo Slim in a World Full of Fat People*, Preston has been at ease in the spotlight since 1972, when he won the third WSOP championship

game and immediately embarked on a tour of television chat shows and personal appearances. This had the effect of putting professional poker in the public eye, but also served to introduce one of the game's most colourful characters to the rest of the world.

Always sporting his trademark Stetson, Preston looks every inch the Texan cowboy, although he was actually born in Arkansas, moving to Amarillo with his family when he was a child. He took up poker in his twenties, unusually late in life compared to contemporaries such as Johnny Moss and Doyle Brunson, and has the distinction of having played against presidents Lyndon Johnson and Richard Nixon in his time. Remarkably, in a case of mistaken identity, he was kidnapped while in Colombia to help promote the opening of a new casino. The kidnap resulted, rather bizzarely, in Preston playing poker against drug lord Pablo Escobar. Preston is less of a feature on the tournament circuit these days. As he nears his 80th year, he has declared himself "pokered out" after 50 years of sometimes intense competition that has brought him fame, riches and no less than four WSOP bracelets.

JOHNNY CHAN AND STU UNGAR

Johnny 'Orient Express' Chan

After dropping out of university in Houston, where he was studying hotel and restaurant management, Johnny Chan took up professional gambling in the late 1970s. Originally from Canton in China, he had been brought to the United States by his family in 1968 after spending a few years in Hong Kong, but it was in Las Vegas that he made his reputation as a consummate poker player. Initially, his opponents underestimated his skill, although Chan himself admits that his early successes were counterbalanced by too many occasions when he would chase his losses. Once he addressed this, his game moved to another level and enabled him to win the WSOP world championship in both 1987 and 1988, replicating Doyle Brunson's feat of successive titles a decade earlier. A remarkable hat-trick of titles was denied him by Phil Hellmuth in 1989, when the self-styled poker brat beat Johnny Chan into

second place. By then, his place in poker folklore was assured, courtesy of a cameo appearance in the film *Rounders*, which reinforced his status as the best player in the world.

Outside poker, Chan has invested his money in a fast-food franchise and acts as a consultant to several casinos, harbouring ambitions that he may one day open his own establishment. But it is high-stakes poker that brings out the best in him, a point proven when he claimed his tenth WSOP bracelet in 2005 by winning the US$2,500 pot-limit Texas Hold 'em championship, equalling another of Doyle Brunson's career achievements.

Stu 'The Kid' Ungar

Winner of the WSOP championship event on three occasions, Stu Ungar is regarded by many as the best poker player of all time, although his reputation as an

Above: The Las Vegas Strip, more formally known as Las Vegas Boulevard South, is the four-mile-long stretch of road running from McCarran Airport in the south to the Stratosphere Hotel Casino in the north. The majority of the city's largest resort hotels and casinos are located there.

Left: Johnny 'Orient Express' Chan, pictured at the WSOP in 2002. Originally from Canton in China, Johnny Chan arrived in the United States with his family in 1968 and looked set for a career in the family restaurant business. A trip to Las Vegas changed that and by 1987 Chan had become WSOP world champion, a title he successfully defended in 1988. A remarkable hat-trick of victories was denied him in 1989 when Chan finished second to Phil Hellmuth.

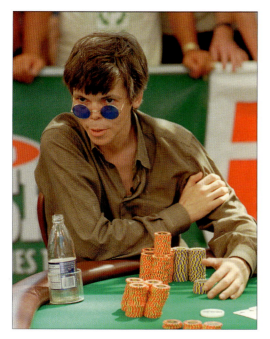

Left: Stu Ungar, at the final table of the 1997 WSOP world championship, a tournament he won to claim the US$1 million top prize. After his previous triumphs in 1980 and 1981, his performance in 1997 surprised many people since his hedonistic lifestyle had taken its toll and diminished his skills.

Below: Pictured at the 1980 WSOP are, from left to right, Doyle Brunson, Stu Ungar and Benny Binion's son, Jack. Ungar had just won the world championship event and is seen with his US$365,000 winnings having finally beaten Brunson into second place when his 5-high straight – known as a 'wheel' – proved too good for Texas Dolly's two pairs of aces and sevens.

obsessive gambler is equally legendary. As a child, the New Yorker quickly acquired a head for figures and a skill for playing gin rummy, winning his first tournament at the age of ten. He turned professional at 14, by which time he was regularly beating the best players in New York, and left school soon afterwards when a bookmaker paid his entry fee into a gin rummy tournament, which Ungar won without losing a hand. The US$10,000 first prize, however, was lost in one week at the Aqueduct racetrack, setting a pattern for the rest of his life.

Stu sought the big-money gin games of Miami, although his weakness for betting on the horses and other sports ensured that he was frequently broke. He moved to Las Vegas in 1976, where his uncanny ability to memorize cards during a game of blackjack led to the single-deck shoes, from which the cards were dealt during a game, being dropped by casinos. A successful run at Caesar's Palace was halted by a suspicious manager, at which point, in a fit of pique, Ungar correctly forecast the last 18 cards remaining in the deck. He was simply too good and found himself barred from every casino in Las Vegas, although his card-counting ability did win him US$100,000 from casino owner and designer Bob Stupak in 1977. Stupak

had privately challenged Ungar to forecast the rank of each card from the last three decks held in a six-deck shoe, a feat Ungar duly managed.

In 1980, he entered his first WSOP championship and won the main event aged just 24, repeating the feat the next year to seal his reputation and his nickname of 'The Kid'. However, Ungar's self-destructive appetite for cocaine and amphetamines ultimately led to his demise and contributed to his regular bouts of poverty. By 1997, he was considered a spent force, but entered the WSOP after fellow professional, Billy Baxter, paid his US$10,000 entry fee. Ungar's third victory saw him split the US$1 million prize equally with his sponsor.

Just over a year later, Ungar was found dead in a Las Vegas motel room, having suffered heart failure directly attributable to his lifetime of drug abuse. Reputed to have won and lost over US$30 million in all, Ungar's attitude to life is summed up by his remark on winning the 1980 WSOP world championship. Asked what he would do with the money, Ungar giggled as he replied: "Gamble it!" Ungar played 30 major no-limit Hold 'em tournaments in which the buy-in or entry fee was at least US$5,000, managing to win ten, a remarkable strike rate unmatched by any other tournament player.

THE HENDON MOB

Four of the best poker players in the UK, who have been friends since the early 1990s are otherwise known as the 'Hendon Mob'. Brothers Barny and Ross Boatman took part in a regular game organized by Joe Beevers in Hendon where they met Ram Vaswani. The four soon decided to pool their collective resources and tackle the best in the world. Bright, articulate and with a reputation for honourable conduct, they regularly featured on UK television's *Late Night Poker*, raising their profile and prompting them to set up their own poker website, www.thehendonmob.com, which provides news of their exploits. Like Dave Ulliott, the members of the Hendon Mob are heavily involved in promoting the game and regularly participate in televised tournaments specifically devised to exploit the current widespread interest in poker.

BARNY 'THE HUMOUR' BOATMAN

The elder of the two brothers, Barny Boatman spent time in various occupations prior to becoming a full-time poker professional, working as a teacher, computer programmer and legal advisor away from the table.

Early success in tournament poker came at London's Grosvenor Victoria Casino, when he won a small seven-card stud event before graduating at the highest level by finishing 16th of 512 entrants at the 2000 WSOP championship event. Since then, he has regularly reached the final table in tournament events and is frequently called upon as an expert pundit to help commentate on televised poker. He also contributes to various articles in poker magazines.

ROSS BOATMAN

Unlike his colleagues in the Hendon Mob, whose celebrity status is entirely attributable to their poker skills, Ross Boatman is also an actor who has worked his way up from fringe theatre productions to appearances in film and on television. Most notably, he played the character of Kevin Medhurst in the popular UK drama series *London's Burning* during the 1990s. His best performance in *Late Night Poker* saw him finish as runner-up in the second series, but he, too, has since enjoyed success elsewhere by finishing among the prizes on the European and World Poker

Above: Actor Ross Boatman, one of the two brothers in the 'Hendon Mob'. Familiar on British television for his role in the series *London's Burning*, he also featured in films *Bring Me the Head of Mavis Davis* (1997) and *Hard Men* (1996).

Right: Three members of the 'Hendon Mob' pose with poker commentator Jesse May (far right) in 2003. Barny Boatman (left), Ram Vaswani (second left) and Joe Beevers have, with Ross Boatman, been at the forefront of efforts to popularize the game in the UK.

Tours, as well as reaching 34th spot in the 2002 WSOP world championship game. Boatman's first love remains acting, but he admits that his poker is definitely more profitable, with over US$1 million so far accrued in tournament prize money.

JOE 'THE ELEGANCE' BEAVERS

Beevers was introduced to cards by his father who educated him sufficiently to ensure that his prowess at blackjack led to a ban from several London casinos. After completing a degree in finance and accounting, he worked in London for Citibank before turning his attentions to full-time poker, enabling him to become the first of the Hendon Mob to win money at the WSOP in 1996. That was in a pot-limit Texas hold 'em event but he later improved upon that by finishing among the prizes at the 2005 championship event itself, after which he married his wife, Claire, at the Bellagio in Las Vegas, and they became parents in February. In 2006, Beevers managed prize-money finishes in three WSOP tournaments, matching his achievement of the previous year, and he concluded 2007 in fine style with victories in the Great British Poker Tour Grand Final and the Ladbrokes Poker Million event. In 2006, Beevers managed to finish among the prize money in three WSOP tournaments, matching his achievement of the previous year.

Above left: Simon 'Aces' Trumper (left), John Duthie (centre) and Barny Boatman at the Hilton London Metropole Hotel. Trumper is a familiar face on UK television having won Channel 4's *Late Night Poker* in series two, while John Duthie won the first Poker Million in 2000. Boatman has twice been the top-placed British finisher in the WSOP world championship.

Above top right: Ram 'Crazy Horse' Vaswani, so called because of his use of both controlled and erratic styles of play, is the youngest in the Hendon Mob. He makes a living through tournament play, from which he has earned over US$3 million.

Above bottom right: Joe 'The Elegance' Beevers, poised to begin play. He competed in all six *Late Night Poker* tournaments on UK television and reached the final on three occasions.

RAM 'CRAZY HORSE' VASWANI

The youngest of the Hendon Mob four, Ram Vaswani turned his back on a budding professional snooker career when it became apparent that playing professional poker was likely to prove more lucrative. Like the others in the Hendon Mob, Vaswani performed consistently well on *Late Night Poker* without managing to win a series, but he has regularly reached the final table of many tournaments on the European circuit. Over in Las Vegas, he finally managed to win a WSOP bracelet with his triumph in the US$1,500 Limit Texas Hold 'em Shootout tournament. Vaswani remains a confident player and he is likely to be extremely successful – he has over US$3 million in tournament prize money to his name already.

MONEYMAKER, STRAUS AND TOMKO

CHRIS MONEYMAKER

An accountant by trade, Moneymaker hit the headlines when he won the world championship at the World Series of Poker in 2003, having entered the competition via an online satellite tournament. An initial US$40 stake to enter one of these preliminary competitions set him on course to working his way through a series of further satellite tournaments until he emerged with the US$10,000 entry fee for the world championship game itself. After outlasting 838 other players, he finally walked away with the US$2.5 million first prize. Although his victory advertised the ability of online poker players and justified their dreams of similar success, Moneymaker stresses that skill as a card player and not luck is still of the utmost importance. Indeed, his advice to budding professionals is to "have a day job", as even the best players must endure losing streaks. Moneymaker currently runs his own company producing poker paraphernalia and continues to feature on the tournament circuit.

JACK 'TREETOPS' STRAUS

Often referred to as 'Treetops' on account of his being 6ft 6in tall, Jack Straus enjoyed a reputation as an accomplished cash game player with a distinctively creative style. Like Doyle Brunson, Straus had played basketball at university but it was at poker that he excelled, winning the WSOP world championship in 1982, six years before dying of a heart attack while contesting yet another high-stakes game. Well respected and regarded as something of a gentle giant, he had a reputation for telling hugely entertaining poker tales, some of them a little taller than others.

Yet one of his most striking tales in poker lore, which happened in a high-stakes, no-limit Texas Hold 'em game, provides evidence of Straus's creativity at the table. Playing well and feeling confident, he decided to raise with any two cards before the flop, the moment when the first three community cards are revealed. Unfortunately his hand of 7, 2 'offsuit', meaning simply that he had two cards of differing suits, is recognized as

Above: Jack 'Treetops' Straus wins the 1982 WSOP world championship having famously recovered from holding just a single US$500 chip. The Texan was renowned as a fearless gambler on horse racing and other sports, while at poker he was widely respected for his cash game skills. He died of a heart attack at the Bicycle Club in 1988 while playing poker.

Left: Chris Moneymaker plays the final hand of the WSOP world championship tournament at Binion's Horseshoe in May, 2003. The US$2.5 million prize in the foreground was his a few moments later when he secured a full house of fours over fives to beat Sam Farha. Rather than pay US$10,000 for guaranteed entry to the tournament, Moneymaker won his way through several preliminary satellite tournaments.

the worst starting hand in the game and did not justify the move. One player was willing to call the raise but Straus's situation seemed to improve when the flop came 7, 3, 3, giving him two pairs, albeit of low rank. Straus bet again but his opponent raised US$5,000, suggesting that he held a higher pair than sevens in his hand already. Straus decided to call anyway. The fourth community card – the 'turn' – was another 2 and Straus immediately bet US$18,000, despite the fact that it had not improved his hand at all and still left him trailing. His opponent hesitated, giving Straus the chance to make him a proposition. In exchange for a single US$25 chip, Straus offered to reveal either one of his personal 'hole cards', those held face down on the table and obscured from view, after which his opponent could decide whether to continue in the hand or fold his cards and concede defeat over the fate of the pot. After a moment's contemplation, his opponent tossed him a chip and pointed to one of Straus's cards, revealed to be the 2. At this, his opponent considered the implications of Straus's unorthodox move and concluded that the other card, logically, also must have been a 2, making a full house. He thought long enough to convince himself he was now behind, with a very poor chance of winning the hand, and duly folded in the face of the psychological pressure applied by Straus's incredibly subtle bluff.

Left: "The guy who invented poker was bright, but the guy who invented the chip was a genius". This quote from Jules Weintraub, who organized trips to Las Vegas for the wealthy, highlights how gambling for chips detaches players from the sums involved.

STRAUS VERSUS TOMKO

As tournament play was not considered Jack Straus's forte, his win in the 1982 WSOP world championship was a surprise, not least to Straus himself judging by his amazed look when he won the final hand. Dewey Tomko's pair of fours led after the turn card, but a 10 on the river – the fifth and final community card – gave Straus the better pair and he claimed the title along with US$520,000 in prize money.

What makes the triumph stand out is that Straus had been reduced to a solitary US$500 chip earlier in the tournament, inadvertently leaving it under a napkin when he pushed his chips into the pot to call a bet. Thinking he had gone all-in by betting all his remaining chips, but without yet announcing it, he lost the hand and noticed the lucky chip as he rose to leave the table. He was permitted to continue and a few days later emerged as a most remarkable winner.

DEWEY TOMKO
♦ ♣ ♥ ♠

After finishing second to Jack 'Treetops' Straus in the 1982 WSOP world championship game, Dewey Tomko repeated the achievement when runner-up to Spain's Carlos Mortensen in 2001. Despite just missing out on the most prestigious title, Tomko possesses three WSOP bracelets in recognition of his tournament wins which began in 1979 with victory in the US$1,000 no-limit Texas Hold 'em event. Prior to that, Tomko had been a kindergarten teacher who discovered that regular participation in all-night poker sessions was financially more rewarding than holding down a job. The move to professional poker was a natural progression for someone who had been making money at the game since the age of 16. The pool halls of Pittsburgh, in Tomko's native Pennsylvania, offered sufficient poker action for him to pay for his college education and laid the foundations for his highly successful career in the game. Married with three children, Tomko has achieved overall tournament winnings of US$5 million, which, given that tournament victories have been a rare occurrence for him since 1985, is a testament to his ability to reach the prize-money places on a regular basis.

Above: Dewey Tomko is a poker all-rounder having won WSOP titles at no-limit Texas Hold 'em, pot-limit Omaha, and deuce-to-seven draw, one of the popular lowball poker variations at which Tomko is a specialist.

WOMEN POKER PLAYERS

Although the majority of tales from the poker tables of the world invariably concern the exploits of men, the last two decades have seen women making a significant impact on the professional game as they dispel a few myths regarding their innate ability to play at the highest level. Sexism is still encountered, even by some of the more famous players, but this is giving way to respect, as tournament results speak for themselves.

Names from American history such as Belle Siddons, Annie Oakley, Calamity Jane and 'Poker Alice' Iver, all of them respected players, underline the fact that women's historical relationship with poker extends well beyond dealing the cards and acting as promo girls. Professionals such as Cyndy Violette, Jennifer Harman and Melissa Hayden are just a few of the women who have quickly worked their way to the top of the money lists, while Hollywood actress Jennifer Tilly's victory in the 2005 WSOP ladies-only US$1,000 no-limit Texas Hold 'em tournament can only have helped broaden poker's appeal.

ANNIE DUKE

One woman who has earned a reputation as one of the best poker players in the world over the past decade is Annie Duke. She entered the World Series of Poker (WSOP) for the first time in 1994 and finished thirteenth in her maiden tournament, knocking out her brother, Howard Lederer, along the way. He had been playing tournament poker for a couple of years when he introduced Duke to the game in 1992. She tried her hand in Las Vegas and, on the back of her initial success, returned home to her husband armed with the means to supplement their household income. She gained experience playing in some of the tougher clubs and bars of Billings, Montana, but, after winning US$70,000 from her first tournament in Las Vegas, she accepted her brother's advice to capitalize on her ability and play professionally. That Duke made the right decision was apparent when, in 2004, she eliminated several poker legends on her way to victory in the WSOP no-limit Hold 'em Tournament of Champions, where she claimed the US$2 million

Above: Annie Oakley (1860–1926), a respected poker player, became an American celebrity courtesy of her shooting ability with a rifle. She found widespread fame as part of 'Buffalo Bill' Cody's touring show.

Right: Annie Duke at the WSOP world championship in 2005. Her most notable success to date came in the 2004 WSOP Tournament of Champions when she beat Chan, Hellmuth, Brunson and a host of other legendary poker players to win the US$2 million first prize.

prize. Currently acting as a consultant for an online poker site, she is in demand among Hollywood's glitterati as a poker coach and stars in her own television series. Her autobiography, *Annie Duke: How I Raised, Folded, Bluffed, Flirted, Cursed and Won Millions at the World Series of Poker*, was published in 2005.

KATHY LIEBERT

Currently the top female earner on the tournament circuit, with over US$3 million in prize money won, Kathy Liebert needs little guidance on the intricacies of managing financial risk. Born in 1967, Liebert grew up in New York and obtained a degree in business and finance before working as an analyst for a company in New Jersey. Boredom soon set in and she decided to travel, financing her trip across country with the returns from her successful stock investments. Initially, she indulged her interest in poker by playing low-limit games in Colorado, but eventually Liebert arrived in Las Vegas and, upon the recommendation of a friend, started to take the game seriously.

Since then, she has developed a growing reputation as one of the most ruthless players on tour and someone who enjoys all aspects of tournament play.

Above: Betty Carey, described by 'Amarillo Slim' Preston as the best woman poker player he had ever seen. A heads-up challenge between the two ended inside ten minutes as Carey emerged victorious.

Yet, despite her obvious talent, Liebert is content to enter satellite tournaments rather than pay the full entry fee to the bigger events, simply because it helps to keep costs down. Equally, she demonstrated a winner's mentality touched with business acumen when she triumphed in the first PartyPoker Million event in 2002, beating Beri Kecherian and Phil Hellmuth. She cut a deal with them, which saw her first prize reduced, but improved her place money prospects at a time when victory was far from certain.

Above: Tiffany Williamson, on her way to 15th place in the 2005 WSOP world championship and a prize of US$400,000. The corporate lawyer from South Carolina had only been playing poker for a year having learned the game while working in London. Her performance in the main event was the best by a woman since Annie Duke's 10th-place finish in 2000.

KATHY LIEBERT
♦ ♣ ♥ ♠

Above: Kathy Liebert, now a resident of Las Vegas, achieved five prize-money finishes at the 2006 WSOP, her best showing yet at poker's annual showpiece event.

Born in Tennessee though raised on Long Island, New York, Kathy Liebert made her mark on the professional poker scene with victory in the PartyPoker Million tournament in 2002. Two years later she won a fixed-limit Texas Hold 'em event at the WSOP to claim her first gold bracelet. Her career earnings from poker to date amount to over US$3 million.

MYTHS AND LEGENDS

Given the confrontational nature of poker and the stakes for which players sometimes compete, many stories have emerged over the years reflecting the best, and the worst, of human nature. Every ambassador for the game proclaims the virtues of coolness under pressure, grace in defeat and modesty in victory, and many of poker's legendary tales feature exhibitions of these qualities. Yet there are others that tell of drastic and unorthodox strategies employed at the poker table in the face of extreme intimidation. In 19th-century America, playing poker could be a serious and potentially deadly pursuit.

JIM BOWIE

Poker on the Mississippi riverboats was notorious for attracting hustlers who viewed it as a means of earning a living amid America's harsh, speculative culture. Indeed, being a successful professional card player was synonymous with being a cheat, although not all prospered. One group of players had cause to reconsider their profession in 1832 when inviting a wealthy but evidently naive young man to join them in a poker game during one particular steamboat journey. After predictably losing his entire fortune, the man was sufficiently distraught to be contemplating suicide when he was encountered by Jim Bowie, later

to die at the Alamo, a famous battle between the Republic of Mexico and rebel Texan forces fighting for independence. Suspecting that the man had been duped in an unfair game, Bowie watched the remaining poker players in action for a while until he was confident that someone was cheating. His surveillance paid off and, after pulling a knife on the suspect to force him into revealing his deception, Bowie collected the cash from the table and split the proceeds with the young man.

'BUFFALO BILL' & 'WILD BILL' HICKOK

Many of the myths surrounding the Wild West stem from the activities of one of its most famous figures, William 'Buffalo Bill' Cody, whose travelling stage show entertained the public for 30 years with fanciful tales of an era that was coming to an end. One story about Cody concerns the occasion when he was challenged to a game of poker by a man who freely proclaimed his contempt for the famous 'Buffalo Bill'. Cody agreed, but insisted that the game should end in a duel, the winner having the first opportunity to shoot his opponent from ten yards. Cody won the game, but his adversary immediately tried to draw his pistol, at which point a certain 'Wild Bill' Hickok pressed a gun to the man's head, judged him a cheat,

Right: James Bowie (1796–1836), aka Jim Bowie, who was a 19th-century pioneer and soldier, and is now immortalized as one of the most colourful folk heroes of Texas history. Born in Kentucky, he spent most of his youth in Louisiana, where he first acquired a reputation for his bold and fearless disposition. Bowie took a prominent part in the Texas Revolution and was killed in the siege of the Alamo. He is also known for the style of knife he carried, which came to be known as the 'Bowie knife'.

Below: 'Buffalo Bill' Cody and Annie Oakley perform a quadrille during the 'Wild West Show'. Though hugely popular at the time, these shows were also responsible for peddling many enduring myths concerning life on the frontier.

Left: William 'Buffalo Bill' Cody, a former scout and buffalo hunter who devised the Wild West Show in 1883. He earned his nickname while working for a railroad company which employed him to kill buffalo in order to feed the labourers laying the track. A keen poker player, Cody even found time for a game while on his deathbed.

THE DEAD MAN'S HAND

Above and right: When 'Wild Bill' Hickok was shot dead, his hand comprised two pairs, black aces and eights, though the identity of the odd remaining card – the 'kicker' – is subject to debate. His killer, Jack McCall, testified that the card was the J diamonds, but Deadwood's museum has a 5 diamonds which it claims is Hickok's real kicker.

and consequently hanged him. The legendary pair, friends for some years, were keen poker players and 'Buffalo Bill' Cody is even reputed to have played one last game when told he had just hours to live.

THE DEAD MAN'S HAND

Although he arguably saved 'Buffalo Bill' Cody's life in the interests of fair play, James Butler Hickok was not averse to threatening opponents in a similar fashion when losing a game himself. He worked as a stagecoach driver and scout before his reputation for marksmanship and his uncompromising nature led to him becoming a US marshal. As befits a man nicknamed 'Wild Bill', he is credited with taking part in the first recognized Wild West gunfight when he shot dead Davis J. Tutt in July 1865. Hickok also played professional poker, but in one drunken game he ruthlessly cheated an opponent named McDonald out of a large pot. He claimed a full house to beat McDonald's three jacks but, just as his hand was

revealed to include merely a pair of aces with a six, Hickok drew his pistol and his knife. Faced by the additional six, in the shape of the six-shot revolver, and an ace in the hole – the knife – McDonald wisely chose to concede the hand.

Most famously, 'Wild Bill' Hickok was playing poker when he was shot dead in a saloon bar in Deadwood, South Dakota, in August 1876. A cattle herder named Jack McCall, who was drinking at the bar with his gun concealed, slowly approached the table and shot Hickok in the back of the head. The cards held by 'Wild Bill' at the time showed two pairs – aces and eights, all black – which have been known ever since as the 'Dead Man's Hand'.

THE BUCK STOPS HERE

Poker is considered such a quintessentially American game it is hardly surprising that several presidents are known to have enjoyed playing it. 'Amarillo Slim' revealed that he played with Lyndon B. Johnson on occasion, as well as with the Texan's successor, Richard M. Nixon, a man who diligently applied himself to learning everything about the game while serving in the US Navy. Reluctant to risk any money until he felt confident in his ability, Nixon played poker continuously for months with a friend who was prepared to teach him the strategies required to win. Only then was Nixon prepared to gamble for real, and the education stood him in good stead – his winnings from poker partially financed the early stages of his political career. Perhaps the most famous of all poker-playing presidents, however, is Harry S. Truman, the man credited with coining the phrase "the buck stops here" – 'the buck' being another term for the dealer button – while in office. This president, who took the decision to deploy atomic weapons against Japan in 1945, often sought refuge in poker's familiar rhythms when under pressure. Indeed, while considering whether or not to use the bomb, Truman spent many hours relaxing at sea playing poker with members of the press, all the while contemplating one of the most significant decisions in history.

ERROL FLYNN LOSES AN ISLAND
♦ ♣ ♥ ♠

A film star of the 1930s and 40s, Flynn was a renowned drinker, womanizer and gambler, who once lost an entire island in a game of poker. A journey to Jamaica aboard his yacht in 1947 led to Flynn purchasing Navy Island, a haven lying just off Port Antonio that he planned to develop into a holiday resort. But, as he partied away the declining years of his career, Flynn's love of poker meant this ambition would remain unfulfilled, when he gambled away ownership of the island during what he described as "a bad poker night".

POKER AND THE STARS

The film industry, responsible in many ways for popularizing poker, has also been a rich source of stories concerning the stars and their poker exploits. Steve McQueen's familiarity with the game made him a natural for the role of poker hustler Eric Stoner in *The Cincinnati Kid*. As such an integral part of American culture, poker has traditionally been a popular diversion for crews during filming, with McQueen and his co-stars in *The Magnificent Seven*, for instance, famously pictured playing the game. Charles Bronson, another to appear in the classic Western, often sat in

Above: President Harry S. Truman's poker table, complete with cards and a poker chip carousel, is one of the exhibits at the Little White House Museum. Truman played poker while deliberating over whether or not he should order the dropping of an atomic bomb on Japan in 1945.

Right: Errol Flynn in relaxed mood. The film star's attachment to poker cost him his dream of developing an exclusive holiday resort in Jamaica – the island he bought was gambled away in a poker game.

on 24-hour sessions with the likes of Lee Marvin and Telly Savalas while filming *The Dirty Dozen* in London. They were regularly joined by comedian and Oscar-winning director Woody Allen, who was in London filming *Casino Royale* at the time. Such was the reported disorganization behind the scenes of that production that Allen was content to play marathon poker sessions instead.

In fact, Telly Savalas was well respected as a player by the professionals in Los Angeles and Las Vegas, regularly participating in the WSOP and once finishing 21st in the no-limit world championship game. Of the current crop of Hollywood actors famed for their poker skills, Tobey Maguire and Ben Affleck have both won major tournament prizes, with Affleck victorious in the prestigious California State Poker Championship of 2004. This achievement came after Affleck had sought poker lessons from professional player Annie Duke. His next project is reportedly a comedy concerning the poker scene that will feature David Schwimmer, another keen player. Other stars currently making an impact in high-profile poker tournaments are James Woods and Jennifer Tilly, both of whom have managed to win money at the WSOP.

JOHN WAYNE WINS A DOG
♦ ♣ ♥ ♠

American icon John Wayne was typical of many film stars in that he often indulged his fondness for poker with the rest of the crew during breaks in filming, although one game in 1953 saw him win a remarkable pot, even by Hollywood standards. During production of the Western adventure *Hondo*, a drunken poker session resulted in Rudd Weatherwax, owner of Hollywood's canine legend Lassie, losing his faithful collie to the man known as 'Duke'. However, on sobering up the next day, noted dog lover Wayne duly returned the animal to its owner. This is perhaps not surprising – his nickname derived from that given to a pet dog he once owned some years earlier.

Left: The Magnificent Seven enjoy a game of poker while filming in 1960. Robert Vaughn (left) looks on as Yul Brynner (centre left) makes a move. To Brynner's left are Brad Dexter, Charles Bronson and James Coburn. Playing poker during a break in filming remains almost traditional in Hollywood.

POKER ON FILM

Images of American culture and society have been a fixture of film throughout the history of the moving picture and, naturally, poker has featured in many scenes during that time. Usually, the game provides a context for developing characters and furthering the plot, whether in Westerns, gangster films or more contemporary dramas. For example, in the 1965 Sergio Leone Western *For a Few Dollars More*, Clint Eastwood's first scene as the poncho-wearing bounty hunter sees him interrupt a saloon-bar poker game in pursuit of his quarry. He wins the hand, shoots four bandits and pockets a US$2,000 reward, neatly summarizing the qualities of the so-called 'man with no name'.

In a more contemporary setting, the 1968 comedy *The Odd Couple*, starring Walter Matthau and Jack Lemmon, centres on the relationship between two friends who play in a regular poker game. Developed from a Neil Simon stage play, the story unfolds during a number of scenes in which poker is revealed as the bond tying the characters together.

Similarly, *A Streetcar Named Desire*, made in 1951, was adapted from a Tennessee Williams play originally visualized as a single act with a poker game at its core. In the event, the brooding menace present in Marlon Brando's portrayal of Stanley Kowalski is revealed during a couple of games with his friends, poker being exhibited as a typical medium for very masculine expressions of anger and frustration.

GANGSTERS AND CASINOS

Many portrayals of poker as a man's game emanate from the gangster genre of films, which is often tied in with the exploits of the Mafia in Las Vegas. Martin Scorsese's 1990 film *Goodfellas* featured the leading characters in a poker scene, while in *Casino*, made in 1995, the emphasis was on the criminal activity in one of the larger Las Vegas gambling joints. The Rat Pack's association with Las Vegas prompted the production of *Ocean's Eleven* in 1960, a popular caper movie that saw Frank Sinatra, Dean Martin, Sammy Davis Jr and the rest attempting to rob five casinos simultaneously. Later, of course, the film was remade with George Clooney cast in the lead role, supported by a few keen poker-player actors including Matt Damon, Brad Pitt, Don Cheadle and Elliott Gould. For Gould, this represented familiar territory – in 1974 he had teamed up with George Segal to play a couple of gamblers heading for a make-or-break poker game in *California Split*, directed by the acclaimed director Robert Altman. The film also featured a cameo appearance by 1972 WSOP world champion 'Amarillo Slim', which served to heighten his own profile and that of poker as well. In addition to these occasions when poker has been portrayed on film, however, there are a handful of productions that stand out for the manner in which the game itself, and the people who play it, are central to proceedings.

Above: Robert De Niro as Sam 'Ace' Rothstein, the gangster who runs a casino for the Mafia in 1970s Las Vegas, as depicted in Martin Scorsese's *Casino* (1995).

Left: While Henry Hill (Ray Liotta, left) looks on, Tommy DeVito (Joe Pesci) holds all the aces at the poker table in this scene from *Goodfellas* (1990).

Left: A scene from *A Big Hand for the Little Lady* (1966) in which Mary, played by Joanne Woodward, takes over at the poker table after her husband dies of a heart attack half way through a crucial hand. As the pot develops, Mary's entire fortune depends on the outcome of the game.

Below: Elliott Gould in the 1974 film *California Split*, directed by Robert Altman. Gould and co-star George Segal play a couple of gamblers in search of that elusive big win. Their adventures take them from racetrack to casino as they make their way to Reno for the decisive poker game.

A BIG HAND FOR THE LITTLE LADY

This light-hearted Western, directed by Fielder Cook in 1966 and starring Henry Fonda and Joanne Woodward, turns on the poker game that Fonda's character, Meredith, simply cannot resist. The pair of them are on the way to California to start a new life with their son but, while stopping in Laredo, Meredith discovers that a big game featuring some of the wealthiest players around is about to start. His wife is appalled at the prospect of seeing their life savings disappear, knowing her husband to be a dreadful player, but she sits in on the game anyway. Things go from bad to worse until, with a winning hand finally in his grasp, Meredith dies of a heart attack, leaving his widow to take his place. At this point she faces a big bet and, in an unlikely twist, dashes to the bank to negotiate a loan using the cards as collateral. This enables her to call the bet and produce the required happy ending.

Although satisfying the need for drama, this type of situation is highly unlikely to arise in reality since the majority of games are played for table stakes. This rule ensures that only the chips on the table may be bet during the play of any hand. Players who do not possess enough to call a bet may still commit their remaining chips to the pot and retain interest in the outcome. Should their hand prove best, they can claim from their opponents an amount equal to the total number of chips they have invested in the pot.

TABLE STAKES
♦ ♣ ♥ ♠

The table stakes ruling prohibits players from introducing additional funds to the game during the play of a hand. A player who does not have enough chips to match the current level of betting may still contest the hand by going all-in, the term used when committing all one's remaining chips to the pot. If the player loses, then it may be possible to buy more chips to continue in the game, but this must be done in a break between hands, not during play itself.

THE CINCINNATI KID

Probably the most iconic of all poker films, *The Cincinnati Kid*, directed by Norman Jewison in 1965, features Steve McQueen as Eric Stoner, a young and ambitious poker player in 1930s New Orleans. Confident that he has the ability to be the best, Stoner seeks a confrontation with the acknowledged master of the game – Lancey Howard, or 'The Man' – memorably played by Edward G. Robinson. The stakes are high, though it is not just the money that drives the young pretender, but the status that comes from beating the man regarded as the best poker player around in order to be acknowledged as the new champion. The final scene sees the two men playing a no-limit game of five-card stud which, though it fulfils the need for dramatic tension, stretches credibility in the eyes of experienced players. Stoner bets his way, round by round, towards a hand of three aces and two tens. Yet, despite visibly trailing at every stage, Howard continues to pour cash into the pot and capitalizes on some outrageous fortune to win with a queen-high straight flush (8, 9, 10, J, Q) in diamonds. At this point he utters the immortal line: "Gets down to what it's all about, doesn't it? Making the wrong move at the right time."

KALEIDOSCOPE

An easygoing romantic drama, directed by Jack Smight, made at the height of the 'Swinging Sixties', in 1966. This stylish film features Warren Beatty as the suave Barney Lincoln, a card-playing jetsetter with a secret – he cheats. In an elaborate scheme, Lincoln breaks into the Kaleidoscope factory and etches marks into the metal plates that are used for printing the playing cards used in continental Europe's casinos. Now able to identify the cards face down from the patterns he has doctored, Lincoln embarks on a lucrative gambling

Above: The defining scene from *The Cincinnati Kid* (1965) as Steve McQueen (left) and Edward G. Robinson (right) confront each other in the game that will determine which of them emerges with the reputation for being the best poker player in the country. Shelley Winters (centre) is the dealer.

Left: The iconic Steve McQueen as Eric Stoner in *The Cincinnati Kid*, contemplating his strategy as he engages in another big-money poker game. The film involves him testing his skills at the table as well as having to cope with a complicated love life involving his girlfriend (Tuesday Weld) and his mentor's wife (Ann-Margret).

spree, with nobody suspecting the reason for his success. Unfortunately, his girlfriend is the daughter of a Scotland Yard inspector and, when his ruse is eventually uncovered, he is blackmailed by police into challenging a poker-playing gangster to a game. All he has to do is win to keep up the financial pressure on the crook, a suspected drug smuggler. Predictably, Lincoln's true poker skills are then tested to the full when the cards of another manufacturer are used rather than his preferred Kaleidoscope decks. The undercover cheat must therefore hold his nerve in a quest for redemption.

Above: Teddy KGB (John Malkovich) looking menacingly confident at the poker table in *Rounders* (1998). The film helped rejuvenate interest in the game and inspired a new generation of players, including 2003 WSOP world champion Chris Moneymaker, to take poker seriously.

ROUNDERS

This is the film, directed by John Dahl in 1998, credited with putting poker back on the map and inspiring a new generation of players. The 2003 WSOP world champion Chris Moneymaker is among those claiming to have become much more interested in the game after watching this film. Matt Damon plays a law student, Mike McDermott, who turns his back on poker after losing all his money to the notorious 'Teddy KGB', portrayed with customary relish by John Malkovich. However, when his friend is released from jail and needs help repaying a loan of US$15,000 from Teddy, McDermott comes to the rescue. He returns to the card rooms to put his skills to the test, jeopardizing his relationship with his girlfriend in the process.

As with so many other poker-related films, some of the scenes are a little too contrived to retain credibility, even with a respected card player like Matt Damon heading the cast and a cameo appearance by twice world champion Johnny Chan. Nevertheless, it sheds light on the world of the low-level poker professional and is notable for this essential piece of advice from the main character. "Listen, here's the thing. If you can't spot the sucker in the first half hour at the table, then you are the sucker."

Right: Matt Damon as law student Mike McDermott in *Rounders* (1998). Having quit poker following a defeat to Teddy KGB (John Malkovich), McDermott returns to the tables in order to help a friend repay a loan. The film featured a cameo appearance by Johnny Chan, at the time the WSOP world champion, though the story mainly concerns the low-level professional game.

POKER ON TELEVISION

As already noted, the combined power of television and the Internet over the past decade has helped poker attain a higher profile than at any time in its history. More people then ever before are playing the game and television has been quick to capitalize on this interest, providing poker programming to cater for an expanding audience. This development in televised poker has helped many of the most successful tournament players become household names. Promoted by supermodels and played by film stars, poker is now perceived as a respectable and even glamorous gambling medium that offers the chance, albeit a slim one, for anyone to win a fortune.

MORALITY TALES

Dramatic representations of poker games on the small screen have, naturally, been a staple of numerous television series set in the Wild West, though the game is generally less visible in contemporary settings. Popular Western shows such as *Bonanza*, *Rawhide*, *The Virginian* and, of course, *Maverick* have all employed poker as a means of imparting a few moral concepts, particularly the idea that cheats should never prosper. Westerns apart, one latter-day character certainly identified with poker is the iconic US Army schemer Sergeant Bilko, played by Phil Silvers, who preferred fleecing his men in a game to supervising their duties in the motor pool. More recently, an episode of the long-running comedy series *Friends* was devoted to a

poker game, while suggestions that poker may well remain popular in the future are present in various episodes of *Star Trek: The Next Generation*. Additionally, in the original *Star Trek* series, Captain James T. Kirk is confronted by a stubborn and powerful opponent in an episode entitled 'The Corbomite Maneuver', and has to deploy a poker-inspired bluff to save the USS *Enterprise* from destruction. On the back of the game's current popularity, however, the potential for a drama series centred entirely on poker has finally been realized with *Tilt*, written by the team responsible for the film *Rounders*. Michael Madsen plays Don 'The Matador' Everest, whose status is under threat from a group of young poker tyros intent on taking him down as the WSOP approaches. But Las Vegas has a

Above: Alex Brenes (left) from Costa Rica, playing in the televised World Cup Poker Tournament in 2005. This team competition features heads-up poker as players duel against each other, one on one, as shown here. Costa Rica went on to win this event to retain the title secured in the inaugural competition the previous year.

Left: John Duthie, winner of the first Poker Million event on the Isle of Man in 2000, is the driving force behind the European Poker Tour (EPT) established in 2004. Inspired by the World Poker Tour (WPT) on American television, the EPT featured six events during the 2006/07 season, concluding with the grand final in Monte Carlo.

few surprises in store for the budding champions. It remains to be seen whether the series will inspire others of a similar nature, but the audience for poker is currently well served by the prolific amount of real tournament play on offer via television.

Above left: Mike Sexton, the WPT's expert presenter and commentator, achieved a victory in the 2006 no-limit Texas Hold 'em Tournament of Champions in Las Vegas. His prize for winning was US$1 million.

Above: Andrew Rogers sits calmly with a monitor checking his heart rate, lower right, as he takes part in the Mansionpoker.net Poker Dome Challenge at the Tropicana Resort and Casino in Las Vegas in June 2006.

WORLD POKER TOUR

Now an established part of the cable television scene, the World Poker Tour (WPT) was instigated in 2002 by attorney and television producer Stephen Lipscomb. Interest from the Travel Channel saw the establishment of several tournaments under the WPT brand, with highlights of the various games shown during 2003. By February 2004, American network television was sufficiently interested in the viewing figures for NBC to broadcast a special WPT 'Battle of Champions' event. It performed surprisingly well in direct competition with the CBS network's pre-Superbowl coverage and confirmed poker as a truly legitimate televised spectacle. After seven successful seasons, the WPT continues to grow in popularity, its programmes currently presented by WSOP winner Mike Sexton and Hollywood home-game sensation, Vincent Van Patten.

EUROPEAN POKER TOUR

In the UK, the surprise success of Channel 4's *Late Night Poker*, first broadcast in 1999 and revived in 2008, has generated more televised tournament poker, with an audience for the game existing throughout Europe. Following the example of the WPT, television director John Duthie, a competitor on *Late Night Poker* himself, sought support from online site PokerStars.com and instigated the European Poker Tour (EPT) in 2004. The opening season featured six tournaments, but the EPT has quickly grown to become the most prestigious poker circuit in Europe and is now broadcast in over 40 countries. Apart from being the EPT's chief executive, Duthie also acts as a pundit during the series, a role for which he is eminently suited since he won the Poker Million event in 2000. Interestingly, Duthie came second to the WPT's Mike Sexton in the 2003 European Heads-Up Championship held in Paris.

POKER IN PRINT

Those currently interested in poker and its culture have a wealth of literature from which to glean knowledge of the game. R.F. Foster's *Practical Poker*, published in 1905, was the first serious attempt to record all that was known about poker at the time, but the last 40 years have seen the publication of many more books on the subject. The majority are concerned with teaching readers how to play poker and develop their skills in order to win consistently. Many contemporary professionals have written or endorsed such books, building on the work of some influential poker theorists of the past. For those who wish to know about the poker players themselves, 'Amarillo Slim' and Annie Duke are just two of the big names to have autobiographies currently on the bookshelves. In addition, poker-playing writers Al Alvarez, Anthony Holden and James McManus have all written critically acclaimed accounts of their experiences in the world of professional poker.

LITERARY REFERENCES

Perhaps the most famous writer to have included poker tales within his literary work is Mark Twain, a keen advocate of the game he encountered while working on the Mississippi as a steamboat pilot. Indeed, the creator of Tom Sawyer and Huckleberry Finn once stated: "There are few things so unpardonably neglected in our country as poker ... It is enough to make you blush." In *The Professor's Yarn*, Twain tells the story of a poker player who manages to even the score against some cheats, a familiar plotline in many gambling tales. Following Twain's example, other writers such as Damon Runyon and Dashiel Hammett incorporated poker in their work, either as a feature of their characters' lives or as a useful plot device. More recently, ubiquitous poker commentator and pundit Jesse May has also written *Shut Up and Deal*, a fictional tale set in American poker rooms of the 1990s.

Above: Damon Runyon, the celebrated journalist and author whose short stories set in Prohibition-era New York vividly describe a world populated by gangsters, actors and gamblers. The famous musical *Guys and Dolls* was inspired by two of his stories.

Right: *Friend in Need* (aka *Passing the Ace Under the Table*) by Cassius Marcellus Coolidge, one of nine depictions of dogs playing poker for which the artist was commissioned in 1903. Two of the original oil paintings from the much-imitated series were sold at auction in 2005 for US$590,000.

Left: Annie Duke secured her reputation as one of the foremost professional poker players in the world with victory in the 2004 WSOP Tournament of Champions, and with it a US$2 million prize.

Below: Mark Twain, born Samuel Langhorne Clemens in 1835, is famed for his portrayals of life on the Mississippi river, the route by which poker spread throughout America. Of the game itself, Twain wrote: "There are few things so unpardonably neglected in our country as poker."

A LIFE IN POKER

Given the sometimes colourful nature of their exploits, it is hardly surprising that a number of professionals are cashing in on their fame while trying to broaden the game's appeal. For example Phil Hellmuth, arguably the best tournament player in the world, is planning an autobiography, entitled *Poker Brat*, while *Amarillo Slim in a World Full of Fat People*, published in 2003, recounts Thomas Preston's eventful gambling career. Unsurprisingly, given his nihilistic approach to life, the late Stu Ungar is also the subject of a biography by Nolan Dalla and Peter Alson, entitled *One of a Kind: The Rise and Fall of Stuey 'The Kid' Ungar, the World's Greatest Poker Player*. Offering a different perspective on the game is literary critic Al Alvarez's account of the 1981 WSOP, *The Biggest Game in Town*. His analysis of the tournament, linked to the stories behind the players, makes it almost essential reading for anyone interested in the game. In a similar vein, Andy Bellin's *Poker Nation* and Anthony Holden's *Big Deal: One Year as a Professional Poker Player* offer two more interpretations of time spent playing cards for a living.

POKER TUITION

Following the success of Frank R. Wallace's 1968 book *Advanced Concepts of Poker*, the 1970s saw a steady growth in the number of publications containing advice on how to play the game. The authoritative musings of top players and theorists revealed the analytical and mathematical skills employed at the poker table by the game's most successful exponents. One of the most influential is David Sklansky's *Hold 'Em Poker*, first published in 1976. He has subsequently written several other books on the game and also contributed to *Doyle Brunson's Super System: A Course in Power Poker*, another 1970s classic that covers a selection of the most popular variations. A guide to WSOP tournament strategy emerged in 1995, written by 1983 WSOP world champion Tom McEvoy while, from the next generation, Phil Hellmuth's *Play Poker Like the Pros*, published in 2003, explains the principles behind successful play. Some focus on one variation, others highlight the ploys to be adopted in a range of poker scenarios, but they represent a mere fraction of the literature available to those seeking to improve their understanding of the game.

HOW TO PLAY

THERE ARE MANY VARIATIONS OF POKER, BUT THE OVERALL OBJECTIVE OF THE GAME REMAINS THE SAME: TO WIN THE MONEY OR GAMING CHIPS FROM THE OTHER PLAYERS. WHETHER A NOVICE OR A PRO, THERE ARE MANY OPPORTUNITIES TO TAKE PART IN A GAME, IT IS EASY TO PLAY A GAME AT HOME WITH FRIENDS OR ONLINE, AND THERE ARE MANY CLUBS AND CASINOS WHICH WILL OFTEN HAVE ORGANISED GAMES AND TOURNAMENTS.

Evidence concerning the origins of poker may be limited but what is certainly clear is that the game possesses qualities that make it immensely enjoyable to play. Most commentators regard poker as being a simple game to learn but one which may take a lifetime to master. For the newcomer, poker's lexicon of terms, added to the wide variety of poker games in existence, can make the journey of discovery seem a daunting prospect. The aim of this chapter, therefore, is to guide beginners through the practical aspects of play while also noting other considerations to be taken into account when sitting at the poker table, from choosing a game and learning the general sequence of play to understanding the betting structures.

Right: Another hand commences as the dealer distributes the cards to those involved in the game. The number of cards received by each player will depend on the poker variation being played since the first thing to understand about the game is that poker is really a term that applies to a huge family of vying games. Though each variation has its own basic rules and betting structure, this chapter covers those facets common to all poker games which a newcomer needs to understand before settling down to play.

POKER RULES AND REGULATIONS

Poker encompasses a range of hugely popular vying card games in which players bet against each other regarding the relative merits of the cards in their hand. All poker hands must consist of five cards only, although, in most forms of poker, players may be permitted to select these five from several more cards available to them during play. The term hand also applies to each game, typically of a few minutes duration, extending from the deal to the showdown.

RANKINGS, SUITS AND ACES

Binding the hundreds of poker variations together is the ranking of poker hands, a hierarchical list of the 2,598,960 different five-card combinations it is possible to draw from a standard 52-card deck. These rankings are based on the likelihood of being dealt any particular hand, with the most valuable – the royal flush (or royal straight flush) – being that regarded as the least likely to occur. Two other key components of poker are that the suits are of equal value and aces may count as both the highest or lowest card in any suit during the course of play.

One anomaly is that, beyond universal acceptance of the ranking of hands, there are no official rules of play in existence for any of poker's many variations. This situation gives rise to confusion among players new to the game. Unlike most organized professional sports, poker has no established international federation or governing body to ratify the rules, resolve disputes and generally protect the integrity of the game. In tournament poker, however, this may change over time. The World Poker Association was launched in March 2006, and is an organization that aims to establish uniform codes of conduct governing playing rules and etiquette on the global tournament circuit.

Right: The dealer button, sometimes referred to as 'the buck', is used to show which player is acting as the dealer for each particular hand. Buttons are most commonly used in commercial card rooms which employ dealers to control the action.

Royal flush (or royal straight flush). The highest-ranked hand in poker, consisting of an ace-high straight in any one of the four suits. All suits are ranked equally.

Straight flush. The second-best hand in poker, consisting of five cards of the same suit in sequential order. If two or more players hold a straight flush, the high card determines the winner.

Four of a kind. Four cards of one rank supplemented by any additional card. If two or more players hold four of a kind, the highest rank wins.

Full house. Three cards of one rank plus two of another. The value of the hand is determined by the three cards of the same rank meaning, for example, that K, K, K, J, J beats Q, Q, Q, A, A.

Flush. Five cards of the same suit not in sequential order. Competing flushes are determined by the high card, then the second highest and so on. An ace-high flush in diamonds comprising A, J, 10, 5, 2, beats an ace-high flush in spades consisting of A, J, 9, 8, 7, for example.

Straight. Five cards of differing suits in sequential order. Again, when there are competing straights, the high card determines the winner.

Three of a kind. Three cards of one rank plus two other unmatched cards.

Two pairs. A hand comprising two cards of one rank, two cards of another rank and one odd card, known as the 'kicker'. If two or more players possess two pairs, the high pair dictates the value of the hand, followed by the second pair and ultimately the kicker. So A, A, 2, 2, Q beats K, K, Q, Q, 5 and A, A, 10, 10, Q beats A, A, 10, 10, J.

One pair. Two cards of the same rank plus three unmatched cards. The rank of the pair determines the value of the hand but, should two players both show a pair of the same rank, then the remaining cards come into play. So, 5, 5, A, K, 2, beats 5, 5, A, 10, 8.

High card. A hand comprising five assorted cards, all of differing ranks and suits. Its value is dictated by the highest card.

OBJECT OF THE GAME

Poker is a gambling game, of course, and the objective is to win money, usually represented by gaming chips, from the other players at the table. The chips staked during each hand of play constitute the pot and this is claimed by the winner at the conclusion of the hand. The winner is determined by either one of two methods: a player who makes a bet that is unmatched by any opponent can win the pot without having to reveal his cards; alternatively, if two or more players match bets to the conclusion of the hand, they then reveal their cards at the showdown and the holder of the best poker hand claims the spoils.

THE GAMBLING ELEMENT

For any poker session to be meaningful and fulfilling, it must involve gambling for stakes that are of value to the players. Whether that means playing for pennies around the kitchen table or paying the US$10,000 entry fee for the World Series of Poker championship tournament is entirely dependent on a player's resources and motivation. Both experienced players and novices are sensibly advised to select a game at which the stake levels are not so high as to create hardship in the event of a heavy loss. Since one of the key factors required to play good poker is discipline, recognizing one's own skill level and the stakes for which one can afford to play is an important step in the right direction. For the beginner this is crucial advice given that the majority of players will inevitably lose money as they effectively pay for their education during their early games.

A DECK OF CARDS
♦ ♣ ♥ ♠

Any standard deck of 52 cards will suffice for an informal game of poker, but it is recommended that a fresh deck is used to underline the integrity of the game, this being common practice in casinos and clubs. In home games, having two easily distinguishable decks in operation is a good idea since this helps to maintain a steady rhythm to proceedings. The spare deck can be shuffled and cut during the play of a hand so that it is immediately ready for dealing the next. Players may request that the deck be changed at any time, perhaps because cards have become inadvertently marked or spoiled during play.

CHIPS, STAKES AND BUY-INS

Before learning the standard playing procedure for any of poker's many variations, prospective players should consider why they wish to engage in a game. This means contemplating whether playing poker is to be purely a social pleasure or a serious pursuit. Poker, by design, generates competition, so it is important for players to be aware of their own attitudes towards winning and losing, since both are inevitable consequences of play. Being fully engaged in a game can provide a player with a vast range of mental and emotional challenges. For those serious enough to consider earning a living from poker, controlling one's emotions and staying focused on the task in hand is an essential skill.

STAKES

Most poker is played socially for modest stakes, enabling players to appreciate the aesthetics of the game without fearing imminent financial ruin. The essence of poker is in the gambling, which is why it is important for players to compete at stake levels within their means. This is crucial, for the cash sums at stake should not distract players from their primary task, which is to assess opponents, absorb the nuances of play and decide when to make a move. Understanding the character as well as the betting habits of an opponent is crucial to becoming a successful poker player.

THE BUY-IN

Every venue staging a game possesses a set of house rules governing play. These cover the technical issues concerning the betting structures of the poker variations dealt in the establishment, as well as points of etiquette on acceptable behaviour at the table. For example, the minimum amount of money required to sit in on a game – the 'buy-in' – will be stipulated, and there may also be a rule forbidding players from discussing the play of a hand in progress. These rules vary from one card room to the next, and players should take individual responsibility for checking them prior to sitting in on a game. Anybody planning to host a poker game should also devise a basic set of rules governing issues such as the length of each session, the poker variations to be played and any restrictions to be observed regarding the minimum or maximum bet.

Above: Modern-day poker, often played in casinos, can have a very different etiquette to a private game, but is equally exciting.

Right: During the 19th century, poker was largely a private, social pursuit, although high-stake games were liable to turn ugly.

Left: Cards are kept close to the chest and sneaky pocketing of early winnings is strictly off-limits – chips must remain on show and in circulation throughout a game. All casinos have their own unique colourful designs or at least a logo on their poker chip sets.

Below: Betting with chips rather than money helps players lose their gambling inhibitions, and keeps the game running smoothly.

This helps to prevent unnecessary disputes and creates the proper context for poker so that a session balances the social and competitive demands of the participants.

CHIPS

Poker chips are special tokens representing a fixed amount of money. Especially in card rooms and casinos, poker chips are also known as checks. Each casino has a unique set of chips, even if the casino is part of a larger company. This distinguishes a casino's chips from others, since each chip and token on the gaming floor has to be backed up with the appropriate amount of cash. Durable gaming chips enhance any poker session, since they are cleaner and easier to use than cash, thus quickening proceedings and adding credibility to the game. Using chips does separate players, conceptually at least, from the notion of betting for real cash sums. Novices need to take this effect into account when learning the game, but it can prove beneficial during play. Detaching oneself from the monetary value of the chips at the table helps to reduce inhibitions when betting, which, within the context of the game, is considered essential in enabling a player to make calculated and rational decisions.

CHIP MANAGEMENT
♦ ♣ ♥ ♠

One of the key conventions in poker is that players must ensure that their chips are clearly visible to all at the table during play. Purposely trying to obscure them, by perhaps stacking high-denomination chips behind rows of lower-value chips, is a breach of etiquette. Chips in play at the table must remain in circulation for the duration of the game, with players not permitted to pocket any substantial winnings to protect themselves against a losing session. Also, any player may ask an opponent how many chips they have left when considering a betting decision, often seen in tournament play when one player may consider betting a sufficient amount to force an opponent to bet all-in, if calling.

Left: The colour of plain chips is determined by the denomination. For example 1s are white, 50s are orange, 100s are black, 500s are purple and 1000s are burgundy. The number is embedded so it does not rub off during normal play.

WHERE TO PLAY

The upsurge in poker's popularity has provided experienced players and newcomers alike with an increased range of opportunities to indulge their passion. Online poker leads the way in offering players ready access to a game from the comfort of their own homes. The benefit of this is that newcomers can learn quickly, and in private, before venturing out to test their skills in public. However, poker in the virtual environment denies players the chance to read anything into their opponents' play that may be conveyed through body language, so maintaining a 'poker face' – a face that reveals no thoughts or emotions – is of less importance. For those who relish the face-to-face battles inherent in play, this lack of social interaction at the table reduces the appeal of the game considerably.

HOME GAMES

The culture of the home game as a means of entertaining friends or colleagues is an established part of poker. Popularly regarded as an excuse for men to gather on a regular basis, away from the distractions of work and family, the numbers of women who similarly engage in home games renders this image somewhat anachronistic. Overall, the home game is considered the preserve of the amateur player for whom money won or lost is of secondary importance to the social act of participating.

Instigating a regular game requires planning in order to address the potentially contentious issues that may arise during play. Declaring what variation of poker to play, how the betting is to be structured and how much is required to buy in to the game is essential. Also, it is advisable to set a time limit on participation so that everyone who is playing is immediately aware of when play will finish. Players who intend to leave the game before the agreed conclusion are usually expected to make this clear, as a matter of courtesy. Anyone who habitually sits in for a few hands before departing hastily with a quick profit is soon likely to prove an unwelcome participant in a primarily social game. Practical concerns such as the seating available, the decks of cards to be used and

Above: A home poker game in progress, perhaps typically conveying the image of poker as primarily a masculine pursuit. Owing to the explosion in media coverage of poker, the popularity of the game is such that many more people are once again enjoying the social benefits that come with sitting at a table to play cards with a few friends.

Left: Teenagers having fun playing poker, demonstrating that the game has aspects that make it appealing to people of all ages and doesn't need to involve money changing hands. Card games have long been a source of amusement for friends and family, of course, with many of today's professionals acquiring a taste for poker long before leaving school.

enforce the rules and even provide refreshments, this pleasure comes at a cost. Poker has never been considered an especially profitable game for casinos because, unlike in blackjack and roulette, players compete against each other and not the house. Instead, a fee, known as the 'rake', is levied in one of two ways. In small-stakes cash games, the house dealer may take a cut from each pot, this being anything from two to ten per cent of the amount staked. Alternatively, there may be a set hourly charge for the facilities, this being more likely in games contested by so-called 'high-rollers' – gamblers who play for large stakes.

ONLINE POKER

The proliferation of online poker sites over the last ten years has undoubtedly provided a boost to the game's popularity. Anyone possessing a computer and access to the Internet is now able to sit in at a game within minutes, and millions of people worldwide have been seduced into doing just that. The major sites such as PartyPoker, PokerStars and PokerRoom offer several different poker variations at stake levels ranging from a few cents to hundreds of dollars, the US dollar being the common currency in operation at most sites. It is also possible to play poker online at no cost, since 'play money' games are provided, primarily to encourage newcomers to learn the game inexpensively before trying their luck at the real money tables.

sufficient chips to accommodate all players must be considered. Also, having clear house rules covering acceptable poker play and etiquette will maintain the integrity of the game, making it more enjoyable for all.

CASINOS AND CLUBS

Home games may be the natural medium for occasional poker players, but, for those who take the game a little more seriously, playing poker in a casino or at a club will undoubtedly prove appealing. Obviously, with staff on hand to organize the games,

Above: The scene at a casino poker table in Las Vegas, popularly regarded as the poker capital of the world. Anyone who takes their game seriously will gravitate towards a club or casino in order to gain experience, learn from others and perhaps even make a regular income from their favoured pastime.

Right: Online poker is one of the success stories of the 21st century with millions of players taking advantage of the Internet to participate in a game from the comfort of home. However, not everybody views such convenient access to gambling opportunities as being personally or socially beneficial.

CHOOSING A GAME

The many variations of poker are testament to the curiosity and resourcefulness exhibited by players in the past as they sought fresh ways to make the game ever more satisfying. Some developments were introduced by sharp players with a keen mathematical knowledge and a desire to make their poker playing more lucrative. Others sprung from a need to include more players in proceedings. The number of cards available to each player, the scale of the betting, and the frequency of betting rounds must all be considered, but the degree of flexibility offered by poker means that one can formulate a game for every occasion.

THE NUMBER OF PLAYERS

In amateur games, assessing which variation to play is most likely to be influenced by the number of players wishing to participate as well as their individual tastes. On the assumption that one deck of cards must suffice and that discarded cards are not to be recycled during play, choosing the right game can prove challenging. Texas Hold 'em may be appealing for several reasons, but furnishing players with only two cards at the deal makes it a more inclusive game than some others. Between two and twenty players could play, although casinos, both real and online, limit participation to a maximum of ten players as this is much more manageable. As a general guide, draw poker suits up to six players, stud poker should be limited to no more than eight players, and Omaha, like Texas Hold 'em, may accommodate up to ten players at a sitting.

THE STAKES

Choosing the correct stake level for a game should be governed by two factors: the minimum amount of the buy-in and the betting structure involved. Players are advised to begin with at least one hundred times the value of the minimum bet and this is commonly the upper limit placed on the buy-in for online cash games. To voluntarily buy in for fewer chips than

Above: The basic equipment required for a poker game remains a table, a deck of cards and some chips. Depending on the variation played, poker can accommodate from two to twenty players although something between six and ten players is generally the norm. Fewer than six players can make a game uncompetitive while more than ten players at a table can make it almost unmanageable.

Left: A hand of draw poker comes to a conclusion with the 'showdown' as the players in contention for the chips in the centre of the table – the pot – reveal their cards to determine the winner. The game is the oldest recognized form of poker and is usually the first variation that anyone learns to play.

one's opponents is immediately disadvantageous since a player doing so will soon be pressurized by those in a superior chip position. Equally important is the betting structure of the game. 'Fixed-limit' poker is probably the most popular since it provides players with a means of estimating potential gains and losses during the progress of a hand. This is because, as the term implies, the maximum bet permitted is set at a fixed amount. It therefore represents a less risky prospect than playing 'pot-limit' or 'no-limit' poker, betting structures that permit players to bet all their chips on a single hand. These structures favour the experienced player whereas the style of poker that is most popular among casual players is one incorporating low stakes, strict limits on the maximum bet permitted, and several betting rounds to help build a substantial pot.

TABLE STAKES

A 'table stakes' game is one in which players can only bet with the chips in front of them during the play of a hand. This prevents them from buying more chips during a prolonged betting confrontation. Any player wanting to 'call' – or match – a bet made by an opponent when lacking sufficient chips may still invest in the pot by betting 'all-in' with the remainder. Subsequent bets from other players are kept apart from the original, or main, pot and constitute what is termed a 'side pot', upon which the all-in player has no claim. The rule is applied universally in formal poker and safeguards players from being frozen out of a game in the face of deliberately heavy or intimidating betting by opponents.

Above right: The deck of cards should be shuffled prior to the deal of each hand with care being taken not to expose any cards. The dealer for the next hand will shuffle the cards first before asking the player to the immediate right to cut the deck. Knowing how to shuffle the cards quickly and efficiently is a skill in itself, and it helps to keep the rhythm of the game flowing.

Right: The situation after the 'flop' in Texas Hold 'em for one lucky player who has made a royal flush. Players are dealt two personal cards – hole cards – to start the game. The flop is the moment when the first three of a maximum five community cards are revealed. An unbeatable hand is known as a 'lock hand' or 'the nuts'.

DEALER'S CHOICE
♦ ♣ ♥ ♠

A popular means of deciding which poker variation to play is to adopt a policy of 'dealer's choice', whereby the dealer for each hand specifies the game, the procedure and any special rules that may apply. Prevalent in home games where having fun may be more important than winning money, this is the likeliest source of poker variations involving wild cards – nominated cards, twos (deuces) for example, or the joker perhaps, that can be counted as a card of any other value in order to improve the quality of a hand.

GENERAL SEQUENCE OF PLAY

Although every poker variation possesses its own specific pattern of play, there are practical elements common to all. Each hand begins with the deal, progresses through a series of betting rounds and ends with the winner claiming the pot, either by making a bet unmatched by any opponent, or by revealing the best poker hand at the end of the final betting round, known as the 'showdown'. The betting itself is usually initiated before the deal, when some or all players, depending on the variation played, make a nominal compulsory bet to ensure that there is a pot to be contested at every deal.

THE DEAL

To begin the game, the nominated dealer must thoroughly shuffle the deck, taking care not to inadvertently expose any card in the process. Usually, the player to the dealer's right then cuts the cards by lifting the top portion of the deck and placing it on the table, at which point the dealer places the remaining cards on top. The dealer then distributes the cards from the top of the deck with each player

receiving one card each, in turn, beginning with the player on the dealer's immediate left. A clockwise distribution around the table follows until each player has the requisite number of cards for the poker variation being played. In draw poker, for example, each player receives a starting hand of five cards all dealt face down. Yet in five-card stud, players receive just two cards with which to begin play, the first dealt face down and the second, face up. This second card, the first exposed, or 'up' card in a player's hand, is known as the 'door card'.

BETTING ROUNDS

The betting rounds, or betting intervals as they are sometimes called, are those occasions when players must make a decision as to whether they continue in the hand or not. Depending on the poker variation being played, making a bet may be optional or obligatory. In seven-card stud, for example, the player showing the lowest door card after the deal is obliged to make a nominal bet known as the 'bring-in'. Anyone else wishing to continue in the hand must

Above: A player makes a bet in a game of five-card stud. This poker variation begins with each player receiving two cards, one face down and one face up, prior to the opening betting round.

Left: A casino poker game in progress in which a professional dealer deals the cards, clockwise around the table. The game is Texas Hold 'em. The players each receive two cards before the first betting round begins.

Left: When betting, players should clarify their aims by announcing 'call' or 'raise', for example, since their betting actions alone may not be obvious to opponents at the table. Also, the chips that constitute a bet should be placed on the table immediately in front of the player, making it clear to everybody how the betting is progressing.

Below: To the victor, the spoils as the showdown reveals who has the best hand. The showdown occurs when two or more players have matched bets in the final round, after which they display their cards to decide the winner. The only other way in which a player can win the pot during the game is by making a bet that nobody else calls. In this event, the bettor claims the chips without showing the winning hand.

then put chips into the pot. Yet in Texas Hold 'em, after the 'flop' (the dealing of the first three cards to the board), has been revealed, all players remaining in the hand may opt not to bet. This is known as checking and at this point, the next card, known as the 'turn card', is dealt to the table. In general, the evolution of poker has seen players receiving more cards and having to negotiate more betting rounds for three key reasons. First, to increase the potential size of the pot on offer and thus encourage more players to remain involved in each hand; second, to counteract the caution exhibited by extremely conservative players averse to risk; and third, to increase the levels of skill, deception and subterfuge required to win.

DEALER'S ROLE
♦ ♣ ♥ ♠

During the play of each hand, the dealer is responsible for distributing the cards and ensuring the game is played in accordance with the rules. This involves monitoring play to ensure that everyone acts in turn, bets when required and conducts themselves with appropriate regard for poker etiquette. In casinos and clubs, dealers are often provided as part of the service and can be expected to manage the game smoothly and efficiently. In home games, although proceedings may be more informal, the dealer should be similarly managing the progress of the hand in play, even when no longer competing for the pot.

DETERMINING THE WINNER

In poker there are two methods for determining the winner of each hand. If, at the conclusion of all betting rounds, there are two or more players who have matched stakes, they are required to reveal their cards and the best poker hand on display wins the pot. This is called the showdown. In the event of a tie, the pot is divided equally between those players possessing winning hands of the same value. The other method of winning the pot involves making a bet that no opponent matches. Should this be the case, then the player making the bet can take the pot without revealing the winning hand.

BETTING TERMS EXPLAINED

To obtain the most from poker it is important to understand the meanings of the betting terms used during play. The phrases will be familiar to anyone who has seen poker on television, but for those completely new to the game, the key terms regarding the betting or action at the table are explained here.

ANTES AND BLINDS

Compulsory bets called 'antes' are made before the deal of each hand, to guarantee that there is something in the pot to generate competition. Ordinarily, the sums involved are small, relative to the stake levels in operation during the game, and the number of players compelled to pay the ante, or 'ante-up' as it is known, varies depending on the form of poker played. Generally speaking, the more betting rounds there are to be negotiated to the showdown, the smaller the antes required. In Texas Hold 'em and its close poker relative Omaha, the compulsory bets before the deal are known as the 'blinds'. Almost invariably, the two

players to the dealer's immediate left are required to make these bets which, as the term suggests, should be made before they see any cards.

CALLING AND FOLDING

In order to 'call' a bet, also referred to as 'seeing' a bet, a player must simply match the amount bet by the previous player to have acted in the betting round. For example if the first player to act puts 50 chips in the pot, then all other players have the option of calling that bet of 50 chips to retain their interest. Should they not wish to match the bet, then they must 'fold' – or 'pass' – by discarding their cards. In doing so, they relinquish any claim on the pot and any chips they may have already committed to it.

BETS AND RAISES

Two of the key elements of poker are 'bets' and 'raises' because they increase the cost to opponents of staying in a hand and suggest strength on the part of the

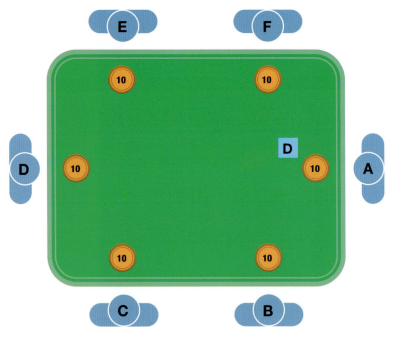

Right: Draw and stud poker variations require all players to pay a nominal sum – the ante – into the pot before the deal. Here, player A is the dealer, as indicated by the dealer button (D), and everybody has 'anted-up' by contributing 10 chips each to the pot. The size of the ante varies depending on the stake levels, but it is usually less than the minimum bet permitted once the cards have been dealt. In this instance, the minimum bet in the first round may be set at 25 chips, for example.

player making them. The term bet specifically refers to the action made by the first player to put chips in the pot during each betting round. Subsequent bets during the round are then referred to as calls or raises. To make a raise involves a player matching the previous bet and then, in most cases, making a bet of at least equal value. For example, if the bet stands at 50 chips, anyone wishing to raise can ordinarily expect to bet at least 100 chips – 50 chips to call the outstanding bet and a further 50 chips to increase the betting level.

THE CHECK

Provided no betting – compulsory or voluntary – has yet taken place during a betting round, players may 'check' rather than bet when it is their turn to act. By checking, a player defers a decision to bet but remains in the hand. If an opponent subsequently makes a bet then, of course, players who previously checked must, when the action returns to them, choose whether to fold, call or raise; checking at this stage is no longer an option. Games played for small stakes will often feature informal rules to restrict or prohibit checking, since it is a tactic favoured by conservative players.

BETTING STATEMENTS

When making a betting decision, all players are encouraged to be clear and precise about their intentions. In this regard, verbally announcing "fold", "call" or "raise" keeps everyone informed as the action moves around the table. Most importantly, the intention to call or raise should be stated before a player commits chips to the pot. This is to discourage 'string bets', which occur when a player, while slowly adding chips to the pot, deliberately delays announcing the scale of the bet in order to study the reactions of opponents.

MUCKING A HAND
♦ ♣ ♥ ♠

The 'muck' is the pile of discarded cards that accrue during the play of each hand. As players fold, they 'muck their hand' by placing their cards face down with the other discards. Responsibility for ensuring folded hands are properly mucked falls upon the dealer; only players still contesting the pot should have cards in front of them on the table.

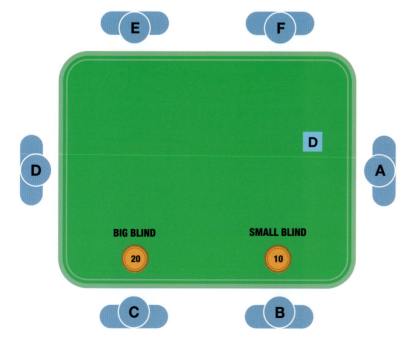

Left: In Texas Hold 'em and Omaha, the two players to the dealer's left make compulsory bets before the deal, these being known as the blinds. Here, the dealer is again player A meaning that player B must pay the small blind – 10 chips – while player C is forced to bet the big blind, typically double the small blind, of 20 chips. After the deal, player D will be the first to make an active decision on whether to contest the hand.

BIG BLIND 20

SMALL BLIND 10

BETTING STRUCTURES

U nderstanding the betting structure in place and how that affects the style of the game is absolutely imperative when opting to play poker. As with the number of poker variations, several betting structures have been developed over the years to suit the tastes, temperaments and financial means of different players. Cautious players tend to favour the small-stakes, fixed- and spread-limit games in which profits are not so lucrative, but losses can be more easily controlled. Those who prefer a more volatile game are inexorably drawn to pot-limit and no-limit poker where the rewards are potentially high, but the risk of heavy losses is also greater.

FIXED-LIMIT

This betting structure applies traditionally to home or social games and its popularity has ensured that it is widely available in casinos and online. In fixed-limit games, all bets are fixed at a level constituting both the maximum and the minimum permissible. Ordinarily, this level may be doubled in the latter betting rounds

of a hand. In a game of five-card stud, for example, bets and raises may be restricted to 100 chips in the first two betting rounds, and to 200 chips in the final two rounds. This would be indicated as a 100/200 fixed-limit game.

SPREAD-LIMIT

This style of betting differs slightly from fixed-limit poker in that bets may be made for any amount between the specified upper and lower limits. In a 100/300 spread-limit game, therefore, a player may bet any sum from 100 to 300 chips. Any subsequent raises are capped at a maximum of 300 chips. Games with several betting rounds may have an increase in the limit applying for the later rounds. A 100/300/500/1,000 Texas Hold 'em game, for instance, might have maximum bets and raises limited to 300 chips for the first two betting rounds while on the 'turn' and the 'river' – respectively the fourth and fifth community cards dealt to the board – the upper limit would rise to 500 and 1,000 chips respectively.

Above: Chips lined up prior to a tournament. Poker tournaments continue to increase in popularity and, in these, each player is credited with the same number of chips before play commences.

Right: A close-up shot of the moment when the winner rakes in the chips from a big pot. Though inexperienced players tend to think that profitable poker is linked to winning plenty of pots, the key to success is in regularly winning the few really big pots that might be contested during a session. Players who achieve this are generally much more selective in the quality of hands they play.

POT-LIMIT

This betting structure is most popular among experienced players, but it can be difficult to follow and potentially very expensive for beginners. In pot-limit poker, minimum bets are structured as they are in fixed-limit poker, but the maximum bet is limited only by the size of the pot. For example, assuming the antes total 100 chips, in the opening betting round of a 100/200 game, player A as the first player to act might make the minimum bet of 100 chips, making the pot total 200. Player B must then call for 100 to stay in the game, but, if considering a pot-size raise, that player can raise by a further 300 chips, matching the antes of 100, player A's bet of 100 and player B's own call of 100. With the pot now at 600, player C is faced with a minimum call of 400 chips to match player B's bet and boost the pot to 1,000 chips. If choosing to raise the maximum allowed, player C may bet an additional 1,000 chips, making a bet of 1,400 in total and increasing the pot to

2,000 chips. This illustrates just how rapidly pots can grow in an aggressive pot-limit game and emphasizes the need for cool judgement under pressure.

NO-LIMIT

This betting style is applicable in many tournaments, has a minimum betting structure in place in common with fixed-limit poker, but the maximum bet permitted is limited only by the number of chips at a player's disposal. Pushing one's entire chip stack into the pot and betting all-in is a powerful play when in a dominant position during the game, and exudes desperation when short stacked. But this facet of no-limit poker helps create serious opportunities to bluff and intimidate opponents. For that reason, it is generally not recommended for inexperienced players, who may understandably baulk at the idea of having to risk all their chips on the very first hand.

Left: In no-limit poker players have the option to bet 'all-in' by committing all their chips to the pot when it is their turn to act, but they do run the risk of losing all their chips on a single hand if called.

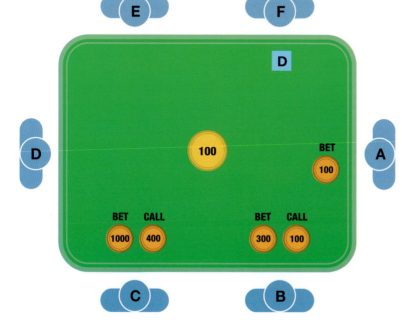

Left: This shows how volatile the betting can be in a game using a pot-limit betting structure. Following player A's initial bet of 100 chips, player B decides to raise by the amount in the pot, the maximum bet permitted. To make the raise requires 400 in total from player B, 100 to call player A's bet, putting 300 chips in the pot, plus 300 to match the pot total. Player C now makes a pot-limit raise as well, betting 400 to cover player B's bet and 1,000 more to match the new total in the pot. The action is then on player D who must bet 1,400 chips merely to call.

THE SHOWDOWN

In poker, there are two ways to win the pot. If a player should make a bet that is not called by any opponent, that player claims the pot and is under no obligation to show the winning hand. Alternatively, if two or more players are still contesting the hand at the end of the final betting round, then those players should reveal their cards simultaneously in what is termed the showdown. The player judged to possess the highest-ranking hand of those on display then wins the pot. If one or more hands are tied, then the chips in the pot are divided equally between the winners.

Above: Amid the excitement of a game it can be all too easy to misread one's hand. This is merely an A-high straight and not, as it might appear, a royal flush.

Above: This A-high flush in hearts is superior to the straight pictured above and shows the value of the showdown. It allows everyone to determine the winner in the event that a player misreads a hand.

Above: At the showdown, it is customary for those players still contesting the pot to reveal their cards face up on the table. The player holding the royal flush in clubs here can be confident of victory.

ACTING IN TURN
♦ ♣ ♥ ♠

It is essential that players remember to act only when it is their turn to do so. Betting out of turn may seem a minor infringement, but it unnecessarily presents opponents with information regarding the potential strength of a hand. Those players whose decision has been pre-empted will obviously modify their betting intentions based on such a mistake, and folding out of turn presents similar advantages to opponents. A player acting first often has little information upon which to base a strategy, but if a couple of opponents fold out of turn, that player's situation immediately improves.

DECLARATIONS

At a showdown between two players, it is quite common for the player calling an opponent's final bet to ask that opponent to reveal his cards first rather than for both hands to be revealed simultaneously. Should the caller recognize that the opponent's hand is superior he may legitimately muck his cards and thus conceal information concerning his own hand. In regular poker, this procedure occurs quite frequently, as experienced players have little difficulty in identifying whether they hold a winning hand.

It is quite possible, however, particularly in poker played with wild cards, for a player to misread the value of a hand and declare that it is higher or lower in value than is actually the case. To avoid this situation it is worth applying the 'cards speak' poker rule such that, when the hands are exposed at the showdown,

Left: Steve McQueen and Robert DoQui discuss play in *The Cincinnati Kid*. Commentating on proceedings at the table and debating the hand in progress, though often tolerated during an informal game, is generally regarded as taboo. Antagonistic or disparaging comments regarding an opponent's play are also discouraged in most card rooms.

Below: Frank Sinatra, as Frankie Machine in United Artists' *The Man with the Golden Arm*, shown in the marathon 36-hour poker session, one of the highlights of director Otto Preminger's production.

the winning hand is adjudicated solely using the cards on display. Players who make mistakes in verbally declaring the value of their hands are thus prevented from winning or losing as a result of their error.

SPLIT-POT, HIGH-LOW GAMES

This popular form of poker involves the players with the highest hand and the lowest hand both claiming a share of the pot. Ideally, players aim to win all the chips, or 'scoop the pot', by holding both the high and low hands simultaneously. When betting is completed but before hands are revealed at the showdown, players must declare whether they are competing for the high hand, low hand or both. This declaration, best made simultaneously, usually involves a procedure as follows. Players take a couple of their chips and place their hands under the table to conceal any activity. At a given signal from the dealer, all competing players then reveal the number of chips in their hand to indicate their declared intention. No chips in the hand symbolizes a low call, one chip indicates a high call and two chips means the player intends to call both high and low. Once again, to avoid confusion over identifying the best hands, both high and low, it is advisable to adopt the cards speak ruling.

ACCEPTABLE TABLE TALK
♦ ♣ ♥ ♠

Debating events during the play of a hand is generally frowned upon, irrespective of whether a player is still participating or awaiting the next deal. Careless comments by players regarding which cards they folded may provide clues to the strength of the hands still in contention for the pot. Making abusive or critical comments regarding an opponent's play while contesting a hand is known as 'coffeehousing'. While it is not necessarily impolite, it is not always considered a breach of etiquette. In America, it is widely accepted as an integral part of poker culture, whereas in Europe, the opposite tends to be true, certainly at a formal level. On the international tournament circuit, currently attracting widespread television coverage, the debate over what constitutes acceptable table talk continues. Some of the more notable professionals who regularly appear on television, among them Phil Hellmuth, Mike 'The Mouth' Matusow and Tony G, are extremely vocal during play. As arch competitors, they are inclined to use every tactic to try and obtain an edge over their opponents which, though it may at times seem unethical, can provide entertaining television for the viewer.

CASH OR RING GAMES

Cash games, or 'ring games' as they are sometimes called, are the mainstay of poker, both in casinos and online. Characteristically, they involve players competing against each other, typically for several hours, in games with constant betting structures. In tournament poker, the betting levels increase as play progresses, to force players into confrontations that might see them eliminated. By contrast, the level of the compulsory bets – the antes and blinds – in cash games remains the same throughout, as do the upper and lower betting limits applicable. This difference is influential in the long-term and short-term strategies players need to implement in order to play profitable cash game poker, but there are many other factors equally worthy of consideration.

ADOPTING THE RIGHT APPROACH

Most regular home games played for cash have their own protocols governing the poker variations played, the minimum and maximum amount of the buy-in, and the level of the betting. Casinos and online poker sites will also have regulations covering these aspects

of the game, while offering a much wider range of cash games to match the personality and the financial means of every player. And since these may be operated around the clock, any one table will see players regularly cashing out to be replaced by others buying in.

Given such choice, a player's first decision concerns which poker variation to play, it being advisable to limit this to the game or games the player understands best. The next factor to consider is the scale of the betting, as determined by the antes or blinds, since this will dictate the size of a player's buy-in. Most experts recommend buying in for the maximum permitted, since this provides a player with the resources to exploit early winning opportunities while offering a safeguard against a run of poor cards.

The next objective is to find a suitable table at which to play. Personal preference will dictate whether a player selects a full-handed game of up to ten players, or opts instead for a short-handed game with as few as two or three opponents. In a full-handed game, having the patience to wait for a strong hand before betting is immensely important, given the

Above: 'Splashing the pot' by dumping your chips in among the others already staked can lead to confusion. Ordinarily, players should each make a bet by placing the required number of chips in a neat stack just in front of them.

Right: Joseph Hachem competing in the WSOP world championship poker tournament which he went on to win. Here he is shown piling up his chips during the event at Binion's Gambling Hall and Hotel in July 2005.

number of players and potentially better hands in opposition. A short-handed game, on the other hand, is likely to feature looser betting, with players more prepared to gamble on marginal hands.

GENERAL ADVICE

Aside from the practical aspects of playing cash game poker, there are also some general points that should be considered by those eager for poker action. Most professionals insist that, to play the game at the highest level, players need to be aware of their own strengths and weaknesses, whether physical, mental or emotional. The reasoning is that without understanding oneself and one's motivation for playing, it is difficult to set clear and realistic poker objectives.

The professionals also advocate some very basic principles for improving play, key among them being not to drink alcohol, to avoid playing when tired or feeling stressed, and never to play with frightened money – that is, money that is reserved for other purposes. Additionally, while rebuying chips may be permissible in a cash game once a player's stack is exhausted, borrowing money from other players in order to do so is rarely, if ever, a good idea.

THE BANKROLL
♦ ♣ ♥ ♠

A player's bankroll is the money set aside specifically for playing poker, which, for the serious player, may represent a substantial capital sum to be invested in the game. Whether siphoned from a regular income or shrewdly accrued from poker itself, the state of this bankroll serves as a barometer for a player's fortunes at the table. Disciplined cash game players adopt a long-term view, regarding the outcome of any single session as incidental to the overriding objective of securing a profit.

Above: The increased popularity of televised tournament poker has led to an increase in the number of regular tournaments held by casinos and card rooms around the world. As players new to the game seek to mimic what they see on television, so the casinos have responded by offering tournaments with low entry fees to attract more players keen to experience tournament play for themselves.

Left: Carlos Mortensen celebrates becoming the 2001 WSOP world champion following his victory in the US$10,000 no-limit Texas Hold 'em tournament at Binion's Horseshoe Hotel and Casino, Las Vegas. As is traditional, the winner's prize is presented on the table, in cash, as photographers capture the scene for posterity. The 29-year-old professional gambler beat Dewey Tomko into second place in order to claim the US$1.5 million prize for winning.

TOURNAMENT PLAY

Tournament play has many attributes that make it appealing, not least of which is that anyone with sufficient money to buy in to a major competition can find themselves competing on level terms against the stars of the contemporary game. Equally, there are a prolific number of online tournaments that, for a very modest outlay, offer the chance to win seats at some of the major events including the US$10,000 WSOP world championship game itself. Lower down the scale, tournament poker provides the opportunity for players to participate in a competitive and possibly profitable game for a fixed fee, making it easier to gauge potential losses. Indeed, there are even freeroll tournaments that require no entry fee at all, although the prizes for winning sometimes consist of tickets to more lucrative tournaments rather than cash.

TOURNAMENT STRUCTURES

A variety of different tournament structures exist, although they are all based on the same knockout principle, by which one player accumulates all the chips as opponents lose theirs and are eliminated. During play, the antes or blinds are increased at regular intervals, thus dictating increases in the minimum bet. This mechanism propels even cautious players into betting action, since the alternative is to witness their chip stacks being eroded by the ever-increasing compulsory bets. The most popular games are well represented and the cost of entering a tournament need be no more than small change. Ordinarily, an additional house charge of up to ten per cent of the entry fee may be levied by the club or casino that plays host. Anyone wishing to contest a US$10 event contributes that sum to the prize pool,

Above: Age Spets (right) competing in the Poker Stars World Cup in 2005, a televised tournament featuring heads-up poker. This format involves two players only, facing each other across the table in poker combat, the object being to acquire all the opponent's chips to win the game.

Left: Dealers take a break during the 2005 WSOP. Often taken for granted by the players, the huge 24-hour casinos of Las Vegas employ an army of dealers, croupiers and waiting staff to meet the needs of their clients. Historically, Vegas dealers have rarely earned extravagant wages and it is customary for players to offer a small tip, known as a 'toke', to the dealer when they win a hand.

the cash that will be divided between the tournament's highest-placed finishers, and pays a further US$1 to the house to cover incidental costs. To win a share of the prize pool itself, a player will usually have to finish within the top ten per cent of all entrants, which, in a field of a thousand or more starters, represents a major examination of anybody's poker skills.

FREEZE-OUTS, REBUYS AND ADD-ONS

In freeze-out tournaments, all players begin with an equal number of chips but they are not allowed to buy any more at all during play. Players who lose all their chips are eliminated from the game. Rebuy tournaments, as the term suggests, are those in which players are permitted to buy additional chips after the game has started, subject to restrictions that vary from one tournament to another. Typically, rebuys are limited to the first hour or two of a tournament and are often only permissible if a player has fallen below a certain number of chips. For example, a player who began with 1,500 chips may only be able to purchase more if falling below this figure during the specified rebuy period. When this ends, it is common for players to have an additional chance to buy more chips, irrespective of their current chip status. This is termed the add-on. Following this, the rebuy tournament proceeds to a conclusion in freeze-out fashion.

CARD HANDLING
♦ ♣ ♥ ♠

A general point of etiquette to remember when playing poker, especially in a formal and competitive environment, is that all those active in a hand should have their cards on the table immediately in front of them. This helps clarify exactly who is still participating in a hand, any folded cards having already been added to the muck.

In stud poker, the structure of the game naturally contrives this situation as it involves cards being dealt face up as well as face down. But many other poker variations involve players being dealt cards face down only. The value of these concealed cards, otherwise known as hole, or 'pocket cards', is unknown to opponents. Players often physically hold their cards to assess their opening hand, but it is recommended that they be replaced on the table as the betting begins.

BASIC POKER SKILLS

HAVING A GOOD GRASP OF THE POKER ODDS IS CRUCIAL FOR ANYONE WHO WANTS TO EXPERIENCE A SUCCESSFUL GAME. ESTIMATING THE PROBABILITIES OF GETTING A WINNING CARD WILL INFLUENCE A PLAYER'S DECISIONS AND JUDGEMENT DURING A GAME.

Understanding and absorbing the practical conventions of poker that govern the rules and patterns of play is obviously the first step along the road to becoming an above-average player. But beyond the mechanical processes of the deal and the betting structures lie the more esoteric elements of poker that make the game so challenging. These are the focus of attention in this chapter, which highlights the various skills that must be employed at the table in order to be competitive. Of course, many social players may consider that participating in an occasional poker game is of more importance than actually winning. Such opponents are regarded as 'fish', 'pigeons' or 'sheep' by the mercenary player who adopts a predatory approach, deploying the skills detailed here. Chief among these skills is an understanding of the theory of probability as it applies to poker, knowledge of which gives the studious player an edge.

Right: Acknowledging that poker is a game of skill in which chance plays a part represents the first step on the way to becoming a better poker player. Anyone wishing to improve their game should always take a little time to consider the implications of any betting decision before committing their chips to the pot. Consistently successful players, while aware of the element of chance, make rational decisions based upon the information available at the table, and that is an acquired skill.

POKER ODDS: THE THEORY

The theory of probability was devised by 17th-century French philosophers and mathematicians Pierre de Fermat and Blaise Pascal after they had responded to a nobleman's query regarding a gambling game played with dice. They realized that it was possible to calculate the likelihood of an event happening by chance when a finite number of potential outcomes existed. To understand this, consider rolling a pair of dice with the aim of hitting a double 6. Each die presents six possible outcomes, so to calculate the total number of outcomes from rolling both involves multiplying the first six possibilities by the second set of six possibilities. This produces 36 potential outcomes in total, of which just one will realize a double 6, making the odds against this happening 35 to 1. Assuming a fair game, probability theory therefore suggests that in 36 rolls of the dice, a double 6 can be expected to materialize once; in 36,000 rolls, a pair of sixes can be expected to appear 1,000 times. This leads to an important point concerning probability in that the greater the sample of repeated events with multiple possible outcomes, the likelier it is that the results will more accurately reflect the probability of their occurrence. It is possible that in 36,000 rolls of the dice, a pair of sixes may result on anything from none to all 36,000 occasions, but the probability is that it will occur 1/36th of the time.

Above: A basic grasp of probability theory is an asset in poker and a simple example of the concept in action can be found when rolling a pair of dice. Each die presents six possible outcomes so the total number of combinations occurring when rolling a pair of dice can be calculated as 6 x 6. The chances of rolling a double 6 are therefore 1 in 36, representing odds of 35 to 1 against this event occurring.

PROFITABLE KNOWLEDGE

Understanding the significance of odds and probabilities in poker is absolutely crucial for anyone wishing to prosper at the game. Possessing such knowledge and applying it judiciously at the poker table inevitably gives a player an advantage over weaker opponents whose decisions are governed by instinct or a profound belief in luck alone. Being able to compare the probability of seeing beneficial cards with the odds of reward offered by the pot – the pot odds – enables a player to judge situations more clinically, something that is particularly useful when the stakes are high. It leads players into the realm of rational and reasoned decision-making which, in the long term, is likely to prove profitable, as they are readily able to distinguish the relative values of poker hands and bet accordingly.

LEARNING THE BASICS

Although a keen knowledge of mathematics is an asset, the key elements of probability theory applicable to poker are simple enough to understand. First, the probability of an event occurring plus the probability of it not occurring must add up to 1. For example a 1 in 10 chance of securing a winning card represents a probability of 0.10 or 10 per cent, while the chances of it not occurring are 0.90 or 90 per cent. Whenever a 1 in 10 chance does present itself, it is sometimes worth recalling that a loss can be expected nine times as often as a win.

To calculate the probability of multiple events occurring in succession, often a requirement in poker, multiply the probability of the first by the probability of the second, then by the probability of the third and so on. The chance of receiving pocket aces – a pair of aces as hole cards – in Texas Hold 'em, therefore, can be expressed as the product of 4/52 x 3/51. Here it is crucial to bear in mind that the second probability is dependent on the player's first card being an ace. The product of 4/52 x 3/51 represents 0.45 per cent and equates to 1 chance in 221 of a pair of aces being dealt. Three aces appearing on the flop – the first three community cards that are dealt face up in the centre of the table all at one time – represents a probability of 4/52 x 3/51 x 2/50, which is 0.018 per cent. That

GIVE IT A WHIRL

Above: In any poker game, the chances that the first card to be dealt to a player will be an Ace are 4/52 = 0.076.

Above: The chances of a player being dealt a pair of pocket Aces in Texas Hold'em may be expressed as 4/52 x 3/51 = 0.0045.

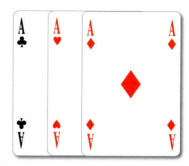

Above: The chance of three Aces making the flop in Hold'em can be calculated as 4/52 x 3/51 x 2/50 = 0.00018, though this bare statistic takes no account of the cards held by any participating player after the deal.

equates to one flop in every 5,555. Computing the probability of either of two events occurring requires that the probability of each be *added* together before subtracting the probability of both taking place. So, if any ace, 7 or heart will offer a winning hand with two cards to come, the subtraction counteracts the possibility of counting the ace and 7 of hearts twice if these cards are among those unseen. Though it may seem daunting for the novice, the ability to make these calculations improves quickly with practice and experience.

CALCULATING PROBABILITIES

By way of illustration, imagine a game of seven-card stud in which, after six cards have been dealt, a player requires one more heart to secure an ace-high flush. If a player has seen 17 cards already – the player's own six cards and 11 others dealt face up to the player's opponents – of which six are hearts, then seven hearts remain among the 35 cards unseen by the player. This outcome has a 1 in 5 (20 per cent) chance of occurring, making the odds against a heart being dealt 4 to 1.

CALCULATING PROBABILITIES

PLAYER A

Right: In this seven-card stud example, a sixth card has been dealt to the three players contesting the hand. Player F shows the best hand and is first to act, betting 100 to make the pot total now 875. To win, Player A needs a heart with the final card to make an ace-high flush. With seven hearts remaining among the 35 unseen cards, he has a 1 in 5 chance of this occurring. A bet of 100 chips to win at least 875, meaning pot odds of nearly 9 to 1, makes calling for 100 a decent option as the odds of reward are greater than the odds against making the flush. Should player B call too, then player A has even better value in gambling on the 5 to 1 chance.

POKER ODDS: THE PRACTICE

Estimating probabilities requires speedy and often rough calculations, though these are usually enough to guide a player's betting decisions during a game. Experience will show that recurring themes arise during a session, leaving any player with three key questions to bear in mind when assessing the chances of winning. First, how many cards are needed to obtain or retain a winning hand? Second, how many unseen and potentially available cards remain to secure such a hand? Third, how many chances are there to be dealt the required cards?

APPLYING THE KNOWLEDGE

Whichever form of poker is played, players will frequently need one or more cards for a winning hand, but the odds against this occurring vary from game to game. In draw poker, a player holding two pairs, aces and sixes, may already hold a winning chance, but drawing a third ace or 6 to make a full house would make victory highly likely. To do so requires drawing one of four cards – the remaining aces and sixes – from among the 47 unseen cards, the probability of which is 4/47, showing odds fractionally better than 11 to 1 against. Yet holding the same hand in five-card stud with one more card to come presents a different betting proposition, as the player will have seen numerous cards face up on the table during play. If 15 opponents' face-up cards have been seen, of which none are aces or sixes,

Above: Professional poker player Carl Olson considers his next move as the hand unfolds. At this level of the game, players are highly skilled in evaluating the number of cards required to win and whether it is cost-effective to pursue them.

PLAYER C

Right: Player C may already have the best hand, with two pairs, in this draw poker game, though there are 4 chances in 47 of drawing an ace or 6 to improve to a full house, reflecting odds of just under 11 to 1.

APPLYING THE KNOWLEDGE

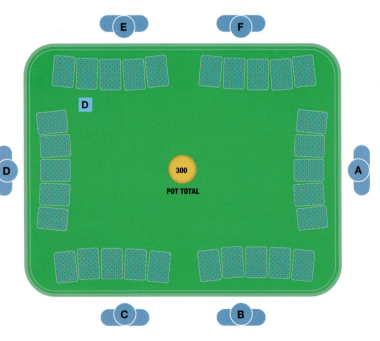

then the player has just 33 unseen cards from which to find a winner. The chances are 4/33, or fractionally more than 1 in 8, that an ace or 6 will be dealt to complete the full house, showing odds of just over 7 to 1. While the scenarios are similar, the odds against hitting a full house are much lower in the five-card stud example, but the player is likely to have negotiated more betting rounds to reach this position.

JUDGING SITUATIONS

Using the concepts of probabilities and pot odds is crucial for serious poker players. Having a rough idea of the odds against securing a winning hand is better than betting blindly. Crucially, players are advised to focus on the chances not just of improving a hand, but of holding the eventual winner. Opponents also receive other cards as the game progresses, and in games such as Texas Hold 'em, a card that strengthens one hand may also improve another quite dramatically. This is a key aspect of community card games, like Hold 'em, in which all players combine exposed cards on the table with their own cards to form the best possible hand. Being aware that a hand can improve but still be beaten by another player is also worth considering.

IMPLIED POT ODDS

Speculative gambles do occasionally pay off in poker, with players confounding the odds by betting when perhaps folding was a likelier option. Even world-class players sometimes bet speculatively, although usually after assessing the implied pot odds on offer during a hand. This means that a player considers the potential pot odds that might arise as a result of subsequent bets during the hand in play. For instance, betting 100 chips into a 500-chip pot may seem inadvisable when the odds against winning are 7 to 1. However, only two more callers would be required to expand the pot to 800 chips and thus improve the pot odds sufficiently to justify the decision. If successful, the player stands to win 700 chips for the bet of 100, accurately reflecting the odds against being dealt a card that can guarantee a winning hand. Given seven additional similar situations, the probability is that the player will be successful once, which will be sufficient to break even. By contrast, if the potential winnings on those seven occasions remain at 500 chips only, then even the single expected success would result in a net loss of 200 chips. This underlines how betting when the odds are favourable is the key to success.

APPLYING THE KNOWLEDGE

PLAYER C

Left: In this five-card stud example, player C also has the two pairs, aces and sixes, but the odds against securing a full house have improved to just over 7 to 1. This is the case because, since no aces or sixes are visible among the other players' hands, player C is now seeking any one of four cards from just 33 remaining unseen to improve to a full house.

CARD READING

Playing successful poker involves interpreting many strands of information that may be available. A grasp of probability theory is important but it can only be confidently implemented when a player is capable of reading the cards on display. This means being able to identify the strength of one's own hand and its chances of being improved, as well as considering the cards that may be held by opponents. Aside from draw poker, most variations involve several cards being revealed during a hand and this information, in addition to the betting patterns in evidence, can help a player to deduce the cards an opponent currently holds or is trying to obtain.

ASSESSING A HAND

When assessing the qualities of any poker hand, players must first have an awareness of the average winning hand required in the poker variation played, this in turn being affected by the number of players competing at the table. For instance, in a full-handed Texas Hold 'em game, meaning one that involves nine or ten players, two pairs or three of a kind represent

decent hands with fair chances of winning, since players hoping to make straights or flushes are often forced out of the betting before their hand materializes. Yet in Omaha, which is structured very similarly to Texas Hold 'em, the prevalence of straights, flushes and full houses is much greater, since players receive four hole cards face down on the table, with which to begin play, not two. Although the players are

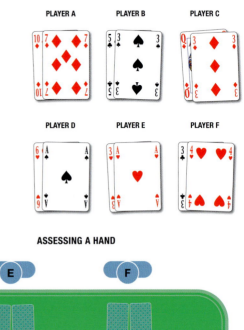

ASSESSING A HAND

Right: Reading the cards is an essential skill, as shown in this example where player A's two pairs, ordinarily a good hand in Texas Hold 'em, are leading but remain vulnerable to a flush. A substantial bet from player D, due to act first, suggesting the flush has already been secured, might be sufficient to encourage player A to fold the leading hand.

required to combine exactly two hole cards with three of the board cards dealt face up to make a hand, the greater number of possible combinations available to each player presents more opportunities to secure a high-ranking poker holding. As a general rule, winning hands naturally tend to be of greater value the more players there are involved in a game.

READING OPPONENTS

Combining information from the cards in play with knowledge of a specific opponent's mannerisms helps a player to gauge the meaning behind events at the table. To this end, it is worth underlining the value in observing as much as possible even after folding a hand. Inferences obtained from the betting of those still contesting the pot can be tested, at no further cost, when the hand is resolved at the showdown. Indeed, most experts recommend that anyone wishing to participate in a game, at a casino or online, should watch the action for a while rather than immediately begin playing. This helps condition a player to the rhythm of a game and provides time to identify whether the potential opponents are strong or weak poker players. Equally, those who play aggressively or

who are inclined to bluff too often may be distinguished from the 'calling stations', these being loose players who do not raise much, and repeatedly call other players' bets, irrespective of their chances of winning. The comments and general behaviour of the players may also provide clues to their current mood. For instance, anybody who seems distracted during play but suddenly starts concentrating on the game may be indicating possession of a good hand.

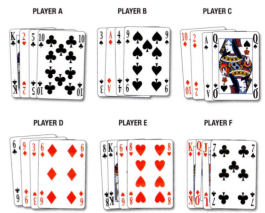

ASSESSING A HAND

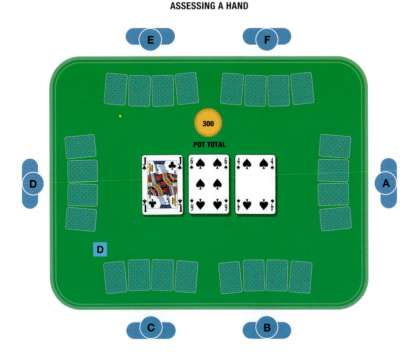

300

POT TOTAL

Left: This Omaha example illustrates that, with more cards in circulation around the table, the chances of at least one player obtaining a flush with a flop such as this are greatly increased. Player C can count the As and Qs for a possible ace-high flush, but must now worry about a pair appearing on the board as this could furnish an opponent, player D for instance, with a full house or even four of a kind.

ATTENTION TO DETAIL

By now it will be evident that keeping abreast of events at the poker table is a prerequisite for success, although regular social games typically include at least one player who always needs prompting when the time to make a betting decision arrives. Other factors that warrant attention, particularly in club and casino games, include the rake (the casino's commission fee), the general house rules and, of course, the betting structures applying to the games themselves. Regrettably, as befits a pastime historically referred to as 'the cheating game', it is worth remembering that not everybody plays fairly. Various sharp practices might be perpetrated by other players, ranging from short-changing the pot to playing with a marked deck of cards. Vigilance is therefore recommended, even if only to police the minor infringements taking place during a game.

THE IMPORANCE OF MEMORY

Many of the lessons to be learned from poker are best absorbed from experience. Being able to benefit from such experience, however, will depend on a good memory, another essential asset possessed by most of the top players. Contrary to popular myth, it is possible to train and develop one's memory, a process that often involves coding information by breaking it down into recognizable patterns. Telephone numbers,

for example, are usually remembered as small groups of numbers rather than as a long string of digits. Similarly, acronyms are commonly employed as shorthand terms for words and phrases. At the poker table, there are many patterns observable during play that, if remembered and understood, may be brought to bear either later in the game or at a subsequent session.

The three prime components to focus on are the cards themselves, the betting habits of opponents, and, most importantly, one's own playing style. Although it is useful to identify the various revealing mannerisms, or 'tells', of opponents, controlling one's own betting moves or gestures is also beneficial. In this respect, adopting a flexible attitude and varying the style of play during a session makes it more difficult for habitual behaviour to be recognized.

Above right: Allan Dyrstad in action at the Poker Stars World Cup in 2005, a tournament featuring heads-up poker – a two-player confrontation. Both players will pay an ante or blind in heads-up games, investing chips in every pot. This is enough to generate the betting action as players cannot afford to wait for good cards. They have to take risks with mediocre hands and this makes such one-to-one poker combat a highly specialized form of the game.

Right: The key to successful poker is to be able to read an opponents' actions from the moment the cards are dealt. At every level, when players fold, call or raise, there is a reason behind their decision. Astute players recognize behaviour patterns that can offer clues, giving them a tactical edge over their opponents.

Left: The 2003 WSOP world champion Chris Moneymaker became the first player to win the main event having qualified via the Internet. Despite not having played in a live tournament of this magnitude before, Moneymaker successfully made the transition from the online game.

Below: Success at poker depends to a degree on a player's ability to deceive opponents regarding the strength or weakness of a hand. Possessing a 'poker face' is considered an asset. However, many players take the precaution of shielding their eyes from opponents when having to contemplate a decision.

ASSESSING A PLAYER'S MOVES

Information obtained from the cards during a game only represents part of the story when playing a hand. Other clues emanate from the actions and mannerisms of other players at the table, and recognizing the significance of these moves is a very helpful skill. In regular poker schools, players will be comfortably familiar with each other's characteristics, but when encountering new opponents, online or in a casino perhaps, it can take time to decipher their actions.

There are some playing styles that can usually be identified after a short while at the table, certainly at amateur games. Beginners are often very difficult to bluff since they are not skilled enough to recognize what an opponent's raise is supposed to imply. Even if having only a remote chance of winning, such players often stay in the pot simply because they enjoy the betting action. Similarly, players known as calling stations will insist on calling bet after bet, either because they overestimate their chances of winning or because they are intrinsically sceptical by nature.

Adjusting one's play to take account of such players, perhaps by adopting a stricter policy on which hands to support, is a sound strategy. Equally important to recognize are the cautious players, the 'rocks', who regularly fold before the betting becomes serious, choosing to preserve their chips for the moment when they can bet aggressively with a very strong hand. It pays to be wary of calling a large bet made by such a player unless possessing a very strong hand oneself.

COUNTING CARDS
♦ ♣ ♥ ♠

It is in stud poker that this skill is most readily applied, since the game features many cards dealt face up to the players. These cards are subsequently turned face down as and when players fold throughout the game. Retaining a clear idea of how many cards have been seen, and their value, is essential for any player wishing to calculate the probability of being dealt the card or cards needed to win.

CONCENTRATION

Being able to draw accurate inferences from play during any session requires high levels of concentration. Assimilating information by memorizing cards in play, assessing fluctuating probabilities and observing the actions of opponents is of great benefit in guiding a player's own decisions. But this can only happen if a player is focused on the game. Aside from the strategic benefits of concentrating on play, it is also conducive to any game for all players to be aware of the basic proceedings, such as who dealt, whose turn it is to bet and how many players remain active in the later betting rounds.

PACING THE GAME

Poker is most enjoyable when played at a decent pace, there being nothing more frustrating for the average player than to fold a hand and then have to wait several minutes for slow, distracted players to resolve the outcome. Casinos will seek to deal 40 or more hands per hour, particularly if the rake is a fraction of every pot, which underlines how most hands take just a couple of minutes to complete. The inherent speed of online poker means that rates of over 60 hands per hour are not uncommon in that form of the game.

Although a quick conclusion to each hand is appreciated by most players, it is also true that the majority will anticipate any poker session lasting several hours. For those earning a living from the game, such time spent playing is simply regarded as work. But for the casual player and professional alike, engaging in a marathon poker session brings with it certain pressures. Pacing oneself to handle the mental and physical challenge is as important as any strategy. Taking advantage of mistakes induced by tiredness or stress is all part of the game, so, to avoid falling victim to this possibility, players should be prepared to take breaks or even cash out of a game if their concentration levels lapse for any reason.

AVOIDING DISTRACTIONS

In emphasizing the skills employed in poker, the guiding principle is to outline how best to minimize losses and maximize winnings while assessing the risks that are a natural element of the game. To that end, intense concentration is sometimes required, which implies that unnecessary distractions be avoided. In home games, television, background music and protracted conversations among friends are common

Above: Playing poker well requires a high degree of disciplined application to the game. Concentrating is essential which means that any distraction could have a negative impact on play. Anyone seriously involved in a game will surely be unwilling to respond to regular mobile phone calls if intent on being competitive.

Left: Clonie Gowen exudes apprehension at the WSOP in 2004. Like most players, even the winner of the 2003 WPT Ladies Night tournament can be unpleasantly surprised at having either misread an opponent's hand or suffered what is known as a 'bad beat'. The latter occurs when an opponent defies the odds to make the winning hand.

Above left: Despite its general popularity, poker has always had to compete for space in casinos with other gambling games such as blackjack, roulette, craps and slot machines. All these, unlike poker, involve fixed-odds payouts for various winning outcomes, meaning that the house can guarantee itself a profit margin.

Above: Mike 'The Mouth' Matusow engages in banter at the poker table while competing in the 2005 WSOP. As his nickname suggests, Matusow chats incessantly during play, a trait that so divides opinion that he is considered both the most entertaining and the most annoying player in the game.

Left: The celebrated illusionists Siegfried and Roy, pictured with one of their trademark white tigers. In 1990 Siegfried Fischbacher (left) and Roy Uwe Ludwig Horn were offered over US$50 million a year to perform at the Mirage Hotel and Casino.

features of a poker session, along with breaks for food and drink. Such elements enhance sociability, of course, but divert attention from the cards and slow up the game. The distractions on offer in the major casinos, by contrast, include slot machines, roulette tables and the sports betting bar, all of which could easily claim a poker player's bankroll during moments of weakness. For the best results in poker, focusing on the task in hand is vital, since not doing so invites failure.

Similar considerations apply at home when playing online poker. The familiarity of the home environment, coupled with the fact that there is no risk of being physically distracted by opponents at the table, can induce a sense of complacency. Surfing the Internet or writing emails while playing at an online poker site is possible for those with a genuine ability to handle multiple tasks, though this is likely to have a negative impact on a player's results.

EXTERNAL PRESSURES

As with any aspect of life, playing poker to the best of one's ability is generally easier and much more enjoyable when not burdened by other serious concerns. Illness, tiredness and emotional stress are all likely to have a negative impact on play, whatever the source of the problem. Such pressures can be expected to inhibit concentration, the effect of which is likely to result in costly mistakes being made. Problems at work or within the home may dull the competitiveness required at the table in order to prosper and, just as importantly, could reduce the pleasure obtained from simply playing the game. Of course, approaching a poker session in a relaxed and positive frame of mind is a sound policy, but there will always be those players who can successfully immerse themselves in a game precisely because this helps them forget their other concerns.

BODY LANGUAGE

Much has already been made of the information to be gained from shrewd observations at the poker table, particularly with regard to the cards in play and the betting patterns of opponents. But assessing other players also involves understanding their mental and emotional state, since this is likely to have an overriding impact on their performance. This becomes easier the more frequently the same players gather together to play, as is the case in regular amateur games. Typical things to note include the postures adopted by opponents and their general demeanour at different stages of the game, as these are likely to reflect their true feelings. Players dispiritedly slumped in their chairs after a series of losing hands might be understandably frustrated. Although unremarkable in itself, this could also advertise the intrusive presence of doubts in their own ability or even a loss of interest in the game, something that could easily be exploited by an aggressive opponent.

There are also a few specific signs of tension or nervousness that might inadvertently betray the strength of an opponent's hand. For example players who bet out of turn because of their eagerness to be involved are probably holding decent cards.

Also, those whose hands literally shake as they make a substantial bet may be revealing excitement at the proximity of victory. Making sense of such clues is another skill that can improve any player's chances of success. Pulling them all together when the adrenaline is flowing represents a serious challenge, but this is definitely one of the reasons poker retains its appeal.

POKER TELLS

Players must deceive each other in order to improve their winning chances, but this practice of deliberate misrepresentation often infringes the moral codes learned since childhood. The internal pressure generated can manifest itself in particular mannerisms that, if witnessed and understood, could give away the strength of a player's hand. These are known as 'tells'. Former world champion Doyle Brunson maintains that the pulse in a man's neck is a good source of information. Often visible when the heart is pounding, this usually betrays a bluff since the heart is more likely to race at the prospect of a deception being uncovered. The reasoning is that a player betting with a strong hand is less likely to fear a call and will be more relaxed at the prospect of this happening.

Above: Paul Wasicka fails to stifle a yawn at the final table of a WSOP tournament in 2006. The world championship extends over several days during which even the most experienced professional will suffer fatigue.

Right: Jac Arama celebrates a win at the Grosvenor Victoria Casino in London. Many players wear sunglasses to obscure their eyes from opponents since our pupils dilate when excited, whether from fear or pleasure.

The denomination of chips used when betting may also offer clues to a player's hand. Low denominations casually added to the pot could suggest weakness from a reluctant caller prepared to speculate only with small change. Alternatively, confident bets with high-denomination chips usually emanate from players who fully expect to reclaim them at the showdown. Admittedly, some of the more obvious tells are easily faked. Feigning indifference when possessing a powerful hand, for example, or staring intently at an opponent when bluffing in order to intimidate the player into folding, require a minimal deployment of acting skills. In addition to reading other players' poker tells, of course, is the need to restrict giving away clues to one's own hand, which is dependent on maintaining consistency in one's actions throughout the game, whether winning or losing.

ONLINE POKER TELLS

Without the ability to see opponents when playing online, the scope for identifying poker tells is obviously restricted, but there are still a few pointers worth considering. Comments typed into the chat box may reveal something of a player's age, mood or skill level, though it is unwise to take them all at face value. More significantly, the speed at which players make their betting decisions can provide clues,

Above: Carl Olson pictured in classically pensive mode with his elbows on the table and his head resting on his hands. Olson's pose is typical of a player keen to avoid betraying the quality of his hand.

especially given that some online players will be competing on several tables at once. Those who repeatedly delay their actions are likely to be distracted by events elsewhere. By contrast, players who ordinarily act promptly but delay in calling a particular bet may be trying to infer that they face a difficult decision when, in fact, they hold a winning hand. Once again, the key is for players to stay focused on events and act consistently themselves, to prevent opponents from reading any significance into their own actions.

Above: Allen Cunningham of Nevada blows on his hands during the latter stages of the 2006 WSOP world championship tournament. He finished fourth behind the winner, Jamie Gold.

Left: Eddie Scharf rubs his head as he contemplates the action at the table. Though this may represent a player being puzzled by the betting, such deliberations can easily be faked. Scharf could well have the best hand and yet be trying to convey an air of indecision.

THE ART OF BLUFFING

Ordinarily, a bluff involves a player with poor cards betting to represent possession of a strong hand, with the aim of causing opponents to fold. Successfully achieving this is undoubtedly one of the most thrilling and rewarding features of a game in which deceiving one's opponents is integral to success. However, there is an art to bluffing that is framed by the nature of the poker variation played, the stakes that are involved and the quality of the players at the table. For instance, in low-stakes, fixed-limit games, it is difficult to execute many bluffs because the cost of calling any bet is rarely enough to force everyone to fold, particularly when the pot is large, relative to the size of the stakes. On the other hand, no-limit poker features more bluffing opportunities, since players can bet sums substantial enough to create real concern in the minds of players holding good but not unbeatable cards. The key to the success of any bluff lies in identifying the right moment to bet against opponents who will understand the message that the bluffer is attempting to convey.

SEEDS OF DOUBT

There are two important benefits to be gained from bluffing in poker. In the short term, a successful bluff can convert a weak hand into a winner, enabling a player to acquire a pot unexpectedly by representing sufficient, though actually non-existent, strength. Obviously, this will not happen every time a player bluffs, yet losing a pot when having a bluff called also offers positive long-term benefits, even as the weakness of a player's hand is revealed. Once a capacity for deception is exposed, doubts surface in the mind of

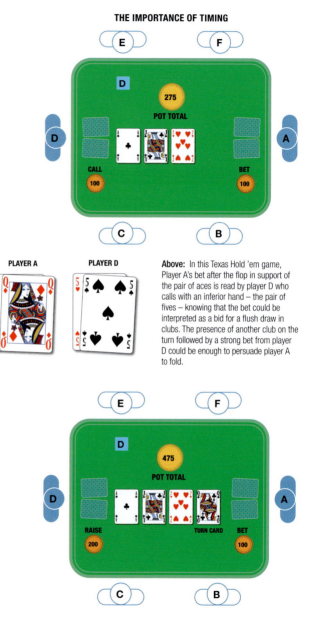

THE IMPORTANCE OF TIMING

Above: In this Texas Hold 'em game, Player A's bet after the flop in support of the pair of aces is read by player D who calls with an inferior hand – the pair of fives – knowing that the bet could be interpreted as a bid for a flush draw in clubs. The presence of another club on the turn followed by a strong bet from player D could be enough to persuade player A to fold.

PLAYER A

PLAYER D

Above: The turn card is the Qc meaning that player A now holds two pairs, aces and queens. However, player A's bet with what is currently the strongest hand is immediately raised by player D to suggest that the flush has been obtained. This has the mark of a credible bluff and may cause player A to fold rather than to try drawing for the full house that might now be assumed necessary to win. The odds against achieving this are 11 to 1, greater than the current pot odds on offer.

SEMI-BLUFFS

Right: Another Texas Hold 'em example shows the concept of the semi-bluff. Player D, who needs a 4 for a straight, bets 100 chips after the flop hoping to take the pot immediately. Player E's call shows possession of a strong hand, a pair of kings, but though player D's initial bluff at the pot did not succeed, a 4 could still come on the turn or the river to give the winning hand.

CALL
100

275
POT TOTAL

BET
100

E   F

D   D   A

C   B

PLAYER D

PLAYER E

each opponent over the meaning behind any subsequent bet from the known bluffer. The second reason for bluffing, therefore, is to enhance the likelihood of opponents contributing chips to a pot they have little or no chance of winning, simply because they wrongly suspect another bluff is being executed.

THE IMPORTANCE OF TIMING

The majority of poker variations involve several cards in play being exposed for all to see, the exception being draw poker and its derivations. This fact creates many viable bluffing scenarios, as players can generate inferences regarding the hand they hold, which are clearly recognizable to opponents. But to do this successfully requires a good sense of timing. For example, as the diagram at the top of the opposite page illustrates, a player holding Ad, Qd in Texas Hold 'em when the flop reveals Ac, Jc, 7h, may bet on the strength of the pair of aces, only to be called by a single opponent. One logical assumption could be that the caller is drawing to a flush in clubs, which, when the turn card is revealed as Qc, presents the player now holding two pairs with a serious problem. If the player bets and is immediately raised by the opponent, the clear inference is that the flush has been secured, leaving the player in need of another ace or queen on the river, the final community card dealt face up to the board, for a full house. The opponent does not need to possess the flush in this situation to stand a chance of taking the pot, since representing it with a bluff, a possibility established by calling on the flop, could easily be enough to win.

SEMI-BLUFFS
♦ ♣ ♥ ♠

Players who bet in the knowledge that their hand cannot win are said to be making 'naked bluffs', which can only succeed when everyone else folds. Distinct from such occasions are those when a player bets in support of a weak hand that has an outside chance of improvement with cards still to come. David Sklansky, poker expert and author of several books on the game, coined the term 'semi-bluff' to describe such situations. Using another Texas Hold 'em example, (above) a player holding 6s, 7s, when the flop is 3h, Kd, 5c, might bluff to take the pot there and then without holding even a pair. Should an opponent call, immediately suggesting a superior hand, there remain two opportunities to hit a 4, offering a 17 per cent chance that the semi-bluffer will be rewarded with a winning straight.

Right: Gus Hansen, known as the 'Great Dane', seen competing in the no-limit Hold 'em tournament at the Danish Poker Championships in 2005. Though only fourth on this occasion, Hansen has earned a reputation as a formidable tournament player since his breakthrough victory in the WPT's Five Diamond Poker Classic in May 2002.

EXERCISING JUDGEMENT

The ability to exercise sound judgement obviously comes with experience, but putting into practice some of the skills briefly described in this chapter will improve anyone's poker game. How much it improves depends upon a player's level of competitiveness and the quality of their observations at the table. Those who have a strong desire to win possess all the incentive they need to take note of patterns emerging during play in order to distinguish the good players from the poor ones. Indeed, one of the key factors to successful poker is being able to identify the right level at which to play in terms of the abilities of opponents and the sums being contested. Being the shrewdest player at a regular game may be enough to earn a modest extra income, something that might satisfy the ambitions of many amateur players. On the other hand, no player should be ashamed to preserve their bankroll by cashing out of a game in which it is evident that the opponents are superior or in which the stakes are simply too high. Accurate judgement exercised in this situation can protect a player against unnecessary losses.

THE IMPORTANCE OF POSITION

Although the importance of a player's position during a betting round varies slightly from one poker variation to another, it is accepted as typically more advantageous to act later, when more information is available. Yet this commonly acknowledged fact can be utilized by players in early positions to work against their opponents. Since it is expected that players will check or bet cautiously the earlier they are to act, a maximum bet from an early position will often be respected as representative of a very strong hand. Bluffing and semi-bluffing opportunities therefore exist in these situations, although, as with any tactical move, it is wise not to employ it indiscriminately.

By the same token, betting in a late position offers greater chances to steal pots from opponents who have shown a marked reluctance to become involved in the action earlier in the round. Since their reticence usually suggests weakness, a player in late position may find that even a modest bet is enough to persuade everyone else to fold.

THE IMPORTANCE OF POSITION

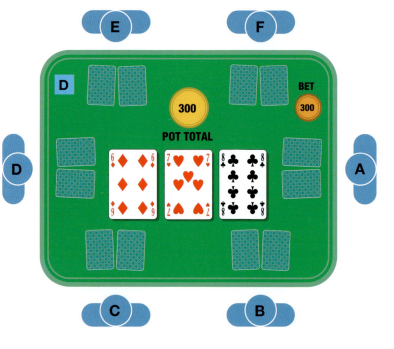

PLAYER F

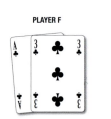

Right: In this no-limit Texas Hold 'em game, each player has paid the minimum of 50 chips to see the flop. As first to act after the flop, player F bluffs with a pot-sized bet of 300. Since a large bet in this situation is generally acknowledged as risky, the aim here is to suggest that a strong hand such as a straight or three of a kind is already held, enough perhaps to intimidate opponents into folding.

ASSESSING CHANCES

Judging one's chances of winning any pot always needs consideration of three key elements to the game, namely the cards in play, the betting patterns of opponents and the odds of probability at work. As each hand lasts only a couple of minutes, however, accurately analysing the fluctuating scenarios presented during a game sometimes calls for educated guesses on the part of each player. Some general patterns of play are repeated sufficiently, however, to make this process a little easier. For example, a player drawing three cards in draw poker can be expected to be retaining a pair, whereas a one-card draw is likely to indicate that a straight or flush is being targeted. In Texas Hold 'em, a pre-flop raise (the matching of or increase on a previous bet before the three community cards are dealt) is rarely considered unless the player holds an ace, king or high-value pair. Similarly, when playing stud poker, it is prudent to accept that any player who continues betting in the face of an opponent's showing pair is likely to hold superior hole cards. Understanding the implications of such betting patterns enables a player to make swift but generally sound assessments of the play before hastily committing chips to the pot.

POT MANAGEMENT

Successful pot management incorporates both attacking and defensive measures, which a player can use to accentuate winning hands and diminish the impact of losing hands. In simple terms, pot management means contributing less in support of hands that will probably lose, and betting in a style that will build a big pot when holding a hand that is virtually certain to prove the best. For instance, needing to draw a card or two to fill in a straight or a flush is a common situation, but the odds against this occurring usually prohibit calling any significantly large bet by an opponent.

The idea, obviously, is to preserve a chance of an unlikely win as cheaply as possible, either by checking or only calling minimum bets. By contrast, when the cards fall favourably enough for a win to appear likely, it pays to disguise the fact by checking, or betting the minimum, to encourage opponents to remain in the pot and thus boost the probable winnings. Raising the pot is a viable strategy in this situation as well, provided an opponent or two can be relied upon to call the bet. Since some opponents will fold, this offers the dual benefit of increasing the pot and reducing the opposition at the same time.

THE IMPORTANCE OF POSITION

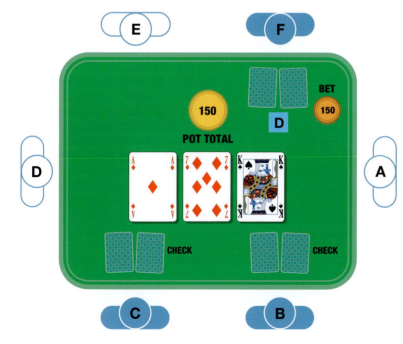

PLAYER F

Left: In this example from a no-limit Texas Hold 'em game, three players have seen the flop and players B and C have both checked. Their reticence enables player F to make a pot-sized bet of 150, representing a stronger hand than a pair of sevens in a bid to try winning – or 'stealing' – the pot from the others.

POKER VIRTUES

Assimilating all the advice on sensible poker play before tackling a game is a rarity, as the majority of players only tend to discover the relevance of such advice through experience. Learning from one's mistakes, however, is certainly a virtue that is as applicable to poker as to any other endeavour. Irrespective of a player's level of ability, exercising patience and some personal discipline also brings its rewards at the poker table. Players who enjoy early success during a session can easily start betting a little more loosely and fritter away hard-earned chips in a misguided effort to capitalize on their skilful play or simple good fortune. This contravenes one of poker's maxims, which states that players should not try to beat opponents, but should, instead, allow their opponents to force the issue by trying to beat them. The more they lose, the more desperate they are likely to become, with the likely result being that they will make increasingly poor decisions as play continues.

PATIENCE

The need for patience becomes unavoidable when each poker session is considered as part of a lifelong poker game. Although it is always preferable to be ahead when any session concludes, this is highly unlikely to occur on every occasion. Nevertheless, this simple fact does not prevent some players from betting loosely and taking more chances than necessary in order to stay involved in the action. Quite often this stems from the mistaken belief that contesting the majority of hands offers a greater chance of success, which is rarely the case.

At the serious end of the scale, the reality is that most successful poker players contest few pots and save their chips for those betting confrontations in which they have the edge. This helps ensure that the pots they do win are much bigger than average, which means they need to win fewer of them to stay ahead. Such strategy is employed by what the professionals refer to as tight-aggressive players, predatory types who bide their time and wait for the right moment to pounce on unwary or impulsive opponents.

DISCIPLINE

Having the discipline to remain patient, perhaps by folding a strong hand in the face of a convincingly large bet, can be a major test. Equally, when the textbook moves consistently fail to achieve the desired

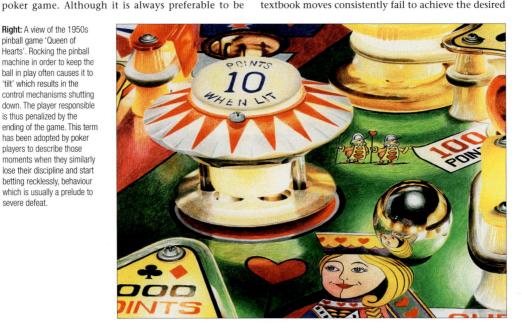

Right: A view of the 1950s pinball game 'Queen of Hearts'. Rocking the pinball machine in order to keep the ball in play often causes it to 'tilt' which results in the control mechanisms shutting down. The player responsible is thus penalized by the ending of the game. This term has been adopted by poker players to describe those moments when they similarly lose their discipline and start betting recklessly, behaviour which is usually a prelude to severe defeat.

Right: Retaining the discipline required to play effectively is a major test of a player's ability. A succession of unlucky defeats can easily cause a player to lose control – to tilt – and make even more costly misjudgements under pressure. In this Texas Hold 'em example, the player holding 8, 9 offsuit has a chance of securing a straight with a 7 or a Q on the turn or river, but to pursue this hand in the face of a bet from an opponent is probably to be avoided. Any Q will simply furnish someone holding an A with a higher straight (A, K, Q, J, 10), while it is also possible an opponent holds A, Q already.

PLAYER'S HOLE CARDS

FLOP

result, it is easy to lose faith and make questionable betting decisions in a bid to recoup short-term losses. This is often the prelude to a player 'tilting', a term borrowed from pinball, where machines that have tilted do not function. It refers to the deterioration in a player's game to the point where ever more frequent losses trigger irrational and usually costly betting decisions. Under such pressure, it is far more likely that players will misjudge the situations confronting them. For example a player holding 8s, 9c in Texas Hold 'em when the flop is 10h, Js, Kd, could easily fall prey to pursuing the 7 or Q that would realize a successful straight draw. Yet a Q on the turn or the river would also complete a higher straight for any opponent holding an A, a detail that is easy to miss if not fully concentrating on the game.

Having the strength of character to walk away from a losing session, rather than throw good money after bad, is another essential poker discipline. During any session itself, the key to maintaining a sound strategy is to have strict standards regarding which starting hands to play, to trust in the odds of probability and to treat each hand on its merits as play develops. In adopting such a disciplined approach, players can expect to reduce losses to a minimum and remain competitive, although a sense of humour is also an asset to cope with any series of bad 'beats'. These are occasions when opponents consistently defy the odds in drawing the cards that they need to win.

A LONG-TERM GAME
♦ ♣ ♥ ♠

Learning the basic poker skills offers the chance to obtain a lifetime of pleasure from the game, whether as an amateur or as a budding professional. Most players will spend more of their disposable income on the game than they are ever likely to recoup, but adopting a patient, disciplined and objective approach will at least help to keep down the cost of their gambling pleasure.

Above: As with so many card games, the skills absorbed from playing poker can be maintained over a lifetime through regular participation in a game. To obtain the most from a session a player needs to possess some semblance of competitiveness, a quality that need not diminish with age.

Right: A player at the 2004 WSOP waits patiently for the right time to make a move. Highest-level tournament poker is sometimes characterized as hours of inaction punctuated by moments of extreme excitement. Lengthy periods of time may be spent waiting for a suitable chance to become involved in a pot, The consequence of making a misjudgement could be elimination from the event.

PRACTICE MAKES PERFECT

To become skilled in any pursuit obviously requires practice as well as experience. Fortunately for the legions of players new to poker, there exist many opportunities to both study the game and put into practice what they have learnt, either live or online. The benefit of online poker sites is that they offer play money tables, which, as the name implies, enable players to warm up for a session before risking any real cash. Beginners use these tables in order to gain experience, and they help condition new users to the configurations of the poker site. The betting strategies exhibited on these tables may be erratic, given that no cash is at stake, but the scenarios enacted help attune a player to the general patterns of the game. However, whether live or online, it is always worthwhile warming up with a few hands dealt out before play, simply to remind oneself of the different possibilities that can emerge.

Right: As with any pursuit, becoming more skilled at poker requires studying the game as well as obtaining playing experience at the table. The concept of the 'poker school' emanates from players regularly convening to enjoy a game and informally analysing each other's play. While this constitutes enough of an education for some players, more serious students of the game will absorb the lessons to be learned from many of the books and websites dedicated to poker.

AVAILABLE RESOURCES

Taking advantage of the vast amount of written and recorded material concerning poker is obviously of benefit to anyone's play, irrespective of their level of experience. Both the World and European Poker Tours were established to help meet the interest in televised poker and these have supplemented the many other tournaments that have appeared on television. The predominant game featured in these is no-limit Texas Hold 'em, so students of that variation are well served, but those wanting guidance on how to play the other popular poker games need only scour the bookshelves or the Internet for information. The majority of professionals who have written about the game, generally offer tips on how to play draw, stud, Omaha and their various high-low derivations, as well as Texas Hold 'em. World champions such as Doyle Brunson, Phil Hellmuth and Tom McEvoy have all offered their

Above: Keeping a record of poker income and expenditure is advisable for those who wish to improve their game. A simple record of wins and losses, complete with notes on which variations were played and the level of stakes involved, can help players to identify their strengths and weaknesses.

own insights into how to play winning poker, although professional gambler David Sklansky and gaming expert John Scarne are two other respected writers whose work covers most aspects of the game.

ANALYSING THE GAME

All players have different motivations behind their wish to play poker, but those who take the game seriously enough to consider improving their techniques can only do so by analysing their previous performances. Remembering each hand contested during a session is improbable, though there are often key hands, usually involving big pots, which can be recalled later when considering why a particular ploy either succeeded or failed. If, despite winning several

sizeable pots during a session, a player still finishes with a loss, an objective review would probably reveal that too many chips are being squandered playing hands that have a poor chance of success. Acknowledging that possibility is a positive step towards eradicating loose and costly betting strategies. A general analysis of the game is central to the concept of the 'poker school', usually involving a regular group of players who not only compete against each other, but discuss the game and help further their poker education as a result.

KEEPING RECORDS

Poker is first and foremost a gambling game with chips and, by extension, cash, being the obvious means by which players can assess their ability. Relatively few people make a substantial living from playing poker, but that does not negate the value of lesser-skilled players monitoring their own performance by keeping accurate records of their play and their finances. Doing so helps players to analyse their game and enables them to build up a picture of their strengths or weaknesses. Making a note of the variations played during a session and recalling which of these proved most successful is obviously useful when deciding which variations to play in future. Similarly, comparing one's performance in tournament poker with that in cash games might highlight which of these best suits an individual's own temperament or playing style. Most of all, keeping a record of play promotes an objective approach and ensures that the game remains at the forefront of any player's mind.

THE POWER OF OBSERVATION
♦ ♣ ♥ ♠

At the poker table there is always plenty of information on offer, which, if observed and interpreted correctly, can give any player an edge during the game. Apart from the visible cards in play, the betting patterns of opponents and how they play certain hands should be mentally noted. Most importantly, players are encouraged to stay focused on the game at all times, even when not participating in a hand. By watching events unfold to the showdown, when competing hands are revealed, it is possible to gain an insight into how others play, what type of hands they are willing to support, and whether they favour a tight or a loose betting style.

Above: Prior to attending any poker game, players may find it worthwhile dealing out a few hands to themselves as a way of warming up. If the session is likely to include several variations then someone who is used to playing Texas Hold 'em may wish to refresh their memory of the subtle differences between that game and Omaha. Winning hands in Omaha are usually of higher value so a quick revision of the impact this might have on play could safeguard a player against making costly mistakes.

POPULAR POKER VARIATIONS

THERE ARE MANY CHALLENGING AND VARIED WAYS OF PLAYING POKER, FROM THE TRADITIONAL GAME OF DRAW POKER, WHICH IS A FUN GAME OFTEN ENJOYED BY FAMILIES, TO EXCITING HIGH-STAKES GAMES OF SKILL AND CONCENTRATION SUCH AS TEXAS HOLD'EM AND OMAHA.

In its earliest recognized form, poker was played with a deck of just 20 cards and was limited to four players, who each received five cards before betting on the strength of their respective hands. Since the introduction of the 52-card deck, the game has undergone a substantial period of evolution, with the simplistic nature of the 'bluffing game' giving way to hundreds of variations on a theme. Bluffing and reading body language take a great deal of practice, but spotting an opponent's tells, will increase any player's chances of success. The purpose of this chapter is to introduce the five most popular and widely played poker variations – draw poker, five-card stud, seven-card stud, Texas Hold'em and Omaha – and explain the basic rules and patterns of play for each, beginning with the oldest recognized form of the game, draw poker.

Right: A typical hand following the deal in draw poker, the oldest form of the game. Players receive five cards each and can expect to see at least a pair, such as the sixes illustrated, in two out of every five deals.

DRAW POKER

Of all poker games, this is likely to be the version familiar to anyone who has ever spent time playing cards with friends or family, and it fits the profile of what is often referred to as 'kitchen-table' or 'penny-ante' poker. It is the traditional game which has been passed down through the generations over the past 150 years. As such, it has historically been the starting point from which keener players go on to discover the many other forms of poker that have emerged since the 19th century.

ORIGINS OF THE GAME

Draw poker became widely recognized as a game in its own right some time after the American Civil War (1861 to 1865) and remains popular to this day, though arguably more as a parlour game played for nominal stakes than as a serious betting medium. Before the draw element was introduced, poker was regularly played as a no-limit betting game with the size of bets and raises unrestricted. This made it far more a test of nerve than a matter of judgement, there being few clues to the composition of an opponent's hand throughout play and numerous opportunities to bluff. The gradual adoption of the draw – allowing players the option to discard cards they do not want in exchange for new cards during a game – and the acceptance of limits on the betting changed poker sufficiently between 1850 and 1900 to secure its immediate future as a game of skill. These developments made draw poker much more appealing to cautious players who wanted to gamble without being reckless. Further discipline was imposed on the game with a restriction that is believed to have originated in Toledo, Ohio. Under this rule, a player

Above: The great game of poker. This illustration, dating from 1884, shows four players participating in a game while a fifth looks on. By this time, draw poker was well established as a popular pastime, a status that was greatly accelerated during the American Civil War which ended in 1865.

POKER HAND PROBABILITIES
♦ ♣ ♥ ♠

Draw poker begins with each player being dealt five cards and, while in the majority of cases players will need to utilize the draw in order to improve their hands, the chances of being dealt a recognized poker hand in those initial five cards are detailed below.

HAND	CHANCE
Royal Flush	1 chance in every 649,740 deals
Straight Flush	1 in 72,193
Four of a Kind	1 in 4,165
Full House	1 in 694
Flush	1 in 509
Straight	1 in 255
Three of a Kind	1 in 47
Two Pairs	1 in 21
One Pair	1 in 2.5
No Pair	1 in 2

Right: Royal Flush – there is one chance in every 649,740 deals that a player will receive this hand in the first five cards dealt.

could only open the betting after the deal if in possession of a hand comprising a pair of jacks or better. Players who wildly gambled on their first five cards, irrespective of what they held, were denied the opportunity to intimidate opponents with an unpredictable and loose betting strategy. The game using this rule became known as 'jackpots' and it was soon adopted as the favoured form of draw poker. It tested a player's mathematical and observational skills to a greater degree and is the form of the game under consideration here.

Number of players

Ordinarily, draw poker is a game best suited to no more than six players, since this represents the maximum viable number that can be satisfactorily accommodated with a single 52-card deck. To avoid the possibility of having to recycle discarded cards at the draw stage, players are typically limited to exchanging no more than three cards in an effort to improve their respective hands. Given the lack of any substantive rules for the game, there are poker schools and online poker rooms that will permit a player to exchange all five

cards at the draw if desired, especially if there are five or fewer participants. This is a questionable tactic and most players with a hand poor enough to warrant being completely replaced are probably best advised to forfeit their ante by folding and awaiting the next deal.

Chip Denominations
♦ ♣ ♥ ♠

The denominations of the coloured chips used in poker vary from one establishment to another but the values indicated here are typical of those used in many casinos and online poker sites.

VALUE	COLOUR
1	White
2	Yellow
5	Red
10	Blue
20	Grey
25	Green
50	Orange
100	Black
250	Pink
500	Purple
1,000	Burgundy
2,000	Light Blue
5,000	Brown

SEQUENCE OF PLAY

Once the compulsory bets have been made, usually with everyone adding an ante to the pot, the dealer deals five cards each, face down, to all players. A round of betting follows, provided at least one player holds a pair of jacks or better. After the betting round, those players who are still competing for the pot may discard the unwanted cards from their hands, subject to any limits in place, and replace them with others from the deck. After the draw, a second round of betting ensues, leading to the conclusion of the hand. A player who makes a bet that is unmatched by any opponent, whether in the first or second betting round, can win the pot without having to expose the winning hand. If two or more players match bets to the end of the game, they reveal their cards in a showdown and the best hand claims the spoils.

ANTES

Draw poker requires all players to ante a nominal sum to create the pot, usually set at between 10 and 20 per cent of the minimum bet for the game. In a 25/50 fixed-limit game for instance, in which bets are set at 25 chips during the first round and 50 in the second, a typical ante would be 5 chips.

An alternative approach for instigating the pot is to have the dealer contribute a sufficient sum to cover the antes for all players since, as the deal moves around the table, the net contribution from each player will remain the same, provided each shares an equal number of deals during the session. These conventions apply in live games, but the online version of draw poker uses the blind betting system, whereby the two players to the dealer's immediate left contribute compulsory bets before the deal, known as the small blind and big blind respectively.

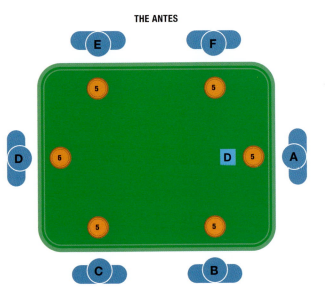

THE ANTES

Above: In this example of a 25/50 fixed-limit draw poker game, each player is required to ante 5 chips to generate the initial pot. After the deal, players may bet and raise in denominations of 25 chips only. During the second round, the bets and raises are set at 50 chips.

THE DEAL

After the cards have been shuffled and cut, the nominated dealer discards or 'burns' the top card before dealing one card at a time to each player in turn, working clockwise around the table, until they have five each. The remainder of the pack is then placed face down in readiness for the draw that follows the first round of betting.

THE DRAW
♦ ♣ ♥ ♠

Should two or more players have matched bets to the conclusion of the first betting round, they next have the option to draw further cards from the deck to improve their hands. Working clockwise, each player may discard up to three cards face down and request replacements from the dealer, who should discard the top card of the deck before commencing the draw to prevent any player gaining an advantage from recognizing the first card dealt. Once the first player has had any discards replaced by the dealer, the next player still involved in the game exercises the option of the draw. This process continues until all remaining players have been accommodated, at which point, the second and final betting round occurs.

In all poker games, it is the dealer's responsibility to direct proceedings during play, ensuring that players act in turn, bet the correct amounts and are aware of the rules. And since accidents do happen, if any card is inadvertently exposed during the deal, it is customary to declare the hand dead. Once the misdeal occurs, the cards should be gathered together by the dealer before being shuffled, cut and dealt once again with no additional antes required.

OPENING THE BETTING

The opportunity to bet passes clockwise around the table, starting with the player to the left of the dealer. Any player unable to meet the requirement of at least a pair of jacks to open the betting must check, but a player whose hand does meet the opening requirements has the choice either to check or to make the first bet. In the original draw poker game of jackpots, the first player to declare possession of a hand comprising a pair of jacks or better was compelled to make the opening bet, but this rule soon lost its appeal and is rarely applied now. Once an opening bet has been made, the remaining players must decide whether to fold, call or raise. If nobody opens the betting, the hand is declared dead, with the pot remaining in place and players obliged to pay a further ante in readiness for the deal. Evidently, with no compulsion to open the betting, even when holding a suitably high pair, a game between extremely cautious players could be stiflingly short of action.

THE DEAL

Above: After the antes have been paid, the dealer discards or "burns" the top card in the deck before distributing cards, face down and one at a time, to each player in turn, until they have five each.

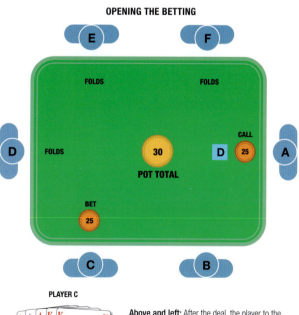

OPENING THE BETTING

PLAYER A

PLAYER B

PLAYER C

Above and left: After the deal, the player to the dealer's left – player B – is the first to act but must check since the opening requirement of holding a pair of jacks or better is not met. The option to bet then passes to player C, who, with a pair of kings, now opens with a bet of 25 chips. Players D, E and F all fold, but the dealer, player A, calls the bet. The action is now on player B, who decides to fold.

FINAL BETTING ROUND

The player who opened the betting is also the first to act in the second round and has the option to fold, check or bet. Should all players decide to check, then each player reveals their hand to determine the winner. Once a player bets then the other active players must decide whether to fold, call or raise. Any player who makes a bet that is not called wins the pot and is under no obligation to show the winning hand. But if one or more opponents call the bet, then all active players should lay their cards face up on the table to determine the winner.

THE SHOWDOWN

There are several conventions that are typically applied at the showdown at the end of the second betting round. If nobody bets and all players check, then the participants should reveal their cards in turn, beginning with the player who opened the betting in the first round, known naturally as the opener. Working clockwise around the table, all active hands are therefore exposed, one at a time, with the winning hand being readily identified. When there has been some action during the second round and a bet or raise is called, then the bettor or raiser is first to reveal their

Above: As player A is dealing, player C is the first to draw further cards. Retaining the pair of kings and the A kicker, player C discards the remainder and draws two additional cards. Player A does the same, retaining the pair of nines and the K.

Right: While showing no improvement on the pair of kings, player C bets the minimum of 50 chips and is called by player A whose hand has improved to three of a kind ('trips'). Player A could have raised as any three of a kind is a strong holding in draw poker, but calling represents a safe option. Player C opened the betting originally and must have been holding a higher pair than player A's nines which could similarly have improved to three of a kind.

cards. In this situation, many callers are reluctant to show their cards if they know they are beaten, thus depriving opponents of any clues to their betting strategy or the quality of hand they are prepared to support. Although accepted as a legitimate ploy, most guides to poker suggest that all active hands should be exposed at the showdown at the request of any player still contesting the pot. To avoid disputes, players could agree to reveal their cards simultaneously. Finally, cards speak at the showdown because, although players normally announce what they are holding, this rule restricts the possibility of players winning – or losing – by wrongly declaring the value of a hand.

SIMILAR VARIATIONS

While jackpots is commonly regarded as the dominant draw poker game, there are numerous other versions played throughout the world. For example in California many players tend to favour incorporating the joker, which is often referred to as 'the bug', to make a 53-card deck using the joker as a wild card. This card may be counted as an ace or as the fifth card needed to complete a straight, a flush or a straight flush, so it has limited value. A player may obtain a hand of five aces, ranked above a royal flush in this game, but may not use the joker to make five of a kind in any other rank below aces.

Outside California, draw poker with the joker wild sees the joker unlimited regarding which card it may represent. Similarly, playing deuces – twos – wild sees the four twos in the deck counting as wild cards of any value, with five of a kind becoming the highest-ranked hand attainable. Involving wild cards in a game can often improve the chances of players obtaining a strong hand, which, in turn, generates more betting action.

Left: A player should expect to be dealt a hand such as this J-high straight only once in every 255 deals. Though not the best possible hand, it is strong enough for a player to 'stand pat' by declining to draw any further cards and therefore constitutes a 'pat hand'.

A PAT HAND
♦ ♣ ♥ ♠

A player who declines to exchange any cards at the time of the draw is said to possess a 'pat hand', with the decision not to draw further cards known as 'standing pat'. Evidently, players who opt to do this cannot help but suggest that they possess a strong hand, a move that is inclined to suppress the opposition's willingness to bet. Very strong hands, therefore, may often secure relatively modest pots. However, standing pat also represents a viable bluffing opportunity that may be sufficient to win a few pots with poor cards. Better still, being caught bluffing in such a situation on occasion increases the possibility that, when the pat hand actually is powerful, it will be paid off with more callers and a bigger pot.

THE SHOWDOWN

Above: Since player A has called player C's bet, the hand is concluded with both players revealing their cards at the showdown. Player A wins the pot of 180 chips with three nines, beating player C's pair of kings. It is worth noting that both players retained their pairs but drew just two cards, not three, when given the chance. To have kept just two cards would have clearly signified to opponents that a pair, and no more, was currently held.

FIVE-CARD STUD

Although draw poker's success as a gambling medium saw it become a hugely popular game during the 19th century, it was not long before poker players devised a variation to extend poker's appeal. Five-card stud emerged to compensate for the perceived deficiencies seen in draw or 'closed' poker by those who felt that the original game offered far too little information upon which to make any betting decisions. Stud or 'open' poker, where players receive the majority of their cards face up, remedied this problem. The game also involved four, not two, betting rounds, which presented the potential for gradually building sizeable pots with players better able to gauge the relative merits of their opponents' hands during play.

ORIGINS OF THE GAME

The first mention of five-card stud appears in the 1864 American version of Hoyle's famous guide to card games, lending credence to the notion that, alongside draw poker, it developed during the American Civil War. Having spread from the states of Ohio, Illinois and Indiana, it grew in popularity among those players who found draw poker to be a stifling game with little scope for implementing subtle betting ploys. The increased number of betting rounds and the exposure of cards during play created a game that encouraged players to stay involved, thus leading to pots that were worth contesting. In draw poker, building a pot large enough to generate interest often involved high antes, a discouraging factor for players unwilling to risk money before seeing their cards.

Despite the opportunities presented by the game to implement viable bluffs and betting strategies, five-card stud declined in popularity following a ruling in 1910 by the Attorney General of California. He declared it a game of chance and thus illegal, while draw poker was adjudged a game of skill and was exempted, in California at least, from the widespread prohibition of other forms of gambling. Though five-card stud continued to be played, it became viewed as a mechanical game lacking dynamism by those

Left: Three poker players in Ohio, *circa* 1870. Draw poker had developed into a game distinct from its European origins by the mid-19th century but, by the time this photograph was taken, five-card stud poker was also increasing in popularity.

Below: These antique ivory poker chips may not be to everybody's taste although the popularity of the game has led to a boom in the sales of poker chip sets which, along with a deck of cards, constitute the basic equipment required for a game. Nowadays most good quality chips are made of clay or, more usually, a heavy durable plastic.

Right: Karl Malden (centre) deals as Steve McQueen and Edward G. Robinson engage in a heads-up, five-card stud confrontation in *The Cincinnati Kid*. Though two players can easily play, there is more cut and thrust when five-card stud is played by eight to ten players.

players who had absorbed the basic, conservative strategies required to reduce potential losses. It was not until the 1950s that stud poker once again overtook draw poker as the most popular variation, but it was the seven-card version, not five-card stud, that had become pre-eminent by then.

NUMBER OF PLAYERS

As there is no draw to consider and many players can be expected to fold before the latter betting rounds, up to ten players can comfortably play five-card stud utilizing a single deck of cards. The game is characterized by low average winning hands and this, allied to some disciplined betting strategy, can make it rather dull if there are five or fewer players. For this reason, experienced five-card stud players prefer games between eight to ten competitors since, with more cards in play, better hands may develop and this is likelier to prompt the betting confrontations that are the essence of poker.

THE CINCINNATI KID
♦ ♣ ♥ ♠

The celebrated showdown in *The Cincinnati Kid* features a high-stakes game of five-card stud, the structure of which lends itself to the building of dramatic tension in a fashion not matched by draw poker. Eric Stoner, played by Steve McQueen, has an A in the hole and a pair of tens showing when he bets US$1,000 and is immediately raised a further US$1,000 by his opponent, who shows Qd, 8d. Lancey Howard, as portrayed by Edward G. Robinson, also possesses the Jd, offering an outside chance of a straight or a flush, but is trailing so badly that most poker commentators believe he ought to have folded. Stoner calls and ultimately the pot increases to US$25,000 by the time of the showdown with Stoner, the eager new kid on the block, showing a full house. Remarkably, the poker master's luck is in and Howard secures a queen-high straight flush (Q, J, 10, 9, 8 of diamonds) to win the pot, retain his status as 'The Man', and break the spirit of the young pretender.

Left: *A Winning Hand*, a poker representation dating from the late 19th century by which time five-card stud had begun to rival draw poker as the most popular form of the game. It is less commonly played today, as shown by its absence from the numerous tournaments staged at the WSOP, although a specific variant of the game called *Sökö* is very popular in Finland. The term derives from 'Minä Sökötän' which, in Finnish, means 'I check'.

SEQUENCE OF PLAY

As in all poker games, five-card stud begins with the dealer shuffling the cards and having the deck cut before, typically, each player antes a nominal amount to instigate the pot. Players receive one card each face down (their first hole card) and a second card each face up before the first round of betting commences. Those paying to remain in the game are dealt a third card, also face up, at which point a second betting round takes place. Should the pot still be contested, a fourth card is dealt face up to each participant before the next betting round when the minimum bet is often doubled. If a fifth card is required to decide the destiny of the pot, then this too is dealt face up to each player, following which the fourth and final betting round occurs. The pot is won by any player making a bet unmatched by an opponent at any stage during the game or, in the event of a showdown, by the player with the best poker hand. Importantly, players who fold during play should turn all their cards face down to indicate they have dropped out of the hand.

THE ANTES AND THE DEAL

Prior to the deal, it is customary for all players to ante a small sum to initiate the pot and confirm their willingness to participate in the hand. In a 25/50 fixed-limit game of five-card stud a nominal ante of 5 or 10 chips will usually be sufficient to generate a pot, particularly if there are as many as ten players in competition. For beginners, a low-stakes, fixed-limit game along these lines is recommended until the nuances of stud poker are understood. However, since good players soon master the rules of sound five-card stud strategy, playing the game for small stakes and with fixed betting limits can render it somewhat

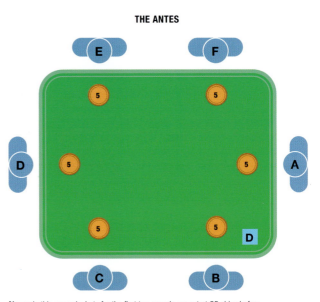

THE ANTES

Above: In this example, bets for the first two rounds are set at 25 chips before rising to 50 chips for the final two rounds. Before then, however, all players must pay the ante, set here at a nominal 5 chips, in order to participate in the game. At this point, the dealer, player B, may then deal the cards.

THE DEAL

Above: Once the antes have been paid, the dealer burns – discards – the top card and then deals one card face down to each player in turn, followed by one card face up, known as the 'door card'. Player E, showing a Q, is compelled to bet first, by virtue of possessing the highest card on display.

formulaic. It is recognized, therefore, that five-card stud benefits more than many other variations from being played as a no-limit or high-limit game. Such betting structures offer players the chance to make large bets, relative to the size of the pot, encouraging creative play from those at the table. Aggressive betting strategies and bluffs are more likely to work when opponents realize that calling a bet may mean going all-in with their remaining chips.

Once the antes have been paid, the dealer burns the top card and then deals one card each, face down, to every player, working clockwise around the table. Each player receives a second card dealt face up. Since the remaining cards to be dealt during the hand will also be face up, it is crucial that players keep their hole cards obscured from opponents.

OPENING THE BETTING

Following the deal, the player holding the highest first face-up card, known as the 'door card', has to make a compulsory opening bet. This may be set at the minimum betting level for the game or may also, like the ante, be a nominal bet for a sum less than the minimum. Using the 25/50 fixed-limit example once again, this means that the opening bet may be set at 25 chips or, to offset the obligation to the opening bettor, reduced to, say, 10 chips. Thereafter, beginning with the player to the opener's left, the other players must decide whether to fold, call or raise. Should the compulsory opening bet – the 'bring-in' – be set at 10 chips, it is possible for players to call for that sum or raise to the stipulated minimum of 25 chips, an act known as 'completing the bet', as the action circulates around the table. Should two or more players hold a door card of the same rank, then the opening bet is made by the first of those to the dealer's left.

Above: The purpose of the ante in poker is to create a pot for which players can compete and to stimulate their interest by ensuring they already have a small investment in the hand. It is also a mechanism for ensuring that cautious players who are reluctant to risk their chips will see their stacks steadily eroded unless they actively try to win a pot now and again.

OPENING THE BETTING

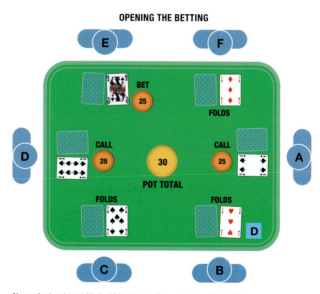

Above: As the player with the highest-value door card, player E bets 25 chips with the Q showing. The remaining players, beginning with player F, must now decide whether to fold, call for 25 or raise by entering 50 chips into the pot. Player F folds, player A calls, then players B and C fold. Finally, player D calls for 25 chips to conclude the betting for this round.

THIRD STREET

At the completion of the first round of betting, those players still contesting the pot receive their third card dealt face up. On 'third street', as it is known, there is sufficient information for players to begin assessing their chances of winning. Assuming a six-player game in which all are still participating, each player will have seen 13 of the 52 cards, representing a quarter of the deck. These are the 12 cards so far dealt face up to each player, plus their own individual hole cards. Possessing a high pair at this stage of the game is generally advantageous, particularly if the hole card is paired with an up card. If the pair is comprised of both up cards, making it an open or showing pair, then the strength of the hand is plain to see. The opening bet in this round is made by the player with the best visible two-card hand and, again, if there are players with hands of the same value then the honour falls to the player nearest the dealer's left. Unlike in the first round, from third street onwards no player is compelled to bet and all players may check, if they wish, prior to receipt of a fourth card. In most forms of limit stud poker, the minimum bet applying to the first two betting rounds is doubled for the latter two rounds. However, if an open pair materializes on third street, the player in possession is permitted to double the bet at this stage of the game, thus protecting the hand by making it more expensive for speculative callers to try outdrawing it.

FOURTH AND FIFTH STREET

Once the betting on third street is complete, a fourth card is dealt, face up, to those still in the game, after which it is the player showing the highest-value hand who has the option to bet first. The final round of betting occurs after

Above: The three players remaining now receive a third card, face up, prior to the next round. With an Ah showing, player D is the first to act in this round, but any bet is optional, so player D may defer a decision by checking. In the event, player D bets 25 chips and is called by both opponents.

Above: On fourth street, the betting levels now double with player D showing a pair of aces, leading player E's pair of queens and therefore facing the first betting decision. Player D bets 50 chips, confident that the pair of aces is leading, but both players E and A call, holding a pair of queens and aces respectively.

the fifth card has been dealt, by which time anyone still contesting the hand is in possession of five cards, one face down and four face up. Betting once again starts with the player in possession of the best visible hand. Obviously, inferences from the betting allied to the visible cards on the table during play mean that players will have a clear idea of what their opponents hold, or are suggesting they hold, during the concluding round.

THE GOLDEN RULES

One of the reasons that five-card stud has succumbed to the popularity of other poker variations is that the application of some simple strategic rules reduces the likelihood of large pots being contested to a showdown. On many occasions, hands fail to progress beyond third street since the pot odds rarely justify players with drawing hands seeking the cards they need to improve, particularly in the face of an open pair.

This represents the first rule of sensible play in that it is very rarely worthwhile to call a significant bet made by a player whose board cards alone outrank one's own hand. Playing a three-card flush or straight with two cards to come, for instance, is rarely advisable and is regarded as folly if an opponent bets with an open pair. The odds against completing the flush or straight are usually far too prohibitive to warrant calling, particularly when the betting levels are set to rise in the next two rounds. Similarly, it is dangerous to continue supporting an open pair after third street when an opponent with a higher-value board card calls a bet. A player showing a pair of tens and with a Q as a hole card, for example, is entitled to be wary if, having bet on third street, an opponent with an A and a K calls or raises. The inference is clearly that the

FIFTH STREET

Above: The players now receive their final card, giving them four cards face up and one – the hole card – face down, so each player is able to gauge the potential strength of their opponents' hands. Player D still shows the best hand and bets while player E, knowing that the queens are beaten, folds. Player A, also holding a pair of aces, calls and wins the pot at the showdown because the 9c is a higher kicker than the 8s held by player D.

opponent's hole card is either an A or a K and that the pair of tens represents little threat. While a disciplined application of these guidelines may help a player to conserve chips, since they are quickly absorbed with experience, they can render a session of five-card stud rather mechanical and somewhat short of serious confrontations.

Above: Showing the Ac as a door card, this player finds that the hole card is another A for the top pair and the best possible starting hand. The odds against this occurring are fractionally over 220 to 1 against though, in five-card stud, the hand presents a strong opportunity to take the pot.

355

SEVEN-CARD STUD

Once poker players had come to terms with the concept of five-card stud, it was not long before a seven-card version of the game materialized. More cards and more betting rounds generated greater interest in this stud variation, which left its five-card precursor behind in terms of popularity. From the beginning of the 20th century until the end of the World War II, during which the game was widely played by US servicemen, seven-card stud gradually acquired a reputation for being a testing but rewarding form of poker. After the war, the players of Las Vegas were similarly in thrall to the game and, up until the 1980s, it was twice as likely to be played in Nevada's casinos as all other variations combined. Only in the last 30 years has Texas Hold 'em managed to challenge seven-card stud as the pre-eminent poker game.

HOW THE GAME DEVELOPED

The game of seven-card stud, also known as 'seven-toed Pete' or 'down the river', is regarded by many as the quintessential poker variation. With each player ultimately receiving seven cards with which to form a hand, three face down and four face up, the game combines aspects of both open and closed poker. There are enough visible cards in circulation throughout play to formulate clear ideas concerning the composition of an opponent's hand, favouring those who are reluctant to bet blindly. However, with each player having three cards unexposed at the showdown, there is also enough scope for subterfuge and for some strong hands to develop away from the prying eyes of opponents. In addition, there are five betting rounds to negotiate, so that even a low-stakes game between

Above: US servicemen take time out to play poker, a pastime that naturally infiltrated military culture from the time of the American Civil War. By the time of World War II, seven-card stud was the preferred game for most servicemen and this played a part in it becoming the most popular poker variation in the immediate post-war era.

THE NUMBER OF PLAYERS

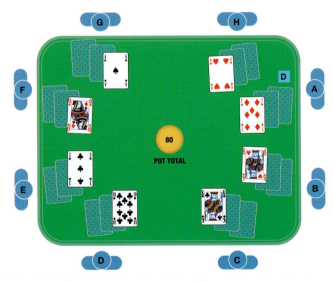

Above: Up to eight players can play seven-card stud and it is common for casinos and card rooms to cater for this number at a sitting. In a typical game, several players will have folded before the latter betting rounds, so the deck is rarely in danger of being exhausted during a single deal. This illustration represents the position after the initial deal when players receive three cards, two face down and one face up. Each has anted 10 chips to the pot and the compulsory bet (known as the 'bring-in bet') falls to player E, who possesses the lowest door card.

conservative players can generate plenty of betting action and large pots. The key to successful seven-card stud is, as ever, to monitor the ever-changing probabilities of receiving the card or cards needed to improve a hand by keeping a close eye on the up cards in play and those already folded during the game. Although difficult to master, seven-card stud maintains its appeal because it is a challenging game that rewards the dedicated application of all poker skills to an extent not replicated by draw poker or five-card stud.

NUMBER OF PLAYERS

Seven-card stud is a game for between two and eight players, with casinos and clubs limiting participation to the higher number, which is the most that can be accommodated using a single deck. Although players may receive up to seven cards, the prospect of the deck becoming exhausted during the play of a hand is remote, since some players can be expected to fold long before the seventh and final card – the river card – is dealt. In low-stakes home games, it is possible that more players will retain their interest in the pot for longer. Therefore, if there is likely to be pressure on the deck during a game of seven-card stud, it is advisable to restrict the number of players to seven at most.

Left: A player takes a look at his hole cards following the deal in a casino game. Note the care taken to restrict any possibility that an opponent might see them and so gain free information. Players can often be sat quite closely together at the table so shielding the cards in this fashion is recommended.

THE FINAL ROUND

Above: This illustrates a typical scene prior to the final betting round of a 25/50 fixed-limit game, with four players having a full complement of seven cards. As will be apparent, estimating what each player holds at this stage from the cards on display and their betting behaviour throughout is a major test of skill and observation. Player A, for example, could hold any value hand between a pair of eights and a Q-high straight flush in hearts. The potential of the hands belonging to players D and G is more easily recognized.

SEQUENCE OF PLAY

Assuming a fixed-limit game, all players typically ante a nominal sum, after which the dealer distributes the cards one at a time to each player in turn until they have three cards, two face down and one face up. After the first betting round, those remaining in the game receive a fourth card, face up, prior to the second round of betting. Further betting rounds ensue after the fifth and sixth cards are dealt, also face up, following which a seventh card is dealt face down to each remaining player. Anyone participating in the game to the showdown now has seven cards from which to make a five-card poker hand, four face up and three face down. The winner, as always, is the player who either makes a bet that is uncalled or who displays the best hand at the showdown once the fifth and final betting round has concluded.

THE ANTES AND THE DEAL

The size of the antes depends on the betting limits applied and the house rules in operation, but a figure approaching 20 per cent of the minimum betting level is quite normal. In a 50/100 fixed-limit game, the ante to be paid by each player will therefore be 10 chips. If seven-card stud is the only game to be played during a session, it is recommended that the dealer pays the antes for each player. This can help speed up the game

and nobody is disadvantaged as the deal circulates around the table one hand at a time. After the antes are in the pot, the dealer burns the top card and deals one card at a time to each player until they have three cards, the first two face down and the third, referred to as the door card, face up. At this point, the first round of betting is ready to commence.

EARLY BETTING ROUNDS

In seven-card stud, the player with the lowest-ranked first exposed card or 'up' card on the board (otherwise termed the door card) is obliged to make a bet known as the 'bring-in'. When two or more players possess the low card, the suits come into play on the only occasion in poker when they are ranked, with clubs counting lowest followed by diamonds, hearts and spades in ascending order of value. A 2c is lower than a 2d, which, in turn, is lower than a 2h. The size of bring-in may vary from one card room to another, but it is typically set at twice the size of the ante. If the ante is 10 chips, the bring-in is likely to be 20 chips, still below the level of the minimum bet. The betting continues clockwise around the table, with the player to the left of the bring-in next to act. This player may fold, call the bring-in or raise the betting to the minimum level for the first two rounds, which, continuing with the 50/100 fixed-limit example, would be 50 chips. If this occurs, it is known as

THE ANTES

Right: In this fixed-limit seven-card stud game, bets for the first two rounds are set at 50 chips before rising to 100 chips for the final three rounds. But first, all players must pay the ante of 10 chips before the cards are dealt. This immediately gives them a stake in what is initially a small pot but, with five betting rounds to go, this can be expected to grow substantially prior to a potential showdown.

'completing the bet' and sets the level for the rest of the round, with bets and raises now in denominations of 50 chips. From fourth street onwards, the first player to bet is the one who shows the best visible hand, and the option to check is available to all players if no bets are made. Also, as in five-card stud, if a player holds an open pair on fourth street, then betting during this round may be doubled to the higher limit – 100 chips in this case – by any player still contesting the hand. Holding the best visible cards does not always imply the best possible hand, but the number of cards to have been displayed at this stage should help players to assess their own chances of winning. Since players who fold will turn their up cards face down to confirm their decision, remembering the cards that have already been dealt is a skill that can help shape this assessment as the hand progresses.

PLAYABLE OPENING HANDS
♦ ♣ ♥ ♠

To win a pot in a full-handed, eight-player game of seven-card stud normally requires a hand of at least two pairs, with straights, flushes and full houses occurring frequently enough at the showdown to make them worth pursuing. It makes sense for players to conduct a quick assessment of their first three cards to determine the chances of making a potential winning hand. Having three of a kind is obviously beneficial, since this may be sufficient to win the pot without any further improvement. It also offers a player the chance to drive opponents holding potential flush and straight draws out of the game with some confident, aggressive betting. High-value pocket pairs (two cards of the same rank) are also worth playing, while other hands that warrant consideration in the early stages of the game are three-card flushes and open-ended three-card straights such as 8, 9, 10, for instance. It is possible for any starting hand to improve sufficiently to win, but the examples detailed here offer by far the best chances of success.

Left: The first three cards dealt in seven-card stud offer a range of opening hands that offer plausible chances of developing into winners. Any three of a kind, such as the three tens seen here, represents an immensely strong starting hand and could easily prove good enough to win even if it fails to improve.

THE DEAL

Left: This shows the position after the deal, with each player having received two cards face down and one – the door card – face up. The player with the lowest door card is now obliged to make a nominal bet known as the bring-in, which, in this case is set at 20 chips – double the ante. Player F, showing a 3h, is therefore compelled to open the betting, or bring it in, for 20 chips. Following player F's compulsory bet of 20 chips, the action moves clockwise around the table, beginning with player A. Players may fold, call the bring-in of 20 chips, or raise the bet to the stipulated minimum of 50 chips, this being known as completing the bet.

FIFTH STREET

The crucial point in seven-card stud for those still involved in the pot comes on fifth street, the moment when a fifth card is dealt to each player, face up, in readiness for the third round of betting. With just two cards to come, everyone should have a sound idea regarding the composition of their opponents' hands and whether or not it is worth continuing to bet against them. This decision is crucial because the betting typically increases on fifth street with the minimum bet for the final three rounds being twice that applicable during the first two. In general, any player who has already secured a high straight or better on fifth street will probably bet modestly to keep opponents interested. The time for a larger bet to build the pot comes on sixth street, when a player's sixth card is dealt and when those still needing cards to win are more likely to call.

INCREASED BETTING LIMITS

From a strategic point of view, this is usually the last moment in a fixed-limit game when a large bet or raise might induce opponents to fold, although this is difficult to achieve in a restrained, low-stakes affair. Although the minimum bet usually doubles on fifth street, anyone with a realistic chance of making a good hand is unlikely to fold in the face of a bet unless there are one or two raises to indicate that much better hands already exist. In pot-limit stud,

Right and above: Following the bring-in, player A calls for 20 chips before player B, with a pair of tens, completes the bet by putting in 50 chips. Players may call or raise in denominations of 50 chips. With the Ac showing, player C calls, as does player D; player E folds. If players F and A both call by adding a further 30 chips to make up the deficit, the first round will be over.

PLAYING A LEADING HAND
♦ ♣ ♥ ♠ ♣

Since most seven-card stud hands are not fully realized until at least the sixth card has been dealt, having a made hand on fifth street is obviously advantageous. A high-ranking straight or better will win around half the hands played in a seven-handed game featuring plenty of callers at the showdown. When holding such a hand it is therefore regarded as sensible to wait until the fourth betting round before making a raise, since those remaining in the pot are more likely to call for the final card, in hope as much as in expectation. The key for any player in a winning position, of course, is to make it costly for opponents to catch the cards they need, and timing such a move is also important in maximizing winning chances. Any player who holds a vulnerable leading hand such as two pairs or a low-ranking straight must consider betting on fifth street to eliminate some of the opposition and reduce the risk of being outdrawn by those with the apparent potential to do so. Should such a move not prove successful in eliminating the majority of opponents, it is usually advisable to sit tight and play the remaining rounds as cheaply as possible.

THE FIRST BETTING ROUND

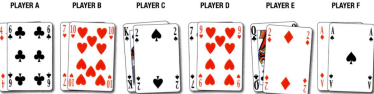

| PLAYER A | PLAYER B | PLAYER C | PLAYER D | PLAYER E | PLAYER F |

players are more inclined to try reducing the field with a big bet on fifth street, relative to the size of the pot. Bluffs and semi-bluffs are much more likely to succeed, especially when a player has three cards to a high-ranking straight or flush showing. A large bet on fifth street from someone in this position may cause opponents to fold potential winning hands because they are unwilling to risk calling even larger subsequent bets when they could already be beaten. Understandably, when the stakes are higher, players tend to be much more selective in which hands they support beyond fifth street.

POT MANAGEMENT

As in all poker games, managing the pot when holding a strong hand in seven-card stud needs a clear assessment of the opposition's visible cards and betting patterns. The style of game is important, since players are more likely to bet to the showdown with speculative hands in a low-stakes, fixed-limit game than they are in pot-limit stud, a game characterized by heavy betting in the closing rounds. Generally, the more players that continue beyond fifth street, the stronger the winning hand is likely to be. A player holding three of a kind or two pairs of high value will usually bet the maximum allowed to encourage those with straight and flush draws to fold.

If possessing a lock hand (a hand that cannot lose), or something close to it, then the strategy normally applied is to bet the minimum required to keep other players in the pot. This helps build the pot gradually by preventing players from receiving cards for free, as well as offering opponents a chance to improve their hand and yet still be trailing. If they do improve, they are more likely to call subsequent bets and raises which further increases the chance of winning a substantially inflated pot.

FOURTH STREET

PLAYER E

Above: Players F and A call the first-round bet, adding a further 30 chips each before the fourth card is dealt. Player C, showing the highest-value up cards, opens the second round by checking with a weak hand. With a pair of sevens, player D bets 50; player F raises, doubling the bet to 100 chips. Player A, who needs two cards for a flush or straight, calls for 100, along with player B, who holds a vulnerable pair of tens. Player C folds, D calls, and the round is over.

FIFTH STREET

PLAYER C

Above: As the fifth card is dealt, player B bets first as he has a pair of jacks, but checks as he cannot show a strong enough hand to drive others out, with the other two jacks already visible. Player D, holding two small pairs, also checks; player F, leading with two pairs of aces and threes, applies further pressure by betting 100. Player A, without a pair, folds. Both players B and D decide to call for 100.

CLOSING ROUNDS

At the completion of the third betting round on fifth street, each remaining player receives a sixth card, face up, and the option to bet passes to the player showing the top-ranked four-card hand. It is not unusual for half the players in a full-handed, fixed-limit game to remain involved at this stage, with every aim of betting to the end. Once the betting is complete, the dealer distributes a seventh and final card, face down, to those still participating. The final betting round then proceeds, with the option to bet, once again, falling to the player with the best visible hand.

SIXTH STREET

The betting action on sixth street depends on the nature of the game and the players involved. In an aggressive pot-limit game, it is rare for more than two players to be in opposition by the sixth card, while a fixed-limit variation is more likely to see three or four players still in contention. At this point, each player has four of their final seven

Right: Player F receives a 5s, face down, which does not improve his full house of threes over aces. Of more concern, both players B and D called when the three threes appeared, so from player F's perspective, player B could have a bigger full house if holding pocket tens, as could player D. Player F opens the betting and is raised by player B, who cannot beat player F's board cards, so can only win by a bluff. Player D folds.

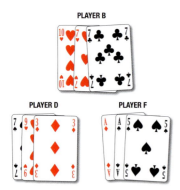

SIXTH STREET

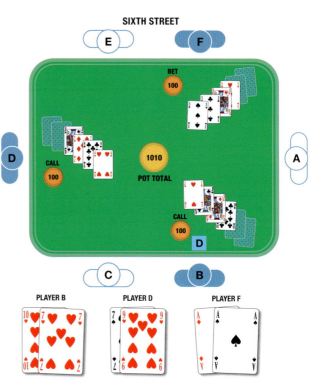

Above: The pot contains 1,010 chips which, with the minimum bet of 100, offers pot odds of 10 to 1. Player F is first to act as he has three threes and bets 100 chips. Players B and D know that player F cannot have another J for a full house, but must fear that the remaining 3 may be among their opponent's hole cards. If deducing that player F instead has a pocket pair for a made full house, both will realize that they may still draw a card for a better hand. One of the two unseen tens will help player B, while player D requires either a 7 or a 9 for a full house.

SEVENTH STREET

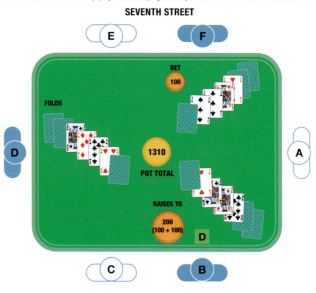

cards face up on the table. In conjunction with the betting patterns they have already exhibited in the previous three rounds, this information offers clues as to the hands each player holds or is hoping to obtain. Having three or four cards of one suit suggests a flush, while someone betting with a four-card straight in view is indicating that the hand is completed by one of their pocket cards. The value of having the strength of one's hand disguised amid those pocket cards, especially with a further down card to come, is thus underlined.

SEVENTH STREET

The seventh and final card is dealt face down to each player once the fourth betting round is complete, providing those still in the hand with three cards face down and four face up. In terms of strategy, a couple of simple guidelines apply during the final betting round, since certain situations can be expected to recur. Players holding an obvious winning hand should bet, particularly if it uses two or all three down cards. Opponents who have played to the showdown will often call with hands that have improved but are inferior.

By contrast, when the strength of a potential winning hand is clearly visible from the up cards, then a bet is rarely advised. An opponent who cannot beat the hand at the showdown will fold, so there is nothing further to be gained from the pot. Someone who can readily beat it will probably raise in the face of a bet, perhaps triggering a reluctant and costly call only to confirm possession of the second-best hand. The problem here is that it is easy for a player to feel justified in calling given the amount committed to the pot. Also, even though the call may be made in expectation of defeat, it can seem a small price to pay just to be certain that an opponent who re-raises a bet on the river is not bluffing.

SIMILAR VARIATIONS

The huge popularity of seven-card stud has given rise to variations that are as challenging as the original. English stud poker follows the structure of seven-card stud as far as fifth street. For the final two rounds, however, players may draw a replacement card from the deck with an up card replaced face up, and a down card replaced face down. More popular variations include the low only game, known as razz, and the high-low, split-pot seven-card stud games, of which there are several. In all cases, straights and flushes are discounted in compiling a low hand with A, 2, 3, 4, 5 – a wheel – the lowest hand attainable. In the split-pot variation, this hand would have a sound chance of winning both high and low to scoop the pot.

PLAYING A DRAWING HAND
♦ ♣ ♥ ♠

A drawing hand in poker is one where a player needs a specific card to complete a legitimate poker hand – four-card straights and flushes are typical examples. A player in this position, with two cards to come, in seven-card stud, will hope to pay the minimum for the chance to catch the card. With two rounds of betting to negotiate, this will be a severe test of skill. In limit poker, players will check or merely call an opponent's bet, rather than raise in this scenario. It is essential to avoid 'drawing dead', which occurs when a player tries drawing a hand that, if obtained, still cannot win.

THE SHOWDOWN

Above: Player B's attempted bluff failed as player F called the raise of an extra 100 chips after player D, with only two pairs, folded. As the betting is now concluded, players B and F expose their seven cards and reveal their poker hands, with player F's full house of threes over aces outranking player B's two pairs, jacks and tens, to claim the pot worth 1,710 chips.

TEXAS HOLD 'EM

Texas Hold 'em, often referred to simply as Hold 'em, is currently the most widely played of all poker variations, having surpassed seven-card stud as the game of choice. This situation has arisen as a direct consequence of the game's exposure on television, which has managed to exploit the entertainment value presented by top-class tournament players in action. Almost invariably, televised poker features no-limit Texas Hold 'em, which lends itself extremely well to the medium and is recognized by professionals as the most demanding of poker games. At a lower level, Texas Hold 'em is played for fixed limits and low stakes, which, naturally, helps maintain the amateur player's interest in a game regarded as simple to learn, but difficult to master.

ORIGINS OF THE GAME

Following the development of stud poker, Texas Hold 'em was one of a number of games that utilized community cards, dealt face up on the table, that could be used by all players to make their respective poker hands. One of the first such community card games was termed 'wild widow' and this gave rise to usage of the word 'widow' to describe the common cards on the table that are available to all. Since players ultimately have seven cards from which to choose their best five, it is accepted that Texas Hold 'em is also a variant of seven-card stud. The game emanated from the southern states of the USA, possibly originating in Robstown, Texas, at the turn of the 20th century, before reaching Dallas around 1925. Hugely popular with southern professionals, it naturally spread to Las Vegas, where, in its fixed-limit guise, it was shaded by seven-card stud in terms of popularity. Then, in 1971, Benny Binion decided that the WSOP World Championship should be a knockout tournament and, with the approval of the experienced players who entered, no-limit Texas Hold 'em was chosen for the main event. From that point onwards, the expansion in tournament play, allied to the volatile characteristics of the game, ensured that Texas Hold 'em maintained its place in the public eye.

Above: A sizeable pot is at stake in this Texas Hold 'em game as the showdown reveals the dealer has made the best possible hand – the nuts – on the river as the ten gives him a royal flush. This outcome is highly improbable, but a hand like this may well be encountered at some stage in a long poker career.

Below: Recognizing the best hand available is crucial in forming a viable Hold 'em strategy. Here, with all five board cards revealed, a 5-high straight would constitute 'the nuts', meaning that a player holding 4, 5 as pocket cards could bet knowing that the hand was unbeatable.

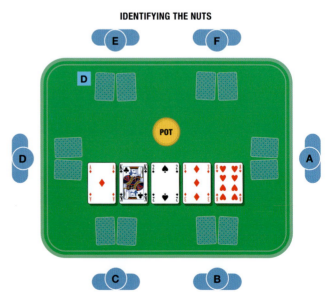

IDENTIFYING THE NUTS

NUMBER OF PLAYERS

Since players are dealt just two cards each, it is feasible to accommodate as many as 20 people in a game. In truth, such a number renders it almost impossible to manage. Clubs and casinos generally limit participants to a maximum of ten, which, even in a tight and cautious game, will create plenty of betting action. Any number between two and ten players can enjoy a competitive game. As with all poker variations, the average value of the winning hand decreases, the fewer players are involved. Consequently, in a full-handed Hold 'em game, this being one featuring the accepted maximum of nine or ten players, a patient and conservative approach is usually recommended. This is particularly the case in cash games when players should expect to fold well over half their hands before the flop. When the game is 'short-handed' with five or fewer players in competition, it is more likely that the betting action will be loose, as players gamble a little more freely in support of marginal hands and bluffs.

Above right: Players receive just two cards in Texas Hold 'em, not much upon which to base the first serious betting decision. A pocket pair represents one of the strongest of the 169 possible two-card combinations that could be dealt, pocket aces most of all. Conversely, holding a hand of 7, 2 'offsuit' (of differing suits), is usually a prelude to folding at the first opportunity.

Right: The value of the nuts changes with each hand, with an A-high flush in hearts being the best possible hand in this example. Anyone holding an A-high straight, by virtue of holding any A and 10, would be concerned at the possibility of an opponent holding a flush. With no pair on board, a full house is impossible.

THE NUTS
♦ ♣ ♥ ♠

A player who holds an unbeatable hand during a poker game is said to hold 'the nuts' or a 'lock hand'. This is advantageous since it allows the player to focus his or her attention on building the pot without fear of losing the hand. In the many open poker variations in which several cards are exposed during play, determining the nuts and the likelihood of someone holding the best possible hand available is therefore a crucial factor when considering whether to bet. According to folklore, the term emanates from the Wild West era, when players were supposedly inclined to bet their wagons and horses on the outcome of a hand. To underline the integrity of such a bet and the strength of belief behind it, the nuts from the wagon wheels would be placed in the pot, a tactic considered inconceivable without possession of an unbeatable hand.

IDENTIFYING THE NUTS

SEQUENCE OF PLAY

To begin the game, each player is dealt two cards face down, these being referred to as 'hole' or 'pocket' cards. A round of betting ensues before the dealer reveals three cards, face up, on the table. This is called the 'flop'. Following the flop, a second betting round occurs and then a fourth card – the 'turn' – is dealt, after which there is further betting. The fifth and final card, known as the 'river', is revealed by the dealer prior to the last round of betting. The objective is to make the best five-card poker hand possible from their two hole cards and the five community cards on the table. Players may discount their hole cards entirely when finalizing their hand, in which case they are said to be 'playing the board', their hand comprising now all five community cards.

THE DEAL AND THE BLINDS

Prior to the deal, the two players to the dealer's left must make compulsory bets, known as 'posting the blinds'. The first player bets the 'small blind', usually set at half the minimum stake of the opening betting round, while the second player makes a full bet known as the 'big blind'.

As the deal moves clockwise around the table, each player faces the prospect of making these forced bets. The deal itself sees players receive two cards each, face down, prior to making their first betting decision. After the blinds, the next player to act may fold, call the big blind or raise. Players cannot check in this round, since the betting has already been opened, courtesy of the blinds. If the betting has not been raised by the time the action returns to the players in the blinds, they may raise if they wish. Although the blinds have late betting positions in the pre-flop betting round, this early advantage is lost after the flop when they will be the first players to act.

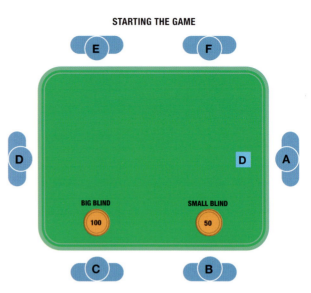

STARTING THE GAME

Above: To start the game, the players to the immediate left of the dealer must post the blinds. Here, the small blind is set at 50 chips, while the big blind is 100 chips, the set level for a bet in the first two rounds of this game, which is a 100/200 fixed-limit example. The dealer is indicated by the dealer button that moves one place to the left after each hand.

Left: A button used to indicate which player is obliged to pay the small blind, a compulsory bet that is paid by the first player to the dealer's left. As the first to act in all betting rounds following the flop, the player in the small blind should be cautious when choosing whether to call any substantial pre-flop bets made by opponents. To do so usually requires possession of a strong starting hand.

IMPORTANCE OF POSITION
♦ ♣ ♥ ♠

In Texas Hold 'em, a player's position relative to the dealer is a crucial factor in any betting decision, since the earlier a player is required to bet during a round, the less information there is to help shape that decision. The dealer, as last to act, has a distinct advantage, because the checks, bets or raises made by opponents can all be taken into account when the time comes to act. Typically, players in early positions are best advised to support only premium hands, while those in the later betting positions may take more chances with poorer quality hands, particularly if the betting is light.

STARTING HANDS

Judging which starting hands to support is crucial in Texas Hold 'em, as each player initially receives just two cards. Any two can win, but being dealt high-ranking cards or a pair is advantageous. High pocket pairs such as aces, kings or queens are strong enough to take the pot at the showdown without help from the board. They are not invincible starting hands, so players holding them often raise the betting before the flop to drive out weaker hands that retain a chance of improving sufficiently to win.

STARTING HANDS
♦ ♣ ♥ ♠

There are 169 possible starting hand combinations in Hold 'em: the most valued are the high pairs of aces, kings and queens. Also strong are the unpaired holdings of A, K; A, Q and A, J, especially if of the same suit. Players with such hands will often raise the betting before the flop to encourage players with weaker hands to fold, thus strengthening their grip on the pot.

PRE-FLOP BETTING

Strategies for betting before the flop vary. In a fixed-limit game for small stakes, many players will pay to see the flop, irrespective of their hole cards, hoping to improve their hands. At the other extreme, high-stakes Texas Hold 'em characteristically sees most hands folded before the flop, especially in the face of the first substantial bet. A player raising the maximum infers possession of a premium hand. Calling such bets in a high-stakes game is risky, unless the caller also holds a viable hand with good chances of improvement.

Right: Once the cards have been dealt, player D folds before player E raises with a strong hand, doubling the bet to 200 chips. Player F folds another weak hand and the dealer calls the 200 with K, Q offsuit. After player B sacrifices the small blind of 50 chips by folding, player C in the big blind calls the raise, by adding 100 chips.

THE DEAL

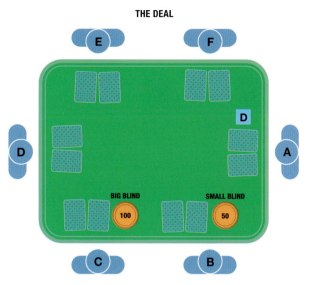

Above: Players receive two cards each from the dealer and must base their initial betting decisions on these alone. Estimating the value of a starting hand based on the likelihood of it proving successful is therefore essential. Here, player E's pair of tens and player C's A, Q suited represent strong hands worthy of support. Player A's K, Q offsuit is not as valuable as it might appear, while the remaining hands are uniformly poor.

PRE-FLOP BETTING

THE FLOP

After the flop, each player is able to see five of the seven cards from which they might ultimately make their respective hands, these being their two hole cards plus the three community cards on the table. This is the key point in the game, as players can visualize the best hand they might achieve if participating in the showdown and, most importantly, assess whether this is likely to prove a winner. Continuing in the game beyond the flop, though, not only depends on the value of the cards, but on the action at the table as the betting round proceeds.

BETTING ON THE FLOP

The player to the dealer's left is first to act and may fold, check or bet. Should all players check, the turn card is dealt, becoming what is known as a 'free' card since nobody has paid to see it. Any post-flop betting strategy must take account of several factors, including a player's position, the betting structure in operation and the number of opponents still in contention. The scale of bets made before the flop also needs to be considered. A raise is usually indicative of a strong two-card holding, particularly if emanating from a player in an early position. For example if a flop comprises As, Ad, Kc and a pre-flop raiser bets again, a natural assumption would be that the player holds an A, a K or possibly both as hole cards. Even an opponent holding a pair of kings for a full house of kings over aces, a very powerful hand, might baulk at calling, for fear of trailing a bigger full house of aces over kings, or possibly even four aces.

Right: Since player C has a good chance of hitting an A-high straight or flush, a bet of 100 tests the strength of the opposition. Player E is leading and calls when another raise may have been in order to emphasize a strong hand. Player A is content simply to call.

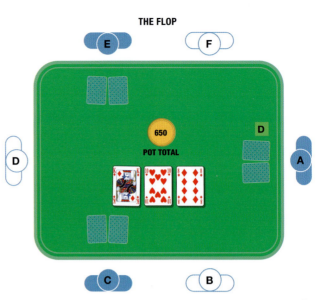

Above: Following the flop, player A as last to act may be confident with the top pair of kings. The flop offers a chance for progress to player C's hand with a better than even-money chance that a straight or a flush will materialize on the next two cards. Player E is leading with three tens.

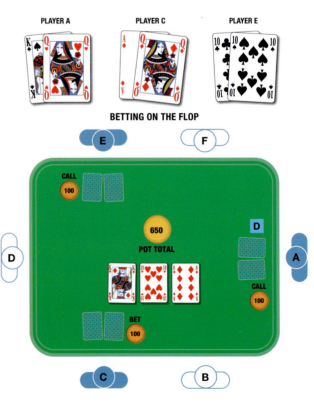

LEADING HANDS

It is rare in Texas Hold 'em for the flop to provide a player with an unbeatable hand, but the flop will normally clarify whether a player possesses a hand that is currently leading. A player holding Kd, Kh when the flop comes Kc, Qs, 6h, would be in a commanding position with three of a kind and a probable winning hand, but danger might still exist if an opponent holds Js, 10s. Needing an A or a 9 for a straight, and with an outside chance of making a flush, such a hand is tempting enough to warrant support. Under these conditions, therefore, it makes sense for the holder of a leading hand to bet, forcing those with 'drawing hands' – those needing a specific card to complete a legitimate poker hand – to pay dearly for their next card. By contrast, when holding a leading hand on the flop that looks unlikely to be beaten, it generally pays to bet lightly, to encourage opponents to stay in the game. Such a strategy conceals the strength of the hand and helps to inflate the pot, thus increasing potential winnings.

DRAWING HANDS

Hands in which a player needs one more card on either the turn or the river in order to improve to a winning position are called drawing hands. Typically, this involves players seeking straights or flushes as these are consistent winners in Texas Hold 'em. Adopting the correct strategy in this situation depends on the probability of hitting a relevant card and the cost of staying in the game, making an awareness of pot odds essential. When the odds against drawing a required card exceed the pot odds available, it is prudent to fold, but if the reverse is true, then it is advisable to stay in the game. Overall, drawing hands are generally pursued only if the cost of doing so is relatively small.

Right: A player with pocket aces peeks at his hole cards once again after the flop to confirm possession of four aces. The hand is definitely guaranteed to win meaning that the player can focus on trying to keep as many opponents involved as possible in order to swell the pot and make a profitable outcome.

THE SIGNIFICANCE OF POT ODDS
♦ ♣ ♥ ♠

Being able to calculate the number of cards that might help a drawing hand or hurt a leading hand is an essential poker skill. It helps a player to distinguish whether the odds of reward for making a bet are justified or not. For example a player who is trailing after the flop may recognize that hitting any one of five cards on the turn or the river will guarantee a winning hand. The odds against this occurring are 4 to 1, so, in this situation, a bet would normally be considered only when the total in the pot offers odds of 4 to 1 or better.

LEADING HANDS AND DRAWING HANDS

Above: In strategic terms, when possessing a leading hand such as the three tens held by player E here, it is generally advisable to bet, forcing those with drawing hands to pay for the privilege of seeing more cards. Conversely, when in player C's position, the usual strategy is to stay in the game as cheaply as possible until or unless a favourable card appears on the turn or the river.

THE TURN AND THE RIVER

In a typical Texas Hold 'em game, the minimum bet doubles after the turn card has been revealed. Those players who continue betting beyond the flop can therefore be assumed to have a reasonable chance of securing the best hand, since the cost of playing has risen. With just one more card to come, identifying the best hand available from the cards in play and estimating the possible hands held by other players is a straightforward task. However, it is also true that a player needs to be realistic in assessing the chances of obtaining a winning hand. This is particularly the case in pot-limit and no-limit Hold 'em, when the scale of the betting tends to increase dramatically in the last two rounds, making it potentially expensive if frequently calling with the second-best hand. Should two or more players match bets after the turn card is exposed, then the dealer reveals the river card, this being the fifth community card on the table and the catalyst for the last round of betting.

THE TURN

Above: The turn card (Kh) has now been revealed, and, with 950 chips already in the pot, the bets and raises in this fixed-limit game are now set at 200 chips each. Player E leads with a full house of tens over kings, while player A has improved to three kings but is still trailing.

PLAYER A **PLAYER C** **PLAYER E**

BETTING ON THE TURN

Above: Having failed to make a straight or a flush, player C checks at this stage. Player E bets 200 chips, indicating that the two kings on the board seem to bear no threat, and player A calls because trip kings is ordinarily a very strong hand in Texas Hold 'em. At this, player C folds, since neither a straight nor a flush will beat the full house that players A and E may possess.

POT MANAGEMENT
♦ ♣ ♥ ♠

Of all the skills common to good poker players, being adept at pot management is one of the most crucial. This means betting in a way that maximizes winning opportunities when holding good cards, but moderating potential losses when holding poor cards. For instance, when possessing a pocket pair in Hold 'em which is matched by a card on the flop to make three of a kind, a large bet might persuade opponents to fold. Since such a hand will usually win, try to build the pot with a minimum bet or a small raise, to keep other players involved.

FINAL BETTING ROUND

At this point in the game, all remaining players can adjudicate their poker hands from the seven cards available to them. Once more, the first active player to the dealer's left has the option to fold, check or bet after the river card has been dealt. If all players check, the winner is determined by a showdown, which also occurs if a player makes a bet that is called by at least one opponent. In terms of strategy, decisions during the final betting round are few. A player holding a powerful hand, if not the nuts, should be aiming to extract as much as possible from opponents who, having sustained their interest to the river card, will often have hands sufficiently strong to tempt them into calling a bet. If the river card does not help a player's hand and an opponent makes a maximum bet, it is often sensible to fold, irrespective of how many chips the player has contributed to the pot already. Above all, the single most important factor to remember in widow games like Hold 'em is that any community card that improves one player's hand may strengthen that of an opponent to an even greater degree.

PLAYING THE BOARD

Occasionally, players who bet through to the river will find that the best poker hand they can make comprises the five community cards alone, their hole cards proving redundant in terms of improving their hand. When this is the case players are said to be 'playing the board'. This is generally a weak position to be in, but, since a player's hole cards are unknown to opponents, it is still possible to bluff at this point in the game, should the opportunity arise. Indeed, for players faced with such a situation, bluffing is normally the only means of claiming the pot, although this should only be contemplated when a player detects weakness in an opponent's hand.

THE RIVER

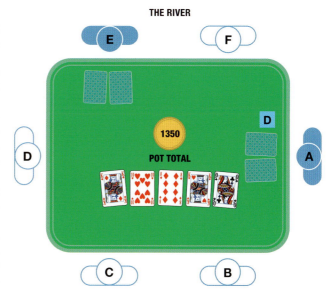

Above: Unluckily for player E, one of only four cards remaining in the deck that could help player A to improve to a winning position has materialized on the river, the Qc now providing player A with a superior full house of kings over queens. This shows how Hold 'em hands can quickly change in value and explains why players with leading hands after the flop often bet aggressively to prevent situations such as this from arising.

THE SHOWDOWN

Above: Player E bets 200 chips in the belief that player A may have three kings but not a full house. But player A has a superior hand and calls to claim the pot of 1,750 chips at the showdown. However, by calling rather than raising, player A misses an opportunity to exploit an unbeatable hand since a raise may have prompted player E to call and so lose even more chips.

OMAHA

This poker variation is one of the more recent examples to have captured the imagination of players, with references to the game almost non-existent prior to 1980, after which it started appearing in the card rooms of Las Vegas. Now it is one of the more popular forms of online poker, regarded as ideal for social players who enjoy a game with loose betting action and high-value winning hands. Although similar to Texas Hold 'em in terms of its betting structure and pattern of play, Omaha differs from its close poker relation in two key respects. First, players are dealt four cards to begin the game instead of two, and they are required to use two, and only two, of their hole cards, with three from the board to make their hands. These differences have a profound effect on the nature of the game. Players experienced in Texas Hold 'em, in which the average winning hand is much lower, sometimes take time to adjust their strategic thinking.

ORIGINS OF THE GAME

Occasionally referred to as Omaha Hold 'em, the game, unsurprisingly, emanates from Nebraska. According to Bob Ciaffone, author of *Omaha Hold'em Poker*, it was normal for players in Omaha to insist that a legitimate Texas Hold 'em hand must include both hole cards and three community cards. This concept was retained in the new variation, where players receive four hole cards, from which any two must form part of their final poker hand. The game first appeared at the WSOP in 1983, when professional gambler and poker theorist David Sklansky won the US$1,000 fixed-limit Omaha contest, taking the first prize of US$25,500. Since

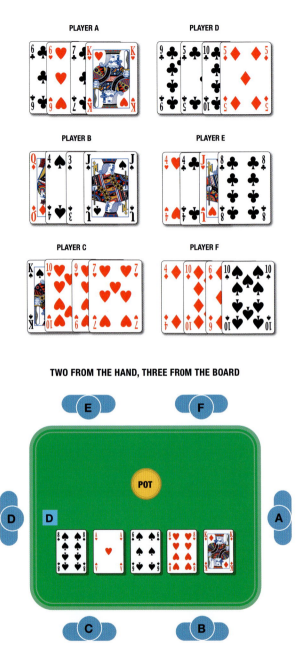

PLAYER A   **PLAYER D**

PLAYER B   **PLAYER E**

PLAYER C   **PLAYER F**

TWO FROM THE HAND, THREE FROM THE BOARD

Above: To form a viable hand in Omaha, players must use two of their pocket cards and three from the board. In this instance, player A makes the winning hand of a full house, sixes over eights, by combining the pocket sixes with the 6 and pair of eights on the board. The apparent full house of sixes over kings is not permissible because this would use three pocket cards and just two board cards. Player B has only a pair of eights since the J-high flush in spades would also require three pocket cards, while player C is similarly unable to make a legitimate straight or flush from what is available.

then, Omaha has become an established part of the poker scene, with a high-low, split-pot variation also having evolved.

NUMBER OF PLAYERS

Between two and ten people can play the game, with card rooms and casinos inclined to cater for the maximum. Some simple arithmetic will confirm that a full-handed, ten-player game will see virtually the whole deck in play during each hand. Since the game is characterized by plenty of calling but little raising before the flop, especially within a fixed-limit betting structure, the number of cards in circulation almost guarantees high-value winning hands. Straights or better win in the majority of cases and players can assume that if the board suggests that a bigger hand than theirs is possible, then an opponent will probably already have it. Poker theorists maintain that success at Omaha is simply a case of finding a lock hand, or the nuts. Only when holding the best possible hand, or facing favourable pot odds in trying to draw to it, should a player consider betting.

LEGITIMATE HANDS

The crucial difference between Omaha and Texas Hold 'em is that players must combine two of their hole cards with three from the board to form their poker hand. Experienced Hold 'em players who are unfamiliar with Omaha sometimes forget this ruling. One of the key implications is that being dealt three or four of a kind is counterproductive, since only two of those cards will be used in the final reckoning. Similarly, holding any four cards of the same suit offers little advantage in securing a flush, since two of the hole cards are redundant and the chances of seeing three more of that suit among the community cards are greatly reduced.

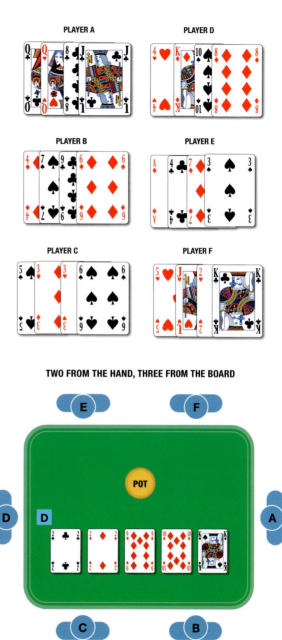

TWO FROM THE HAND, THREE FROM THE BOARD

Above: In this example, player C has the weakest hand, with just two pairs, threes and twos, while the K-high straight held by player A is only fifth best. Players B, D and E are all able to use the three diamonds on the board, with two in their hand, to make flushes, but player E holds the A, 7 of diamonds for the best of these. However, to underline the typically high value of winning hands in Omaha, player F's full house of twos over kings is the best of the six hands dealt.

SEQUENCE OF PLAY

In Omaha, the action begins with the small blind and big blind being posted by the players to the dealer's immediate left, as with Texas Hold 'em. The dealer then deals the cards one at a time to each player, clockwise around the table until everyone has four cards face down prior to the first betting round. The dealer then reveals the flop: three cards face up on the table, which all players can use towards finalizing their hand. A second betting round then takes place, after which the turn card is dealt. Betting limits usually double at this stage of the game, and, following a third betting round, the river card is revealed. This acts as a prelude to the final round of betting. The winner is the player who either makes an unmatched bet during the game or holds the best poker hand at the showdown, comprising exactly two hole cards and three from the board.

THE BLINDS AND THE DEAL

Rather than having every player ante before the deal, Omaha mimics Texas Hold 'em in that the compulsory bets are confined to the two players to the left of the dealer. The first bets the small blind, normally half the minimum stake unit for the first betting round, while the next player must pay the big blind, which is equivalent to a full bet. In a 50/100 fixed-limit game, therefore, the small blind would be 25 chips and the big blind 50. The dealer burns the top card before dealing four cards face down to each player. These hole or pocket cards should be kept hidden from opponents during play.

PLAYABLE OPENING HANDS

As always, the first crucial element of the game comes when players are dealt their opening four cards. Only two of

THE BLINDS AND THE DEAL

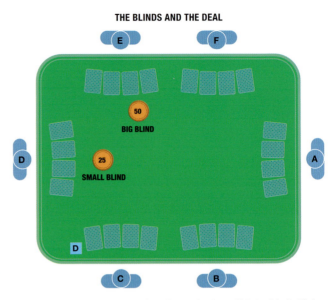

Above: As player C is the dealer, players D and E have to bet the small blind and the big blind, since they are the two players to the dealer's immediate left. This example features a 50/100 fixed-limit Omaha game, so the blinds are set at 25 and 50 chips, respectively. After the blinds have been posted, the cards are dealt one at a time to each player clockwise around the table, beginning with player D, until all players have four cards face down. These are their hole or pocket cards and should remain unseen by opponents.

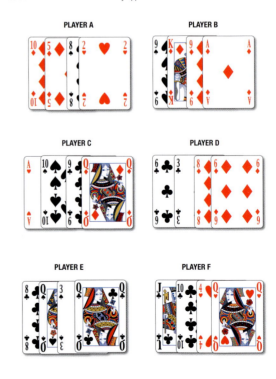

these may be used in forming the eventual hand, but these four cards offer six different combinations of two cards each. The key to successful Omaha play is to recognize when any one of these six two-card combinations may blend with the board cards to provide a winning hand. For example, while high pocket pairs are much less valuable than in Hold 'em, having Ad, As, Kd, Ks is beneficial for several reasons. Should any A or K appear on the flop, the chances of hitting a full house are greatly increased, particularly considering that there is a 50 per cent chance a pair of a lower value will materialize among the five board cards. If the board contains three diamonds or three spades, then the best possible flush would be held, and if any Q, J, 10 should appear, then the player will secure the high straight. The key, therefore, is to support only those opening hands in which four, five or all six two-card combinations offer genuine chances of blending with the board to create a winning hand.

THE FLOP

Once the pre-flop betting round is complete, the dealer burns the top card and reveals the next three cards from the deck, face up in the centre of the table. Since seven cards are available to each player at this point, they should have a clear idea of the best possible hand they can attain and, most importantly, whether this is likely to prove good enough to win. The first player to bet after the flop is the one to the dealer's left, whose options are to check, to bet or to fold. The action then continues clockwise around the table in the usual fashion, as each active player in turn decides whether to remain in the hand or drop out. Should all players check, the dealer reveals the turn card prior to the next betting round.

THE FLOP

Above: All six players called the bet of 50 chips before seeing the flop, generating a pot of 300 chips. The flop itself shows the K, 2 and 4 of clubs, making K-high flushes for players D, E and F. All three have two clubs amid their pocket cards, with player E currently best at this stage by virtue of the Qc. Players A and C have little or no chance of beating a flush, rendering their own prospects of winning remote. Player B, meanwhile, has an outside chance of securing a full house.

Left: A button to help signify that the second player to the dealer's left is compelled to bet the big blind. In Omaha, as in Texas Hold 'em, the big blind is normally the same as the minimum bet for the first two rounds of betting. In a 50/100 game therefore, the big blind will be a compulsory bet of 50 chips.

PRE-FLOP BETTING
♦ ♣ ♥ ♠

In a full-handed game, it is unusual for players to bet aggressively in order to reduce the field before the flop. Few initial holdings are powerful enough to justify a pre-flop raise, which is, in any case, unlikely to eliminate a sufficient number of opponents to greatly help matters. Even the most unpromising of hole cards may ultimately combine with the board cards to produce a strong hand, this being one of the game's most appealing characteristics. Consequently, pre-flop betting is often restrained, with several players calling to see what develops. The net result of this is an increase in the size of the pot and therefore improved pot odds for those still involved as the game unfolds.

THE TURN AND THE RIVER

Following the second round of betting, the dealer reveals the turn card, having previously discarded, or burned, the top card from the deck once again. Typically, the betting limits double at this stage, so any player who has yet to hit the nuts or who has little prospect of doing so should realistically consider folding. The game itself becomes simpler to analyse, however, since players are readily able to identify the likely winning hand and whether they have a chance of obtaining it. In fixed-limit Omaha, betting on the turn to ward off those with drawing hands is rarely successful, although in pot-limit games, this is the moment when those already holding strong but not unbeatable hands will try to exert pressure with pot-sized bets. Once the third-round betting has concluded, the dealer reveals the river card and the final betting round occurs prior to the showdown. The player with the best poker hand comprising two hole cards and three from the board wins the pot. Alternatively, the pot can be won earlier in the game if a player should make a bet that is not called by opponents.

Right: After the turn card, all players decide to check and so the river card, the 5d, is revealed by the dealer, with the pot total remaining at 500 chips. Player D rightly suspects that the low flush comprising Kc, 6c, 4c, 3c, 2c is beaten by either a higher flush or a full house, and checks. Player E holds the best hand, but knows it is not the best possible – the nuts – and also checks. Player F bets 100 chips, the minimum bet having increased for the last two rounds, following which, players B and D fold.

THE TURN

Above: After player D bets 50 chips in support of the flush, players E, F and B call to boost the pot to 500 chips. Players A and C fold. The turn card is revealed as the Ks, giving player B three of a kind and a chance of a full house should an A or 9 appear. Player E's flush is leading.

THE RIVER

PLAYER B	PLAYER D	PLAYER E	PLAYER F

IDENTIFYING THE NUTS

As mentioned earlier, experienced poker players regard Omaha as a game that is consistently won by the player holding the nuts. With this in mind, recognizing the best possible hand available at each stage of the game is an essential skill that can help guard against the costly error of calling with the second-best hand. For example, when a pair appears on the flop, it is highly likely that one or more full houses will already have been secured. Pursuing a flush in this situation is therefore pointless and even drawing for further cards to obtain the best possible full house – known as the nut full house – offers only a 50 per cent chance of success. With no pair on the flop but two or three cards of the same suit evident, then players may assume that a flush is the likeliest winning hand, immediately devaluing any potential for hitting a straight.

OMAHA HIGH-LOW, EIGHT OR BETTER

Evidence of the flexibility of poker and the enthusiasm among players for devising new forms of the game comes in the shape of Omaha high-low, eight or better, a split-pot variation that is arguably more popular than high-only Omaha. The pattern of play is the same, as governed by whichever betting structure is in place, but the pot is divided between the holders of the best high hand and the best low hand. To qualify for the best low hand, however, players must have all five cards of the relevant hand ranked 8 or lower. Also, in compiling a low hand, players can disregard straights and flushes, making the nut low hand a straight of A, 2, 3, 4, 5, known in the game as a 'wheel' or a 'bicycle'. A 5-high straight flush, therefore, could conceivably provide a player with the best low hand and the best high hand simultaneously. This represents the ideal situation, since a player who wins both high and low scoops the pot by taking all the chips bet during the hand. Should no low hand qualify for a share of the pot during a game, the winning high hand takes the entire pot. One of the factors that makes this game so appealing is that, with some players chasing high hands and others aiming low, pots can become so large that even winning a half share represents a good result. However, players need to avoid 'quartering' the pot by tying a hand, either high or low, as the half share of the total pot on offer will be divided in half again.

STRAIGHTS, FLUSHES AND FULL HOUSES
♦ ♣ ♥ ♠

The reason why Omaha is considered a game of straights, flushes and full houses becomes clear when examining statistical facts about the likely composition of the board cards, sometimes referred to as the widow. Half of the time, at least one pair will appear and, when this occurs, a full house or better will be held by someone on two out of every three occasions in a full-handed game. Similarly, the board will contain three or more cards to a flush, 40 per cent of the time, with the result that a flush will be present on around nine out of ten occasions. Seeing three cards on the board that help fill a straight occurs 80 per cent of the time, which, with so many combinations possible among the players' pocket cards, makes a straight almost as likely.

THE SHOWDOWN

Above: Following player F's bet, player E reluctantly calls for 100 chips, despite knowing that the hand could be beaten by a higher flush, a full house or even four kings. At the showdown, the players reveal their cards and player E's Qc proves decisive in securing the pot of 700 chips, with a higher value K-high flush in clubs than that of player F.

POKER STRATEGY

HAVING AN EXCELLENT GRASP OF THE GAME BEING PLAYED AND A STRONG HAND WILL GIVE PLAYERS THE BEST CHANCE OF SUCCESS. CLUES CAN ALSO BE GATHERED FROM OBSERVING OPPONENTS AND READING CARDS.

The various different poker games that have developed over the past two centuries have given rise to many theories regarding poker strategy. To an extent, many of these are extrapolated from the mathematics behind the game, since, with a single deck in use there is always a finite number of possibilities at work, however large. Yet poker is played by and against people, which gives rise to a host of other factors that have to be taken into account when assessing the chances of winning a hand, securing a profitable session, or emerging triumphant from a tournament. The style of the game being played, the betting structure in operation and the stake levels applicable will all influence a player's decisions, as will the characteristics of the opponents themselves. This chapter focuses on the five standard forms of poker, high-only, and outlines some of the key factors that newcomers and experienced recreational players alike must consider if they are intent on improving their poker-playing skills.

Right: A player commits his remaining chips to the pot by betting 'all-in'. This move is a familiar sight to those who have seen poker on television, which almost invariably features no-limit Texas Hold 'em, a game in which players may risk all their chips on a single hand whenever it is their turn to bet.

DRAW POKER

Draw poker begins with all players contributing an ante to the pot. Working clockwise, the dealer deals one card at a time face down until each player has five cards. The option to open the betting falls upon the player to the dealer's left, but only if holding a hand that has a pair of jacks or better. If not, the option moves around the table until someone with a qualifying hand commits chips to the pot. After the first betting round, players may discard up to three unwanted cards and replace them with others from the deck. After the draw, a second round of betting ensues, the first player to act being the player who opened the first betting round. If two or more players match bets in this round, the game ends with the showdown when they reveal their cards to identify who has the winning poker hand. The pot may also be claimed if, during either the first or second round of betting, a player makes a bet and the opponents all fold.

Above: A typical range of hands after the deal in a six-player game where player A is dealer. Players B and C cannot open the betting since their hands do not qualify, but player D can with the pair of kings. A two-card draw for a flush is unlikely to be successful, so player D should keep the kings and discard the other three which are not high enough. Player E has no pair and should fold. Player F could raise any opening bet and take the pot now with two pairs, aces up. A call is safe, as the odds are against anyone improving enough to beat the hand. Betting should prompt players A and B to fold but player C could call to draw one card to a straight – either an A or a 9 will do.

As the original poker variation, draw poker was initially played as a no-limit betting game, which made it suitable as a gambling medium for the wealthy and those who possessed an uncanny ability to bluff. The imposition of limits on the betting broadened the game's appeal, while the adoption of rules governing who opened the betting for each hand further transformed draw poker. With the advent of jackpots, the variation in which a player who opens the betting must possess a pair of jacks or better, draw poker became a much more mechanical game that rewarded sound strategic play. Although still popular in California's card rooms, where for nearly a century it has been the only poker game permitted by law, elsewhere, draw poker has diminished in significance compared to seven-card stud and Texas Hold 'em. Nevertheless, the game provides a solid foundation upon which beginners can gradually expand their poker knowledge, it being the first form of poker most people learn to play. Online poker sites that feature draw poker host games without the requirement for opening the betting with a pair of jacks or better. As such, this deprives players of one of the elements essential to formulating a strategy, namely the certain knowledge that one opponent holds at least a pair of jacks. For this reason, attention here will be focused on jackpots, the draw poker variation that invokes the opening requirement and in which the draw is limited to three cards.

STARTING HANDS

In order to have a clear concept of a good starting hand, it is necessary to contemplate what is ultimately likely to win in a full-handed game of six or even seven players. Anyone dealt two pairs or better in their first five cards immediately possesses a hand that has about an even-money chance of winning without improvement. Two small pairs might prevail, but combining a pair of aces with a lesser pair is preferable. This is because the hand has only an 11 to 1 chance of improving to a full house, assuming a one-card draw, so anyone not holding a pair of aces is vulnerable to opponents who draw two cards to a pair with an A kicker – the highest unpaired side card in that player's hand. They have a 4 to 1 chance of achieving two pairs – with aces up – or better, leaving an opening hand of two low-to-medium pairs as the likeliest to be leading before the draw but trailing afterwards. Holding a pair of aces presents a player with a 3 to 1 chance of improving the hand after a three-card draw and wins frequently enough in its own right to warrant support, particularly in a light betting heat. Pairs lower than jacks are considered risky propositions when calling the opening bet, since such a hand is evidently already trailing. Anyone holding a higher pair has the same chance of improving as the player with the lower or underpair. So a three-card draw to a pair of nines, for example, has a 3 to 1 chance of improvement, generally speaking, and a 7 to 1 chance of becoming three of a kind, known as 'trips'. Yet such improvement may still leave the hand second-best at the showdown, a prospect that is even more likely, given that the opener will occasionally have much better than a pair of jacks.

SEEKING INFORMATION

Players who have developed an understanding for the game soon recognize the inferences to be drawn from the bets made by opponents. Although up to a fifth of all deals may feature no hand good enough to open, when a player does possess such a hand, there is a strong likelihood that another is in circulation. Should the first player to the dealer's left choose to open the betting, taking the earliest position or acting 'under the gun' as it is known, then it is fair to assume that a pair of aces or kings is the minimum hand being advertised. Players opening with anything less in an

early position find it hard to justify calling a subsequent raise, since they are almost bound to need improvement on the draw. In mid and late positions, players are inclined to open with jacks or queens, but will also be wary of anyone who then raises. Such aggression would signify the raiser probably holds at least a pair of aces, and more probably two pairs or three of a kind. In a fixed-limit game, raising with less than a pair of tens is hardly worthwhile, since it is difficult to bet a sufficient amount to prevent the opener from calling with what is, by definition, a better hand. Only a tight player known for only raising with rock-solid hands might perpetrate a successful bluff under such circumstances, underlining the importance of understanding one's opponents and their playing styles.

Above: When dealt two pairs, such as the jacks and eights shown here, a player has an even-money chance of winning even if the hand does not improve. Discarding the 6d in an effort to draw an additional J or 8 for a full house is a logical move, though the odds are against the full house.

Above: Being dealt a pair of aces offers a player the chance to open the betting in any position, even when first to act. But if an opponent should raise an opening bet, they are likely to be holding two pairs or better. So, if choosing to call, the player holding this hand will probably discard the 8h, 5d and hope to find a K or another A to be in with a chance. There is also the possibility that both cards drawn could be a pair to go with the aces.

Above: Whether to play a pair of queens will depend on a player's position at the table. If the option to open has been checked around to a player in late position with this hand, a bet is advisable, if only to collect the antes. If an opponent raises, the player holding the queens must expect to be losing, since the opponent is likely to have at least a higher pair and possibly more. Calling with a fairly good hand is one of the consistent features of the game.

BETTING CLUES

Prior to the draw, the only clues available regarding any player's hand come from the betting. Those with an early advantage will normally bet to emphasize it, the one exception being when a player holding a 'pat hand' – an outwardly strong hand since he or she opted not to exchange any cards at the draw – calls the opener, rather than raising, to encourage others to do likewise and boost the pot. But with only two betting rounds, it is usually best to press home an advantage by forcing opponents either to fold or to inflate the pot in their own efforts to find a winning hand. In a fixed-limit game, therefore, although a player with an average hand – a low pair, perhaps – may call the opener and trust to fortune, anyone who subsequently raises is unlikely to be bluffing. To raise with less than a high pair, which could be vastly inferior to the opener's hand, invites disaster when players need only call one more bet before the draw. Pursuing this strategy will virtually guarantee heavy losses in the long run, since the pot odds will rarely match the odds against securing a winning hand. In other words, when successful, the chips won will not compensate for those lost in the inevitably frequent defeats. Players who favour pot-limit draw poker have a little more scope for a speculative call and the occasional bluff, but in order to beat the odds they will normally have to read their opponents exceptionally well.

PLAYING THE DRAW

Deciding how many cards to draw after the first round of betting is often straight-forward, particularly if the betting itself has offered a few clues as to the potential strength of opponents' hands. Understandably, it is sensible to draw the number of cards needed to

FIG A

Above: When contemplating how many cards to draw, players need to balance the likelihood of improving sufficiently to win against the cost of obtaining more cards. Holding two medium pairs prior to the draw puts a player in a probable winning position, but it is 11 to 1 against drawing to the full house that would make victory almost certain.

FIG B

Above: Players who hold four-card flushes have a 5 to 1 chance of completing the hand, but the one-card draw should only be contemplated when there are several callers in an unraised pot.

FIG C

Above: Any players hoping to draw two cards to complete a straight are trying to beat odds of 22 to 1, making it a speculative play, at best.

maximize the chances of securing the best hand possible, although there is an exception to this rule when a player holds three cards of the same value, also known as 'trips' – a potential winning hand even without improvement. Two-card draws to straights or flushes are rarely worth considering, whether playing a fixed-limit or pot-limit game, while one-card draws for the same hands are best played cheaply against several opponents. The possibility of some vigorous betting in the second round makes the implied pot odds more attractive in this situation, especially as the hand is likely to be a winner if it hits. Against just one opponent, drawing one card to a straight or flush is much less appealing, since the odds of reward rarely justify the risk. To improve upon two pairs requires drawing one card for a full house, but the odds against this occurring are an unattractive 11 to 1. This is why players holding two pairs usually raise the betting in the first round to drive out weak hands and reduce the chance of being outdrawn.

As mentioned earlier, a player holding trips is best advised to draw one card, as opposed to two, even though this reduces the chances of making a full house. Such a move disguises the value of the hand and makes it more likely that an opponent will call a second-round bet with a losing hand, having assumed, wrongly, that the player possesses two pairs or is bluffing with a busted straight or flush. If an opponent decides not to draw further cards or 'stands pat' as it is termed, then anyone holding trips will definitely draw two cards in the expectation that a full house may be necessary to win. Players who are dealt pat hands of a straight or better can usually assume they are in a winning position, leaving them free to concentrate on building the pot.

FIG D

Above: Finding 'trips' – three of a kind – after the deal is something of a rarity, and such a hand is a regular winner. Rather than discard the two odd cards in a bid to improve the hand, it is often worth a player retaining one to help disguise the hand's real strength. Opponents may read a one-card draw as indicative of an attempted straight or flush, or that the player holds two pairs at best.

FIG E

Above: While holding trips is beneficial, being dealt a pat hand such as a 10-high straight should safely see a player claim the pot; extracting the most chips possible from opponents then becomes a matter of pot management.

OBSERVING OPPONENTS

Apart from the information to be gleaned from bets made in the first round, the draw is the only other point in the game when players may gain an insight into the hands held by opponents. Remembering how many cards were drawn and by whom can provide clues to the value of hands in competition for the pot. Discounting an outright bluff, anyone choosing to stand pat with their original five-card hand is obviously confident that they possess a probable winner. Otherwise, players typically draw as many cards as necessary to give themselves the best chance of improving their hands. Those making three-card draws are almost certainly retaining a pair, the value of which can be reasonably estimated if the opener opts to do this. Two-card draws suggest trips or a pair with a high kicker – the highest unpaired side card in that player's hand – since drawing two for either a straight or a flush will bring success on fewer than 1 in 20 occasions, making this an unattractive proposition to most players. Finally, players who draw a single card are perhaps the most difficult to read, since they could be holding anything from a currently worthless four-card straight to a virtually unbeatable four of a kind. Generally, it is best to assume that a player who opens or raises the betting and then draws one card probably has at least two pairs and maybe even trips. In an unraised pot, players drawing one card are more likely to be trying to buy a potentially lucrative flush or straight as cheaply as possible.

Right: Following the opening bet, players A and D fold, but the remainder all call for 25 chips. The fact that no opponent raised could indicate several things: they may each hold a pair that was too low with which to open, leaving them a 4 to 1 chance of improving past a pair of aces; or they may have four-card straights or flushes that they are hoping to fill. At least one opponent may have a powerful hand and be trying to build the pot.

THE DEAL

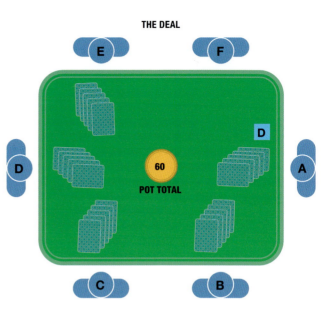

PLAYER F

Above: This example hand of a 25/50 fixed-limit game highlights some of the likely thought processes facing a player throughout a typical game. After the deal, the option to open the betting is checked – or passed – around the table until player F, holding a pair of aces, bets 25 chips. On the assumption that nobody is slow-playing a stronger hand, this high pair may even prove good enough to win without any further improvement.

THE BETTING

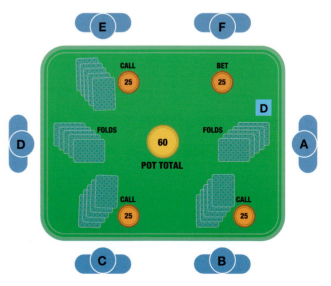

Above: Having opened the betting and indicated that he has at least a high pair, player F keeps the J kicker to disguise the value of the hand. Opponents are then forced to consider that player F may well hold three of a kind. Had the Jc been discarded as well, it would be clear that player F holds a high pair and no more.

ODDS AGAINST

Players who prosper at the game are generally well versed in the probabilities applying at the deal and before the draw. The odds of being dealt a pair of aces or better, for example, are 8 to 1, which emphasizes the need for patience while waiting for a playable hand, as even a pair of jacks and above will only materialize once in every five deals. Against five opponents, a pair of aces has a better-than-even chance of being ahead, which makes it worth playing in most cases. At the other extreme, receiving at least a straight directly from the deal will occur once in every 132 occasions, underlining the rarity of a genuine pat hand. To put this into perspective, a six-player game could see the deal circulate 22 times around the table before anyone is dealt a straight or better. Of the other key opening hands that offer good prospects of winning, two pairs or better will happen once in 13 deals, while a hand of at least three of a kind will appear once in every 35 deals.

ON THE COME
♦ ♣ ♥ ♠

Any player who draws cards to a hand with potential rather than to a hand that is already made is said to be 'on the come'. The term can apply to players with two pairs, for example, who may draw one card to try catching a full house but, in a game where two pairs is often good enough to win, such a holding could be described as a made hand already. It is more usually associated with four-card flushes and straight draws that need one more card to complete the hand. In the best of such situations, namely holding an open-ended straight flush draw, the odds against hitting any one of the 15 cards that will complete – or fill – either a straight or a flush are 2 to 1. At the other extreme, needing one card for an inside straight draw is 11 to 1 against being successful, odds which preclude anything but a cautious betting approach.

THE DRAW

```
        E              F


   D                          D    A

              160
           POT TOTAL


        C              B
```

PLAYER F

Above: Player B draws two cards while players C and E draw one card each. The latter two, by virtue of their betting position and their reluctance to raise earlier, could both be drawing to straights or flushes, but player B's draw is hard to read. If slow-playing trips, it is unlikely that player B would discard two cards, since discarding one would better disguise the hand. As a two-card draw to a flush or a straight is unlikely, it is likely that player B has a medium to high pair with a high kicker. If so, player F is in good shape and discards two.

PURSUING VALUE

Only by comparing the relevant pot odds with the chances of improving a hand sufficiently to win can players ensure that they bet in support of good-value propositions. In fixed-limit games, the implied pot odds before the draw rarely exceed 3 to 1, less than the chance a player holding a low pair has of beating an opponent holding a pair of aces. Opportunities to bet when the pot odds are in favour of drawing a probable winning hand are therefore rare in a game where players with weak hands sensibly fold, leaving two or possibly three players to contest the pot. Players holding a four-card straight or flush are definite underdogs against just a couple of opponents and will be unlikely to win a pot sizeable enough to justify the risk of playing. The situation changes when the opener has several callers, since more bets can be anticipated in the second round, thus increasing the pot odds. A one-card draw to a flush or an open-ended straight has a 5 to 1 chance of completing the hand, which makes this a much more attractive proposition in a multi-handed pot.

FOLLOWING THE DRAW

Betting strategies following the draw are dependent on several factors as players try to assimilate the various strands of information obtained so far. A player opening in early position is advised to bet again in the second round only with an improved hand, otherwise a check is recommended. Anyone who is already beaten will not call a bet, while those who have improved to a possible winning position will call or even raise, perhaps prompting a call from the opener that simply compounds the loss. In fixed-limit poker, the cost of calling is rarely enough to make bluffing in the second round a serious option. Those bluffs that are successful tend to be set

THE DRAW (SECOND-ROUND BETTING)

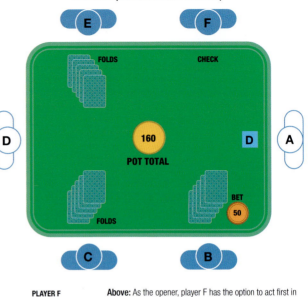

PLAYER F

Above: As the opener, player F has the option to act first in the second round but, having seen no improvement following the draw, the only sensible option is to check. When player B bets 50, player F immediately has doubts that the pair of aces is still strong enough to win, since, if reading player B's hand correctly, it is only 3 to 1 against it having improved from one medium pair to two pairs or better. This would make the bet justifiable in terms of the available pot odds, while a bluff in this situation is unlikely.

Right: A player theatrically tosses his cards away to indicate that he is folding, even though there is a massive pot at stake. Folded hands should always be added face down to the 'muck', this being the pile of discarded cards that accrue during the play of each hand that is the responsibility of the dealer.

up with a strong pre-draw bet or raise, a move that could be enhanced by subsequently not drawing any cards, or 'standing pat' as it is otherwise known. Another general rule is not to bet with anything less than a premium hand, an A-high flush or better, for example, when one or more opponents have drawn one card without previously having raised the pot. Anyone who completes a straight or better will raise any second-round bet, while those who missed their hand will inevitably fold.

STRAIGHTS AND FLUSHES

Holding a straight or a flush, especially A-high, puts a player in a strong position, as such hands can be expected to win, or hold up, on most occasions. How the hand is played after the draw will depend on the circumstances beforehand.

If a made flush is dealt to a player who then opens the betting, then another bet in the second round is almost obligatory. Players who have improved to three of a kind, for instance, may call just to be certain that the opener is not bluffing. Checking merely allows players who fear they have not improved enough to check too, and this reduces the potential winnings.

If an opponent opened, then there are other possibilities for a player with a pat straight or flush. A call will probably keep other players involved, but a raise is not out of the question if the game is loose with plenty of action. When a player successfully draws to a straight or flush, calling the opening second-round bet is generally a sound policy. Those players whose hands remain inferior despite having improved, may well be tempted to call, or perhaps even raise, in the face of perceived weakness. A raise at this point, however, will probably eliminate players who would otherwise call and, once again, reduce the potential winnings.

Above: A player raises the betting by adding more chips to the pot. The raise is an aggressive move, of course, and usually indicates possession of a strong hand although this perception allows players to employ it as a bluffing technique too. When choosing to raise, players should announce their intention clearly before committing their chips to the pot. Adding sufficient chips to call the previous bet and then announcing a raise is known as a string bet and is not permitted.

THE SHOWDOWN

Above: The fact that players C and E quickly folded suggests that they completely missed their draws, leaving player F to decide whether the pot odds, now 4 to 1, justify calling player B's bet. In the event, player F does call, suspecting that player B may hold a lower pair than aces, which did not improve. At the showdown, player B is the winner, but player F's earlier check is vindicated. A bet would surely have been re-raised by player B, meaning that player F would probably have contributed 50 more chips just to confirm defeat.

FIVE-CARD STUD

The pattern of play for five-card stud permits from two to ten players to engage in a game which begins with each player contributing the ante to the pot before being dealt two cards, the first face down and the second face up. The player with the highest-ranking face-up card, otherwise known as the 'door card', opens the first round of betting with a compulsory bet known as the bring-in, following which opponents may fold, call or raise. When the first round of betting is completed, those still involved in the game are dealt a third card, also face up, and a second betting round follows. Again, the player showing the best hand opens the betting with this honour quite often falling to a different player in each round as successive cards are dealt. The game continues with a fourth face-up card being dealt, followed by another betting round and then, if necessary, competing players receive a fifth card face up as a prelude to the final betting round. As ever, the winner is decided either at the showdown when those still involved reveal their hands or by a player making a bet at any stage of the game that is not called by opponents.

Five-card stud represented a major departure from draw poker, the first recognizable form of the game. Although the introduction of betting limits and restrictions on which player opened the betting expanded draw poker's popularity, the paucity of information available upon which to base any betting decisions led to the development of open poker, of which five-card stud is the oldest surviving example. Open poker games are those in which several of the cards in each player's hand are exposed for all to see. In five-card stud, each player ultimately receives one card face down and four face up, if participating to the fourth and final betting round. The structure of the game therefore enables players to modify their strategic thinking after each successive round, as more cards are exposed and the inferences behind opponents'

Below: This is a typical scene after the final card has been dealt. Three players have survived the first three betting rounds and the action is on player F who boasts the best visible hand, a pair of aces. This could be enough to win but, since player A has obviously called on fourth street when both opponents were already showing open pairs, it is possible that player A has a concealed 9 and has successfully completed a J-high straight. This would be enough to beat the others who can only hold three of a kind at most.

As they appear to the opposition   **As they appear to the player**

TYPICAL FINAL-ROUND SCENE

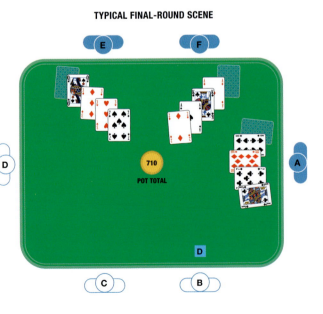

710
POT TOTAL

Above: To be dealt a pair in the first two cards usually provides a player with an immediate advantage, although high-ranking pairs are obviously of more value since they are more likely to win the hand without any improvement required. The odds against being dealt any pair are 16 to 1, but seeing queens or better in the first two cards will happen around once in every 74 deals, while receiving a pair of aces is a 220 to 1 chance.

betting patterns become more apparent. In addition, since there is no draw to put pressure on the deck, five-card stud can accommodate up to ten players, which is the number of participants considered ideal by experienced players and poker professionals. Such a game is likely to create betting confrontations that are essential to an enjoyable session. Adopting a pot-limit or no-limit betting structure will also help to counteract the mechanical facets of five-card stud that are prevalent in a conservative fixed-limit game. Bluffing becomes a more attractive possibility when bigger bets are permitted and the pots can escalate sufficiently to tempt players into staying with hands that might usually be folded in a fixed-limit contest.

STARTING HANDS

In common with all poker variations, judging which opening hands to play and which to fold is the first important element of five-card stud. After the deal, this decision is based upon the receipt of just two cards, of which one is visible to opponents. This might initially seem to present a player with too little information upon which to decide whether to fold or play, but an understanding of the odds affecting the game emphasizes

why this decision is important. Any player who stays to the showdown has an even-money chance of obtaining a pair. In a six-player game, therefore, if all players see five cards the likelihood is that three of them will possess at least a pair, with one of these likely to be queens or better. Possessing a pair of aces or kings gives any competitor an advantage, and the earlier that pair materializes during play, the better. The ideal situation is to be dealt a pair in the first two cards, since a player in this position can exercise more control over the betting. When holding two unmatched cards, the general advice is to be cautious and fold immediately, unless both cards are ranked 10 and above. The only exception to this rule is when a player has a hole card, one that is held face down on the table, that is higher than any door cards (the first exposed or 'up' card) on display. A player can expect to see a pair of aces once in every six deals, so an A in the hole with a 7 showing, for example, presents a player with a fair possibility of making the high pair. If this occurs and there are no other aces or open pairs among opponents' up cards, then the hand has a good chance of winning at the showdown, supposing the player is unable to force opponents to fold beforehand by betting aggressively.

Above: A pair of queens, often referred to as 'ladies', is a strong opening hand in five-card stud. After the deal, a player holding a pair of queens should expect to be leading since only a pair of aces or kings could be beating the hand at this stage. If there are no door cards higher than a Q on show, then the player will be aware of holding an immediate advantage.

THE VALUE OF PAIRS
♦ ♣ ♥ ♠

The value of being dealt a pair in five-card stud can hardly be overstated. Although possessing a pocket A or K to match the door card is desirable, even lower-ranked pairs can be valuable to some extent. In a tight game where players are exercising caution, a raise from a player showing a 7c, for example, may cause the opener and any callers holding higher-value door cards to fold, for fear that a pair has already been secured.

After the deal, a six-player game presents any player with odds of just over 3 to 1 against pairing the high card in this situation, odds that worsen considerably if one of those cards is dealt to an opponent. That unfortunate situation may be enough to induce conservative players to fold. Whether one is dealt a pair or not, in a high-stakes or no-limit game of five-card stud, bluffing with a big first-round bet to suggest a pair is a plausible tactic. However, it is rarely considered by players holding unpaired cards, either of which is ranked below a 10.

DOOR CARDS

Before the first round of betting takes place, the first exposed or 'up' card dealt to each player – the door card – offers the only clue as to the potential of each hand. The player with the highest-value door card opens the betting, but this obligation may fall to a player holding a 7 or an 8 on occasion, in which case several callers can be expected. If the door cards are low, it increases the chance that players will have high-value hole cards – those dealt face down and thus unseen by opponents – which could encourage them to stay in for a round or two. A raise from a player showing a low door card normally indicates a pair is held, and a similar assumption may be wise if the player merely called the opener.

Social players are not always aware of the probabilities at work, so the skill of the opposition needs to be considered when seeking a link between the exposed cards and any bets. Poker is a gambling game, and many players are prepared to pay over the odds for the thrilling, if unlikely, possibility of making a powerful hand.

LIKELY WINNING HANDS

As suggested, the average winning hand in five-card stud is much lower than in other poker variations, with a high pair usually being enough to claim the spoils. Finding such a hand within the first three cards is an advantage, particularly if the pair includes the hole card, as it offers the chance to raise the betting and drive opponents out of the pot. In doing so, many hands with the potential to win will often be folded before they are complete. For example players who hold three-card flushes or straights will hardly ever encounter the pot odds to make it worthwhile to continue with the hand, especially when an opponent has an open pair. Such hands are rarely seen, while even three of a kind has only 1 chance in 35 of being dealt in a

OPEN PAIRS

Left: Three examples of hands after the dealing of the third card face up – third street – all showing an open pair. Typically, the minimum bet for the first two rounds in five-card stud is half that of the last two rounds. Any player holding an open pair on third street, however, is entitled to protect it by doubling the minimum bet, making it more expensive for opponents to try beating the hand. If choosing not to exercise this option, any opponent not showing a pair may also bet at the higher level, if desired.

Below: Workers playing a game of poker in 1940 at the Fort Blanding site, Florida, used by the US army as an infantry replacement training centre during the Second World War. At least eight players are involved making it likely that five-card stud will be one of the poker variations considered for the evening's entertainment. With more cards in circulation the chances of players formulating good hands is increased, thus helping to make the betting action much more competitive.

player's five cards. Since a hand this strong may not materialize until fifth street, the prospect of having to survive three rounds of volatile betting in order to achieve it underlines why hands of such magnitude are seen so infrequently. By contrast, it is difficult to capitalize on trips being held in the first three cards dealt, since the open pair that must be apparent compromises the chances of keeping enough opponents involved in the pot to make the hand pay off.

THIRD STREET

The receipt of the third card – third street – marks the decisive point for most five-card stud hands. Good players will rarely consider going beyond this stage if their hand is outranked by an opponent's visible face-up board cards in play. They adhere to the primary rule, which is that any player who cannot beat the board should fold as a matter of course. An example occurs when an open pair appears, the recommendation being, for any player not yet holding a pair, to fold. Having cards that rank higher than an opponents' cards on the board – also known as 'overcards' – might seem worth playing, but pairing one of these could prove inadequate, especially if several other players stay involved. Sometimes, the opponent showing a pair will already have three of a kind and anyone in this position will happily entertain speculative calls from the unwary.

Sensible third-street play precludes betting in support of causes that may already be lost. This applies to hands such as three-card straights and flushes that are virtually worthless. To underline this, anyone holding As, 10s, 8s, may calculate that they have a slightly better-than-even chance of completing the flush in a six-player game. But these odds only apply if all players stay to the showdown and no other spades appear amid their up cards, a scenario that is unrealistic even in the least competitive of games.

Right: A player takes a look at his hole card to confirm possession of three kings now that the final card has been dealt. Securing three of a kind in five cards will happen, on average, around once in every 35 deals. As in this instance, however, a player may have to wait until the final card to make the hand, so three possibly costly betting rounds will already have been negotiated.

PLAYABLE HANDS

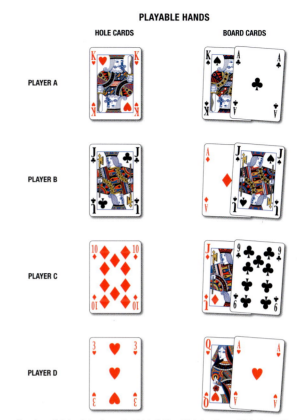

Above: Knowing which hands to play and which to fold on third street is crucial. A player with a pair of kings with an A kicker (the highest unpaired side card) is in a strong position. If no open pairs are visible, this hand will open the betting on third street. Similarly, having an A to support a hidden pair of jacks will intimidate opponents showing a K or a Q. Even if they have a hidden pair, the A will make them wary of calling a bet. Players holding three-card straights and flushes should fold on third street if an opponent bets as the chance of completing the hand is remote.

EFFECTIVE STRATEGIES

The fact that most guidance on how to play five-card stud tends to advocate caution highlights how difficult it is, in limit poker particularly, to manipulate the betting and win large pots. On many occasions, the strength of a player's hand will be clearly apparent from the board cards, making it unlikely that an opponent will call a serious bet. Anyone with an open pair may double the minimum bet on third street in order to protect the hand, but this has two likely outcomes. Opponents with little chance of overtaking the hand will fold, while anyone who calls, let alone raises, is probably already ahead. Even if an opponent with just one up card higher than the open pair bets in the second round, then it is best to assume they have it beaten.

Pairing a mid-ranking hole card is not much better in this situation. For instance, a player who has paired a 9 in the hole with a card dealt face up will feel similarly vulnerable when there are several higher-ranking cards on the board. Any bet from an opponent showing A, Q, for example, will suggest that a third 9 is required to win. In a six-player game, a player will have seen a maximum of 13 cards – their three plus the ten other up cards, assuming everyone is still competing. Provided no other nines have appeared as yet, the chance of making trip nines in the next two rounds is never better than 8 to 1. Added to the fact that an opponent's hand might also improve, most players will fold rather than call in this situation, thus removing the temptation to commit further chips in the later rounds when the minimum bets increase.

Right: Player A cautiously calls the opening bet from player E, because, with two aces on the board already, the chances of either player C or E holding a pair are reduced. The fact that players C and D also decide to call rather than raise means neither has a pair as yet.

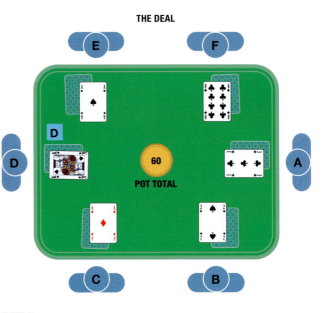

THE DEAL

PLAYER A
Hole card

Above: In this 25/50 fixed-limit game, player A is dealt a pair of threes, which is useful, but no more than that, at present, given the high cards on the table. However, since it is 16 to 1 against any player being dealt a pair in the first two cards, there is a good chance that the pair of threes is currently leading.

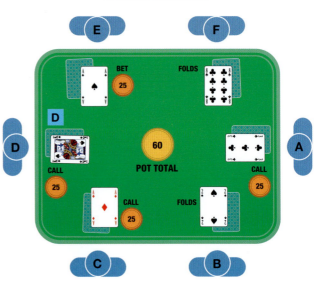

OPENING BETTING ROUND

BLUFFING

Opportunities to bluff in five-card stud do not arise very often in a fixed-limit game, since the cost of calling a bet is rarely prohibitive enough to force all opponents to fold. For a true bluff to be successful, each opponent must relinquish their claim on the pot. In games that involve ten players, there are usually enough cards in circulation to make bluffing with a weak hand on third street a risky proposition, in any case. Any player who has a reputation for tight play might capitalize on this image to perpetrate the occasional bluff, but then all experienced five-card stud players have a tendency to be extremely conservative in their approach. When playing against such opponents, a bluff on third street might be all that is needed to steal a small pot, but this is a manoeuvre best reserved for games with five or fewer players. Those players who wish to promote more bluffing in five-card stud are usually advised to play it as a pot-limit or no-limit game. The larger bets that are allowed have greater potential to intimidate opponents, which makes bluffing a much more viable prospect.

THIRD STREET

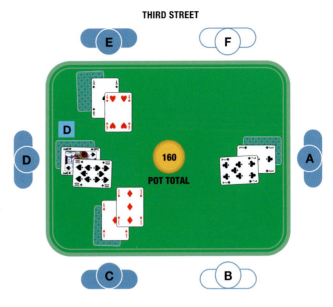

Above: The third card for each player brings no open pairs, but player A's chances of being dealt another 3 are compromised when the 3d is dealt to player C, there now being just one remaining unseen. If, as suspected, players C and E do not have pocket aces, then they may be reluctant to call a bet. But player D still has two overcards – cards higher than player A's threes – and probably represents the biggest danger given the possibility that he has a pocket K or 10 for a higher pair.

Right: Executing a bluff in five-card stud is more likely to succeed when the game is played with no-limit or pot-limit betting. As larger bets are permitted, opponents can be intimidated into folding with a hand such as this one (right).

TIMING A BLUFF
♦ ♣ ♥ ♠

Bluffing is more prevalent in pot-limit and no-limit games because of the greater freedom for players to make large bets. This increases the risk of sacrificing more chips on bluffs that fail, so a player needs to time the move correctly in order to lend any bluff credibility. For example if the opener shows an A after the deal, but is raised by a player whose door card is a lowly 6, then the bet suggests a pair is held. If the raise is big enough, it might take the pot uncontested, but, if not, any improvement in the hand – ideally another 6 – will reinforce the bluff and could persuade anyone holding a high pair to fold in the face of another large bet. Should one or other of the remaining sixes later be dealt to an opponent, the integrity of the bluff may quickly unravel. Players should therefore pay attention to the up cards at each stage, to determine whether the hand they are trying to represent has been compromised by events.

FOURTH STREET

A typical game between six or more reasonable players is likely to feature a maximum of three or four contesting fourth street, and will probably only see a couple continue to the final round. Whichever betting structure is in operation, patience and due caution remain the recommended characteristics to exhibit during play. Players with poor chances of winning usually fold prior to fourth street, when the minimum bet routinely doubles for the remaining two betting rounds. Those who continue in the game can therefore be assumed to have the leading hand or one that has a fair chance of improving to be the best. Each remaining player will have three up cards showing at this stage, which makes an assessment of their ultimate hand's value quite simple

In terms of strategy, any player who is clearly ahead should capitalize on the situation by betting. Should everyone else fold, the player can take the pot, but any opponents who call, evidently do so in the belief that one or more cards in the deck may yet help them win. Offering the chance of a free card by checking in this situation represents poor play no matter how remote the opposition's chances of winning.

At the other end of the spectrum, a player with a trailing hand must realistically compare the pot odds with the odds against drawing a winning card. If the risk is unjustified, as is often the case, a player should fold in response to any bet, remembering that the bettor's hand may also improve. Players who harbour any doubts at all about the merit of their hand after four cards should check, when possible, whether first to act or not. Adopting a cautious approach such as this does, however, present the chance for players acting in late position to try stealing the occasional pot with a bluff.

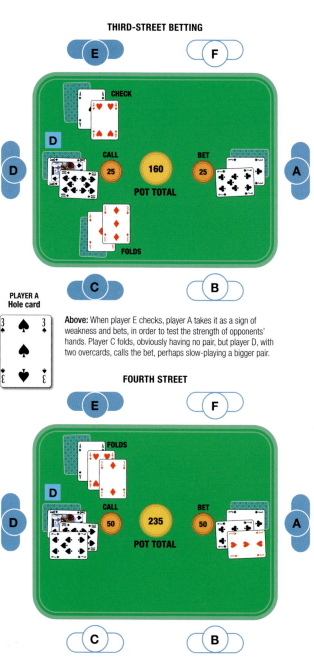

THIRD-STREET BETTING

PLAYER A Hole card

Above: When player E checks, player A takes it as a sign of weakness and bets, in order to test the strength of opponents' hands. Player C folds, obviously having no pair, but player D, with two overcards, calls the bet, perhaps slow-playing a bigger pair.

FOURTH STREET

Above: After player E decided to call the second-round bets, fourth street brings player A trip (three) threes and the option to bet first with a pair of threes showing. Knowing the hand is definitely leading, player A rightly bets, forcing those who may have a winning opportunity to pay for their final card. Player D may make higher trips if holding a pair, but has given no indication yet that a K or 10 is held. It might be assumed that player D's hole card is another high-ranking spade. Player E folds, having no pair and, as player A now knows, no chance of a straight.

READING THE CARDS

Accurately reading the cards is crucial when forming any betting strategy on fourth street. By recalling the up cards previously folded and turned face down during play, as well as the various bets made by opponents in preceding rounds, a player has all the information needed to gauge the actual and potential strength of opposing hands. A player showing Ac, Jd, 9h, for instance, could have a pair of aces, with the possibility of making three of a kind if another A comes on fifth street. But if an A has already appeared among up cards that were folded earlier, the chances of the player fulfilling that potential are obviously reduced. Also, any opponent who does hold a pocket A will know for certain that, with only one remaining A unaccounted for, the player cannot have more than a pair of aces at present. If that is the case, then two pairs are the best the player can achieve, should a J or 9 appear on fifth street. If not, then the best possible hand the player showing Ac, Jd, 9h can hit is three jacks, assuming that the Jd is the only one of that rank to have appeared during the game. Deductive reasoning of this nature should guide betting decisions at this stage of play.

FIFTH STREET

Once the final card has been dealt, there is little mystery concerning the competing hands, since, with only the hole cards obscured from view, their potential value can be quickly estimated. Typically, it is rare for more than two players to reach fifth street, which reduces final-round strategy to a couple of simple rules. A player who has possession of the winning hand should always bet at the first opportunity, in the hope that an opponent will call or even raise, thus boosting the size of the pot. By checking in this situation, a

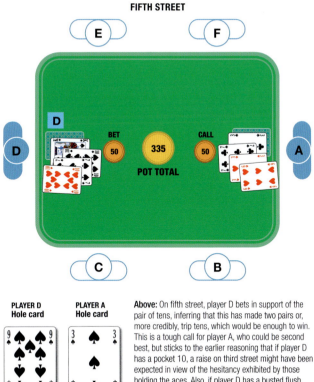

FIFTH STREET

PLAYER D	PLAYER A
Hole card	Hole card

Above: On fifth street, player D bets in support of the pair of tens, inferring that this has made two pairs or, more credibly, trip tens, which would be enough to win. This is a tough call for player A, who could be second best, but sticks to the earlier reasoning that if player D has a pocket 10, a raise on third street might have been expected in view of the hesitancy exhibited by those holding the aces. Also, if player D has a busted flush, then only a bluff can secure the pot. Player A therefore calls and wins with trip threes as player D's bluff, the hole being a 9s, is revealed.

player invites opponents to check, too, and so runs the risk of missing out on additional chips. Should a player be unsure of holding the winning hand, then a check is the best policy. Whether first to act or not, a bet may prompt an opponent to raise, at which point the player either forfeits the additional chips unnecessarily put into the pot or calls, uncomfortably, with what is probably a beaten hand.

Left: A player considers his next move at the table although, in five-card stud, the strategy to be adopted on fifth street is usually straightforward. If it is evident from the board cards that an opponent possesses a weaker hand, a player should bet and hope for a call.

SEVEN-CARD STUD

Seven-card stud starts with each player contributing an ante to the pot prior to the deal. Cards are then dealt one at a time until everyone has three cards, two face down, variously described as hidden, pocket or hole cards, and one face up, known as the door card. The player with the lowest door card opens the betting, typically by making a compulsory bet for a sum less than the usual minimum bet permitted. After the first round, those still in the game each receive a fourth card, face up, prior to the next round of betting. From this point, the first player to act is the one now showing the best visible hand. In this (the second) and subsequent rounds there is no obligation to bet and players may check. Players receive a fifth and sixth card face up, and a seventh card face down with the deal of each punctuated by additional rounds of betting. Players still in the game at the showdown have seven cards from which to make a five-card poker hand, four face up and three face down. The winner is the player who either makes an uncalled bet or who displays the best five-card poker hand once the fifth and final betting round has concluded.

The game of seven-card stud developed from the five-card variation and became popular during the years leading up to World War II. Having travelled the world with the US military, seven-card stud emerged afterwards as the most widely played form of poker and dominated the commercial scene in both Las Vegas and Europe for nearly 40 years. Indeed, up until the 1980s a couple of the more famous Las Vegas casinos offered only seven-card stud in their poker rooms.

Though challenged by Texas Hold 'em for contemporary favouritism, seven-card stud remains a very challenging game which draws upon the whole gamut of any poker player's skills in order to prove rewarding. The five betting rounds help to generate sizeable pots, relative to the stake-levels in operation, and the exposed cards offer a great deal of information as a hand progresses. Yet the fact that players who sustain interest to the showdown will have three of their cards face down still leaves room for doubt in the minds of opposition over the composition of anyone's hand. This creates the opportunity for some imaginative play and leaves the way open for players to consider the occasional bluff, especially in the pot-limit version of

LIKELY WINNING HANDS

FIG 1: TWO PAIRS

| HOLE CARDS | UP CARDS | SEVENTH STREET |

FIG 2: THREE OF A KIND

| HOLE CARDS | UP CARDS | SEVENTH STREET |

Above: The quality of hand required to win at the showdown will be dictated by the nature of the game and the stakes for which players are competing. In high-stakes fixed-limit games, particularly those incorporating the use of substantial antes, players with good starting hands are prone to bet aggressively right away. Such games are therefore likely to see just two or three players involved at any showdown with hands such as two high pairs or three of a kind often proving good enough to win. Fig 1 features two pairs of aces and kings, a hand completed by the 9 kicker (the highest unpaired side card in that player's hand) which could prove decisive in the unlikely event that an opponent also has aces and kings. Fig 2 shows a hand comprising three jacks, the discounted cards in this case being the 3c and 4c.

Below: This picture highlights the fact that, in seven-card stud, a player must count five cards from the seven ultimately available in order to make a viable poker hand. Here, the 8h and 5d are redundant since the player will count the remaining five cards to make a full house of aces over kings.

COST OF INFORMATION
♦ ♣ ♥ ♠

Before the cards are dealt, it must be understood that the level of the antes and bring-in bets may vary from one poker room to another, irrespective of betting limits. Games featuring low antes tend to encourage loose play and can provide rich pickings for a tight, conservative player who is prepared to wait for a strong hand before committing chips to the pot. Players who enjoy being regularly involved in the action should probably play with higher antes as this helps to inflate the pot and capitalize on their good hands, offsetting the losses which come from contesting a high proportion of pots. Many guides to seven-card stud focus on high-stakes games in which tight but aggressive play is the norm. In these, players who are not disciplined enough to fold opening hands may be drawn into situations where their hands improve but still trail that of the aggressor who has two aims in mind. The first is to reduce the field to maybe one opponent, the second is to ensure that players with inferior starting hands pay the maximum amount for the chance to improve. When playing such opponents, calling for a couple of rounds in the expectation of help from the deck can soon reduce a player's chip stack. In social games, the betting is quite restrained with players often content to wait until fifth street before deciding whether to play or fold. The key factor in both types of game is that the betting levels rise on fifth street for the final three rounds, when any player who wants to see extra cards will inevitably pay more for the privilege.

the game. However, this betting structure is most popular among experienced players and those who prefer low-stakes, social poker are more inclined to play fixed- or spread-limit stud.

EARLY CONSIDERATIONS

At the beginning of the game, every player is dealt three cards, the first two are face down and the third – the door card – face up. In common with all poker variations, the decision on which of these opening hands might be worth playing should be determined by an understanding of what is likely to prove to be a winning hand at the showdown. This, in turn, is affected by the culture of the game and whether it is a volatile, low-stakes contest, between loose players, or a tight game between experienced players.

Ordinarily, at least two pairs, probably including aces, will be required to claim victory and three of a kind is often good enough. However, if the cost of betting is not too restrictive, then the likelihood of players chasing straights or better is much greater and could render the average winning hand of two pairs extremely vulnerable. In a low-stakes game, even a player in possession of three eights by fourth street, for example, may not be able to bet a sufficiently large amount to dissuade opponents from calling with inferior hands that still hold the potential for substantial improvement. It is therefore worth remembering that when four or five players stay to see a fifth card, the rank of the winning hand will quite often be higher than two pairs or three of a kind.

Below: A restrained low-stakes game which features little in the way of forceful betting prior to fifth street could easily see several players willing to continue to the showdown. When the betting is light, more players remain involved and initially unpromising hands are given the chance to develop into winners. Strong hands such as straights, flushes and full houses are more likely to occur, although sometimes a solitary pair will still win.

BETTER THAN AVERAGE HANDS
ACE-HIGH STRAIGHT

HOLE CARDS	UP CARDS	SEVENTH STREET

ACE-HIGH FLUSH

HOLE CARDS	UP CARDS	SEVENTH STREET

FULL HOUSE – SEVENS OVER KINGS

HOLE CARDS	UP CARDS	SEVENTH STREET

STARTING HANDS

Assessing the value of the first three cards received will very much depend on the style of game. In a tight game, featuring first-round raises and plenty of folding, only the very best starting hands may warrant support, although this may reduce a player's participation to around one in five hands on average. Social games are likely to feature much more leeway regarding which hands to play, but this does not disguise the fact that it is advantageous to start with any one of five key combinations.

The best possible starting hand is three of a kind, or trips, with high pairs of aces, kings or queens are also highly prized. A starting hand featuring a low pocket pair and a high-value door card (the player's first exposed or 'up' card) such as an A or K may also be worth playing as are three-card flushes and open-ended three-card straights.

Being dealt these combinations does not guarantee victory and players must observe the up cards held by opponents as the game unfolds. This is why players bet aggressively with strong hands when the antes are high in order to end the contest quickly and rake in the chips, winning these small pots being crucial to keeping the cost of the antes at bay.

ROLLED-UP TRIPS

There are 22,100 possible three-card combinations available from the standard 52-card deck and the best of these, naturally, is trip aces which will materialize only once in every 5,525 deals on average. Although such a hand is very powerful, the fact is that any three of a kind may well win even without improvement, and the probability of being dealt 'rolled-up trips' – three of a kind in the first three cards – is rated at 424 to 1. The great benefit of seeing such a hand is that its strength is hidden during the early part of the game,

ROLLED-UP TRIPS

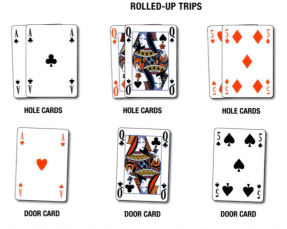

HOLE CARDS   HOLE CARDS   HOLE CARDS

DOOR CARD   DOOR CARD   DOOR CARD

Above: Being dealt any three of a kind presents a player with a huge advantage since the hand will often be enough to win on its own while also having an excellent chance of improving to a full house. But the odds against receiving any three of a kind in the first three cards are 424 to 1, while finding a pair of aces in the hole to match the door card for trip aces will happen about once in every 5,525 deals. When a player holds such a starting hand, a winning outcome should be expected with the main concern being to manage the pot for the maximum possible gain.

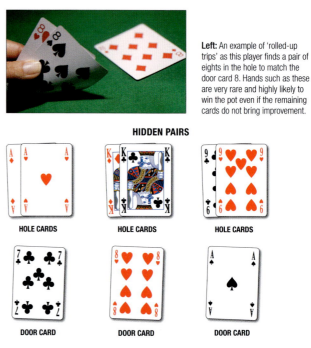

Left: An example of 'rolled-up trips' as this player finds a pair of eights in the hole to match the door card 8. Hands such as these are very rare and highly likely to win the pot even if the remaining cards do not bring improvement.

HIDDEN PAIRS

HOLE CARDS   HOLE CARDS   HOLE CARDS

DOOR CARD   DOOR CARD   DOOR CARD

Above: Any pair dealt in the first three cards is helpful but holding a high pair – aces or kings – will give a player an early advantage. Having the pair concealed enhances that advantage as it allows a player to bet in a fashion that disguises the strength of the hand. Someone holding pocket aces and showing a 7 can justifiably call any first-round bet or raise by an opponent and should certainly make the first raise if acting from an early betting position. Opponents may suspect the hand is better than a pair of sevens but they will be wary of other possibilities.

although playing low trips can be problematic. A player in possession of three threes may well bring in the betting and find that a couple of opponents showing a K and an A respectively both put in a raise. Since they have to be credited with at least a high pair each, a further raise with just a 3 showing will alert them to danger and even a call will put them on their guard.

In most cases, professionals advocate supporting a strong opening hand with maximum bets since underplaying it to keep opponents involved can backfire. However, on rare occasions when rolled-up trips materialize, players can usually afford to bet the minimum and keep opponents involved in the action until the time is right to strike with a large bet. Although opposition hands may improve sufficiently to threaten the early advantage obtained from holding trips, the odds against this hand itself improving to a full house with four cards still to come are only just over two to one. Given that it may also improve to something higher than a full house, it is almost certain that a player dealt trips in the first three cards is going to play to the showdown unless there is strong evidence to suggest an opponent has a higher-ranking full house or better.

SPLIT PAIRS

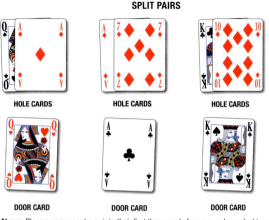

| HOLE CARDS | HOLE CARDS | HOLE CARDS |

| DOOR CARD | DOOR CARD | DOOR CARD |

Above: Players can expect a pair in their first three cards from around one deal in every five. On many occasions this will feature the door card matching a hole card for a 'split pair' which, although beneficial in the case of high pairs, makes disguising the hand difficult. Ordinarily, any first-round bet from a player showing an A, K or Q will be interpreted as representing a pair, allowing scope for a bluff when a player holds just a high card and no pair. By contrast, a player who does hold a split pair of aces but simply calls the bring-in from an early betting position may lull opponents into sensing weakness. Should one of them raise the betting, a subsequent call or re-raise from the player holding the door card A will dispel that notion immediately.

Right: Another decent starting hand in the shape of a split pair, a K in the hole being matched with a door-card K. If no other kings are showing amid opponents' door cards and aces are also absent from the board, a solid bet in the first round is certainly justifiable.

PAIRS
♦ ♣ ♥ ♠

The chances of being dealt a pair among the first three cards in seven-card stud are fractionally less than 5 to 1, although it is around 25 to 1 against receiving jacks or better. While they offer potential for improvement, players must weigh up the merits of holding a hidden pair or a split pair, the former meaning that both paired cards are dealt face down while a split pair, as the name suggests, is one in which the door card matches a hole card. Obviously, it is easier to play deceptively when holding pocket aces and showing a 7 than it is if one of the aces is a door card. Opponents will expect a bet in support of the A on display and will be wary of becoming too involved given the potential for it to be paired with a hole card. In this situation, it can be assumed that any opponents who do call to see fourth street are holding reasonable hands. Nevertheless, they could only be leading a pair of aces and a 7 kicker, in this instance, if holding three of a kind or the other pair of aces with a higher-ranking odd card. A maximum bet when the aces are hidden and the 7 is showing might flush out those opponents holding decent hands without them having a clear idea of the strength truly represented by the first-round bet.

THREE-CARD STRAIGHTS

Open-ended three-card straights, such as 7, 8, 9 or J, Q, K, offer attractive potential as starting hands as the chances of converting them into a full straight are around 6 to 1. Players can expect to see three cards to a straight regularly, maybe as often as one in six deals, making them appealing hands to play in a restrained betting game which regularly features four or five players paying for a fifth card.

In an eight-handed game, each player can see ten cards following the deal, these being their own three cards and the seven door cards in front of their opponents. If holding the 7, 8, 9 combination, for example, any 5, 6, 10 or J on fourth street immediately increases a player's chances of making the straight. Improvement is also ensured if a 7, 8 or 9 is dealt to make a pair which means that up to 25 cards in the deck have the potential to help the hand. However, several of those cards could already be visible on the table and this is the key factor in deciding how far to proceed in a bid to complete the straight. If an opponent with a 10 showing chooses to raise the betting, it would be realistic to assume at least a pair of tens is being

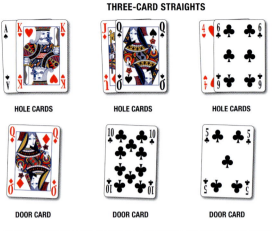

HOLE CARDS   HOLE CARDS   HOLE CARDS

DOOR CARD   DOOR CARD   DOOR CARD

Above: Opening hands of three cards to a straight often occur and an open-ended combination such as a 10, J, Q offers multiple chances for improvement, with the odds for a straight being completed after seven cards of around 6 to 1. Higher-ranking three-card combinations of 10 and above offer the potential for an A-high straight. Pairing any of these with subsequent cards could allow a player to take the pot before a showdown. This is less likely when a player holds low-ranking cards such as 4, 5, 6 and makes one or even two low pairs. But, should a straight come by fifth street, perhaps with a 7 and a 3, the hand may still be a poor betting option if an opponent seems to be drawing to a higher-ranking straight or a flush. If fourth and fifth street bring no improvement to a hand such as this, it is probably best to fold at the first large bet.

Left: Three suited picture cards such as the K, Q, J are generally worth support, especially if the game features little in the way of aggressive betting in the early rounds. The combination is such that half the remaining cards in the deck offer the potential to improve the hand. This is usually enough of an incentive to bet for at least a couple of rounds.

LOW PAIRS, BIG KICKERS
♦ ♣ ♥ ♠

Though they can be more dangerous to play, medium or low pocket pairs still have the same potential for improvement as pairs of aces or kings. The problem is that a player holding the low pair must improve when up against such cards, a prospect made easier if the kicker (the highest-value unpaired card in their hand) is of a high rank. For example an opening bet from an opponent showing a K, and so probably representing a pair, is worth calling if a player holds pocket tens with an A kicker. Such a call implies possession of a reasonable hand, possibly a pair of aces, and could enable the player to see another card or two quite cheaply against the probable pair of kings. Should an A materialize on fourth street to provide an open pair, the player will act first while the opponent holding kings ponders whether any bet indicates trip aces, and not just the pair on display. If a 10 is dealt instead, then a well-disguised three of a kind is secured along with an opportunity to dominate the betting, provided the opponent has not been dealt another K. As with the three-card flush and straight examples, deciding whether to support an opening hand with a small pair is generally based on the possibility of catching a good card on fourth street. If this fails to happen and opponents' hands clearly improve, it is wiser to fold than to continue betting. This helps to avoid the disastrous possibility of improving sufficiently to play to the showdown with what remains the second-best hand.

represented. Immediately, this reduces the prospects of making anything better than a 9-high straight since half the tens in the deck could already be out. On top of that, even pairing a 7, 8 or 9 on fourth street will still leave the player trailing and would make further participation in the hand inadvisable.

THREE-CARD FLUSHES

Flushes outrank straights and the chances of being dealt three assorted cards of the same suit are correspondingly longer at around 24 to 1. Though a flush is a likely winner, disguising a flush draw can be more difficult with each round making it vital that, in pursuing the hand, a player is well aware how many cards of the relevant suit are already in play.

A player holding Kh, 10h, 6h, for instance, has a 5 to 1 chance of making the flush, an appealing prospect after the deal though these odds assume no knowledge of the opposition's cards. If there are hearts among the door cards on the table, then the odds against completing the hand obviously lengthen. As with the straight draw, there are four rounds in which to hit the two hearts that will make the hand but, if missing them on fourth and fifth street, the rising cost of trying to catch them could become prohibitive. For this reason, though three-card flushes have a fair chance of developing into winning hands, they are rarely worth pursuing beyond fourth street in the face of aggressive betting from an opponent.

Drawing hands such as flushes and straights are generally played cautiously, with solid players recognizing that support should be confined to those comprising high-ranking cards only. These provide insurance since pairing aces, kings or queens when drawing to flushes and straights can offer another route to victory should the initial promise of the hand not be realized.

THREE-CARD FLUSHES

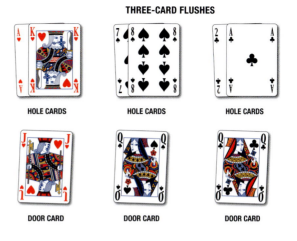

HOLE CARDS **HOLE CARDS** **HOLE CARDS**

DOOR CARD **DOOR CARD** **DOOR CARD**

Above: Holding three cards to a flush after the deal offers scope for staying in a hand, though a player will hope to draw the cards needed to complete the flush cheaply. Calling an opponent's first-round raise is justified if a player holds an A, but help must materialize quickly in the face of aggressive betting to warrant further participation. If two or more cards of the relevant suit are among the opposition's door cards, any attempt to pursue the flush draw should be entertained with caution. High cards are of more value because they present alternative chances to win if the flush draw is derailed.

LOW PAIRS WITH BIG KICKER

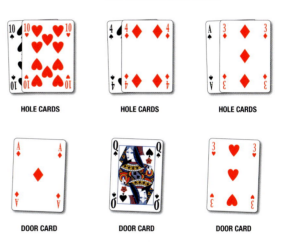

HOLE CARDS **HOLE CARDS** **HOLE CARDS**

DOOR CARD **DOOR CARD** **DOOR CARD**

Above: Though not without potential, starting hands that feature both hidden and split low pairs are immediately vulnerable and will usually need a helpful card on fourth street to encourage a player to continue in all but the lightest of betting heats. To this end, having a high-ranking kicker – ideally an A – to supplement the pair is preferable since pairing the kicker for two pairs could transform a modest hand into a likely winner. For example should a player with a split pair of threes and an A in the hole catch another A on fourth street, the hand could already be strong enough to win while its true value can be disguised if betting remains light. Slow-playing the hand is possible though a raise should be considered if any open pairs lower than aces are visible after four cards.

THIRD-STREET STRATEGY

A common mistake players frequently make is to overestimate the value of their starting hands, following which they bet modestly to keep several opponents involved in the game to help swell the pot. There are so many possibilities at work in seven-card stud that opponents with the weakest of hands can improve past, for example, a high-value opening pair. Consequently, players who are dealt a premium hand of a high pair, and possibly even three high cards offering powerful straight and flush potential, should bet aggressively in the opening round to advertise strength and encourage opponents to fold. The exception to this is when a player holds trips since the time to exert pressure in this case is on fifth street, when the betting levels rise and opponents with drawing hands may feel they are committed to the pot. For example a player who is dealt three nines when there are two or three higher up cards visible should sit tight and just call any opening-round bets whenever possible. Raising in the opening round may be justified from a late betting position if opponents possessing higher door cards – their first exposed or 'up' cards – have so far been content to call. They may think the raise represents an attempt to steal the pot with a pair of nines, in which case their higher-ranking up cards could tempt them into staying for another round or two. However, if an opponent showing an A, for example, has already raised the betting, a re-raise will be read as confirmation of trip nines. This may be enough to take the pot, but calling the raise is a better option in this situation since the meaning behind the bet is more difficult to interpret. By generating an element of doubt in the minds of opponents, the player is more likely to maximize the profit on a probable winning hand.

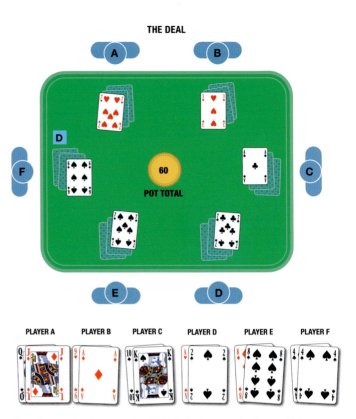

THE DEAL

Above: The scene following the deal in a 50/100 fixed-limit seven-card stud game, with the pot already comprising an ante of 10 chips from each player. Player E's pocket eights is the best hand at present while player F also has a pair in the hole, although the fours are clearly weak. Player C, with high-ranking cards to support the A on display, is in a good position to pressurize opponents given the lack of any door cards higher than his 10 in the hole.

ALL-IN
♦ ♣ ♥ ♠

One of the key elements of table-stakes poker is that players can never be priced out of a hand when they have insufficient chips to call an opponent's bet. In this situation, players may push all their chips into the pot and declare that they are 'all-in' or, if preferred, 'tapped-out'. Should they hold the winning hand at the showdown, they may only claim from their opponents a sum equal to that which they have staked. So a player calling all-in for 100 chips when the bet is 200 may only claim 100 chips from each of those who made the full bet. The rest of the chips constitute a side pot that is contested by the other players. In no-limit poker, the all-in bet can be a powerful tactical ploy, since players are permitted, at their turn, to bet all their chips at any stage of the game.

DOOR CARDS

Assessing the potential of any three-card starting hand is the most crucial factor in deciding whether to take part after the deal. To this end, knowing which hands are likely to secure an early advantage is important, but there are, as always, other factors to bear in mind. The most obvious source of these comes in the value of the opponents' door cards since these must always have an influence on any player's strategy.

Holding a concealed pair of aces with a J as the door card is a good opening hand, but its potential for improvement would obviously be compromised if the two remaining aces in the deck were visible among the opposition's up cards. Possession of the top pair at the outset normally confers an advantage and offers a player the chance to bet aggressively to reduce the competition. The danger in not doing so is that more picture cards will be dealt to opponents in subsequent rounds, perhaps creating an open pair or two, at which point a reassessment of the strength of the pair of aces will be needed. By fifth street, it may be clear that two pairs will not be enough to win and that the chances of catching the K, Q and 10 needed for a straight have all but evaporated.

Again, it is worth stressing that players must keep a watchful eye on the up cards as they are dealt, remember any that have been folded, and constantly re-calculate the changing value of the cards in their possession.

DISGUISING A HAND
♦ ♣ ♥ ♠

One of the better drawing hands to be dealt is a three-card flush which features a low-ranking door card with two higher cards in the hole, particularly when one of those is the A. Pairing the A in this instance could be the springboard for further investment in the hand since it gives insurance against the flush itself not materializing by offering another chance to secure the pot. If there are any cards of the relevant suit already on the board then the flush draw becomes less likely, but the potential for disguising the merit of the hand is high when no other cards of that suit are visible. For instance, with the Ac, Kc in the hole and the 8c as a door card, calling a raise in the opening round from an opponent showing a lower door card than an A or K gives away few clues regarding the hand held, most opponents being likely to credit the player with a pair of eights at best. Indeed, a re-raise at this point could have opponents thinking that a high pocket pair is held, rather than two other clubs, such that another club on fourth street could seem quite innocuous.

Should this happen, the chances of converting the four-card flush into a five-card hand are about even money which will normally be enough to persuade a player to stay to the showdown, provided the flush still appears to be a probable winner.

FIRST-ROUND BETTING

Right: Player B makes the compulsory – or forced – bet known as the bring-in by virtue of holding the lowest door card. To offset this obligation, the bring-in is set at 25 chips, not 50. Player C immediately 'completes the bet' by betting 50 chips and raising the level to the accepted minimum for the first two betting rounds. Player D folds because with one A and two sevens already in play, his own hand of A, 2, 7 is rendered worthless. The remainder all call, including player B who contributes the additional 25 chips to make up the betting.

FOURTH STREET

The arrival of fourth street sees another card dealt face up to those players still in the game while the opening bet in this round, and all subsequent rounds, is the preserve of the player showing the best hand. Importantly, the player in this position is not obliged to bet and may check if desired, a privilege not extended to the holder of the low card in the previous betting round.

In terms of strategy, how to respond to events after the fourth card is dealt depends on the nature of the game. Tight but aggressive opponents assumedly have a promising hand and if fourth street brings them obvious improvement, they are likely to press home the advantage with a bet or, when in late position, a raise. Defending against such strong play in a serious-money game is only advised with a hand that is either already powerful or, as in the case of a flush draw, has multiple opportunities to become a winner with any one of several cards.

In a similar vein, although more liberties are taken by players in low-stakes games regarding which hands to play as far as fifth street, they must still consider their chances of making a better-than-average hand. Since more players are

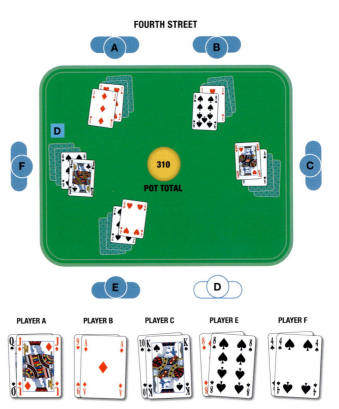

FOURTH STREET

POT TOTAL

310

PLAYER A	PLAYER B	PLAYER C	PLAYER E	PLAYER F

Above: Fourth street brings help in the shape of a pair for both players B and C and, with no pair on the board at present, they may feel this has given them an advantage. In player C's case, the K provides the top pair and a good opportunity to exert more pressure on opponents given the apparent lack of danger represented among the other cards visible on the table. For those holding the pocket pairs there may be just enough incentive to see a fifth card, but player A is definitely in trouble.

Right: Holding a hand such as this open-ended straight-flush draw on fourth street will tempt most players to continue betting given that any club will make a flush while any 9 or 4 will complete a straight, and possibly even a straight flush. These all have the potential to emerge as winning hands at the showdown.

likely to continue to the showdown, when players remaining in the hand reveal their cards to determine the winner, the opportunity for back-door straights and flushes to develop increases, meaning that even two pairs will not be good enough on many occasions.

PREMIUM HANDS

Identifying the most promising hands on fourth street logically follows the same criteria as that applied after the deal. Anyone holding three of a kind – trips – of whatever rank is in a strong position, although this may be weakened from a betting perspective if an open pair on fourth street matches a player's hole card. A player with an open pair of kings who raised the betting in the previous round, for example, will alert the opposition to the likely presence of trip kings, a very powerful hand. An opening bet is likely to win the pot immediately, thus reducing the profitability of the hand, while exercising the option to check will typically result in everyone else checking since they will, quite rightly, suspect a trap is being set. Though trip kings is still likely to be the leading hand after five cards and will usually go on to win, this tactic does offer a chance for opponents to improve at no cost, which rarely constitutes good poker.

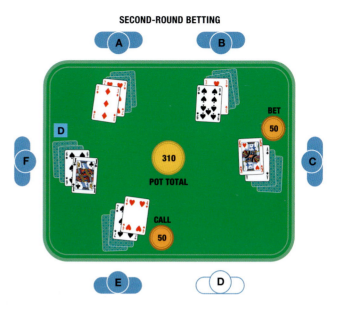

SECOND-ROUND BETTING

Above: Player C duly opens the betting and is called by player E who has the pair of eights and is hoping to find some help on fifth street for the minimum cost. However, with several cards that may complete a low-ranking straight already in play, this is a questionable decision. Realistically, only an 8 for three of a kind will instil any confidence in player E's hand.

Holding any two pairs on fourth street is another good position to be in although, once again, it is better to have two up cards of different rank matching the two in the hole. This conceals the strength of the hand while having an open pair combined with a hidden pair is evidently much more revealing. Other hands that almost demand to be played are high-ranking four-card flushes and open-ended straights, along with three-card flushes and straights that are supplemented by a high pair.

CONTROLLED AGGRESSION
♦ ♣ ♥ ♠

When holding well-disguised high-ranking trips on fourth street, or two high pairs including aces, the key to maximizing the advantage comes from keeping opponents involved in the pot. Because the strength of the hand is concealed, a player can normally afford to check the betting and offer a free card, or make a minimum bet to induce others to call. Controlling the urge to raise on fourth street paves the way for more aggressive betting in the later rounds when the stakes rise. One or two opponents may have improved sufficiently by then to feel committed to the pot with drawing hands that would still not be good enough to win even if completed. By contrast, players who hold low-ranking trips or two pairs usually cannot afford to exercise such restraint on fourth street and are generally advised to bet or raise the maximum when the chance comes. In this situation, the objective is to force opponents with drawing hands to fold, particularly those with high-ranking but, as yet, unpaired door cards.

STRATEGIC PLOYS

For the most part, the strategies applied in the opening betting rounds of a seven-card stud game are similar to those in other poker variations. Players who believe they have the lead should bet accordingly and force opponents to pay more for a chance to take the pot.

The exception to this policy comes when a player holds a distinctly powerful hand that is likely to win without progress. Chances such as this do not arise very often, so players need to exercise a degree of flexibility when betting on fourth street. This is unavoidable since the number of cards in play and the permutations that result prevent any dogmatic approach to the game beyond this stage.

Most guides to seven-card stud highlight a range of hands that, by fourth street, have the potential to become winners. Apart from some of the examples already described, even a hand comprising three cards ranked 10 or higher, but with no pair, is sometimes worth playing. The decision on whether to do so, however, will be dictated by the betting patterns exhibited and the number of open cards already seen. Holding 4s, 10c, Jd, Kh, for example, can only be appealing if there are few cards of the same rank or higher in play. If an array of different picture cards is on display and the betting is heavy, then the value of the hand is considerably diminished since a flush is already impossible and a straight may be very unlikely. This highlights the importance of interpreting the information on offer at the table, rather than relying on a rigid concept of which hands to play.

Right: A hand such as this has limited potential to improve with two cards needed for a straight and a flush already impossible by virtue of holding a card in each suit. Only if the betting is very light and the opposition's face-up cards are of medium-to-low rank should a player persevere. If fifth street brings no help, ideally via a Q, then a decision to fold would be wise.

RAISING IN LATE POSITION

Above: As the second-round betting continues, player F also makes a poor decision by calling given that player E has been dealt a 4, one of the few cards that could immediately improve player F's hand. The pot continues to grow, however, making it difficult to resist taking a chance on another card. Player A's hand is folded but player B makes a raise in late position with the pair of nines. The suggestion that two pairs or possibly three nines have been secured is designed to test the character of the opposition.

STEALING THE POT

In low-stakes fixed-limit games, the chances of stealing the pot on fourth street with a raise are limited. It is usually not possible to bet a sufficient amount to force everyone else to fold. Pot-limit stud, however, offers players a little more leeway when making such a move. This is because a pot-sized bet is hard to call, even at this stage, for opponents holding marginal hands such as small pairs, or three-card flushes and straights. Trying a bluff along these lines is best when in a late betting position and the action has been checked around the table, inferring no one has great faith in their cards. If successful, it enables a player to cover the cost of the antes for several more rounds.

If the bluff is uncovered, this is far from disastrous as it shows a willingness to take a chance with a weak hand which may bring reward later. A bet in a similar situation when holding a strong hand is more likely to be called by opponents who have seen a player's tendency to bluff. Such hands have a greater chance of being paid off by opponents too suspicious to take the hint.

BUILDING THE POT

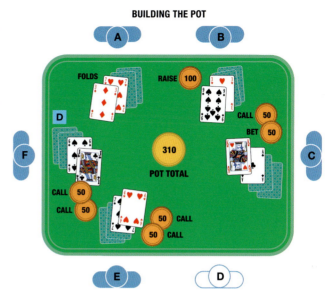

Above: Following player B's raise, player C could re-raise to try driving players E and F out of the pot but, respectful of the bet from player B, decides that the call is a better option. This allows players E and F to follow suit with a call, ensuring that the pot continues to grow and presenting the first player to act in the next round with immediate pot odds of a tempting 7 to 1.

FREE CARDS
♦ ♣ ♥ ♠

Securing more cards as cheaply as possible is vital when holding a viable hand. One way to do this is to raise the betting on fourth street with a hand that is trailing but has potential. Assuming the bet is called but nobody has any obvious help on fifth street, the opposition could warily check the betting around and allow sixth street to be dealt for free. The extra bet on fourth street, which amounts to a semi-bluff, will have saved the player from making a bet at the increased level in the next round. The winning chance of the hand can then be re-assessed with just one more card to come and two further betting rounds to negotiate.

Above: Player B pairs the pocket 9 on fourth street and, acting last, decides to raise given the lack of aggression exhibited in the second round of betting. Although three opponents call the raise, a move such as this is enough to keep them on their guard since they will be aware it could signify three nines are already held.

FIFTH STREET

When playing seven-card stud there are two critical points at which a player must decide whether to participate in a hand, these being after the deal and then again on fifth street. Being able to distinguish a promising opening hand from a poor one is essential, but such promise usually needs to show signs of fulfilment by fifth street for a player to consider any further betting. Since the minimum bet doubles from the third round onwards, players still needing to draw cards for a probable winning hand can expect to pay dearly when trying to catch them. An experienced opponent with a leading hand will certainly ensure this is the case.

Assuming a player has a pair of aces and a four-card straight, holding Ac, Qc in the hole and Kc, Js, Ad on the board, the decision on whether to proceed or not will depend on the strength of hand it is possible to achieve and the likelihood of it occurring. If the four tens, several picture cards and a handful of clubs remain unseen, then the number of live cards available to improve the hand beyond a pair of aces makes participation on fifth street highly likely.

However, these possibilities will be of less interest should an opponent who raised in the opening round with a 7 showing now possess a board comprising trip sevens. If the remaining 7 is in play, a pocket pair is the obvious inference to be drawn from the original raise meaning that a full house must now be suspected. The player holding the pair of aces, expecting the straight and flush draws to be redundant, would need to draw live cards on sixth and seventh streets to improve, though the odds against hitting a full house are 39 to 1. Obtaining a royal flush or four of a kind under these circumstances is highly improbable even if the relevant cards have yet to appear on the table.

Above: Once the fifth card has been dealt, the betting levels rise making this the critical moment in the game. Anyone who bets at this point is likely to continue to the showdown, especially when a fixed-limit betting structure is in operation, as in this example. The size of the pot often becomes too big to resist if players can see they have a chance, however remote, of making the winning hand. Player C acts first once more here with the best hand showing – still the A-high – with the two high pairs of kings and tens well disguised.

Below: On the face of it this appears to be an attractive hand on fifth street since the pair of aces is supplemented by high-ranking cards. Any 10 will complete a straight while pairing the K, Q or J for two high pairs might just prove enough. But whether to bet or not at this stage will very much depend on how many of these key cards have already been seen in play during the hand.

PROMISING POSITIONS

Although it is possible that a lowly pair of twos on fifth street could blossom into four of a kind by the time of the showdown, there are many more promising positions to be in at this point in the game. The general consensus among poker critics is that any hand of aces up or better has to be played, with disguised high pairs and trips remaining very strong hands. Players who have already completed straights will obviously expect to continue in the hand unless an opponent's up cards and betting suggest that a higher straight or a flush is likely to be held. Finding such a hand in five cards will normally guarantee the lead but it can still be difficult to fend off speculative opponents with drawing hands in a low-stakes, fixed-limit game.

The escalating size of the pot, relative to the cost of a bet, will often encourage opponents to call in the third round even though they know they are trailing. In pot-limit stud, by contrast, a player with a made straight can advertise the fact with a pot-sized raise, thus making it much more expensive to call for those opponents still needing additional cards to win.

Below: Any player holding two medium or low pairs on fifth street, like the eights and fours shown here, could be leading but remains vulnerable if unable to force opponents to fold. This is true in fixed-limit poker when the size of the permitted bet may not be intimidating enough to prevent several of them from calling.

CALLING THE OPENER

Above: The 6c presents player E with a small chance of hitting a straight although the 5 dealt to player F does not help. A raise now might be enough to suggest to opponents that the straight is already made but, with so many chips already in the pot, player E realizes that even a bet of 200 will be unlikely to dissuade them from calling. Consequently, player E simply calls for 100.

COMPROMISING SITUATIONS
♦ ♣ ♥ ♠

As might be expected, there is a wide variety of hands that can prove tempting for a player to support from fifth street onwards, the most dangerous being leading hands that are still likely to need improvement in order to prevail. A player holding two medium or low pairs, perhaps holding 9c, 8s, 4h, 8d, 4c, will not feel secure unless dealt another 8 or 4, the chances of which depend upon how many of those remaining are still live. Opponents with higher open pairs or who have previously represented possession of a concealed high pair, could easily have several cards in play that will win them the pot.

A solitary pair of aces is another hand that could frequently be leading after five cards, and most players will probably pursue it to the river – the seventh and final card dealt – if the board suggests no obvious threat. When up against four or five opponents, however, a high pair will rarely be enough to win on its own, though the odds of improvement to two pairs are good at less than 2 to 1. Hitting three of a kind is a 14 to 1 chance which, in itself, is probably less significant in determining whether to bet than the size of the pot and the amount a player has already contributed to it.

WINNING POSITIONS

Having a strong hand after five cards obviously helps a player to determine how best to play the remaining three betting rounds. Anyone holding a high-ranking straight, a flush or possibly even a full house will not only be in a strong position to win but can escalate the betting if necessary to ward off potentially dangerous opposition.

The typical strategy to adopt when in this situation is to check, if opening the betting, or call, if this privilege falls to an opponent who decides to bet. This move is used to keep other opponents active in the game such that they will be more likely to call a big bet or raise on sixth street even if, by now, they know they are trailing. By delaying a big bet when holding a made hand, it is possible that an opponent's hand will improve sufficiently to win. On the whole, however, provided a player's assessment of developments throughout play is sound, such occurrences will be rare enough that slow-playing a hand in this way will regularly prove profitable.

VULNERABLE LEADING HANDS

To be in possession of an invulnerable five-card hand on fifth street is unusual in the extreme. A more likely situation is that a player who currently leads will see plenty of evidence to suggest that this advantage could be temporary. Under these circumstances, an aggressive betting posture is generally advised in a bid to eliminate potentially dangerous opponents. For instance, a player with Ac, Jd in the hole and Jh, 8c, As on the board could easily be leading with two

Above: A player holding two pairs, aces and jacks, can expect to be in a very competitive position on fifth street with a hand that might prove good enough to win at the showdown. An aggressive betting posture is recommended unless there is any reason to suspect that an opponent may have the hand beaten already. Someone showing an open pair, for example, just might have a third card of the same rank for three of a kind.

A COSTLY DECISION?

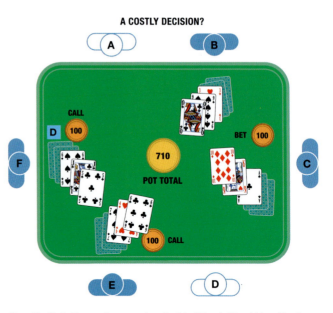

Above: The third betting round now sees player F call for 100, a decision which could easily prove costly given the improvement surely needed to win. By avoiding any aggressive betting moves so far, player F is advertising no strength at all and must be aware by now that a pair of fours is not enough. A flush might yet come good but this requires two of the remaining six unseen clubs in the deck (remember, player D folded the 7c earlier) on sixth and seventh street.

high pairs if the opposition's up cards reveal no obvious threat. Though a maximum bet is advised, any raise from an opponent would have to be taken very seriously and would call for a re-evaluation of the situation.

Unless the hand improves on sixth street, a more cautious approach will then be required since another maximum bet could trigger the same response from the opponent who is, at the very least, likely to call anyway with one card to come. Though the opponent may be bluffing with a weaker hand than that implied by the raise on fifth street, the warning signs are there to suggest that the player may need an A or J to win. In order to draw a relevant card, the player will want to keep the cost of doing so as cheap as possible, which means checking if in an early betting position and just calling if the opponent bets first.

TWO CARDS TO COME

Assuming a player has identified that any drawing hand still has the chance to win with two cards to come, the strategy from fifth street onwards is to see those cards for the minimum outlay. Opponents will be attempting to make this as difficult as possible, a tactic that is much easier to achieve in pot-limit stud than in the fixed-limit game. Nevertheless, even when the likely cost of continuing to the showdown can be readily calculated, playing a drawing hand presents a challenge if there are several opponents still in contention. In these circumstances the best policy is to check or call but definitely not raise, particularly when in an early betting position. The danger of being drawn into a protracted betting war with the worst hand is far too great when in this situation and can result in the size of the pot tempting a player to continue unjustifiably in relation to the chances of actually winning.

STILL IN CONTENTION

710
POT TOTAL

Above: After the exploratory raise in the previous round, player B just calls on this occasion, first because the Q has brought no improvement to the hand and, second, because the other three players remain involved. More importantly, even if player B pairs the A on sixth street, this could still prove inadequate given that player C could have paired the A and a higher card than a 9.

DRAWING DEAD
♦ ♣ ♥ ♠

All players strive to avoid persevering with a hand after fifth street when no available cards can improve it sufficiently to win – a situation known as 'drawing dead'. The number of hidden cards and a subtle betting strategy can help opponents to lay traps for the unwary. Novices often fail to spot the potential difficulty ahead when chasing drawing hands that, even if completed, could fall short of the mark. For example a player might continue betting on a straight draw, needing just one card to complete the hand, when an opponent with three diamonds showing has bet. A call may see the straight completed on sixth street and tempt the player into staying to the showdown where it will too often be beaten by the opponent's made flush or an equally successful draw for an even stronger hand.

Left: An open-ended straight draw after five cards might lure a player into drawing dead. Though a K or an 8 will complete the straight, it may not be worth pursuing if an opponent is showing three diamonds and has bet to infer that one hole card is also a diamond. Receiving a K on sixth street is devalued if the opponent is dealt a fourth diamond since the flush is almost certainly complete.

SIXTH STREET

Even in a fairly loose fixed-limit game it is unusual for there to be many more than three players still contesting the pot on sixth street. A combination of the cards on display and the inferences drawn from the betting is generally enough to have caused anyone without a realistic chance of winning to fold beforehand.

Those at the table will have a fair idea of the quality of hands still in play and, for the players remaining in contention, the considerations are quite simple. A player who possesses what is clearly a winning, if not unbeatable, hand will be aiming to extract as many chips as possible from opponents who are now likely to stay to the showdown. Betting in a bid to eliminate them is extremely difficult at this stage, even in pot-limit stud where a sizeable bet may be interpreted as a bluff. Conversely, a player who holds a good hand but is uncertain whether it is strong enough to take the pot will hope to see seventh street for the minimum cost. This is only worthwhile if the cards that can improve a hand into a likely winner are available. This calculation is reasonably simple given that between a third and half the deck may, by now, have been exposed during play.

EXTRA BETS

In fixed-limit stud there is little likelihood that a player can bet strongly enough to prevent any opponents on sixth street from calling for the final card. Anyone still taking part at this stage will have a reasonably accurate idea of the quality of hands apparently in opposition. As such, they will be more concerned with how their sixth card improves their prospects than with deciphering the subtleties of any betting move.

A player who is confident of leading on sixth street should bet, or raise if appropriate, in the expectation of being

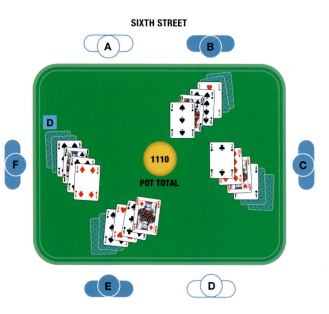

SIXTH STREET

1110

POT TOTAL

Above: After persisting with by far the worst hand, player F now takes the lead on sixth street with trip fours and just one card to come. Player B, meanwhile, has now found two pairs but knows that nines and threes, with four players competing, is unlikely to be good enough at the showdown. Players C and E both draw blanks.

| PLAYER B | PLAYER C | PLAYER E | PLAYER F |

called. Checking not only offers opponents a free opportunity to form a better hand, but also reduces the potential winnings on those occasions when the leading hand on sixth street retains its status at the showdown. The whole strategy for a player who is confident of being ahead is to try to induce as many extra bets from opponents as possible.

Checking and then raising a subsequent bet made by an opponent, a tactic known as 'checkraising', is sometimes worth considering but only if the player with the leading hand is confident that one or more opponents will bet on the strength of their cards. If so, then the player who initially checked can raise in the knowledge that anyone who has bet on sixth street will probably call the raise, rather than fold, even if they now suspect they are behind. The size of the pot relative to the amount required to call almost ensures this eventuality and satisfies the raiser's strategic aim of generating extra bets to maximize the profit on winning hands.

SEVENTH STREET

By seventh street a player's strategy in a fixed-limit game will be influenced by the number of opponents still involved and the player's position in the betting sequence. The final betting round will often be contested heads-up by just two players, in which case there is limited scope for subtle betting moves.

A player who is confident of victory and is set to act first should always bet to pressurize an opponent into calling with a beaten hand. Most opponents will do so in this situation provided there is still the slimmest of chances they might win, if only to indicate that they cannot be bluffed out of a pot at the end. When the player acting first harbours serious doubts about holding a successful hand, then a check is the only viable decision. There is nothing to be gained by betting since an opponent will fold if clearly beaten, but will probably raise if ahead, leading to the likely but unnecessary loss of additional chips when the player feels obliged to call.

In the same scenario against two or more opponents, a check is advised. Any bet with a weak hand is likely to be wasted since a caller will probably have a better hand. Also, there is always the risk that the bet could be raised and even re-raised. Then the player either folds, losing one bet, or calls with a good chance of losing even more last-round bets.

By checking first instead of betting, opponents may fear a checkraise move and might also check, so the showdown would come at no further cost. Likewise, any unraised bet in the final round might make a call justified in this position to trigger the showdown because the potential loss would be limited to a single additional bet. This provides a timely reminder that minimizing losses in poker is as important to long-term success as consistently winning large pots during a session.

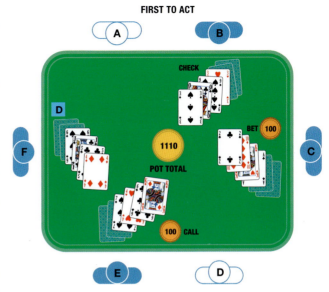

FIRST TO ACT

Above: In the fourth round player B is first to act because of the pair of threes showing and he checks, hoping to see seventh street for free. If the others remember player B's raise on fourth street and think it represented three nines, they might not bet for fear that player B is planning a checkraise with a full house. However, player C bets in support of the two pairs, kings and tens, although the K dealt to player E has reduced the chance of making a full house. Player E calls.

MORE AGGRESSION

Above: Player F now raises in support of the trip fours, a move that could represent to the opposition that the 4d has helped to complete a straight rather than three of a kind. Player B is now thinking that a full house is required to win, meaning that any of the nines and threes that are among the 31 cards he has yet to see must come on seventh street. The odds against this are about 7 to 1, making a call now almost obligatory as the pot odds are roughly the same.

TOURNAMENT PLAY

Many poker players remain puzzled that despite its immense popularity, seven-card stud was passed over in favour of Texas Hold 'em as the game played for the WSOP world championship in the early 1970s. While the latter has come to dominate the tournament scene ever since, its rise to prominence owes much to the predilections of the professionals who contested those early contests. Their preference for the game is thought to have influenced Benny Binion's decision to adopt it for the WSOP.

However, pot-limit and fixed-limit seven-card stud tournaments soon became a fixture of the month-long WSOP event, while Europe's annual Poker EM, held in Vienna, is one of the most prestigious seven-card stud tournaments outside America. Pot-limit seven-card stud events are popular with experienced players, making them a risky prospect for the novice. For those considering a fixed-limit tournament, here are a few basic guidelines that may prove helpful.

EARLY STAGES

At the start of a multi-table tournament with seven or eight players per table, a cautious approach in support of only the best opening hands is the typical strategy. Anyone holding a strong hand will bet aggressively in the first round to capitalize on the early advantage by encouraging opponents to fold. To counter such aggression, only playing the best starting hands and drawing hands is therefore advisable to protect one's chip stack.

Any player holding a high pair after three cards is almost bound to continue to at least fifth street before re-assessing the situation, and will likely continue to bet aggressively until this stage to whittle away the opposition. With this in mind, only drawing hands featuring high-value cards should be considered an alternative since they offer

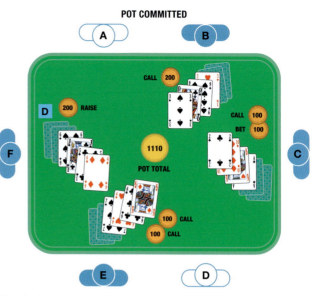

Above: The fourth round ends when players C and E call for the additional 100 chips. Both are under the impression that player F may well have formed a small straight and that they are likely to need help from the final card to emerge victorious. For player C, this means that only a K or a 10 will help while player E cannot be sure that a 5 will provide a straight good enough to win. However, having come this far, player E feels 'pot committed' and will obviously be reluctant to fold at this point for the sake of a few more chips with so much already invested in the pot.

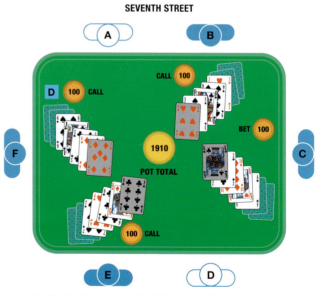

Above: Player B retains the honour to bet first in the final round but checks again, convinced that the two pairs are not enough. Player C, by contrast, bets 100 in support of the full house of kings over tens which is expected to prove the winner. For players E and F the moment of reckoning has arrived. Both have improved their low pairs into three of a kind, but the decision to keep calling in the earlier rounds has come back to haunt them. They call, as does player B.

other chances to win. A player holding As, Ks, 8s, for example, is justified in calling a raise from an opponent who has a Q showing and is representing a high pair since pairing the A or K may be enough to win, even if the flush does not materialize. Players must be wary of pursuing drawing hands blindly during the early stages of a tournament risking a regular loss of chips when survival is of most importance.

MIDDLE STAGES

A tricky element of tournament play is that participants have no knowledge of their opponents' abilities or playing styles, so conservative play is sensible during the early stages. At a table of very conservative opponents, a player may be able to adopt a loose style by supporting marginal hands. For example a raise in late position to represent a large pocket pair when showing a 9 on third street could set up a winning bet on fourth street if another 9 or a picture card is dealt. A cautious opponent will suspect two pairs or three of a kind and will probably fold in the face of a possible full house developing unless there is a realistic chance of beating such a hand. Similarly, if there is plenty of action at the table with several players staying until fifth street, then it is wise to restrict one's involvement to hands which offer the most winning potential.

Apart from gauging the opponents' strength, another key factor governing strategy at this stage of the tournament will be the size of a player's chip stack. If low on chips, opponents are likely to raise with lesser hands than usual as they try to fashion a heads-up scenario that may eliminate the player from the event. Despite the pressure of being short on chips, having the patience to wait for a prime starting hand before committing oneself to a pot offers the best chance of surviving to the later stages.

SHOWDOWN

2310
POT TOTAL

Above: The showdown confirms that player C has won with the full house to claim the pot of 2,310 chips. This example shows the hands that can occur in seven-card stud, especially when several players stay to the showdown. Two pairs and three of a kind are often good enough to win, but the chances of these hands holding up is greater if the field is reduced by fifth street.

PLAYER B   PLAYER C   PLAYER E   PLAYER F

THE FINAL TABLE
♦ ♣ ♥ ♠

Stack size at the final table is the crucial in determining strategy. During the tournament, players in the leading chip positions can avoid getting involved in hands, while short-stacked opponents try to claw their way back into contention. Players with just enough chips for a handful of bets need to be similarly selective in which hands they play. The difference is that when dealt a reasonable hand, they must bet aggressively straight away. A player has a better chance of winning when all-in on third street against one rival than betting all-in on fifth street against two or three. By the time the tournament is down to the last three or four players, the average value of the winning hand will drop while play is likely to be more aggressive. Stealing the antes with the first raise is a typical ploy and more bluffing is apparent, especially when a player's board cards suggest a strong hand.

The key to success at this stage lies in a player's ability to judge the situation and the opposition as much as the quality of hand to support.

TEXAS HOLD 'EM

Texas Hold 'em begins with the first player to the left of the dealer making a compulsory bet known as the small blind, after which the next player bets the big blind, usually set at the same level of the minimum bet for the first round, while the small blind is generally half this sum. The cards are dealt one at a time, face down, until each player has two cards which are referred to as their hole or pocket cards. A round of betting follows before the dealer reveals three cards, face up, on the table. This is called the 'flop'. Following the flop, a second betting round takes place and then a fourth card – the 'turn' – is dealt face up next to the flop, after which there is further betting, with the minimum bet permitted typically doubling at this point. The fifth and final face-up card, known as the 'river', is revealed by the dealer prior to the last round of betting. The objective is for players to make the best five-card poker hand possible from their two hole cards and the five community cards revealed on the table. Players may, if they wish, discount their hole cards entirely when finalizing their hand, in which case they are said to be 'playing the board', their hand comprising all five community cards.

If there is one poker variation that has contributed to the recent resurgence of interest in the game, it is without doubt Texas Hold 'em, often referred to simply as Hold 'em. The game is thought to have originated in Robstown, Texas, early in the 20th century, and was widespread in the southern states of America, although it was eclipsed in terms of popularity by seven-card stud. This state of affairs existed until Benny Binion decided to employ Texas Hold 'em as the variation to decide the WSOP World Champion in the early 1970s. The publicity surrounding the event created a demand for more poker tournaments and Texas Hold 'em established itself as the game of choice for such knockout events.

THE MOST POPULAR GAME

The legendary Johnny Moss once said that "chess is to checkers what Hold 'em is to draw or stud", underlining the complexities of the game that have made it so appealing to millions of players worldwide. Although the basic concepts of Texas Hold 'em are simple enough to grasp, playing it well takes courage, cunning and skill, particularly in pot-limit games (where maximum bets can be no higher than the total in the pot) or no-limit games (where players can bet all their chips at any time during play). These are the favoured betting structures for Texas Hold 'em tournaments, which have helped the game establish itself as a cultural phenomenon in the 21st century.

Television coverage of the tournament circuit and patronage from the stars of show business and sport has generated a stylish and fashionable image for the game that is attracting ever more interest. Consequently, Texas Hold 'em has acquired the status given to chess and bridge, with a wealth of books, feature articles and websites offering serious analytical appraisals of the game and how best to play it. In short, Texas Hold 'em is big business, while at the recreational level, it has revived interest in forming card schools and poker clubs, as newcomers to the game aim to discover the secrets behind its popularity.

Left: Johnny Moss, the first WSOP world champion and the man whose poker battle with Nicholas 'Nick the Greek' Dandolos in 1949 stimulated Benny Binion's desire to initiate the WSOP. Moss always considered Texas Hold 'em to be a more complex game than either draw or stud poker.

ONLINE IMPACT

Draw poker is traditionally the game to which beginners are exposed first, but in the Internet age, this situation is rapidly changing. Media coverage of Texas Hold 'em, together with the upsurge of interest that ensued, has coincided with the growth, since 1998, of online gaming sites that have been perfectly placed to meet the demand for ready access to poker. Texas Hold 'em attracts more players than any other online poker variation, and the ubiquitous nature of the game at present makes it likely that the next generation of poker players will cut their teeth on this game rather than on draw or stud.

Not all players appreciate the impact of the medium on the game itself, believing it to encourage poor poker habits in line with the speed at which decisions are made. Turbo tournaments, in which the blinds – the compulsory bets made by the two players to the immediate left of the dealer – are raised every two or three minutes, are popular at the lower-stake levels and will often be completed within the hour. However, the suggestion is that much of that popularity comes from the greater propensity for luck, rather than skill, to play a part. Bad calls do win on occasions and a poor player may need to be lucky just once with an all-in call in order to eliminate someone whose reading of the game is superior. For online players, the key point is that they should be open-minded in their analysis and not misread a lucky winning streak as evidence of skill.

Above: Behind the scenes at the TV production room during the *Ladbrokes Poker Million Masters* in 2004. Broadcast by Sky Sports in the UK, the event has become an integral part of the TV company's schedule since its inception in 2002. Each player's hand is always visible on camera, allowing the director to piece the action together in a suitably dramatic fashion to enhance a viewer's interest.

TELEVISED TOURNAMENTS
♦ ♣ ♥ ♠

After enthusiastic but limited attempts to convey the WSOP to a television audience during the 1970s, poker truly made its mark on the TV schedules from the late 1990s onwards. Cameras beneath the table enabled viewers to see the players' cards and, since tournaments almost invariably feature Texas Hold 'em, the game quickly became part of the mainstream consciousness. The enthusiasm for online gaming sites to sponsor tournaments staged for television has seen interest expand to the point where there are channels solely dedicated to broadcasting poker. Texas Hold 'em is the principal poker variation driving this interest, inspiring more viewers to play and improve their poker skills.

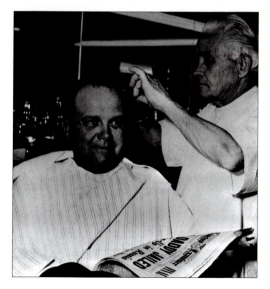

Left: Benny Binion, getting his hair cut for his court appearance, is the founder of legendary Binion's Horseshoe Casino, where all WSOP events were held until 2005. In 1964, he regained control of the Horseshoe Casino after selling his interest to cover his legal costs defending himself from tax evasion charges. As a convicted criminal, Benny could no longer hold a licence to run a gambling establishment. His sons Jack and Ted took over the operation of the casino. Benny remained on the payroll as a consultant.

STARTING HANDS

In Texas Hold 'em, players are dealt just two cards at the start of play, yet even with so little initial information upon which to base a betting decision, this is still perhaps the most crucial moment of the game. Successful cash game players will probably see less than a third of all flops, and maybe as few as a fifth if they are strict in their choice of starting hands. Poorer players are usually much less disciplined in which hole cards they support, trusting in possibilities rather than probabilities. To an extent, this approach is conditioned by the factors motivating them to play; by definition, recreational or social players are keener to take part in the action and to view losses as the price paid for their entertainment.

Which of the 169 potential two-card combinations are worth playing depends on the likely value of the winning hand, as in all forms of poker. In Texas Hold 'em, a single high pair will often win the pot and hands such as two pairs or three of a kind (trips) are highly likely to do so, especially when the hand incorporates both hole cards. A player who holds pocket eights when a third 8 appears on the flop, the moment when the first three community cards are revealed, is in a powerful position due to the concealed strength of the hand. This is an obvious advantage compared to holding a pocket 8 that matches two eights on the flop when the implication behind any bet is much more easily read by opponents.

A straight or better will usually be good enough to win, but many hands of such potential are folded before they have a chance to be realized. This happens because unless the flop brings immediate promise of making the hand, the cost of drawing the cards for a straight or a flush, for example, can be made prohibitively expensive, relative to the odds against success.

STARTING HANDS

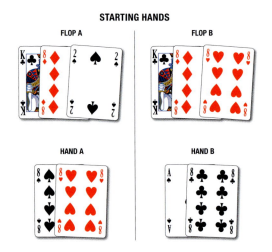

Above: Making three of a kind – trips – on the flop using a pocket pair and one board card, as here in hand A, puts a player in a better position than when making a similar hand with a pair on the board, as is shown in hand B. In the first example, only a player holding a pair of kings could be any threat, but an opponent holding A, K may bet in the belief that the top pair is leading. Whether a call or raise should follow depends on the willingness of the player holding trips to allow any opponents a chance to improve their hands before making a maximum bet. While making trips using just one pocket card is generally strong, any bet in support of the hand immediately suggests possession of either a K or an 8, which will normally be enough to end the hand.

Above: This hand of 7, 2 offsuit is popularly regarded as the worst possible two-card starting hand to be dealt in Texas Hold 'em and most players in receipt of these cards fold immediately. If dealt them while in the big blind, a player might choose to see the flop provided the betting has not been raised. Only if the flop then brings a minimum of two pairs could the player contemplate becoming seriously involved in any subsequent betting.

Right: In Texas Hold 'em, pairs of aces, kings or queens are seen as premium starting hands and players can raise before the flop, whichever betting structure is in operation. Medium pairs such as nines, eights and sevens are best played cheaply in the hope of hitting trips, and similarly for lower pairs. However, so many cards could appear on the flop to counterfeit a hand such as a pair of fours that players should beware of supporting them too strongly.

POCKET PAIRS

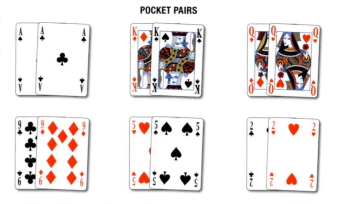

POCKET PAIRS

A pair will often be enough to take the pot, so being dealt a pair in the first two cards is advantageous, but players must beware of becoming too attached to the hand. Some pocket pairs are more valuable than others, with tens and above seen as playable wherever a player is sat in relation to the dealer. Pairs ranked 9 and below will usually need help from the board in the form of a matching card to prove successful, with the odds against making trips on the flop in the region of 8 to 1 against. This could justify calling a bet to see a cheap flop, but anyone with a pair lower than tens may find calling an opponent's raise much more difficult.

A raise is typically indicative of high cards being held, if not paired, meaning that any A, K, Q, J or 10 on the flop – any one of 20 cards – could immediately leave a player with pocket nines, for instance, trailing to a bigger pair. By contrast, a player who has pocket aces or kings has the chance to raise or re-raise any first-round bets, to defeat opponents and consolidate the early advantage.

This is crucial, since, while a pair of aces is the best possible hand before the flop, occurring once in every 220 deals, the board could supply a mixture of cards to help opponents. The more players who see the flop, the more card combinations are in play to blend with the board and render the aces second best. This is why most players advocate playing premium pocket pairs, such as aces, kings and queens, as aggressively as possible arguing that opponents must be made to bet heavily for a shot at beating them.

TOUCHING CARDS
♦ ♣ ♥ ♠

Two cards that are consecutive in rank – 'touching cards' – are valuable in Texas Hold 'em because, on 80 per cent of occasions, the board will contain at least three cards that could help form a straight, which, if held, is often good enough to win the pot. Two touching cards such as J, 10, for example, will fit with four different three-card combinations to form a straight, these being A, K, Q; K, Q, 9; Q, 9, 8 and 9, 8, 7. By comparison, even a hand such as A, 10 can only make a straight if K, Q, J appears on the board. Hands such as A, K and K, Q, although offering reduced chances of making the straight, are compensated by their potential for making the high pair, which is often enough to win at the showdown. Lower down the scale, hands such as 10, 9 and 5, 4 are generally regarded as poor starting hands and players who choose to play them usually do so when pre-flop betting is light. The inherent problem in playing low connecting cards is that when they do make straights, they may be at the wrong end of the spectrum. If the board contains 6, 7, 8, for example, then the player holding the 5, 4 has the low or 'ignorant end' of the straight and is outranked by anyone with 10, 9 or 9, 5. Similarly, K, Q, J on the board provides a straight for a player with 10, 9, but a holding of A, 10 will prove superior.

Above: Hands that feature touching cards offer straight opportunities given that the five board cards will include three cards to a straight 80 per cent of the time. A hand such as the A, K can only make a straight with the Q, J, 10 on the board but the high-ranking cards are beneficial. The 9, 8 combination, however, will blend with four different three-card combinations to make a straight, although there is the potential for it to be second best. The Q, J, 10 combination to form one possible straight could easily form a higher example for a player holding A, K or K, 9.

SUITED CARDS

Holding two suited cards after the deal offers a player possibilities of a flush, although these are best realized when just three cards of the relevant suit are on the board, rather than four. Holding Ks, Qs is much more beneficial if the board reads Ad, 9s, 8s, 6d, 4s, rather than Ad, 9s, 8s, 6s, 4s. In the first instance, it is plausible that an opponent contesting the pot holds the As and a card of a different suit, thus the resulting flush represents the best hand. But with four spades on the board, an opponent with the As would obviously take the pot. This underlines another benefit in holding the A in any suit, and highlights the possibilities of playing any A-suited combination, although the A, 9; A, 8; A, 7 and A, 6 hands are weaker. They do not offer the added benefit of blending with a three-card combination on the board to make a straight.

Flushes are strong hands in Texas Hold 'em, but they have to be played with a degree of caution, since players will often have to see the turn and the river card in order to fill them. A flush draw can be expensive for a player to pursue when an opponent has read the hand correctly. Although there is a 40 per cent chance that the five board cards will feature at least three of the same suit, there are four suits, reducing the relevant chances of any suited pairing matching the board to 1 in 10. Furthermore, the chances of a flush being made on the flop when in possession of suited hole cards are fractionally less than 1 per cent but, although such a hand is powerful, exploiting it to the full can be testing, especially without the A. Betting with such a hand will usually win the pot, making a small profit, however slow-playing it always runs the risk of someone else securing a higher-value flush or, if the board subsequently pairs, a full house.

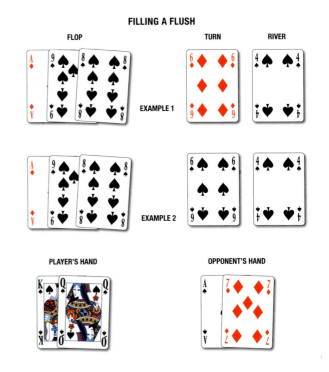

FILLING A FLUSH

FLOP | EXAMPLE 1 | TURN | RIVER

EXAMPLE 2

PLAYER'S HAND | OPPONENT'S HAND

Above: This illustration highlights the potential problems that arise when holding suited pocket cards but not the A. In the first example, the player holding Ks, Qs has two chances to hit a winning spade although the opponent, who holds the leading hand on the flop and the turn with a pair of aces, could make it expensive to stay in the game. In the second example, the turn card puts the player in front with a flush but even an all-in bet might not persuade the opponent holding the As to fold, with potentially disastrous consequences if the river brings a fourth spade.

Above: An opening hand of K, 9, often referred to as 'Lassie' or 'Rin-Tin-Tin'. The hand is more valuable when suited, as in this example, but it can be tricky to play it well. Doyle Brunson is one professional who dislikes it because too many of the cards that might help it develop into a strong hand are likely to do the same for an opponent. Pairing the K, for instance, is of no help if someone else holds a K with a higher kicker, which is a very plausible prospect.

PLAYING MEDIUM PAIRS

FLOP A

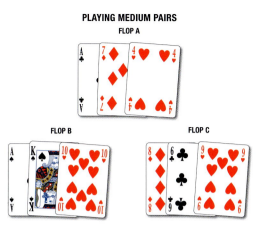

FLOP B   FLOP C

PLAYER'S HAND

Left: A medium pair is worth the occasional call before the flop when the pot is unraised, since there is around an 8 to 1 chance to secure trips immediately, as in example A. However, if the flop consists of three higher cards, an underpair has little value and should be folded if an opponent bets. Occasionally, as in example C, the hand will not directly improve but will generate additional potential to help make a strong hand. Indeed, a post-flop bet or raise may be enough to win the pot, such are the visible threats apparent.

MARGINAL HANDS

The dubious potential of mid-ranking pairs has already been explained, as they can too often become impotent after the flop. A hand such as a pair of sevens can be played when in the big blind since, if nobody raises, a player in that position can check the betting and see the flop at no further cost having already committed the required chips in the pot. If there is no help from the flop in the shape of a 7 or a low straight-draw possibility, the hand should probably be folded in the face of the first bet.

Touching cards ranked J or lower, even if suited, pose similar problems. Whether to play them will depend on the opposition and the situation in a game, but they are rarely powerful enough to call any pre-flop raise. The flops that can help marginal hands are less likely to appear and the danger is that when they do, an opponent's hand may improve even more.

POOR PROSPECTS

More than half the possible two-card combinations are simply never worth playing by anyone with pretensions to being a profitable player. Picture cards with unsuited low cards such as Kh, 2d or Js, 6c have little merit when one considers the composition of the board. They need very specific flops to fall in order to warrant continued support. For example a player holding Kh, 2d when the flop is Kd, 10s, 7c has a top pair but with a very weak kicker. If an opponent bets, the obvious conclusion is that a pair of kings is being represented, it being unusual for a player, holding 9s, 8d for instance, to open the betting in pursuit of a straight draw. This is terminal for the K, 2 since any opponent holding a K cannot hold a kicker lower than 2 and so cannot be losing, making it difficult to withstand any aggressive move. Similar comments apply to a pair of twos that can only be confidently supported after the flop should another 2 be dealt.

POTENTIAL DANGER

FLOP A   FLOP B

FLOP C   PLAYER'S HAND

Above: A weak hand such as K, 2 offsuit needs too much help from the board to be seriously competitive. Flop A offers two pairs, which could warrant a maximum post-flop bet to dissuade callers who fear trips. Yet it could still lose to another poor starting hand of K, 7. Flop B is more dangerous because holding a top pair with a weak kicker is inviting trouble. Any opponent who holds a K with a better kicker is immediately in front, and K, J offsuit could be in opposition. Even making trips as shown in flop C could see the K, 2 against the final K with a higher kicker.

BEFORE THE FLOP

Having assessed the promise of their opening two cards, players have to consider the other factors at work when deciding whether to bet or fold before the flop. Of these, the number of opponents, their position relative to the dealer, and the nature of the game will be the most vital.

A restrained, low-stakes fixed-limit game between ten players may well see five or six calling to see the flop if it is habitually unraised. By contrast, pot-limit and no-limit Texas Hold 'em could see sizeable raises before the flop, as players try to test the resolve of their opponents and reduce the competition. Only by understanding the context of a particular game can a player form a strategy for the hand in progress.

When betting to see the flop, players should be clear on what they need in order to win, while retaining the discipline to fold if the flop brings no encouragement. Loose players are inclined to see too many flops with poor or marginal hands, the likely result of this indiscriminate policy being a steady reduction in their chips as the game unfolds.

EARLY BETTING DECISIONS

How to proceed once the cards are dealt will depend on the character of the players and their motives. This underlines the value of observing, to build up a picture of the hands opponents play and the betting moves they make. In a tight game featuring plenty of folding before the flop, it can pay to be flexible regarding which starting hands to support. A raise before the flop, with a marginal hand, may even be enough to steal the blinds occasionally in a game where opponents are reluctant to play with anything less than excellent cards. They are more likely to respect a pre-flop raise and assume it indicates a high pair or A, K until it is proved otherwise.

In a hectic game where several players routinely see the flop, a more patient strategy is prudent. Playing only the stronger starting hands would conserve chips for those times when a player wishes to maximize the return on investment, having found a winner. Opponents who are preoccupied with their own game may not notice the implications behind a cautious player's participation in the hand until it is too late.

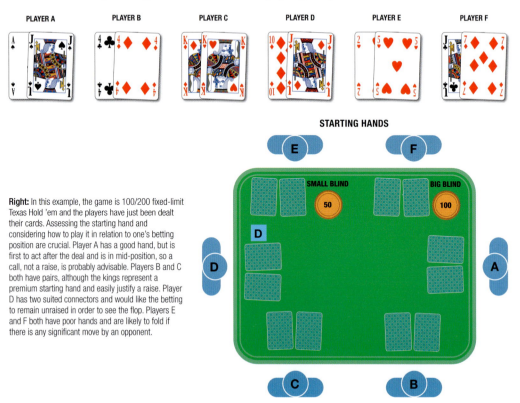

Right: In this example, the game is 100/200 fixed-limit Texas Hold 'em and the players have just been dealt their cards. Assessing the starting hand and considering how to play it in relation to one's betting position are crucial. Player A has a good hand, but is first to act after the deal and is in mid-position, so a call, not a raise, is probably advisable. Players B and C both have pairs, although the kings represent a premium starting hand and easily justify a raise. Player D has two suited connectors and would like the betting to remain unraised in order to see the flop. Players E and F both have poor hands and are likely to fold if there is any significant move by an opponent.

POSITIONAL PLAY

In Texas Hold 'em, a player's position during the betting round is more significant than in any other poker game. The earlier a player has to act, the more difficult it is to control the betting given the lack of information upon which to base any decision. This affects the quality of the starting hand a player can expect to support before the flop, with hands that are virtually unplayable in an early betting position becoming much more attractive when on the dealer button. The dealer is always last to act in the betting rounds that succeed the flop and so has much more information from opponents regarding the quality of their hands. For example, when holding K, J offsuit and seated next to the big blind (who is in second position, clockwise from the dealer), a call might seem reasonable, but the player is vulnerable to subsequent raises from opponents. Since the initial reaction would be to assume such opponents hold a high pair or an A with a good kicker – A, K; A, Q; A, J, for example – the potential of the K, J is immediately devalued. The decision is whether to fold for the loss of a single bet or risk another bet in the knowledge that the hand is probably already losing. The problem in doing this is that cards that may help on the flop could easily improve an opponent's hand as well in this situation. Pair the K alone and an opponent with A, K or K, Q is still ahead, while a flop of K, J, 10 for two pairs could be losing to someone with A, Q for a straight.

Holding the same hand on the dealer button, however, offers much more scope, since, if nobody raises, a call will probably be enough to see the flop. This allows the player to gauge the inferences behind opponents' post-flop bets without having to risk any further chips. Premium hands such as the high pairs and A, K can be played in any position, almost without exception. As a general rule, the earlier a player's position relative to the dealer, the stronger the starting hand is normally required to be.

Below: A pair of twos, sometimes called deuces or ducks. While being dealt a pair in Hold 'em is generally advantageous, a pair of twos should be played as inexpensively as possible since making trips on the flop is the likeliest route to victory. Calling a pre-flop raise with them is unwise and, if failing to hit three of a kind on the flop, the hand is probably worthless.

PRE-FLOP BETTING

Right: Player A's decision to err on the side of caution by calling encourages player B to call with the pair of fours, although a raise from player A might well have seen the small pair folded instead. Player C has the chance to raise but decides instead to disguise the strength of the hand with a call. This is a questionable move since it could easily allow one of the weaker hands to improve past it. Player D now has the chance to call as well and player F checks on the big blind, leaving five players to see the flop. Player E's hand is too poor to be worth calling for the extra 50 chips and is folded.

PLAYING THE FLOP

Although deciding which starting hands to play is crucial, it is the flop that defines whether or not such decisions were justified. Strong two-card holdings can easily be compromised while poor hands will, on occasion, become unbeatable, given the right flop. When each player can see five of the seven cards from which they will ultimately form their hand, they can quickly deduce the best that they can achieve and, most importantly, whether that will be enough to win the pot. However, it is rare for a player to hold the nuts at this stage, from which it can be understood that leading hands may yet be beaten, while weak hands could still improve sufficiently to win.

This volatility is what makes Texas Hold 'em such an appealing and challenging game to play. In terms of strategy, factors such as position, the betting structure in use and the playing styles of opponents are still of paramount importance. But with more information now available in the form of the flop, players are able to calculate how many of the cards remaining unseen might help or hamper their chances of victory. Any post-flop strategy, therefore, should always begin with an assessment of the probabilities that emerge from the cards in play. Only then can the actions of opponents be viewed from the proper perspective as each player attempts to outwit the others and secure the pot.

STRONG PLAY

Each deal offers a completely different scenario, so knowing how best to exploit any given situation depends on a player's ability to assimilate all the information available and act accordingly. Skilful players are better able to strike a balance between aggression and caution after the flop and choose a strategy that fits the specific situation. In this regard, strong play may involve folding a good hand in response to a large bet as much as managing the pot when holding a guaranteed winner. For example a player holding pocket kings who raised before the flop and elicited one caller will be extremely wary if the

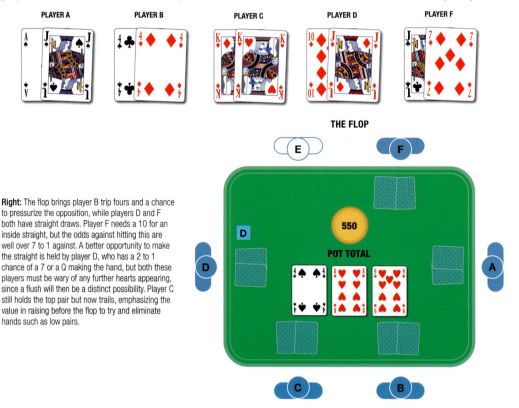

Right: The flop brings player B trip fours and a chance to pressurize the opposition, while players D and F both have straight draws. Player F needs a 10 for an inside straight, but the odds against hitting this are well over 7 to 1 against. A better opportunity to make the straight is held by player D, who has a 2 to 1 chance of a 7 or a Q making the hand, but both these players must be wary of any further hearts appearing, since a flush will then be a distinct possibility. Player C still holds the top pair but now trails, emphasizing the value in raising before the flop to try and eliminate hands such as low pairs.

flop shows an A but no K. Any bet from the opponent surely indicates possession of an A and good players will fold the kings there and then. However appealing the hand was after the deal, it is no stronger in this situation than any other pocket pair lower than aces.

Conversely, raising before the flop to represent an A and then putting in a big bet when one materializes on the flop is powerful play, particularly if opponents are known to call pre-flop raises with marginal hands. Unless they can beat a pair of aces, calling a bet in this situation is extremely difficult for anyone without an A, even if they have the potential to improve their hand. Given that the typical policy in Texas Hold 'em is to bet with leading hands and force opponents to pay for the cards that may win them the pot, the occasional bluff representing an A can be a positive move when used sparingly.

Above: A pair of aces in the hole, sometimes called 'pocket rockets', is the best starting hand available in Texas Hold 'em. Despite the initial advantage enjoyed when holding pocket aces, success cannot be guaranteed which is why most players dealt the hand will raise before the flop as with any other high-ranking pair.

Right: Player F is first to act and checks, as does player A, who has two overcards to the flop but little encouragement to pursue the hand further. Any significant betting might be enough to prompt a fold, given the straight and flush draws made possible by the flop. Player B bets with the three fours, but knows this may still not be enough to force opponents out of the game. Were this a pot-limit or no-limit game, then a much bigger bet would be possible to drive out any drawing hands, but, as it stands, player C is able to call, in the belief that the pair of kings could still be winning. This also allows player D to call, since the current pot odds of over 7 to 1 exceed the 3 to 1 against drawing one of the six cards that will make the straight, these being the Q and 7 in any suit but hearts.

WEAK PLAY

Instances of weak play are not always restricted to players in possession of poor hands, either before or after the flop. Most experts would advocate raising before the flop with a pair of aces in a ten-player game, for example, since to enable several opponents the opportunity to see the flop cheaply decreases the hand's effectiveness. Any pair on the flop could easily provide an opponent with three of a kind and render the aces impotent. This highlights one of the guiding principles of Texas Hold 'em, which determines that players should never become emotionally attached to a powerful starting hand that is diminished in strength after the flop.

On the whole, however, weak play generally consists of players making the wrong decision in relation to the current state of their hand. Those who decide not to bet when in a leading position always run the risk of allowing an opponent to overtake them at negligible cost. Nevertheless, the poorest betting strategy is to continue calling opponents' bets when the possibility of obtaining the card or cards required to win simply does not justify remaining involved in the hand. Pots that are won on the occasions when a player is lucky enough to draw the relevant cards will very rarely compensate for the amount of money lost in similar circumstances during the game.

POST-FLOP BETTING

ASSESSING CHANCES

The three community cards on the flop provide the most immediate opportunity for a player to evaluate the chances of success prior to the beginning of the second betting round. Those players who are in the later positions have time to factor their opponents' betting decisions into the equation once the action is under way, but the cards themselves provide the earliest clues regarding whether to play or not.

On occasions where the flop offers no help at all, the usual recommendation is to fold at the first sign of any betting. A hand of 9d, 9s, for instance, is unlikely to withstand a flop of Ad, Kh, 10c when an opponent bets to indicate possession of at least a high pair. Apart from the possibility of someone holding another A, K or 10 (constituting nine cards), the appearance of a Q or J on the board (a further eight cards) would simply enhance the possibility of a straight being made. In this situation, while the pair of nines may be winning, it is highly unlikely with so many cards in the deck working unfavourably. Only seeing nines on the turn and river – when the fourth and fifth and final community cards are dealt respectively – can guarantee victory and the odds against this are 1,000 to 1, so the rational decision would be to fold. This example illustrates that a player should always be assessing the probability of a hand improving enough to win the pot, rather than for it merely to improve.

CALCULATING OUTS

On the vast majority of occasions, the flop will not furnish a player with the nuts, and, when it does, the board cards will probably nullify any attempt to capitalize on the hand. To take an extreme example, a player holding a pair of queens when the flop is Q, Q, 7 faces an obvious problem in persuading opponents to call a bet. Consequently, players will typically have to calculate the number of outs – cards that can help them keep or obtain the winning hand – available in the deck. For the most part, players who require help from the board will typically be seeking just one of several cards on either the turn or the river.

The more cards that help, the better the opportunities with the tipping point being 13 or 14 cards, since having this many working in a player's favour offers an even-money chance of success. Those drawing to flushes or open-ended straights usually have eight or nine cards that will make the hand, the odds against which are 2 to 1. Any player with 14 or more unseen cards in the deck that will help secure victory is favourite to win.

Below: While player F folded, the escalating size of the pot tempted player A to call on the flop and the turn card – Ks – now offers the chance of an unlikely winning flush. It also illustrates the dynamic nature of Texas Hold 'em, with the lead changing hands once again, as well as highlighting the need for players with leading hands to bet aggressively in an effort to eradicate such potential threats. Player C is now in a very strong position, but may still not be able to bet enough to induce the others to fold.

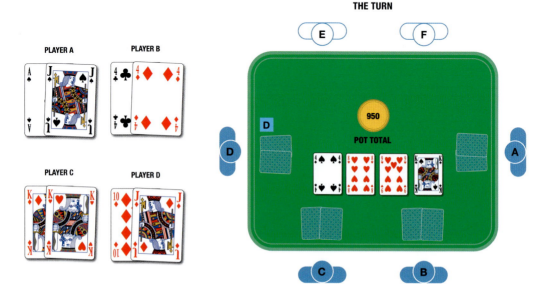

COMMON ERRORS

Mistakes made by players after the flop tend to fall into two categories. They either overvalue their hands and call optimistically despite their poor chance of winning, or they simply pay too little attention to the betting and fail to grasp the implications behind it. This can befall those with leading hands as well as those who need cards to win. Anyone holding Jc, Jd when the flop reads As, Jh, 9c, for example, may be inclined to slow-play the hand, since trip jacks is very strong and would be second only to a player with pocket aces. However, should any K, Q, 10, 8 or 7 be seen on the turn, then an opponent could conceivably make a straight. That is a total of 20 unseen cards that could beat the hand, while any A could do the same if an opponent has an A with the remaining J for a bigger full house.

With so many cards promising potential danger, a maximum bet is advised to force opponents out of the pot. Waiting until the turn card before betting could prove too late to have any effect, by which time the promise of the trip jacks has dissolved.

Above: The scene after the flop as a player hits three Js. Despite the apparent strength of the hand, any one of 20 cards on the turn could conceivably provide an opponent with a straight. In recognition of this, it would be best for the player holding the jacks to bet the maximum now to encourage opponents with straight draws to fold. If the bet is big enough, even players who have paired the A on the flop may think twice before calling.

BETTING ON THE TURN

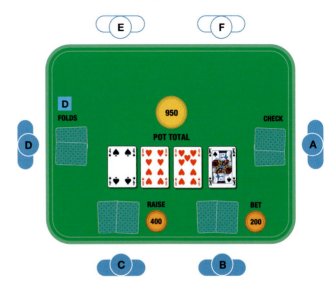

Right: Undeterred by the calls in the previous round, player B bets 200, this being the minimum for the final two rounds, but is raised by player C, whose bet indicates that the K has proved helpful. For player D, the cost of calling is too prohibitive, since the pot is now offering less than 4 to 1 when the chance of hitting a winning card on the river has risen to over 10 to 1 against. This is because only four cards – the Q and 7 in clubs and diamonds – can now secure a potential winning hand without filling a flush. Player A, however, has a 4 to 1 chance of catching another spade for the nut flush, but must be concerned that, with two evidently strong hands in play, a call of 400 chips may yet be raised again by players B and C.

LEADING HANDS

Holding a leading hand after the flop is obviously advantageous, but playing the hand correctly in order to realize its winning potential is still a challenging proposition. On the occasions when a player makes a powerful hand on the flop, such as a full house or a straight flush, the objective is to manage the pot and extract as much as possible from opponents. In this case, checking on the flop, and perhaps on the turn card, is often the only way to induce a bet from opponents, who, if their hands have improved, might assume that the board has not helped other players at all.

Making an unbeatable hand – the nuts – on the flop is a rare occurrence, and most leading hands, no matter how strong, remain vulnerable to defeat. A player with Kc, Qs, for instance, will probably be leading if the flop cards are Kd, 8d, 7s, but if several opponents call a bet advertising the pair of kings, then it is likely that straight and flush draws are being pursued at least. If so, the high pair could be beaten by any one of 29 cards that could complete an opponent's straight or flush, added to which any A, 8 or 7 in suits other than diamonds could also threaten defeat. With up to 80 per cent of the cards working against the pair of kings, the likelihood is that the hand will lose in a showdown. If some aggressive betting on the flop cannot eliminate all opposition under these circumstances, then caution is definitely advocated as the game progresses.

DRAWING HANDS

Whether in possession of a leading hand or one that is trailing, requiring one of several cards to bring about certain victory after the flop is an integral part of Texas Hold 'em. The term 'drawing hands', however, is usually associated with those players who need one card on the turn or river in order to improve sufficiently past a leading hand to win. Players holding suited or connecting cards repeatedly encounter this situation as they try to draw the one card needed to complete a flush or a straight.

In general, the strategy behind playing such hands is to remain in the game as cheaply as possible, since, with two chances to hit the required card, there are obviously two more possibly expensive betting rounds to negotiate. Yet the potential for straights and flushes and full houses when there is a pair on the flop, is all too apparent to those with leading hands. Opponents currently holding the best hand can be expected to try forcing out the drawing hands by betting, so a keen eye on the existing and implied pot odds is advisable when in this situation.

By way of warning, it should be emphasized that more chips are lost by players fruitlessly pursuing drawing hands than in any other aspect of the game. This covers not just hands that fail to improve, but those that do realize their potential, only to secure the runner-up position.

Right: In the event, both players A and B call the raised bet of 400 chips, the former still hoping the flush draw will materialize while the latter is working on the assumption that player C has made no more than two pairs. The river gives player A the nuts since the A-high flush in spades is the best possible hand now available given the board cards, the chances against which were 24 to 1 against occurring when the flop was revealed. Now a bet from player A is absolutely essential, since it is the only way of tempting opponents into putting more chips into a pot they cannot win. Checking in the hope of being able to re-raise later runs the risk of seeing everyone do the same; the pot will still be won, but the profit will be reduced.

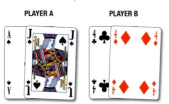

PLAYER A   PLAYER B

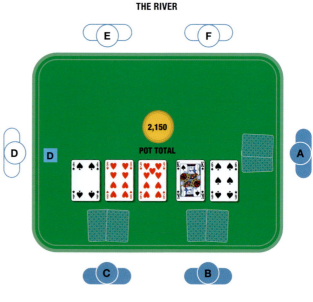

THE RIVER

2,150

POT TOTAL

CHASING HANDS

Hands that need two cards to realize their potential – chasing hands – should ordinarily be folded unless everyone checks on the flop. Expecting two cards to fall conveniently on the turn and river is extremely optimistic and players in such situations should usually fold if there is any significant betting. A player holding Qh, Jh when the flop is Kd, 5s, 6h, for example, would be ill-advised to pursue the flush, since there is only a four per cent chance of the next two cards bringing running hearts. Odds of 24 to 1 against this occurring virtually guarantee that the pot odds will never justify supporting a chasing hand.

When they do win, it is usually in a light betting heat in which all players have poor hands. An example would be when a player holds Kc, 9c and the flop reads Qs, 4c, 8d. Should nobody bet on the flop and the turn card is the Jc, then the player has a 4 to 1 chance of seeing another club on the river for the flush, odds which might justify a third-round call if the pot odds are appealing.

Above: An example of a typical chasing hand with the player holding Q, J suited realistically needing help on both the turn and the river cards to offer a possible winning opportunity. Two more hearts will provide a flush while an A and 10 or 10 and 9 will complete a straight, and these are hands that could easily prove best. Unless there is little or no betting after the flop, chasing two cards for a winning hand is rarely worthwhile since the pot odds rarely justify it.

THE CONCLUSION

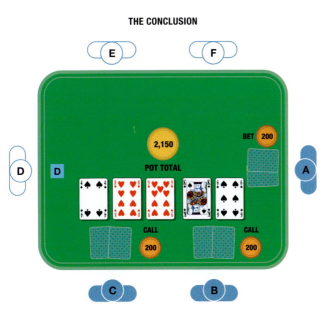

Left: Player A bets with impunity, knowing that players B and C must have reasonably strong hands and might call just to be certain a bluff is not being executed. Both are aware that player A initially checked on the flop and the turn but later called the bets made in both rounds, indicating that a flush could now be held. However, with both of them holding trips, they decide to call, with player C, particularly, regretting that the earlier advantage could not be pressed home. Had the game been a no-limit contest, an all-in move by player C after the K appeared on the turn may well have forced player A out of the hand.

PLAYER C

POST-FLOP STRATEGIES

Players who are sufficiently enamoured of their cards to consider betting will visualize the potential for winning. To achieve this, players will require their visions to be coloured by some strategic thinking concerning the probability of various outcomes during play. Although an assessment of the cards on display is important, the style and betting structure of the game, as well as the quality of the opposition will also influence any viable strategy.

Irrespective of the cards and probabilities in play, it is always easier to call a bet from a serial bluffer in a fixed-limit game than it is to call a raise by someone who normally folds nine hands in every ten while playing pot-limit Texas Hold 'em. For champion Doyle Brunson, the key elements in any post-flop strategy are the intangible qualities of patience and self-discipline, particularly when playing fixed-limit Texas Hold 'em. The pot-limit and no-limit games do permit greater licence to prosecute bold post-flop play via large raises and credible bluffs, but having the patience to wait – for the right cards against the right opponent and when in the right position – remains an asset.

VARYING APPROACHES

The fluid and volatile nature of Texas Hold 'em provides enough uncertainty over the outcome of most hands that players need to adopt a range of varied strategic approaches when playing the flop. In early position with the leading hand, the recommendation is generally to bet. Allowing opponents free cards is only advisable when a player is confident they can do little damage. If the flop offers a probable winning hand, however, a checkraise after the flop may be in order when one or two opponents can confidently be expected to bet. If they fold after the raise, the pot is won, but

THE DEALER BUTTON STEAL

PLAYER C

Above: When a pot is unraised before the flop and the action is checked around to the dealer afterwards, it will often mean that the flop has helped nobody much at all. Should opponents show weakness in this way, a bet from player C, in this instance, could be enough to take the pot. By representing an A in the hole to make the high pair, opponents who have no A and no help from the flop will find it immensely difficult to justify calling. Such a move is more likely to succeed when the player can bet substantially in order to underline the threat, making this a more viable tactic in pot-limit or no-limit Texas Hold 'em.

Above: A cashier at the Commerce Casino in Los Angeles counts out an equal number of chips for each player participating in the World Poker Tour Invitational event. Exposure to the styles and techniques of the top professionals via televised events such as this has helped confirm Texas Hold 'em as the poker game of choice for most players.

should the motive behind the raise be doubted, they will probably call and may well feel committed to the pot thereafter, despite the chance of drawing to a beaten hand.

In later positions, players have the opportunity to take a few liberties on occasions, especially when betting is light. Should the action be checked around the table, for example, the player on the dealer button may be able to steal the pot with a finely judged bet. If a flop of Ah, 9d, 4c invokes no response from others, then a bet to represent an A in the hole for the top pair is perfectly reasonable, provided nobody had raised before the flop. Here, a 'feeler' bet will win the pot or expose the fact that any caller probably has an A, which, if combined with a weak kicker, could explain the previous reluctance to bet.

The key to which strategy or betting style to adopt lies in closely observing the opposition. In a game featuring several cautious players, a little loose play can reap benefits by playing on their fears. Equally, in a game with inexperienced or loose players inclined to call at every opportunity, a more conservative and studied approach is recommended.

BLUFFING IN THE BIG BLIND

PLAYER D

Above: When Texas Hold 'em is played as a pot-limit or no-limit game, the chance to make bigger bets can help to make bluffs more likely to be respected than in the fixed-limit variation. Here, everyone has called the minimum bet of 100 chips before the flop. A check from player C when the flop is revealed could allow player D to infer possession of a strong hand such as trips or two pairs. Having paid the big blind and been allowed to see the flop for no extra cost, the other players know that player D could have any two cards. A hand such as 8, 5 or 5, 2, which would ordinarily have been folded, could have made two pairs, while 3, 4 – another poor hand – could make an open-ended straight draw. Players holding an A could easily believe that pairing it on the turn might also fill a straight for their opponent in the big blind.

BLUFFING OPPORTUNITIES
♦ ♣ ♥ ♠

As mentioned previously, bluffing on the flop in a fixed-limit game is hampered by the inability of players to bet sufficient amounts to intimidate opponents into laying down their hands. In this respect, carving out a reputation as someone who only raises with a top-quality hand can help a player to sneak through an occasional bluff, perhaps, when the risk of being called is generally high. Other betting structures, however, do improve the chances of bluffs being successful, since larger bets are permitted – the impact of this is twofold. First, any pot-sized bet after the flop makes the cost of calling more expensive, and second, the pot odds facing anyone wishing to call are immediately rendered much less attractive. Since a bet from a player in early position usually advertises strength, a pot-sized bluff by the player in the big blind becomes a possibility. Assuming there were no pre-flop raises, a forceful bet from the big blind when the flop reads 8c, 5h, 2s, for example, could easily persuade opponents with high cards to fold. Having already paid the obligatory bet to see the flop, but no more, opponents know that the player could have made a pair or even two pairs with cards that ordinarily would have been folded, such as 8, 5 or 5, 2. Even someone holding an overpair to the board will be wary of calling, given that any 8, 5 or 2 on the turn just might provide the big blind with three of a kind. Opportunities such as this may be rare, but there are times when they can be exploited, especially when opponents are betting timidly.

THE ART OF DECEPTION

The ability to deceive opponents is an integral part of the game, which is why bluffing and varying one's betting style is so vital. The aim is to create doubt in the minds of opponents regarding the meaning behind any bet. If a bluff fails, opponents may consider it the tactic of a loose and reckless player, an image that may be exploited later when a strong hand develops.

In Texas Hold 'em, the capacity for the flop to offer potential to several players generates many opportunities to practise the art of deception. For example a flop of Ad, 3d, 10s presents the chance of a high straight, a low straight or a flush being realized, added to which anyone matching the board with their hole cards for a pair of aces, two pairs or three of a kind will almost certainly be keen to see the turn. Representing any one of these hands with a call or even a small raise could lay the foundations for success. Should any A, 10 or 3 be dealt on the turn, then a large bet would signal three of a kind or a full house has been made, making it difficult for those still needing a card to call. If the card is the 10d specifically, even someone with a made flush might baulk if having to call a large bet against a possible full house, while any opponents still drawing to a straight will definitely think they are beaten.

Using the flop in this way enables players to pick up pots occasionally, without necessarily having the cards to win. The one danger lies in representing a hand that is already held by an opponent, since betting as though holding pocket aces, for example, will prove costly should an opponent actually have pocket aces.

Right: Marlon Brando shuffles the deck in *A Streetcar Named Desire* (1951). Adapted from the Tennessee Williams play, the film features several scenes in which Stanley Kowalski (Brando) and his friends play poker.

CHECKRAISING OPPORTUNITIES

PLAYER E

Above: By checking in early position after the flop, player E with a K-high straight has induced a bet and two calls from opponents and can now consider a raise with what is currently the best possible hand. Should everyone then fold, the manoeuvre will have successfully obtained a few more chips than might have been the case if player E had bet in turn. Alternatively, anyone who subsequently calls the raise will still be trailing and will need further help from the board, leaving player E in a strong position to manage the pot. The checkraise can also be a viable bluffing tactic if the board cards offer the credible threat of a made hand.

CHECKRAISING

While many players deem checkraising, or 'sandbagging' – the latter a tactic of slow-playing a strong hand, perhaps by checkraising – to be an underhand ploy, the fact remains that it is a perfectly legitimate ploy in a game premised, after all, on deception. As an aid to pot management, it allows a player who holds a strong hand in an early position to lure opponents into betting more than intended. Should a check be followed by a bet and a couple of calls from others at the table, a raise might be enough to win straight away. At the very least it might persuade one or two opponents to fold, thus reducing the field and leaving the checkraiser in good shape for the turn, with probably the best hand.

In pot-limit and no-limit Texas Hold 'em, the checkraise is a more powerful bluffing tool than in the fixed-limit game, but players have to be sure that conditions are right. The potential offered by the flop must act as a guide, for it is the board cards that a player must use to engender fear in opponents. For instance, players in late positions will frequently try to pick up the pot if the action has been checked to them, even with a modest hand. If the flop suggests the potential for a much better hand to exist, a checkraise in early position may be sufficient to convince opponents that it is already held. A flop of Qs, 9h, 8c, for example, would make a straight for someone holding J, 10 but, if the betting is checked around, anyone holding a hand such as A, Q or A, 9 may bet in the belief they are leading. By checking and then raising with a large bet to imply possession of the straight, opponents with such hands are instantly put onto the back foot. Even if the bluff is called, any K, J or 10 on the turn followed by a large bet can reinforce belief in the opponents' minds that the straight has definitely been achieved.

SLOW-PLAYING A HAND

PLAYER F

Above: Deceiving opponents is an essential element of Texas Hold 'em, so being able to disguise the strength of a hand is a tactical move that can pay dividends. In this example, player F resisted the urge to raise before the flop with the pair of kings and has generated a family pot in which everybody remains involved. By checking on the flop, the hope is that others will sense weakness and bet with hands far inferior to the trip kings. Slow-playing the hand in this fashion, therefore, is a tactic that can increase its profitability as opponents inflate the pot with little or no chance of winning.

Left: A pocket pair of jacks which is best regarded as a medium pair only. Notoriously tricky to play, pocket jacks can be played aggressively from late position if nobody is keen to raise the pot. Calling with a pair of jacks when an opponent has already raised is much more testing, though, since any A, K or Q on the flop will often have made a higher pair.

SLOW-PLAYING A HAND
♦ ♣ ♥ ♠

When holding an exceptionally strong hand on the flop, players are best advised to slow-play it by simply checking or calling as needed to keep opponents involved. A flop of Kh, 6d, 4c when holding pocket kings, for example, is unlikely to have helped many opponents given that the cards needed for a straight draw are so low. Here, the player with trip kings can probably allow opponents to see the turn card cheaply and reserve bigger bets for the last two betting rounds. While an opponent may strike lucky, there remains a 30 per cent chance that the trip kings could still improve to a full house or four of a kind, which would be highly unlikely to lose.

THE TURN

The revealing of the turn card, or 'fourth street' as it sometimes known, clarifies the situation even more, as players face the same considerations as on the flop. The difference lies in the fact that with just one card to come, assessing one's own hand and comparing it with the best that might result on the river, the last card, is much simpler.

Equally, calculating the pot odds when considering whether to bet or not is a straightforward task. Crucially, it must be remembered that any card that helps one player may improve an opponent's hand as well. The danger in this situation is that, having survived as far as the turn card, it is very easy to become committed to the pot and see the hand through to the showdown. Despite believing it is a probable loser, the amount in the pot and the proximity to claiming it can all too easily prompt a player into casting good money after bad.

PLAYING THE TURN

As ever, discipline and realism are needed at this point in the game, irrespective of how many chips a player has already contributed to the pot. The fact that the minimum bet on the turn and the river is double that of the previous two rounds should encourage players to be circumspect regarding their chances.

Once again, how to play the turn is dependent on a player's position, the number of opponents and the betting that has already occurred. A maximum bet when clearly leading is advisable, to put pressure on opponents with drawing hands who, although tempted by the pot odds on offer, will need to improve on the river to win. In most cases, some doubt will remain over the ultimate result. For instance, if a flop of 4h, Ac, Jh is supplemented with the 6h on the turn, then a player holding Ah, Js is in a reasonable position with the

TRAPPING AN OPPONENT
♦ ♣ ♥ ♠

Opportunities to trap opponents by inducing them to place a bet when they are already losing do not occur very frequently, so it is essential to take advantage of such opportunities when they arise. For the most part, this will involve sitting tight on a winning hand in the hope that an opponent improves sufficiently to risk making a bet. A player seated in early position who checks on the flop with Ks, Qh when the board displays 10s, Kd, Kc ideally wants an opponent to possess As, Jd, for example, to complete a straight should the Qc appear on the turn. By indicating weakness with another check, anyone who has made a straight could well be tempted to walk into the trap by betting. If that is the case, a call will suffice to see the river card, following which a bet is recommended, in the hope that the opponent with the straight has misread the situation and calls, or raises, suspecting a bluff.

PLAYING THE TURN

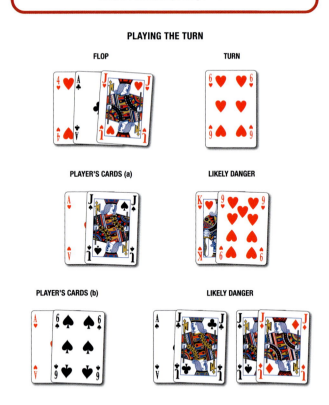

Above: The quality of a hand depends on the flop, but doubt over the final outcome can still exist once the turn card is revealed. The A, J offsuit for the top two pairs and the nut flush draw is still vulnerable if a bet on the flop is called, indicating that an opponent may have two hearts. The possibility of a flush draw having been made on the turn is high, but the player holding A, J still has 11 cards that can win, with the aces, jacks and remaining hearts all helping.

top two pairs and odds of about 3 to 1 against making the nut flush or a full house. Only an opponent who has already made a flush – which could yet be beaten – is likely to call, or more likely raise, any bet in this situation.

By contrast, if the player holds Ah, 6s instead, given the same board cards, then the options are less promising, especially if the betting on the flop indicated that one opponent may also have an A while another was drawing to the flush. Now only another heart on the river can guarantee success, since an A, 6 or a J could give an opponent a better full house. Therefore, choosing whether to bet in this situation must be guided by the inferences drawn from earlier play.

READING THE BETTING

While players are naturally inclined to focus on their own prospects of winning, the clues on offer from the betting of opponents are ignored only by the foolhardy. Whatever the standard of the game, players bet for a reason and deducing the rationale behind their strategy is all part of the challenge presented by Texas Hold 'em. For example if a flop of 10s, 2c, 5c generated only light betting, but a player in early position bets after the turn card is revealed as the 4c, then a flush is surely indicated.

Should that player hold Ac, Jc for the nut flush and be raised by an opponent, then the natural conclusion, however unlikely, is that a straight flush has been secured with pocket cards of 6c, 3c. An opponent with a lower-ranking flush may have called, but would probably credit the player with possession of the Ac for a flush draw at least, making the hand vulnerable.

Any player trying to draw to the flush without the Ac, meanwhile, is likely to fold. The danger for the player

Above: A sizeable pot develops as the game unfolds. In a fairly loose Texas Hold 'em game that features several players regularly paying to see the turn card, substantial pots can develop. As the minimum bet doubles after the turn, players must be certain in their own minds that contributing more chips to the pot is justified by the strength of their cards, not merely the size of the pot on offer.

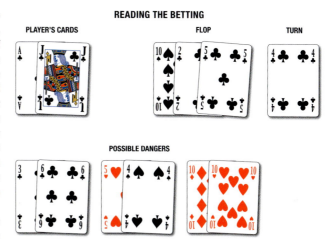

Above: Clues to the strength of an opponent's hand will usually arise from the betting and, on occasions, players have to accept that the improbable can happen. A player holding Ac, Jc, for example, would normally expect to take the pot if a third club should appear on the turn. But if the betting up to this point has been light, players with weak starting hands could still be in contention. Should a bet supporting the A-high flush be called, it is possible that an opponent could be drawing to a full house. However, a raise from an opponent would logically indicate that an unlikely straight flush has been achieved with the 3c, 6c.

with the Ac, Jc in this example comes from calling the raise while potentially already losing, only to see the 3c, 6c, 7c or 8c on the river. Judging by the betting, a straight flush for the opponent would then seem highly likely, not just possible.

THE RIVER

Typically, it is rare for more than three players to be contesting the pot by the time the river card is dealt, whichever betting structure is in place. Players should expect that anyone still in opposition at this stage must like something about the board cards, even if to win they may yet need to execute an impressive bluff.

Once the final card is revealed, players are able to see exactly what their hand comprises and also the potential hands available to opponents. Yet the best hand may still not win depending on the perceived threats held by the board cards and the nature of the betting throughout play. Unless holding the nuts, calling a large bet with a hand that is a potential but not guaranteed winner can test the nerves of even the most experienced player. Whether such a call would be justified depends on the likelihood of the hand proving the best and, as usual, whether the pot odds favour a call even if it is likely to lose. Clues are available from the cards and the previous betting rounds, and play on the river often hinges upon a correct reading of the game. In this regard, knowledge of opponents' playing styles is often crucial, although sitting in on a game with total strangers, as when playing online, understandably makes this more difficult.

AVAILABLE OPTIONS

There are not too many options available on the river. A player holding what seems to be a winning hand must concentrate on pot management by doing what it takes to encourage opponents to contribute more chips. In early position during a pot-limit or no-limit game, a small bet relative to those of previous rounds might be enough to goad an opponent into calling, just to prove that the hand represented is actually

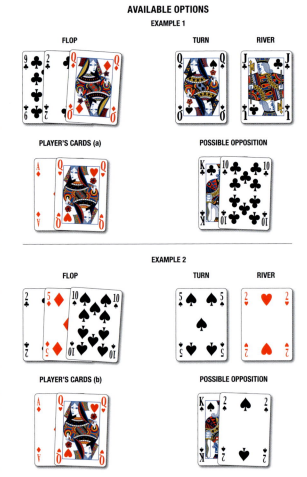

AVAILABLE OPTIONS

EXAMPLE 1

FLOP TURN RIVER

PLAYER'S CARDS (a) POSSIBLE OPPOSITION

EXAMPLE 2

FLOP TURN RIVER

PLAYER'S CARDS (b) POSSIBLE OPPOSITION

Above: Clues from the previous betting rounds will help to make a decision on the river, especially when a strong hand may have been beaten on the river. In example 1, the player holding three queens would have to fear that an opponent had completed a flush if the opponent had previously called a large bet after the turn card. In example 2, holding the A in a light betting heat may be enough to win when the board reveals two low pairs and a medium kicker. But a lack of earlier betting action may ensure the final round is contested by several players, any of which could hold a vital low card such as a 2 to make an unlikely full house.

FISH, GEESE AND SHEEP
♦ ♣ ♥ ♠

Those unable to read a game are considered weak players with 'fish', 'geese' and 'sheep' being just a few of the common terms used by experienced players to refer to them. The challenge for novices is to improve with experience, to avoid continually making the right move at the wrong time. Competent amateur players may be regarded as 'fish' when they move up to a higher level and start competing with the sharks of the professional poker world.

JUDGEMENT CALLS
♦ ♣ ♥ ♠

Playing the river when not holding the best possible hand is a common experience for all Texas Hold 'em players, although this is often due to the inclination of many to keep calling bets from the flop onwards with hands that improve just enough to put them in further trouble. A player holding Ad, 3d, for instance, may have stayed to the end, having seen the board cards revealed as As, 8s, Kh, 6c and finally 3s. But if an opponent has matched bets all the way, it is unsafe to assume that two pairs of aces and threes will be enough to win. If the betting has been at the minimum level throughout, then the opponent probably has an A, could already have two higher pairs and might conceivably have played for the flush draw holding Ks, Qs. Sometimes, however, the river card may simply complete a nondescript board, which makes it possible for a player with, perhaps, just an A-high, to steal the pot by betting first. Judging whether to try this move will depend on how confident a player is that small bets and checks in previous rounds confirm that nobody has a hand good enough to call such a bet.

held. A bet is advised in a fixed-limit game, as there is no point in allowing opponents to check and thus miss the chance of winning a few more chips.

When in a later position, playing the leading hand is more straightforward, since a bet or raise can always be made in confidence. Hands that are made on or before the river but could easily be beaten are more difficult to play. Having three of a kind by the turn when the river card puts a third club on the board, for example, is an awkward position to be in if it is plausible an opponent has pursued the flush all along.

Similarly, a board of two pairs and a low kicker will sometimes generate little action and be won by a player holding an A. It is difficult to call a large bet with the highest kicker when the prospect of encountering a slow-played full house looms. Players will then sometimes have to rely on their instincts concerning the opposition as much as the odds at work.

The river card will often signal the failure of some players to draw the card needed for a straight or a flush. Folding is the usual option here, unless the board holds the promise of a bluff. These are more likely to succeed in games that permit large bets, since, in fixed-limit Texas Hold 'em, the cost of calling is simply not enough to force opponents to surrender the chips already bet.

Left: Once the river card has been dealt to the board, a player who holds the nuts should definitely bet, the real test being to stake just enough that opponents with inferior hands are tempted to call for fear of being bluffed. If the bet is too big, the opposition may well fold leaving the winner of the hand with a smaller profit than might have been the case.

JUDGEMENT CALLS

FLOP	TURN	RIVER

PLAYER'S CARDS   **POSSIBLE OPPOSITION**

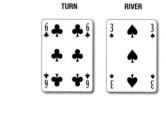

Above: This example illustrates the problems that can result by the river when playing an A with a low kicker. The A on the flop for a high pair offered promise, but if any bet on the flop or the turn was called, then any one of several credible hands could be in opposition. An opponent with an A and a higher kicker could easily have made two better pairs, while a flush is equally possible. In this instance, the improvement for the A, 3 could lead to a player calling a bet with a beaten hand.

KNOW YOUR OPPONENTS

Successful Texas Hold 'em players are obviously aware of the opportunities presented by various starting hands and the board cards as they are revealed. What separates the excellent players from those of average ability, however, is their aptitude for quickly gauging an opponent's playing style and reacting accordingly. Indeed, the very best players will alternate their style throughout a session to confuse and unsettle opponents, many of whom are prone to make predictable moves governed by their personality. Such players generally fall into one of four recognizable categories, irrespective of the stake level at which they normally play poker.

KNOW YOUR SOLID PLAYERS

Solid players, often known as 'rocks', are those who have the discipline and patience to fold the majority of hands and cautiously wait for an unbeatable hand – the nuts – or something very close to it, before committing too many chips to the pot. Conscious of their playing position at all times and the chip stacks in front of their opponents, they have a tendency to play only the highest-ranking starting hands and support them vigorously unless there are enough loose players at the table to justify setting a trap. In fixed-limit games, such players will play the percentages and seize upon mistakes.

KNOW YOUR TIGHT-AGGRESSIVE PLAYER

At high-stakes tournament level, most solid players will adopt a tight-aggressive mode of play, folding anything but the best starting hands and pressurizing opponents with large pre-flop raises. On those occasions when their strategy backfires, however, such players will still retain the discipline to fold rather than chase their losses.

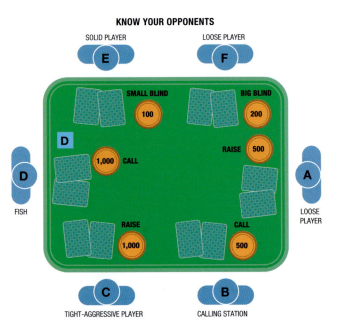

KNOW YOUR OPPONENTS

Above: Each individual's style of play has a bearing on any game. After the deal in this no-limit Texas Hold 'em contest, player A raises out of position with a low pair, in keeping with an enterprising approach, while player B cannot resist calling, due to a desire to be in the action. Player C, with a strong hand, takes advantage by raising again with the pair of queens, only to be called by inexperienced player D, who is unable to read the implications of previous bets. The solid player E will be prepared to fold the A, 9 suited for the loss of the small blind, but a loose player on the big blind could call the further 800 chips for the remote chance of winning.

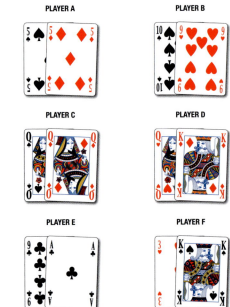

KNOW YOUR LOOSE PLAYERS

Those who play poker for social rather than financial reasons are likely to indulge in a much looser style of play. A desire to stay in the action characterizes such players, and their enthusiasm for Texas Hold 'em will make them likely to call a raise when holding a small pair or 8, 7 suited in the small blind, for example, after which they may disregard the pot odds for an outside chance of winning.

Other examples of loose play include raising repeatedly when out of position and calling in contradiction of the evidence on display when needing cards to win. Such players tend to have volatile periods of good and bad fortune, and their hands are difficult to read, making them dangerous opponents.

KNOW YOUR CALLING STATIONS

For a player with pretensions to winning, knowing the 'calling stations' – these being players who repeatedly call other players' bets, irrespective of their chances of winning – is crucial. These players will frequently upset the odds by drawing unlikely winning hands. Being suspicious by nature, they find it difficult to release any chance of winning a pot, even in the face of particularly antagonistic betting. No matter how big the raise or how unlikely their chances of winning, calling stations will play sheriff as they insist on verifying that the raiser has the hand being represented.

The tendency to call, irrespective of the pot odds or inferences on offer during play, is very common among novices. They are often insufficiently familiar with the nuances of the game to understand the inferences behind a bet, which makes them very difficult to bluff. Should a player not realize that an opponent is unable to interpret the meaning behind large bets, valuable chips could be lost when bluffs are repeatedly called.

IMPACT ON THE BETTING

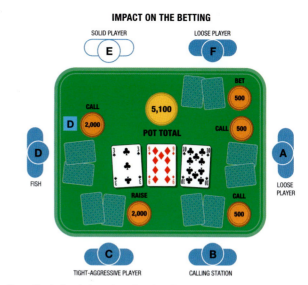

Above: After the flop, the loose players in early position press their case by betting in defiance of the pre-flop raise by player C who again tries to force the opposition out of the pot. However, player D sees a possible straight materializing and calls another big raise, unaware that the pot odds are vastly inferior to the chances of catching a J, one of which – Jc – could make someone else a flush. With over 10,000 chips in the pot, players F, A and B may yet contribute more, as the potential rewards for winning override their concerns at being beaten.

SAME HANDS, DIFFERENT APPROACH

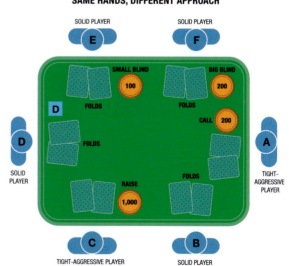

Above: By way of contrast with the first two examples, here the same pre-flop situation is replicated, but in a game between solid and experienced players. A flat call from player A with the low pair is raised by player C, who, content to pick up the pot right now, presses home the early advantage with the pair of queens. Player D reads this as indicative of a high pair and knows that if player C has kings or queens, then chances of improvement are low. Player E will fear that player C has an A with a bigger kicker, undermining the A, 9 suited. Both players fold, as does player F, so player A faces a hard call for 800 chips with a hand that should probably be folded.

BETTING STRUCTURES

Although much of the expert guidance available on how to play Texas Hold 'em is relevant, whichever betting structure is in place, each has sufficient impact on the culture of the game to warrant consideration. The stakes are important too, emphasizing that anyone buying in to a game ought to play at a stake level commensurate with their financial means. Players who participate in games for money that they cannot afford to lose are rarely able to focus entirely on their poker and run the risk of compounding their error with poor play. Contrasting betting structures were devised to satisfy the tastes of different players and their various gambling preferences, with three in particular emerging as the most popular.

FIXED-LIMIT

This is the betting structure favoured by the majority of recreational cash game players, although there are numerous professionals who grind out a living playing fixed-limit Texas Hold 'em in the casinos and card rooms of the world. In the resort casinos of Las Vegas and Atlantic City, the small-stakes limit games are frequently populated by 'rounders' – itinerant gamblers who play only premium hands and sit patiently waiting for the tourists to make mistakes.

Therein lies a clue as to the best way to play fixed-limit Texas Hold 'em, which is a game of position, and percentages. It favours conservative players who are reluctant to gamble wildly, since the scale of any betting during a hand is easier to predict. This helps players to calculate the upper limit of any possible losses while devising their betting strategy.

Right: In no-limit Texas Hold 'em the daunting prospect of throwing away all of one's chips in a single hand is always present.

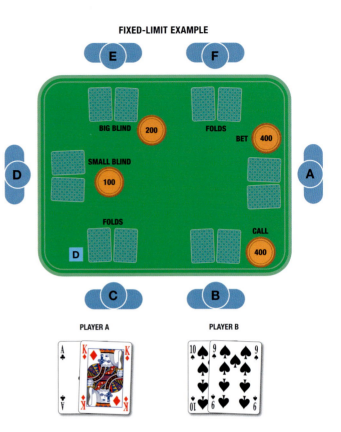

FIXED-LIMIT EXAMPLE

PLAYER A   **PLAYER B**

Above: Raising before the flop with A, K offsuit is a perfectly legitimate tactic, whichever betting structure is in place, but the difficulties of pressing home the advantage in a fixed-limit game are illustrated here. Player B only has to call twice the minimum bet to stay in the game, while those players in the blinds could well call, even with mediocre hands, to see if the flop brings any help. Player A's attempt to reduce the field to perhaps one opponent, over whom the A, K will probably be a favourite to win, is thus hampered by the limit on the size of raise permitted.

In general, players are advised to apply rigid standards to the quality of hands they play, relative to their betting position. Pre-flop raises are less common in this form of the game, since it is difficult to force up to nine opponents to fold for the cost of a single bet. Following the flop, a checkraise in early position may suggest enough threat to cause opponents to fold, but bluffing in this position is rather hazardous. Indeed, bluffing is best kept to a minimum, as players are restricted from betting the sums needed to intimidate the opposition.

POT-LIMIT

Popular with both professionals and amateurs, pot-limit Texas Hold 'em allows the freedom for players to bet more aggressively in support of their strong hands, to reduce the opposition and improve their chances of winning. Pots can quickly escalate in size, but a typical game with blinds set at a nominal level often features several players willing to see the flop. Making a pre-flop raise may encourage some opponents to fold, but the serious action normally begins after the flop has been revealed, since this is when most players are able to define their chances. If they are good, then the betting can be expected to increase, although it may not be until the turn card is dealt that the pot-sized bets start to appear.

So, while the cost of seeing the flop may be relatively small, players are often happy to call with modest hands because the prospect of picking up a very large pot when the flop fits is that much greater than in the fixed-limit game.

Left: A player bets all-in before the flop having decided that, with just a few chips remaining, the hole cards justify taking the risk. Most often seen in no-limit games where making an all-in bet can be an aggressive tactic, players may still find themselves going all-in during fixed-limit games when they have fewer chips than required to make the minimum bet.

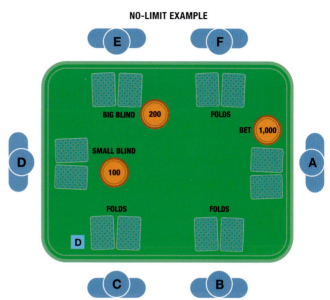

NO-LIMIT EXAMPLE

PLAYER B

Above: By way of contrast, when there is no limit on the maximum bet, player A is better able to represent strength in an effort to dissuade opponents from calling. Player B's 10, 9 suited may have been worth a call of 400 chips in the fixed-limit example, but calling a pre-flop bet of 1,000 chips is much more difficult with the same hand. Unless the players in the blinds have at least a medium pair, they will probably surrender the pot, enabling player A to pick up the blinds with this aggressive move.

NO-LIMIT TEXAS HOLD 'EM
♦ ♣ ♥ ♠

No-limit Texas Hold 'em is the most prominent of all tournament poker games and is regarded by many professionals as the most challenging variation currently being played. While it obviously suits the tournament format, the fact that players only ever stand to lose what may be a modest entry fee can disguise the inherent difficulties of playing it well as a cash game. For anyone hoping to make a modest bankroll stretch over several hours, buying in to a no-limit Texas Hold 'em game promises only anxiety and tension when an entire stack of chips could be lost in one hand. A tight or aggressive style is regarded as the most effective in the long term, which requires folding the majority of hands and betting aggressively, perhaps with a pre-flop raise, when holding premium cards. Having the patience to withstand such aggression from opponents while hoping to see cheap flops and light betting could lead to plenty of inactivity. Yet aggression is definitely an asset in the no-limit game, meaning that anyone who is not prepared to risk their entire chip stack on one hand is probably better suited to fixed-limit Texas Hold 'em.

TOURNAMENT PLAY

Prior to the inception of the WSOP in 1970, tournament poker was virtually unknown, but this situation has changed dramatically. The success of the knockout format and the concept of the winner taking all permeated Las Vegas casinos and soon spread to the rest of the world. By the end of the 20th century, television had realized the potential for tournament poker to offer keen entertainment. No-limit Texas Hold 'em has since emerged as the most widespread tournament game, but fixed-limit and pot-limit Texas Hold 'em tournaments are also a key part of the professional circuit, as well as being popular in poker rooms, both real and online.

A NEW CHALLENGE

Although the basic concepts behind sound Texas Hold 'em play are relevant to tournaments, players must adjust their strategic thinking, to take account of the different context. The search for a definitive winner and the systematic increases in the blinds force players into taking a few more risks than might be the case in a cash game. The ebbs and flows of competition, and the corresponding impact on a player's chip stack, trigger many decisive confrontations as competitors try to keep themselves in contention for a share of the prize money.

Critics consider that luck plays too big a part in tournament poker and that the public's affection for knockout games owes much to a desire for quick and decisive results. For cash game devotees who take a long-term view of their work, constantly raising the blinds in order to provoke the inevitable confrontations is anathema, because hands that would ordinarily be folded, frequently have to be played during a tournament. Some players are highly skilled at both forms of the game, and there are enough successful tournament professionals who consistently finish in the money to suggest that, at the highest level at least, luck remains no substitute for skill and experience.

CHOOSING A TOURNAMENT

The phenomenal success of world-class tournaments, is partly because anyone who wishes to enter usually has only to pay the required entry fee. This could run into thousands of dollars since many of the events cost upwards of US$1,000, with the fee for entering the WSOP world championship game currently set at US$10,000. That does not prevent the tournament from attracting up to 8,000 players for a competition that takes the best part of a week to complete.

TYPICAL TOURNAMENT SET-UP

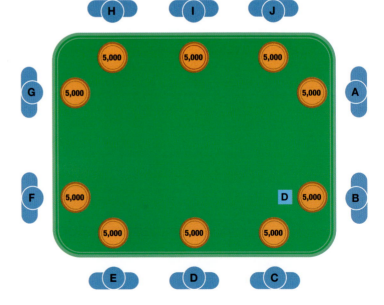

Right: This represents the typical scene at the beginning of a tournament, with up to ten players seated at the table and each starting with, in this case, 5,000 chips. A single-table tournament would feature a maximum of ten players, but a multi-table tournament featuring one hundred entrants would see this scene replicated on nine other tables as play commences. The dealer button (D), which is moved clockwise round the table after each deal, indicates that player B will be the nominal dealer for the first hand. Card rooms will often employ a professional dealer to conduct proceedings, leaving the players free to concentrate on play.

PRIZE STRUCTURES
♦ ♣ ♥ ♠

The prize structure in the formative years of tournament play was often a simple case of the winner taking all. Gradually, as tournament poker grew in popularity, the prize pools on offer led to a more equitable distribution of cash prizes, with the top 10 per cent of entrants now likely to win sufficient to cover their entry fee at least. To claim the more substantial prizes, however, still requires a player to finish in the top three or four per cent which is, understandably, a major challenge. The breakdown of the prize pool varies according to the numbers involved, the winner often claiming 50 per cent in events comprising less than 50 players, but only 25 per cent in those featuring 200 players or more. Although obviously more difficult to win, it is the prospect of turning a few dollars into a few thousand that makes large-scale, multi-table tournaments so appealing.

At a lower level, regular tournaments for players with tighter budgets exist, with online poker rooms offering the tournament experience for pocket-money entrance fees. The tournaments are varied in terms of style and structure. Daily or weekly competitions in real and online card rooms are supplemented by sit 'n' go tournaments, satellites, freerolls, qualifiers, turbo tournaments and single-table or multi-table events. There are also freeze-out or rebuy tournaments, meaning that, in terms of consumer choice, there is likely to be a tournament structure to suit every Texas Hold 'em player. Deciding which one to play will depend on a player's own personal tastes and financial means.

Above: A stack of chips as used in the European Poker Championships. Specifically branded chips are common in casinos and the idea extends to tournament events as well. Apart from the obvious promotional aspects associated with such branding, there is a practical purpose behind the use of exclusive chips since it prevents players from introducing chips from one establishment into a game at another.

Left: Joe Hachem from Melbourne, Australia, kisses a stack of US$100 bills having won the first prize of US$7.5 million at the WSOP world championship in 2005. Entries for the event have increased massively over the last decade, fuelled by thousands of online qualifiers, leading to a corresponding increase in the top prize. The US clampdown on online gaming in late 2006 led to a small reduction in entries for the WSOP world championship games of 2007 and 2008.

EARLY STAGES

Since no-limit Texas Hold 'em is the most popular tournament game, the general considerations detailed here will focus on the situations encountered in such an event, although many of the comments will apply equally well to pot-limit and fixed-limit contests. Also, any reference to cash sums will be in US dollars, this being the common currency of poker the world over.

The entry fees involved have an impact, with it being likely that players will play more loosely in a freeroll tournament in which there is no entry fee at all than they would having paid US$1,000 for the privilege of competing. In a similar vein, tournaments that offer the chance to rebuy chips during the first hour or two of play also invite players to take chances early on in the game. A successful all-in bet could double or triple a player's chip stack to secure an advantage, which is a tempting move, given that immediate elimination from the tournament is not at stake.

Freeze-out tournaments, the main focus of attention here, are generally characterized by most players easing themselves into the game as they assess their opponents. However, even these will include a minority of players who play aggressively from the start.

STEALING THE BLINDS

The difference between cash games and tournaments is that the blinds will rise at specified intervals of anything between two minutes and a couple of hours. Players who sit waiting for a perfect hand to materialize risk being anted away before having a chance to act. Irrespective of whether playing in a single or multi-table tournament, the need to put in the occasional pre-flop raise to steal the blinds must be considered. Successful moves such as this, whether they are bluffs or not, help to keep a player's chip stack intact while covering the cost of the compulsory bets as the deal moves round the table.

While the blinds are modest at the start, the need to pressurize the blinds when there is little interest before the flop is a recurring theme during play as they increase in scale. Since this tactic is common, combating such a move when in the big blind, for example, usually needs possession of a good starting hand to justify a call. If one opponent repeatedly targets a specific player in this situation, a substantial re-raise might put them off doing so for a while. In tournament play, timing is everything, since one wrong move can devastate a player's chip stack, if not guarantee elimination.

EARLY STAGES

Right: This shows the situation in a typical tournament after the betting has already risen through a couple of levels. The total number of chips currently held by each player is indicated, all having started the tournament with 5,000 chips. The player in seat D has been eliminated, with player E having profited from the early action. Player C is under the most pressure, because, with the blinds having risen from 25 (small) and 50 (big) to 100 and 200, for example, the minimum bet represents more than one-twelfth of the player's total chip count. As players are eliminated during a multi-table tournament, others are moved from adjoining tables to occupy vacated seats. This keeps the ratio of players per table consistent and enables the organizers to gradually reduce the number of tables in operation.

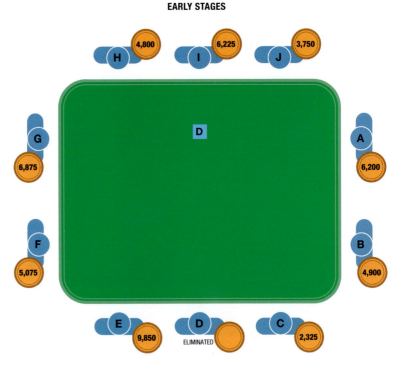

SURVIVAL OF THE FITTEST

At the beginning of a tournament, each player receives an equal number of chips, the objective being to amass the total in play by eliminating all opposition. Events in which the blind levels are raised every 15 minutes or less do not provide much scope for players to remain patient. However, while some aggression is required, players should still be wary of fighting early betting wars when dealt only fair starting hands. Those who are intent on pursuing a death-or-glory policy can usually be left to eliminate each other as the tournament settles into its rhythm.

No tournament is ever won within the first few hands, so surviving until the later stages of the game should be uppermost in players' minds. This is certainly true in events with much longer intervals between the increased betting levels. The general advice is for players to monitor the level of the average chip stack and stay ahead of that figure. In online tournaments, such information is updated after each hand, but at a multi-table event in a real card room, a quick glance at the other tables for an assessment of the opposition's chip standing might be necessary. There is no suggestion that a player holding a premium hand should never

consider betting aggressively. Good opportunities to double-up with an all-in bet will occur, but only by exercising a high degree of selectivity over which hands to play – and when – will a player maintain interest in a competition.

Above: Jeff Williams, the American student who won the 2006 EPT Grand Final in Monte Carlo having qualified via satellite tournaments on the PokerStars online site. Though experienced tournament professionals often have the edge in big events, the proliferation of online poker tournaments means that Internet players can rapidly develop the skills required.

STEALING THE BLINDS

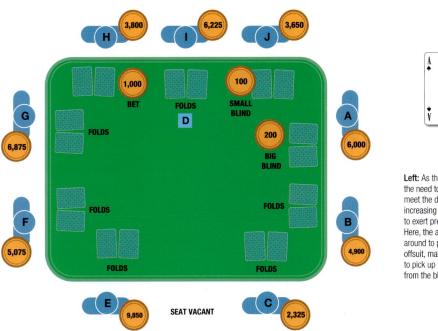

PLAYER H

Left: As the tournament develops, the need to accumulate chips to meet the demands of the ever-increasing blinds prompts players to exert pressure when they can. Here, the action has been folded around to player H, who, with A, Q offsuit, makes a large bet, hoping to pick up the 300 chips on offer from the blinds without a contest.

MIDDLE STAGES

As the tournament nears its middle stages, with as many as half the original starters already eliminated, the strategy to adopt very much depends on how many chips a player still holds. Being the chip leader is obviously beneficial, but holding a better-than-average chip position should at least help a player fend off the pressure of the ever-increasing blinds.

By now, the big blind could easily be as much as a fifth of the original starting stack, emphasizing the need to keep picking up pots on a regular basis. A run of poor cards in the face of aggressive betting can make this prospect exceedingly difficult, so making a few bluffs is almost unavoidable.

Under normal circumstances, many of the loose and reckless players will have been knocked out by this stage. As a result, the more astute players who are left may be more susceptible to a credible bluff, since they have a sharper awareness of the inferences behind any bet. Also, as the possibility of claiming a prize draws closer for those managing to avoid elimination, players are sometimes prone to becoming more defensive, which presents another situation to be exploited.

CHIP COUNT

From the middle stages onwards, it becomes essential for players to monitor their opponents' chip positions as well as their own. Assuming that to finish in the prizes means making the final table, a keen eye on the chip counts will help guide a player's tactical and strategic thinking as the number of opponents dwindles. Anyone in the top third has the chance to fold a succession of hands and avoid confrontations, while short-stacked opponents battle against each other. Also, the possibility of intimidating opponents with the occasional large raise to force them all-in if they call is another available tactic.

Short-stacked players can expect to be pressurized all the time as the blinds eat into their reserves. In this position there may not be time to wait for a large

PLAYER A

Right: The ability to change gear during the middle stages of a tournament is a major asset. This means that players may start to bet with lower-ranking starting hands than usual when they have an above-average chip count and the advantage of position. For those low on chips, pressure will come from all quarters and they may have little option but to go all-in with a poor hand. Here, for example, player J makes a substantial raise that threatens each of those still to act with elimination in this hand, given that there are three further betting rounds to negotiate. Player B, in particular, has a limited number of opportunities to survive, given the big blind is approaching, but decides to fold the J, 8 offsuit on this occasion. The action now is on player D, who has an uncomfortable decision to make with the pair of sevens.

pair or A, K before pushing all the remaining chips into the pot, so opportunities with lesser hands have to be taken. Certainly, when a player is down to no more than five times the big blind, every hand must be considered in terms of its all-in potential, although the need to double-up one's stack may arise sooner than that. Another point to bear in mind is that the chip leaders may also fold in the face of aggression from mid-ranking players, since they could well be reluctant to sacrifice valuable chips with a place at the final table beckoning.

CHANGING GEAR

The ability to vary one's style of play is an asset in any form of poker, but being able to change gear during a tournament can help improve or stabilize a player's chip position. A burst of aggressive play featuring pre-flop and post-flop raises may be enough to win a few blinds and reluctant calls from opponents locked into a tight, conservative pattern. Winning enough to cover the blinds for another three or four circuits of the table will typically give a player 30 or more additional hands to consider and time to see more opponents eliminated.

This strategy is more effective when implemented by someone who has previously exhibited all the traits of a sound but cautious player. When short-stacked, such a ploy may smack of desperation, but for those within reach of the prize-money spots, it offers the chance to exploit any timidity in opponents, regardless of their chip position. It does mean being less selective over which starting hands to play, bringing with it the risk of being caught out by a strong hand. However, if the strategy is unsuccessful but still leaves a player with a manageable chip stack, consolidating for a while by reverting to caution once more remains an option.

As the tournament moves towards its conclusion, the value of a player's hole cards may be less significant to any betting strategy than the current chip positions of opponents. If three short-stacked opponents go all-in before the flop, even a large pair such as kings or aces may be worth folding. Competing against several opponents with a high pair simply increases the combined chances that one of them will beat the hand. Winning the pot could mean knocking out three opponents, but losing it could see just two of them eliminated, while the other emerges with a more substantial chip stack than need have been the case.

TACTICAL DECISIONS

PLAYER J

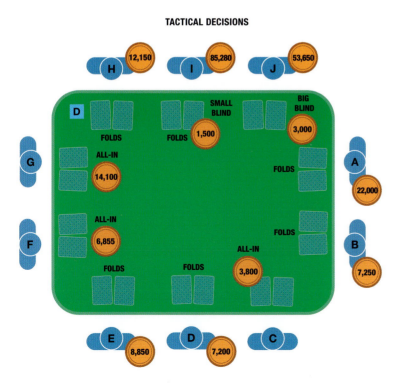

Left: As the pressure mounts, the need for discipline from those within touching distance of the final table increases. In this separate example, ordinarily player J would consider the pair of jacks worthy of a bet and, having already bet 3,000 chips in the big blind, a further bet of 11,100 to call player G could establish a chance to knock out three players in one hand. But a win for player G would see the pair of them in a similar chip position. Under the circumstances, a fold may be better, since a win for player G would still leave that opponent trailing player J by over 20,000 chips, which remains a significant advantage. This highlights how the value of the cards themselves may become less important compared to the other strategic concerns that develop throughout the tournament.

THE END GAME

To reach the final table in any regular multi-table tournament, a player is likely to have prospered on several different tables, for a number of hours, against up to nine opponents at a time. Despite the fact that luck may well have played a part at some stage of the competition, it is the players with the skill to capitalize upon their fortune rather than relying on luck alone who will usually reach the prize-money spots. The difference between first place and tenth, however, will still be represented by a huge variation in the prizes available. Having successfully made it to the final table, plotting a strategy towards ultimate victory will again be dependent on the chips at a player's disposal.

Players who have short stacks will be highly aware that every hand could be their last and should bet all-in while they have enough chips to make the risk worthwhile. By allowing the stack to dwindle, a player might be faced with having to win a succession of all-in bets to find a way back into the game and, since many such confrontations provide no better than an even-money chance of winning, achieving this is exceedingly difficult.

CHANGING FORTUNES

Players with medium-sized chip stacks still need to exercise caution as the tournament reaches its final stages. Should the chip leader start bullying opponents with aggressive raises, it is best to avoid confrontations for as long as possible in the hope that those with shorter stacks succumb to the pressure. Raising a bet from an opponent with many more chips can only be confidently considered while holding an excellent hand.

As the eliminations continue and the number of players falls to four or five, the increased blinds will circulate the table much quicker. Players in the blinds can expect opponents to try stealing them with ever-larger bets, although judging what cards they hold becomes more of a challenge. With fewer players, the value of the average winning hand decreases and more risks are therefore taken with marginal starting hands.

Large pots contested by two players will develop repeatedly and fortunes can change rapidly. Having half as many chips as the leader when in an all-in battle will see the players swap positions should the low stack triumph, underlining that a tournament is never won until the final opponent has been eliminated.

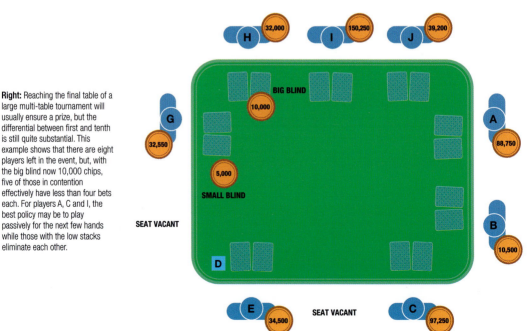

THE FINAL TABLE

Right: Reaching the final table of a large multi-table tournament will usually ensure a prize, but the differential between first and tenth is still quite substantial. This example shows that there are eight players left in the event, but, with the big blind now 10,000 chips, five of those in contention effectively have less than four bets each. For players A, C and I, the best policy may be to play passively for the next few hands while those with the low stacks eliminate each other.

HEADS-UP

When there are only two players left competing heads-up at the table both will be assured of a prize usually well in excess of their entry fee. To secure victory, however, requires each player to pressurize the other with large bets, frequent bluffs and the willingness to support some weak starting hands.

Against one opponent, J, 7 offsuit represents the average hand and will win on half the occasions it is played. Holding a card higher than a J therefore offers a decent opportunity, while being dealt an A or any pair could easily warrant an all-in bet, whether having the majority or minority of chips.

Aggression is very important, since the blinds by this stage are usually so high that folding on two or three successive occasions can seriously weaken a player's chip position. Even when holding a substantial lead, with perhaps 80 per cent of the chips, a player cannot afford to fold too often, while losing to an all-in bet from an opponent on two successive occasions will see the lead change hands.

Generally, good heads-up play involves pressing home any perceived advantage as forcefully as possible in what amounts to an archetypal poker confrontation. Practising heads-up play is advisable, since there is no doubt that some players respond to the challenge of one-to-one combat much better than others. Ultimately, with almost every hand being contested, the conclusion to several hours of intense competition could be swift, with the winning hand often ranked lower than a pair. This may seem a little anti-climactic, given the quality of hands that will have been played to reach the last two, but both winner and runner-up will have successfully shown a consummate range of poker skills to be contesting the concluding hand of the tournament.

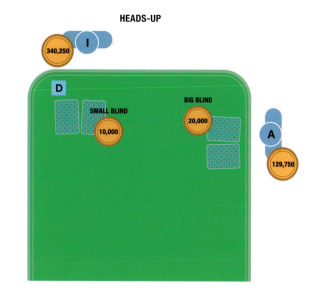

HEADS-UP

Above: When just two players are left, a heads-up situation exists, with the size of the blinds ensuring that almost every pot is worth contesting, irrespective of the cards held by each player. Ordinarily, a player either raises before the flop, or folds, since merely calling a bet invites an aggressive move from the opponent. This is the point at which a player's nerve is truly tested.

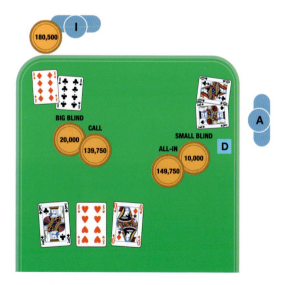

RAPIDLY CHANGING FORTUNES

Above: Even a substantial chip lead at this stage of the game can soon be eradicated, with player I on the verge of winning here, having called player A's all-in bet from the small blind. Both have above-average hands and the flop, although favouring the chip leader, still provides player A with an outside chance to double up and take the lead. Any of the four remaining kings and queens in the deck will make a better full house and prompt another deal.

OMAHA

In Omaha, the action begins with the small blind and big blind being posted by the players to the dealer's left, just as in Texas Hold 'em. The dealer deals the cards one at a time to each player, clockwise around the table until everyone has four cards face down prior to the first betting round. Once the first-round betting is complete, the dealer reveals the flop which consists of three cards face up on the table which all players can use towards finalizing their hand. A second betting round takes place after which the turn card is dealt. Betting limits usually double at this stage of the game and, after a third betting round, the river card is revealed. This acts as a prelude to the final round of betting. The winner is the player who either makes an unmatched bet during the game or who holds the best poker hand at the showdown, of two hole cards and three from the board.

Below: When assessing which starting hands to play, consideration must be given to the likely possibilities presented by the board cards when they are all revealed. Half of the time, at least one pair will be present, as in the first example, making four of a kind a possibility and a full house almost certain. Players will usually need at least a straight to win and ample opportunities exist, since, as in the second example, three cards or more to a straight will appear on four out of every five occasions. However, flushes are regular winners, too, with three or more cards to a flush on the board occurring 40 per cent of the time as shown in the third example.

WHAT TO EXPECT FROM THE BOARD

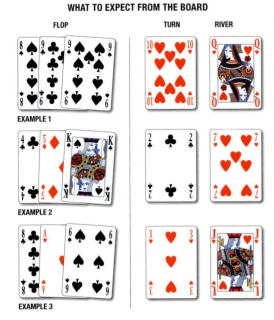

FLOP   TURN   RIVER

EXAMPLE 1

EXAMPLE 2

EXAMPLE 3

Almost unheard of before the 1980s, Omaha – Omaha Hold 'em if preferred – is one of the most popular games played at home and online, and is firmly rooted on the professional circuit. Omaha tournaments reflect the most common betting structures applied to the game, though they are often played for high stakes. The pot-limit variation allows players room to manoeuvre, since the capacity to make pot-sized bets and raises creates bluffing opportunities. Fixed-limit Omaha tends to reward knowledgeable and often conservative players in the long run.

The game shares the same basic structure as Texas Hold 'em, with players receiving four hole cards, not two, prior to the five board cards being revealed. Also, their hands must comprise two hole cards and three from the board. These differences completely change the nature of the game and the strategies that should be applied in the search for success. The major factors to consider are reading the cards, understanding the odds and observing opponents. Acknowledging the impact of the betting structure – pot-limit or fixed-limit – on a player's strategic thinking is also important and this will be reflected in the following analysis of the game.

CRUCIAL CONSIDERATIONS

The starting point when considering any poker strategy is to contemplate the end of the game in order to understand the quality of hand that is likely to prevail. In draw poker or five-card stud, this may be as little as a pair of queens, while in Texas Hold 'em, two pairs and three of a kind are frequent winners. This is prone to confuse even experienced Texas Hold 'em players who are new to Omaha, a game in which a hand such as trip aces will very rarely prove good enough.

The minimum hand normally required to win at Omaha is a straight, but flushes and full houses are so frequent that even a straight is quite weak. Generally, it will win only when the board cards make a full house or flush impossible to achieve. Before assessing the relative merits of any starting hand, it is pertinent to consider the likely outcome on the board once the five community cards – the widow – have been revealed.

There are three key issues to remember, beginning with the fact that half the time at least one pair will appear, making a full house very likely. Second, at least

Above: Players receive four cards in Omaha prior to the first betting round and this represents a fairly good starting hand given that it comprises high-ranking cards and offers chances of a straight. It is, however, compromised by containing four hearts since this obviously reduces the number of available hearts in the deck with which the player could make a flush.

three cards of one suit will be seen in four out of every ten widows, emphasizing the potential for flushes. Third, 80 per cent of the time, three cards that fit a straight will be present, underlining why this is the minimum rank that hand players should be aiming to achieve.

STARTING HANDS

Armed with a knowledge of what hands are likeliest to win at the showdown, players are better able to assess the quality of hand required to justify competing for the pot. After the deal, any four cards that offer realistic chances of full houses, flushes and straights are worth consideration, but Omaha is renowned as a game that is usually won by the best possible hand – the nuts. High-ranking cards, therefore, especially aces, have greater value because they offer players the chance to hit the best straights, flushes and full houses available. Given how often these hands occur, it is always preferable to have the nut flush when there is no pair on the board to indicate a full house might exist.

GOOD STARTING HANDS

Above: A good hand in Omaha is one in which all six two-card combinations offer a chance to fit the board cards to make a winning hand, with at least a straight required. High-ranking pocket cards are best, but their value is not as significant before the flop as in Texas Hold 'em. Both examples favour the highest-value straights, flushes and full houses and should be played.

FAIR STARTING HANDS

Above: Any hand that offers four or more viable combinations is certainly worthy of consideration. Here, the Ad, Qh, Qs, 7s offers full house and A-high straight possibilities, although the flush potential of the Qs, 7s combination is weak. Should the board feature three spades not including the A or K, then the Q-high flush is in danger of being outranked. The second example has fair straight and full house potential, but both the K, 8 combinations will need help from the board.

POOR STARTING HANDS

Above: Opening hands of low-ranking cards or less than three working combinations should be folded. A pair of nines may contribute to a full house, but it could be second-best, even if a 9 appears. To complete the full house would need a pair on the board and anything higher than a 9 – a pair of kings for example, will lose to anyone with a K and one other card matching the board. The straight potential of the 4, 3 combination is almost worthless, since a 5, 6, 7 on the board will lose to anyone holding 8, 4 or 9, 8. Similar problems apply to the other featured hand.

Good starting hands offer the most viable two-card combinations, of which there are six in all; the more of these that might fit any potential widow, the better the prospects of securing a playable hand. For instance, being dealt two pairs, such as Ad, As, 7h, 7c, is good, but holding Kd, Kc, Qd, Qc is arguably better. In the first case, the six combinations offer opportunities for a full house or even four of a kind, but the aces and sevens cannot be combined to make a straight. Having four different suits in the hand also rules out a flush. The second example, however, supplements the full house and four-of-a-kind potential, with the possibilities of high-ranking flushes and straights, offering more chances of success.

PRE-FLOP STRATEGY

Before taking a closer look at the strategic possibilities that are presented by the first four cards, it is first worth highlighting other aspects of the game of Omaha that will have an influence on a player's betting decisions. In a high-stakes game featuring plenty of aggressive betting, players are far more likely to raise before the flop in an attempt to reduce the opposition. It is therefore a good policy to support only hands that offer multiple possibilities of winning. At a lower level, in fixed-limit home games, for example, pre-flop raises are much less likely, since the majority of players are inclined to call whatever cards are in their possession.

Essentially, this is what makes Omaha such a popular game, since social players enjoy the fact that even the most unpromising combination of hole cards will come good on the odd occasion. However, although players in a typical fixed-limit game will call to see perhaps half of all flops even with marginal hands, this does present them with the temptation of chasing hands that are destined to be second best. Pots can quickly escalate when there are several players involved, and this can encourage some of them to remain in the hand mistakenly pursuing value.

A constant appraisal of the odds and probabilities at work throughout the game remains the foundation for a disciplined approach to Omaha, and enables players to exploit those opponents who are always keen to be involved in the action.

Above: A player commits chips to the pot before the flop even though the hole cards displayed do not offer the greatest promise. Of the six two-card combinations available to the player, only two – the A, K and 6, 6 – have any merit in a hand that cannot make a flush because the cards are of four different suits. Unless the flop fits perfectly, the hand should probably be folded if an opponent bets in the second round.

Left: This example shows a strong starting hand which, because of the high value of the cards, has the potential to blend with a variety of flops to put the player in a good position. If the first three community cards are 9d, Ah, Qd then multiple opportunities open up for the player in the shape of straights, flushes and possibly even a full house.

Right: Irrespective of a starting hand, once the flop is dealt it is crucial to understand the implications behind the board cards, and identify what may form the nuts when all five are revealed. Anyone holding 9, 8 in the first example will have the best hand, with a straight, but a player with the A, K; A, Q or K, Q of clubs has the nut flush draw and the potential to hit a royal flush. The second example makes a full house probable and a player holding pocket kings will feel that kings over sixes will be enough, although the nuts at this stage is four sixes. Should nobody hold pocket sixes, then a further 6 on the board, or two aces, could yet see the hand beaten. Gauging the likelihood of that should always guide a player's betting strategy.

BE GUIDED BY THE FLOP

EXAMPLE 1

EXAMPLE 2

SEEKING THE NUTS

The safest policy when contemplating Omaha is to remember that, once all the board cards have been shown, the winner in any showdown is likely to possess the nuts. This will not always be the case, but it should be at the forefront of any player's mind when holding a strong but not unbeatable hand and it should also be the guiding principle when assessing the options presented after the deal.

A good hand is one where the first four cards combine to offer six viable two-card hands. Having two high pairs including aces is good since four of a kind and nut full house prospects exist, along with the chance of making a high straight. Flushes are also regular winners, so holding the A plus one other card of a particular suit again guarantees the nut flush if three or more cards of that suit are among the board cards. This is a better position to be in than when dealt four spades, as the reduced number of spades left in the deck makes a flush in that suit less likely. Similarly, when holding four cards in a sequence such as K, Q, J, 10, the hand is always stronger if two cards each from two suits are present to add flush and straight flush potential to that of making a straight.

PROBLEMS WITH MARGINAL HANDS

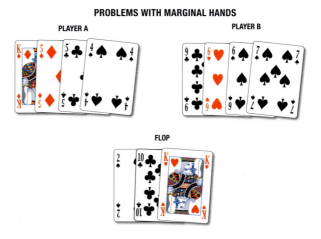

PLAYER A   PLAYER B

FLOP

Above: Players with marginal hands need to be cautious when the board cards offer potential. Player A cannot use the K and the pair of fives simultaneously and has only a pair of kings, a weak hand on the flop. To make a winning hand requires two kings or two fives in the last two cards; should a K and 5 or K and 4 appear, the full house could lose to a player holding K, 10.

Left: The hole cards shown here represent a poor hand since only the Kc, Qc combination holds any real promise. Nevertheless, if the game features light betting and no pre-flop raises, as is customary when poker is played socially, hands such as these are much more likely to be retained than folded. A pair of eights on the flop, in this case, could then change the complexion of the hand altogether.

MORE COMBINATIONS
♦ ♣ ♥ ♠

Omaha games can feature up to ten players, this being the normal number for a cash game staged by a casino or online poker site. This many participants ensures that 40 cards – almost 80 per cent of the deck – are in play immediately after the deal and with each player forming six two-card combinations from their hole cards, 60 of these exist before the betting begins. This contributes to the typically high value of winning hands and underlines why players should always be trying to attain the best hand possible. However, while hands featuring high pairs, suited cards or connecting cards are favourable, even two-card combinations with modest potential regularly confound expectations. This is particularly true in fixed-limit Omaha games, when players with one decent two-card hand will often call to see the flop and find that their least valuable cards – 'rags' – suddenly become significant. For example a player holding Kc, Qc, 8d, 3s, would realistically expect only the K, Q combination to offer any chance of winning, but if the flop is 8h, 3d, Ks, then nine cards from the unseen 45 in the deck provide the player with a 38 per cent chance of achieving a full house. Any K, 8 or 3 will suffice, along with any two of the remaining three queens, although not all of these necessarily constitute the nuts. Should the turn and river cards be Kd and Ad, a player with a pair of aces or A, K would win, but the example does highlight the impact of having many more two-card combinations in play.

POST-FLOP STRATEGY

Whatever the potential of a player's hole cards, the flop is the moment in the game when a hand's strength is clarified. Ideally, players will already have a mental picture of the cards they would prefer to see, although the principal consideration at this stage is the same as in Texas Hold 'em. In order to continue in the hand, players need to be confident that they have either the best hand or a realistic chance of achieving it.

This means identifying, first, which hand is likely to constitute the nuts and, second, whether it is possible to obtain it, given the cards at a player's disposal. Careless or inexperienced players are frequently seduced by the merits of a good hand only to discover, to their cost, that it is ultimately not good enough. As ever, a quick assessment of how many cards might make or break a hand, and the odds against them appearing, is crucial in determining whether to bet.

A player already holding the nuts can obviously focus on pot management and do whatever is required to keep opponents interested. They will often have sufficient scope for improvement to feel justified in calling a minimum bet to see the turn card. Loose players may even be prepared to call a raise in a fixed-limit game if they are slow to recognize that the nuts may already have been acquired. On the other hand, a check by the player holding a lock hand, which is essentially a hand that cannot lose, is likely to keep more opponents involved until later in the game, when the betting levels rise.

The aim then is to bet at the higher level and hope that opponents' hands have improved enough to call to see the final card. Should they do so, there is every chance they may call again in the fourth betting round, thus enhancing the profit made by slow-playing the nuts.

Above: Comic actor W.C. Fields keeps his cards close to his chest during a game. During his days in vaudeville in the early 20th century, Fields learned to play poker with some of the hustlers he met while touring, although golf was his preferred gambling medium. He did, however, develop some card tricks to supplement the skills he employed in his juggling act of the time.

COUNTING OUTS

FLOP

PLAYER A

PLAYER B

Above: These contrasting hands show the differing fortunes encountered as players consider the cards that can convert a hand into a winner. Player A has six chances of making a full house on the turn and 8 or 9 chances – depending on whether the turn card is an 8 – of filling it on the river, offering combined odds of just over 2 to 1 against. Player B has the best hand, but must assume that any pair on the board would be terminal. Of the unseen cards, 36 from the 45 remaining are good, and if the turn card pairs one of player B's hole cards, then 33 from the 44 in the deck are favourable. So player B has a 60 per cent chance of surviving both rounds.

READING THE CARDS

Once the flop has been revealed, players must note the possibilities presented by the three community cards. Any pair that appears will make it extremely likely that a full house or better will ultimately take the pot. Up to a third of all Omaha hands are won by full houses and half of these are likely to have been secured on the flop. Players with trips should therefore be wary of drawing to a full house that will not prove to be the best possible.

A flop featuring three cards of the same suit – Qc, 7c, 2c, for example – will stifle any betting from those who cannot beat a flush. A player holding the nut flush – perhaps Ac, 8c – should bet the maximum, since any caller is bound to be drawing for a full house and must be forced to pay for any of the cards that might complete it. When two cards to a flush appear on the flop, a player with the nut flush draw should also bet and hope for a couple of callers. When the flush is completed, the profits made will compensate for losses that occur when an opponent does hit a full house.

WHO IS FAVOURITE?

THE FLOP	PLAYER'S HAND

Above: After the flop, the key number for players to bear in mind is 13, since possessing this many outs for the best possible hand offers an even-money chance of victory. In this example, the player with the A-high straight can be certain of winning if any one of 15 cards appears on the turn or river, making the player a slight favourite to prevail.

Right: The player pictured here in possession of an A-high flush after the flop is in the perfect position to bet. Though holding the best hand, should either the turn or the river bring a card to pair one of those on the flop, it may be beaten by an opponent with a full house. A bet now would make it clear that the nut flush has been obtained which, if not sufficient to take the pot straight away, at least defines any callers as being in pursuit of a full house.

THE TURN

Since the flop offers so much information to the wary player, anyone still competing for the pot when the turn card is revealed must believe they have a potential winning hand, even if it has only an outside chance of success. After the turn card is dealt, the likely nature of the nuts should be apparent to all those still engaged in the game. This helps keep the basic analysis required to a minimum, since a player would only have three serious questions to consider before deciding whether a bet is warranted at this stage: do I have the best possible hand at the table, is it possible to obtain it, and does someone else already have it?

A player who is already in possession of the nuts should simply try to build the pot, while a player who identifies that the nut hand is still obtainable is justified in calling any opponent's bet when the pot odds are favourable. Meanwhile, those who recognize that their chances of catching a winning card on the river are poor in relation to the pot odds would probably do best to fold.

Above all, players must beware of calling a bet on the turn for a card that will improve their hand but not guarantee the win. Calling in the hope of making a K-high flush, for example, is usually the quickest way to discover an opponent has an A-high flush.

ESTIMATING PROBABILITIES ON THE TURN

Allowing the rules of probability to influence one's betting decisions is not always straightforward, even if it is generally advisable. With just one final community card to come, however, calculating the odds against seeing specific cards on the river, when the final community card is dealt, is relatively simple. Players who have leading hands will be considering how many cards might blend with the board to provide an opponent with a winning hand, while those drawing for cards will be making similar calculations regarding their own chances. Each hand represents a different puzzle, so players must be aware of the fluctuating probabilities apparent from one hand to the next. For example a player holding Ah, Kd, 10h, 10s when the board reads 3h, 8h, 4c, 5s has nine hearts remaining to make the nut flush, at odds of 4 to 1 against.

However, this would not be the best possible hand available if either the 4h or 5h completed the flush, because, by pairing the board, they could provide an opponent with a full house. To obtain the nuts and be certain of victory, the player must rely on the other seven hearts, at odds of just over 5 to 1 against. Should the board read 3h, 6h, 4c, 5s instead, then the chances of holding the nut hand if a heart appears on the river are reduced further. Although

PLAYER C

HOLE CARDS

Right: To help visualize some of the strategic thinking that applies to Omaha, this example of a 100/200 fixed-limit game will highlight the betting decisions of player C in the big blind. The starting hand is good, with a high pair, a couple of connecting cards and two spades, offering multiple possibilities.

THE DEAL

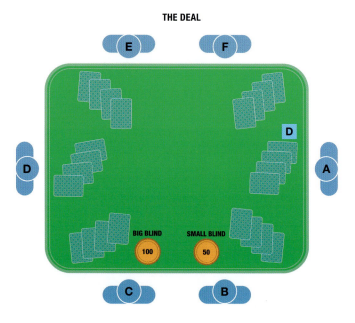

nine hearts still remain, the 2, 4, 5, and 7 all threaten danger, since they have the potential to complete a low straight flush, while the full house options still exist. With only five cards that will guarantee the best hand, the player faces odds of 8 to 1 against this occurring.

AIMING STRAIGHT
♦ ♣ ♥ ♠

A straight is the minimum hand normally required to win the pot, although it can be difficult to exploit, given the frequency with which flushes and full houses occur in Omaha. Prior to the flop, the best chance of obtaining the hand arises when a player has a sequence of four consecutive hole cards, since this can complete up to 20 different straights, given the right board cards. A hand such as 9, 8, 7, 6, for instance, can make a Q-high straight with a Q, J, 10, or a 7-high straight with 5, 4, 3, and can work with 18 other three-card combinations to produce straights valued between these examples. On the flop, should there be no pair and no two cards of the same suit, there is an even-money possibility that a straight will ultimately win. However, players should still guard against finishing with anything less than the best possible straight available.

Left: A sequence of middle-ranking cards such as this is certainly worth playing if the pre-flop betting is light. There are 20 possible three-card combinations that could appear on the board to make a straight while the two hearts also offer flush possibilities. Despite the potential for making a strong hand, the low rank of the cards can cause problems. If the flop brought Q, J, 10, for example, the 9, 8 in the hole completes a straight, but this will be outranked by anyone holding K, 9 or A, K.

FIRST-ROUND BETTING

Left: Omaha characteristically features several players calling to see the flop, since even the weakest hand could quickly develop into an almost certain winner. For this reason, pre-flop raising in fixed-limit games is rare since it is unlikely to reduce the field sufficiently to make it worth the extra bet. Here, the remaining players all call the big blind (player C), who decides not to raise the betting further.

CALL, BET OR RAISE?

The flop may be the most crucial phase of the game, but the moment the turn card is revealed also prefaces a serious decision for those still contesting the pot. Players who can clearly see they have little chance of winning will probably fold, certainly in a fixed-limit game when it is normally impossible to bet enough to successfully bluff drawing hands out of contention.

Those whose hands still retain realistic prospects of taking the pot, by contrast, face a test of nerve and discipline as the serious betting begins. Not only is the minimum bet doubled on the turn in a typical Omaha game, but the likelihood is that players who bet now are probably committing themselves to further betting on the river. More bets generate bigger pots and this can tempt players into pursuing too many lost causes. Repeatedly finishing as the runner-up in these situations can reduce confidence as well as chip stacks.

In deciding whether to call, bet or even raise after the turn card has been dealt, good players will consider the pot odds on offer in light of the betting patterns throughout the game. Although betting without the best hand is usually ill advised, it is not always certain that an opponent already has it, with the clues behind this assessment coming from bets in the previous rounds. Despite the methodical approach recommended for playing Omaha successfully, being able to read an opponent's hand from the nature of the betting is a clear asset.

Right: As first person to act, player B surely indicates either a straight draw, two pairs or possession of a pocket pair – sevens or nines – that would make three of a kind. If this is so, then player C's winning full house possibilities are reduced, since the 7 or a 9 that could complete it might now give player B four of a kind. If player B has a Q, 9 or 9, 7, then the odds of 3 to 1 for securing a full house, although not the nuts, may well prompt a bet, too, given the pot odds. Player C's raise is a strong move and will have opponents pondering what the bet implies. Players F and B call the raise.

THE FLOP

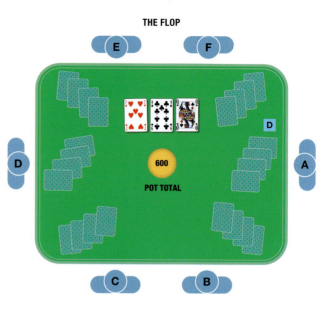

PLAYER C
HOLE CARDS

Above: The flop of 7, 9, Q is ideal for player C, who has the best hand with trip queens, and is just under 2 to 1 to make a full house or 'quads' (four of a kind) come the river card. Since the pot odds offer 6 to 1, maintaining interest in the hand is justified and a raise might eliminate a couple of opponents who missed the flop. Any 5, 6, 8, 10, J or K – 23 of the remaining 44 cards (player C has a K) – can fill a straight on the turn, however, and an opponent who does so will probably bet to try warding off draws for flushes and full houses.

SECOND BETTING ROUND

PASSIVE OR AGGRESSIVE?

One of the things that makes Omaha such an enjoyable poker variation is that the many cards in circulation, particularly in a ten-player game, generate plenty of possibilities to make very strong hands. Betting tends to be lighter in the first two rounds, whether the game is fixed- or pot-limit poker, but becomes heavier from the turn onwards.

In pot-limit games, this is when the larger bets materialize, as players try to ward off those who, although possibly behind, still have chances to win. Such bets at this stage shrink the pot odds considerably, making speculative calls less attractive to opponents.

Yet large pots can still develop in fixed-limit poker, even though successful players are usually cautious and pragmatic. A couple of aggressive players who, on occasion, like to buck the odds with an irresponsible raise, can trigger an avalanche of betting in fixed-limit games. Since there are normally three or four raises per round before the betting level is capped, large pots can soon develop if a betting war breaks out. Under such circumstances, the implied pot odds on offer might tempt even the most passive player into calling for the river card if any chance of winning exists.

SIMPLE DECISIONS

Players whose betting on the turn is governed by the probabilities at work can expect to save themselves plenty of chips if they are strictly disciplined in their approach. The key is counting exactly how many of the unseen cards can help them either retain or acquire the winning hand. With four cards on the board and four in the hand, each player knows the value of eight cards. Simply, if half the remaining 44 cards will provide a player with a winning hand, then the chances are evidently even that this will happen, making any bet or call almost obligatory.

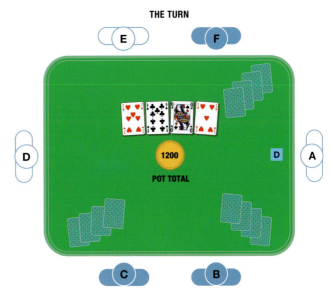

THE TURN

1200

POT TOTAL

Above: The 5h on the turn does not improve player C's hand but can do little either for any opponent holding a pair of nines or sevens in the hole. It does help fulfil a low straight for any opponent holding 8, 6, which is plausible given that these two cards could feature in the hand of someone also holding a high pair such as aces or kings, for example.

If only 11 cards will confirm the hand as a winner, then the odds against it occurring are 3 to 1, which might discourage a player from calling a bet in a very tight game. Players with fewer than 11 cards working for them should definitely be sure that the pot odds on offer will justify staying for the river, in the face of any bet.

Above: The pair of sevens supplemented by the A, 10 suited represents a fair starting hand and it is just one combination that could plausibly be held by player B in the game illustrated on these pages. From player C's perspective, player B's bet into a flop showing 7, 9, Q could easily be construed as representing trip sevens though this is a hand player C has well covered at present with the trip queens.

THE RIVER

The card that completes the deal and removes all doubt regarding the value of a player's hand and how it compares with the best available, is the river card. At this point it is worth reiterating the golden rule of Omaha, which underlines how the game essentially amounts to a search for the nuts. Any player who does not hold the best possible hand available after the river card may safely assume that an opponent probably does.

If the betting patterns suggest exactly that, then there is little sense in a player calling a last-round bet, however modest, in order to confirm what is already suspected. This applies to both fixed- and pot-limit games, although players are more likely to support potentially strong hands on the flop or the turn in pot-limit Omaha with large bets, offering clues to the value of their cards. Having been called as far as the river, a modest final-round bet by a player who had raised in the previous round should create suspicion in the mind of an opponent who has failed to make a lock hand. The possibility exists that the opponent is being trapped into parting with a few more chips by a player with the nuts.

PLAYER C
HOLE CARDS

Right: Three players are still competing as the river card falls, giving player C the nuts with four of a kind. Although opponents may have read the betting patterns correctly and put player C on pocket queens, the pair on the board could have made someone a full house that may induce them to bet. Although four of a kind is not uncommon in Omaha, players find it difficult to fold a hand as good as a full house. Once player B checks, player C has no option but to bet and hope for a call to swell the pot. With the best hand, there is no point checking and allowing opponents a free showdown.

THIRD BETTING ROUND

Above: The raise from Player C after the flop causes player B to check this time round after the turn card is dealt, either to re-examine the possibilities presented by the board or, perhaps, to set a trap. Player C bets the minimum, reasoning that player B could be slow-playing a straight by holding an 8 and 6, but that it is still more likely he has three of a kind. If this is the case, then another 7 or 9 on the river could be disastrous for player C since either card could conceivably furnish player B with four of a kind. In the event, players F and B both call, but do not raise, indicating possession of hands that probably still require improvement.

THE RIVER

READING OPPONENTS

Identifying the contrasting levels of players' skills is an essential element of successful poker, as is assessing their motivations. While Omaha strategy involves some inflexible rules, players are still challenged psychologically to decipher the meaning behind any bet after the river card has been dealt.

Having survived three rounds of betting, players hope their efforts have been worthwhile, even when evidence from the cards alone suggests this is unlikely. But the winning hand is not always the best possible, especially when several low cards are featured in the widow. Potential lock hands may have been folded, leaving perhaps the most aggressive players to fight over the spoils with reasonable but not outstanding cards. A player facing an awkward decision on the river should reconsider the scale and timing of previous bets. Players who raised on the flop, for example, may have done so in order to eliminate several dangers to a weak leading hand. If the hand implied by that bet does not appear to have been strengthened by the turn and river cards, the bet could have been a semi-bluff that failed to pay off.

Large bets from players after the turn card ordinarily imply that they hold the nut hand or are strong favourites to do so on the river. But since the inference is easily understood by experienced Omaha players, some may choose to capitalize on this awareness by occasionally prosecuting a bluff.

POT MANAGEMENT

Players lucky enough to have a winning opportunity early in the hand are in prime position to control the betting. They can exercise more choice in whether to raise a pot and eliminate potential threats or conceal the value of their cards by calling along with several opponents. The time for setting a trap may arise later, when an opponent stumbles across a good hand that is destined to lose. For example a player holding Ac, Ah, Jd, 8d will appreciate the promise presented by a flop of 10d, As, 9d. In early position, a check may be in order to see how many opponents also like the flop, with anyone holding trips, two pairs and draws for high flushes likely to bet or call the minimum.

If a call will then suffice to see the turn card, the hand may be underrated by opponents who might have expected a player holding trip aces to have advertised the fact already. Should the turn card be the Ad, prompting a bet from the player now holding four aces, anyone with a full house – by matching a pair of tens, perhaps – may call a bet for fear of being bluffed out of a win. All the time they are drawing dead while the player with the top hand is patiently encouraging them to build the pot. In this position, the player would like to see a 10 or a 9 on the river, since that could give an opponent a lower-ranking four of a kind that would prove very difficult to fold, despite the implications behind the player's betting becoming more clear.

FINAL BETTING ROUND

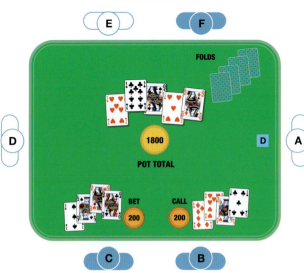

Left: Player C's bet is enough to persuade player F to fold, but player B calls the 200 only to discover that the full house of nines over queens is outranked. This is a common mistake among Omaha players, who are often sufficiently seduced by the size of the pot that they will commit more chips despite knowing they could be beaten. In pot-limit games, players may be more inclined to bluff without the nuts, but, even when suspecting a bluff, calling a large bet with a beatable hand is a tough decision.

ONLINE POKER

THERE ARE MANY ADVANTAGES OF ONLINE POKER. A PLAYER CAN ACCESS USEFUL INFORMATION SUCH AS THE AVERAGE POT SIZE OR THE BETTING LEVEL PREFERRED. THERE ARE OF COURSE DISADVANTAGES TOO: MOST NOTICEABLE IS A GREATER DIFFICULTY IN READING THE OPPONENTS' TELLS.

The huge surge of interest in poker during the past decade is attributable almost entirely to the increased publicity for the game generated by television and the Internet. As the intricacies of tournament-style Texas Hold 'em entertained and inspired television viewers, so online poker sites emerged to offer convenient and ready access to a game. PlanetPoker started the trend in 1998 and there are now over 600 online gaming companies offering access to the top 40 poker networks, generating revenue of over US$100 billion per year. Such sums have attracted many of the world's leading companies from the betting industry and beyond, all establishing their own online poker rooms in their eagerness for a piece of the increasingly lucrative action. However, this rapid growth has brought with it some concern over the morality of gambling online, as well as prompting investigations into its legality. These issues and some basic details regarding the online poker experience are the subject of this chapter.

Right: The upsurge in interest in the game of poker can be squarely placed on the shoulders of rapid developments in the media. As soon as poker tournaments started being televised, the game's legendary players became more widely known and the subsequent inundation of poker guidebooks helped generate even more publicity for the game. The Internet not only offers access to virtually everything there is to know about poker, but also acts as a barometer of poker's global popularity.

THE LAW AND ONLINE POKER

The speed at which online poker has developed as a hugely popular global gambling medium has, to some extent, left the machinations of the law far behind in many countries, and the extensive reach of the Internet has thrown these differences into stark relief.

For the most part, governments of nations in Europe, South America, Asia and around the Caribbean have either adopted a pragmatic approach by legalizing online gambling, or have actively welcomed gaming companies by licensing their operations. However, in America, home to over half of online poker players, the confusion surrounding the legality of Internet betting came to a head in October 2006. Repeated attempts by right-wing Republicans to lobby for an outright ban proved successful when President George W. Bush signed the Safe Port Act, enacting a law that ostensibly aimed to improve American port security. A late amendment to the bill meant that the Unlawful Internet Gambling Enforcement Act was simultaneously incorporated into the legislation. The principal thrust of this additional act is to restrict financial institutions from processing transactions to and from the now outlawed Internet gaming sites on behalf of their clients. Consequently, the cloud of illegality that has enveloped online poker has left American players effectively prevented from utilizing their online betting accounts and reduced their opportunities to play. Needless to say, both the online gaming companies and the vast army of online poker players are working towards overturning this legislation, their primary argument being that poker is a game of skill and not pure chance.

Above: The security and integrity of online casino operations is becoming increasingly trustworthy thanks to the fierce competition between companies offering the service. It is in their interests to make the financial dealings as simple and secure as possible. This includes offering players the option to restrict their involvement in games by means of responsible game settings.

Right: Collusion can be a problem in both real world and virtual poker rooms, and involves two or more players working together to gain an unfair advantage. However, online casino companies operate sophisticated security software that is designed to police collusive behaviour or fraudulent activity by monitoring playing patterns.

Above: Jeff Markley, vice president of Online Operations for Bluff Media, owner of America's largest poker magazine, peruses three online casino screens in his office following the successful passage of the Unlawful Internet Gaming Act in 2006. Within a week, gamblers in America had withdrawn thousands of dollars from their web accounts and access to online poker, casinos and sports-betting on some sites was blocked.

REGULATIONS

Unsurprisingly, considering America's current responses to online gaming, very few countries are prepared to provide licences to online casinos and poker rooms, with most operations being concentrated in places such as Costa Rica, Gibraltar, Malta and countries dotted around the Caribbean. The UK, with one eye on the potential tax revenues that might accrue, has legalized the establishment of online gaming sites, and this move is considered likely to instil more confidence in the industry among consumers.

Although it is true that reputable companies pay their host country a sizeable licensing fee and subject their operations to official scrutiny, the fact remains that the industry itself is mostly self-regulating. Several organizations monitor online gaming, of which the Interactive Gaming Council, Online Players' Association and Gambling Commission are perhaps most respected. In a competitive market, the vast majority of operators recognize that customer satisfaction is of paramount importance and promote the integrity of their businesses. Some rogue elements do still exist, and it is incumbent on the consumer to exercise a degree of caution when selecting an Internet site at which to play.

ONLINE SECURITY

Although one cannot be assured of the security of online poker sites in view of the rapidly changing world of computer technology, the majority can be trusted to handle financial transactions and keep personal details confidential. The digital encryption methods are the same as those used by the world's financial institutions and it is in the interests of the operators to ensure that security is watertight.

The better sites monitor the virtual tables for signs of players cheating by colluding with each other during a game. Two or three players could gain a seat at the same table and communicate with each other about their respective hands remotely. High-stakes games are more likely to be targeted by cheats, but the better poker sites operate systems that identify suspect betting patterns. Players who suspect cheating can always alert the operator's customer support section. It may not compensate any immediate losses, but it will prompt the most reputable online poker rooms to investigate.

GETTING STARTED

The online poker market is immensely competitive, with literally hundreds of sites offering the chance for players to indulge their passion. Three years after the launch of PlanetPoker, PartyPoker became the dominant force in the industry on the back of a major advertising campaign in 2003 that helped it command almost half the total revenues generated by the online game. Following the implementation of the Unlawful Internet Gambling Enforcement Act in October 2006, however, PartyPoker's decision to withdraw its services to American customers led to PokerStars assuming the mantle of busiest poker site. Here, the big-money tournaments are renowned as being among the toughest to win. It is also the site from which which both Chris Moneymaker and Greg Raymer emerged to become WSOP world champions and, not surprisingly, it has a reputation for attracting solid and experienced players.

Other online poker rooms worthy of mention are Full Tilt Poker, Titan Poker and Pacific Poker, since these are also well regarded within the industry. Many of the sites are endorsed by poker professionals, while Doyle Brunson is just one player to exploit his reputation for integrity by creating his own online poker room.

REGISTRATION

Logging on to a preferred site is a straightforward process for anyone familiar with accessing the Internet. In order to play, however, it is necessary to register with the operator, which will involve submitting an email address, selecting a username and creating a password. An account number will be issued, although it is not always necessary to make an immediate cash deposit in order to be able to play, since there are usually play money tables in operation. Details of the account and access to the virtual poker tables can only be obtained by submitting the relevant username and password. It is not unusual for players to have accounts with several online poker rooms, so it is advisable to keep a separate record of the account numbers and passwords for each. The majority of sites require players to download the necessary software before being able to play, but several still offer the chance to play within a web browser.

Below: Four of the more established online gaming sites available today. There are over 140 sites catering for players seeking a game in the comfort of their own home. The astonishing growth in online poker is a 21st-century phenomenon, the first online card room opening just before the millennium.

Below: Poker is growing fast in Germany, with nearly 300,000 players logging on to gaming sites, despite a change to German law in January 2008 effectively banning online betting. Deutsche Poker Tour is a free online poker league whose members play on poker sites to gain points that will enable them to compete for the huge prize pool on offer at the league championship.

Above: Armed with a low-grade personal computer (PC), a 56K modem and access to a telephone line, it is possible to play poker games with people all over the world. The benefit that online poker offers the novice is the chance to practise, without the trouble of finding a card room or organizing a game.

THE VIRTUAL POKER ROOM

Rival sites differ cosmetically in terms of their graphics and presentation but access to the desired games and ancillary services is generally organized along very similar lines. Drop-down menus and clearly labelled tabs indicate the poker variations available, the stake levels that apply and the betting structures that are in operation. Distinguishing between cash games and tournaments is simple and there are a range of statistical details available for each table in operation including such key information as the average pot size and the number of hands dealt per hour. This can help a player to identify whether a game is tight or loose which is useful in formulating an initial strategy.

Once seated at a table, of course, a player must actively click on the relevant button to join a game at which point such elements as the deal and the payment of antes is automated. The options available to each player when a betting decision needs to be made are clearly displayed and only require the press of a button or a click of the mouse to check, bet or fold.

POKERBOTS
♦ ♣ ♥ ♠

All serious poker players are keen on having an edge over their opponents, and online players are no different. To this end, many are inclined to employ pokerbots, these being computer software programs that can access a game in progress and provide a player with a range of useful information. Pokerbots can read all the face-up cards and calculate pot odds as well as make recommendations on which hands to play and when to bet. In this regard, they can save a player time in making a decision, although it might be argued that this stunts the development of an individual's own ability to read a game. Some pokerbots can be programmed to play automatically, but their success rates are rather limited.

Modest returns at low-stakes games have been recorded, but, given the rigid strategies often employed by the pokerbots, this success is often attributed to the poor quality of the players that contest such games. Experienced players are better able to manipulate a hand when playing a predictable opponent, and, as yet, no pokerbot program is able to understand the subtleties of bluffing and checkraising to pose a serious threat.

ONLINE GAMES

Despite some variations from one card room to another, the mainstays of online poker are Texas Hold 'em, Omaha and seven-card stud, along with the split-pot games Omaha/8 and seven-card stud high/low. Draw poker is also available at some sites as is the Hold 'em derivative, crazy pineapple, a game in which players are dealt three cards rather than two, one of which must be discarded following the flop and the conclusion of the second betting round. Such is the scale of American influence on the game that the majority of sites trade in US dollars, irrespective of their registered location.

The betting structures operated are the staples of fixed-limit, pot-limit and no-limit, with the former recommended as the most likely to appeal to the beginner. Games for real money exist at levels ranging from a few cents up to hundreds of dollars and should easily match the means of anybody who wishes to play. Of course, the key difference when playing poker in a virtual card room compared to the live experience is that the pace of events is much quicker. Each hand may take less than a minute to complete and players rarely have the luxury of sitting back for more than 30 seconds to contemplate a decision.

Left: A leading Japanese online poker guide, featuring reviews of all major poker rooms, top lists, strategy advice for both beginners and advanced players as well as poker rules. It also offers daily freerolls and tournament schedules. The nation of 128 million is looking to lift its ban on casinos to increase tourist arrivals and revive its gaming industry. Japan's ruling party is holding talks with global gaming companies including Harrah's Entertainment Inc. to operate the nation's first casinos after 2010.

Right: Juega Poker Ya is one of Spain's leading online poker gaming sites offering freeroll and satellite tournaments. Thousands of budding Spanish poker players are queuing up to learn how to play in the hope of emulating the success of Spanish poker star Carlos Mortensen, World Poker Champion in 2001. Poker is similar to the popular Spanish gambling game Mus, another game of skill and psychology where players try to outwit their opponents.

Left: There are many online poker gaming sites in Russia, though Malta-based company Red Star Poker, which opened in June 2005, filled the crucial void of providing instruction and customer service in both Russian and English. Upon downloading the necessary gaming software, players may participate in satellite tournaments with international players.

Above: An online poker gaming site in Slovenia. Casinos in Slovenia are attracting gamblers from Italy, where tight marketing restrictions and high tax rates have hampered growth in the industry. In 2004, over 87 per cent of all visits to Slovenian casinos were made by foreigners.

Above: An Israeli poker portal, in Hebrew. Gambling is currently illegal in Israel, but there are efforts to reverse that. The Israeli government is sitting on a proposal that would allow casinos to be built in Eilat, the country's principal holiday city. A formal decision has yet to be made, but many groups of investors are already vying for building contracts.

HOW MANY PLAYERS?

In keeping with the standard tables in the card rooms and casinos of the world, online poker tables typically have space for nine or ten players. Texas Hold 'em and Omaha are the games most likely to accommodate the maximum per table, while seven-card stud games are usually limited to eight players. All these games, are also staged with lower limits on the number of participants, with heads-up contests widely available and many Texas Hold 'em tables limited to three, four or five players. The impact of having fewer competitors is that the blinds circulate the table quicker, of course, and this keeps players involved in the action. With the standard of the average winning hand also being reduced, such short-handed games tend to be loose betting affairs and appeal to those who perhaps do not have the patience or inclination to fold a succession of hands while watching others compete.

THE RAKE

This is the fee charged by the online poker room for providing the facilities to play. To enter a US$10 tournament, for example, players are usually required to pay US$11, of which US$10 goes into the prize pool with the additional US$1 being claimed by the operator. A levy of ten per cent is typical for the lower-stakes games although it is often reduced in more expensive tournaments.

The fees that are charged in cash games differ quite considerably from site to site with levels varying from five to ten per cent of each pot at the lowest stake levels. A cap is often placed on the rake if a pot exceeds

PLAY-MONEY POKER
♦ ♣ ♥ ♠

Once registered to an online poker site, players will normally be credited with chips that may be used in play-money games only. These offer an ideal opportunity for novices to learn how to play at no expense and so represent a valuable educational resource. Experienced players may also find them useful as a means of warming up prior to sitting in on a real money game. Obviously, with nothing at stake, the games tend to be fairly loose affairs, but that does not diminish their potential for helping a player focus on the key facets of the game prior to playing for real.

a certain size but the poker room's cut could easily be a dollar or more for every hand. Since 60 hands per hour is a fairly common rate of play per table, the scale of the potential income to be accrued becomes apparent given the thousands of virtual tables simultaneously staging a game at any one time.

From a consumer's perspective it is obviously worth checking the rake charts that are published by the majority of reputable online poker rooms. A comparison between the different rates applicable at the preferred betting levels will certainly prove worthwhile for anyone considering playing for several hours a week. Even those who win consistently may be paying more for the privilege than need be the case.

CASH GAMES

One of the great advantages of online poker is the sheer wealth of information available to players who wish to engage in a cash game. Those with some experience of the medium will consider the statistics for each table at the betting level they favour, taking into account such information as the average pot size and, at Texas Hold 'em tables, how many players are seeing the flop, usually expressed in percentage terms. A loose table can be identified as one where at least half the players are regularly calling to see the flop, probably with some modest hands among them. Such a game would be a very attractive proposition for an experienced poker player who is able to exercise more discipline in selecting which hands to support. Games with a minimum bet of US$1 or more can normally be expected to attract reasonably good players, whereas the levels below this appeal more to those who treat their poker casually.

Understanding the likely quality of opposition is a key consideration, of course, with many online players content to compete without a solid appreciation of strategy and the nuances of a particular game. Identifying these players can certainly help, but unsophisticated opponents pose problems in that they are difficult to bluff, being unable to understand the implications behind a strong bet. Similarly, any calling stations or maniacs at the table who are content to play many hands cannot beat the odds in the long run but will, on occasions, strike it lucky by hitting the cards they need to win. Such players are hazardous, but not as daunting as those who sit patiently, folding hand after hand while waiting for the cards that will justify a large bet. Becoming involved in betting confrontations with tight, aggressive players should only be considered when holding an exceptionally good hand.

STAKE LEVELS

A minimum and maximum buy-in normally applies at whichever table one chooses to play, particularly in pot-limit and no-limit games, while in fixed-limit, poker players may be able to buy in for their entire bankroll. Ordinarily, the upper limit is one hundred times the minimum bet and it is recommended that players always buy in for the maximum permitted. Maintaining a chip stack that is well in excess of the average pot size at the table is essential to ward off pressure from the chip leaders and to ensure that, in the event of holding a winning hand, a player can capitalize on it to best advantage. Topping up one's chip stack where permitted is therefore advisable,

Left: There has been a huge upsurge in people playing poker online globally and the Eastern European nation, Croatia, is no exception. On land, the country boasts 12 casinos, of which four are located in Zagreb, the capital city. The largest casino in the country, Miro hotel and casino Minera in Plovanija, has 34 gaming tables and 250 video poker or other gaming machines.

Right: An online poker gaming website in Chinese. ESPN, an American cable TV network dedicated to sports-related programming is the major broadcaster of poker. The sports network now airs in China and has exposed 1.3 billion people to the game. The first to feel these benefits will be the online gaming sites.

Left: A Polish online poker website. Poland's poker community is small, but its poker players are among the best. Team Poland beat Team America to win the third annual PokerStars televised World Cup of Poker 2006 event, claiming the top prize of US$100,000. The free tournament began online with 39 nations around the globe battling for the right to represent their countries.

Middle right: Sweden's leading portal about poker and related information. The site offers reviews of poker rooms, articles, rules, tournaments and a poker forum.

Right: Land-based casino gambling in France is highly restricted and the only choice is state-managed operations, but the nation's online casino business is now in full swing.

although there is little point in continually doing so at a table where an opponent has amassed a chip lead of perhaps two or three times the maximum buy-in.

Similarly, players should be incredibly confident in their ability to consider joining a table where one opponent already has such an advantage. It is usually indicative of having played well for several hours, and confronting an in-form opponent with the means to make intimidating bets is inadvisable in the extreme.

ONLINE POKER TELLS

The ability to read opponents in order to assess the meaning behind any bet is an asset and, to this end, deciphering clues from a player's body language can often be helpful. However, distinctive physical mannerisms are quite obviously not visible when playing online, although there are still some clues available to the keen observer regarding opponents' styles and attitudes.

Messages in the chat box, if taken at face value, might prove a good indicator of an opponent's mood, given that many players could easily be tired, bored or even drunk. During a game there are some who take the maximum permitted time to make a decision, which

could be the result of a poor connection, but could also indicate that the individual concerned is either a novice or is playing several tables simultaneously. If the latter is suspected, the opponent may be restricting play to aggressive support for premium starting hands at each table as that is a much easier strategy to manage. Any bet or raise from such an opponent would evidently merit respect under these circumstances. Similarly, an opponent who raises a bet almost instantaneously usually indicates possession of a good hand, the speed of the response suggesting maximum confidence. Conversely, an opponent who takes much more time than usual in playing one particular hand may be consciously trying to disguise its true value.

Online poker rooms do offer the facility for players to make notes about their opponents while games are in progress, and many offer a statistical breakdown of one's own play during any session. However, the speed of the games themselves and the tendency for virtual tables to experience a high turnover of players makes it difficult to read opponents. Taking note of new players joining the table and adjusting one's strategy accordingly is crucial to success at the online game.

ONLINE TOURNAMENTS

The inspiration provided by the spectacle of televised tournament poker is undoubtedly responsible for the popularity of the knockout game in online poker rooms. While trying to make a regular profit from cash games requires a long-term strategy and a consistently disciplined approach, the appeal of tournament poker is that a single victory could realize a dramatic profit for a few hours' work. In addition, because the entry fees are always stipulated, it is possible to know in advance the maximum loss that will be incurred if a player is knocked out before reaching the prize-money positions.

One other aspect of tournaments that makes them so appealing to the new generation of poker players is that luck has the potential to undermine the strategies of opponents who are regarded as more skilful. One bad beat and the loss of a substantial pot can seriously undermine a good player's attempts to win a tournament as easily as those of a novice. However, it must be remembered that the very best professionals regularly finish in the prize money in live tournaments so there is no reason to suppose that experienced online tournament players are not similarly successful, particularly in the high-stakes contests.

TOURNAMENT STRUCTURES

The very nature of online poker permits a greater range of tournament styles and structures than might be found in a typical card room, such are the benefits of having a computer program in control of proceedings. The single-table sit 'n' go tournaments for between five and ten players are especially popular, since they rarely take more than an hour to complete at most. Indeed, if played as high-speed turbo tournaments, they may be resolved in less than half that time.

At the other end of the scale, the multi-table tournaments hosted by online poker rooms can take several hours to complete, making them more appealing to players with time on their hands. Texas Hold 'em is the preferred game for most online tournament players, although other popular variations are also played in tournament format using the standard range of betting structures.

STRATEGIC CONSIDERATIONS

In terms of actual tournament strategy, the basic advice is for players to be cautiously disciplined during the early stages while taking stock of opponents, only betting when in possession of a very good hand. All

Left: The computer age may soon be creeping into card rooms, and taking jobs from dealers. Here a game of Texas Hold 'em is being played on the new PokerPro dealer-free electronic poker tables at the Hollywood Park Casino in Inglewood, California. The electronic tables require no dealers, as the players select all their actions via the touch screen in front of them. The casino unveiled its e-poker room in October 2006, making it the first casino in California to feature e-poker tables which combine the speed and accuracy of online poker with the personal player interaction of traditional 'brick and mortar' casino poker.

Left and below: All Aussie Poker is an Australian online poker resource, offering a range of poker-related services; Mega poker is its Dutch equivalent. Type in 'online poker' to almost any search engine and and you will score a barrage of hits.

Below right: The convenience and anonymity associated with playing online poker has led to women representing roughly 40 per cent of the card-room clientele, compared to just 5 per cent in real life card rooms and casinos.

players start with the same number of chips, but this selective approach can help to conserve a player's resources while opponents knock each other out.

From the middle stages onwards, players need to be selectively more aggressive in order to withstand the increasing betting levels, this being easier for those in healthy chip positions, of course. Varying one's playing style to accommodate the changing fortunes of opponents is a requirement at this point, and those with the largest stacks are obviously in a position to take a few more risks with moderate hands without necessarily damaging their overall prospects.

By the time the tournament reaches its final stages, betting choices are often dictated by the size of a player's chip stack as much as by the cards themselves. Those in the lead will be pressurizing those with fewer chips and on the verge of elimination in order to move one step nearer the top prize. Understandably, it is this level of volatility at the business end of the event that makes tournament poker so exciting for regular participants.

PRIZES
♦ ♣ ♥ ♠

Prize money is normally distributed among the leading ten per cent of players in any tournament, though some events are organized on a 'winner takes all' basis. A single-table tournament of ten players will usually see the first three rewarded, the winner taking 50 per cent of the prize pool. A US$10 event will see the winner claiming US$50, the runner-up US$30 and third-place US$20. Multi-table events featuring 1,000 entrants could see the winner's share reduced to 25 per cent of the total prize pool, to accommodate payments for the top 100 finishers. Assuming a US$10 event once more, the first prize would still amount to US$2,500, which is an attractive sum for a modest outlay. However, beating up to 1,000 opponents in a hugely competitive environment is obviously a major achievement and not something that many poker players are regularly able to repeat.

CASINOS AND CLUBS

CASINOS CAN BE A GREAT PLACE TO PLAY POKER AS THEY WILL FREQUENTLY HAVE ORGANISED TOURNAMENTS. THE GAMES ON OFFER WILL REFLECT THE CURRENT TRENDS, AND THERE ARE OFTEN FACILITIES FOR PLAYERS TO HOLD THEIR OWN PRIVATE GAMES.

The recent popularity of playing online poker over the last decade has created an increased demand for the game in the world's foremost casinos, although many of the smaller establishments are still reluctant to provide poker facilities. From a purely commercial perspective, the cost of operating a poker table is rarely as profitable for the house as a range of other gambling games such as roulette, craps or the ubiquitous slot machines. In these, of course, players bet against the house rather than each other, assuring the casinos of a regular and predictable stream of income. However, despite the fact that the rake from a poker table may never match the revenue of a dozen slot machines that could easily take its place, consumer demand has helped prompt a change of approach. For those new to the experience, this chapter highlights some of the key factors to bear in mind when playing poker in a commercial card room.

Right: In poker, the cards are shuffled prior to the deal of each hand. The players will normally shuffle and deal in home games and smaller clubs, while in casinos it is more likely that a dealer will be employed specifically to manage this aspect of the game. A professional dealer can help to speed up proceedings, leaving players free to concentrate on their poker strategies although this luxury comes at a price in the form of the casino rake, a fee often levied on each pot to cover the costs of the dealer and other facilities.

WHAT TO EXPECT

Players who are used to enjoying poker in home games against friends, particularly for modest stakes, are entitled to be intimidated when they first venture into a dedicated poker room. Of course, the setting will differ from one card room to another, with the glitz and glamour of the palatial hotel-casinos in Las Vegas not replicated in small, urban poker clubs. There may be five tables in operation or 50, but the fact remains that anyone who takes a seat in a commercial card room for the first time, to play poker against complete strangers, is likely to feel nervous.

The unfamiliar environment, the potential distractions and the need to keep stock of developments at the table can all conspire to disrupt a player's concentration. This, of course, can prove costly, so those considering a visit to a card room are well advised to familiarize themselves with the venue for a while before engaging in a game. There will always be members of staff on hand to answer any questions concerning the facilities on offer and the general rules that apply to specific games. Most poker commentators suggest that it is always a good idea to watch a game in progress for a while rather than take a seat immediately, should one be available. This helps acclimatize a player to the environment and offers the chance to gauge the quality of the opposition and the style of the games in progress.

Above: The Bellagio hotel and casino, Las Vegas, was inspired by the Lake Como resort of Bellagio in Italy. It was the most expensive hotel ever built when opened in 1998, having cost over US$1.6 billion. Many professional poker players prefer to play there, due in part to the high table limits.

HOUSE RULES

Every poker room will have a manager, cashiers and a set of rules governing the games, as well as points of general etiquette. Larger operations will, of course, employ several dealers and have staff on hand to deal with any disputes as they arise. Although a degree of consistency is common in card rooms operating in close proximity to each other, there are often variations governing the betting limits, the permitted buy-ins and the structures of the games. Few people are likely to play poker in a formal setting without having some experience of the game, but it is still incumbent upon the individual to be aware of the different regulations in operation.

It is also worth remembering that experienced players prefer a fairly swift pace to proceedings and, because of the rake and the potential for earning tips, dealers are inclined to meet this demand. Inexperienced players can soon become a nuisance to opponents and dealers alike if they continually struggle to follow events and delay the game by seeking continual guidance on what options are available to them. This underlines how harshly competitive the game can be when played in a commercial setting and confirms the need for proper preparation on the part of any prospective participant.

Left: Laser light show at the Las Vegas Golden Nugget casino-hotel. The world's largest gold nugget on display, the Hand of Faith, is in the lobby. Weighing 876 troy ounces (27.2kg) and 46 centimetres (18 inches) in length, it was found near the Golden Triangle in Australia in 1980.

Right: The famous 'Welcome to Las Vegas' sign, located just to the south of the Las Vegas Strip. Betty Willis and Ted Rogich created the sign, characteristic of the Googie architecture movement popular at the time, for Clark County, Nevada. The back of the sign reads 'Drive Carefully and Come Back Soon'. When seen up close, the circles on which the letters of the word 'WELCOME' appear reveal themselves to be silver dollars.

LAS VEGAS

Poker's long association with Las Vegas has helped it develop a magnetic appeal that attracts players from all over the world. The choice of games and venues on offer is staggering, with over 50 dedicated card rooms catering for their needs. Many, such as the Bellagio, the Mirage and Caesar's Palace, are located in the plush casinos of the Las Vegas Strip, while Binion's Horseshoe, the former home of the WSOP, is in the downtown area, along with the Golden Nugget. Although each poker room has its own unique personality, there are aspects common to all, with relaxed dress codes the norm and, increasingly, a ban on smoking at the poker tables. Not surprisingly, many of the world's best poker players live and work in Las Vegas and anyone seriously considering a visit can expect fierce competition in whichever room they choose to play.

BINION'S, LAS VEGAS
♦ ♣ ♥ ♠

For many, this is the only place to play poker, such is the casino's famous association with the WSOP, instigated by the venue's original owner, Benny Binion. Originally known as Binion's Horseshoe, the casino was rebranded following a change of ownership, while the WSOP has moved to Harrah's Rio Casino, having outgrown its original home. Situated at 128 East Fremont, Binion's has 14 tables in a room regarded as spacious by casino standards, with the usual roster of Texas Hold 'em, seven-card stud and Omaha. Betting limits are among the lowest in town, with US$2/$4 fixed-limit Texas Hold 'em on offer, while the minimum buy-in for a no-limit game is US$100, the blinds being set at US$1 and US$2. No-limit Texas Hold 'em tournaments are organized daily, the buy-ins starting at US$50 – although the cost rises to US$150 on Friday and Saturday evenings. Basic lessons in how to play Texas Hold 'em are held at 11am each day.

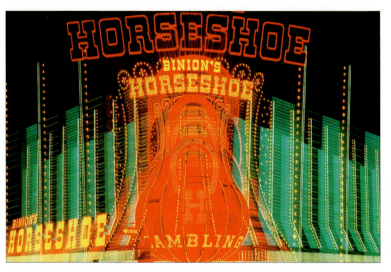

Right: Binion's Horsehoe casino, located in the centre of Fremont Street, where two million light bulbs and 540,000 watts of sound transform the canopy into the world's largest animated light show every night. Although it is most famous for its gaming, the Horseshoe has other popular attractions, including the Poker Hall of Fame wall inside, which honours the greatest players in the history of poker.

THE CASINO RAKE

As mentioned earlier, while poker clubs do exist, many established international casinos have at times been reluctant to offer players the facilities required to pursue their preferred gambling interest. The resurgence of interest in the game has encouraged a change of heart in many cases, but the services provided by any commercial card room do come at a price, of course. This takes the form of the 'rake', sometimes referred to as the 'cut', the 'vigorish' or 'vig'. It is usually set at a minimum of three per cent, and could be as high as ten per cent of every pot contested, although there will usually be a cap on the rake once any pot exceeds a certain level.

Given that it is often customary for the winner of each pot to tip the dealer, it soon becomes evident how difficult it is to make money from the game. This is particularly the case at the lower-stake levels, where, even when capped, the rake can seem a relatively big slice of the smaller pots usually contested. Winning an

average number of pots may not be enough to break even unless players limit themselves to playing hands that promise an early advantage. Exerting this discipline requires folding on most occasions, perhaps making for a gruelling session. However, it is the only way that any player can realistically hope to beat both the opposition and the house cut.

Above: A waitress serves poker players at Binion's casino. With food and drink constantly on offer during play, casinos do have ways other than gambling to extract money from visitors' pockets. The casino environment is geared towards cutting you off from the outside world and the level of concentration required to play well is difficult to sustain for long. It is advisable to regulate your time at the table and take regular breaks for refreshment.

Left: Among the signature attractions at Caesar's Palace hotel-casino, located on the Las Vegas Strip between the Bellagio and the Mirage, is the Colosseum theatre, where Céline Dion and Elton John have been regular performers. It was specifically built for the Dion show, *A New Day*, a spectacular produced by former Cirque du Soleil director Franco Dragone. Despite having some of the highest ticket prices for any show in the city, with seats as high as US$200 each, the show regularly sold out.

Right: To win when playing in poker games where the house takes a cut, a player must not only beat opponents, but also the financial drain of the rake. The rake represents a fee for the facilities, and it's also customary to tip the dealer when you win the pot. So even a winning session does not come without some expense.

GAMES AND FACILITIES

The poker variations on offer in casinos tend to reflect current trends, with Texas Hold 'em, seven-card stud and Omaha most prominent, although other games are generally available on request. The split-pot and low-only games such as Omaha/8, razz, lowball and seven-card stud/8 are also popular, although not as widely available. Larger establishments sometimes offer separate rates for a private room or table at which players may engage in whichever game they choose. Typically, hiring such a facility is usually conditional on it being in use for a minimum of, perhaps, six hours.

Aside from poker, of course, casinos offer many other gambling facilities that have proved the downfall of many successful poker players. Even the late Stu Ungar, three times a world champion, had a reputation for leaving a casino broke on occasions, despite having won substantial sums at the poker table. In terms of ancillary services, players will often find themselves waited on while playing poker, since staff will be on hand to take orders for drinks and perhaps even food. Play for long enough and there is a chance that complimentary refreshments will be offered, but this service is not universally available.

Above: One of several slot machine halls inside the Golden Nugget casino-hotel. Casinos operate to make money and they are generally very good at it. Given that the space occupied by one poker table could easily accommodate perhaps a dozen machines, simple economics have contributed to the game being marginalized by casinos in the past.

AVIATION CLUB DE FRANCE, PARIS
♦ ♣ ♥ ♠

Situated at 10, Avenue de Champs-Elysées, the Aviation Club de France in Paris is regarded as one of the most stylish casinos in the world. It was established in 1907 primarily to cater for baccarat players but is now readily associated with poker courtesy of the Grand Prix de Paris, a Texas Hold 'em tournament that ranks among the most prestigious in Europe and constitutes part of the World Poker Tour. The card room offers a wide range of cash games including Omaha, seven-card stud and their high-low variations, along with Texas Hold 'em. It also boasts its own hybrid of Hold 'em in which players are dealt four cards, one of which must be discarded before the flop while a second must be mucked before the turn card is revealed. Buying in to a game can cost from €50 to €10,000 and the betting structures, starting at €2/€4 for fixed-limit tables, vary according to the minimum buy-in but include fixed-, pot- and no-limit games. Daily €50 no-limit Hold 'em tournaments are staged each morning and afternoon, and on Saturday evenings there is a similar event for which the buy-in is €250. In common with many of Europe's prominent casinos, the Aviation Club insists that its patrons dress smartly, declining to admit anyone wearing a t-shirt or trainers.

THE PLAYERS

While the number of regular players who attend a home game may vary, in a casino the likelihood is that cash game tables will have from seven to ten players at a time competing against each other. If this represents a greater number of opponents than an individual is used to facing, then it is worth remembering that a more conservative approach will be required to garner any success. This is particularly important when bearing in mind that some of these opponents may be very good players indeed, added to which the house rake is an ever-present obstacle to negotiate. The standard of opposition very much depends on the location of the poker room, the stake levels in operation and, perhaps, even the time of day chosen to play. Peak times tend to be during the evenings and at weekends, of course, when games are likely to represent far tougher propositions.

PROS, SEMI-PROS AND TOURISTS

The nature of the opposition varies from one card room to another, so a little research is advisable when considering a visit to a commercial establishment. Online reviews of specific venues can help players identify those that may best suit their financial means and skills. This is certainly a useful tool for anyone thinking of playing in Las Vegas or Atlantic City, although not all locations are as saturated with poker rooms as these hotbeds of tourism.

Wherever a player's chosen card room is situated, the likelihood is that there will be a regular clientele for whom poker is a major source of income. Such professionals, given their experience, will normally play at the higher-stakes tables, but they can be found playing lower-stakes cash games too. They may be passing the time waiting for a seat at a bigger game to

Above: Many of the largest hotel, casino and resort properties in the world are located on 'The Strip'– four miles of boulevard that has been designated an All-American Road. New casinos design their facades to attract walk-up customers and many of these entrances have become attractions themselves.

Left: Professional Danish poker player Mads Andersen, winner of the four-day EPT Scandinavian Open 2006, which saw him take home €341,000 in winnings. The Dane had to work hard for the money, with the final table lasting a record 10 hours. Before making his mark in the poker world, Andersen was a former World Backgammon Champion.

become available or, having endured a run of bad fortune, may be trying to restore their bankroll by capitalizing on the inexperience of casual players. Such tourists commonly make the mistake of playing a little too loosely in their eagerness to become involved in the action, perhaps replicating the style of play in their regular home games. By trying to force the issue in this fashion, inexperienced players make the task of the patient professionals and semi-professionals that much easier. The latter will know that by waiting for a top-quality hand before betting, they will almost certainly find a caller or two who is immediately at a disadvantage and so likely to lose the pot.

Anybody considering a poker holiday of some form, particularly to Las Vegas, should approach the experience with a realistic set of expectations. The prospect of an average player winning a fortune at the poker table is unlikely given the typical standard of competition. Indeed, conventional wisdom suggests that poker tourists should budget for losses at the table as they would for any other leisure entertainment. Anyone who breaks even over a few sessions while managing to combat the ravages of the rake can then be satisfied that they have skills of a competent player.

Above: Tourists enjoying the nightlife in Las Vegas, marketed as 'the entertainment capital of the world', also commonly known as 'sin city' due to the popularity of legalized gambling, availability of alcohol at any time, and various forms of adult entertainment. The city's image has made it a popular setting for films and television programmes.

Below: Increasing numbers of casinos offer table card games where there are alternative ways to play and win. Three card poker is an exciting stud poker game where players may bet against the dealer or bet on the value of their own three-card hand or bet both. Bonus payouts may be had for certain wagers against the dealer.

CONCORD CARD CASINO, VIENNA
♦ ♣ ♥ ♠

The Concord Card Casino, located on the Geiselbergstrasse in Vienna, has only been open since 1993 and boasted Europe's largest poker room until the opening of the UK's Dusk till Dawn club in 2007. No-limit Texas Hold 'em, pot-limit Omaha and fixed-limit seven-card stud account for the bulk of the games played, with the casino acknowledging that many more young players are taking seats at its 30 poker tables. Fixed-limit Hold 'em is also on offer at stakes of €3/€6 and above, while seven-card stud games are available on request. Tournaments are organized each evening with buy-ins from €24. The Concord stages several high-stakes tournaments during the year, the most prestigious being the Austrian Poker Championship, part of Vienna's Spring Poker Festival held in March, and the European Poker Masters. Both competitions require a buy-in of €3,000. The Concord has no membership policy although it insists that players dress relatively smartly and do not wear jeans or t-shirts.

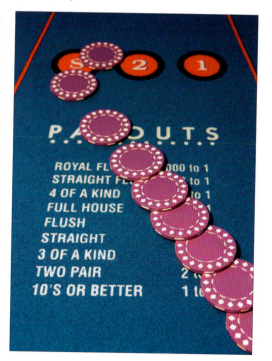

THE CASINO ENVIRONMENT

Casino profitability is dependent upon keeping customers comfortably entertained for as long as possible, since the longer they stay, the more likely it is that they will lose money. Windows and clocks are noticeable by their absence and, with air-conditioning systems that help maintain a constant temperature, the whole casino experience is geared towards separating clients from any connection with the outside world.

Poker players may benefit from preferential facilities in some establishments, but many poker rooms compete for space with other gambling attractions. Consequently, it is quite common for a busy room with plenty of tables in operation to generate a great volume of noise, which, along with the distractions emanating from other gaming tables, can test a player's powers of concentration. Technological developments have seen the larger, more prestigious poker rooms striving to improve their booking systems in an effort to help operations run more smoothly, but regular poker players can be tough customers to please.

PLAYING CONDITIONS

Anyone seriously contemplating a game of poker normally expects to spend several hours engaged in competition, even if moving from one table to another during a session. With this in mind, the conditions of play with regard to the poker room itself become more significant. The large oval tables could host ten players who are all sat in close proximity to each other, which, if the scene is replicated throughout the room, can make the experience slightly claustrophobic. If this in itself is not too intimidating, then confronting opponents wearing hats or sunglasses to obscure their facial expressions may seem slightly disconcerting. In terms of physical well-being, an occasional break from even the most comfortable seat will be needed and poker rooms with toilet facilities nearby always score highly with reviewers.

At the tables, competent dealers will ensure a steady pace to the game, with some venues even possessing automatic shuffling machines to help reduce the inevitable pause between hands. There will rarely be time for players to indulge in a weighty discussion on the outcome of a hand before the next is dealt, such inquests being of little interest to those who were not involved, in any case.

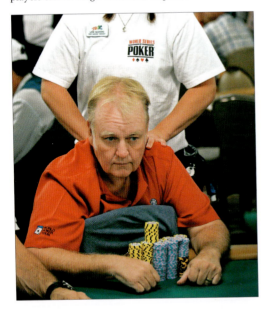

Above: American Russ Hamilton receiving a massage during the Hold 'em main event in the 2005 World Series of Poker. Hamilton, who started playing poker when he was seven, won in 1994, claiming a US$1 million prize. Since it was the 25th anniversary, he also won his weight in silver.

Above: Inside the Casino Barrière de Deauville, France, during the French Open tournament of 2005. In the annals of James Bond history, it is said that Ian Fleming, the spy's creator, modelled the gambling salon of his novel *Casino Royale* on the baize tables and spinning roulette wheels in Deauville.

DISTRACTIONS

Coming to terms with an unfamiliar environment, speed of play at the table and the quality of the opposition is a major challenge, given the other potential distractions in a card room. It can be difficult to ignore the general level of background noise arising from adjacent tables and the steady stream of players coming and going from the facility. Also, spectators may sometimes stop by to see how play is progressing, either because they are checking out the competition at a table for which they would like a seat or, perhaps, because they are friendly with one of the players competing in the game. If waiting staff are on hand to provide table service as well, the potential level of disruption to a player's concentration becomes apparent.

Coping with these factors is a test of character, of course, but if a player feels uncomfortable at any time, it is always best to take a break or change tables if possible. Anything that creates a degree of stress while playing is bound to have an impact on an individual's performance, which will inevitably detract from the experience of playing in a dedicated poker room.

TRUMP TAJ MAHAL, ATLANTIC CITY
♦ ♣ ♥ ♠

Recently voted 'best casino' by *Casino Player* magazine readers, the Trump Taj Mahal boasts Atlantic City's biggest poker room and has played host to the US Poker Championships for the past 10 years. Tables are dedicated to Texas Hold 'em, Omaha and seven-card stud, along with their high-low variants, and there are free daily lessons teaching newcomers. Stake levels begin at US$1/$3 for seven-card stud and US$2/$4 for pot-limit Texas Hold 'em, while there are no-limit Texas Hold 'em tournaments staged each day. The minimum buy-in is for US$50 plus US$15, and the events start at various times during the day, with the betting levels rising every 20 minutes. Opened in 1990 and built to rival anything on offer in Las Vegas, the Trump Taj Mahal is a major attraction for holidaymakers, as well as poker tourists, drawn to the east coast of America.

Above: The trademark sunglasses that professional poker player Greg Raymer wore when he won the 2004 World Series of Poker tournament. The holographic lizard eyes began as a joke during a big hand in the 2002 WSOP, but it seemed to have a desirable effect, distracting his opponent. Since then, Raymer has worn the glasses in all the major poker tournaments that he has played.

Right: A lit fountain shimmers at night in front of a large neon sign at the Trump Taj Mahal casino resort in Atlantic City, New Jersey. The hotel and casino underwent a US$250 million renovation, which included the addition of a new hotel tower, luxurious spas, five-star dining, and a shuttle.

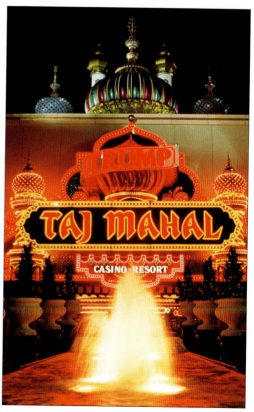

KEY ADVICE

Putting into practice the principles outlined so far is always going to be difficult the first time a player tackles casino poker. However, while it may take a while to adjust to the different conditions, there are several key factors worth remembering that can help alleviate any initial stress. Perhaps the most obvious is to choose a game at a comfortable stake level that is relative to the size of a player's bankroll. If successfully adopting a more cautious attitude, it is possible that a player could see the deal circulate the table several times before winning a hand. Having sufficient chips to cover the antes or blinds while, perhaps, losing the odd contested pot is therefore essential to enable a player to sustain interest throughout such a lean spell.

Should a game at the right level not be available, then it is better to play for lower stakes, rather than joining a game that is, in all conscience, beyond one's means. A profitable session against players of similar ability might provide the impetus to move up a grade, and this situation is certainly more likely to enhance a player's confidence than dropping down a level, having already lost a substantial chunk of one's bankroll. Understanding the routines of a chosen poker variation is also vital, of course, since playing an unfamiliar game is likely to prove a costly exercise in education without some prior knowledge of even the most basic strategies to adopt.

Above: A tired-looking actor Tobey Maguire reacting to losing during a game of Texas Hold 'em at the World Series of Poker in Las Vegas in 2005. Casinos are designed to shake cash from your pockets and can wear you down if you do not take regular breaks. Exhausted players would do well to remember that a game will always be happening somewhere tomorrow.

BUDGETING TIME

Presented with an opportunity to play poker at any time, day or night, it is easy for players to fall into the trap of over-indulging their interest. Maintaining the levels of concentration required to play studiously and competently is a tall order for even the most accomplished professionals. Knowing when to walk away from the table is therefore as much a part of disciplined poker play as anything a player may need to exhibit while in competition. One lapse in concentration could undo plenty of good work earlier in the session, so regular breaks are also advisable when intending to play for several hours at a time.

This is particularly important if, having played well, an individual suffers a bad beat that wipes out any short-term gains already accrued. Controlling the anger or frustration experienced following an unlucky loss can test the mettle of almost any player, but only the very best are able to accept the result calmly and not allow it to prejudice their subsequent betting patterns. The crucial thing to

Above: Edgar Skjervold at the EPT Monte Carlo event in 2006. Skjervold, a 30-year-old financial analyst from Oslo, Norway, is part of a group of Norwegian players who have burst upon the poker scene in recent years. He shot to prominence after winning the World Championship of Online Poker in 2004, taking home US$424,945, the largest internet cash prize in history.

Right: Chips from the Grosvenor Victoria casino. A highlight of The Vic's poker calendar is the annual Grosvenor Grand Prix, an event which features a collection of big buy-in tournaments and attracts players from all over Europe to compete for millions of pounds in prize money.

Left: Among the largest and oldest of the casinos in the UK, The Vic as it is known, featured a classic upset during The Poker Classics, held there in April 2005, when the relatively unknown Andy Church placed first among nearly two hundred players, including many who are well known on the circuit.

avoid in such circumstances is the type of reckless play that signifies a player is 'on tilt' – this is characterized by betting more heavily on marginal hands to try and compensate for earlier perceived injustices. Should any player suspect that their game is deteriorating along these lines, it is well worth remembering that a fresh opportunity to play is rarely long in coming, such is the widespread access to poker now available.

GROSVENOR VICTORIA CASINO, LONDON
♦ ♣ ♥ ♠

London's Grosvenor Victoria Casino, often referred to as 'The Vic', is a popular haunt for many of the city's top poker players and it regularly stages high-stakes tournaments, some occasionally recorded for television. Its two card rooms offer 20 poker tables and there are daily no-limit Texas Hold 'em tournaments at stake levels ranging from £30, plus administration fees. Inexpensive rebuy tournaments for beginners are a feature of Friday nights and such games are an increasingly common part of the casino scene, such is the demand for the game in the UK. Anyone wishing to enter the Grosvenor Victoria will have to register for free membership by producing some form of personal identification. However, players are permitted to enter the premises promptly, having registered, rather than being forced to wait for 24 hours before sampling the action, as was the case until the UK removed this legal stipulation in 2005. Along with most of the country's casinos, a 'smart casual' dress code is *de rigueur*.

Above: English Roland 'the Sheep' de Wolfe at the final table of the EPT event in Dublin in 2006. He went on to win the tournament and the top prize of €554,300 (US$737,208) in the no-limit Texas Hold 'em event.

Above: The final table during the European Poker Tour's second season held in London in October 2005 at the Grosvenor Victoria Casino. American Noah Jefferson and Norwegian Jonas Helness watch as British player Mark Teltscher checks his cards. Teltscher went on to win the £3,000 (US$5,900) no-limit Hold 'em main event, taking home £280,000 (US$552,000).

CASH GAMES AND TOURNAMENTS

LARGE CASH PRIZES ARE A GREAT INCENTIVE FOR MANY PLAYERS TO TAKE PART IN A TOURNAMENT. THE ENTRY FEES CAN VARY GREATLY, FROM NO ENTRY FEE TO UP TO US$10,000.

As a gambling medium, poker has always been premised upon the idea of players vying with each other for sums of cash or some other meaningful currency. Since its early days, however, poker has developed into a wide range of different games with a variety of betting structures to match. Up until the 1970s, poker remained conceptually a cash game, with players buying in for a stipulated maximum or minimum sum prior to a session. But the success of the WSOP and the exposure of poker on television have increased the popularity of tournament poker, which has also been given a phenomenal boost by the advent of online gambling sites. This has led to distinctive differences in the strategies and approaches to be adopted when playing cash game poker as opposed to a tournament. The purpose of this chapter is to identify some of those differences and outline the key facets of both forms of the game.

Right: A player rakes in the chips at the conclusion of a hand. Whether playing a cash game or a tournament, winning a hand and claiming the pot is every player's objective as the cards are being dealt. Those new to the game often mistakenly believe that winning at poker is predicated upon winning a majority of hands played during a session. Experienced players know, however, that the key to long-term success lies in winning the few hands that generate big pots. This holds true for both cash games and poker tournaments even if strategies applied in one form of the game may not always be advisable in the other.

CASH GAMES

Cash games, or ring games if preferred, are the mainstay of poker and involve players gambling with the money at their disposal, usually in the form of chips obtained from the acting cashier. The stake levels and betting limits of the various games differ, of course, and players will naturally gravitate towards those that suit them best.

Typically, in a formal card room, there will be a minimum buy-in required of perhaps as little as five times the maximum bet, offering the scope for playing at minimal cost. However, most experts recommend that players should not consider sitting in on any game with less than forty times the maximum bet. This is premised on the assumption that any fulfilling poker session will most probably last for several hours during which time a sustained run of poor cards or bad beats is almost inevitable.

In games where a maximum buy-in also applies, players may be allowed to rebuy chips during a pause in play to maintain their stacks at that level. Taking advantage of this possibility is also advised as a very positive strategy for two reasons. First, under table-stakes rules, players can only bet with the chips currently on the table, with any rebuys to be conducted at the conclusion of the hand. Betting all-in when holding the nuts is much more profitable with a large stack than with a small one, should a big pot develop, therefore it makes sense to keep as many chips as possible available for such an eventuality. This obviously involves avoiding games in which the buy-in could immediately absorb a player's entire bankroll. The second reason for doing so is simply to maintain a credible defence against opponents who bet aggressively to intimidate those short on chips. Without the

Above: Actor Lou Diamond Phillips playing poker at the Celebrity World Poker Tour held at the Commerce Casino in Los Angeles, USA. A popular spectator sport, celebrity poker has many actors among its leading lights. The cash winnings are often donated to charity.

Left: Rhett Butler (Clark Gable) keeps a cool head while playing poker in the film of *Gone with the Wind*. In real life too, containing one's emotions is an essential part of playing the game well.

Left: Jamie Gold of Malibu, California, becomes the new World Series of Poker champion, winning US$12 million in Las Vegas, Nevada, 11 August 2006. The prize of US$12 million is the largest ever won in television or sport. The top 12 players competing in this tournament became millionaires.

Below: When playing cash games, you need to decide what sort of bankroll you are willing to commit. It is not advisable to play in games that are either too big or too small for your bankroll. If you do so, your emotions may well get in the way of your ability to think logically.

resources to make the occasional re-raise, players run the risk of being anted away in the face of aggressive betting while they are waiting for a competitive hand. It is difficult to be successful if, when such as hand is held, a player does not have the resources to capitalize upon it to the fullest extent.

THE LONG-TERM STRATEGY

Although poker is rooted in competition, the risks that must be taken in order to win will very often lead to defeat. This applies during every hand of every session, which means that players must very quickly come to terms with losing and how it can affect their decisions. Having the discipline to control one's emotional reactions while playing poker is an asset, since it is all too easy to tilt, following a succession of losing hands. By allowing frustration or anger to guide one's play, it is likely that any losses will be compounded by poor betting decisions. Not every session will prove profitable and being able to walk away from the table while losing is a test of character that confronts every poker player.

Such a prospect is easier to accept when each individual session is considered merely one of countless others to be played during a lifetime. By setting realistic targets and keeping a record of performances, regular players who hope to improve their game, and perhaps even make it profitable, are better able to put losing sessions into perspective.

THE BANKROLL
♦ ♣ ♥ ♠

Managing the bankroll is of the utmost importance for a poker player, this being the cash specifically reserved for playing the game. Very few poker players are sponsored and the majority of full-time professionals are entirely reliant upon their ability to win in order to earn an income. Should their bankroll become exhausted, they have no immediate means of buying in to another game, which is one of the reasons why the best players are ruthless and clinical in their approach; they cannot afford to adopt any other attitude. Most players, however, will simply allocate a proportion of their income to poker in much the same way as they would for any other leisure interest. For the amateur, the test of discipline comes in treating the bankroll in the same way as a professional, since that is the surest way of promoting a competitive instinct.

ADOPTING THE RIGHT APPROACH

The reasons for playing poker are as many and varied as the people who enjoy the game, although purists insist that players should always strive to be as tough, ruthless and competitive as possible in order to do themselves justice. Each individual may have contrasting motives for playing, but all should consider some basic questions concerning how long they may wish to play, the nature of the opposition, and the potential cost involved. Only when these questions are satisfactorily answered can they hope to feel at ease and ready to play their best. Similarly, approaching the game in a positive frame of mind is obviously advantageous, with players who are tired, jaded or otherwise distracted by external pressures unlikely to exploit their true ability.

HOME GAMES

Regular games conducted at home between friends or colleagues have the potential to be as harshly competitive as any casino session involving poker's high-rollers. On the whole, though, such games are typically social events played for sums that are rarely large enough to endanger long-lasting friendships. Food, drink and conversation are as much a part of such events as playing cards, and this should be taken into account when devising even the vaguest of strategies.

Winning may not be the most pressing concern for the amateur player but nobody deliberately sets out to lose. Observing opponents to gather an appreciation of their playing styles and levels of ability remains an important skill. This is particularly true when invited to play in a regular home game for the first time, since even good friends may reveal personal characteristics in their poker that had previously never surfaced during the relationship.

CLUBS AND CASINOS

Buying in to a table operated by a club or casino can be a daunting experience for the novice player who is better acquainted with the home game. Although the stake levels may offer clues regarding the ability of the opposition, engaging in competition with strangers still requires a degree of self-confidence in one's own skill. Choosing the correct level at which to play is crucial, of course, and a disciplined approach to the time that is to be spent playing during a session is also important. Also, in formal card rooms there is always the rake to consider, this being the fee levied by the house for operating the game. The fee could be charged on an hourly basis, either per table or per player, or it could simply be that the dealer takes a few

Above: The home is where most poker is played. Using chips brings credibility to the game. Apart from being easier to use than cash, they help speed up the action.

Right: Extreme Poker is an initiative that is taking the game to exhilarating frontiers, no matter how strange. Poker professional Rob Varkonyi (far left) competes against other players during the second Extreme Poker tournament, held atop the vast ice fields of the Arctic Sea in Kemi, Finland, in March 2006.

Left: Swede Christer Johansson (far left), ultimate winner of the World Poker Tour (WPT) first season Grand Prix de Paris event in 2003, playing heads-up at the final table with Frenchman Claude Cohen (centre), considered by many to be France's top player. Christer took home the €500,000 (US$659,450) first prize. Timing in poker is of huge importance and never more so than when competing at the highest level. To be successful in a competitive arena, being able to adjust your style of play and frequently change gear are invaluable skills.

chips from every winning pot up to a maximum of perhaps 10 per cent. With a cut from each pot going to the house and the winner of each reasonable pot customarily tipping the dealer, the pace of the game will also be quicker than in home games, it being in the dealer's interests to ensure that is the case. The combination of all these factors underlines, once more, the need for a realistic assessment of one's ability when deciding to play in public.

QUALITY OF OPPONENTS

Players can expect to encounter opponents of much higher quality in commercial card rooms than they would in their home games. Leaving aside the tournament-level professionals, many other players manage to grind out a living from poker, defying the rake and their opponents in order to do it. For these players and the semi-professionals who supplement their regular income with profitable stints at the table, poker is simply a job requiring a high degree of application. Those they prey upon are the tourists, occasional poker players whose bankrolls, perhaps, exceed their abilities but who enjoy the chance to pit their wits against the best. Although it is a much more impersonal experience, the same considerations still apply for those who play online.

KEEPING COUNT
♦ ♣ ♥ ♠

So much advice concerning sound poker play emphasizes the benefits of analysing performance, as well as exercising discipline and patience. These virtues are also important for the serious player who wishes to improve with experience. Keeping a mental record of one's play in certain scenarios is an asset when studying the game away from the table. Players should also keep accurate financial records of their poker. Ultimately, money is simply a means of keeping score, with a good poker player being one who, year after year, regularly makes a profit. Only by being honest with themselves and making an accurate note of poker income and expenditure can players expect to be objective about their overall performance.

Left: It can be argued that the televising of poker tournaments has already given poker playing a whole new air of respectability, which is sure to attract a lot of people to try it.

TOURNAMENT PLAY

Inspired by television coverage of tournament poker and the potential prize money on offer for winning, many more players are developing a taste for this form of the game. Whereas a commercial cash game in a 24-hour club or casino may, in theory, continue indefinitely as players come and go from the table, a tournament is structured to ensure a definitive winner at the end of the event. To this end, the antes and blinds in tournaments progressively increase, whereas in cash poker, they remain at a constant level as dictated by the terms of the game. Each betting level may apply for a matter of minutes or a matter of hours, depending on the nature and scale of the tournament, but the principle is always the same, with the objective for each player, of course, being to win all the chips in play.

KNOCKOUT POKER

The major difference between cash games and tournaments is, of course, the knockout element that sees players eliminated when they run out of chips. To last the distance, players are compelled to engage in betting confrontations, which means they have to implement different strategies and contrasting styles of play at the various stages of the tournament.

In a cash game, tight players can usually allow the deal to circulate the table a couple of times while waiting for a playable hand, without the antes seriously damaging their chip stacks. Although commendable as a general long-term playing strategy, the nature of knockout poker precludes maintaining this patient approach throughout a tournament. During the early stages, when survival is of primary concern, patience is certainly required, but, as the antes increase and opponents acquire more chips, players must bet forcefully and be prepared to take greater risks.

Above: American Joe Bartholdi, winner of the 2006 WPT no-limit Hold 'em US$25,000 buy-in championship sits amid bundles of cash after winning US$3.7 million – the biggest pot ever in the tournament's history up to that point. Bartholdi outlasted a field of 605 players to claim the first place prize. The victory came after years of mixed fortunes due to experiencing difficulty maintaining a stable bankroll.

Left: An enormous poster for Full Tilt Poker, found outside the game room at the 2005 WSOP. The online gaming site is well known for having a huge team of poker professionals on its advertising team (Phil Ivey, Chris 'Jesus' Ferguson, Howard Lederer, Mike Matusow, to name but a few). The site has excellent reviews for its software: its website was designed by professional players. Full Tilt's advertising campaigns have taken promotion of the game to a new level.

ENTRY FEES AND PRIZES

For tournaments, entry fees vary dramatically, with the events held at the WSOP, for example, generally costing US$500 and upwards, while the World Championship game itself requires a buy-in of US$10,000. At the lower end of the scale, casinos and clubs stage tournaments for much smaller entry fees and such games are also a very popular element of online poker. There are even freeroll tournaments that require no entry fee but usually result in the winner being offered a seat in a more prestigious competition. Satellite tournaments are similar in nature, with players paying a small fee for the chance to win a place in the next round of the main event.

The great benefit of playing tournament poker compared to cash games is that players can be certain at the outset of the maximum they stand to lose. In order to win, however, it is possible they may have to outlast several hundred opponents, which is obviously a major challenge. The prize money is usually allocated to those who finish in the top ten per cent of entrants, but the lion's share of the cash tends to be reserved for the top three or four per cent, the winner perhaps claiming between a quarter and a half of the entire prize pool.

TYPES OF TOURNAMENT

Most of the popular variations are played in tournament fashion and all can be conducted as fixed-pot or no-limit contests. The number of competitors may range from the 8,000-strong entry for the WSOP World Championship, the most celebrated of all multi-table tournaments, to a private heads-up contest between just two players. Single-table tournaments exist that offer players a better chance of victory for a much smaller top prize, of course, and many of these are known as sit 'n' go events. Players simply pay the required fee and, when all seats are taken, the tournament immediately begins. These differ from the regular diarized competitions for which players may enter some time in advance.

One other key factor for players to bear in mind is the distinction between freeze-out and rebuy tournaments. In the former, all players start with the same number of chips for their fixed fee and play until they either lose them all or win the tournament. Subject to certain conditions, players may purchase more chips during a rebuy tournament, with the opportunity to do this typically restricted to the first hour or two of the event. After that, the tournament continues as a freeze-out competition.

Above left: Eventual winner of the WSOP 2006 championship, Jamie Gold (centre), focuses on a hand as the players compete to be in the final nine. It stands to reason that at this stage, players must be observant to pick up clues from the table. The prospect of reaching the final table beckons, and with it a share of the prize pool, so players may tighten up their play to protect their chip position.

Left: Pack of cards on display at the WSOP championship in 2004. Like any major sporting event, the WSOP has corporate sponsors which pay fees to market themselves as an official sponsor or licensee and exclusively use the WSOP insignia and cross-promote with their events. In addition to Harrah's properties and cable TV networks dedicated to sports broadcasting, the major sponsors have included Miller Brewing, Pepsi, GlaxoSmithKline/Bayer and Nintendo.

Tournament Strategy

A single-table event with rapidly increasing betting levels may be over in a matter of minutes, while most multi-table tournaments comprising thirty or more entrants could easily last for several hours. The likely duration of the tournament will therefore have a bearing on strategy, as only those who finish in the top ten per cent typically win a share of the prize pool.

During the early stages, survival is very much the primary concern and players are advised to adopt a tight and cautious approach while they evaluate the opposition. Judgement of starting hands is crucial and, whichever poker variation is being played, avoiding unnecessary and potentially costly confrontations early on in the tournament is generally advisable. There will always be those who prefer to gamble from the outset, in an attempt to gain an early advantage, but playing a conservative game while reckless opponents knock each other out is arguably a better long-term strategy.

Having evaded an early exit, however, players can still expect the pressure to build as the tournament develops. The regular increases in the minimum betting level ensure this as players find themselves having to contest pots with hands they might ordinarily fold. Those who are short of chips can expect to see large and intimidating bets emanating from the chip leaders as the proximity of the prize-money places draws near.

Distinguishing features

Recognizing distinctive betting patterns among opponents is always important at the poker table. This is no less true in a tournament and is an asset at a single-table event in which players only vacate their seats when they are eliminated. Distinguishing the cautious strategists from the loose gamblers is relatively straightforward under these circumstances.

Multi-table tournaments present a different challenge, however, since players will be moved between tables, to equalize numbers as others are

Above: British player Arshad Hussain, at the EPT 2006 grand final held in Monte Carlo. The dramatic final stages of the tournament ended with Hussain in a heads-up showdown against American political science student Jeff Williams, who went on to win the big event taking home €900,000 (US$1,078,000). Arshad had spent nothing to reach Monte Carlo after winning an online satellite tournament and took home €492,000 (US$592,607) for his second place.

Left: Players try their luck during the early stages of the WSOP 2006 held at the Rio hotel and casino, in Las Vegas. The enormous scale of the tournament can be intimidating for amateur players, and ten- or eleven-handed games mean that space at tables is tight.

Left: Players at the WSOP 2006 final table. As has become customary at the final table of WSOP events, the prize money is brought out by armed security guards and put on display. The previously unknown American player Jamie Gold completely dominated the table and went on to win US$12 million without ever being seriously challenged.

Below: 'Diamond' Carlo Citrone, British professional poker player and commentator, enjoys a massage at the table during the 2005 World Series of Poker where he made it to the final table. Citrone ultimately collected US$59,175 in cash for coming 8th out of a total of 1,072 players.

eliminated and tables are taken out of action. Having acquired a healthy chip lead at one table and profited from the opportunity to intimidate the short stacks, a player could be moved to another table where an opponent or two may have many more chips. If this is the case, a player once again needs to take stock of the opposition and their betting styles to discover whether the leaders have been skilfully shrewd or simply lucky. Of course, as the tournament progresses towards the final table and the antes or blinds increase, betting patterns tend to be dictated by the chips at a player's disposal more than any other factor.

MONITORING CHIP STACKS

The need to keep abreast of developments elsewhere is an element of multi-table tournament play that is not replicated in cash games. The technology behind online tournaments facilitates hand-by-hand updates, allowing contestants to gauge their progress against opponents at other tables. Outside the world of the virtual casino, however, players may have to take the occasional break from their own game in order to regroup their thoughts and check the progress of opponents at other tables.

In a freeze-out contest, the total number of chips in play is constant, so calculating the current average is a straightforward matter of dividing the chip total by the number of players remaining. Maintaining an above-average chip stack during the earlier stages of a tournament can provide the foundation for more attacking play as short-stacked opponents are threatened by the prospect of elimination. However, it is worth remembering that from the middle stages onwards, the average stack may be some way short of the chip leader if one player has managed to attain a dominant lead.

495

HOW TO WIN

The greater the number of competitors, the more difficult any tournament is to win, of course, and it is true that players may have to rely on good fortune at key moments to a greater extent than when contesting a cash game. Armed with a sound strategy and a consistent approach in the selection of which hands to support, players are more likely to finish ahead on a regular basis if restricting their poker to the cash game format.

Tournament poker, however, calls for more risks to be taken in order both to survive and to prosper. The size of a player's chip stack will dictate the frequency and scale of those risks, with players who are down to ten times the minimum bet or less faced with the prospect that every hand could be their last. Those in good shape have more options from which to choose, since they can contest a few more multi-handed pots with low-ranking cards if opponents choose not to raise the betting. Alternatively, there is always the option to sit back for a while and wait patiently while opponents jostle for position by eliminating each other. Anyone who has improved on their starting stack by judiciously sticking to a tight game plan is also in a better position to bluff from the

middle stages onwards as the cost of participating in a hand inevitably increases. Opponents will be wary of calling such a solid player and this provides the opportunity to pick up some valuable chips from some weakly contested pots.

STAY ALERT

The key to absorbing all the information available while playing poker is concentration, whatever form of the game is being played. In tournaments, taking stock of the opposition, their playing styles and the fluctuations in stack sizes requires a high degree of mental application. Accomplishing this as well as monitoring events at the surrounding tables demands that competitors stay alert. As the average chip count increases, for example, players should be acutely aware that they need to win a few pots to stay ahead of the game. The danger with playing too tightly and falling well behind is that a player may eventually face betting all-in with such limited resources that even winning the hand may be of little benefit. Being alert to the possibility of this happening and adjusting one's play accordingly can therefore prevent a player from having to implement increasingly desperate strategies.

Above: In 2006, British newspaper columnist, author and TV presenter Victoria Coren beat 397 others to win £500,000 (US$976,200) in the EPT event in London.

Above: Former investment banker Rob Varkonyi winning the WSOP in 2002. The American became a celebrity and professional poker player after his surprise victory. Phil Hellmuth said that the odds against Varkonyi winning were so high that he would shave his head if he won.

Above: Norwegian Bjorn-Erik Glenne was crowned winner of the European Poker Tour event in Barcelona in 2006, beating 480 players to claim the €691,000 prize (US$875,000). The former marketing manager is the first Norwegian to win an EPT event. Glenne is also a high-ranking chess player and enjoys substantial success online.

Left: Chris Moneymaker at the final table of the 2003 WSOP. He earned his way into the championship event by playing in an online poker tournament at a cost of US$40 and went on to win the first prize of US$2.5 million, despite the fact it was his first experience of a 'live' poker tournament.

From the chip leader's perspective, choosing the right time to pressurize a short-stacked opponent is no less challenging. While intimidating the opposition with large bets is a viable option, it is still best to do so when in possession of a strong hand. Inducing all-in calls or raises from opponents short on chips can easily backfire if betting with a marginal hand, since being vulnerable does not preclude them from having excellent cards. Similarly, calling a short-stacked opponent's all-in bet is easier to justify when holding a decent hand, there being little profit from continually calling in such situations simply because one has the chips to spare.

CHANGE GEAR

The ability to change gear by varying one's betting patterns and general approach is required in both cash games and tournaments. In the former, adopting a contrasting style to that prevalent among the opposition can be beneficial, with tight play best at a table of loose players, and more expansive play possible when the opposition is ultra-conservative.

Responding in a similar way during a tournament is a good policy in the early stages, but the need to change gear is dictated by the increasing betting levels and the unavoidable impact they have on each competitor's play. Acquiring chips to withstand the ravages of the antes and blinds means players will often have to contemplate betting with a poor hand. Taking a positive stance and betting aggressively in this situation is generally a better policy than passively calling and hoping for the best. Having to adopt this more forceful approach on occasions is probably the greatest distinguishing factor between tournaments and cash games, where a consistently patient strategy can prove rewarding. As a result, individuals who regularly play tournament poker should adjust their thinking accordingly when reverting to a cash game.

ODDS TABLES

Having an understanding of the odds and probabilities in poker is essential for anyone wishing to be successful at the game. It will give you a definite advantage over your opponents and help you work out your strategy for the rest of the game. Use the odds tables given here to decide on your play. For a detailed analysis of odds and probabilities turn to pages 322 to 325 of this book.

TEXAS HOLD 'EM: Odds Against Receiving Specific Starting Hands

Pair of Aces	220 to 1
Pair of Aces or Kings	119 to 1
Pair of Tens or better	43 to 1
Any Pair	16 to 1
Ace King suited	331 to 1
Ace King offsuit	110 to 1
Any two suited cards	3.25 to 1
Any hand with a pair or an Ace	4 to 1

SEVEN-CARD STUD: Odds Against Receiving Specific Starting Hands

Three Aces	5,524 to 1
Three Queens or better	1, 841 to 1
Three Tens or better	1,104 to 1
Any three of a kind (Trips)	424 to 1
Pair of Aces	76 to 1
Pair of Queens or better	25 to 1
Pair of Tens or better	14 to 1
Three cards to a straight flush	85 to 1
Three cards to a flush	24 to 1
Three cards to a straight	5 to 1

DRAW POKER: Odds Against Improvement Following the Draw

Player Holds	Result	
One pair – draws three cards	Any improvement	5 to 2
	Two Pairs	5 to 1
	Three of a Kind (Trips)	8 to 1
	Full House	97 to 1
	Four of a Kind (Quads)	360 to 1
One pair plus a kicker – draws two cards	Any improvement	3 to 1
	Two Pairs	5 to
	Trips	12 to 1
	Full House	120 to 1
Two pairs – draws one card	Full House	11 to 1
Trips – draws two cards	Any improvement	9 to 1
	Full House	15 to 1
	Quads	23 to 1
Trips plus a kicker – draws one card	Any improvement	11 to 1
	Full House	15 to 1
	Quads	46 to 1
Open-ended straight draw – draws one card	Improvement to Straight	5 to 1
Inside straight draw – draws one card	Improvement to Straight	11 to 1
Four-card flush – draws one card	Improvement to Flush	4 to 1
Open-ended four-card straight flush – draws one card	Improvement to Straight Flush	23 to 1

TEXAS HOLD 'EM: On the Flop

Player holds	Result	
A Pair	Quads	407 to 1
	Full House	136 to 1
	Trips	7.5 to 1
Two unpaired cards	Full House	1087 to 1
	Trips	73 to 1
	Two Pairs (using both hole cards)	48 to 1
	Any Two Pairs	24 to 1
	Pair	2 to 1
Two suited cards	Flush completed	118 to 1
	Four-card Flush	7.5 to 1
	Three-card Flush	1.4 to 1

RECOMMENDED BOOKS

There are countless books on individual card games and aspects of card play. The following books are a personal selection. Some are more useful than others, but all of them are worth a read. David Parlett's website (*www.davidparlett.co.uk*) repays investigation, particularly if you are interested in more arcane historical games. Equally, the Pagat web site (*www.pagat.com*) is an indispensable, instant on-line reference. *Mentored* by John McLeod, a leading member of the International Playing Card Society, is also a treasure trove of information.

Alvarez, Al, *The Biggest Game in Town* (Houghton Mifflin, Boston, 1983)

Andrews, Joseph P., *The Complete Win at Hearts* (Bonus Books, 2000)

Bellin, Andy, *Poker Nation: A High-Stakes, Low-Life Adventure into the Heart of Gambling* (Yellow Jersey Press, London, 2003)

Brunson, Doyle, *Doyle Brunson's Super System: A Course in Power Poker* (B & G Publishing, Las Vegas, 1978)

Buttler, Frank, Buttler, Simon, *Cribbage* (Weidenfeld & Nicolson, 2000)

Dalla, Nolan, and Alson, Peter, *The Man Behind the Shades: The Rise and Fall of Stuey 'The Kid' Ungar, Poker's Greatest Player* (Phoenix, London, 2006)

Fletcher, Iain, *The Rough Guide to Poker* (Rough Guides Ltd, London, 2005)

Frey, Richard L., Culbertson, Ely, *How to Play Canasta* (Kessinger Publishing, 2007)

Fry, Sam, *Gin Rummy* (Dover, 1978)

Gibson, Walter B., *Hoyle's Modern Encyclopaedia of Card Games* (Robert Hale, 1987)

Hellmuth Jr, Phil, *Play Poker Like the Pros* (HarperCollins, New York, 2003)

Johnson, Herman, *Bid Whist* (Author House, 2003)

Kantor, Eddie, *Bridge for Dummies* (Hungry Minds Inc., 2006)

Klinger, Ron, Kambites, Andrew, Husband, Pat, *Basic Bridge* (Cassell, 2001)

Marcus, Richard, *The Great Casino Heist* (Constable & Robinson Ltd, London, 2005)

McEoy, Tom, *Tournament Poker* (Cardoza, New York, 1995)

McNally, Brian, *How to Play Poker and Win* (Macmillan, London, 2000)

Mendelson, Paul, *Texas Hold 'em Poker* (Elliot Right Way Books, 2005)

Morehead, Albert, Mott-Smith, Geoffrey, *Complete Book of Solitaire and Patience Games* (Foulsham, 1996)

Parlett, David, *A History of Card Games* (OUP, 1990)

Parlett, David, *A–Z of Card Games* (OUP, 2004)

Parlett, David, *Card Games for Everyone* (Hodder & Stoughton, 1983)

Pottage, Julian, *The Bridge Player's Bible* (Barron's Educational, 2006)

Regal, Barry, *Card Games for Dummies* (Hungry Minds Inc., 2005)

Robson, Andrew, *Bridge* (HarperCollins, 2007)

Scarne, John, *Scarne's Encyclopaedia of Card Games* (Harper Reference, 1995)

Scarne, John, *Scarne's Guide to Modern Poker* (Pocket Books, New York, 1980)

Scharf-Cohen, Leo E., Scharf-Cohen, Robert, *Cohen's Complete Book of Gin Rummy* (Ace Books, 1973)

Schüssler, Thomas G., *Skat* (Südwest Verlag, 2004)

Sharvik, Andrea, Sharvik, Dan, *Playing Poker to Win* (How To Books, 2006)

Sklansky, David, *Hold 'em Poker* (Two Plus Two Publishing LLC, Henderson, 1978)

Steiner, Peter O., *Thursday-Night Poker: How to Understand, Enjoy – and Win* (Random House, New York, 1996)

The Diagram Group, *Card Games* (HarperCollins, 1977)

Wilson, Des, *Swimming with the Devilfish…under the surface of professional poker* (Macmillan, London, 2006)

Wilson, Greg, *Bezique* (Robert Hale, 1998)

Wolpin, Stewart, *The Rules of Neighbourhood Poker According to Hoyle* (New Chapter Press, New York, 1990)

Yarnold, Stuart, *Online Poker in Easy Steps* (Computer Step, Southam, 2005)

Magazines & Periodicals

Inside Edge (Dennis Publishing, London)

Poker Player (Dennis Publishing, London)

WPT Poker: The Official World Poker Tour Magazine (Future Publishing, Bath)

GLOSSARY

Ace in the hole A slang expression referring to the ace playing card a player has as a hole card (or face-down card) in a game of stud poker.

Aces High The term used when the Ace is the highest-ranked card in each suit. When it is the lowest-ranked, the term is **Aces Low**.

Aces up The term used to indicate that a player possesses a pair of aces coupled with a pair of lower rank.

Action The betting activity at the poker table.

Add-on A purchase of more chips (optional) at the end of the rebuy period in a tournament.

All-in Wagering all one's remaining chips in a single bet.

Ante A compulsory bet made by one or more players before the deal.

Ante-up Put one's ante in the pot.

Alliance A partnership between players that lasts for only one deal.

Ante In gambling games, the opening stake that all players must make before or at the start of each deal.

Auction Bidding to establish which suit should be trumps, how many tricks the bidders undertake to win and other basic conditions of a particular game.

Back-door flush Securing a flush against the odds when the turn and river cards fall favourably in community card games like Texas Hold 'em and Omaha.

Back-door straight Securing a straight in the same manner as above.

Bad beat This occurs when a strong hand is beaten by an inferior hand that improves against the odds.

Bankroll Stake money. It can refer to a player's stake during a single session or to the total amount allocated solely for the purpose of playing poker over an extended period.

Bet Putting chips in the pot.

Betting intervals The occasions during play when bets are permitted.

Bicycle The lowest possible straight comprising A, 2, 3, 4, 5.

Bid The offer to win a certain number of tricks in exchange for choosing conditions of play, for example, what the trump suit will be. If a bid is not overcalled by a higher one, then it becomes a contract.

Big slick Slang term for hole cards of A, K when dealt in Texas Hold 'em.

Blank A card that is valueless.

Blind Compulsory bet, or ante, made in games such as Texas Hold 'em and Omaha. Usually, the player to the immediate left of the dealer bets the small blind and the next player to act bets the big blind, generally set at twice the level of the small.

Bluff The act of deception: making a strong bet to disguise a weak hand.

Board card The visible, face-up cards in play during stud poker, and the community cards revealed during Texas Hold 'em and Omaha.

Boat Another term for a full house.

Boodle In the game Michigan, cards from a separate pack placed on a layout on which bets (gambling chips or counters) are staked.

Book In Bridge and Whist, the first six tricks won by a side, which are recorded 'below the line'. In collecting games, a set of four cards of the same rank.

Bring-in The forced bet made in the first round of betting by the player who is dealt the lowest card showing.

Bug A single wild card in play; typically the joker is played as the wild card.

Bump To raise the betting in the pot.

Burn The discarding of the top card from the deck by the dealer, in order to guard against cheating.

Buy-in The fee required to sit in at a poker game.

Call Matching a bet already made to maintain interest in the hand.

Caller A player who makes a call bet.

Call the blind Matching the bet amount of the blinds. These are bets made by the two players sitting directly to the dealer's left to start the action on the first round of betting.

Card-points The point-scoring values of specific cards, principally in point-trick games. These points are different to the nominal face values.

Card sharp A person who is known to cheat at cards.

Calling station A passive and loose player who does not raise much and who repeatedly calls other players' bets, irrespective of his chances of winning.

Cards speak The means of adjudicating a decision at the showdown. In wild card games it prevent players from wrongly declaring the value of their hand.

Carte blanche A hand containing no court cards.

Carte rouge A hand in which every card counts towards a scoring combination.

Cash game The mainstay of poker games in casinos and online, involving players competing against each other, typically for several hours, in games with constant betting structures.

Cash in Exchanging chips for cash at the end of a session.

Chasing hand Hands that need two cards to realize their potential.

Check The act of deferring a betting decision while remaining in the hand. A player can only check if no bet has yet been made during the betting round.

Checkraise This describes the tactic of checking in a betting round and then raising a subsequent bet made by an opponent.

Chips Coloured counters used to represent cash sums at the poker table. Each colour represents a different denomination.

Coffeehousing Making abusive or critical comments about an opponent's hand while contesting a hand.

Combination Set of scoring cards that match each other in rank or by suit.

Community cards Cards dealt during a game that are common to all players.

Court cards The King, Queen and Jack of each suit, as opposed to the numbered or 'pip' cards. They are also sometimes referred to as picture cards.

Cut To divide a pack of playing cards by lifting a portion from the top, to establish who deals first.

Deadwood The penalty cards remaining in opponents' hands when a player goes out.

Deal The distribution of cards to the players at the beginning of a game and the play ensuing between one deal and the next.

Dealer's choice A style of play, popular in home games, whereby each successive dealer nominates which poker variation will apply for the hand that they deal.

Declare To state the contract or conditions of play (for example, the trump suit or number of tricks intended, etc.). To reveal your hand and score for achieving a particular combination of cards.

Declarer The highest bidder in an auction, who then tries to fulfil his contract.

Deuce Slang term used to describe any of the four twos in the deck.

Discard A card that a player has rejected and placed on a discard pile. To throw away a worthless or unwanted card to a trick.

Door card The first exposed card in a player's hand in stud games.

Down the river Another name for the game of seven-card stud.

Draw To take or be dealt one or more cards from a stock or discard pile. The word also applies generally to the need for a player to hit specific cards to secure a viable hand.

Drawing dead To be unable to beat an existing hand in play despite having more cards to come.

Drawing hand A hand that needs one more relevant card on the turn or river to improve sufficiently past a leading hand to win.

Dummy A full hand of cards dealt to the table, or, in Bridge, to one of the players (who has to spread them face up on the table at a certain point in the game), with which the declarer plays as well as with his own hand.

Elder/Eldest The player who is obliged to lead, bid or make the opening bet first, usually the person seated to the left of the dealer in left-handed games, or seated to the right in right-handed games.

Exchange To discard cards and receive the same number of replacements or to add cards to a hand and then discard the same number.

Family pot A pot contested by all, or nearly all, the players in the game.

Fifth street Simply the fifth card dealt in stud poker games, or the fifth card dealt to the board in community card games.

Fish Poor players.

Fixed-limit A betting structure that stipulates a fixed amount to be bet during each round. For example in a US$5/$10 fixed-limit game of Texas Hold 'em, bets and raises during the first two betting rounds must be in US$5 increments. During the final two rounds bets and raises are in US$10 increments.

Floorman A casino or card room employee who officiates over proceedings and arbitrates in disputes.

Flop The first three community cards revealed, simultaneously, in Texas Hold 'em and similar games.

Flush A hand of cards that are all of the same suit.

Fold To discard one's cards and take no further part in a particular hand. Also called passing or mucking one's hand.

Follow suit To play a card of the same suit as the last one played.

Forced bet An obligatory bet that is set at a fixed amount.

Four of a kind Four cards of the same rank (number) supplemented by an additional card.

Fourth street The fourth card dealt in stud poker games, or the fourth community card dealt to the board.

Free card A card seen by players for no extra cost.

Freeze-out A style of tournament in which all players begin with an equal amount in chips which cannot be replenished during the game.

Freeroll A chance to win something at no risk or cost.

Full-handed game A poker game that involves nine or ten players.

Full house A hand comprising three cards of one rank and two of another.

Game The whole series of deals, or the target score. For example, 'game is 500 points'.

Game points Card points that are won to fulfill a particular bid.

Geese Poor players.

Go out To play the last card of a hand.

Gut straight draw When the middle card of a straight sequence is needed to make the hand: a hand of 6, 7, 9, 10 needs an 8 to secure the straight.

Hand The play that takes place between one deal and the next. The term also describes the cards each individual player holds during the games.

Head To play a higher card than any so far played to the trick.

Heads-up A confrontation between two Poker players, typically the last two players left competing at a Poker tournament table.

Hidden pair Two cards of the same rank dealt face down in a player's starting hand.

High card Simply the highest card counting in a player's hand when no pair or better is obtained.

High hand The best hand in any round of poker.

High-low A term used for split pot poker games, where the total stakes bet during the playing of each hand are divided equally between the highest and lowest hands still standing at the time of the showdown.

High roller A gambler who plays for large stakes. Extreme high rollers are also referred to as 'whales'.

Holdout machine A device designed to help a cheater conceal cards and then reintroduce them to the game at a later point, i.e., to hold them out.

Hole cards The cards dealt face down to each player which remain unseen by the other players, up to the point of any showdown or until the end of the game.

Honours Cards that attract bonus scores or extra payments if they are held in hand and, occasionally, if captured in play.

Ignorant end The lower end of a straight in community card games.

Inside straight draw The situation faced when needing the second or fourth card in a sequence to make a straight, for example, when holding 8, 10, J, Q and requiring a 9 to complete the hand.

Jackpots A prize fund awarded to a player who meets a set of predetermined requirements. Some casinos will give a jackpot to someone who gets four of a kind or higher and loses. The game 'jackpots' refers to a form of draw poker in which a player needs to have at least a pair of jacks to open the betting.

Joker An extra card supplied with the standard 52-card pack that is often used as a wild card.

Kicker The highest value card in a player's hand apart from a stronger holding. Should a player hold 9, 9, A, K, 7 – a pair of nines – then the kicker is the A. The kicker is significant in a situation where two players have the same value pair, or even two pairs. For example a hand of 9, 9, Q, 10, 2 loses to the earlier example because the Q kicker is outranked by the A.

Kitty Another term for the pool or pot of chips that are being played for.

Knock In Rummy, a player uses this to signify that all his cards are melded. In Poker, knocking can be used to signify that a player will make no more bets.

Laying off The playing of cards to opponents' melds on the table in Rummy games.

Lead The first card to be played or the action of playing the first card.

Lock hand A hand that cannot lose.

Loose player Someone who contests many pots, often betting against the odds.

Main pot A pot contested by interested parties to the point when a player is all-in. Any further betting, excluding the all-in player, is entered in a side pot.

Maker The player who names the trump suit.

Maniac An unpredictable player.

Marriage A meld of the King and Queen of the same suit.

Meld A group of cards of the same rank or in sequence that attracts scores.

Misdeal To deal cards incorrectly, in which case they must be collected, shuffled and dealt again.

Misère A contract to lose every trick in a hand, otherwise termed a *Null*.

Muck The pile of discarded cards that accrues during the play of a hand.

Naked bluff A bet made by players in the knowledge that their hand cannot win unless all other players fold.

No-limit The betting structure, often used in knockout tournaments, that allows players to bet all their chips at any time during the game when it is their turn to act.

Null A contract to lose every trick in a hand, or a card carrying no point value in point-trick games.

Nut flush The 'nuts' represents the best possible hand, so the nut flush is the best possible flush obtainable.

Nut full house The best full house available in a poker hand.

Nuts The best available poker hand from the cards in play.

Offsuit Term used to describe hole cards of differing suits, most often applicable in Texas Hold 'em.

On the come A situation occurring when a player draws cards to a hand with potential rather than one that is already made.

Open-ended straight Four cards in a sequence requiring a high or low card to complete the five-card straight. For example when holding 8, 9, 10, J either a 7 or a Q will make the hand.

Openers A minimum hand required in some poker variations in order to open the betting: a pair of Js in some draw poker games, for instance.

Out A card required to transform a losing hand into a winner.

Ouverte A contract played with one's hand of cards spread face up on the table for everyone to see.

Overcall To bid higher than the previous bidder.

Overcard A card higher than any card on the board. For example a player with A, Q as hole cards when the flop is J, 7, 3, has two overcards.

Overtrick A trick taken in excess of the number a player is contracted to take.

Pair Two cards of the same rank.

Pass To miss a turn when it comes to bidding or playing without dropping out of play. To fold a hand.

Pat hand In draw poker, a hand dealt to a player who then opts not to exchange any cards at the draw, the impression that the hand is already strong.

Pigeons Poor players.

Plain suit Any suit other than the trump suit.

Play the board When a player's best poker hand comprises the five community cards on the board in Texas Hold 'em or Omaha.

Pocket card The two cards dealt to you at the beginning of a Hold 'em hand that no one else is entitled to see.

Pocket pair Two cards of the same rank in a starting hand.

Pocket rockets A pair of aces face down in the hole.

Poker face An expressionless facial appearance revealing no thoughts or emotions.

Pool/Pot This is a sum of money or a number of chips, to which the players contribute before play starts or throughout play and which is taken by the eventual winner.

Post the blinds When you post a bet, you place your chips in the pot. The blinds are compulsory bet(s) made by the two players sitting directly to the dealer's left before any cards are dealt, which will start the action on the first round of betting.

Pot The collective total of chips staked during each individual hand for which players compete.

Pot-limit A betting structure in which the maximum bet can be no higher than the total currently in the pot.

Pot odds The amount of money in the pot compared to the amount you must put in the pot to continue playing. If there is US$60 in the pot and a player bets US$6, to raise the pot total to US$66, it costs a player US$6 to call, making the pot odds 11:1.

Pre-flop raise A raise made before the first three community cards are revealed in Texas Hold 'em and similar games.

Prial Three cards of the same rank; a triplet.

Quads Four cards of the same rank. Four of a kind.

Quint In Piquet, a set of five cards. In Quinto, the Five of every suit, and every pair of cards in a suit that totals five. In this game, the Joker is known as the Quint Royal.

Quitting time An agreed-upon time to end a poker game (curfew).

Rag A worthless card or hand.

Raise To increase the betting level, usually by calling the previous bet and then wagering at least the same amount or more again.

Rank A card's denomination and its relative trick-taking power (for example, 'Ace ranks above King').

Rake The fee charged by a club or casino for staging a poker game. Typically it involves a small deduction being made from each pot.

Razz Seven-card stud game in which the lowest hand claims the pot.

Read To assess the strength of an opponent's hand.

Rebuy tournament A style of tournament in which all players are permitted to buy additional chips after the game has started.

Renege To fail to follow suit to the card led, but legally, in accordance with the rules of the game.

Revoke To fail to follow suit, when able and required to do so. It usually incurs a penalty if detected.

Ring game A 'live' cash game that is not a tournament.

River The final card dealt in some poker games.

Rock A tight, cautious player who only plays premium hands.

Rolled-up trip Three cards of the same rank held by a player after the deal in seven-card stud.

Round A division of play in which every player participates in dealing, bidding, playing a trick, etc. the same number of times (usually once).

Rounder A person who travels all over the country to earn a living through gambling.

Royal flush The highest ranking poker hand consisting of 10, J, Q, K, A all of one suit.

Rubber In partnership games, a match usually consisting of three games and thus won by the side winning two.

Ruff In games of Bridge, playing a trump card on a trick that was led with a plain suit. In Gleek, it is the highest card value a player holds in a single suit.

Run Term for a straight sequence.

Rush Experienced when cards fall favourably enough for a player to win several pots in a short space of time.

Sandbagging The practice of slow-playing a strong hand, perhaps by checkraising, in order to trap opponents into betting.

Satellite tournament A mini-tournament to gain an entry into a larger tournament.

See To call a bet.

Semi-bluff A bet made in support of a weak hand that still retains the possibility of becoming an outright winner.

Sequence A run of three or more cards of the same suit in numerical order.

Set Another term for three of a kind.

Seventh street The seventh card dealt in poker games, most commonly seven-card stud.

Shark A good, crafty player often posing as a fish early in the game.

Sheep Poor players.

Shoe A box from which cards are dealt in some card games.

Short-handed game A poker game that involves only a few players.

Showdown The moment when players remaining in the hand reveal their cards to determine the winner at the conclusion of all betting.

Side bet Any bet made outside the pot.

Side pot Chips bet by players competing separately from the main pot, usually after another player has made an all-in bet.

Sixth street The sixth card dealt in seven-card stud, prefacing the fourth round of betting.

Slam A bid to win every trick in a hand.

Slow-play To bet very lightly, or check, in order to disguise a strong hand of cards and encourage opponents to remain in the pot.

Solo A contract played with the hand as dealt without exchanging any cards, or, played alone against the other players. The soloist is the player who elects to play alone.

Split pair Two cards of the same face or number value, one dealt face down and one face up in a starting hand.

Split-pot A pot shared by players who, at the showdown, reveal hands of equal value. Also describes high-low games in which the spoils are divided between the highest and lowest ranking hands.

Spread-limit A betting structure featuring a lower and upper limit. Players may bet any amount within these limits during the game.

Stake The amount of money or chips a player is willing to play with during a game, or the amount a player needs to be included in a game.

Stand pat To not draw any cards in a draw game.

Steal A bluffing bet that succeeds in causing opponents to fold.

Stock The cards that are not dealt immediately to the players, but may be dealt or drawn later on during the game.

Straight Five cards of differing suits in a sequence, for example, 5, 6, 7, 8, 9. Also called a run.

Straight flush Five cards of the same suit in a sequence.

String bet Placing chips in the pot as if to call before announcing a raise. The delay in stating the true nature of the bet helps the perpetrator gather extra information from opponents' reactions and is considered to be unacceptable.

Sucker A very poor player. Also, can be used to refer to an innocent victim in a crooked game.

Suit The internationally recognized suits are Hearts, Clubs, Diamonds and Spades. There are also local ones found in German, Italian and Spanish games.

Table stakes A style of game in which players may only bet the chips available to them during a hand. If additional chips are needed to continue in the game, these may be bought between the playing of hands, not during the game.

Talon The undealt portion of the pack put aside for use later in a game; the same as the stock.

Tap-out To bet all one's chips.

Tapped-out To be out of chips and in Tap city.

Tell An involuntary mannerism that may reveal the strength of a player's hand. A 'tell' is unknown to the player with the tell.

Third street Simply the third card dealt in stud poker games.

Three of a Kind Three cards of the same rank.

Tight player Someone who plays cautiously and only with strong hands.

Tilt Players are described as 'on tilt' when they lose control of their emotions and bet irrationally and without discipline.

Toke A tip for the card room dealer.

Touching cards Two cards that are consecutive in rank: a J, 10 for example.

Trey The Three of any suit.

Trick A round of cards, consisting of one card from each player in turn, played according to the rules of the particular game.

Trips Three cards of the same value, abbreviated from triplets.

Trump A suit that outranks all the others. A trump card always beats any card from a plain suit.

Turn The fourth community card dealt in Texas Hold 'em and Omaha.

Turn-up A card, also called the upcard, turned up at the start of play to determine which suit is trumps and, depending on the game, at other times during play for a variety of reasons.

Two pairs A hand consisting of two different pairs.

Underdog The least likely hand to win the pot, often shortened to 'dog'.

Under the gun Being the first person to act, being in the earliest position.

Undertrick A trick which is less than the number bid or contracted.

Up card A card that is dealt face up.

Upcard The turn-up card.

Void Having no cards of a specified suit in the hand.

Vole The winning of every trick; same as slam.

Vulnerable In Bridge, this describes a partnership, which, having won one game towards the rubber, is subject to increased scores or penalties.

Waste pile A pile of unwanted cards, usually dealt face up.

Wheel The lowest possible straight: A, 2, 3, 4, 5. Also called a bicycle.

Widow A card or cards common to all hands. It can be a hand of cards dealt to the table face down usually at the start of play which players may exchange their cards with during the game.

Wild card A card that can stand in for any other card, either played freely or subject to certain restrictions, depending on the game.

Younger/Youngest The player last in turn to play at the beginning of a game.

INDEX

Acknowledgements

The Publisher would like to thank the following for kindly supplying photographs for this book:

Akg images 207 (tr), 262 (br), 297 (tr); **Alamy** 18 (br), 35 (tr), 40 (br), 74 (bl), 135 (br), 162 (br), 180 (br), 188 (br), 200 (br), 212 (br), 236 (br), 239 (tr, cl), 247 (br), 305 (t, b) 452 (b); **Bridgeman Art Library** 10 (bl, bc, br), 26 (br), 32 (cl), 34 (br), 72 (br), 102 (br), 129 (br), 197 (tr), 250 (br); **BBco** 150 (br), 218 (br), 248 (b), 251 (b); **Bridgewater Book company** 259 (b); **Corbis** 16 (tr), 17 (tr), 105 (t), 106 (tr), 108 (bl, br), 131 (tr), 136 (br), 147 (tr), 157 (cl), 167 (br), 174 (bl), 215 (bl), 240 (tr), 255 (t), 258 (cr, b), 260 (bl, br), 261 (t, cr), 262 (bl), 263 (tr), 264 (bl), 265 (tr), 266 (cl, b), 267 (cr, b), 268 (cr), 270 (bl), 271 (cl, b), 273 (tr), 275 (tl, tr), 284 (bl, br), 285 (bl), 286 (br), 287 (tl), 288 (bl), 292 (b), 296 (cl), 302 (bl, br), 303 (tl), 304 (bl), 306 (tr, bl). 309 (cr), 315 (tl, tr), 316 (br), 317 (bl), 330 (br), 331 (tl, cl), 338 (b), 339 (cr), 340, 345 (t), 351 (b), 353, 356, 357, 417 (bl), 430, 443 (bl), 451,454, 464 (br), 477, 478 (b), 479 (t), 480 (br), 481 (t), 482 (bl), 483 (br), 488 (bl, br), 489 (tl), 492 (cr), 493 (cl); **Dover Publications Inc.** 18 (tl), 26 (tl), 34 (tl), 40 (tl), 50 (tl), 58 (tl), 86 (tl), 102 (tl), 110 (tl), 116 (tl), 126 (bl), 129 (tl), 136 (tl), 162 (tl), 177 (b), 179 (tr), 180 (tl), 188 (tl), 189 (br), 200 (tl), 208 (tl), 212 (tl), 220 (tl), 232 (tl), 242 (tl), 249 (t); **Empics** 265 (bl), 277 (tr), 279 (tl), 281 (tl main), 282 (bl), 295 (tr), 328 (tr), 331 (tr), 332 (bl), 395, 465, 494 (bl), 484 (tr),490 (br); **Getty** 10, 11 (tr), 134 (tr), 220 (br), 263 (tl), 270 (cr), 296 (br), 333 (bl, br), 390, 467 (tl), 472, 495 (tl); **Golden Nugget casino** 476 (bl), 479 (bl); **iStock photography** 3, 8 (t), 11 (br), 53 (br), 86 (br), 88 (b), 254, 255 (br), 283 (tr), 300, 307 (cr, b), 308 (bl, br), 312 (br), 313, 314, 317 (tc), 319 (br), 322, 328 (b), 341 (tl, br), 345 (b), 350 (bl, br), 364, 366, 369, 375, 386, 387, 418, 420, 423, 425, 433, 437, 477 (t), 490 (bl); **Jupiter Images** 3; **The Kobal collection** 232 (br), 288 (br), Warner Bros 289 (tr), United artists 289 (b), Warner Bros 290 (bl), Universal (289 br), Warner Bros 291 (t), Columbia/Persky-Bright/Reno 291 (cr), MGM/Filmways 292 (cr), Miramax/John Clifford 293 (cl), Miramax/ John Clifford 293 (b), MGM/ Filmways 351 (tr), Warner Bros 433; **Mary Evans picture library** 17, 134 (bl), 135, 151, 208, 209, 242,

344 (t); **The Picture Desk** 16 (bl), 17 (bl), 50 (br), 60 (tr), 110 (br), 116 (br), 131 (tr); **Photo library** 473 (cr), 481 (br); **Photos.com** 169 (tr), 303 (tr), 304 (tr), 435; **Pokerimages.com** 264 (br), 268 (tl), 269 (t), 272, 273 (b), 274 (bl), 276 (bl, br), 278 (bl), 279 (tr), 280 (bl, br), 281 (tr, tcr), 282 (br), 283 (b), 285 (t, br), 294 (cr, bl), 295 (tl), 297 (tl), 312 (cl), 318 (cr, bl), 319 (tl), 324, 328 (cr), 329 (tl), 330 (bl), 332 (br), 333 (tr), 339 (br), 416, 417 (tr), 443 (tr), 445, 476 (t), 478 (tr), 480 (bl), 482, (br), 483 (bl), 484 (b), 485 (tl, tr, bl, br), 489 (tr), 491 (br), 492 (bl), 494 (cr), 496 (bl, br), 497 (tl, tr); Top foto 274 (tr), 277 (tl), 278 (cr), 286 (bl), 317 (cr), 335; **Robert Abbot** 58 (br); **Topfoto** 199 (bl).

www.pokerroom.com 464, 465;
www.pacificpoker.com 466;
www.partypoker.com 466; www.pokerstars.com 466; www.deutschepokertour.com 467;
www.pokerguide.jp 468; www.juegapokerya.com 468; www.redstarpoker.com 468;
www.slo-poker.com 469; www.poker.org.il 469;
www.poker.com.hr 470; www.ecardroom.cn 470;
www.poker24.pl 471; www.spelapoker.se 471;
www.poker.fr 471; www.allaussiepoker.com 473;
www.megapoker.nl 473.

All other photos by Andrew Perris.
Artwork by Virginia Zeal.

Every effort has been made to obtain permission to reproduce copyright material, but there may be cases where we have been unable to trace a copyright holder. The publisher will be happy to correct any omissions in future printings.